Cloud Computing

To Vera Rae and Luke Bell

Contents

Preface

The idea that computing may be organized as a public utility, like water and electricity, was formulated in the 1960s by John McCarthy, a visionary computer scientist who championed mathematical logic in artificial intelligence. Four decades later, utility computing was embraced by major IT companies such as Amazon, Apple, Google, HP, IBM, Microsoft, and Oracle.

Cloud computing is a movement started sometime during the middle of the first decade of the new millennium. The movement is motivated by the idea that information processing can be done more efficiently on large farms of computing and storage systems accessible via the Internet. In this book we attempt to sift through the large volume of information and dissect the main ideas related to cloud computing.

Computer clouds support a paradigm shift from local to network-centric computing and network-centric content, when computing and storage resources are provided by distant data centers. Scientific and engineering applications, data mining, computational financing, gaming and social networking, and many other computational and data-intensive activities can benefit from cloud computing. Storing information "on the cloud" has significant advantages and was embraced by cloud service providers. For example, in 2011 Apple announced the *iCloud*, a network-centric alternative for content such as music, videos, movies, and personal information. Content previously confined to personal devices such as workstations, laptops, tablets, and smart phones need no longer be stored locally, can be shared by all these devices, and is accessible whenever a device is connected to the Internet.

The appeal of cloud computing is that it offers scalable and elastic computing and storage services. The resources used for these services can be metered and the users can be charged only for the resources they use. Cloud computing is a business reality today as increasing numbers of organizations are adopting this paradigm.

Cloud computing is cost effective because of the multiplexing of resources. Application data is stored closer to the site where it is used in a manner that is device and location independent; potentially, this data storage strategy increases reliability as well as security. The maintenance and security are ensured by service providers; the service providers can operate more efficiently due to economy of scale.

Cloud computing is a technical and social reality today; at the same time, it is an emerging technology. At this time one can only speculate how the infrastructure for this new paradigm will evolve and what applications will migrate to it. The economic, social, ethical, and legal implications of this shift in technology, whereby users rely on services provided by large data centers and store private data and software on systems they do not control, are likely to be significant.

Cloud computing represents a dramatic shift in the design of systems capable of providing vast amounts of computing cycles and storage space. During the previous four decades, one-of-a-kind systems were built with the most advanced components available at the time at a high cost; but today clouds use off-the shelf, low-cost components. Gordon Bell argued in the early 1990s that one-of-a-kind systems are not only expensive to build, but the cost of rewriting applications for them is prohibitive [45].

Cloud computing reinforces the idea that computing and communication are deeply intertwined. Advances in one field are critical for the other. Indeed, cloud computing could not emerge as a feasible alternative to the traditional paradigms for data-intensive applications before the Internet was able to support high-bandwidth, low-latency, reliable, low-cost communication; at the same time, modern networks could not function without powerful computing systems to manage them. High-performance switches are critical elements of both networks and computer clouds.

There are virtually no bounds on composition of digital systems controlled by software, so we are tempted to build increasingly complex systems. The behavior and the properties of such systems are not always well understood; thus, we should not be surprised that computing clouds will occasionally exhibit an unexpected behavior and system failures.

The architecture, the coordination algorithms, the design methodology, and the analysis techniques for large-scale complex systems like computing clouds will evolve in response to changes in technology, the environment, and the social impact of cloud computing. Some of these changes will reflect the changes in the Internet itself in terms of speed, reliability, security, capacity to accommodate a larger addressing space by migration to IPv6, and so on. In December 2011, 32.7% of the world population, of slightly less than 7 billion, were Internet users, according to www.internetworldstats.com/stats.htm. The 528% growth rate of Internet users during the period 2000–2011 is expected to be replicated if not exceeded in the next decade. Some of these new Internet users will discover the appeal of computing clouds and use cloud services explicitly, whereas a very large segment of the population will benefit from services supported by computing clouds without knowing the role the clouds play in their lives.

A recent posting on *ZDNet* reveals that *EC2* was made up of 454,600 servers in January 2012; when one adds the number of servers supporting other *AWS* services, the total number of Amazon systems dedicated to cloud computing is much larger. An unofficial estimation puts the number of servers used by Google in January 2012 close to 1.8 million; this number was expected to be close to 2.4 million by early 2013.

The complexity of such systems is unquestionable and raises questions such as: How can we manage such systems? Do we have to consider radically new ideas, such as self-management and self-repair, for future clouds consisting of millions of servers? Should we migrate from a strictly deterministic view of such complex systems to a nondeterministic one? Answers to these questions provide a rich set of research topics for the computer science and engineering community.

The cloud movement is not without skeptics and critics. The critics argue that cloud computing is just a marketing ploy, that users may become dependent on proprietary systems, that the failure of a large system such as the cloud could have significant consequences for a very large group of users who depend on the cloud for their computing and storage needs. Security and privacy are major concerns for cloud computing users.

The skeptics question what a cloud actually is, what is new, how does it differ from other types of large-scale distributed systems, and why cloud computing could be successful when grid computing had only limited success. The CEO of Oracle said, "I think the Internet was the last big change. The Internet is maturing. They don't call it the Internet anymore. They call it cloud computing." In 2012, the Oracle Cloud was announced; the website of the company acknowledges: "Cloud computing represents a fantastic opportunity for technology companies to help customers simplify IT, that often-baffling and always-changing sector of the corporate world that's become increasingly valuable in today's global economy."

A very important question is whether, under pressure from the user community, the current standardization efforts spearheaded by the National Institute of Standards and Technology (NIST), will succeed. The alternative, the continuing dominance of proprietary cloud computing environments, is likely to have a negative impact on the field. The three cloud delivery models, Software as a Service (SaaS), Platform as a Service (PaaS), and Infrastructure as a Service (IaaS), will continue to coexist for the foreseeable future. Services based on SaaS will probably be increasingly popular because they are more accessible to lay people, whereas services based on IaaS will be the domain of computer-savvy individuals. If the standardization effort succeeds, we may see PaaS designed to migrate from one infrastructure to another and overcome the concerns related to vendor lock-in.

This book attempts to provide a snapshot of the state of the art of a dynamic field likely to experience significant developments in the near future. The first chapter is an informal introduction to network-centric computing and network-centric content, to the entities involved in cloud computing, the paradigms and the services, and the ethical issues. Chapter 2 is a review of basic concepts in parallel and distributed computing; the chapter covers a range of subjects, from the global state of a process group to causal history, atomic actions, modeling concurrency with Petri nets, and consensus protocols.

The next two chapters address questions of interest for the users of cloud computing. The cloud infrastructure is the subject of Chapter 3; we discuss the cloud services provided by Amazon, Google, and Microsoft, then we analyze the open-source platforms for private clouds, service-level and compliance-level agreements, and software licensing. Next we cover the energy use and the social impact of large-scale data centers and the user experience. Chapter 4 discusses cloud applications; after a brief review of workflows we analyze coordination using the *Zookeeper* and then the MapReduce programming model. The applications of clouds in science and engineering, biology research, and social computing are then discussed, followed by a presentations of benchmarks for high-performance computing on a cloud.

Chapters 5 through 9 cover the architecture, algorithms, communication, storage, and cloud security. Chapter 5 is dedicated to virtualization; we discuss virtual machines, virtual machine monitors, architectural support for virtualization, and performance and security isolation and illustrate the concepts with an in-depth analysis of *Xen* and *vBlades* and with a performance comparison of virtual machines. Chapter 5 closes with a discussion of virtual machine security and software fault isolation.

Resource management and scheduling are the topics of Chapter 6. First, we present a utility model for cloud-based Web services, then we discuss the applications of control theory to scheduling, two-level resource allocation strategies, and coordination of multiple autonomic performance mangers. We emphasize the concept of resource bundling and introduce combinatorial auctions for cloud resources. Next, we analyze fair queuing, start-time fair queuing, and borrowed virtual time scheduling algorithms and cloud scheduling subject to deadlines.

Chapter 7 presents several aspects of networking pertinent to cloud computing. After a brief discussion of the evolution of the Internet we review basic ideas regarding network resource management strategies, interconnects for warehouse-scale computers, and storage area networks. Then we overview content delivery networks and analyze in some depth overlay networks and their potential applications to cloud computing. Finally, we discuss epidemic algorithms.

In Chapter 8 we discuss storage systems. First, we review the early distributed file systems of the early 1980s: the Network File System developed by Sun Microsystems, the Andrew File System developed at Carnegie Mellon University as part of the Andrew project, and the Sprite Network File System developed at University of California Berkeley as a component of the Unix-like distributed operating system called Sprite. Then we present the General Parallel File System developed at IBM in the early 2000s. The in-depth discussions of the Google File System, the *Bigtable*, and the *Megastore* illustrate the new challenges posed to the design of datastores by network-centric computing and network-centric content and the shift from traditional relational database systems to databases capable of supporting online transaction-processing systems.

Cloud security is covered in Chapter 9. After a general discussion of cloud security risks, privacy, and trust, the chapter analyzes the security of virtualization and the security risks posed by shared images and by the management operating system. The implementation of a hypervisor based on microkernel design principles and a trusted virtual machine monitor are then presented.

Chapter 10 presents topics related to complex systems and self-organization. The chapter starts with an introduction to complex systems, followed by an analysis of the relationship between abstractions and the physical reality. A review of the possible means to quantify complexity is followed by a discussion of emergence and self-organization. The discussion of the complexity of computing and communication systems starts with presentation of composability bound and scalability, followed by other means to cope with complexity, including modularity, layering, and hierarchy. Finally we discuss the challenges posed by systems of systems.

The last chapter of the book, Chapter 11, is dedicated to practical aspects of application development. Here we are only concerned with applications developed for the Amazon Web Services (AWS). The chapter starts with a discussion of security-related issues and the practical means of clients to connect to cloud instances through firewalls. The chapter provides recipes for using different AWS services; two AWS applications, one related to trust management in a cognitive network and the other to adaptive data streaming to and from a cloud are discussed in detail.

More than 385 references are cited in the text. Many references present recent research results in several areas related to cloud computing; others are classical references on major topics in parallel and distributed systems. A glossary covers terms grouped in several categories, from general to services, virtualization, desirable attributes, and security.

The history notes at the end of many chapters present the milestones in a particular field; they serve as reminders of how recently important concepts, now considered classical in the field, have been developed. They also show the impact of technological developments that have challenged the community and motivated radical changes in our thinking.

The contents of this book reflect a series of lectures given to graduate classes on cloud computing. The applications discussed in Chapter 11 were developed by several students as follows: Tim Preston contributed to 11.3; Shameek Bhattacharjee to 11.4, 11.10, and 11.11; Charles Schneider to 11.5; Michael Riera to 11.6 and to 11.13; Kumiki Ogawa to 11.7; Wei Dai to 11.8; Gettha Priya Balasubramanian to 11.9; and Ashkan Paya to 11.2.

The author is grateful to several students who contributed ideas, suggested ways to improve the manuscript, and helped identify and correct errors: David Adams, Ragu N. Aula, Surbhi Bhardwaj, Solmaz Gurkan, Brendan Lynch, Kyle Martin, Bart Miller, Ganesh Sundaresan, and Paul Szerlip. Special thanks to Ramya Pradhan and William Strickland for their insightful comments and suggestions. The author wants to express his appreciation for the constant guidance and help provided by Steve Elliot and Lindsay Lawrence from the publisher, Morgan Kaufmann. We also acknowledge Gabriela Marinescu's effort during the final stages of manuscript preparation.

Supplemental Materials

Supplemental materials for instructors or students can be downloaded from Elsevier: http://store.elsevier.com/product.jsp?isbn=9780124046276

Foreword

This book is a timely, comprehensive introduction to cloud computing. The phrase *cloud computing*, which was almost never used a decade ago, is now part of the standard vocabulary. Millions of people around the world use cloud services, and the numbers are growing rapidly. Even education is being transformed in radical ways by cloud computing in the form of massive open online courses (MOOCs). This book is particularly valuable at this time because the phrase *cloud computing* covers so many different types of computing services, and the many people participating in conversations about clouds need to be aware of the space that it spans. The introductory material in this book explains the key concepts of cloud computing and is accessible to almost everybody; such basic, but valuable, information should be required reading for the many people who use some form of cloud computing today.

The book provides a signal service by describing the wide range of applications of cloud computing. Most people are aware of cloud services such as email and social networks, but many are not familiar with its applications in science and medicine. Teams of scientists, collaborating around the world, find that cloud computing is efficient. This book will help people dealing with a variety of applications evaluate the benefit of cloud computing for their specific needs.

This book describes the wide range of cloud services available today and gives examples of services from multiple vendors. The examples are particularly helpful because they give readers an idea of how applications work on different platforms. The market for cloud computing is dynamic, and as time goes on new vendors and new platforms will become available. The examples provided in the book will help readers develop a framework for understanding and evaluating new platforms as they become available.

Cloud computing is based on many decades of work on parallel and distributed computing systems. This book describes some of the central ideas in this work as it applies to cloud computing. Relatively few books integrate theory with applications and with practical examples from a variety of vendors; this book is an excellent source for the increasing numbers of students interested in the area.

Server farms consume an increasing amount of the nation's energy. Sustainability requires mechanisms for server farms to provide the same quality of cloud services while reducing the amount of energy required. This book discusses this important issue as well as other critical issues such as security and privacy. Indeed, this is an excellent single source for the range of critical issues in cloud computing. The wide span of material covered, from the introductory to the advanced; the integration of theory and practice; the range of applications; and the number of examples the book includes make this an excellent book for a variety of readers.

K. Mani Chandi
Simon Ramo Professor and Professor of Computer Science,
California Institute of Technology

CHAPTER

Introduction

1

The last decades have reinforced the idea that information processing can be done more efficiently centrally, on large farms of computing and storage systems accessible via the Internet. When computing resources in distant data centers are used rather than local computing systems, we talk about *network-centric computing* and *network-centric content*. Advancements in networking and other areas are responsible for the acceptance of the two new computing models and led to the *grid computing* movement in the early 1990s and, since 2005, to *utility computing* and *cloud computing*.

In *utility computing* the hardware and software resources are concentrated in large data centers and users can pay as they consume computing, storage, and communication resources. Utility computing often requires a cloud-like infrastructure, but its focus is on the business model for providing the computing services. *Cloud computing* is a path to utility computing embraced by major IT companies such as Amazon, Apple, Google, HP, IBM, Microsoft, Oracle, and others.

Cloud computing delivery models, deployment models, defining attributes, resources, and organization of the infrastructure discussed in this chapter are summarized in Figure 1.1. There are three cloud delivery models: *Software-as-a-Service* (SaaS), *Platform-as-a-Service* (PaaS), and *Infrastructure-as-a-Service* (IaaS), deployed as public, private, community, and hybrid clouds.

The defining attributes of the new philosophy for delivering computing services are as follows:

- Cloud computing uses Internet technologies to offer elastic services. The term *elastic computing* refers to the ability to dynamically acquire computing resources and support a variable workload. A cloud service provider maintains a massive infrastructure to support elastic services.
- The resources used for these services can be metered and the users can be charged only for the resources they use.
- Maintenance and security are ensured by service providers.
- Economy of scale allows service providers to operate more efficiently due to specialization and centralization.
- Cloud computing is cost-effective due to resource multiplexing; lower costs for the service provider are passed on to the cloud users.
- The application data is stored closer to the site where it is used in a device- and location-independent manner; potentially, this data storage strategy increases reliability and security and, at the same time, it lowers communication costs.

Cloud computing is a technical and social reality and an emerging technology. At this time, one can only speculate how the infrastructure for this new paradigm will evolve and what applications will migrate to it. The economical, social, ethical, and legal implications of this shift in technology, in which users rely on services provided by large data centers and store private data and software on systems they do not control, are likely to be significant.

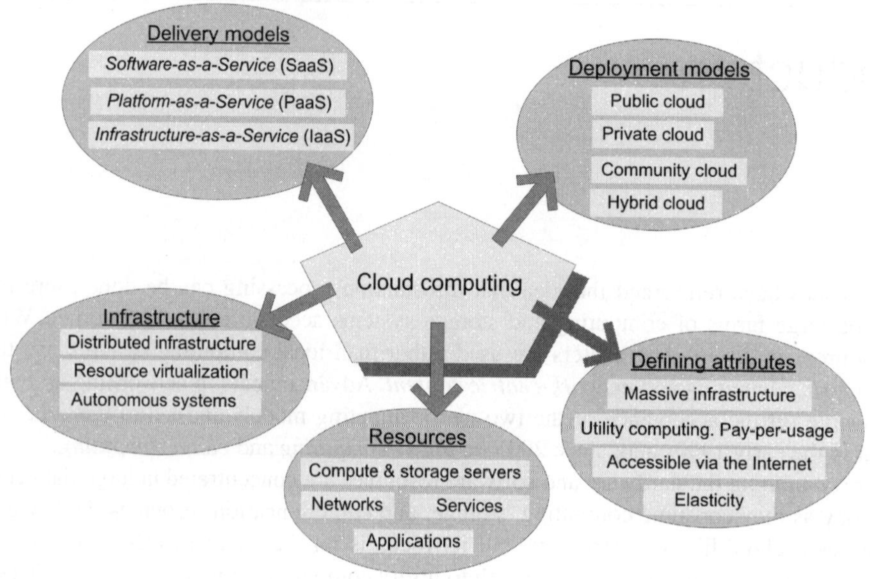

FIGURE 1.1

Cloud computing: Delivery models, deployment models, defining attributes, resources, and organization of the infrastructure.

Scientific and engineering applications, data mining, computational financing, gaming, and social networking as well as many other computational and data-intensive activities can benefit from cloud computing. A broad range of data, from the results of high-energy physics experiments to financial or enterprise management data to personal data such as photos, videos, and movies, can be stored on the cloud.

In early 2011 Apple announced the *iCloud,* a network-centric alternative for storing content such as music, videos, movies, and personal information; this content was previously confined to personal devices such as workstations, laptops, tablets, or smartphones. The obvious advantage of network-centric content is the accessibility of information from any site where users can connect to the Internet. Clearly, information stored on a cloud can be shared easily, but this approach raises major concerns: Is the information safe and secure? Is it accessible when we need it? Do we still own it?

In the next few years, the focus of cloud computing is expected to shift from building the infrastructure, today's main front of competition among the vendors, to the application domain. This shift in focus is reflected by Google's strategy to build a dedicated cloud for government organizations in the United States. The company states: "We recognize that government agencies have unique regulatory and compliance requirements for IT systems, and cloud computing is no exception. So we've invested a lot of time in understanding government's needs and how they relate to cloud computing."

In a discussion of technology trends, noted computer scientist Jim Gray emphasized that in 2003 the cost of communication in a wide area network had decreased dramatically and will continue to do so. Thus, it makes economical sense to store the data near the application [144] – in other words, to store it in the cloud where the application runs. This insight leads us to believe that several new classes of cloud computing applications could emerge in the next few years [25].

As always, a good idea has generated a high level of excitement that translated into a flurry of publications – some of a scholarly depth, others with little merit or even bursting with misinformation. In this book we attempt to sift through the large volume of information and dissect the main ideas related to cloud computing. We first discuss applications of cloud computing and then analyze the infrastructure for the technology.

Several decades of research in parallel and distributed computing have paved the way for cloud computing. Through the years we have discovered the challenges posed by the implementation, as well as the algorithmic level, and the ways to address some of them and avoid the others. Thus, it is important to look back at the lessons we learned from this experience through the years; for this reason we start our discussion with an overview of parallel computing and distributed systems.

1.1 Network-centric computing and network-centric content

The concepts and technologies for network-centric computing and content evolved through the years and led to several large-scale distributed system developments:

- The Web and the semantic Web are expected to support composition of services (not necessarily computational services) available on the Web.[1]
- The Grid, initiated in the early 1990s by National Laboratories and Universities, is used primarily for applications in the area of science and engineering.
- Computer clouds, promoted since 2005 as a form of service-oriented computing by large IT companies, are used for enterprise computing, high-performance computing, Web hosting, and storage for network-centric content.

The need to share data from high-energy physics experiments motivated Sir Tim Berners-Lee, who worked at the European Organization for Nuclear Research (CERN) in the late 1980s, to put together the two major components of the World Wide Web: HyperText Markup Language (HTML) for data description and HyperText Transfer Protocol (HTTP) for data transfer. The Web opened a new era in data sharing and ultimately led to the concept of network-centric content.

The semantic Web[2] is an effort to enable laypeople to more easily find, share, and combine information available on the Web. In this vision, the information can be readily interpreted by machines, so machines can perform more of the tedious work involved in finding, combining, and acting upon information on the Web. Several technologies are necessary to provide a formal description of concepts, terms, and relationships within a given knowledge domain; they include the Resource Description Framework (RDF), a variety of data interchange formats, and notations such as RDF Schema (RDFS) and the Web Ontology Language (OWL).

[1]The Web is dominated by unstructured or semistructured data, whereas the semantic Web advocates inclusion of semantic content in Web pages.

[2]The term *semantic Web* was coined by Tim Berners-Lee to describe "a web of data that can be processed directly and indirectly by machines." It is a framework for data sharing among applications based on the Resource Description Framework (RDF). The semantic Web is "largely unrealized," according to Berners-Lee.

Gradually, the need to make computing more affordable and to liberate users from the concerns regarding system and software maintenance reinforced the idea of concentrating computing resources in data centers. Initially, these centers were specialized, each running a limited palette of software systems as well as applications developed by the users of these systems. In the early 1980s major research organizations such as the National Laboratories and large companies had powerful computing centers supporting large user populations scattered throughout wide geographic areas. Then the idea to link such centers in an infrastructure resembling the power grid was born; the model known as network-centric computing was taking shape.

A *computing grid* is a distributed system consisting of a large number of loosely coupled, heterogeneous, and geographically dispersed systems in different administrative domains. The term *computing grid* is a metaphor for accessing computer power with similar ease as we access power provided by the electric grid. Software libraries known as *middleware* have been furiously developed since the early 1990s to facilitate access to grid services.

The vision of the grid movement was to give a user the illusion of a very large virtual supercomputer. The autonomy of the individual systems and the fact that these systems were connected by wide-area networks with latency higher than the latency of the interconnection network of a supercomputer posed serious challenges to this vision. Nevertheless, several "Grand Challenge" problems, such as protein folding, financial modeling, earthquake simulation, and climate and weather modeling, run successfully on specialized grids. The Enabling Grids for Escience project is arguably the largest computing grid; along with the LHC Computing Grid (LCG), the Escience project aims to support the experiments using the Large Hadron Collider (LHC) at CERN which generate several gigabytes of data per second, or 10 PB (petabytes) per year.

In retrospect, two basic assumptions about the infrastructure prevented the grid movement from having the impact its supporters were hoping for. The first is the heterogeneity of the individual systems interconnected by the grid; the second is that systems in different administrative domains are expected to cooperate seamlessly. Indeed, the heterogeneity of the hardware and of system software poses significant challenges for application development and for application mobility. At the same time, critical areas of system management, including scheduling, optimization of resource allocation, load balancing, and fault tolerance, are extremely difficult in a heterogeneous system. The fact that resources are in different administrative domains further complicates many already difficult problems related to security and resource management. Although very popular in the science and engineering communities, the grid movement did not address the major concerns of the enterprise computing communities and did not make a noticeable impact on the IT industry.

Cloud computing is a technology largely viewed as the next big step in the development and deployment of an increasing number of distributed applications. The companies promoting cloud computing seem to have learned the most important lessons from the grid movement. Computer clouds are typically homogeneous. An entire cloud shares the same security, resource management, cost and other policies, and last but not least, it targets enterprise computing. These are some of the reasons that several agencies of the US Government, including Health and Human Services (HHS), the Centers for Disease Control (CDC), the National Aeronautics and Space Administration (NASA), the Navy's Next Generation Enterprise Network (NGEN), and the Defense Information Systems Agency (DISA), have launched cloud computing initiatives and conduct actual system development intended to improve the efficiency and effectiveness of their information processing needs.

The term *content* refers to any type or volume of media, be it static or dynamic, monolithic or modular, live or stored, produced by aggregation, or mixed. *Information* is the result of functions applied to content. The creation and consumption of audio and visual content are likely to transform the Internet to support increased quality in terms of resolution, frame rate, color depth, and stereoscopic information, and it seems reasonable to assume that the Future Internet[3] will be content-centric. The content should be treated as having meaningful semantic connotations rather than a string of bytes; the focus will be the information that can be extracted by content mining when users request named data and content providers publish data objects. Content-centric routing will allow users to fetch the desired data from the most suitable location in terms of network latency or download time. There are also some challenges, such as providing secure services for content manipulation, ensuring global rights management, control over unsuitable content, and reputation management.

Network-centric computing and network-centric content share a number of characteristics:

- Most applications are data-intensive. Computer simulation becomes a powerful tool for scientific research in virtually all areas of science, from physics, biology, and chemistry to archeology. Sophisticated tools for computer-aided design, such as Catia (Computer Aided Three-dimensional Interactive Application), are widely used in the aerospace and automotive industries. The widespread use of sensors contributes to increases in the volume of data. Multimedia applications are increasingly popular; the ever-larger media increase the load placed on storage, networking, and processing systems.
- Virtually all applications are network-intensive. Indeed, transferring large volumes of data requires high-bandwidth networks; parallel computing, computation steering,[4] and data streaming are examples of applications that can only run efficiently on low-latency networks.
- The systems are accessed using *thin clients* running on systems with limited resources. In June 2011 Google released Google Chrome OS, designed to run on primitive devices and based on the browser with the same name.
- The infrastructure supports some form of workflow management. Indeed, complex computational tasks require coordination of several applications; composition of services is a basic tenet of Web 2.0.

The advantages of network-centric computing and network-centric content paradigms are, at the same time, sources for concern; we discuss some of them:

- Computing and communication resources (CPU cycles, storage, network bandwidth) are shared and resources can be aggregated to support data-intensive applications. Multiplexing leads to a higher resource utilization; indeed, when multiple applications share a system, their peak demands for resources are not synchronized and the average system utilization increases. On the other hand, the management of large pools of resources poses new challenges as complex systems are subject to phase transitions. New resource management strategies, such as self-organization, and decisions based on approximate knowledge of the state of the system must be considered. Ensuring quality-of-service (QoS) guarantees is extremely challenging in such environments because total performance isolation is elusive.

[3]The term *Future Internet* is a generic concept referring to all research and development activities involved in the development of new architectures and protocols for the Internet.

[4]Computation steering in numerical simulation means to interactively guide a computational experiment toward a region of interest.

- Data sharing facilitates collaborative activities. Indeed, many applications in science, engineering, and industrial, financial, and governmental applications require multiple types of analysis of shared data sets and multiple decisions carried out by groups scattered around the globe. Open software development sites are another example of such collaborative activities. Data sharing poses not only security and privacy challenges but also requires mechanisms for access control by authorized users and for detailed logs of the history of data changes.
- Cost reduction. Concentration of resources creates the opportunity to pay as you go for computing and thus eliminates the initial investment and reduces significantly the maintenance and operation costs of the local computing infrastructure.
- User convenience and elasticity, that is the ability to accommodate workloads with very large peak-to-average ratios.

It is very hard to point out a single technological or architectural development that triggered the movement toward network-centric computing and network-centric content. This movement is the result of a cumulative effect of developments in microprocessor, storage, and networking technologies coupled with architectural advancements in all these areas and, last but not least, with advances in software systems, tools, programming languages, and algorithms to support distributed and parallel computing.

Through the years we have witnessed the breathtaking evolution of solid-state technologies which led to the development of multicore and many-core processors. Quad-core processors such as the AMD Phenom II X4, the Intel i3, i5, and i7 and hexa-core processors such as the AMD Phenom II X6 and Intel Core i7 Extreme Edition 980X are now used in the servers populating computer clouds. The proximity of multiple cores on the same die allows the cache coherency circuitry to operate at a much higher clock rate than would be possible if the signals were to travel off-chip.

Storage technology has also evolved dramatically. For example, solid-state disks such as RamSan-440 allow systems to manage very high transaction volumes and larger numbers of concurrent users. RamSan-440 uses DDR2 (double-data-rate) RAM to deliver 600,000 sustained random input/output operations per second (IOPS) and over 4 GB/s of sustained random `read` or `write` bandwidth, with latency of less than 15 microseconds, and it is available in 256 GB and 512 GB configurations. The price of memory has dropped significantly; at the time of this writing the price of a 1 GB module for a PC is approaching $10. Optical storage technologies and Flash memories are widely used nowadays.

The thinking in software engineering has also evolved and new models have emerged. The *three-tier model* is a software architecture and a software design pattern. The *presentation tier* is the topmost level of the application; typically, it runs on a desktop PC or workstation, uses a standard graphical user interface (GUI) and displays information related to services such as browsing merchandise, purchasing products, and managing shopping cart contents. The presentation tier communicates with other tiers by sending the results to the browser/client tier and all other tiers in the network. The *application/logic tier* controls the functionality of an application and may consist of one or more separate modules running on a workstation or application server; it may be multitiered itself, in which case the architecture is called an *n-tier architecture*. The *data tier* controls the servers where the information is stored; it runs a relational database management system (RDBMS) on a database server or a mainframe and contains the computer data storage logic. The data tier keeps data independent from application servers or processing logic and improves scalability and performance. Any of the tiers can be replaced independently; for example, a change of operating system in the presentation tier would only affect the user interface code.

1.2 Peer-to-peer systems

The distributed systems discussed in Chapter 2 allow access to resources in a tightly controlled environment. System administrators enforce security rules and control the allocation of physical rather than virtual resources. In all models of network-centric computing prior to utility computing, a user maintains direct control of the software and the data residing on remote systems.

This user-centric model, in place since the early 1960s, was challenged in the 1990s by the peer-to-peer (P2P) model. P2P systems can be regarded as one of the precursors of today's clouds. This new model for distributed computing promoted the idea of low-cost access to storage and central processing unit (CPU) cycles provided by participant systems; in this case, the resources are located in different administrative domains. Often the P2P systems are self-organizing and decentralized, whereas the servers in a cloud are in a single administrative domain and have a central management.

P2P systems exploit the network infrastructure to provide access to distributed computing resources. Decentralized applications developed in the 1980s, such as Simple Mail Transfer Protocol (SMTP), a protocol for email distribution, and Network News Transfer Protocol (NNTP), an application protocol for dissemination of news articles, are early examples of P2P systems. Systems developed in the late 1990s, such as the music-sharing system Napster, gave participants access to storage distributed over the network, while the first volunteer-based scientific computing, SETI@home, used free cycles of participating systems to carry out compute-intensive tasks.

The P2P model represents a significant departure from the client-server model, the cornerstone of distributed applications for several decades. P2P systems have several desirable properties [306]:

- They require a minimally dedicated infrastructure, since resources are contributed by the participating systems.
- They are highly decentralized.
- They are scalable; the individual nodes are not required to be aware of the global state.
- They are resilient to faults and attacks, since few of their elements are critical for the delivery of service and the abundance of resources can support a high degree of replication.
- Individual nodes do not require excessive network bandwidth the way servers used in case of the client-server model do.
- Last but not least, the systems are shielded from censorship due to the dynamic and often unstructured system architecture.

The undesirable properties of peer-to-peer systems are also notable: Decentralization raises the question of whether P2P systems can be managed effectively and provide the security required by various applications. The fact that they are shielded from censorship makes them a fertile ground for illegal activities, including distribution of copyrighted content.

In spite of its problems, the new paradigm was embraced by applications other than file sharing. Since 1999 new P2P applications such as the ubiquitous Skype, a Voice-over-Internet Protocol (VoIP) telephony service,[5] data-streaming applications such as Cool Streaming [386] and BBC's online video

[5]Skype allows close to 700 million registered users from many countries around the globe to communicate using a proprietary VoIP protocol. The system developed in 2003 by Niklas Zennström and Julius Friis was acquired by Microsoft in 2011 and nowadays is a hybrid P2P and client-server system.

service, content distribution networks such as CoDeeN [368], and volunteer computing applications based on the Berkeley Open Infrastructure for Networking Computing (BOINC) platform [21] have proved their appeal to users. For example, Skype reported in 2008 that 276 million registered Skype users have used more than 100 billion minutes for voice and video calls. The site `www.boinc.berkeley.edu` reports that at the end of June 2012 volunteer computing involved more than 275,000 individuals and more than 430,000 computers providing a monthly average of almost 6.3 petaFLOPS. It is also reported that peer-to-peer traffic accounts for a very large fraction of Internet traffic, with estimates ranging from 40% to more than 70%.

Many groups from industry and academia rushed to develop and test new ideas, taking advantage of the fact that P2P applications do not require a dedicated infrastructure. Applications such as *Chord* [334] and *Credence* [366] address issues critical to the effective operation of decentralized systems. *Chord* is a distributed lookup protocol to identify the node where a particular data item is stored. The routing tables are distributed and, whereas other algorithms for locating an object require the nodes to be aware of most of the nodes of the network, *Chord* maps a key related to an object to a node of the network using routing information about a few nodes only.

Credence is an object reputation and ranking scheme for large-scale P2P file-sharing systems. Reputation is of paramount importance for systems that often include many unreliable and malicious nodes. In the decentralized algorithm used by *Credence*, each client uses local information to evaluate the reputation of other nodes and shares its own assessment with its neighbors. The credibility of a node depends only on the votes it casts; each node computes the reputation of another node based solely on the degree of matching with its own votes and relies on like-minded peers. *Overcite* [337] is a P2P application to aggregate documents based on a three-tier design. The Web front-ends accept queries and display the results while servers crawl through the Web to generate indexes and to perform keyword searches; the Web back-ends store documents, meta-data, and coordination state on the participating systems.

The rapid acceptance of the new paradigm triggered the development of a new communication protocol allowing hosts at the network periphery to cope with the limited network bandwidth available to them. *BitTorrent* is a peer-to-peer file-sharing protocol that enables a node to download/upload large files from/to several hosts simultaneously.

The P2P systems differ in their architecture. Some do not have any centralized infrastructure, whereas others have a dedicated controller, but this controller is not involved in resource-intensive operations. For example, Skype has a central site to maintain user accounts; users sign in and pay for specific activities at this site. The controller for a BOINC platform maintains membership and is involved in task distribution to participating systems. The nodes with abundant resources in systems without any centralized infrastructure often act as *supernodes* and maintain information useful to increasing the system efficiency, such as indexes of the available content.

Regardless of the architecture, P2P systems are built around an *overlay network*, a virtual network superimposed over the real network. Methods to construct such an overlay, discussed in Section 7.10, consider a graph $G = (V, E)$, where V is the set of N vertices and E is the set of links between them.

Each node maintains a table of *overlay links* connecting it with other nodes of this virtual network, each node being identified by its IP address. Two types of overlay networks, unstructured and structured, are used by P2P systems. Random walks starting from a few bootstrap nodes are usually used by systems desiring to join an unstructured overlay. Each node of a structured overlay has a unique key that determines its position in the structure; the keys are selected to guarantee a uniform distribution in a very large name space. Structured overlay networks use *key-based routing* (KBR); given a starting node v_0 and a key k, the function $KBR(v_0, k)$ returns the path in the graph from v_0 to the vertex with key k. Epidemic algorithms discussed in Section 7.12 are often used by unstructured overlays to disseminate network topology.

1.3 Cloud computing: an old idea whose time has come

Once the technological elements were in place, it was only a matter of time until the economical advantages of cloud computing became apparent. Due to the economy of scale, large data centers – centers with more than 50,000 systems – are more economical to operate than medium-sized centers that have around 1,000 systems. Large data centers equipped with commodity computers experience a five to seven times decrease of resource consumption, including energy, compared to medium-sized centers [25]. The networking costs, in dollars per Mbit/s/month, are $95/13 = 7.1$ times larger, and the storage costs, in dollars per Gbyte/month, are $2.2/0.4 = 5.7$ times larger for medium-sized centers. Medium-sized centers have a larger administrative overhead – one system administrator for 140 systems versus one for 1,000 systems for large centers.

Data centers are very large consumers of electric energy to keep servers and the networking infrastructure running and for cooling. For example, there are 6,000 data centers in the United States and in 2006 they reportedly consumed 61 billion KWh, 1.5% of all electric energy in the U.S., at a cost of $4.5 billion. The power demanded by data centers was predicted to double from 2006 to 2011. Peak instantaneous demand was predicted to increase from 7 GW in 2006 to 12 GW in 2011, requiring the construction of 10 new power plants. In the United States the energy costs differ from state to state; for example 1 KWh costs 3.6 cents in Idaho, 10 cents in California, and 18 cents in Hawaii. Thus, data centers should be placed at sites with low energy cost.

The term *computer cloud* is overloaded, since it covers infrastructures of different sizes, with different management and different user populations. Several types of cloud are envisioned:

- *Private cloud.* The infrastructure is operated solely for an organization. It may be managed by the organization or a third party and may exist on or off the premises of the organization.
- *Community cloud.* The infrastructure is shared by several organizations and supports a specific community that has shared concerns (e.g., mission, security requirements, policy, and compliance considerations). It may be managed by the organizations or a third party and may exist on premises or off premises.
- *Public cloud.* The infrastructure is made available to the general public or a large industry group and is owned by an organization selling cloud services.
- *Hybrid cloud.* The infrastructure is a composition of two or more clouds (private, community, or public) that remain unique entities but are bound together by standardized or proprietary technology that enables data and application portability (e.g., cloud bursting for load balancing between clouds).

A private cloud could provide the computing resources needed for a large organization, such as a research institution, a university, or a corporation. The argument that a private cloud does not support utility computing is based on the observation that an organization has to invest in the infrastructure and a user of a private cloud pays as it consumes resources [25]. Nevertheless, a private cloud could use the same hardware infrastructure as a public one; its security requirements will be different from those for a public cloud and the software running on the cloud is likely to be restricted to a specific domain.

A natural question to ask is: Why could cloud computing be successful when other paradigms have failed? The reasons that cloud computing could be successful can be grouped into several general categories: technological advances, a realistic system model, user convenience, and financial advantages. A nonexhaustive list of reasons for the success of cloud computing includes these points:

- Cloud computing is in a better position to exploit recent advances in software, networking, storage, and processor technologies. Cloud computing is promoted by large IT companies where these new technological developments take place, and these companies have a vested interest in promoting the new technologies.
- A cloud consists of a homogeneous set of hardware and software resources in a single administrative domain. In this setup, security, resource management, fault tolerance, and quality of service are less challenging than in a heterogeneous environment with resources in multiple administrative domains.
- Cloud computing is focused on enterprise computing; its adoption by industrial organizations, financial institutions, healthcare organizations, and so on has a potentially huge impact on the economy.
- A cloud provides the illusion of infinite computing resources; its elasticity frees application designers from the confinement of a single system.
- A cloud eliminates the need for up-front financial commitment, and it is based on a pay-as-you-go approach. This has the potential to attract new applications and new users for existing applications, fomenting a new era of industrywide technological advancements.

In spite of the technological breakthroughs that have made cloud computing feasible, there are still major obstacles for this new technology; these obstacles provide opportunity for research. We list a few of the most obvious obstacles:

- *Availability of service.* What happens when the service provider cannot deliver? Can a large company such as General Motors move its IT to the cloud and have assurances that its activity will not be negatively affected by cloud overload? A partial answer to this question is provided by service-level agreements (SLAs).[6] A temporary fix with negative economical implications is *overprovisioning*, that is, having enough resources to satisfy the largest projected demand.
- *Vendor lock-in.* Once a customer is hooked to one provider, it is hard to move to another. The standardization efforts at National Institute of Standards and Technology (NIST) attempt to address this problem.
- *Data confidentiality and auditability.* This is indeed a serious problem; we analyze it in Chapter 9.
- *Data transfer bottlenecks.* Many applications are data-intensive. A very important strategy is to store the data as close as possible to the site where it is needed. Transferring 1 TB of data on a 1 Mbps network takes 8 million seconds, or about 10 days; it is faster and cheaper to use courier service and send data recoded on some media than to send it over the network. Very high-speed networks will alleviate this problem in the future; for example, a 1 Gbps network would reduce this time to 8,000 s, or slightly more than 2 h.

[6]SLAs are discussed in Section 3.8.

- *Performance unpredictability.* This is one of the consequences of resource sharing. Strategies for performance isolation are discussed in Section 5.5.
- *Elasticity, the ability to scale up and down quickly.* New algorithms for controlling resource allocation and workload placement are necessary. Autonomic computing based on self-organization and self-management seems to be a promising avenue.

There are other perennial problems with no clear solutions at this time, including software licensing and system bugs.

1.4 Cloud computing delivery models and services

According to the NIST reference model in Figure 1.2 [260], the entities involved in cloud computing are the *service consumer*, the entity that maintains a business relationship with and uses service from service providers; the *service provider*, the entity responsible for making a service available to service consumers; the *carrier*, the intermediary that provides connectivity and transport of cloud services between providers and consumers; the *broker*, an entity that manages the use, performance, and delivery of cloud services and negotiates relationships between providers and consumers; and the *auditor*, a party that can conduct independent assessment of cloud services, information system operations, performance, and security of the cloud implementation. An *audit* is a systematic evaluation of a cloud system that measures how well it conforms to a set of established criteria. For example, a security audit evaluates

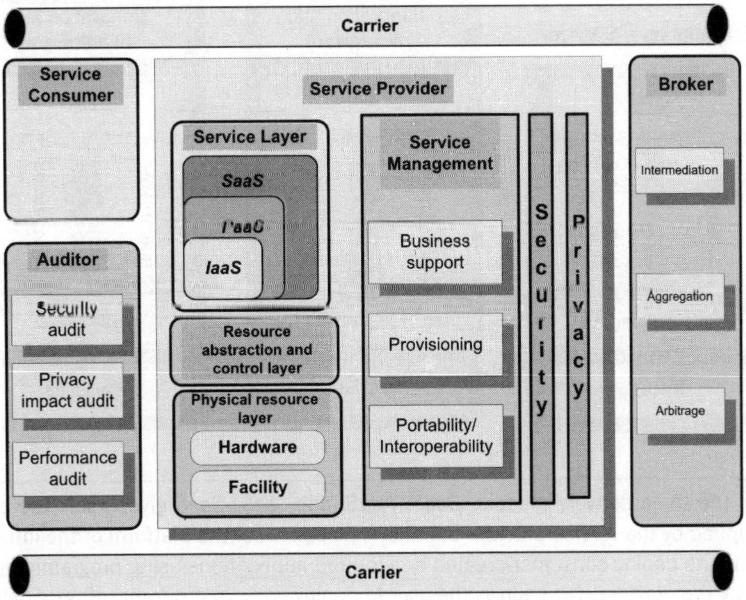

FIGURE 1.2

The entities involved in service-oriented computing and, in particular, in cloud computing, according to NIST. The carrier provides connectivity among service providers, service consumers, brokers, and auditors.

cloud security, a privacy-impact audit evaluates cloud privacy assurance, and a performance audit evaluates cloud performance.

We start with the observation that it is difficult to distinguish the services associated with cloud computing from those that any computer operations center would include [332]. Many of the services discussed in this section could be provided by a cloud architecture, but note that they are available in noncloud architectures as well.

Figure 1.3 presents the structure of the three delivery models, *SaaS*, *PaaS*, and *IaaS*, according to the Cloud Security Alliance [98].

Software-as-a-Service (SaaS) gives the capability to use applications supplied by the service provider in a cloud infrastructure. The applications are accessible from various client devices through a thin-client

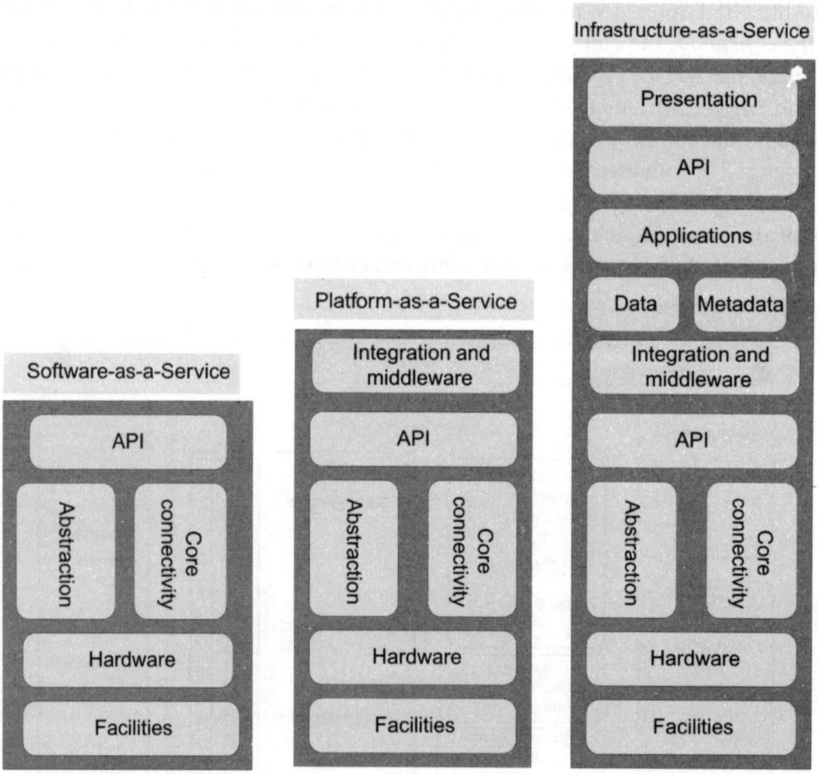

FIGURE 1.3

The structure of the three delivery models, *SaaS*, *PaaS*, and *IaaS*. *SaaS* gives users the capability to use applications supplied by the service provider but allows no control of the platform or the infrastructure. *PaaS* gives the capability to deploy consumer-created or acquired applications using programming languages and tools supported by the provider. *IaaS* allows the user to deploy and run arbitrary software, which can include operating systems and applications.

interface such as a Web browser (e.g., Web-based email). The user does not manage or control the underlying cloud infrastructure, including network, servers, operating systems, storage, or even individual application capabilities, with the possible exception of limited user-specific application configuration settings. Services offered include:

- Enterprise services such as workflow management, groupware and collaborative, supply chain, communications, digital signature, customer relationship management (CRM), desktop software, financial management, geo-spatial, and search [32].
- Web 2.0 applications such as metadata management, social networking, blogs, wiki services, and portal services.

The *SaaS* is not suitable for applications that require real-time response or those for which data is not allowed to be hosted externally. The most likely candidates for *SaaS* are applications for which:

- Many competitors use the same product, such as email.
- Periodically there is a significant peak in demand, such as billing and payroll.
- There is a need for Web or mobile access, such as mobile sales management software.
- There is only a short-term need, such as collaborative software for a project.

Platform-as-a-Service (PaaS) gives the capability to deploy consumer-created or acquired applications using programming languages and tools supported by the provider. The user does not manage or control the underlying cloud infrastructure, including network, servers, operating systems, or storage. The user has control over the deployed applications and, possibly, over the application hosting environment configurations. Such services include session management, device integration, sandboxes, instrumentation and testing, contents management, knowledge management, and Universal Description, Discovery, and Integration (UDDI), a platform-independent Extensible Markup Language (XML)-based registry providing a mechanism to register and locate Web service applications.

PaaS is not particulary useful when the application must be portable, when proprietary programming languages are used, or when the underlaying hardware and software must be customized to improve the performance of the application. The major *PaaS* application areas are in software development where multiple developers and users collaborate and the deployment and testing services should be automated.

Infrastructure-as-a-Service (IaaS) is the capability to provision processing, storage, networks, and other fundamental computing resources; the consumer is able to deploy and run arbitrary software, which can include operating systems and applications. The consumer does not manage or control the underlying cloud infrastructure but has control over operating systems, storage, deployed applications, and possibly limited control of some networking components, such as host firewalls. Services offered by this delivery model include: server hosting, Web servers, storage, computing hardware, operating systems, virtual instances, load balancing, Internet access, and bandwidth provisioning.

The *IaaS* cloud computing delivery model has a number of characteristics, such as the fact that the resources are distributed and support dynamic scaling, it is based on a utility pricing model and variable cost, and the hardware is shared among multiple users. This cloud computing model is particulary useful when the demand is volatile and a new business needs computing resources and does not want to invest in a computing infrastructure or when an organization is expanding rapidly.

A number of activities are necessary to support the three delivery models; they include:

1. Service management and provisioning, including virtualization, service provisioning, call center, operations management, systems management, QoS management, billing and accounting, asset management, SLA management, technical support, and backups.
2. Security management, including ID and authentication, certification and accreditation, intrusion prevention, intrusion detection, virus protection, cryptography, physical security, incident response, access control, audit and trails, and firewalls.
3. Customer services such as customer assistance and online help, subscriptions, business intelligence, reporting, customer preferences, and personalization.
4. Integration services, including data management and development.

This list shows that a service-oriented architecture involves multiple subsystems and complex interactions among these subsystems. Individual subsystems can be layered; for example, in Figure 1.2 we see that the service layer sits on top of a resource abstraction layer, which controls the physical resource layer.

1.5 Ethical issues in cloud computing

Cloud computing is based on a paradigm shift with profound implications for computing ethics. The main elements of this shift are: (i) the control is relinquished to third-party services; (ii) the data is stored on multiple sites administered by several organizations; and (iii) multiple services interoperate across the network.

Unauthorized access, data corruption, infrastructure failure, and service unavailability are some of the risks related to relinquishing the control to third-party services; moreover, whenever a problem occurs, it is difficult to identify the source and the entity causing it. Systems can span the boundaries of multiple organizations and cross security borders, a process called *deperimeterization*. As a result of deperimeterization, "not only the border of the organization's IT infrastructure blurs, also the border of the accountability becomes less clear" [350].

The complex structure of cloud services can make it difficult to determine who is responsible in case something undesirable happens. In a complex chain of events or systems, many entities contribute to an action, with undesirable consequences. Some of them have the opportunity to prevent these consequences, and therefore no one can be held responsible – the so-called "problem of many hands."

Ubiquitous and unlimited data sharing and storage among organizations test the self-determination of information, the right or ability of individuals to exercise personal control over the collection, and use and disclosure of their personal data by others; this tests the confidence and trust in today's evolving information society. Identity fraud and theft are made possible by the unauthorized access to personal data in circulation and by new forms of dissemination through social networks, which could also pose a danger to cloud computing.

Cloud service providers have already collected petabytes of sensitive personal information stored in data centers around the world. The acceptance of cloud computing therefore will be determined by privacy issues addressed by these companies and the countries where the data centers are located. Privacy is affected by cultural differences; though some cultures favor privacy, other cultures emphasize community, and this leads to an ambivalent attitude toward privacy on the Internet, which is a global system.

The question of what can be done proactively about ethics of cloud computing does not have easy answers; many undesirable phenomena in cloud computing will only appear in time. However, the need for rules and regulations for the governance of cloud computing is obvious. The term *governance* means the manner in which something is governed or regulated, the method of management, or the system of regulations. Explicit attention to ethics must be paid by governmental organizations providing research funding for cloud computing; private companies are less constrained by ethics oversight and governance arrangements are more conducive to profit generation.

Accountability is a necessary ingredient of cloud computing; adequate information about how data is handled within the cloud and about allocation of responsibility are key elements for enforcing ethics rules in cloud computing. Recorded evidence allows us to assign responsibility; but there can be tension between privacy and accountability, and it is important to establish what is being recorded and who has access to the records.

Unwanted dependency on a cloud service provider, the so-called *vendor lock-in*, is a serious concern, and the current standardization efforts at NIST attempt to address this problem. Another concern for users is a future with only a handful of companies that dominate the market and dictate prices and policies.

1.6 Cloud vulnerabilities

Clouds are affected by malicious attacks and failures of the infrastructure (e.g., power failures). Such events can affect Internet domain name servers and prevent access to a cloud or can directly affect the clouds. For example, an attack at Akamai on June 15, 2004 caused a domain name outage and a major blackout that affected Google, Yahoo!, and many other sites. In May 2009 Google was the target of a serious denial-of-service (DoS) attack that took down services such Google News and Gmail for several days.

Lightning caused a prolonged downtime at Amazon on June 29 and 30, 2012; the *AWS* cloud in the Eastern region of the United States, which consists of 10 data centers across four availability zones, was initially troubled by utility power fluctuations, probably caused by an electrical storm. A June 29, 2012 storm on the East Coast took down some Virginia-based Amazon facilities and affected companies using systems exclusively in this region. *Instagram*, a photo sharing service, was one of the victims of this outage, according to `http://mashable.com/2012/06/30/aws-instagram/`.

The recovery from the failure took a very long time and exposed a range of problems. For example, one of the 10 centers failed to switch to backup generators before exhausting the power that could be supplied by *uninterruptible power supply* (UPS) units. *AWS* uses "control planes" to allow users to switch to resources in a different region, and this software component also failed. The booting process was faulty and extended the time to restart *EC2* (*Elastic Computing*) and *EBS* (*Elastic Block Store*) services. Another critical problem was a bug in the elastic load balancer (ELB), which is used to route traffic to servers with available capacity. A similar bug affected the recovery process of the Relational Database Service (RDS). This event brought to light "hidden" problems that occur only under special circumstances.

A recent paper [126] identifies stability risks due to interacting services. A cloud application provider, a cloud storage provider, and a network provider could implement different policies, and the unpredictable interactions between load-balancing and other reactive mechanisms could lead to dynamic instabilities. The unintended coupling of independent controllers that manage the load, the power consumption, and the elements of the infrastructure could lead to undesirable feedback and instability similar to the ones experienced by the policy-based routing in the Internet Border Gateway Protocol (BGP). For example, the load balancer of an application provider could interact with the power optimizer of the infrastructure provider. Some of these couplings may only manifest under extreme conditions and be very hard to detect under normal operating conditions, but they could have disastrous consequences when the system attempts to recover from a hard failure, as in the case of the *AWS* 2012 failure.

Clustering the resources in data centers located in different geographical areas is one of the means used today to lower the probability of catastrophic failures. This geographic dispersion of resources could have additional positive side effects; it can reduce communication traffic and energy costs by dispatching the computations to sites where the electric energy is cheaper, and it can improve performance by an intelligent and efficient load-balancing strategy. Sometimes a user has the option to decide where to run an application; we shall see in Section 3.1 that an *AWS* user has the option to choose the regions where the instances of his or her applications will run, as well as the regions of the storage sites. System objectives (e.g., maximize throughput, resource utilization, and financial benefits) have to be carefully balanced with user needs (e.g., low cost and response time and maximum availability).

The price to pay for any system optimization is increased system complexity, as we shall see in Section 10.7. For example, the latency of communication over a wide area network (WAN) is considerably larger than the one over a local area network (LAN) and requires the development of new algorithms for global decision making.

1.7 Major challenges faced by cloud computing

Cloud computing inherits some of the challenges of parallel and distributed computing discussed in Chapter 2; at the same time, it faces major challenges of its own. The specific challenges differ for the three cloud delivery models, but in all cases the difficulties are created by the very nature of utility computing, which is based on resource sharing and resource virtualization and requires a different trust model than the ubiquitous user-centric model we have been accustomed to for a very long time.

The most significant challenge is security [19]; gaining the trust of a large user base is critical for the future of cloud computing. It is unrealistic to expect that a public cloud will provide a suitable environment for all applications. Highly sensitive applications related to the management of the critical infrastructure, healthcare applications, and others will most likely be hosted by private clouds. Many real-time applications will probably still be confined to private clouds. Some applications may be best served by a hybrid cloud setup; such applications could keep sensitive data on a private cloud and use a public cloud for some of the processing.

The *SaaS* model faces similar challenges as other online services required to protect private information, such as financial or healthcare services. In this case a user interacts with cloud services through a well-defined interface; thus, in principle it is less challenging for the service provider to close some of the attack channels. Still, such services are vulnerable to DoS attack and the users are fearful of malicious insiders. Data in storage is most vulnerable to attack, so special attention should be devoted to the protection of storage servers. Data replication necessary to ensure continuity of service in case of storage system failure increases vulnerability. Data encryption may protect data in storage, but eventually data must be decrypted for processing, and then it is exposed to attack.

The *IaaS* model is by far the most challenging to defend against attacks. Indeed, an *IaaS* user has considerably more degrees of freedom than the other two cloud delivery models. An additional source of concern is that the considerable resources of a cloud could be used to initiate attacks against the network and the computing infrastructure.

Virtualization is a critical design option for this model, but it exposes the system to new sources of attack. The trusted computing base (TCB) of a virtual environment includes not only the hardware and the hypervisor but also the management operating system. As we shall see in Section 9.7, the entire state of a virtual machine (VM) can be saved to a file to allow migration and recovery, both highly desirable operations; yet this possibility challenges the strategies to bring the servers belonging to an organization to a desirable and stable state. Indeed, an infected VM can be inactive when the systems are cleaned up, and it can wake up later and infect other systems. This is another example of the deep intertwining of desirable and undesirable effects of basic cloud computing technologies.

The next major challenge is related to resource management on a cloud. Any systematic rather than ad hoc resource management strategy requires the existence of controllers tasked to implement several classes of policies: admission control, capacity allocation, load balancing, energy optimization, and last but not least, to provide QoS guarantees.

To implement these policies the controllers need accurate information about the global state of the system. Determining the state of a complex system with 10^6 servers or more, distributed over a large geographic area, is not feasible. Indeed, the external load, as well as the state of individual resources, changes very rapidly. Thus, controllers must be able to function with incomplete or approximate knowledge of the system state.

It seems reasonable to expect that such a complex system can only function based on self-management principles. But self-management and self-organization raise the bar for the implementation of logging and auditing procedures critical to the security and trust in a provider of cloud computing services. Under self-management it becomes next to impossible to identify the reasons that a certain action that resulted in a security breach was taken.

The last major challenge we want to address is related to interoperability and standardization. Vendor lock-in, the fact that a user is tied to a particular cloud service provider, is a major concern for cloud users (see Section 3.5). Standardization would support interoperability and thus alleviate some of the fears that a service critical for a large organization may not be available for an extended period of time. But imposing standards at a time when a technology is still evolving is not only challenging, it can be counterproductive because it may stifle innovation.

From this brief discussion the reader should realize the complexity of the problems posed by cloud computing and understand the wide range of technical and social problems cloud computing raises. If successful, the effort to migrate the IT activities of many government agencies to public and private clouds will have a lasting effect on cloud computing. Cloud computing can have a major impact on education, but we have seen little effort in this area.

1.8 Further reading

A very good starting point for understanding the major issues in cloud computing is the 2009 paper "Above the clouds: a Berkeley view of cloud computing" [25]. A comprehensive survey of peer-to-peer systems was published in 2010 [306]. Content distribution systems are discussed in [368]. The BOINC platform is presented in [21]. *Chord* [334] and *Credence* [366] are important references in the area of peer-to-peer systems.

Ethical issues in cloud computing are discussed in [350]. A recent book covers topics in the area of distributed systems, including grids, peer-to-peer systems, and clouds [173].

The standardization effort at NIST is described by a wealth of documents [259–267] on the Web site `http://collaborate.nist.gov`.

1.9 History notes

John McCarthy was a visionary in computer science; in the early 1960s he formulated the idea that computation may be organized as a public utility, like water and electricity. In 1992 Gordon Bell was invited to and delivered an address at a conference on parallel computations with the provocative title *Massively parallel computers: why not parallel computers for the masses?* [45]; he argued that one-of-a-kind systems are not only expensive to build, but the cost of rewriting applications for them is prohibitive.

Google Inc. was founded by Page and Brin, two graduate students in computer science at Stanford University; in 1998 the company was incorporated in California after receiving a contribution of $100, 000 from the co-founder and chief hardware designer of Sun Microsystems, Andy Bechtolsheim.

Amazon *EC2* was initially released as a limited public beta cloud computing service on August 25, 2006. The system was developed by a team from Cape Town, South Africa. In October 2008 Microsoft announced the *Windows Azure* platform; in June 2010 the platform became commercially available. *iCloud*, a cloud storage and cloud computing service from Apple Inc., stores content such as music, photos, calendars, and documents and allows users to access it from Apple devices. The system was announced on June 6, 2011. In 2012 the Oracle Cloud was announced (see `www.oracle.com/us/corporate/features/oracle-cloud/index.html`)

1.10 Exercises and problems

Problem 1. Mobile devices could benefit from cloud computing; explain the reasons you think that this statement is true or provide arguments supporting the contrary. Discuss several cloud applications for mobile devices, then explain which one of the three cloud computing delivery models, *SaaS*, *PaaS*, or *IaaS*, would be used by each one of the applications and why.

Problem 2. Do you believe that the homogeneity of large-scale distributed systems is an advantage? Discuss the reasons for your answer. What aspects of hardware homogeneity are the most relevant in your view, and why? What aspects of software homogeneity do you believe are the most relevant, and why?

Problem 3. Peer-to-peer systems and clouds share a few goals but not the means to accomplish them. Compare the two classes of systems in terms of architecture, resource management, scope, and security.

Problem 4. Compare the three cloud computing delivery models, *SaaS*, *PaaS*, and *IaaS*, from the point of view of application developers and users. Discuss the security and the reliability of each model. Analyze the differences between *PaaS* and *IaaS*.

Problem 5. *Overprovisioning* is the reliance on extra capacity to satisfy the needs of a large community of users when the average-to-peak resource demand ratio is very high. Give an example of a large-scale system using overprovisioning and discuss whether overprovisioning is sustainable in that case and what its limitations are. Is cloud elasticity based on overprovisioning sustainable? Give arguments to support your answer.

Problem 6. Discuss the possible solution for stabilizing cloud services mentioned in [126] inspired by BGP (Border Gateway Protocol) routing [145,359].

Problem 7. An organization debating whether to install a private cloud or to use a public cloud (e.g., the *AWS*) for its computational and storage needs asks for your advice. What information will you require to come to your recommendation, and how will you use each one of the following items? (a) The description of the algorithms and the type of the applications the organization will run; (b) the system software used by these applications; (c) the resources needed by each application; (d) the size of the user population; and (e) the relative experience of the user population; and (f) the costs involved.

Problem 8. A university is debating the question in Problem 7. What will be your advice, and why? Should software licensing be an important element of the decision?

Problem 9. An IT company decides to provide free access to a public cloud dedicated to higher education. Which one of the three cloud computing delivery models, *SaaS*, *PaaS*, or *IaaS*, should it embrace, and why? What applications would be most beneficial for the students? Will this solution have an impact on distance learning? Why or why not?

CHAPTER

Parallel and Distributed Systems

2

Cloud computing is based on a large number of ideas and the experience accumulated since the first electronic computer was used to solve computationally challenging problems. In this chapter we overview parallel and distributed systems concepts that are important to understanding the basic challenges in the design and use of computer clouds.

Cloud computing is intimately tied to parallel and distributed computing. Cloud applications are based on the client-server paradigm with relatively simple software, a *thin client*, running on the user's machine while the computations are carried out on the cloud. Many cloud applications are data-intensive and use a number of instances that run concurrently. Transaction processing systems, such as Web-based services, represent a large class of applications hosted by computing clouds; such applications run multiple instances of the service and require reliable and in-order delivery of messages.

The concepts introduced in this section are very important in practice. Communication protocols support coordination of distributed processes and transport information through noisy and unreliable communication channels that may lose messages or deliver duplicate, distorted, or out-of-order messages. To ensure reliable and in-order delivery of messages, the protocols stamp each message with a sequence number; in turn, a receiver sends an acknowledgment with its own sequence number to confirm the receipt of a message. The clocks of a sender and a receiver may not be synchronized, so these sequence numbers act as logical clocks. Timeouts are used to request the retransmission of lost or delayed messages.

The concept of consistent cuts and distributed snapshots are at the heart of *checkpoint-restart* procedures for long-lasting computations. Indeed, many cloud computations are data-intensive and run for extended periods of time on multiple computers in the cloud. Checkpoints are taken periodically in anticipation of the need to restart a software process when one or more systems fail; when a failure occurs, the computation is restarted from the last checkpoint rather than from the beginning.

Many functions of a computer cloud require information provided by *monitors*, system components that collect state information from the individual systems. For example, controllers for cloud resource management, discussed in Chapter 6, require accurate state information; security and reliability can only be implemented using information provided by specialized monitors. Coordination of multiple instances is a critical function of an application controller.

2.1 Parallel computing

As demonstrated by nature, the ability to work in parallel as a group represents a very efficient way to reach a common target; human beings have learned to aggregate themselves and to assemble man-made devices in organizations in which each entity may have modest ability, but a network of entities can organize themselves to accomplish goals that an individual entity cannot. Thus, we should not be surprised that the thought that individual systems should work in concert to solve complex applications was formulated early on in the computer age.

Parallel computing allows us to solve large problems by splitting them into smaller ones and solving them concurrently. Parallel computing was considered for many years the "holy grail" for solving data-intensive problems encountered in many areas of science, engineering, and enterprise computing; it required major advances in several areas, including algorithms, programming languages and environments, performance monitoring, computer architecture, interconnection networks, and last but not least, solid-state technologies.

Parallel hardware and software systems allow us to solve problems demanding more resources than those provided by a single system and, at the same time, to reduce the time required to obtain a solution. The speed-up measures the effectiveness of parallelization; in the general case the *speed-up* of the parallel computation is defined as

$$S(N) = \frac{T(1)}{T(N)}, \tag{2.1}$$

with $T(1)$ the execution time of the sequential computation and $T(N)$ the execution time when N parallel computations are carried out. Amdahl's Law[1] gives the potential speed-up of a parallel computation; it states that the portion of the computation that cannot be parallelized determines the overall speed-up. If α is the fraction of running time a sequential program spends on nonparallelizable segments of the computation, then

$$S = \frac{1}{\alpha}. \tag{2.2}$$

To prove this result, call σ the sequential time and π the parallel time and start from the definitions of $T(1)$, $T(N)$, and α:

$$T(1) = \sigma + \pi, \quad T(N) = \sigma + \frac{\pi}{N}, \quad \text{and} \quad \alpha = \frac{\sigma}{\sigma + \pi}. \tag{2.3}$$

Then

$$S = \frac{T(1)}{T(N)} = \frac{\sigma + \pi}{\sigma + \pi/N} = \frac{1 + \pi/\sigma}{1 + (\pi/\sigma) \times (1/N)}. \tag{2.4}$$

But

$$\pi/\sigma = \frac{1 - \alpha}{\alpha}. \tag{2.5}$$

Thus, for large N

$$S = \frac{1 + (1 - \alpha)/\alpha}{1 + (1 - \alpha)/(N\alpha)} = \frac{1}{\alpha + (1 - \alpha)/N} \approx \frac{1}{\alpha}. \tag{2.6}$$

Amdahl's law applies to a *fixed problem size*; in this case the amount of work assigned to each one of the parallel processes decreases when the number of processes increases, and this affects the efficiency of the parallel execution.

[1] Gene Amdahl is a theoretical physicist turned computer architect who contributed significantly to the development of several IBM systems, including System/360, and then started his own company, Amdahl Corporation. His company produced high-performance systems in the 1970s. Amdahl is best known for Amdahl's Law, formulated in 1960.

When the problem size is allowed to change, Gustafson's Law gives the *scaled speed-up* with N parallel processes as

$$S(N) = N - \alpha(N-1). \tag{2.7}$$

As before, we call σ the sequential time; now π is the *fixed parallel time per process*; α is given by Equation 2.3. The sequential execution time, $T(1)$, and the parallel execution time with N parallel processes, $T(N)$, are

$$T(1) = \sigma + N\pi \quad \text{and} \quad T(N) = \sigma + \pi. \tag{2.8}$$

Then the scaled speed-up is

$$S(N) = \frac{T(1)}{T(N)} = \frac{\sigma + N\pi}{\sigma + \pi} = \frac{\sigma}{\sigma + \pi} + \frac{N\pi}{\sigma + \pi} = \alpha + N(1-\alpha) = N - \alpha(N-1). \tag{2.9}$$

Amdahl's Law expressed by Equation 2.2 and the *scaled speed-up* given by Equation 2.7 assume that all processes are assigned the same amount of work. The scaled speed-up assumes that the amount of work assigned to each process is the same, regardless of the problem size. Then, to maintain the same execution time, the number of parallel processes must increase with the problem size. The scaled speed-up captures the essence of efficiency, namely that the limitations of the sequential part of a code can be balanced by increasing the problem size.

Coordination of concurrent computations could be quite challenging and involves overhead, which ultimately reduces the speed-up of parallel computations. Often the parallel computation involves multiple stages, and all concurrent activities must finish one stage before starting the execution of the next one; this *barrier synchronization* further reduces the speed-up.

The subtasks of a parallel program are called *processes*, whereas *threads* are lightweight subtasks. Concurrent execution could be very challenging (e.g., it could lead to *race conditions*, an undesirable effect in which the results of concurrent execution depend on the sequence of events). Often, shared resources must be protected by *locks* to ensure serial access. Another potential problem for concurrent execution of multiple processes or threads is the presence of deadlocks; a *deadlock* occurs when processes or threads competing with one another for resources are forced to wait for additional resources held by other processes or threads and none of the processes or threads can finish. The four *Coffman conditions* must hold simultaneously for a deadlock to occur:

1. *Mutual exclusion.* At least one resource must be nonsharable, and only one process/thread may use the resource at any given time.
2. *Hold and wait.* At least one process/thread must hold one or more resources and wait for others.
3. *No preemption.* The scheduler or a monitor should not be able to force a process/thread holding a resource to relinquish it.
4. *Circular wait.* Given the set of n processes/threads $\{P_1, P_2, P_3, \ldots, P_n\}$, P_1 should wait for a resource held by P_2, P_2 should wait for a resource held by P_3, and so on and P_n should wait for a resource held by P_1.

There are other potential problems related to concurrency. When two or more processes or threads continually change their state in response to changes in the other processes, we have a *livelock* condition; the result is that none of the processes can complete its execution. Very often processes/threads running concurrently are assigned priorities and scheduled based on these priorities. *Priority inversion* occurs when a higher-priority process or task is indirectly preempted by a lower-priority one.

Concurrent processes/tasks can communicate using messages or shared memory. Multicore processors sometimes use shared memory, but the shared memory is seldom used in modern supercomputers because shared-memory systems are not scalable. Message passing is the communication method used exclusively in large-scale distributed systems, and our discussion is restricted to this communication paradigm.

Shared memory is extensively used by the system software; the stack is an example of shared memory used to save the state of a process or thread. The kernel of an operating system uses control structures such as processor and core tables for multiprocessor and multicore system management, process and thread tables for process/thread management, page tables for virtual memory management, and so on. Multiple application threads running on a multicore processor often communicate via the shared memory of the system. Debugging a message-passing application is considerably easier than debugging a shared memory application.

We distinguish *fine-grain* from *coarse-grain* parallelism; in the former case relatively small blocks of the code can be executed in parallel without the need to communicate or synchronize with other threads or processes, while in the latter case large blocks of code can be executed in parallel. The speed-up of applications displaying fine-grain parallelism is considerably lower than that of coarse-grained applications; indeed, the processor speed is orders of magnitude higher than the communication speed, even on systems with a fast interconnect.

In many cases, discovering parallelism is quite challenging, and the development of parallel algorithms requires a considerable effort. For example, many numerical analysis problems, such as solving large systems of linear equations or solving systems of partial differential equations (PDEs), requires algorithms based on domain decomposition methods.

Data parallelism is based on partitioning the data into several blocks and running multiple copies of the same program concurrently, each running on a different data block – thus the name of the paradigm, Same Program Multiple Data (SPMD).

Decomposition of a large problem into a set of smaller problems that can be solved concurrently is sometimes trivial. For example, assume that we want to manipulate the display of a three-dimensional object represented as a *3D* lattice of $(n \times n \times n)$ points; to rotate the image we would apply the same transformation to each one of the n^3 points. Such a transformation can be done by a geometric engine, a hardware component that can carry out the transformation of a subset of n^3 points concurrently.

Suppose that we want to search for the occurrence of an object in a set of n images, or of a string of characters in n records; such a search can be conducted in parallel. In all these instances the time required to carry out the computational task using N processing elements is reduced by a factor of N.

A very appealing class of applications of cloud computing is numerical simulations of complex systems that require an optimal design; in such instances multiple design alternatives must be compared and optimal ones selected based on several optimization criteria. Consider for example the design of a circuit using field programmable gate arrays (FPGAs). An FPGA is an integrated circuit designed to be configured by the customer using a hardware description language (HDL), similar to that used for an application-specific integrated circuit (ASIC). Because multiple choices for the placement of components and for interconnecting them exist, the designer could run concurrently N versions of the design choices and choose the one with the best performance, such as minimum power consumption. Alternative optimization objectives could be to reduce cross-talk among the wires or to minimize the overall noise. Each alternative configuration requires hours or maybe days of computing; hence, running them concurrently reduces the design time considerably.

The list of companies that aimed to support parallel computing and ended up as casualties of this effort is long and includes names such as Ardent, Convex, Encore, Floating Point Systems, Inmos, Kendall Square Research, MasPar, nCube, Sequent, Tandem, and Thinking Machines. The difficulties of developing new programming models and the effort to design programming environments for parallel applications added to the challenges faced by all these companies.

From the very beginning it was clear that parallel computing requires specialized hardware and system software. It was also clear that the interconnection fabric was critical for the performance of parallel computing systems. We now take a closer look at parallelism at different levels and the means to exploit it.

2.2 Parallel computer architecture

Our discussion of parallel computer architectures starts with the recognition that parallelism at different levels can be exploited. These levels are:

- *Bit-level parallelism.* The number of bits processed per clock cycle, often called a word size, has increased gradually from 4-bit processors to 8-bit, 16-bit, 32-bit, and, since 2004, 64-bit. This has reduced the number of instructions required to process larger operands and allowed a significant performance improvement. During this evolutionary process the number of address bits has also increased, allowing instructions to reference a larger address space.
- *Instruction-level parallelism.* Today's computers use multi-stage processing pipelines to speed up execution. Once an n-stage pipeline is full, an instruction is completed at every clock cycle. A "classic" pipeline of a Reduced Instruction Set Computing (RISC) architecture consists of five stages[2]: instruction fetch, instruction decode, instruction execution, memory access, and `write` back. A Complex Instruction Set Computing (CISC) architecture could have a much large number of pipelines stages; for example, an Intel Pentium 4 processor has a 35-stage pipeline.
- *Data parallelism or loop parallelism.* The program loops can be processed in parallel.
- *Task parallelism.* The problem can be decomposed into tasks that can be carried out concurrently. A widely used type of task parallelism is the Same Program Multiple Data (SPMD) paradigm. As the name suggests, individual processors run the same program but on different segments of the input data. Data dependencies cause different flows of control in individual tasks.

In 1966 Michael Flynn proposed a classification of computer architectures based on the number of *concurrent control/instruction* and *data streams*: Single Instruction, Single Data (SISD), Single Instruction, Multiple Data (SIMD), and (Multiple Instructions, Multiple Data (MIMD).[3]

The SIMD architecture supports vector processing. When an SIMD instruction is issued, the operations on individual vector components are carried out concurrently. For example, to add two vectors

[2]The number of pipeline stages in different RISC processors varies. For example, ARM7 and earlier implementations of ARM processors have a three-stage pipeline: fetch, decode, and execute. Higher performance designs, such as the ARM9, have deeper pipelines: Cortex-A8 has 13 stages.

[3]Another category, Multiple Instructions Single Data (MISD), is a fourth possible architecture, but it is very rarely used, mostly for fault tolerance.

$(a_1, a_2, \ldots, a_{50})$ and $(b_1, b_2, \ldots, b_{50})$, all 50 pairs of vector elements are added concurrently and all the sums $(a_i + b_i)$, $1 \leqslant i \leqslant 50$ are available at the same time.

The first use of SIMD instructions was in vector supercomputers such as the CDC Star-100 and the Texas Instruments ASC in the early 1970s. Vector processing was especially popularized by Cray in the 1970s and 1980s by attached vector processors such as those produced by the FPS (Floating Point Systems), and by supercomputers such as the Thinking Machines CM-1 and CM-2. Sun Microsystems introduced SIMD integer instructions in its VIS instruction set extensions in 1995 in its UltraSPARC I microprocessor; the first widely deployed SIMD for gaming was Intel's MMX extensions to the *x86* architecture. IBM and Motorola then added AltiVec to the POWER architecture, and there have been several extensions to the SIMD instruction sets for both architectures.

The desire to support real-time graphics with vectors of two, three, or four dimensions led to the development of graphic processing units (GPUs). GPUs are very efficient at manipulating computer graphics, and their highly parallel structures based on SIMD execution support parallel processing of large blocks of data. GPUs produced by Intel, Nvidia, and AMD/ATI are used in embedded systems, mobile phones, personal computers, workstations, and game consoles.

An MIMD architecture refers to a system with several processors that function asynchronously and independently; at any time, different processors may be executing different instructions on different data. The processors can share a common memory of an MIMD, and we distinguish several types of systems: Uniform Memory Access (UMA), Cache Only Memory Access (COMA), and Non-Uniform Memory Access (NUMA).

An MIMD system could have a distributed memory; in this case the processors and the memory communicate with one another using an interconnection network, such as a hypercube, a `2D` torus, a `3D` torus, an omega network, or another network topology. Today most supercomputers are MIMD machines, and some use GPUs instead of traditional processors. Multicore processors with multiple processing units are now ubiquitous.

Modern supercomputers derive their power from architecture and parallelism rather than the increase of processor speed. The supercomputers of today consist of a very large number of processors and cores communicating via very fast custom interconnects. In mid-2012 the most powerful supercomputer was a *Linux*-based IBM Sequoia-BlueGene/Q system powered by Power BQC 16-core processors running at 1.6 GHz. The system, installed at Lawrence Livermore National Laboratory and called Jaguar, has a total of 1,572,864 cores and 1,572,864 GB of memory, achieves a sustainable speed of 16.32 petaFLOPS, and consumes 7.89 MW of power.

More recently, a Cray XK7 system called Titan, installed at the Oak Ridge National Laboratory (ORNL) in Tennessee, was coronated as the fastest supercomputer in the world. Titan has 560,640 processors, including 261,632 Nvidia K20x accelerator cores; it achieved a speed of 17.59 petaFLOPS on the Linpack benchmark. Several most powerful systems listed in the "Top 500 supercomputers" (see `www.top500.org`) are powered by the Nvidia 2050 GPU; three of the top 10 use an InfiniBand [4] interconnect.

The next natural step was triggered by advances in communication networks when low-latency and high-bandwidth wide area networks (WANs) allowed individual systems, many of them multiprocessors,

[4] InfiniBand is a switched fabric communications link used in high-performance computing and in datacenters.

to be geographically separated. Large-scale distributed systems were first used for scientific and engineering applications and took advantage of the advancements in system software, programming models, tools, and algorithms developed for parallel processing.

2.3 Distributed systems

A *distributed system* is a collection of autonomous computers that are connected through a network and distribution software called *middleware*, which enables computers to coordinate their activities and to share the resources of the system. A distributed system's users perceive the system as a single integrated computing facility.

A distributed system has several characteristics: Its components are autonomous, scheduling and other resource management and security policies are implemented by each system, there are multiple points of control and multiple points of failure, and the resources may not be accessible at all times. Distributed systems can be scaled by adding additional resources and can be designed to maintain availability even at low levels of hardware/software/network reliability.

Distributed systems have been around for several decades. For example, distributed file systems and network file systems have been used for user convenience and to improve reliability and functionality of file systems for many years. Modern operating systems allow a user to *mount* a remote file system and access it the same way a local file system is accessed, yet with a performance penalty due to larger communication costs. The *remote procedure call* (RPC) supports inter-process communication and allows a procedure on a system to invoke a procedure running in a different address space, possibly on a remote system. RPCs were introduced in the early 1970s by Bruce Nelson and used for the first time at Xerox; the Network File System (NFS) introduced in 1984 was based on Sun's RPC. Many programming languages support RPCs; for example, Java Remote Method Invocation (Java RMI) provides a functionality similar to that of *UNIX* RPC methods, and XML-RPC uses XML to encode HTML-based calls.

The middleware should support a set of desirable properties of a distributed system:

- *Access transparency.* Local and remote information objects are accessed using identical operations.
- *Location transparency.* Information objects are accessed without knowledge of their location.
- *Concurrency transparency.* Several processes run concurrently using shared information objects without interference among them.
- *Replication transparency.* Multiple instances of information objects are used to increase reliability without the knowledge of users or applications.
- *Failure transparency.* The concealment of faults.
- *Migration transparency.* The information objects in the system are moved without affecting the operation performed on them.
- *Performance transparency.* The system can be reconfigured based on the load and quality of service requirements.
- *Scaling transparency.* The system and the applications can scale without a change in the system structure and without affecting the applications.

2.4 Global state of a process group

To understand the important properties of distributed systems, we use a model, an abstraction based on two critical components: processes and communication channels. A *process* is a program in execution, and a *thread* is a lightweight process. A thread of execution is the smallest unit of processing that can be scheduled by an operating system.

A process is characterized by its *state*; the state is the ensemble of information we need to restart a process after it was suspended. An *event* is a change of state of a process. The events affecting the state of process p_1 are numbered sequentially as $e_i^1, e_i^2, e_i^3, \ldots$, as shown in the *space-time diagram* in Figure 2.1(a). A process p_1 is in state σ_i^j immediately after the occurrence of event e_i^j and remains in that state until the occurrence of the next event, e_i^{j+1}.

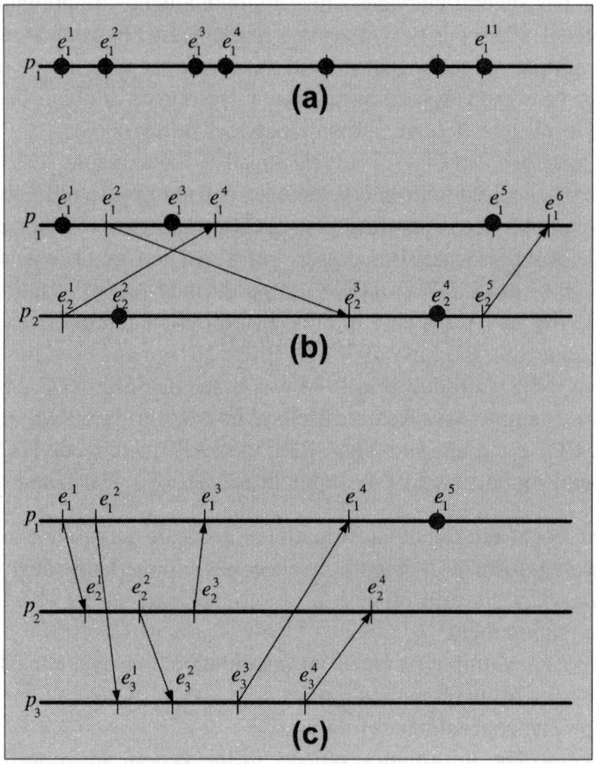

FIGURE 2.1

Space-time diagrams display local and communication events during a process lifetime. Local events are small black circles. Communication events in different processes are connected by lines originating at a *send* event and terminated by an arrow at the *receive* event. (a) All events in the case of a single process p_1 are local; the process is in state σ_1 immediately after the occurrence of event e_1^1 and remains in that state until the occurrence of event e_1^2. (b) Two processes p_1 and p_2; event e_1^2 is a communication event, p_1 sends a message to p_2; event e_2^3 is a communication event, process p_2 receives the message sent by p_1. (c) Three processes interact by means of communication events.

A *process group* is a collection of cooperating processes; these processes work in concert and communicate with one another to reach a common goal. For example, a parallel algorithm to solve a system of partial differential equations (PDEs) over a domain D may partition the data in several segments and assign each segment to one of the members of the process group. The processes in the group must cooperate with one another and iterate until the common boundary values computed by one process agree with the common boundary values computed by another.

A *communication channel* provides the means for processes or threads to communicate with one another and coordinate their actions by exchanging messages. Without loss of generality, we assume that communication among processes is done only by means of *send* (m) and *receive* (m) communication events, where m is a message. We use the term *message* for a structured unit of information, which can be interpreted only in a semantic context by the sender and the receiver. The *state of a communication channel* is defined as follows: Given two processes p_i and p_j, the state of the channel, $\xi_{i,j}$, from p_i to p_j consists of messages sent by p_i but not yet received by p_j.

These two abstractions allow us to concentrate on critical properties of distributed systems without the need to discuss the detailed physical properties of the entities involved. The model presented is based on the assumption that a channel is a unidirectional bit pipe of infinite bandwidth and zero latency, but unreliable; messages sent through a channel may be lost or distorted or the channel may fail, losing its ability to deliver messages. We also assume that the time a process needs to traverse a set of states is of no concern and that processes may fail or be aborted.

A *protocol* is a finite set of messages exchanged among processes to help them coordinate their actions. Figure 2.1(c) illustrates the case when communication events are dominant in the local history of processes, p_1, p_2, and p_3. In this case only e_1^5 is a local event; all others are communication events. The particular protocol illustrated in Figure 2.1(c) requires processes p_2 and p_3 to send messages to the other processes in response to a message from process p_1.

The informal definition of the state of a single process can be extended to collections of communicating processes. The *global state of a distributed system* consisting of several processes and communication channels is the union of the states of the individual processes and channels [34].

Call h_i^j the history of process p_i up to and including its j-th event, e_i^j, and call σ_i^j the local state of process p_i following event e_i^j. Consider a system consisting of n processes, $p_1, p_2, \ldots, p_i, \ldots, p_n$ with $\sigma_i^{j_i}$ the local state of process p_i; then the global state of the system is an n-tuple of local states

$$\Sigma^{(j_1,j_2,\ldots,j_n)} = \left(\sigma_1^{j_1}, \sigma_2^{j_2}, \ldots, \sigma_i^{j_i}, \ldots, \sigma_n^{j_n}\right). \tag{2.10}$$

The state of the channels does not appear explicitly in this definition of the global state because the state of the channels is encoded as part of the local state of the processes communicating through the channels.

The global states of a distributed computation with n processes form an n-dimensional lattice. The elements of this lattice are global states $\Sigma^{(j_1,j_2,\ldots,j_n)}\left(\sigma_1^{j_1}, \sigma_2^{j_2}, \ldots, \sigma_n^{j_n}\right)$.

Figure 2.2(a) shows the lattice of global states of the distributed computation in Figure 2.2(b) This is a two-dimensional lattice because we have two processes, p_1 and p_2. The lattice of global states for the distributed computation in Figure 2.1(c) is a three-dimensional lattice, and the computation consists of three concurrent processes, p_1, p_2, and p_3.

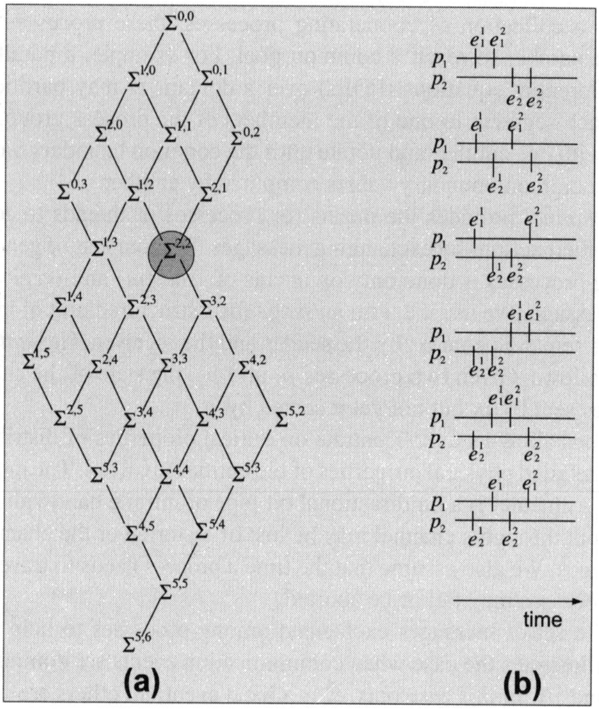

FIGURE 2.2

(a) The lattice of the global states of two processes with the space-time diagrams in Figure 2.2(b). Only the first two events for each thread are shown in Figure 2.2(b). (b) The six possible sequences of events leading to the state $\Sigma^{(2,2)}$.

The initial state of the system in Figure 2.2(b) is the state before the occurrence of any event and it is denoted by $\Sigma^{(0,0)}$; the only global states reachable from $\Sigma^{(0,0)}$ are $\Sigma^{(1,0)}$ and $\Sigma^{(0,1)}$. The communication events limit the global states the system may reach; in this example the system cannot reach the state $\Sigma^{(4,0)}$ because process p_1 enters state σ_4 only after process p_2 has entered the state σ_1. Figure 2.2(b) shows the six possible sequences of events to reach the global state $\Sigma^{(2,2)}$:

$$\left(e_1^1, e_1^2, e_2^1, e_2^2\right), \left(e_1^1, e_2^1, e_1^2, e_2^2\right), \left(e_1^1, e_2^1, e_2^2, e_1^2\right), \left(e_2^1, e_2^2, e_1^1, e_1^2\right), \left(e_2^1, e_1^1, e_1^2, e_2^2\right), \left(e_2^1, e_1^1, e_2^2, e_1^2\right). \tag{2.11}$$

An interesting question is how many paths does it take to reach a global state. The more paths exist, the harder it is to identify the events leading to a state when we observe an undesirable behavior of the system. A large number of paths increases the difficulty of debugging the system.

We conjecture that in the case of two threads in Figure 2.2(b) the number of paths from the global state $\Sigma^{(0,0)}$ to $\Sigma^{(m,n)}$ is

$$N_p^{(m,n)} = \frac{(m+n)!}{m!n!}. \tag{2.12}$$

We have already seen that there are six paths leading to state $\Sigma^{(2,2)}$; indeed,

$$N_p^{(2,2)} = \frac{(2+2)!}{2!2!} = \frac{24}{4} = 6. \tag{2.13}$$

To prove Equation 2.12 we use a method resembling induction; we notice first that the global state $\Sigma^{(1,1)}$ can only be reached from the states $\Sigma^{(1,0)}$ and $\Sigma^{(0,1)}$ and that $N_p^{(1,1)} = (2)!/1!1! = 2$. Thus, the formula is true for $m = n = 1$. Then we show that if the formula is true for the $(m-1, n-1)$ case it will also be true for the (m, n) case. If our conjecture is true, then

$$N_p^{[(m-1),n]} = \frac{[(m-1)+n]!}{(m-1)!n!}. \tag{2.14}$$

and

$$N_p^{[m,(n-1)]} = \frac{[m+(n-1)]!}{m!(n-1)!}. \tag{2.15}$$

We observe that the global state $\Sigma^{(m,n)}$, $\forall (m,n) \geqslant 1$ can only be reached from two states, $\Sigma^{(m-1,n)}$ and $\Sigma^{(m,n-1)}$ (see Figure 2.3), thus:

$$N_p^{(m,n)} = N_p^{(m-1,n)} + N_p^{(m,n-1)}. \tag{2.16}$$

It is easy to see that indeed,

$$\begin{aligned}\frac{[(m-1)+n]!}{(m-1)!n!} + \frac{[m+(n-1)]!}{m!(n-1)!} &= (m+n-1)!\left[\frac{1}{(m-1)!n!} + \frac{1}{m!(n-1)!}\right] \\ &= \frac{(m+n)!}{m!n!}.\end{aligned} \tag{2.17}$$

This shows that our conjecture is true; thus, Equation 2.12 gives the number of paths to reach the global state $\Sigma^{(m,n)}$ from $\Sigma^{(0,0)}$ when two threads are involved. This expression can be generalized for the case of q threads; using the same strategy, it is easy to see that the number of path from the state $\Sigma^{(0,0,\ldots,0)}$ to the global state $\Sigma^{(n_1,n_2,\ldots,n_q)}$ is

$$N_p^{(n_1,n_2,\ldots,n_q)} = \frac{(n_1+n_2+\cdots+n_q)!}{n_1!n_2!\ldots n_q!}. \tag{2.18}$$

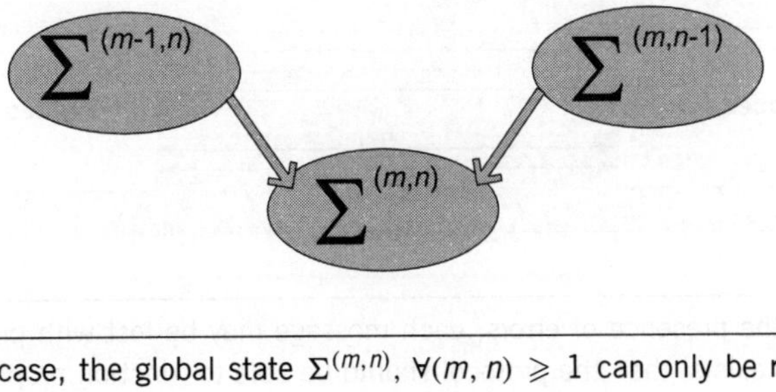

FIGURE 2.3

In the two-dimensional case, the global state $\Sigma^{(m,n)}$, $\forall (m,n) \geqslant 1$ can only be reached from two states, $\Sigma^{(m-1,n)}$ and $\Sigma^{(m,n-1)}$.

Indeed, it is easy to see that

$$N_p^{(n_1,n_2,\ldots,n_q)} = N_p^{(n_1-1,n_2,\ldots,n_q)} + N_p^{(n_1,n_2-1,\ldots,n_q)} + \cdots + N_p^{(n_1,n_2,\ldots,n_q-1)}. \quad (2.19)$$

Equation 2.18 gives us an indication of how difficult it is to debug a system with a large number of concurrent threads.

Many problems in distributed systems are instances of the *global predicate evaluation problem* (GPE), where the goal is to evaluate a Boolean expression whose elements are functions of the global state of the system.

2.5 Communication protocols and process coordination

A major concern in any parallel and distributed system is communication in the presence of channel failures. There are multiple modes for a channel to fail, and some lead to messages being lost. In the general case, it is impossible to guarantee that two processes will reach an agreement in case of channel failures (see Figure 2.4.)

Given two processes p_1 and p_2 connected by a communication channel that can lose a message with probability $\epsilon > 0$, no protocol capable of guaranteeing that two processes will reach agreement exists, regardless of how small the probability ϵ is.

The proof of this statement is by contradiction. Assume that such a protocol exists and it consists of n messages; recall that a protocol is a finite sequence of messages. Since any message might be lost with probability ϵ, the protocol should be able to function when only $n-1$ messages reach their destination, the last one being lost. Induction on the number of messages proves that indeed no such protocol exists; indeed, the same reasoning leads us to conclude that the protocol should function correctly with $(n-2)$ messages, and so on.

In practice, error detection and error correction allow processes to communicate reliably though noisy digital channels. The redundancy of a message is increased by more bits and packaging a message as a code word; the recipient of the message is then able to decide if the sequence of bits received is a valid code word and, if the code satisfies some distance properties, then the recipient of the message is able to extract the original message from a bit string in error.

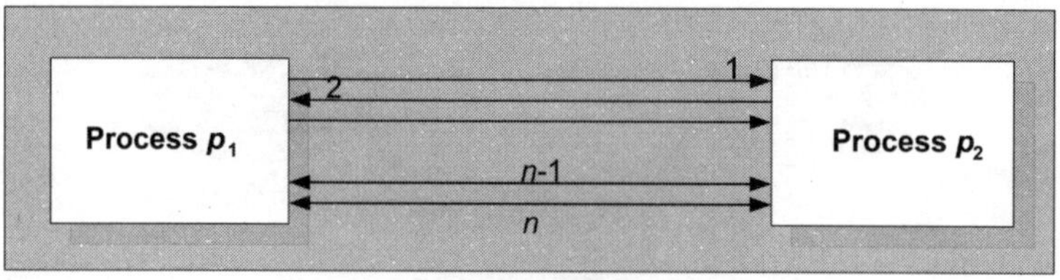

FIGURE 2.4

Process coordination in the presence of errors; each message may be lost with probability ϵ. If a protocol consisting of n messages exists, then the protocol should be able to function properly with $n-1$ messages reaching their destination, one of them being lost.

Communication protocols implement not only *error control* mechanisms, but also flow control and congestion control. *Flow control* provides feedback from the receiver; it forces the sender to transmit only the amount of data the receiver is able to buffer and then process. *Congestion control* ensures that the offered load of the network does not exceed the network capacity. In store-and-forward networks, individual routers may drop packets when the network is congested and the sender is forced to retransmit. Based on the estimation of the *round-trip-time* (RTT), the sender can detect congestion and reduce the transmission rate.

The implementation of these mechanisms requires the measurement of *time intervals*, the time elapsed between two events; we also need a *global concept of time* shared by all entities that cooperate with one another. For example, a computer chip has an *internal clock*, and a predefined set of actions occurs at each clock tick. Each chip has an *interval timer* that helps enhance the system's fault tolerance; when the effects of an action are not sensed after a predefined interval, the action is repeated.

When the entities communicating with each other are networked computers, the precision of the clock synchronization is critical [205]. The event rates are very high and each system goes through state changes at a very fast pace; modern processors run at a 2–4 GHz clock rate. That explains why we need to measure time very accurately; indeed, we have atomic clocks with an accuracy of about 10^{-6} seconds per year.

An isolated system can be characterized by its *history*, expressed as a sequence of events, each event corresponding to a change of the state of the system. Local timers provide relative time measurements. A more accurate description adds to the system's history the time of occurrence of each event as measured by the local timer.

Messages sent by processes may be lost or distorted during transmission. Without additional restrictions regarding message delays and errors, there are no means to ensure a perfect synchronization of local clocks and there are no obvious methods to ensure a global ordering of events occurring in different processes. Determining the global state of a large-scale distributed system is a very challenging problem.

The mechanisms described here are insufficient once we approach the problem of cooperating entities. To coordinate their actions, two entities need a common perception of time. Timers are not enough. Clocks provide the only way to measure distributed duration, that is, actions that start in one process and terminate in another. *Global agreement on time* is necessary to *trigger actions* that should occur concurrently (e.g., in a real-time control system of a power plant, several circuits must be switched on at the same time). Agreement on *the time when events occur* is necessary for distributed recording of events – for example, to determine a precedence relation through a temporal ordering of events. To ensure that a system functions correctly, we need to determine that the event causing a change of state occurred before the state change – for instance, the sensor triggering an alarm has to change its value before the emergency procedure to handle the event is activated. Another example of the need for agreement on the time of occurrence of events is in replicated actions. In this case several replicas of a process must log the time of an event in a consistent manner.

Time stamps are often used for event ordering using a global time base constructed on local virtual clocks [235]. The Δ-protocols [94] achieve total temporal order using a global time base. Assume that local virtual clock readings do not differ by more than π, called *precision* of the global time base. Call g the *granularity of physical clocks*. First, observe that the granularity should not be smaller than the precision; given two events a and b occurring in different processes, if $t_b - t_a \leqslant \pi + g$ we cannot tell which one occurred first [361]. Based on these observations, it follows that the order discrimination of clock-driven protocols cannot be better than twice the clock granularity.

System specification, design, and analysis require a clear understanding of *cause-effect relationships*. During the system specification phase we view the system as a state machine and define the actions that cause transitions from one state to another. During the system analysis phase we need to determine the cause that brought the system to a certain state.

The activity of any process is modeled as a sequence of *events*; hence, the binary relation cause-effect relationship should be expressed in terms of events and should express our intuition that *the cause must precede the effects*. Again, we need to distinguish between local events and communication events. The latter events affect more than one process and are essential for constructing a global history of an ensemble of processes. Let h_i denote the local history of process p_i and let e_i^k denote the k-th event in this history.

The binary cause-effect relationship between two events has the following properties:

1. Causality of local events can be derived from the process history:

$$\text{if} \quad e_i^k, e_i^l \in h_i \quad \text{and} \quad k < l \quad \text{then} \quad e_i^k \rightarrow e_i^l. \tag{2.20}$$

2. Causality of communication events:

$$\text{if} \quad e_i^k = send(m) \quad \text{and} \quad e_j^l = receive(m) \quad \text{then} \quad e_i^k \rightarrow e_j^l. \tag{2.21}$$

3. Transitivity of the causal relationship:

$$\text{if} \quad e_i^k \rightarrow e_j^l \quad \text{and} \quad e_j^l \rightarrow e_m^n \quad \text{then} \quad e_i^k \rightarrow e_m^n. \tag{2.22}$$

Two events in the global history may be unrelated. If so, neither one is the cause of the other; such events are said to be *concurrent events*.

2.6 Logical clocks

A *logical clock (LC)* is an abstraction necessary to ensure the clock condition in the absence of a global clock. Each process p_i maps events to positive integers. Call $LC(e)$ the local variable associated with event e. Each process time stamps each message m sent with the value of the logical clock at the time of sending, $TS(m) = LC(send(m))$. The rules to update the logical clock are specified by the following relationship:

$$LC(e) = \begin{cases} LC + 1 & \text{if} \quad e \text{ is a local event or a } send(m) \text{ event} \\ \max(LC, TS(m) + 1) & \text{if} \quad e = receive(m). \end{cases} \tag{2.23}$$

The concept of logical clocks is illustrated in Figure 2.5 using a modified *space-time diagram* in which the events are labeled with the logical clock value. Messages exchanged between processes are shown as lines from the sender to the receiver; the communication events corresponding to sending and receiving messages are marked on these diagrams.

Each process labels local events and sends events sequentially until it receives a message marked with a logical clock value larger than the next local logical clock value, as shown in Equation 2.23.

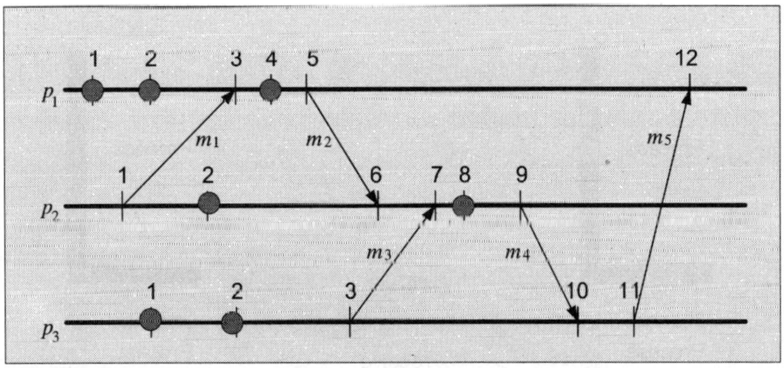

FIGURE 2.5

Three processes and their logical clocks. The usual labeling of events as $e_1^1, e_1^2, e_1^3, \ldots$ is omitted to avoid overloading the figure; only the logical clock values for the local and communication events are marked. The correspondence between the events and the logical clock values is obvious: $e_1^1, e_2^1, e_3^1 \rightarrow 1$, $e_1^5 \rightarrow 5$, $e_2^4 \rightarrow 7$, $e_3^4 \rightarrow 10$, $e_1^6 \rightarrow 12$, and so on. Global ordering of all events is not possible; there is no way to establish the ordering of events e_1^1, e_2^1 and e_3^1.

It follows that logical clocks do not allow a global ordering of all events. For example, there is no way to establish the ordering of events e_1^1, e_2^1, and e_3^1 in Figure 2.5. Nevertheless, communication events allow different processes to coordinate their logical clocks; for example, process p_2 labels the event e_2^3 as 6 because of message m_2, which carries the information about the logical clock value as 5 at the time message m_2 was sent. Recall that e_i^j is the j-th event in process p_i.

Logical clocks lack an important property, *gap detection*; given two events e and e' and their logical clock values, $LC(e)$ and $LC(e')$, it is impossible to establish if an event e'' exists such that

$$LC(e) < LC(e'') < LC(e'). \tag{2.24}$$

For example, for process p_1 there is an event, e_1^4, between the events e_1^3 and e_1^5 in Figure 2.5; indeed, $LC(e_1^3) = 3$, $LC(e_1^5) = 5$, $LC(e_1^4) = 4$, and $LC(e_1^3) < LC(e_1^4) < LC(e_1^5)$. However, for process p_3, the events e_3^3 and e_3^4 are consecutive, though $LC(e_3^3) = 3$ and $LC(e_3^4) = 10$.

2.7 Message delivery rules; causal delivery

The communication channel abstraction makes no assumptions about the order of messages; a real-life network might reorder messages. This fact has profound implications for a distributed application. Consider for example a robot getting instructions to navigate from a monitoring facility with two messages, "turn left" and "turn right," being delivered out of order.

Message receiving and message delivery are two distinct operations; a *delivery rule* is an additional assumption about the channel-process interface. This rule establishes when a message received is actually delivered to the destination process. The receiving of a message m and its delivery are two distinct

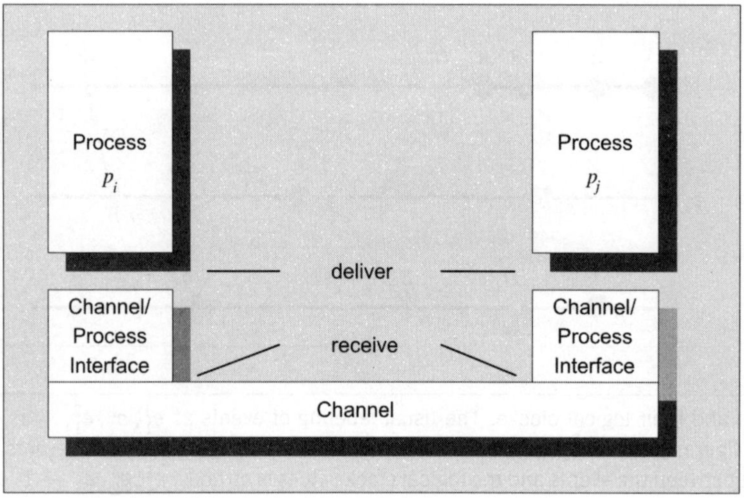

FIGURE 2.6

Message receiving and message delivery are two distinct operations. The channel-process interface implements the delivery rules (e.g., FIFO delivery).

events in a causal relation with one another. A message can only be delivered after being received (see Figure 2.6)

$$receive(m) \rightarrow deliver(m). \tag{2.25}$$

First In, First Out (*FIFO*) *delivery* implies that messages are delivered in the same order in which they are sent. For each pair of source-destination processes (p_i, p_j), FIFO delivery requires that the following relation should be satisfied:

$$send_i(m) \rightarrow send_i(m') \Rightarrow deliver_j(m) \rightarrow deliver_j(m'). \tag{2.26}$$

Even if the communication channel does not guarantee FIFO delivery, FIFO delivery can be enforced by attaching a sequence number to each message sent. The sequence numbers are also used to reassemble messages out of individual packets.

Causal delivery is an extension of the FIFO delivery to the case when a process receives messages from different sources. Assume a group of three processes, (p_i, p_j, p_k) and two messages m and m'. Causal delivery requires that

$$send_i(m) \rightarrow send_j(m') \Rightarrow deliver_k(m) \rightarrow deliver_k(m'). \tag{2.27}$$

When more than two processes are involved in a message exchange, the message delivery may be FIFO but not causal, as shown in Figure 2.7 where we see that

- $deliver(m_3) \rightarrow deliver(m_1)$, according to the local history of process p_2.
- $deliver(m_2) \rightarrow send(m_3)$, according to the local history of process p_1.
- $send(m_1) \rightarrow send(m_2)$, according to the local history of process p_3.

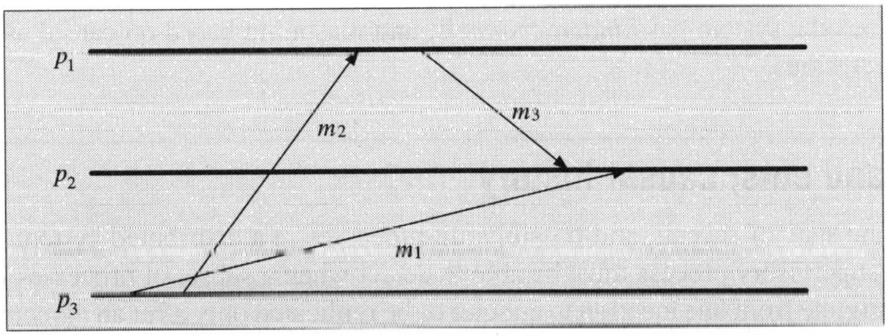

FIGURE 2.7

Violation of causal delivery when more than two processes are involved. Message m_1 is delivered to process p_2 after message m_3, though message m_1 was sent before m_3. Indeed, message m_3 was sent by process p_1 after receiving m_2, which in turn was sent by process p_3 after sending message m_1.

- $send(m_2) \rightarrow deliver(m_2)$.
- $send(m_3) \rightarrow deliver(m_3)$.

The preceding transitivity property and the causality relations imply that $send(m_1) \rightarrow deliver(m_3)$.

Call $TS(m)$ the *time stamp* carried by message m. A message received by process p_i is *stable* if no future messages with a time stamp smaller than $TS(m)$ can be received by process p_i. When logical clocks are used, a process p_i can construct consistent observations of the system if it implements the following delivery rule: *Deliver all stable messages in increasing time-stamp order.*

Let's now examine the problem of *consistent message delivery* under several sets of assumptions. First, assume that processes cooperating with each other in a distributed environment have access to a *global real-time clock*, that the message delays are bounded by δ, and that there is no clock drift. Call $RC(e)$ the time of occurrence of event e. A process includes $RC(e)$ in every message it sends, where e is the send-message event. The delivery rule in this case is: *At time t deliver all received messages with time stamps up to $(t - \delta)$ in increasing time-stamp order.* Indeed, this delivery rule guarantees that under the bounded delay assumption the message delivery is consistent. All messages delivered at time t are in order and no future message with a time stamp lower than any of the messages delivered may arrive.

For any two events, e and e', occurring in different processes, the so-called *clock condition* is satisfied if

$$e \rightarrow e' \Rightarrow RC(e) < RC(e'), \quad \forall e, e'. \tag{2.28}$$

Often, we are interested in determining the set of events that caused an event knowing the time stamps associated with all events; in other words, we are interested in deducing the causal precedence relation between events from their time stamps. To do so we need to define the so-called strong clock condition. The *strong clock condition* requires an equivalence between the causal precedence and the ordering of the time stamps

$$\forall e, e', \quad e \rightarrow e' \equiv TS(e) < TS(e'). \tag{2.29}$$

Causal delivery is very important because it allows processes to reason about the entire system using only local information. This is only true in a closed system where all communication channels are known; sometimes the system has *hidden channels*, and reasoning based on causal analysis may lead to incorrect conclusions.

2.8 Runs and cuts; causal history

Knowledge of the state of several, and possibly all, processes in a distributed system is often needed. For example, a supervisory process must be able to detect when a subset of processes is deadlocked; a process might migrate from one location to another or be replicated only after an agreement with others. In all these examples a process needs to evaluate a predicate function of the global state of the system.

We call the process responsible for constructing the global state of the system the *monitor*. A monitor sends messages requesting information about the local state of every process and gathers the replies to construct the global state. Intuitively, the construction of the global state is equivalent to taking snapshots of individual processes and then combining these snapshots into a global view. Yet, combining snapshots is straightforward if and only if all processes have access to a global clock and the snapshots are taken at the same time; hence, the snapshots are consistent with one another.

A *run* is a total ordering R of all the events in the global history of a distributed computation consistent with the local history of each participant process; a run

$$R = \left(e_1^{j_1}, e_2^{j_2}, \ldots, e_n^{j_n}\right) \tag{2.30}$$

implies a sequence of events as well as a sequence of global states.

For example, consider the three processes in Figure 2.8. We can construct a three-dimensional lattice of global states following a procedure similar to the one in Figure 2.2, starting from the initial state $\Sigma^{(000)}$ and proceeding to any reachable state $\Sigma^{(ijk)}$ with i, j, k the events in processes p_1, p_2, p_3, respectively. The run $R_1 = (e_1^1, e_2^1, e_3^1, e_1^2)$ is consistent with both the local history of each process and

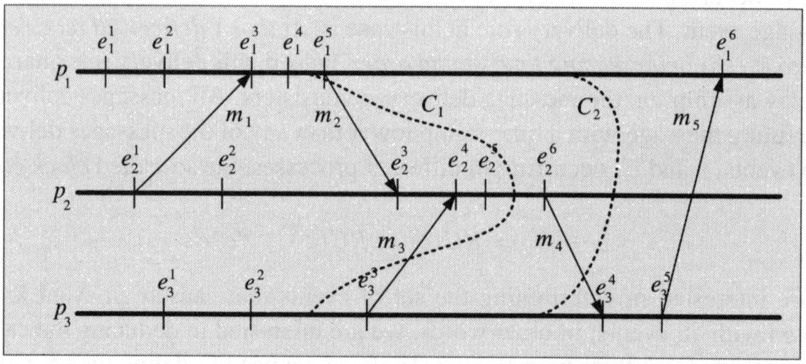

FIGURE 2.8

Inconsistent and consistent cuts. The cut $C_1 = (e_1^4, e_2^5, e_3^2)$ is inconsistent because it includes e_2^4, the event triggered by the arrival of the message m_3 at process p_2, but does not include e_3^3, the event triggered by process p_3 sending m_3. Thus, the cut C_1 violates causality. On the other hand, $C_2 = (e_1^5, e_2^6, e_3^3)$ is a consistent cut; there is no causal inconsistency because, it includes event e_2^6, the sending of message m_4, without the effect of it, the event e_3^4 receiving the message by process p_3.

the global history; this run is valid, and the system has traversed the global states

$$\Sigma^{000}, \Sigma^{100}, \Sigma^{110}, \Sigma^{111}, \Sigma^{211}. \tag{2.31}$$

On the other hand, the run $R_2 = (e_1^1, e_1^2, e_3^1, e_1^3, e_3^2)$ is invalid because it is inconsistent with the global history. The system cannot ever reach the state Σ^{301}; message m_1 must be sent before it is received, so event e_2^1 must occur in any run before event e_1^3.

A *cut* is a subset of the local history of all processes. If h_i^j denotes the history of process p_i up to and including its j-th event, e_i^j, then a cut C is an n-tuple

$$C = \{h_i^j\} \text{ with } i \in \{1, n\} \text{ and } j \in \{1, n_i\}. \tag{2.32}$$

The frontier of the cut is an n-tuple consisting of the last event of every process included in the cut. Figure 2.8 illustrates a *space-time diagram* for a group of three processes, p_1, p_2, p_3, and it shows two cuts, C_1 and C_2. C_1 has the frontier (4, 5, 2), frozen after the fourth event of process p_1, the fifth event of process p_2, and the second event of process p_3, and C_2 has the frontier (5, 6, 3).

Cuts provide the necessary intuition to generate global states based on an exchange of messages between a monitor and a group of processes. The cut represents the instance when requests to report individual states are received by the members of the group. Clearly not all cuts are meaningful. For example, the cut C_1 with the frontier (4, 5, 2) in Figure 2.8 violates our intuition regarding causality; it includes e_2^4, the event triggered by the arrival of message m_3 at process p_2 but does not include e_3^3, the event triggered by process p_3 sending m_3. In this snapshot p_3 was frozen after its second event, e_3^2, before it had the chance to send message m_3. Causality is violated and the system cannot ever reach such a state.

Next we introduce the concepts of consistent and inconsistent cuts and runs. A cut closed under the *causal precedence relationship* is called a *consistent cut*. C is a consistent cut if and only if for all events

$$\forall e, e', (e \in C) \wedge (e' \rightarrow e) \Rightarrow e' \in C. \tag{2.33}$$

A consistent cut establishes an "instance" of a distributed computation. Given a consistent cut we can determine if an event e occurred before the cut.

A run R is said to be consistent if the total ordering of events imposed by the run is consistent with the partial order imposed by the causal relation; for all events, $e \rightarrow e'$ implies that e appears before e' in R.

Consider a distributed computation consisting of a group of communicating processes $G = \{p_1, p_2, \ldots, p_n\}$. The *causal history of event e*, $\gamma(e)$, is the smallest consistent cut of G including event e

$$\gamma(e) = \{e' \in G | e' \rightarrow e\} \cup \{e\}. \tag{2.34}$$

The causal history of event e_2^5 in Figure 2.9 is:

$$\gamma\left(e_2^5\right) = \left\{e_1^1, e_1^2, e_1^3, e_1^4, e_1^5, e_2^1, e_2^2, e_2^3, e_2^4, e_2^5, e_3^1, e_3^2, e_3^3\right\}. \tag{2.35}$$

This is the smallest consistent cut including e_2^5; indeed, if we omit e_3^3, then the cut (5, 5, 2) would be inconsistent; it would include e_2^4, the communication event for receiving m_3, but not e_3^3, the sending of m_3. If we omit e_1^5, the cut (4, 5, 3) would also be inconsistent and it would include e_2^3 but not e_1^5.

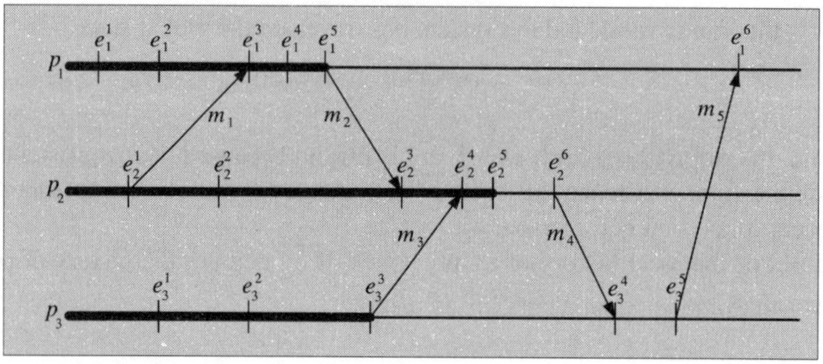

FIGURE 2.9

The causal history of event e_2^5, $\gamma(e_2^5) = \left\{e_1^1, e_1^2, e_1^3, e_1^4, e_1^5, e_2^1, e_2^2, e_2^3, e_2^4, e_2^5, e_3^1, e_3^2, e_3^3\right\}$ is the smallest consistent cut including e_2^5.

Causal histories can be used as clock values and satisfy the strong clock condition, provided that we equate clock comparison with set inclusion. Indeed,

$$e \rightarrow e' \equiv \gamma(e) \subset \gamma(e'). \tag{2.36}$$

The following algorithm can be used to construct causal histories:

- Each $p_i \in G$ starts with $\theta = \emptyset$.
- Every time p_i receives a message m from p_j it constructs

$$\gamma(e_i) = \gamma(e_j) \cup \gamma(e_k) \tag{2.37}$$

with e_i the *receive* event, e_j the previous local event of p_i, e_k the *send* event of process p_j.

Unfortunately, this concatenation of histories is impractical because the causal histories grow very fast.

Now we present a protocol to construct consistent global states based on the monitoring concepts discussed in this section. We assume a fully connected network; recall that given two processes p_i and p_j, the state $\xi_{i,j}$ of the channel from p_i to p_j consists of messages sent by p_i but not yet received by p_j. The snapshot protocol of Chandy and Lamport consists of three steps [72]:

1. Process p_0 sends to itself a "take snapshot" message.
2. Let p_f be the process from which p_i receives the "take snapshot" message for the first time. Upon receiving the message, the process p_i records its local state, σ_i, and relays the "take snapshot" along all its outgoing channels without executing any events on behalf of its underlying computation. Channel state $\xi_{f,i}$ is set to empty, and process p_i starts recording messages received over each of its incoming channels.
3. Let p_s be the process from which p_i receives the "take snapshot" message after the first time. Process p_i stops recording messages along the incoming channel from p_s and declares channel state $\xi_{s,i}$ as those messages that have been recorded.

Each "take snapshot" message crosses each channel exactly once, and every process p_i has made its contribution to the global state. A process records its state the first time it receives a "take snapshot"

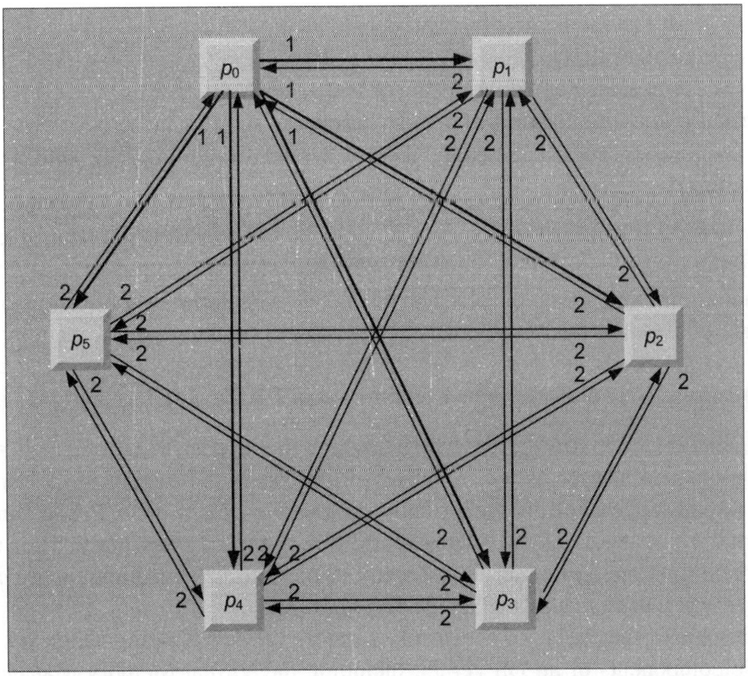

FIGURE 2.10

Six processes executing the snapshot protocol.

message and then stops executing the underlying computation for some time. Thus, in a fully connected network with n processes, the protocol requires $n \times (n-1)$ messages, one on each channel.

For example, consider a set of six processes, each pair of processes being connected by two unidirectional channels, as shown in Figure 2.10. Assume that all channels are empty, $\xi_{i,j} = 0, i \in \{0, 5\}$, $j \in \{0, 5\}$, at the time when process p_0 issues the "take snapshot" message. The actual flow of messages is:

- In step 0, p_0 sends to itself the "take snapshot" message.
- In step 1, process p_0 sends five "take snapshot" messages, labeled (1) in Figure 2.10.
- In step 2, each of the five processes p_1, p_2, p_3, p_4, and p_5 sends a "take snapshot" message labeled (2) to every other process.

A "take snapshot" message crosses each channel from process p_i to p_j, $i, j \in \{0, 5\}$ exactly once and $6 \times 5 = 30$ messages are exchanged.

2.9 Concurrency

Concurrency means that several activities are executed simultaneously. Concurrency allows us to reduce the execution time of a data-intensive problem, as discussed in Section 2.1. To exploit concurrency, often we have to take a fresh look at the problem and design a parallel algorithm. In other instances we can still use the sequential algorithm in the context of the SPMD paradigm.

Concurrency is a critical element of the design of system software. The kernel of an operating system exploits concurrency for virtualization of system resources such as the processor and the memory. *Virtualization*, covered in depth in Section 5.1, is a system design strategy with a broad range of objectives, including:

- Hiding latency and performance enhancement (e.g., schedule a ready-to-run thread when the current thread is waiting for the completion of an I/O operation).
- Avoiding limitations imposed by the physical resources (e.g., allow an application to run in a virtual address space of a standard size rather than be restricted by the physical memory available on a system).
- Enhancing reliability and performance, as in the case of RAID systems mentioned in Section 3.5.

Sometimes concurrency is used to describe activities that appear to be executed simultaneously, though only one of them may be active at any given time, as in the case of processor virtualization, when multiple threads appear to run concurrently on a single processor. A thread can be suspended due to an external event and a context switch to a different thread takes place. The state of the first thread is saved and the state of another thread ready to proceed is loaded and the thread is activated. The suspended thread will be reactivated at a later point in time.

Dealing with some of the effects of concurrency can be very challenging. Context switching could involve multiple components of an OS kernel, including the Virtual Memory Manager (VMM), the Exception Handler (EH), the Scheduler (S), and the Multilevel Memory Manager (MLMM). When a page fault occurs during the fetching of the next instruction, multiple context switches are necessary, as shown in Figure 2.11.

Concurrency is often motivated by the desire to enhance system performance. For example, in a pipelined computer architecture, multiple instructions are in different phases of execution at any given time. Once the pipeline is full, a result is produced at every pipeline cycle; an n-stage pipeline could potentially lead to a speed-up by a factor of n. There is always a price to pay for increased performance, and in this example it is design complexity and cost. An n-stage pipeline requires n execution units, one for each stage, as well as a coordination unit. It also requires careful timing analysis in order to achieve the full speed-up.

This example shows that the management and coordination of the concurrent activities increase the complexity of a system. The interaction between pipelining and virtual memory further complicates the functions of the kernel; indeed, one of the instructions in the pipeline could be interrupted due to a page fault, and the handling of this case requires special precautions, since the state of the processor is difficult to define.

In the early days of computing, concurrency was analyzed mostly in the context of the system software; nowadays concurrency is a ubiquitous feature of many applications. *Embedded systems* are a class of concurrent systems used not only by the critical infrastructure but also by the most diverse systems, from ignition in a car to oil processing in a refinery, from smart meters to coffee makers. Embedded controllers for reactive real-time applications are implemented as mixed software/hardware systems [294].

Concurrency is exploited by application software to speed up a computation and to allow a number of clients to access a service. Parallel applications partition the workload and distribute it to multiple

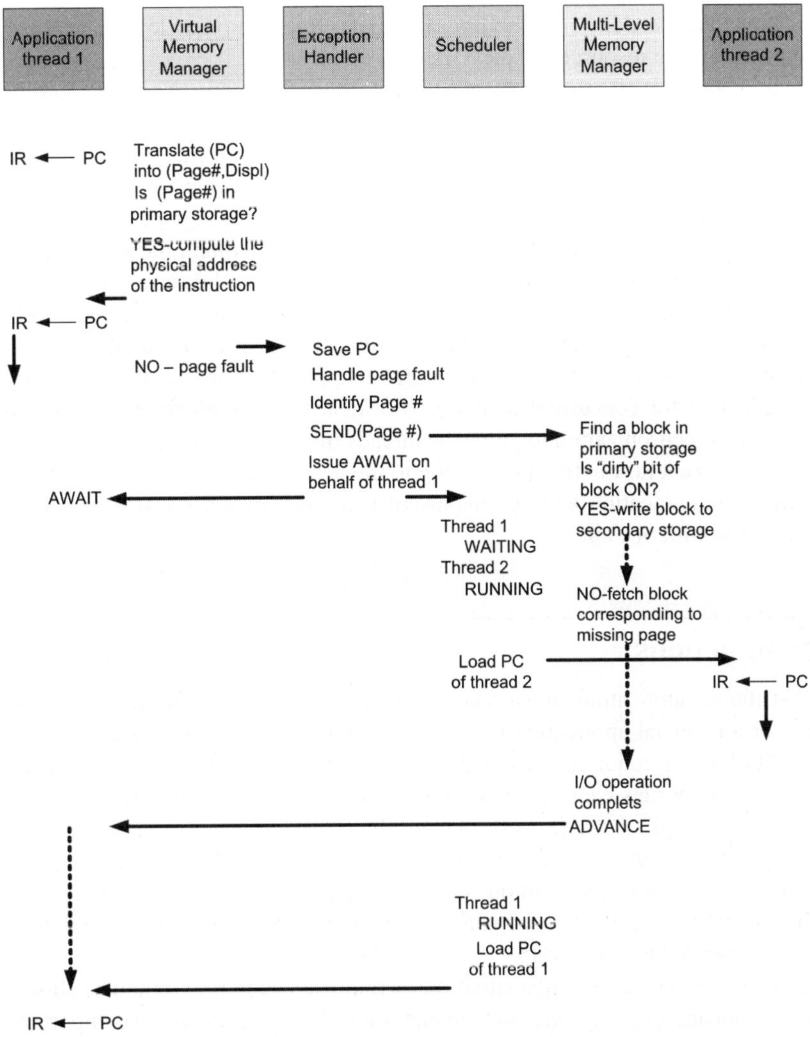

FIGURE 2.11

Context switching when a page fault occurs during the instruction fetch phase. The VMM attempts to translate the virtual address of a next instruction of thread 1 and encounters a page fault. Then thread 1 is suspended waiting for an event when the page is brought into the physical memory from the disk. The Scheduler dispatches thread 2. To handle the fault, the Exception Handler invokes the MLMM.

threads running concurrently. Distributed applications, including transaction management systems and applications based on the client-server paradigm discussed in Section 2.13, use concurrency extensively to improve the response time. For example, a Web server spawns a new thread when a new request is received; thus, multiple server threads run concurrently. A main attraction for hosting Web-based applications is the cloud elasticity – the ability of a service running on a cloud to acquire resources as needed and to pay for these resources as they are consumed.

Communication channels allow concurrent activities to work in concert and to coordinate. Communication protocols allow us to transform noisy and unreliable channels into reliable ones that deliver messages in order. As mentioned earlier, concurrent activities communicate with one another via shared memory or via message passing. Multiple instances of a cloud application, a server and the clients of the service it provides, and many other applications communicate via message passing. The Message Passing Interface (MPI) supports both synchronous and asynchronous communication, and it is often used by parallel and distributed applications. Message passing enforces modularity, as we see in Section 2.13, and prevents the communicating activities from *sharing their fate*; a server could fail without affecting the clients that did not use the service during the period the server was unavailable.

The communication patterns in the case of a parallel application are more structured, whereas patterns of communication for concurrent activities of a distributed application are more dynamic and unstructured. Barrier synchronization requires the threads running concurrently to wait until all of them have completed the current task before proceeding to the next. Sometimes one of the activities, a coordinator, mediates communication among concurrent activities; in other instances individual threads communicate directly with one another.

2.10 Atomic actions

Parallel and distributed applications must take special precautions for handling shared resources. For example, consider a financial application in which the shared resource is an account record. A thread running on behalf of a transaction first accesses the account to `read` the current balance, then updates the balance, and finally, writes back the new balance. When a thread is interrupted before being able to complete the three steps of the process, the results of the financial transactions are incorrect if another thread operating on the same account is allowed to proceed. Another challenge is to deal with a transaction involving the transfer from one account to another. A system crash after the completion of the operation on the first account will again lead to an inconsistency – the amount debited from the first account is not credited to the second.

In these cases, as in many other similar situations, a multistep operation should be allowed to proceed to completion without any interruptions, and the operation should be *atomic*. An important observation is that such atomic actions should not expose the state of the system until the action is completed. Hiding the internal state of an atomic action reduces the number of states a system can be in; thus, it simplifies the design and maintenance of the system. An atomic action is composed of several steps, each of which may fail; therefore, we have to take additional precautions to avoid exposing the internal state of the system in case of such a failure.

The discussion of the transaction system suggests that an analysis of atomicity should pay special attention to the basic operation of updating the value of an object in storage. Even to modify the contents of a memory location, several machine instructions must be executed: load the current value in a register, modify the contents of the register, and store back the result.

Atomicity cannot be implemented without some hardware support; indeed, the instruction sets of most processors support the *test-and-set* instruction, which writes to a memory location and returns

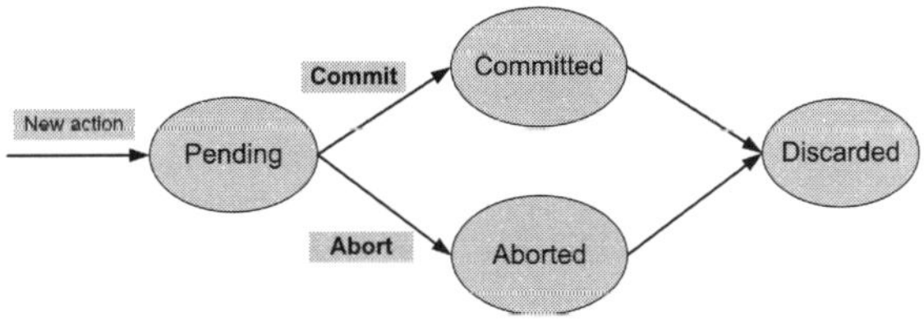

FIGURE 2.12

The states of an *all-or-nothing* action.

the old content of that memory cell as noninterruptible operations. Other architectures support *compare-and-swap*, an atomic instruction that compares the contents of a memory location to a given value and, only if the two values are the same, modifies the contents of that memory location to a given new value.

Two flavors of atomicity can be distinguished: *all-or-nothing* and *before-or-after* atomicity. *All-or-nothing* means that either the entire atomic action is carried out, or the system is left in the same state it was before the atomic action was attempted. In our examples a transaction is either carried out successfully, or the record targeted by the transaction is returned to its original state. The states of an *all-or-nothing* action are shown in Figure 2.12.

To guarantee the all-or-nothing property of an action we have to distinguish preparatory actions that can be undone from irreversible ones, such as the alteration of the only copy of an object. Such preparatory actions are as follows: allocation of a resource, fetching a page from secondary storage, allocation of memory on the stack, and so on. One of the golden rules of data management is never to change the only copy; maintaining the history of changes and a log of all activities allows us to deal with system failures and to ensure consistency.

An all-or-nothing action consists of a *pre-commit* and a *post-commit* phase; during the former it should be possible to back up from it without leaving any trace, whereas the latter phase should be able to run to completion. The transition from the first to the second phase is called a *commit point*. During the *pre-commit* phase all steps necessary to prepare the post-commit phase – for example, check permissions, swap in main memory all pages that may be needed, mount removable media, and allocate stack space – must be carried out; during this phase no results should be exposed and no irreversible actions should be carried out. Shared resources allocated during the pre-commit phase cannot be released until after the commit point. The commit step should be the last step of an all-or-nothing action.

A discussion of storage models illustrates the effort required to support all-or-nothing atomicity (see Figure 2.13). The common storage model implemented by hardware is the so-called *cell storage*, a collection of cells each capable of holding an object (e.g., the primary memory of a computer where each cell is addressable). Cell storage does not support all-or-nothing actions. Once the content of a cell is changed by an action, there is no way to abort the action and restore the original content of the cell.

To be able to restore a previous value we have to maintain a *version history* for each variable in the cell storage. The storage model that supports all-or-nothing actions is called *journal storage*. Now the cell storage is no longer accessible to the action because the access is mitigated by a *storage manager*. In addition to the basic primitives to `read` an existing value and to `write` a new value in cell storage, the storage manager uniquely identifies an action that changes the value in cell storage and, when the

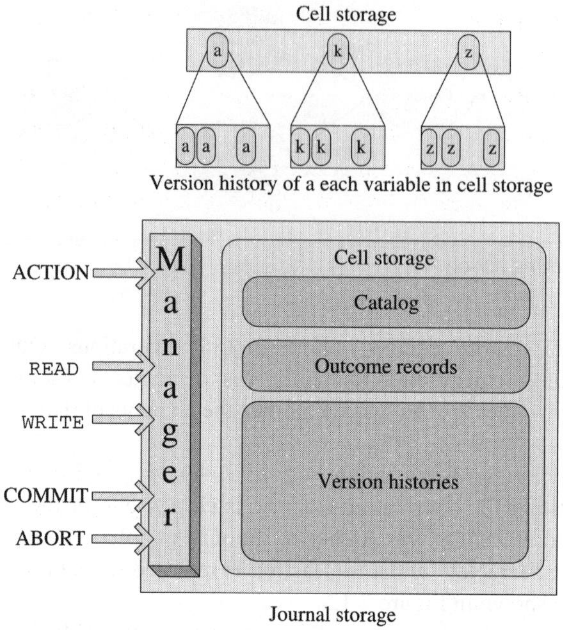

FIGURE 2.13

Storage models. Cell storage does not support all-or-nothing actions. When we maintain version histories, it is possible to restore the original content, but we need to encapsulate the data access and provide mechanisms to implement the two phases of an atomic all-or-nothing action. Journal storage does precisely that.

action is aborted, is able to retrieve the version of the variable before the action and restore it. When the action is committed, then the new value should be written to the cell.

Figure 2.13 shows that for a journal storage, in addition to the version histories of all variables affected by the action, we have to implement a catalog of variables and maintain a record to identify each new action. A new action first invokes the *Action* primitive; at that time an outcome record uniquely identifying the action is created. Then, every time the action accesses a variable, the version history is modified. Finally, the action invokes either a *Commit* or an *Abort* primitive. In the journal storage model the action is atomic and follows the state transition diagram in Figure 2.12.

Before-or-after atomicity means that, from the point of view of an external observer, the effect of multiple actions is as though these actions have occurred one after another, in some order. A stronger condition is to impose a sequential order among transitions. In our example the transaction acting on two accounts should either debit the first account and then credit the second one or leave both accounts unchanged. The order is important because the first account cannot be left with a negative balance.

Atomicity is a critical concept in our efforts to build reliable systems from unreliable components and, at the same time, to support as much parallelism as possible for better performance. Atomicity allows us to deal with unforseen events and to support coordination of concurrent activities. The unforseen event could be a system crash, a request to share a control structure, the need to suspend an activity, and so on; in all these cases we have to save the state of the process or of the entire system to be able to restart it at a later time.

Because atomicity is required in many contexts, it is desirable to have a systematic approach rather than an ad hoc one. A systematic approach to atomicity must address several delicate questions:

- How to guarantee that only one atomic action has access to a shared resource at any given time.
- How to return to the original state of the system when an atomic action fails to complete.
- How to ensure that the order of several atomic actions leads to consistent results.

Answers to these questions increase the complexity of the system and often generate additional problems. For example, access to shared resources can be protected by locks, but when there are multiple shared resources protected by locks, concurrent activities may deadlock. A *lock* is a construct that enforces sequential access to a shared resource; such actions are packaged in the *critical sections* of the code. If the lock is not set, a thread first locks the access, then enters the critical section, and finally unlocks it; a thread that wants to enter the critical section finds the lock set and waits for the lock to be reset. A lock can be implemented using the hardware instructions supporting atomicity.

Semaphores and monitors are more elaborate structures ensuring serial access. Semaphores force processes to queue when the lock is set and are released from this queue and allowed to enter the critical section one by one. Monitors provide special procedures to access the shared data (see Figure 2.14).

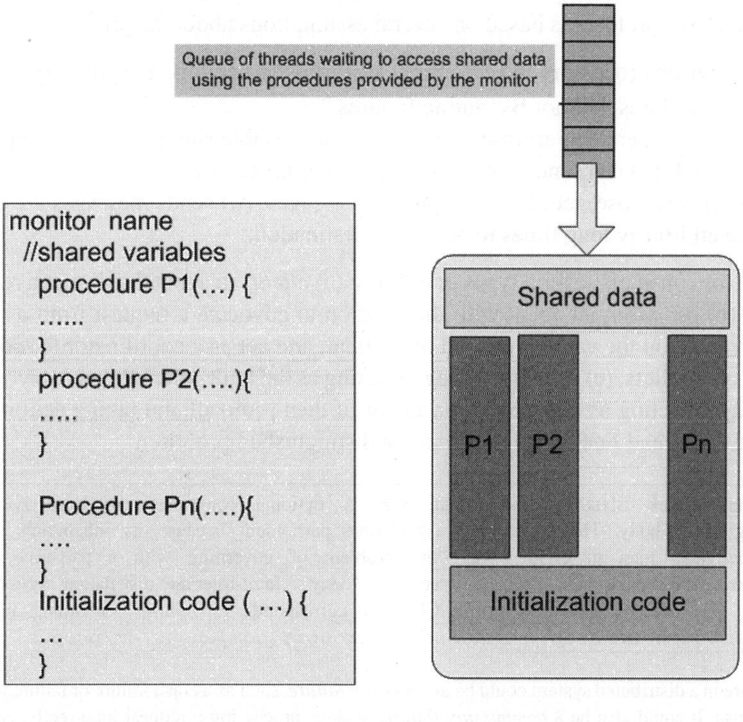

FIGURE 2.14

A monitor provides special procedures to access the data in a critical section.

The mechanisms for the process coordination we described require the cooperation of all activities, the same way traffic lights prevent accidents only as long as drivers follow the rules.

2.11 Consensus protocols

Consensus is a pervasive problem in many areas of human endeavor; consensus is the process of agreeing to one of several alternatives proposed by a number of agents. We restrict our discussion to the case of a distributed system when the agents are a set of processes expected to reach consensus on a single proposed value.

No fault-tolerant consensus protocol can guarantee progress [123], but protocols that guarantee freedom from inconsistencies (safety) have been developed. A family of protocols to reach consensus based on a finite state machine approach is called *Paxos*.[5]

A fair number of contributions to the family of Paxos protocols are discussed in the literature. Leslie Lamport has proposed several versions of the protocol, including *Disk Paxos, Cheap Paxos, Fast Paxos, Vertical Paxos, Stoppable Paxos, Byzantizing Paxos by Refinement, Generalized Consensus and Paxos,* and *Leaderless Byzantine Paxos*. He has also published a paper on the fictional part-time parliament in Paxos [206] and a layman's dissection of the protocol [207].

The *consensus service* consists of a set of n processes. *Clients* send requests to processes and propose a value and wait for a response; the goal is to get the set of processes to reach consensus on a single proposed value. The *basic Paxos* protocol is based on several assumptions about the processors and the network:

- The processes run on processors and communicate through a network; the processors and the network may experience failures, but not Byzantine failures.[6]
- The processors: (i) operate at arbitrary speeds; (ii) have stable storage and may rejoin the protocol after a failure; and (iii) can send messages to any other processor.
- The network: (i) may lose, reorder, or duplicate messages; (ii) sends messages are asynchronously that may take arbitrarily long times to reach the destination.

The *basic Paxos* considers several types of entities: (a) *client,* an agent that issues a request and waits for a response; (b) *proposer,* an agent with the mission to advocate a request from a client, convince the acceptors to agree on the value proposed by a client, and act as a coordinator to move the protocol forward in case of conflicts; (c) *acceptor*, an agent acting as the fault-tolerant "memory" of the protocol; (d) *learner,* an agent acting as the replication factor of then protocol and taking action once a request has been agreed upon; and finally, (e) the *leader,* a distinguished proposer.

[5]Paxos is a small Greek island in the Ionian Sea. A fictional consensus procedure is attributed to an ancient Paxos legislative body. The island had a part-time parliament because its inhabitants were more interested in other activities than in civic work; "the problem of governing with a part-time parliament bears a remarkable correspondence to the problem faced by today's fault-tolerant distributed systems, where legislators correspond to processes and leaving the Chamber corresponds to failing," according to Leslie Lamport [206]. (For additional papers see `http://research.microsoft.com/en-us/um/people/lamport/pubs/pubs.html`.)

[6]A Byzantine failure in a distributed system could be an *omission failure*, such as a crash failure or failure to receive a request or to send a response. It could also be a *commission failure*, such as processing a request incorrectly, corrupting the local state, and/or sending an incorrect or inconsistent response to a request.

A *quorum* is a subset of all acceptors. A proposal has a proposal number pn and contains a value v. Several types of requests flow through the system: *prepare, accept*.

In a typical deployment of an algorithm, an entity plays three roles: proposer, acceptor, and learner. Then the flow of messages can be described as follows [207]: "Clients send messages to a leader; during normal operations the leader receives the client's command, assigns it a new command number i, and then begins the i-th instance of the consensus algorithm by sending messages to a set of acceptor processes." By merging the roles, the protocol "collapses" into an efficient client/master/replica-style protocol.

A proposal consists of a pair, a unique proposal number and a proposed value, (pn, v); multiple proposals may propose the same value v. A value is chosen if a simple majority of acceptors have accepted it. We need to guarantee that at most one value can be chosen; otherwise there is no consensus. The two phases of the algorithm are described here.

Phase I

1. *Proposal preparation:* A proposer (the leader) sends a proposal $(pn = k, v)$. The proposer chooses a proposal number $pn = k$ and sends a *prepare message* to a majority of acceptors requesting:
   a. that a proposal with $pn < k$ should not be accepted;
   b. the $pn < k$ of the highest number proposal already accepted by each acceptor.
2. *Proposal promise:* An acceptor must remember the highest proposal number it has ever accepted as well as the highest proposal number it has ever responded to. The acceptor can accept a proposal with $pn = k$ if and only if it has not responded to a prepare request with $pn > k$; if it has already replied to a prepare request for a proposal with $pn > k$, then it should not reply. Lost messages are treated as an acceptor that chooses not to respond.

Phase II

1. *Accept request:* If the majority of acceptors respond, the proposer chooses the value v of the proposal as follows:
   a. the value v of the highest proposal number selected from all the responses;
   b. an arbitrary value if no proposal was issued by any of the proposers.

   The proposer sends an *accept request* message to a quorum of acceptors including $(pn = k, v)$.
2. *Accept:* If an acceptor receives an *accept message* for a proposal with the proposal number $pn = k$, it must accept it if and only if it has not already promised to consider proposals with a $pn > k$. If it accepts the proposal, it should register the value v and send an *accept* message to the proposer and to every learner; if it does not accept the proposal, it should ignore the request.

The following properties of the algorithm are important to show its correctness: (1) A proposal number is unique; (2) any two sets of acceptors have at least one acceptor in common; and (3) the value sent out in Phase II of the algorithm is the value of the highest numbered proposal of all the responses in Phase I.

Figure 2.15 illustrates the flow of messages for the consensus protocol. A detailed analysis of the message flows for different failure scenarios and of the properties of the protocol can be found in [207]. We only mention that the protocol defines three safety properties: (1) nontriviality, the only values that can be learned are proposed values; (2) consistency, at most one value can be learned; and (3) liveness, if a value

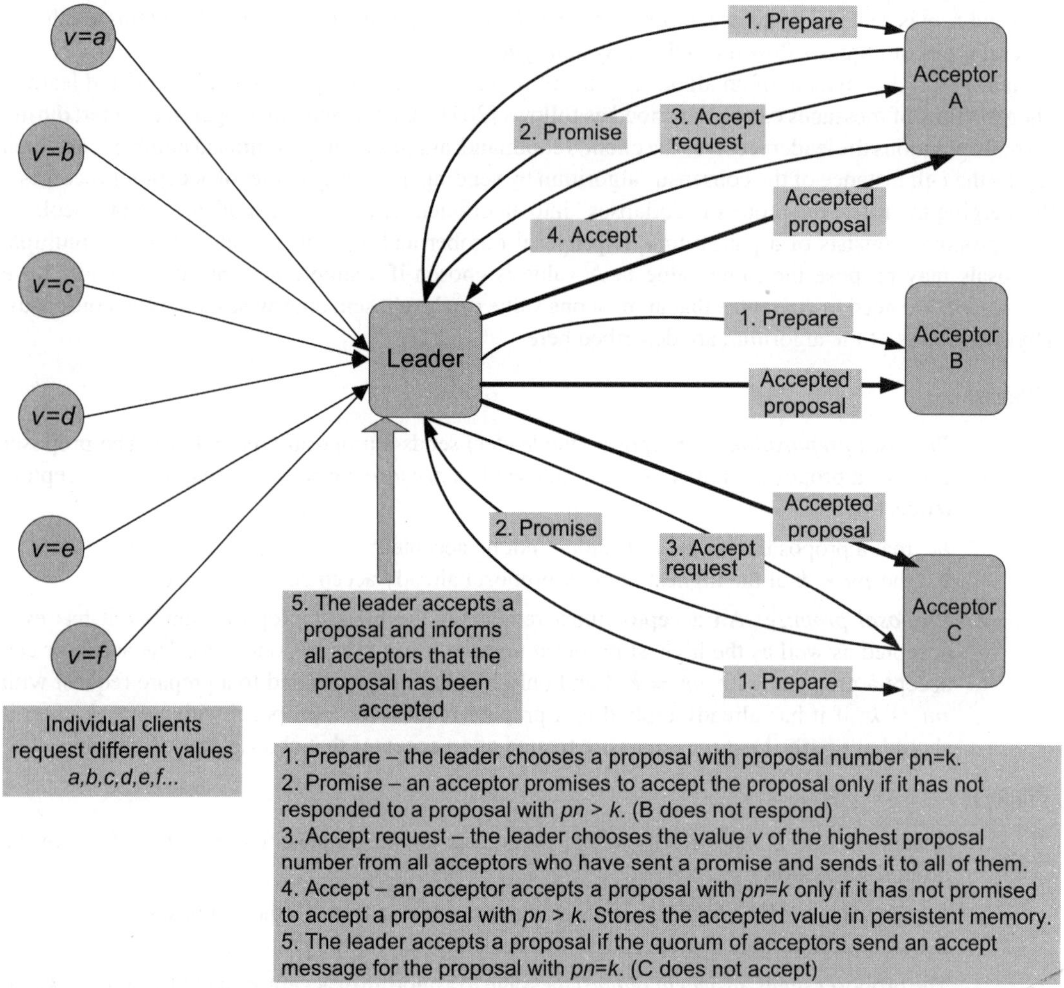

FIGURE 2.15

The flow of messages for the Paxos consensus algorithm. Individual clients propose different values to the leader, who initiates the algorithm. Acceptor A accepts the value in the message with proposal number $pn = k$; acceptor B does not respond with a promise, while acceptor C responds with a promise but ultimately does not accept the proposal.

v has been proposed, eventually every learner will learn some value, provided that sufficient processors remain non-faulty. Figure 2.16 shows the message exchange when there are three actors involved.

In Section 4.5 we present a consensus service, the *ZooKeeper*, based on the Paxos protocol. In Section 8.7 we discuss *Chubby*, a locking service based on the algorithm.

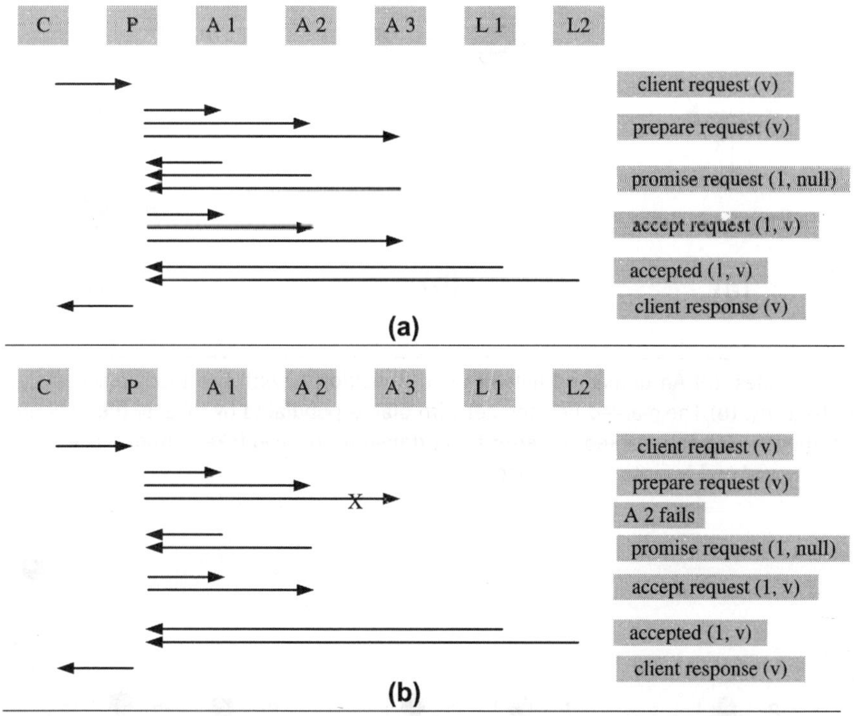

FIGURE 2.16

The basic Paxos with three actors: proposer (P), three acceptors (A1, A2, A3), and two learners (L1, L2). The client (C) sends a request to one of the actors playing the role of a proposer. The entities involved are (a) successful first round when there are no failures and (b) successful first round of Paxos when an acceptor fails.

2.12 Modeling concurrency with Petri nets

In 1962 Carl Adam Petri introduced a family of graphs, the so-called Petri nets (PNs) [291]. PNs are bipartite graphs populated with tokens that flow through the graph that are used to model the dynamic rather than static behavior of systems (e.g., detecting synchronization anomalies).

A *bipartite graph* is one with two classes of nodes; arcs always connect a node in one class with one or more nodes in the other class. In the case of Petri nets the two classes of nodes are *places* and *transitions*; thus, the name place-transition (P/T) nets is often used for this class of bipartite graphs. Arcs connect one place with one or more transitions or a transition with one or more places.

To model the dynamic behavior of systems, the places of a Petri net contain tokens. Firing of transitions removes tokens from the *input places* of the transition and adds them to its *output places* (see Figure 2.17).

Petri nets can model different activities in a distributed system. A *transition* may model the occurrence of an event, the execution of a computational task, the transmission of a packet, a logic statement, and so on. The *input places* of a transition model the pre-conditions of an event, the input data

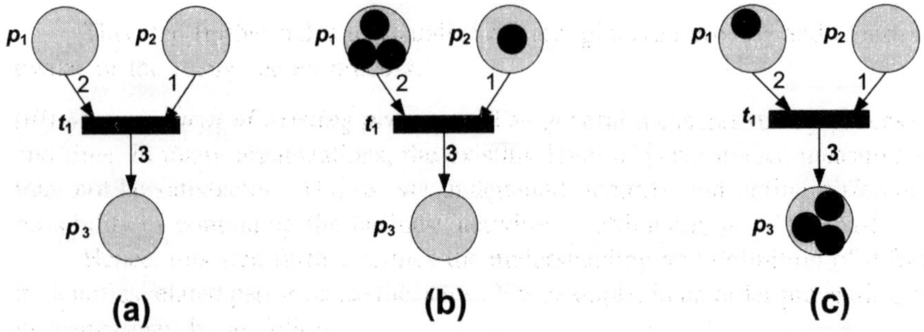

FIGURE 2.17

Petri nets, firing rules. (a) An unmarked net with one transition t_1 with two input places, p_1 and p_2, and one output place, p_3. (b) The marked net, the net with places populated by tokens; the net before firing the enabled transition t_1. (c) The marked net after firing transition t_1. Two tokens from place p_1 and one from place p_2 are removed and transported to place p_3.

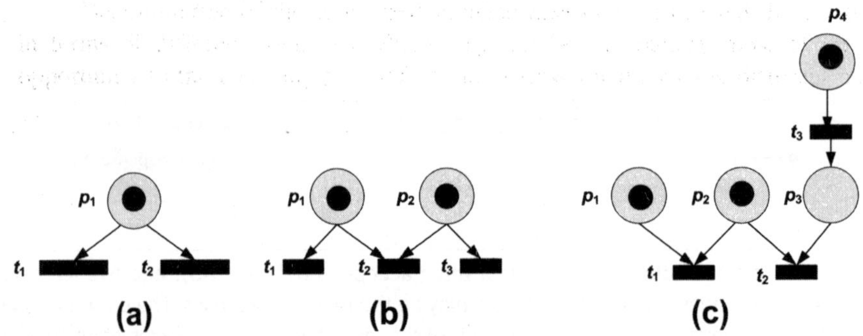

FIGURE 2.18

Petri nets modeling. (a) Choice: Only one of transitions t_1, or t_2 may fire. (b) Symmetric confusion: Transitions t_1 and t_3 are concurrent and, at the same time, they are in conflict with t_2. If t_2 fires, then t_1 and/or t_3 are disabled. (c) Asymmetric confusion: Transition t_1 is concurrent with t_3 and is in conflict with t_2 if t_3 fires before t_1.

for the computational task, the presence of data in an input buffer, or the pre-conditions of a logic statement. The *output places* of a transition model the post-conditions associated with an event, the results of the computational task, the presence of data in an output buffer, or the conclusions of a logic statement.

The distribution of a token in place of a PN at a given time is called the *marking* of the net and reflects the state of the system being modeled. PNs are very powerful abstractions and can express both concurrency and choice, as we can see in Figure 2.18.

Petri nets can model concurrent activities. For example, the net in Figure 2.18(a) models conflict or choice; only one of the transitions t_1 and t_2 may fire, but not both. Two transitions are said to be *concurrent* if they are causally independent. Concurrent transitions may fire before, after, or in parallel with each other; examples of concurrent transitions are t_1 and t_3 in Figure 2.18(b) and (c).

When choice and concurrency are mixed, we end up with a situation called *confusion*. *Symmetric confusion* means that two or more transitions are concurrent and, at the same time, they are in conflict with another one. For example, transitions t_1 and t_3 in Figure 2.18(b) are concurrent and, at the same time, they are in conflict with t_2. If t_2 fires, either one or both of them will be disabled. *Asymmetric confusion* occurs when a transition t_1 is concurrent with another transition t_3 and will be in conflict with t_2 if t_3 fires before t_1, as shown in Figure 2.18(c).

The concurrent transitions t_2 and t_3 in Figure 2.19(a) model concurrent execution of two processes. A *marked graph* can model concurrency but not choice; transitions t_2 and t_3 in Figure 2.19(b) are concurrent, so there is no causal relationship between them. Transition t_4 and its input places p_3 and p_4 in Figure 2.19(b) model synchronization; t_4 can only fire if the conditions associated with p_3 and p_4 are satisfied.

Petri nets can be used to model *priorities*. The net in Figure 2.19(c) models a system with two processes modeled by transitions t_1 and t_2; the process modeled by t_2 has a higher priority than the one modeled by t_1. If both processes are ready to run, places p_1 and p_2 hold tokens. When the two processes are ready, transition t_2 will fire first, modeling the activation of the second process. Only after t_2 is activated will transition t_1 fire, modeling the activation of the first process.

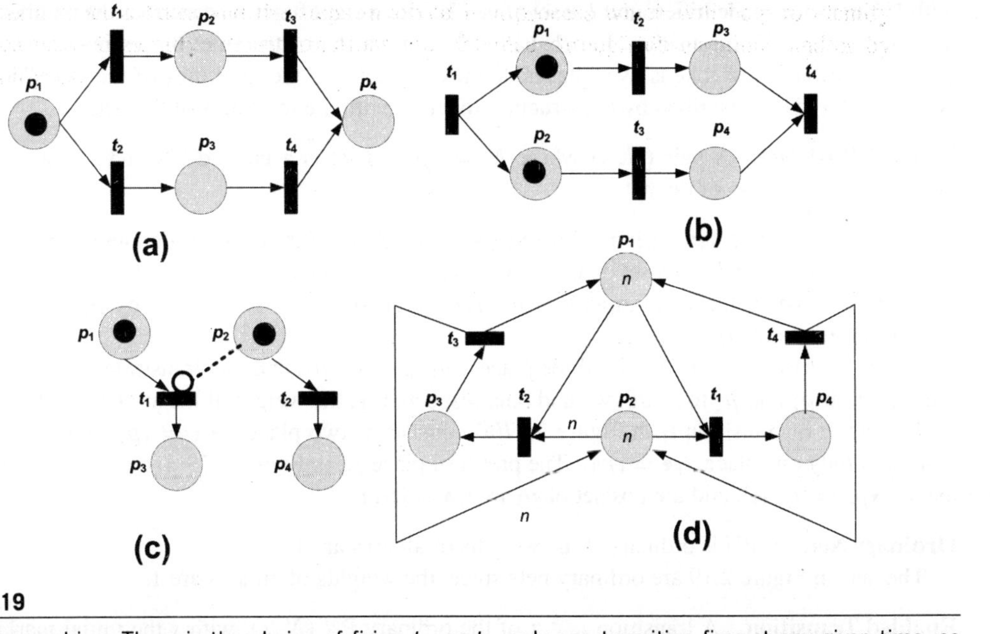

FIGURE 2.19

(a) A state machine. There is the choice of firing t_1, or t_2; only one transition fires at any given time, so concurrency is not possible. (b) A *marked graph* can model concurrency but not choice; transitions t_2 and t_3 are concurrent, so there is no causal relationship between them. (c) An extended net used to model priorities; the arc from p_2 to t_1 is an inhibitor arc. The process modeled by transition t_1 is activated only after the process modeled by transition t_2 is activated. (d) Modeling exclusion; transitions t_1 and t_2 model writing and, respectively, reading, with n processes to a shared memory. At any given time only one process may `write`, but any subset of the n processes may `read` at the same time, provided that no process writes.

Petri nets are able to model *exclusion*. For example, the net in Figure 2.19(d), models a group of n concurrent processes in a shared-memory environment. At any given time only one process may `write`, but any subset of the n processes may `read` at the same time, provided that no process writes. Place p_3 models the process allowed to `write`, p_4 the ones allowed to `read`, p_2 the ones ready to access the shared memory, and p_1 the running tasks. Transition t_2 models the initialization/selection of the process allowed to `write` and t_1 of the processes allowed to `read`, whereas t_3 models the completion of a `write` and t_4 the completion of a `read`. Indeed, p_3 may have at most one token, whereas p_4 may have at most n. If all n processes are ready to access the shared memory, all n tokens in p_2 are consumed when transition t_1 fires. However, place p_4 may contain n tokens obtained by successive firings of transition t_2.

After this informal discussion of Petri nets we switch to a more formal presentation and give several definitions.

Labeled Petri Net. A tuple $N = (p, t, f, l)$ such that:

- $p \subseteq U$ is a finite set of *places*,
- $t \subseteq U$ is a finite set of *transitions*,
- $f \subseteq (p \times t) \cup (t \times p)$ is a set of directed arcs, called *flow relations*, and
- $l : t \rightarrow L$ is a labeling or a weight function,

with U a universe of identifiers and L a set of labels. The weight function describes the number of tokens necessary to enable a transition. Labeled PNs describe a static structure; places may contain *tokens*, and the distribution of tokens over places defines the state, or the markings of the PN. The dynamic behavior of a PN is described by the structure together with the markings of the net.

Marked Petri Net. A pair (N, s) where $N = (p, t, f, l)$ is a labeled PN and s is a bag[7] over p denoting the markings of the net.

Preset and Postset of Transitions and Places. The preset of transition t_i denoted as $\bullet t_i$ is the set of input places of t_i, and the postset denoted by $t_i \bullet$ is the set of the output places of t_i. The preset of place p_j denoted as $\bullet p_j$ is the set of input transitions of p_j, and the postset denoted by $p_j \bullet$ is the set of the output transitions of p_j.

Figure 2.17(a) shows a PN with three places, p_1, p_2, and p_3, and one transition, t_1. The weights of the arcs from p_1 and p_2 to t_1 are two and one, respectively; the weight of the arc from t_1 to p_3 is three.

The preset of transition t_1 in Figure 2.17(a) consists of two places, $\bullet t_1 = \{p_1, p_2\}$, and its postset consist of only one place, $t_1 \bullet = \{p_3\}$. The preset of place p_4 in Figure 2.19(a) consists of transitions t_3 and t_4, $\bullet p_4 = \{t_3, t_4\}$, and the postset of p_1 is $p_1 \bullet = \{t_1, t_2\}$.

Ordinary Net. A PN is ordinary if the weights of all arcs are 1.

The nets in Figure 2.19 are ordinary nets since, the weights of all arcs are 1.

Enabled Transition. A transition $t_i \in t$ of the ordinary PN (N, s), with s the initial marking of N, is *enabled* if and only if each of its input places contain a token, $(N, s)[t_i > \Leftrightarrow \bullet t_i \in s$. The notation $(N, s)[t_i >$ means that t_i is enabled.

---

[7] A bag $\mathcal{B}(\mathcal{A})$ is a multiset of symbols from an alphabet, $\mathcal{A}$; it is a function from $\mathcal{A}$ to the set of natural numbers. For example, $[x^3, y^4, z^5, w^6 | P(x, y, z, w)]$ is a bag consisting of three elements x, four elements y, five elements z, and six elements w such that the $P(x, y, z, w)$ holds. P is a predicate on symbols from the alphabet. x is an element of a bag A denoted as $x \in A$ if $x \in \mathcal{A}$ and if $A(x) > 0$.

The marking of a PN changes as a result of transition firing; a transition must be enabled in order to fire.

Firing Rule. The firing of the transition t_i of the ordinary net (N, s) means that a token is removed from each of its input places and one token is added to each of its output places, so its marking changes $s \mapsto (s - \bullet t_i + t_i \bullet)$. Thus, firing of transition t_i changes a marked net (N, s) into another marked net $(N, s - \bullet t_i + t_i \bullet)$.

Firing Sequence. A nonempty sequence of transitions $\sigma \in t^*$ of the marked net (N, s_0) with $N = (p, t, f, l)$ is called a *firing sequence* if and only if there exist markings $s_1, s_2, \ldots, s_n \in \mathcal{B}(p)$ and transitions $t_1, t_2, \ldots, t_n \in t$ such that $\sigma = t_1, t_2, \ldots, t_n$ and for $i \in (0, n)$, $(N, s_i)t_{i+1} >$ and $s_{i+1} = s_i - \bullet t_i + t_i \bullet$. All firing sequences that can be initiated from marking s_0 are denoted as $\sigma(s_0)$.

Reachability. The problem of finding whether marking s_n is reachable from the initial marking s_0, $s_n \in \sigma(s_0)$. Reachability is a fundamental concern for dynamic systems; the reachability problem is decidable, but reachability algorithms require exponential time and space.

Liveness. A marked Petri net (N, s_0) is said to be *live* if it is possible to fire any transition starting from the initial marking, s_0. The absence of deadlock in a system is guaranteed by the liveness of its net model.

Incidence Matrix. Given a Petri net with n transitions and m places, the incidence matrix $F = [f_{i,j}]$ is an integer matrix with $f_{i,j} = w(i, j) - w(j, i)$. Here $w(i, j)$ is the weight of the flow relation (arc) from transition t_i to its output place p_j, and $w(j, i)$ is the weight of the arc from the input place p_j to transition t_i. In this expression $w(i, j)$ represents the number of tokens added to the output place p_j and $w(j, i)$ the ones removed from the input place p_j when transition t_i fires. F^T is the transpose of the incidence matrix.

A marking s_k can be written as an $m \times 1$ column vector, and its j-th entry denotes the number of tokens in place j after some transition firing. The necessary and sufficient condition for transition t_i to be enabled at a marking s is that $w(j, i) \leqslant s(j)\ \forall s_j \in \bullet t_i$, the weight of the arc from every input place of the transition, be smaller or equal to the number of tokens in the corresponding input place.

Extended Nets. PNs with inhibitor arcs; an *inhibitor arc* prevents the enabling of a transition. For example, the arc from p_2 to t_1 in the net in Figure 2.19(a) is an inhibitor arc; the process modeled by transition t_1 can be activated only after the process modeled by transition t_2 is activated.

Modified Transition Enabling Rule for Extended Nets. A transition is not enabled if one of the places in its preset is connected with the transition with an inhibitor arc and if the place holds a token. For example, transition t_1 in the net in Figure 2.19 (c) is not enabled while place p_2 holds a token.

Based on their structural properties, Petri nets can be partitioned in several classes:

- State machines are used to model finite state machines and cannot model concurrency and synchronization.
- Marked graphs cannot model choice and conflict.
- Free-choice nets cannot model confusion.
- Extended free-choice nets cannot model confusion but they do allow inhibitor arcs.
- Asymmetric choice nets can model asymmetric confusion but not symmetric ones.

This partitioning is based on the number of input and output flow relations from/to a transition or a place and by the manner in which transitions share input places. The relationships between different classes of Petri nets are illustrated in Figure 2.20.

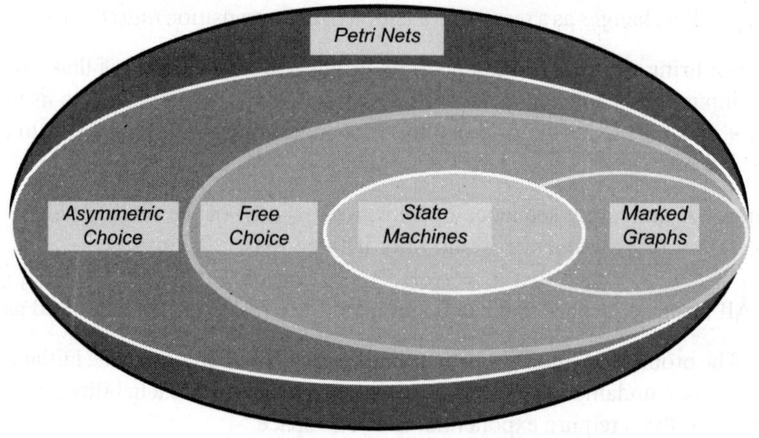

FIGURE 2.20

Classes of Petri nets.

State Machine. A Petri net is a *state machine* if and only if $\forall t_i \in t$ then $(|\bullet t_i| = 1 \wedge |t_i \bullet| = 1)$. All transitions of a state machine have exactly one incoming and one outgoing arc. This topological constraint limits the expressiveness of a state machine, so no concurrency is possible. For example, the transitions t_1, t_2, t_3, and t_4 of the state machine in Figure 2.19(a) have only one input and one output arc, so the cardinality of their presets and postsets is one. No concurrency is possible; once a choice was made by firing either t_1, or t_2, the evolution of the system is entirely determined. This state machine has four places p_1, p_2, p_3, and p_4 and the marking is a 4-tuple (p_1, p_2, p_3, p_4); the possible markings of this net are $(1, 0, 0, 0)$, $(0, 1, 0, 0)$, $(0, 0, 1, 0)$, $(0, 0, 0, 1)$, with a token in places p_1, p_2, p_3, or p_4, respectively.

Marked Graph. A Petri net is a *marked graph* if and only if $\forall p_i \in p$ then $(|\bullet p_i| = 1 \wedge |p_i \bullet| = 1)$. In a marked graph each place has only one incoming and one outgoing flow relation; thus, marked graphs do no not allow modeling of choice.

Free Choice, Extended Free Choice, and Asymmetric Choice Petri Nets. The marked net, (N, s_0) with $N = (p, t, f, l)$ is a *free-choice net* if and only if

$$(\bullet t_i) \cap (\bullet t_j) = \emptyset \Rightarrow |\bullet t_i| = |\bullet t_j| \quad \forall t_{i,j} \in t. \tag{2.38}$$

N is an *extended free-choice net* if $\forall t_i, t_j \in t$ then $(\bullet t_i) \cap (\bullet t_j) = \emptyset \Rightarrow \bullet t_i = \bullet t_j$.
N is an *asymmetric choice net* if and only if $(\bullet t_i) \cap (\bullet t_j) \neq \emptyset \Rightarrow (\bullet t_i \subseteq \bullet t_j)$ or $(\bullet t_i \supseteq \bullet t_j)$, $\forall t_i, t_j \in t$.

In an extended free-choice net, if two transitions share an input place they must share all places in their presets. In an asymmetric choice net, two transitions may share only a subset of their input places.

Several extensions of Petri nets have been proposed. For example, colored Petri nets (CPSs) allow tokens of different colors, thus increasing the expressivity of the PNs but not simplifying their analysis. Several extensions of Petri nets to support performance analysis by associating a random time with each transition have been proposed. In case of stochastic Petri nets (SPNs), a random time elapses between the time a transition is enabled and the moment it fires. This random time allows the model to capture the service time associated with the activity modeled by the transition.

Applications of stochastic Petri nets to performance analysis of complex systems is generally limited by the explosion of the state space of the models. Stochastic high-level Petri nets (SHLPNs) were introduced in 1988 [219]; they allow easy identification of classes of equivalent markings even when the corresponding aggregation of states in the Markov domain is not obvious. This aggregation could reduce the size of the state space by one or more orders of magnitude, depending on the system being modeled.

2.13 Enforced modularity: the client-server paradigm

Modularity. Modularity is a basic concept in the design of man-made systems. A complex system is made of components, or modules, with well-defined functions. Modularity supports the separation of concerns, encourages specialization, improves maintainability, reduces costs, and decreases the development time of a system. Hence, it is no surprise that the hardware as well as the software systems are composed of modules that interact with one another through well-defined interfaces.

In this section we are only concerned with software modularity. We distinguish *soft modularity* from *enforced modularity*. The former means to divide a program into modules that call each other and communicate using shared memory or follow the procedure call convention. The steps involved in the transfer of the flow of control between the caller and the callee are: (i) The caller saves its state, including the registers, the arguments, and the return address, on the stack; (ii) the callee loads the arguments from the stack, carries out the calculations, and then transfers control back to the caller; (iii) the caller adjusts the stack, restores its registers, and continues its processing.

Soft modularity hides the details of the implementation of a module and has many advantages. Once the interfaces of the modules are defined, the modules can be developed independently, and a module can be replaced with a more elaborate or a more efficient one as long as its interfaces with the other modules are not changed. The modules can be written using different programming languages and can be tested independently.

Soft modularity presents a number of challenges. It increases the difficulty of debugging; for example, a call to a module with an infinite loop will never return. There could be naming conflicts and wrong context specifications. The caller and the callee are in the same address space and may misuse the stack (e.g., the callee may use registers that the caller has not saved on the stack, and so on). A strongly typed language may enforce soft modularity by ensuring type safety at compile or at run time, it may reject operations or function classes that disregard the data types, or it may not allow class instances to have their classes altered. Soft modularity may be affected by errors in the run-time system, errors in the compiler, or by the fact that different modules are written in different programming languages.

The Client-Server Paradigm. The ubiquitous client-server paradigm is based on enforced modularity; this means that the modules are forced to interact only by sending and receiving messages. This paradigm leads to a more robust design where the clients and the servers are independent modules and may fail separately. Moreover, the servers are stateless; they do not have to maintain state information. The server may fail and then come up without the clients being affected or even noticing the failure of the server. The system is more robust since it does not allow errors to propagate. Enforced modularity makes an attack less likely because it is difficult for an intruder to guess the format of the messages or the sequence numbers of segments when messages are transported by Transport Control Protocol (TCP).

Last but not least, resources can be managed more efficiently; for example, a server typically consists of an ensemble of systems: a *front-end* system that dispatches the requests to multiple *back-end* systems that process the requests. Such an architecture exploits the elasticity of a computer cloud infrastructure. The larger the request rate, the larger the number of back-end systems activated.

The client-server paradigm allows systems with different processor architecture (e.g., 32-bit or 64-bit), different operating systems (e.g., multiple versions of operating systems such as *Linux*, *Mac OS*, or *Microsoft Windows*), different libraries and other system software to cooperate. The client-server paradigm increases flexibility and choice; the same service could be available from multiple providers, or a server may use services provided by other servers, a client may use multiple servers, and so on.

System heterogeneity is a blessing in disguise. The problems it creates outweigh its appeal. It adds to the complexity of the interactions between a client and a server because it may require conversion from one data format to another (e.g., from *little-endian* to *big-endian* or vice versa), or it may require conversion to a canonical data representation. There is also uncertainty in terms of response time because some servers may be more performant than others or may have a lower workload.

A major difference between the basic models of grid and cloud computing is that the former do not impose any restrictions regarding heterogeneity of the computing platforms. On the other hand, a computer cloud is a collection of homogeneous systems, systems with similar architecture and running under the same or very similar system software.

The clients and the servers communicate through a network that itself can be congested. Transferring large volumes of data through the network can be time consuming; this is a major concern for data-intensive applications in cloud computing. Communication through the network adds additional delay to the response time. Security becomes a major concern because the traffic between a client and a server can be intercepted.

Remote Procedure Call (RPC). RPC is often used for the implementation of client-server systems interactions. The RPC standard is described in RFC 1831. To use an RPC, a process may use special services `PORTMAP` or `RPCBIND`, available at port 111, to register and for service lookup. RPC messages must be well structured; they identify the RPC and are addressed to an RPC demon listening at an RPC port. *XDP* is a machine-independent representation standard for RPC.

RPCs reduce the so-called *fate sharing* between caller and callee but take longer than local calls due to communication delays. Several RPC semantics are implemented:

- **At least once.** A message is resent several times and an answer is expected. The server may end up executing a request more than once, but an answer may never be received. These semantics are suitable for operations free of side effects.
- **At most once.** A message is acted on at most once. The sender sets up a time-out for receiving the response; when the time-out expires, an error code is delivered to the caller. These semantics require the sender to keep a history of the time stamps of all messages because messages may arrive out of order. These semantics are suitable for operations that have side effects.
- **Exactly once.** It implements the *at most once* semantics and requests an acknowledgment from the server.

Applications of the Client-Server Paradigm. The large spectrum of applications attests to the role played by the client-server paradigm in the modern computing landscape. Examples of popular applications of the client-server paradigm are numerous and include the World Wide Web, the Domain Name System (DNS), *X-windows*, electronic mail [see Figure 2.21(a)], event services [see Figure 2.21(b)], and so on.

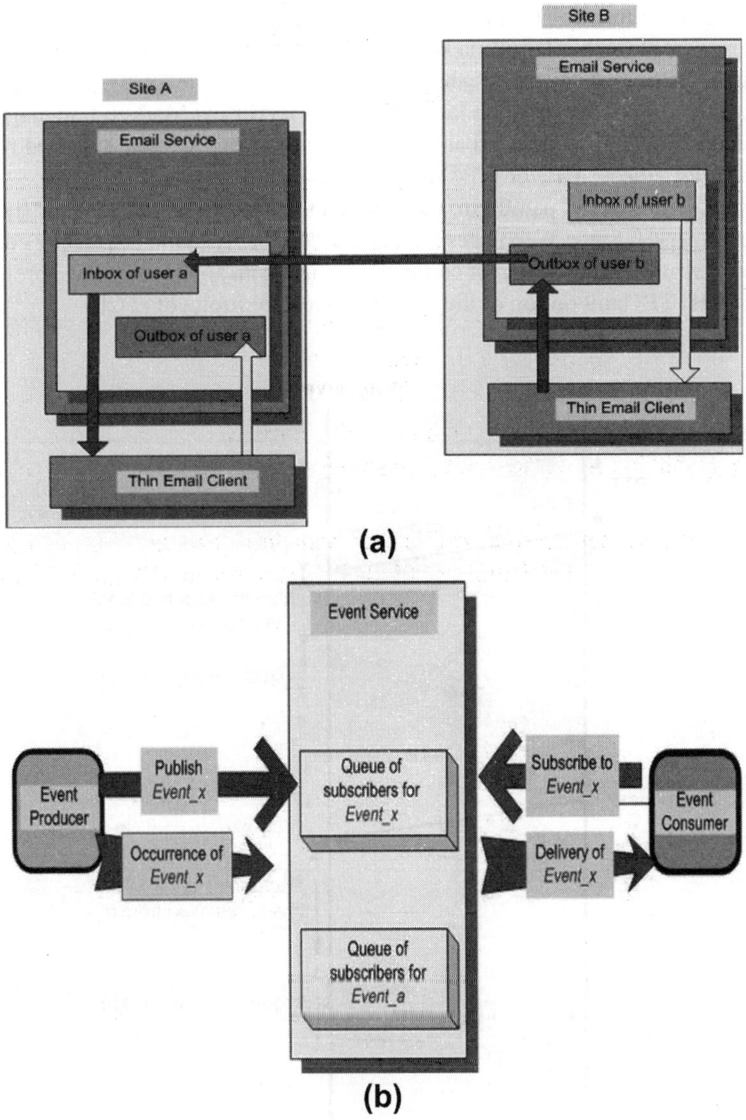

FIGURE 2.21

(a) Email service. The sender and the receiver communicate asynchronously using inboxes and outboxes. Mail demons run at each site. (b) An event service supports coordination in a distributed system environment. The service is based on the *publish/subscribe* paradigm; an event producer *publishes* events and an event consumer *subscribes* to events. The server maintains queues for each event and delivers notifications to clients when an event occurs.

The World Wide Web illustrates the power of the client-server paradigm and its effects on society. As of June 2011 there were close to 350 million Web sites. The Web allows users to access *resources* such as text, images, digital music, and any imaginable type of information previously stored in a digital format. A *Web page* is created using a description language called Hypertext Markup Language (HTML). The information in each Web page is encoded and formatted according to some standard (e.g., GIF, JPEG for images, MPEG for videos, MP3 or MP4 for audio, and so on).

The Web is based on a "pull" paradigm; the resources are stored at the server's site and the client pulls them from the server. Some Web pages are created "on the fly"; others are fetched from disk. The client, called a *Web browser*, and the server communicate using an application-level protocol HyperText Transfer Protocol (HTTP) built on top of the Transport Control Protocol (TCP).

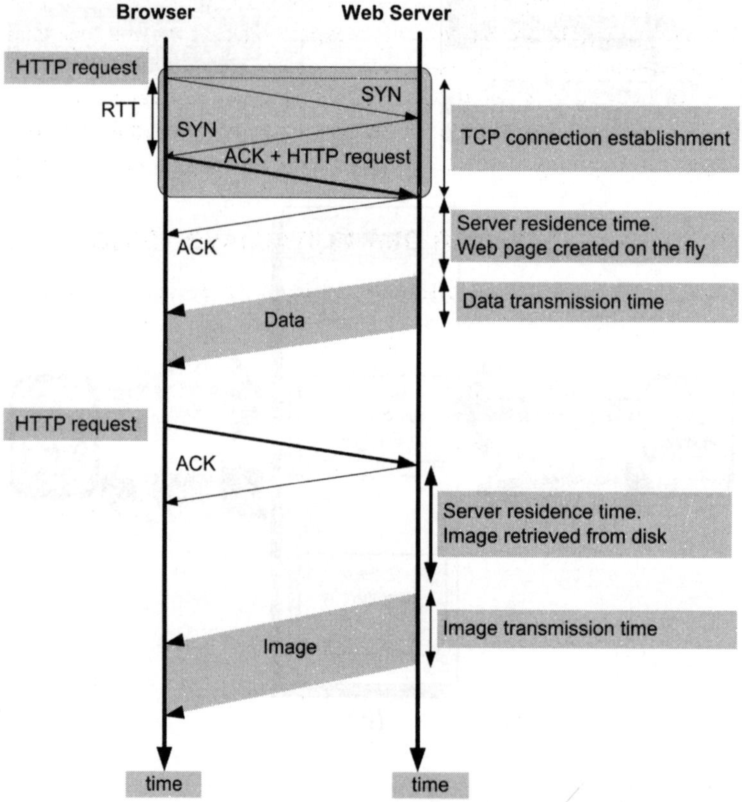

FIGURE 2.22

Client-server communication, on the World Wide Web. The *three-way handshake* involves the first three messages exchanged between the client and the server. Once the TCP connection is established, the HTTP server takes its time to construct the page to respond the first request. To satisfy the second request, the HTTP server must retrieve an image from the disk. The *response time* includes the *round-trip-time* (RTT), the server residence time, and the data transmission time.

The Web server, also called an *HTTP server*, listens at a well-known port, port 80, for connections from clients. Figure 2.22 shows the sequence of events when a client sends an HTTP request to a server to retrieve some information and the server constructs the page on the fly; then it requests an image stored on the disk. First a TCP connection between the client and the server is established using a process called a *three-way handshake*; the client provides an arbitrary initial sequence number in a special segment with the SYN control bit on. Then the server acknowledges the segment and adds its own arbitrarily chosen initial sequence number. Finally the client sends its own acknowledgment ACK as well as the HTTP request, and the connection is established. The time elapsed from the initial request until the server's acknowledgment reaches the client is the RTT.

The *response time*, defined as the time from the instance the first bit of the request is sent until the last bit of the response is received, consists of several components: the RTT, the *server residence time*, the time it takes the server to construct the response, and the data transmission time. RTT depends on the network latency, the time it takes a packet to cross the network from the sender to the receiver; the data transmission time is determined by the network bandwidth. In turn, the server residence time depends on the server load.

Often the client and the server do not communicate directly but through a proxy server, as shown in Figure 2.23. Proxy servers can provide multiple functions; for example, they may filter client requests

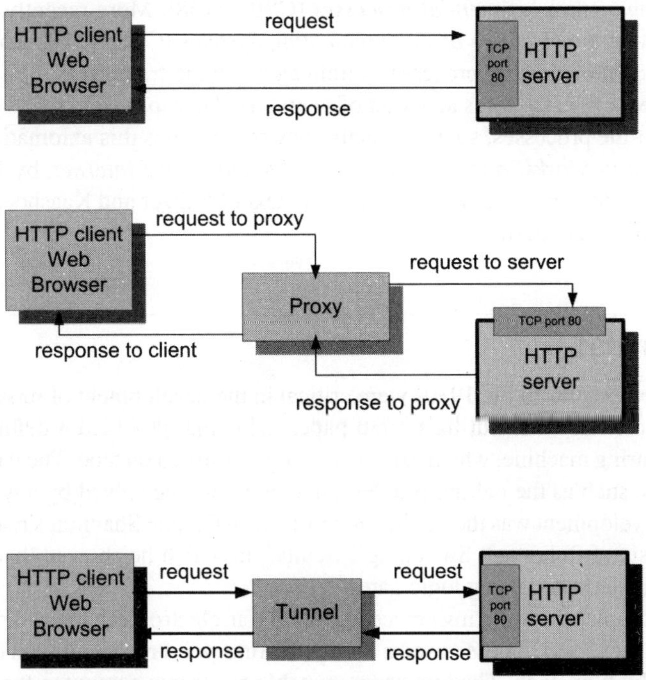

FIGURE 2.23

A client can communicate directly with the server, it can communicate through a proxy, or it may use tunneling to cross the network.

and decide whether or not to forward the request based on some filtering rules. The proxy server may redirect the request to a server in close proximity to the client or to a less loaded server. A proxy can also act as a cache and provide a local copy of a resource rather than forward the request to the server.

Another type of client-server communication is *HTTP tunneling*, used most often as a means for communication from network locations with restricted connectivity. Tunneling means encapsulation of a network protocol. In our case HTTP acts as a wrapper for the communication channel between the client and the server (see Figure 2.23).

2.14 Further reading

Seminal papers in distributed systems have been authored by Mani Chandy and Leslie Lamport [72], by Leslie Lamport [205–207], Hoare [168], and Milner [244]. The collection of contributions with the title *Distributed systems*, edited by Sape Mullender, includes some of these papers.

Petri nets were introduced in [291]. An in-depth discussion of concurrency theory and system modeling with PNs can be found in [292]. The brief discussion of distributed systems leads to the observation that the analysis of communicating processes requires a more formal framework. Hoare realized that a language based on execution traces is insufficient to abstract the behavior of communicating processes and developed *communicating sequential processes* (CSPs) [168]. More recently, Milner initiated an axiomatic theory called the *Calculus of Communicating Systems* (CCS) [244]. *Process algebra* is the study of concurrent communicating processes within an algebraic framework. The process behavior is modeled as a set of equational axioms and a set of operators. This approach has its own limitations, the real-time behavior of the processes, so true concurrency still escapes this axiomatization.

The text *Computer networks: a top-down approach featuring the internet*, by J. A. Kurose and K. W. Ross is a good introduction to networking. A recent text of Saltzer and Kaashoek [312] covers basic concepts in computer system design.

2.15 History notes

Two theoretical developments in the 1930s were critical in the development of modern computers. The first was the publication of Alan Turing's 1936 paper [354] that provided a definition of a universal computer, called a Turing machine, which executes a program stored on tape. The paper also proved that there were problems, such as the halting problem, that could not be solved by any sequential process. The second major development was the publication in 1937 of Claude Shannon's master's thesis at MIT, "A Symbolic Analysis of Relay and Switching Circuits," in which he showed that any Boolean logic expression can be implemented using logic gates.

The first Turing complete[8] computing device was the *Z3*, an electromechanical device built by Konrad Zuse in Germany in May 1941. The *Z3* used a binary floating-point representation of numbers and was program-controlled by film stock. The first programmable electronic computer, the *ENIAC*, built at the Moore School of Electrical Engineering at the University of Pennsylvania by a team led by John Prosper

[8] A Turing complete computer is equivalent to a universal Turing machine except for memory limitations.

Eckart and John Mauchly, became operational in July 1946 [239]. Unlike the *Z3*, the *ENIAC* used a decimal number system and was program-controlled by patch cables and switches.

John von Neumann, the famous mathematician and theoretical physicist, contributed fundamental ideas for modern computers [60,362,363]. His was one of the most brilliant minds of the 20th century, with an uncanny ability to map fuzzy ideas and garbled thoughts to crystal-clear and scientifically sound concepts. John von Neumann drew the insight for the stored-program computer from Alan Turing's work[9] and from his visit to University of Pennsylvania; he thought that the *ENIAC* was an engineering marvel but was less impressed with the awkward manner of "programming" it by manually connecting cables and setting switches. He introduced the so-called "von Neumann architecture" in a report published in the 1940s; to this day he is faulted by some because he failed to mention in this report the sources of his insight.

Von Neumann led the development at the Institute of Advanced Studies at Princeton of the *MANIAC*, an acronym for Mathematical and Numerical Integrator and Computer. The *MANIAC* was closer to modern computers than any of its predecessors; it was used for sophisticated calculations required by the development of the hydrogen bomb, nicknamed "Ivy Mike" and secretly detonated on November 1, 1952, over an island that no longer exists in the South Pacific. In a recent book [110] science historian George Dyson writes: "The history of digital computing can be divided into an Old Testament whose prophets, led by Leibnitz, supplied the logic, and a New Testament whose prophets led by von Neumann built the machines. Alan Turing arrived between them."

Third-generation computers were built during the 1964–1971 period; they made extensive use of integrated circuits (ICs) and ran under the control of operating systems. *MULTIX* (Multiplexed Information and Computing Service) was an early time-sharing operating system for the GE 645 mainframe, developed jointly by MIT, GE, and Bell Labs [91]. It had numerous novel features and implemented a fair number of interesting concepts, such as a hierarchical file system, access control lists for file information sharing, dynamic linking, and online reconfiguration.

The development of the *UNIX* system was a consequence of the withdrawal of Bell Labs from the *MULTIX* project in 1968. *UNIX* was developed in 1969 for a DEC PDP minicomputer by a group led by Kenneth Thompson and Dennis Ritchie [304]. According to [303], "the most important job of *UNIX* is to provide a file-system." The same reference discusses another concept introduced by the system: "For most users, communication with *UNIX* is carried on with the aid of a program called the Shell. The Shell is a command line interpreter: it reads lines typed by the user and interprets them as requests to execute other programs."

The first microprocessor, the Intel 4004, announced in 1971, performed binary-coded decimal (BCD) arithmetic using 4-bit words. It was followed in 1971 by the Intel 8080, the first 8-bit microprocessor, and by its competitor, Motorola 6800, released in 1974. The first 16-bit multichip microprocessor, the IMP-16, was announced in 1973 by National Semiconductor. The 32-bit microprocessors appeared in 1979; the widely used Motorola MC68000 had 32-bit registers and supported 24-bit addressing. Intel's 80286 was introduced in 1982. The 64-bit processor era was inaugurated by the AMD64, an architecture called *x86-64*, backward-compatible with Intel *x86* architecture. Dual-core processors appeared in 2005; multicore processors are ubiquitous in today's servers, PCs, tablets, and even smartphones.

[9] Alan Turing came to the Institute of Advanced Studies at Princeton in 1936 and got his Ph.D. there in 1938. John von Neumann offered him a position at the Institute, but as war was approaching in Europe, Turing decided to go back to England.

2.16 Exercises and problems

Problem 1. Nonlinear algorithms do not obey the rules of scaled speed-up. For example, it was shown that when the concurrency of an $\mathcal{O}(N^3)$ algorithm doubles, the problem size increases only by slightly more than 25%. Read [326] and explain this result.

Problem 2. Given a system of four concurrent threads t_1, t_2, t_3, and t_4, we take a snapshot of the consistent state of the system after 3, 2, 4, and 3 events in each thread, respectively; all but the second event in each thread are local events. The only communication event in thread t_1 is to send a message to t_4 and the only communication event in thread t_3 is to send a message to t_2. Draw a space-time diagram showing the consistent cut; mark individual events on the thread t_i as e_i^j.

How many messages are exchanged to obtain the snapshot in this case? The snapshot protocol allows application developers to create a checkpoint. An examination of the checkpoint data shows that an error has occurred, and it is decided to trace the execution. How many potential execution paths must be examined to debug the system?

Problem 3. The run time of a data-intensive application could be days or possibly weeks, even on a powerful supercomputer. Checkpoints are taken periodically for a long-running computation, and when a crash occurs, the computation is restarted from the latest checkpoint. This strategy is also useful for program and model debugging; when one observes wrong partial results, the computation can be restarted from a checkpoint where the partial results seem to be right.

Express η, the *slowdown due to checkpointing*, for a computation when checkpoints are taken after a run lasting τ units of time and each checkpoint requires κ units of time. Discuss optimal choices for τ and κ.

The checkpoint data can be stored locally, on the secondary storage of each processor, or on a dedicated storage server accessible via a high-speed network. Which solution is optimal and why?

Problem 4. What is in your opinion the critical step in the development of a systematic approach to all-or-nothing atomicity? What does a systematic approach mean? What are the advantages of a systematic versus an ad hoc approach to atomicity?

The support for atomicity affects the complexity of a system. Explain how the support for atomicity requires new functions or mechanisms and how these new functions increase the system complexity. At the same time, atomicity could simplify the description of a system; discuss how it accomplishes this task.

Support for atomicity is critical for system features that lead to increased performance and functionality, such as virtual memory, processor virtualization, system calls, and user-provided exception handlers. Analyze how atomicity is used in each one of these cases.

Problem 5. The Petri net in Figure 2.19(d) models a group of n concurrent processes in a shared-memory environment. At any given time only one process may `write`, but any subset of the n processes may `read` at the same time, provided that no process writes. Identify the firing sequences, the markings of the net, the postsets of all transitions, and the presets of all places. Can you construct a state machine to model the same process?

Problem 6. Explain briefly how the *publish/subscribe* paradigm works and discuss its application to services such as bulletin boards, mailing lists, and so on. Outline the design of an event service based on this paradigm, as in Figure 2.21(b). Can you identify a cloud service that emulates an event service?

Problem 7. Tuple spaces can be thought of as an implementation of a distributed shared memory. Tuple spaces have been developed for many programming languages, including *Java*, *LISP*, *Python*, *Prolog*, *Smalltalk*, and *TCL*. Explain briefly how tuple spaces work. How secure and scalable are the tuple spaces you are familiar with, such as *JavaSpaces*?

Problem 8. Consider a computation consisting of n stages with a barrier synchronization among the N threads at the end of each stage. Assuming that you know the distribution of the random execution time of each thread for each stage, show how you could use order statistics [99] to estimate the completion time of the computation.

Problem 9. In Section 3.7 we analyze cloud computing benchmarks and compare them with the results of the same benchmarks performed on a supercomputer. This is not unexpected; discuss the reasons that we should expect the poor performance of fine-grain parallel computations on a cloud.

CHAPTER

Cloud Infrastructure

3

In this chapter we give an overview of the cloud computing infrastructure at Amazon, Google, and Microsoft as of mid-2012. These cloud service providers support one or more of the three cloud computing delivery models discussed in Section 1.4: *Infrastructure-as-a-Service* (IaaS), *Platform-as-a-Service* (PaaS), and *Software-as-a-Service* (SaaS). Amazon is a pioneer in *IaaS*, Google's efforts are focused on *SaaS* and *PaaS* delivery models, and Microsoft is involved in *PaaS*.

Private clouds are an alternative to public clouds. Open-source cloud computing platforms such as *Eucalyptus* [269], *OpenNebula*, *Nimbus*, and *OpenStack* can be used as a control infrastructure for a private cloud. We continue our discussion of the cloud infrastructure with an overview of service level agreements (SLAs) and the responsibility sharing between users and cloud service providers, followed by a brief discussion of software licensing, energy consumption, and ecological impact of cloud computing. We conclude with a section covering user experiences with current systems.

Several other IT companies are also involved in cloud computing. IBM offers a cloud computing platform, *IBMSmartCloud*, which includes servers, storage, and virtualization components for building private and hybrid cloud computing environments. In October 2012 it was announced that IBM had teamed up with AT&T to give customers access to IBM's cloud infrastructure over AT&T's secure private lines.

In 2011 HP announced plans to enter the cloud computing club. Oracle announced its entry to enterprise computing in the early 2012. The Oracle Cloud is based on Java, SQL standards, and software systems such as Exadata, Exalogic, WebLogic, and Oracle Database. Oracle plans to offer application and platform services. Some of these services are Fusion HCM (Human Capital Management), Fusion CRM (Customer Relation Management), and Oracle Social Network; the platform services are based on Java and SQL.

3.1 Cloud computing at Amazon

Amazon introduced a computing platform that has changed the face of computing in the last decade. First, it installed a powerful computing infrastructure to sustain its core business, e-commerce, selling a variety of goods ranging from books and CDs to gourmet foods and home appliances. Then Amazon discovered that this infrastructure could be further extended to provide affordable and easy-to-use resources for enterprise computing as well as computing for the masses.

In mid-2000 Amazon introduced *Amazon Web Services* (AWS), based on the *IaaS* delivery model. In this model the cloud service provider offers an infrastructure consisting of compute and storage servers interconnected by high-speed networks that support a set of services to access these resources. An application developer is responsible for installing applications on a platform of his or her choice and managing the resources provided by Amazon.

It is reported that in 2012, businesses in 200 countries used the *AWS*, demonstrating the international appeal of this computing paradigm. A significant number of large corporations as well as start-ups take advantage of computing services supported by the *AWS* infrastructure. For example, one start-up reports that its monthly computing bills at Amazon are in the range of $100,000, whereas it would spend more than $2,000,000 to compute using its own infrastructure, without benefit of the speed and flexibility offered by *AWS*. The start-up employs 10 engineers rather than the 60 it would need to support its own computing infrastructure ("Active in cloud, Amazon reshapes computing," *New York Times*, August 28, 2012).

Amazon Web Services. Amazon was the first provider of cloud computing; it announced a limited public beta release of its Elastic Computing platform called *EC2* in August 2006. Figure 3.1 shows the palette of *AWS* services accessible via the *Management Console* in late 2011 [13–18].

Elastic Compute Cloud (EC2)[1] is a Web service with a simple interface for launching instances of an application under several operating systems, such as several *Linux* distributions, *Microsoft Windows* Server 2003 and 2008, *OpenSolaris*, *FreeBSD*, and *NetBSD*.

An instance is created either from a predefined *Amazon Machine Image* (AMI) digitally signed and stored in *S3* or from a user-defined image. The image includes the operating system, the run-time environment, the libraries, and the application desired by the user. AMI images create an exact copy of the original image but without configuration-dependent information such as the *hostname* or the MAC address. A user can: (i) Launch an instance from an existing AMI and terminate an instance; (ii) start and stop an instance; (iii) create a new image; (iv) add tags to identify an image; and (v) reboot an instance.

EC2 is based on the *Xen* virtualization strategy discussed in detail in Section 5.8. In *EC2* each virtual machine or instance functions as a virtual private server. An instance specifies the maximum amount of resources available to an application, the interface for that instance, and the cost per hour.

A user can interact with *EC2* using a set of SOAP messages (see Section 4.3) and can list available AMI images, boot an instance from an image, terminate an image, display the running instances of a user, display console output, and so on. The user has root access to each instance in the elastic and secure computing environment of *EC2*. The instances can be placed in multiple locations in different regions and availability zones.

EC2 allows the import of virtual machine images from the user environment to an instance through a facility called *VM import.* It also automatically distributes the incoming application traffic among multiple instances using the *elastic load-balancing* facility. *EC2* associates an *elastic IP address* with an account; this mechanism allows a user to mask the failure of an instance and remap a public IP address to any instance of the account without the need to interact with the software support team.

Simple Storage System (S3) is a storage service designed to store large objects. It supports a minimal set of functions: `write`, `read`, and `delete`.

S3 allows an application to handle an unlimited number of objects ranging in size from one byte to five terabytes. An object is stored in a *bucket* and retrieved via a unique developer-assigned key. A bucket can be stored in a region selected by the user. *S3* maintains the name, modification time, an access control list, and up to four kilobytes of user-defined metadata for each object. The object names

[1] Amazon *EC2* was developed by a team led by C. Pinkham, including C. Brown, Q. Hoole, R. Paterson-Jones, and W. Van Biljon, all from Cape Town, South Africa.

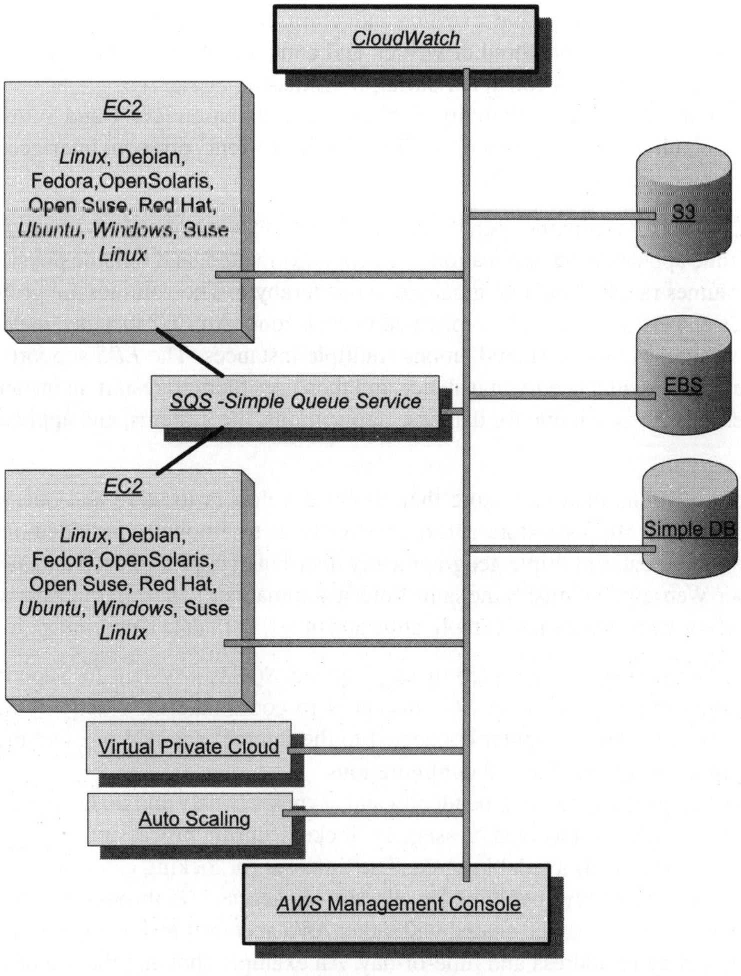

FIGURE 3.1

Services offered by *AWS* are accessible from the *AWS Management Console*. Applications running under a variety of operating systems can be launched using *EC2*. Multiple *EC2* instances can communicate using *SQS*. Several storage services are available: *S3*, *Simple DB*, and *EBS*. The *Cloud Watch* supports performance monitoring; the *Auto Scaling* supports elastic resource management. The *Virtual Private Cloud* allows direct migration of parallel applications.

are global. Authentication mechanisms ensure that data is kept secure; objects can be made public, and rights can be granted to other users.

S3 supports `PUT`, `GET`, and `DELETE` primitives to manipulate objects but does not support primitives to copy, rename, or move an object from one bucket to another. Appending to an object requires a `read` followed by a `write` of the entire object.

S3 computes the *MD5*[2] of every object written and returns it in a field called *ETag*. A user is expected to compute the *MD5* of an object stored or written and compare this with the *ETag*; if the two values do not match, then the object was corrupted during transmission or storage.

The *Amazon S3 SLA* guarantees reliability. *S3* uses standards-based REST and SOAP interfaces (see Section 4.3); the default download protocol is HTTP, but BitTorrent[3] protocol interface is also provided to lower costs for high-scale distribution.

Elastic Block Store (EBS) provides persistent block-level storage volumes for use with Amazon *EC2* instances. A volume appears to an application as a raw, unformatted, and reliable physical disk; the size of the storage volumes ranges from one gigabyte to one terabyte. The volumes are grouped together in availability zones and are automatically replicated in each zone. An *EC2* instance may mount multiple volumes, but a volume cannot be shared among multiple instances. The *EBS* supports the creation of snapshots of the volumes attached to an instance and then uses them to restart an instance. The storage strategy provided by *EBS* is suitable for database applications, file systems, and applications using raw data devices.

Simple DB is a nonrelational data store that allows developers to store and query data items via Web services requests. It supports store-and-query functions traditionally provided only by relational databases. *Simple DB* creates multiple geographically distributed copies of each data item and supports high-performance Web applications; at the same time, it automatically manages infrastructure provisioning, hardware and software maintenance, replication and indexing of data items, and performance tuning.

Simple Queue Service (SQS) is a hosted message queue. *SQS* is a system for supporting automated workflows; it allows multiple Amazon *EC2* instances to coordinate their activities by sending and receiving *SQS* messages. Any computer connected to the Internet can add or `read` messages without any installed software or special firewall configurations.

Applications using *SQS* can run independently and asynchronously and do not need to be developed with the same technologies. A received message is "locked" during processing; if processing fails, the lock expires and the message is available again. The time-out for locking can be changed dynamically via the *ChangeMessageVisibility* operation. Developers can access *SQS* through standards-based *SOAP* and Query interfaces. Queues can be shared with other *AWS* accounts and *anonymously*; queue sharing can also be restricted by IP address and time-of-day. An example showing the use of message queues is presented in Section 4.7.

CloudWatch is a monitoring infrastructure used by application developers, users, and system administrators to collect and track metrics important for optimizing the performance of applications and for increasing the efficiency of resource utilization. Without installing any software, a user can monitor approximately a dozen preselected metrics and then view graphs and statistics for these metrics.

When launching an Amazon Machine Image (AMI), a user can start the *CloudWatch* and specify the type of monitoring. *Basic Monitoring* is free of charge and collects data at five-minute intervals for up

[2]MD5 (Message-Digest Algorithm) is a widely used cryptographic hash function; it produces a 128-bit hash value. It is used for checksums. SHA-i (Secure Hash Algorithm, $0 \leqslant i \leqslant 3$) is a family of cryptographic hash functions; SHA-1 is a 160-bit hash function that resembles MD5.

[3]BitTorrent is a peer-to-peer (P2P) communications protocol for file sharing.

to 10 metrics; *Detailed Monitoring* is subject to a charge and collects data at one-minute intervals. This service can also be used to monitor the latency of access to *EBS* volumes, the available storage space for *RDS DB* instances, the number of messages in *SQS*, and other parameters of interest for applications.

Virtual Private Cloud (VPC) provides a bridge between the existing IT infrastructure of an organization and the *AWS* cloud. The existing infrastructure is connected via a virtual private network (VPN) to a set of isolated *AWS* compute resources. *VPC* allows existing management capabilities such as security services, firewalls, and intrusion detection systems to operate seamlessly within the cloud.

Auto Scaling exploits cloud elasticity and provides automatic scaling of *EC2* instances. The service supports grouping of instances, monitoring of the instances in a group, and defining *triggers* and pairs of *CloudWatch alarms and policies*, which allow the size of the group to be scaled up or down. Typically, a maximum, a minimum, and a regular size for the group are specified.

An *Auto Scaling group* consists of a set of instances described in a static fashion by *launch configurations*. When the group scales up, new instances are started using the parameters for the `runInstances` *EC2* call provided by the launch configuration. When the group scales down, the instances with older launch configurations are terminated first. The monitoring function of the *Auto Scaling* service carries out *health checks* to enforce the specified policies; for example, a user may specify a *health check for elastic load balancing* and then *Auto Scaling* will terminate an instance exhibiting a low performance and start a new one. Triggers use *CloudWatch* alarms to detect events and then initiate specific actions; for example, a trigger could detect when the CPU utilization of the instances in the group goes above 90% and then scale up the group by starting new instances. Typically, triggers to scale up and down are specified for a group.

Several new *AWS* services were introduced in 2012; some of them are in a beta stage at the time of this writing. Among the new services we note: *Route 53*, a low-latency DNS service used to manage user's DNS public records; *Elastic MapReduce (EMR)*, a service supporting processing of large amounts of data using a hosted *Hadoop* running on *EC2* and based on the *MapReduce* paradigm discussed in Section 4.6; *Simple Workflow Service (SWF)*, which supports workflow management (see Section 4.4) and allows scheduling, management of dependencies, and coordination of multiple *EC2* instances; *ElastiCache*, a service enabling Web applications to retrieve data from a managed in-memory caching system rather than a much slower disk-based database; *DynamoDB*, a scalable and low-latency fully managed NoSQL database service; *CloudFront*, a Web service for content delivery; and *Elastic Load Balancer*, a cloud service to automatically distribute the incoming requests across multiple instances of the application. Two new services, the *Elastic Beanstalk* and the *CloudFormation*, are discussed next.

Elastic Beanstalk, a service that interacts with other *AWS* services, including *EC2, S3, SNS, Elastic Load Balance*, and *Auto Scaling*, automatically handles the deployment, capacity provisioning, load balancing, *Auto Scaling*, and application monitoring functions [356]. The service automatically scales the resources as required by the application, either up, or down based on default Auto Scaling settings. Some of the management functions provided by the service are: (i) deployment of a new application version (or rollback to a previous version); (ii) access to the results reported by *CloudWatch* monitoring service; (iii) email notifications when application status changes or application servers are added or removed; and (iv) access to server login files without needing to login to the application servers.

The *Elastic Beanstalk* service is available to developers using a *Java* platform, the *PHP* server-side description language, or *.NET* framework. For example, a Java developer can create the application using any Integrated Development Environment (IDE) such as *Eclipse* and package the code into a Java Web Application Archive (a file of type ".war") file. The ".war" file should then be uploaded to the *Elastic Beanstalk* using the *Management Console* and then deployed, and in a short time the application will be accessible via a URL.

CloudFormation allows the creation of a *stack* describing the infrastructure for an application. The user creates a template, a text file formatted as in *Javascript Object Notation* (JSON), describing the resources, the configuration values, and the interconnection among these resources. The template can be parameterized to allow customization at run time, (e.g., to specify the types of instances, database port numbers, or RDS size). A template for the creation of an *EC2* instance follows:

```
{
  "Description" : "Create instance running Ubuntu Server 12.04 LTS
                   64 bit AMI
   "Parameters" : {
        "KeyPair" : {
             "Description" : "Key Pair to allow SSH access to the instance",
             "Type" : "String"
        }
  },
  "Resources" : {
        "Ec2Instance" : {
             "Type" : "AWS::EC2::Instance",
             "Properties" : {
                   "KeyName" : {"Ref" : "KeyPair"},
                   "ImageId" : "aki-004ec330"
             }
        }
  },
  "Outputs" : {
        "InstanceId" : {
             "Description" : "The InstanceId of the newly created
             instance",
             "Value" : { "Ref" : "Ec2InstDCM"}
        }
  },
  "AWSTemplateFormatVersion" : "2012-03-09"
}
```

The Amazon Web Services Licensing Agreement (AWSLA) allows the cloud service provider to terminate service to any customer at any time for any reason and contains a covenant not to sue Amazon or its affiliates for any damages that might arise out of the use of *AWS*. As noted in [133], the AWSLA prohibits the use of "other information obtained through *AWS* for the purpose of direct marketing, spamming, contacting sellers or customers." It prohibits *AWS* from being used to store any content

Table 3.1 Amazon data centers are located in several regions; in each region there are multiple availability zones. The billing rates differ from one region to another and can be roughly grouped into four categories: low, medium, high, and very high.

Region	Location	Availability Zones	Cost
US West	Oregon	us-west-2a/2b/2c	Low
US West	North California	us-west-1a/1b/1c	High
US East	North Virginia	us-east-1a/2a/3a/4a	Low
Europe	Ireland	eu-west-1a/1b/1c	Medium
South America	Sao Pauló, Brazil	sa-east-1a/1b	Very high
Asia/Pacific	Tokyo, Japan	ap-northeast-1a/1b	High
Asia/Pacific	Singapore	ap-southeast-1a/1b	Medium

that is "obscene, libelous, defamatory or otherwise malicious or harmful to any person or entity." It also prohibits *S3* from being used "in any way that is otherwise illegal or promotes illegal activities, including without limitation in any manner that might be discriminatory based on race, sex, religion, nationality, disability, sexual orientation, or age."

Users have several choices for interacting with and managing *AWS* resources from either a Web browser or from a system running *Linux* or *Microsoft Windows*:

1. The *AWS* Web Management Console, available at `http://aws.amazon.com/console/`; this is the easiest way to access all services, but not all options may be available in this mode.
2. Command-line tools; see `http://aws.amazon.com/developertools.`
3. AWS SDK libraries and toolkits provided for several programming languages, including Java, PHP,[4] C#, and Obj C.
4. Raw REST requests (see Section 4.3 for a discussion of architectural styles for cloud applications).

Regions and Availability Zones. Today Amazon offers cloud services through a network of data centers on several continents, (see Table 3.1[5]). In each *region* there are several *availability zones* interconnected by high-speed networks; regions communicate through the Internet and do not share resources.

An availability zone is a data center consisting of a large number of servers. A server may run multiple virtual machines or instances, started by one or more users; an instance may use storage services, *S3*, *EBS)*, and *Simple DB*, as well as other services provided by *AWS* (see Figure 3.2). A cloud interconnect allows all systems in an availability zone to communicate with one another and with systems in other availability zones of the same region.

Storage is automatically replicated within a region; *S3* buckets are replicated within an availability zone and between the availability zones of a region, whereas *EBS* volumes are replicated only within the

[4]PHP evolved from a set of Perl scripts designed to produce dynamic Web pages called Personal Home Page Tools into a general-purpose server-side scripting language. The code embedded into an HTML source document is interpreted by a Web server with a PHP processor module, which generates the resulting Web page.

[5]In November 2012 Amazon announced a new region, Asia Pacific-Sydney.

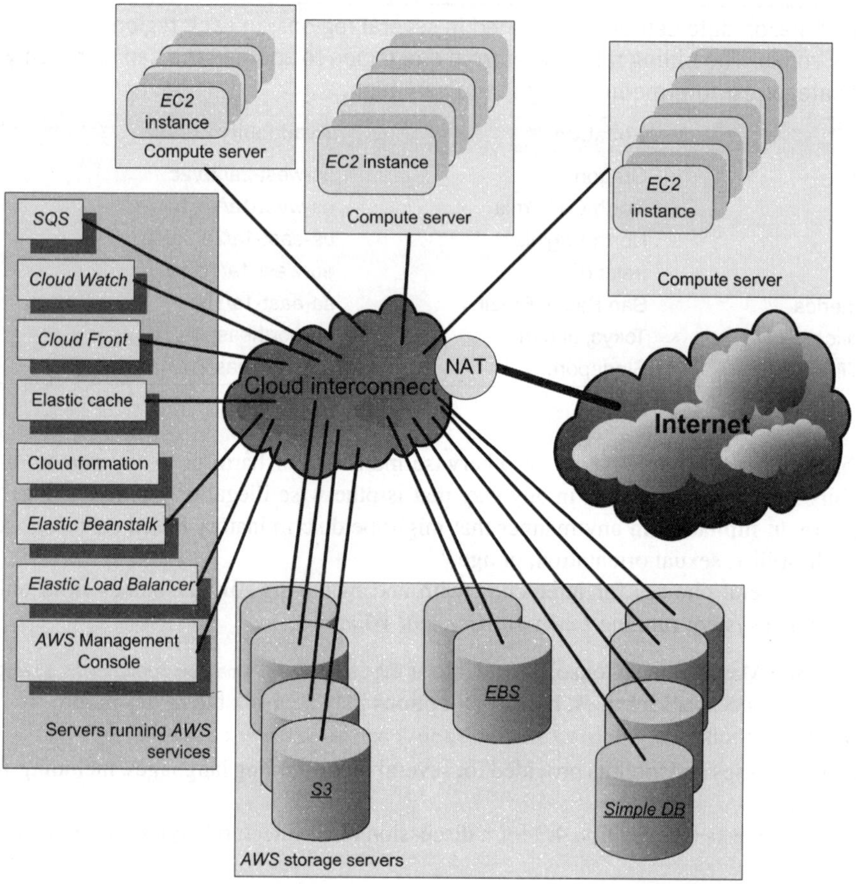

FIGURE 3.2

The configuration of an availability zone supporting *AWS* services. A cloud interconnect supports high-speed communication among compute and storage servers in the zone. It also supports communication with servers in other availablity zones and with cloud users via a Network Address Translation (NAT). NAT maps external IP addresses to internal ones. Multitenancy increases server utilization and lowers costs.

same availability zone. Critical applications are advised to replicate important information in multiple regions to be able to function when the servers in one region are unavailable due to catastrophic events.

A user can request virtual servers and storage located in one of the regions. The user can also request virtual servers in one of the availability zones of that region. The *Elastic Compute Cloud (EC2)* service allows a user to interact and to manage the virtual servers.

The billing rates in each region are determined by the components of the operating costs, including energy, communication, and maintenance costs. Thus, the choice of the region is motivated by the desire to minimize costs, reduce communication latency, and increase reliability and security.

An *instance* is a virtual server. The user chooses the region and the availability zone where this virtual server should be placed and selects from a limited menu of instance types: the one that provides the resources, CPU cycles, main memory, secondary storage, communication, and I/O bandwidth needed by the application.

When launched, an instance is provided with a *DNS name*. This name maps to a *private IP address* for internal communication within the internal *EC2* communication network and a *public IP address* for communication outside the internal Amazon network, (e.g., for communication with the user that launched the instance). Network Address Translation (NAT) maps external IP addresses to internal ones.

The public IP address is assigned for the lifetime of an instance and it is returned to the pool of available public IP addresses when the instance is either stopped or terminated. An instance can request an *elastic IP address*, rather than a public IP address. The elastic IP address is a static public IP address allocated to an instance from the available pool of the availability zone. An elastic IP address is not released when the instance is stopped or terminated and must be released when no longer needed.

The Charges for Amazon Web Services. Amazon charges a fee for *EC2* instances, *EBS* storage, data transfer, and several other services. The charges differ from one region to another and depend on the pricing model; see `http://aws.amazon.com/ec2/pricing` for the current pricing structure.

There are three pricing models for *EC2* instances: on-demand, reserved, and spot. *On-demand instances* use a flat hourly rate, and the user is charged for the time an instance is running; no reservation is required for this most popular model. For *reserved instances* a user pays a one-time fee to lock in a typically lower hourly rate. This model is advantageous when a user anticipates that the application will require a substantial number of CPU cycles and this amount is known in advance. Additional capacity is available at the larger standard rate. In case of *spot instances*, users bid on unused capacity and their instances are launched when the market price reaches a threshold specified by the user.

The *EC2* system offers several instance types:

- *Standard instances.* Micro (StdM), small (StdS), large (StdL), extra large (StdXL); small is the default.
- *High memory instances.* High-memory extra-large (HmXL), high-memory double extra-large (Hm2XL), and high-memory quadruple extra-large (Hm4XL).
- *High CPU instances.* High-CPU extra-large (HcpuXL).
- *Cluster computing.* Cluster computing quadruple extra-large (Cl4XL).

Table 3.2 summarizes the features and the amount of resources supported by each instance. The resources supported by each configuration are main memory, virtual computers (VCs) with a 32- or 64-bit architecture, instance memory (I-memory) on persistent storage, and I/O performance at two levels: moderate (M) or high (H). The computing power of a virtual core is measured in *EC2 compute units (CUs)*.

A main attraction of Amazon cloud computing is the low cost. The dollar amounts charged for one hour of running Amazon's services under *Linux* or *Unix* and *Microsoft Windows* in mid-2012 are summarized in Table 3.3. There are no charges for data transfers from the user's site to the Amazon network or within the Amazon network; the charges for data transfer from the *AWS* network to the outside world depend on the region. For example, the charges for the US West (Oregon) region are shown in Table 3.4.

An Evaluation of Amazon Web Services. In 2007 Garfinkel reported the results of an early evaluation of Amazon Web Services [133]. The paper reports that *EC2* instances are fast, responsive, and

Table 3.2 The nine instances supported by *EC2*. The cluster computing `cl4XL` (quadruple extra-large) instance uses two Intel Xeon X5570, Quad-Core Nehalem Architecture processors. The instance memory (I-memory) refers to persistent storage; the I/O performance can be moderate (M) or high (H).

Instance Name	API Name	Platform (32/64-bit)	Memory (GB)	Max *EC2* Compute Units	I-Memory (GB)	I/O (M/H)
StdM		32 and 64	0.633	1 VC; 2 CUs		
StdS	`m1.small`	32	1.7	1 VC; 1 CU	160	M
StdL	`m1.large`	64	7.5	2 VCs; 2 × 2 CUs	85	H
StdXL	`m1.xlarge`	64	15	4 VCs; 4 × 2 CUs	1,690	H
HmXL	`m2.xlarge`	64	17.1	2 VCs; 2 × 3.25 CUs	420	M
Hm2XL	`m2.2xlarge`	64	34.2	4 VCs; 4 × 3.25 CUs	850	H
Hm4XL	`m2.4xlarge`	64	68.4	8 VCs; 8 × 3.25 CUs	1,690	H
HcpuXL	`c1.xlarge`	64	7	8 VCs; 8 × 2.5 CUs	1,690	H
Cl4XL	`cc1.4xlarge`	64	18	33.5 CUs	1,690	H

Table 3.3 The charges in dollars for one hour of Amazon's cloud services running under *Linux* or *Unix* and under *Microsoft Windows* for several *EC2* instances.

Instance	*Linux/Unix*	*Windows*
StdM	0.007	0.013
StdS	0.03	0.048
StdL	0.124	0.208
StdXL	0.249	0.381
HmXL	0.175	0.231
Hm2XL	0.4	0.575
Hm4XL	0.799	1.1
HcpuXL	0.246	0.516
Cl4XL	0.544	N/A

Table 3.4 Monthly charges in dollars for data transfer out of the US West (Oregon) region.

Amount of Data	Charge $
First 1 GB	0.00
Up to 10 TB	0.12
Next 40 TB	0.09
Next 100 TB	0.07
Next 350 TB	0.05

very reliable; a new instance could be started in less than two minutes. During the year of testing, one unscheduled reboot and one instance freeze were experienced. No data was lost during the reboot, but no data could be recovered from the virtual disks of the frozen instance.

To test the *S3* service, a bucket was created and loaded with objects in sizes of 1 byte, 1 KB, 1 MB, 16 MB, and 100 MB. The measured throughput for the 1-byte objects reflected the transaction speed of *S3* because the testing program required that each transaction be successfully resolved before the next was initiated. The measurements showed that a user could execute at most 50 non-overlapping *S3* transactions. The 100 MB probes measured the maximum data throughput that the *S3* system could deliver to a single client thread. From the measurements, the author concluded that the data throughput for large objects was considerably larger than for small objects due to a high transaction overhead. The write bandwidth for 1 MB data was roughly 5 MB/s, whereas the `read` bandwidth was five times lower at 1 MB/s.

Another test was designed to see if concurrent requests could improve the throughput of *S3*. The experiment involved two virtual machines running on two different clusters and accessing the same bucket with repeated 100 MB `GET` and `PUT` operations. The virtual machines were coordinated, with each one executing one to six threads for 10 min and then repeating the pattern for 11 h. As the number of threads increased from one to six, the bandwidth received by each thread was roughly cut in half and the aggregate bandwidth of the six threads was 30 MB/s, about three times the aggregate bandwidth of one thread. In 107,556 tests of *EC2*, each one consisting of multiple `read` and `write` probes, only six `write` retries, three `write` errors, and four `read` retries were encountered.

3.2 Cloud computing: the Google perspective

Google's effort is concentrated in the area of *Software-as-a-Service* (SaaS). It is estimated that the number of servers used by Google was close to 1.8 million in January 2012 and was expected to reach close to 2.4 million in early 2013 [289].

Services such as *Gmail, Google Drive, Google Calendar, Picasa*, and *Google Groups* are free of charge for individual users and available for a fee for organizations. These services are running on a cloud and can be invoked from a broad spectrum of devices, including mobile ones such as iPhones, iPads, Black-Berrys, and laptops and tablets. The data for these services is stored in data centers on the cloud.

The *Gmail* service hosts emails on Google servers and, provides a Web interface to access them and tools for migrating from Lotus Notes and Microsoft Exchange. *Google Docs* is Web-based software for building text documents, spreadsheets, and presentations. It supports features such as tables, bullet points, basic fonts, and text size; it allows multiple users to edit and update the same document and view the history of document changes; and it provides a spell checker. The service allows users to import and export files in several formats, including Microsoft Office, PDF, text, and OpenOffice extensions.

Google Calendar is a browser-based scheduler; it supports multiple calendars for a user, the ability to share a calendar with other users, the display of daily/weekly/monthly views, and the ability to search events and synchronize with the Outlook Calendar. Google Calendar is accessible from mobile devices. Event reminders can be received via SMS, desktop popups, or emails. It is also possible to share your calendar with other Google Calendar users. *Picasa* is a tool to upload, share, and edit images; it provides 1 GB of disk space per user free of charge. Users can add tags to images and attach locations to photos using *Google Maps*. *Google Groups* allows users to host discussion forums to create messages online or via email.

Google is also a leader in the *Platform-as-a-Service* (PaaS) space. AppEngine is a developer platform hosted on the cloud. Initially it supported only Python, but support for Java was added later and detailed documentation for Java is available. The database for code development can be accessed with Google Query Language (GQL) with a SQL-like syntax.

The concept of *structured data* is important to Google's service strategy. The change of search philosophy reflects the transition from unstructured Web content to structured data, data that contains additional information, such as the place where a photograph was taken, information about the singer of a digital recording of a song, the local services at a geographic location, and so on [227].

Search engine crawlers rely on hyperlinks to discover new content. The *deep Web* is content stored in databases and served as pages created dynamically by querying HTML forms. Such content is unavailable to crawlers that are unable to fill out such forms. Examples of *deep Web* sources are sites with geographic-specific information, such as local stores, services, and businesses; sites that report statistics and analysis produced by governmental and nongovernmental organizations; art collections; photo galleries; bus, train, and airline schedules; and so on. Structured content is created by labeling; *Flickr* and *Google Co-op* are examples of structures where labels and annotations are added to objects, images, and pages stored on the Web.

Google Co-op allows users to create customized search engines based on a set of *facets* or categories. For example, the facets for a search engine for the database research community available at `http://data.cs.washington.edu/coop/dbresearch/index.html` are `professor`, `project`, `publication`, `jobs`.

Google Base is a service allowing users to load structured data from different sources to a central repository that is a very large, self-describing, semi-structured, heterogeneous database. It is self-describing because each item follows a simple schema: (item type, attribute names). Few users are aware of this service. *Google Base* is accessed in response to keyword queries posed on *Google.com*, provided that there is relevant data in the database. To fully integrate Google Base, the results should be ranked across properties. In addition, the service needs to propose appropriate refinements with candidate values in select menus; this is done by computing histograms on attributes and their values during query time.

Google Drive is an online service for data storage that has been available since April 2012. It gives users 5 GB of free storage and charges $4 per month for 20 GB. It is available for PCs, MacBooks, iPhones, iPads, and Android devices and allows organizations to purchase up to 16 TB of storage.

Specialized structure-aware search engines for several interest areas, including travel, weather, and local services, have already been implemented. However, the data available on the Web covers a wealth of human knowledge; it is not feasible to define all the possible domains and it is nearly impossible to decide where one domain ends and another begins.

Google has also redefined the laptop with the introduction of the *Chromebook*, a purely Web-centric device running *Chrome OS*. Cloud-based applications, extreme portability, built-in *3G* connectivity, almost instant-on, and all-day battery life are the main attractions of this device with a keyboard.

Google adheres to a bottom-up, engineer-driven, liberal licensing and user application development philosophy, whereas Apple, a recent entry in cloud computing, tightly controls the technology stack, builds its own hardware, and requires application developers to follow strict rules. Apple products, including the iPhone, the iOS, the iTunes Store, *Mac OS X*, and iCloud, offer unparalleled polish and effortless interoperability, but the flexibility of Google results in more cumbersome user interfaces for the broad spectrum of devices running the Android OS.

Google as well as the other cloud service providers must manage vast amounts of data. In a world where users would most likely desire to use multiple cloud services from independent providers, the question of whether the traditional data base management services (DBMSs) are sufficient to ensure interoperability comes to mind. A DBMS efficiently supports data manipulations and query processing but operates in a single administrative domain and uses well-defined schema. The interoperability of data management services requires *semantic integration* of services based on different schemas. An answer to the limitations of traditional DBMS is the so-called *dataspaces* introduced in [127]; dataspaces do not aim at data integration but rather at data coexistence.

3.3 *Microsoft Windows Azure* and online services

Azure and *Online Services* are, respectively, *PaaS* and *SaaS* cloud platforms from Microsoft. *Windows Azure* is an operating system, *SQLAzure* is a cloud-based version of the SQL Server, and *Azure AppFabric* (formerly .NET Services) is a collection of services for cloud applications.

Windows Azure has three core components (see Figure 3.3): *Compute*, which provides a computation environment; *Storage* for scalable storage; and *Fabric Controller*, which deploys, manages, and monitors applications; it interconnects nodes consisting of servers, high-speed connections, and switches.

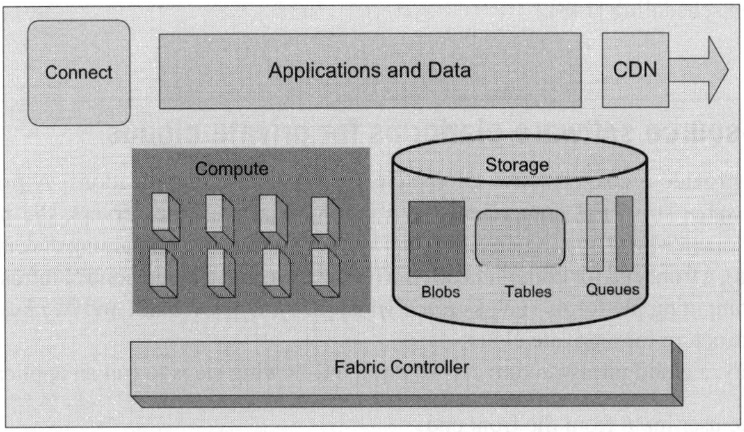

FIGURE 3.3

The components of *Windows Azure*: *Compute*, which runs cloud applications; *Storage*, which uses blobs, tables, and queues to store data; *Fabric Controller*, which deploys, manages, and monitors applications; CDN, which maintains cache copies of data; and *Connect*, which allows IP connections between the user systems and applications running on *Windows Azure*.

The *Content Delivery Network* (CDN) maintains cache copies of data to speed up computations. The *Connect* subsystem supports IP connections between the users and their applications running on *Windows Azure*. The API interface to *Windows Azure* is built on REST, HTTP, and XML. The platform includes five services: *Live Services, SQL Azure, AppFabric, SharePoint*, and *Dynamics CRM*. A client library and tools are also provided for developing cloud applications in Visual Studio.

The computations carried out by an application are implemented as one or more *roles*; an application typically runs multiple *instances of a role*. We can distinguish (i) Web role instances used to create Web applications; (ii) Worker role instances used to run Windows-based code; and (iii) VM role instances that run a user-provided Windows Server 2008 R2 image.

Scaling, load balancing, memory management, and reliability are ensured by a *fabric controller*, a distributed application replicated across a group of machines that owns all of the resources in its environment – computers, switches, load balancers – and it is aware of every *Windows Azure* application. The fabric controller decides where new applications should run; it chooses the physical servers to optimize utilization using configuration information uploaded with each *Windows Azure* application. The configuration information is an XML-based description of how many Web role instances, how many Worker role instances, and what other resources the application needs. The fabric controller uses this configuration file to determine how many VMs to create.

Blobs, tables, queues, and drives are used as scalable storage. A blob contains binary data; a container consists of one or more blobs. Blobs can be up to a terabyte and they may have associated metadata (e.g., the information about where a JPEG photograph was taken). Blobs allow a *Windows Azure* role instance to interact with persistent storage as though it were a local NTFS[6] file system. Queues enable Web role instances to communicate asynchronously with Worker role instances.

The Microsoft Azure platform currently does not provide or support any distributed parallel computing frameworks, such as *MapReduce, Dryad*, or *MPI*, other than the support for implementing basic queue-based job scheduling [148].

3.4 Open-source software platforms for private clouds

Private clouds provide a cost-effective alternative for very large organizations. A private cloud has essentially the same structural components as a commercial one: the servers, the network, virtual machines monitors (VMMs) running on individual systems, an archive containing disk images of virtual machines (VMs), a front end for communication with the user, and a cloud control infrastructure. Open-source cloud computing platforms such as *Eucalyptus* [269], *OpenNebula*, and *Nimbus* can be used as a control infrastructure for a private cloud.

Schematically, a cloud infrastructure carries out the following steps to run an application:

- Retrieves the user input from the front end.
- Retrieves the disk image of a VM from a repository.
- Locates a system and requests the VMM running on that system to set up a VM.

[6]New Technology File System (NTFS) is the standard file system of the *Microsoft Windows* operating system starting with *Windows NT 3.1*, *Windows 2000*, and *Windows XP*.

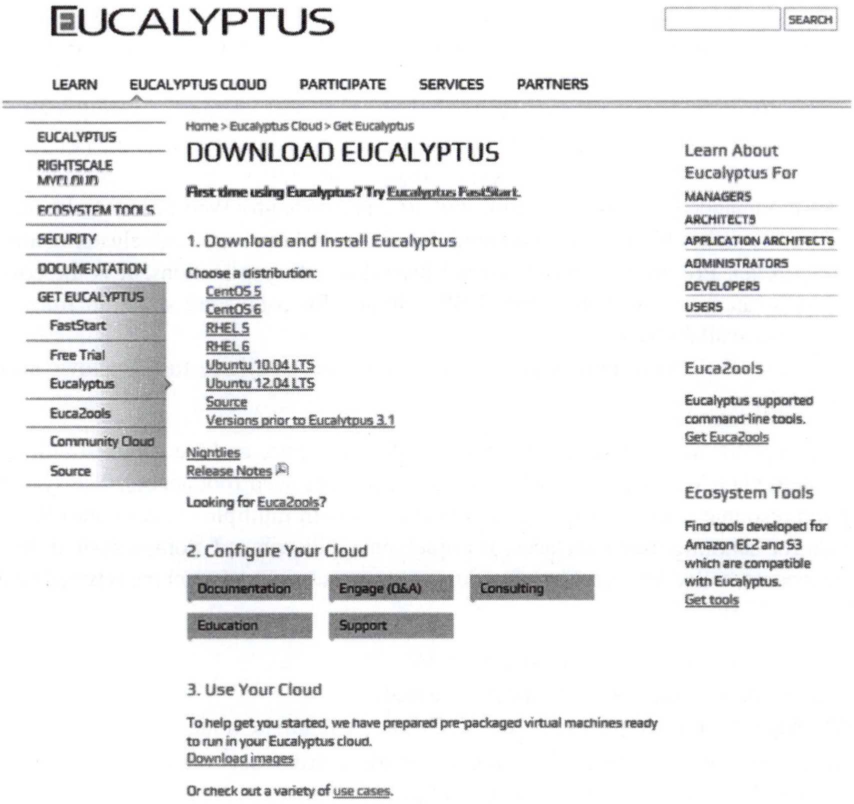

FIGURE 3.4

Eucalyptus supports several distributions and is well-documented software for private clouds.

- Invokes the DHCP[7] and the IP bridging software to set up a MAC and IP address for the VM.

We discuss briefly the three open-source software systems, *Eucalyptus*, *OpenNebula*, and *Nimbus*.

Eucalyptus (`www.eucalyptus.com`) can be regarded as an open-source counterpart of Amazon's EC2, (see Figure 3.4). The systems supports several operating systems including CentOS 5 and 6, RHEL 5 and 6, *Ubuntu* 10.04 LTS, and 12.04 LTS.

The components of the system are:

[7]The Dynamic Host Configuration Protocol (DHCP) is an automatic configuration protocol; it assigns an IP address to a client system. A DHCP server has three methods of allocating IP addresses. (1) Dynamic allocation: A network administrator assigns a range of IP addresses to DHCP, and each client computer on the LAN is configured to request an IP address from the DHCP server during network initialization. The request-and-grant process uses a lease concept with a controllable time period, allowing the DHCP server to reclaim (and then reallocate) IP addresses that are not renewed. (2) Automatic allocation: The DHCP server permanently assigns a free IP address to a client from the range defined by the administrator. (3) Static allocation: The DHCP server allocates an IP address based on a table with MAC address/IP address pairs, which are manually filled in; only clients with a MAC address listed in this table will be allocated an IP address.

- *Virtual machine.* Runs under several VMMs, including *Xen, KVM*, and *Vmware*.
- *Node controller.* Runs on every server or node designated to host a VM and controls the activities of the node. Reports to a cluster controller.
- *Cluster controller.* Controls a number of servers. Interacts with the node controller on each server to schedule requests on that node. Cluster controllers are managed by the cloud controller.
- *Cloud controller.* Provides the cloud access to end users, developers, and administrators. It is accessible through command-line tools compatible with *EC2* and through a Web-based Dashboard. Manages cloud resources, makes high-level scheduling decisions, and interacts with cluster controllers.
- *Storage controller.* Provides persistent virtual hard drives to applications. It is the correspondent of *EBS*. Users can create snapshots from EBS volumes. Snapshots are stored in *Walrus* and made available across availability zones.
- *Storage service (Walrus).* Provides persistent storage and, similarly to *S3*, allows users to store objects in buckets.

The system supports a strong separation between the user space and the administrator space; users access the system via a Web interface, whereas administrators need root access. The system supports a decentralized resource management of multiple clusters with multiple cluster controllers, but a single head node for handling user interfaces. It implements a distributed storage system, the analog of Amazon's *S3* system, called *Walrus*. The procedure to construct a virtual machine is based on the generic one described in [323]:

- The *euca2ools* front end is used to request a VM.
- The VM disk image is transferred to a compute node.
- This disk image is modified for use by the VMM on the compute node.
- The compute node sets up network bridging to provide a virtual network interface controller (NIC)[8] with a virtual Media Access Control (MAC) address.[9]
- In the head node the DHCP is set up with the MAC/IP pair.
- VMM activates the VM.
- The user can now `ssh`[10] directly into the VM.

The system can support a large number of users in a corporate enterprise environment. Users are shielded from the complexity of disk configurations and can choose their VM from a set of five configurations for available processors, memory, and hard drive space set up by the system administrators.

Open-Nebula (`www.opennebula.org`) is a private cloud with users actually logging into the head node to access cloud functions. The system is centralized and its default configuration uses NFS (Network File System). The procedure to construct a virtual machine consists of several steps: (i) the user signs into the head node using `ssh`; (ii) the system uses the `onevm` command to request a VM; (iii) the VM

[8]An NIC is the hardware component connecting a computer to a LAN. It is also known as a network interface card, network adapter, or LAN adapter.

[9]A MAC address is a unique identifier permanently assigned to a network interface by the manufacturer.

[10]Secure Shell (`ssh`) is a network protocol that allows data to be exchanged using a secure channel between two networked devices. `ssh` uses public-key cryptography to authenticate the remote computer and allow the remote computer to authenticate the user. It also allows remote control of a device.

Table 3.5 A side-by-side comparison of *Eucalyptus*, *OpenNebula*, and *Nimbus*.

	Eucalyptus	*OpenNebula*	*Nimbus*
Design	Emulate *EC2*	Customizable	Based on Globus
Cloud type	Private	Private	Public/Private
User population	Large	Small	Large
Applications	All	All	Scientific
Customizability	Administrators and limited users	Administrators and users	All but image storage and credentials
Internal security	Strict	Loose	Strict
User access	User credentials	User credentials	x509 credentials
Network access	To cluster controller	—	To each compute node

template disk image is transformed to fit the correct size and configuration within the NFS directory on the head node; (iv) the `oned` daemon on the head node uses `ssh` to log into a compute node; (v) the compute node sets up network bridging to provide a virtual NIC with a virtual MAC; (vi) the files needed by the VMM are transferred to the compute node via the NFS; (vii) the VMM on the compute node starts the VM; and (viii) the user is able to `ssh` directly to the VM on the compute node.

According to the analysis in [323], the system is best suited for an operation involving a small-to medium-sized group of trusted and knowledgeable users who are able to configure this versatile system based on their needs.

Nimbus (`www.nimbusproject.org`) is a cloud solution for scientific applications based on the Globus software. The system inherits from Globus the image storage, the credentials for user authentication, and the requirement that a running Nimbus process can `ssh` into all compute nodes. Customization in this system can only be done by the system administrators.

Table 3.5 summarizes the features of the three systems [323]. The conclusions of the comparative analysis are as follows: *Eucalyptus* is best suited for a large corporation with its own private cloud because it ensures a degree of protection from user malice and mistakes. *OpenNebula* is best suited for a testing environment with a few servers. *Nimbus* is more adequate for a scientific community less interested in the technical internals of the system than with broad customization requirements.

OpenStack is an open-source project started in 2009 at the National Aeronautics and Space Administration (NASA) in collaboration with Rackspace (`www.rackspace.com`) to develop a scalable cloud operating system for farms of servers using standard hardware. Though recently NASA has moved its cloud infrastructure to *AWS* in addition to Rackspace, several other companies, including HP, Cisco, IBM, and Red Hat, have an interest in *OpenStack*. The current version of the system supports a wide range of features such as application programming interfaces (APIs) with rate limiting and authentication; live VM management to run, reboot, suspend, and terminate instances; role-based access control; and the ability to allocate, track, and limit resource utilization. The administrators and the users control their resources using an extensible Web application called the *Dashboard*.

3.5 Cloud storage diversity and vendor lock-in

There are several risks involved when a large organization relies solely on a single cloud provider. As the short history of cloud computing shows, cloud services may be unavailable for a short or even an extended period of time. Such an interruption of service is likely to negatively impact the organization and possibly diminish or cancel completely the benefits of utility computing for that organization. The potential for permanent data loss in case of a catastrophic system failure poses an equally great danger.

Last but not least, a Cloud Service Provider (CSP) may decide to increase the prices for service and charge more for computing cycles, memory, storage space, and network bandwidth than other CSPs. The alternative in this case is switching to another provider. Unfortunately, this solution could be very costly due to the large volume of data to be transferred from the old to the new provider. Transferring terabytes or possibly petabytes of data over the network takes a fairly long time and incurs substantial charges for the network bandwidth.

This chapter discusses the storage models supported by the cloud infrastructure provided by Amazon, Google, and Microsoft; Chapter 8 covers the architecture of storage systems in general. Reliability is a major concern, and here we discuss a solution that addresses both avoidance of vendor lock-in and storage reliability.

A solution to guarding against the problems posed by the vendor lock-in is to replicate the data to multiple cloud service providers. Straightforward replication is very costly and, at the same time, poses technical challenges. The overhead to maintain data consistency could drastically affect the performance of the virtual storage system consisting of multiple full replicas of the organization's data spread over multiple vendors. Another solution could be based on an extension of the design principle of a RAID-5 system used for reliable data storage.

A RAID-5 system uses block-level stripping with distributed parity over a disk array, as shown in Figure 3.5(a); the disk controller distributes the sequential blocks of data to the physical disks and computes a parity block by bit-wise XOR-ing of the data blocks. The parity block is written on a different disk for each file to avoid the bottleneck possible when all parity blocks are written to a dedicated disk, as is done in the case of RAID-4 systems. This technique allows us to recover the data after a single disk loss. For example, if Disk 2 in Figure 3.5 is lost, we still have all the blocks of the third file, $c1$, $c2$, and $c3$, and we can recover the missing blocks for the others as follows:

$$\begin{aligned} a2 &= (a1) \text{ XOR } (aP) \text{ XOR } (a3) \\ b2 &= (b1) \text{ XOR } (bP) \text{ XOR } (b3)\ . \\ d1 &= (dP) \text{ XOR } (d2) \text{ XOR } (d3) \end{aligned} \quad (39)$$

Obviously, we can also detect and correct errors in a single block using the same procedure. The RAID controller also allows parallel access to data (for example, the blocks $a1$, $a2$, and $a3$ can be `read` and written concurrently) and it can aggregate multiple write operations to improve performance.

The system in Figure 3.5(b) strips the data across four clusters. The access to data is controlled by a proxy that carries out some of the functions of a RAID controller, as well as authentication and other security-related functions. The proxy ensures *before-and-after* atomicity as well as *all-or-nothing* atomicity for data access; the proxy buffers the data, possibly converts the data manipulation commands,

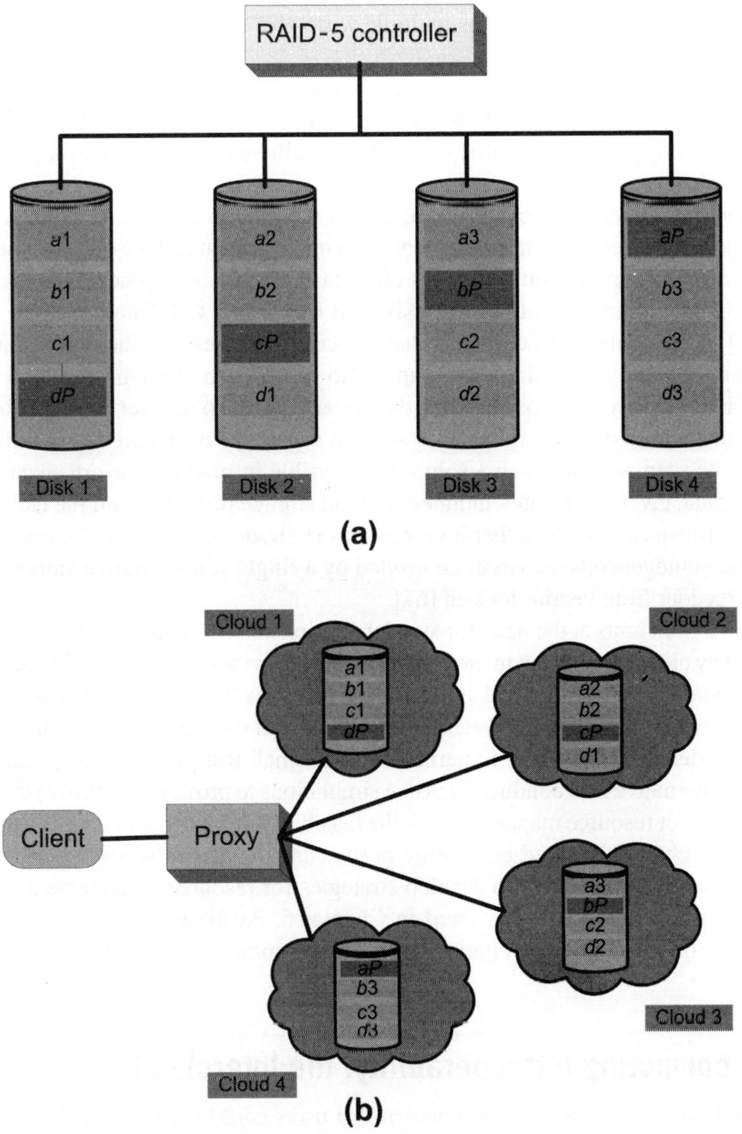

FIGURE 3.5

(a) A (3, 4) RAID-5 configuration in which individual blocks are stripped over three disks and a parity block is added; the parity block is constructed by XOR-ing the data blocks (e.g., $aP = a1 \text{XOR} a2 \text{XOR} a3$). The parity blocks are distributed among the four disks: *aP* is on disk 4, *bP* on disk 3, *cP* on disk 2, and *dP* on disk 1. (b) A system that strips data across four clouds; the proxy provides transparent access to data.

optimizes the data access (e.g., aggregates multiple write operations), converts data to formats specific to each cloud, and so on.

This elegant idea immediately raises several questions: How does the response time of such a scheme compare with that of a single storage system? How much overhead is introduced by the proxy? How could this scheme avoid a single point of failure, the proxy? Are there standards for data access implemented by all vendors?

An experiment to answer some of these question is reported in [5]; the Redundant Array of Cloud Storage (RACS) system uses the same data model and mimics the interface of the *S3* provided by *AWS*. The *S3* system, discussed in Section 3.1, stores the data in *buckets*, each bucket being a flat namespace with *keys* associated with *objects* of arbitrary size but less than 5 GB. The prototype implementation discussed in [5] led the authors to conclude that the cost increases and the performance penalties of the RACS systems are relatively minor. The paper also suggests an implementation to avoid the single point of failure by using several proxies. Then the system is able to recover from the failure of a single proxy; clients are connected to several proxies and can access the data stored on multiple clouds.

It remains to be seen whether such a solution is feasible in practice for organizations with a very large volume of data, given the limited number of cloud storage providers and the lack of standards for data storage. A basic question is whether it makes sense to trade basic tenets of cloud computing, such as simplicity and homogeneous resources controlled by a single administrative authority, for increased reliability and freedom from vendor lock-in [67].

This brief discussion hints at the need for standardization and for scalable solutions, two of the many challenges faced by cloud computing in the near future. The pervasive nature of scalability dominates all aspects of cloud management and cloud applications; solutions that perform well on small systems are no longer feasible when the number of systems or the volume of the input data of an application increases by one or more orders of magnitude. Experiments with small test-bed systems produce inconclusive results. The only alternative is to conduct intensive simulations to prove (or disprove) the advantages of a particular algorithm for resource management or the feasibility of a particular data-intensive application.

We can also conclude that cloud computing poses challenging problems to service providers and to users. The service providers have to develop strategies for resource management subject to quality of service and cost constraints, as discussed in Chapter 6. At the same time, the cloud application developers have to be aware of the limitations of the cloud computing model.

3.6 Cloud computing interoperability: the Intercloud

Cloud interoperability could alleviate the concern that users could become hopelessly dependent on a single cloud service provider, the so-called vendor lock-in discussed in Section 3.5. It seems natural to ask the question whether an Intercloud – a "cloud of clouds," a federation of clouds that cooperate to provide a better user experience – is technically and economically feasible. The Internet is a network of networks; hence, it appears that an Intercloud seems plausible [47–49].

Closer scrutiny shows that the extension of the concept of interoperability from networks to clouds is far from trivial. A network offers one high-level service, the transport of digital information from a source, a host outside a network, to a destination, another host, or another network that can deliver the information to its final destination. This transport of information through a network of networks is feasible because before the Internet was born, agreements on basic questions were reached: (a) how to uniquely identify the source and the destination of the information; (b) how to navigate through a maze of networks; and (c) how to actually transport the data between a source and a destination. The three elements on which agreements were reached are, respectively, the IP address, the IP protocol, and transport protocols such as TCP and UDP.

The situation is quite different in cloud computing. First, there are no standards for storage of processing; second, the clouds we have seen so far are based on different delivery models: *SaaS, PaaS,* and *IaaS*. Moreover, the set of services supported by each of these delivery models is not only large, it is open; new services are offered every few months. For example, in October 2012 Amazon announced a new service, the *AWS GovCloud (US)*.

The question of whether cloud service providers (CSPs) are willing to cooperate to build an Intercloud is open. Some CSPs may think that they have a competitive advantage due to the uniqueness of the added value of their services. Thus, exposing how they store and process information may adversely affect their business. Moreover, no CSP will be willing to change its internal operation, so a first question is whether an Intercloud could be built under these conditions.

Following the concepts borrowed from the Internet, a federation of clouds that does not dictate the internal organization or the structure of a cloud but only the means to achieve cloud interoperability is feasible. Nevertheless, building such an infrastructure seems a formidable task. First, we need a set of standards for interoperability covering items such as naming, addressing, identity, trust, presence, messaging, multicast, and time. Indeed, we need common standards for identifying all the objects involved as well as the means to transfer, store, and process information, and we also need a common clock to measure the time between two events.

An Intercloud would then require the development of an *ontology*[11] for cloud computing. Then each cloud service provider would have to create a description of all resources and services using this ontology. Due to the very large number of systems and services, the volume of information provided by individual cloud service providers would be so large that a distributed database not unlike the Domain Name Service (DNS) would have to be created and maintained. According to [47] this vast amount of information would be stored in Intercloud *root* nodes, analogous to the root nodes of the DNS.

Each cloud would then require an interface, a so-called Intercloud *exchange*, to translate the common language describing all objects and actions included in a request originating from another cloud in terms of its internal objects and actions. To be more precise, a request originated in one cloud would have to be translated from the internal representation in that cloud to a common representation based on the shared ontology and then, at the destination, it would be translated into an internal representation that can be acted on by the destination cloud. This raises immediately the question of efficiency and performance. This question cannot be fully answered now, since an Intercloud exists only on paper, but there is little doubt that performance will be greatly affected.

Security is a major concern for cloud users, and an Intercloud could only create new threats. The primary concern is that tasks will cross from one administrative domain to another and that sensitive information about the tasks and users could be disclosed during this migration. A seamless migration of tasks in an Intercloud requires a well-thought-out trust model.

[11] An ontology provides the means for knowledge representation within a domain. It consists of a set of domain concepts and the relationships among the concepts.

The Public Key Infrastructure (PKI),[12] an all-or-nothing trust model, is not adequate for an Intercloud, where the trust must be nuanced. A nuanced model for handling digital certificates means that one cloud acting on behalf of a user may grant access to another cloud to `read` data in storage, but not to start new instances.

The solution advocated in [48] for trust management is based on dynamic *trust indexes* that can change in time. The Intercloud roots play the role of Certificate Authority, whereas the Intercloud exchanges determine the trust indexes between clouds.

Encryption must be used to protect the data in storage and in transit in the Intercloud. The OASIS[13] Key Management Interoperability Protocol (KMIP)[14] is proposed for key management.

In summary, the idea of an Intercloud opens up a wide range of interesting research topics. The practicality of the concepts can only be discussed after the standardization efforts under way at NIST bear fruit.

3.7 Energy use and ecological impact of large-scale data centers

We start our discussion of energy use by data centers and its economic and ecological impact with a brief analysis of the concept of *energy-proportional systems*. This is a very important concept because a strategy for resource management in a computing cloud is to concentrate the load on a subset of servers and switching the rest of the servers to a standby mode whenever possible [7]. This strategy aims to reduce power consumption and, implicitly, the cost of providing computing and storage services; we analyze this subject in depth in Chapter 6.

The operating efficiency of a system is captured by an expression of "performance per Watt of power." It is widely reported that, during the last two decades, the performance of computing systems has increased much faster than their operating efficiency; for example, during the period 1998–2007, the performance of supercomputers increased by 7,000% whereas their operating efficiency increased by only 2,000%.

In an ideal world, the energy consumed by an idle system should be near zero and should grow linearly with the system load. In real life, even machines whose power requirements scale linearly, use more than half the power when idle than they use at full load (see Figure 3.6) [42].

Energy-proportional systems could lead to large savings in energy costs for computing clouds. An *energy-proportional* system consumes no power when idle, very little power under a light load, and gradually more power as the load increases. By definition, an ideal energy-proportional system is always operating at 100% efficiency. Humans are a good approximation of an ideal energy proportional system; human energy consumption is about 70 W at rest and 120 W on average on a daily basis and can go as high as 1,000–2,000 W during a strenuous, short effort [42].

Different subsystems of a computing system behave differently in terms of energy efficiency. Many processors have reasonably good energy-proportional profiles, but significant improvements in memory

[12]PKI is a model to create, distribute, revoke, use, and store digital certificates. It involves several components: (1) The Certificate Authority (CA) binds public keys to user identities in a given domain. (2) The third-party Validation Authority (VA) guarantees the uniqueness of the user identity. (3) The Registration Authority (RA) guarantees that the binding of the public key to an individual cannot be challenged, the so-called *nonrepudiation*.

[13]OASIS stands for Organization for the Advancement of Structured Information Standards.

[14]The KMIP Specification version 1.0 is available at `http://docs.oasis-open.org/kmip/spec/v1.0/kmip-spec-1.0.html`.

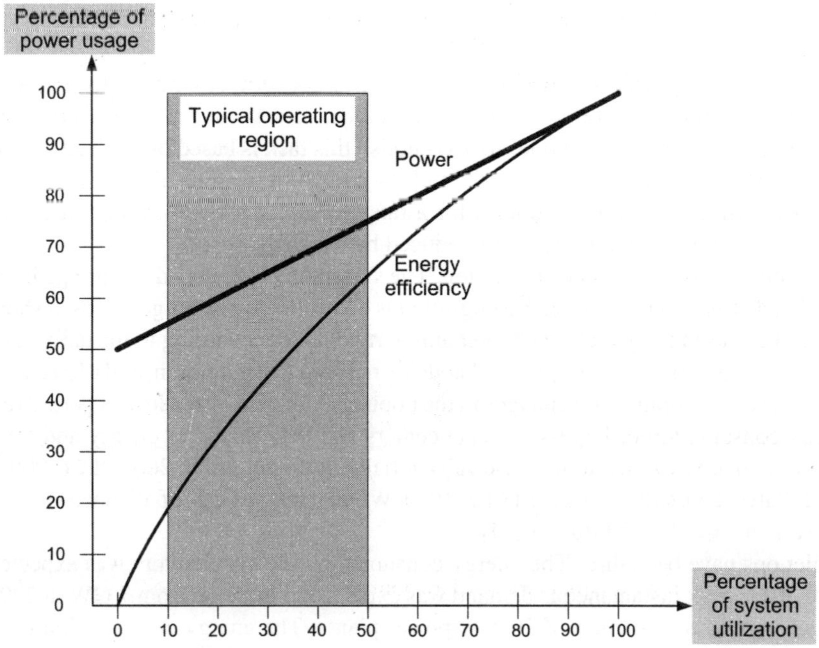

FIGURE 3.6

Even when power requirements scale linearly with the load, the energy efficiency of a computing system is not a linear function of the load; even when idle, a system may use 50% of the power corresponding to the full load. Data collected over a long period of time shows that the typical operating region for the servers at a data center is from about 10% to 50% of the load.

and disk subsystems are necessary. The processors used in servers consume less than one-third of their peak power at very low load and have a dynamic range[15] of more than 70% of peak power; the processors used in mobile and/or embedded applications are better in this respect. According to [42] the dynamic power range of other components of a system is much narrower: less than 50% for dynamic random access memory (DRAM), 25% for disk drives, and 15% for networking switches.

A number of proposals have emerged for *energy-proportional* networks; the energy consumed by such networks is proportional to the communication load. For example, in [6] the authors argue that a data center network based on a flattened butterfly topology is more energy and cost efficient than one using a different type of interconnect.

High-speed channels typically consist of multiple serial lanes with the same data rate; a physical unit is stripped across all the active lanes. Channels commonly operate plesiochronously[16] and are always on, regardless of the load, because they must still send idle packets to maintain byte and lane alignment

[15] The dynamic range in this context is the lower and the upper range of the power consumption of the device. A large dynamic range means that the device is better; it is able to operate at a lower fraction of its peak power when its load is low.

[16] Different parts of the system are almost but not quite perfectly synchronized; in this case, the core logic in the router operates at a frequency different from that of the I/O channels.

across the multiple lanes. An example of an *energy-proportional* network is *InfiniBand*, discussed in Section 3.1.

Energy saving in large-scale storage systems is also of concern. A strategy to reduce energy consumption is to concentrate the workload on a small number of disks and allow the others to operate in a low-power mode. One of the techniques to accomplish this task is based on replication. A replication strategy based on a sliding window is reported in [364]; measurement results indicate that it performs better than LRU, MRU, and LFU[17] policies for a range of file sizes, file availability, and number of client nodes, and the power requirements are reduced by as much as 31%.

Another technique is based on data migration. The system in [158] uses data storage in virtual nodes managed with a distributed hash table; the migration is controlled by two algorithms, a short-term optimization algorithm, used for gathering or spreading virtual nodes according to the daily variation of the workload so that the number of active physical nodes is reduced to a minimum, and a long-term optimization algorithm, used for coping with changes in the popularity of data over a longer period (e.g., a week).

The energy consumption of large-scale data centers and their costs for energy and for cooling are significant now and are expected to increase substantially in the future. In 2006, the 6,000 data centers in the United States reportedly consumed 61×10^9 KWh of energy, 1.5% of all electricity consumption in the country, at a cost of $4.5 billion [364].

The predictions have been dire: The energy consumed by the data centers was expected to double from 2006 to 2011; peak instantaneous demand was expected to increase from 7 GW in 2006 to 12 GW in 2011, requiring the construction of 10 new power plants. The energy consumption of data centers and the network infrastructure is predicted to reach 10, 300 TWh/year[18] in 2030, based on 2010 levels of efficiency [295]. These increases are expected in spite of the extraordinary reduction in energy requirements for computing activities; over the past 30 years the energy efficiency per transistor on a chip has improved by six orders of magnitude.

The effort to reduce energy use is focused on the computing, networking, and storage activities of a data center. A 2010 report shows that a typical Google cluster spends most of its time within the 10–50% CPU utilization range; there is a mismatch between server workload profile and server energy efficiency [6]. A similar behavior is also seen in the data center networks; these networks operate in a very narrow dynamic range, and the power consumed when the network is idle is significant compared to the power consumed when the network is fully utilized.

Many proposals argue that dynamic resource provisioning is necessary to minimize power consumption. Two main issues are critical for energy saving: the amount of resources allocated to each application and the placement of individual workloads. For example, a resource management framework combining a utility-based dynamic virtual machine provisioning manager with a dynamic VM placement manager to minimize power consumption and reduce SLA violations is presented in [358].

The support for network-centric content consumes a very large fraction of the network bandwidth; according to the CISCO VNI forecast, consumer traffic was responsible for around 80% of bandwidth use in 2009 and is expected to grow at a faster rate than business traffic. Data intensity for various activities ranges from 20 MB/minute for HDTV streaming to 10 MB/minute for standard TV streaming,

[17] Least recently used (LRU), most recently used (MRU), and least frequently used (LFU) are replacement policies used by memory hierarchies for caching and paging.

[18] One TWh (Tera Watt hour) is equal to 10^{12} Wh.

1.3 MB/minute for music streaming, 0.96 MB/minute for Internet radio, 0.35 MB/minute for Internet browsing, and 0.0025 MB/minute for ebook reading [295].

The same study reports that if the energy demand for bandwidth is 4 Watts-hour per MB[19] and if the demand for network bandwidth is 3.2 GB/day/person or 2,572 EB/year for the entire world population, then the energy required for this activity will be $1,175$ GW. These estimates do not count very high-bandwidth applications that may emerge in the future, such as 3D TV, personalized immersive entertainment such as Second Life, or massively multiplayer online games.

The power consumption required by different types of human activities is partially responsible for the world's greenhouse gas emissions. According to a recent study [295], the greenhouse gas emissions due to data centers are estimated to increase from 116×10^6 tons of CO_2 in 2007 to 257 tons in 2020, due primarily to increased consumer demand. Environmentally opportunistic computing is a macro-scale computing idea that exploits the physical and temporal mobility of modern computer processes. A prototype called a Green Cloud is described in [376].

3.8 Service- and compliance-level agreements

A *service-level agreement (SLA)* is a negotiated contract between two parties, the customer and the service provider. The agreement can be legally binding or informal and specifies the services that the customer receive rather than how the service provider delivers the services. The objectives of the agreement are:

- Identify and define customers' needs and constraints, including the level of resources, security, timing, and quality of service.
- Provide a framework for understanding. A critical aspect of this framework is a clear definition of classes of service and costs.
- Simplify complex issues; for example, clarify the boundaries between the responsibilities of the clients and those of the provider of service in case of failures.
- Reduce areas of conflict.
- Encourage dialogue in the event of disputes.
- Eliminate unrealistic expectations.

An SLA records a common understanding in several areas: (i) services, (ii) priorities, (iii) responsibilities, (iv) guarantees, and (v) warranties. An agreement usually covers: services to be delivered, performance, tracking and reporting, problem management, legal compliance and resolution of disputes, customer duties and responsibilities, security, handling of confidential information, and termination.

Each area of service in cloud computing should define a "target level of service" or a "minimum level of service" and specify the levels of availability, serviceability, performance, operation, or other attributes of the service, such as billing. Penalties may also be specified in the case of noncompliance with the SLA. It is expected that any service-oriented architecture (SOA) will eventually include middleware supporting SLA management. The *Framework 7* project supported by the European Union is researching this area (see `http://sla-at-soi.eu/`).

[19] In the United States, in 2006, the energy consumed to download data from a data center across the Internet was in the range of 9 to 16 Watts hour per MB.

The common metrics specified by an SLA are service-specific. For example, the metrics used by a *call center* usually are: (i) abandonment rate: percentage of calls abandoned while waiting to be answered; (ii) average speed to answer: average time before the service desk answers a call; (iii) time service factor: percentage of calls answered within a definite time frame; (iv) first-call resolution: percentage of incoming calls that can be resolved without a callback; and (v) turnaround time: time to complete a certain task.

There are two well-differentiated phases in SLA management: the negotiation of the contract and the monitoring of its fulfillment in real time. In turn, automated negotiation has three main components: (i) the *object of negotiation*, which defines the attributes and constraints under negotiation; (ii) the *negotiation protocols*, which describe the interaction between negotiating parties; and (iii) the *decision models* responsible for processing proposals and generating counterproposals.

The concept of compliance in cloud computing is discussed in [55] in the context of the user's ability to select a provider of service. The selection process is subject to customizable compliance with user requirements, such as security, deadlines, and costs. The authors propose an infrastructure called *Compliant Cloud Computing* (C3) consisting of: (i) a language to express user requirements and the compliance level agreements (CLAs) and (ii) the middleware for managing CLAs.

The Web Service Agreement Specification (WS-Agreement) [20] uses an XML-based language to define a protocol for creating an agreement using a predefined template with some customizable aspects. It only supports one-round negotiation without counterproposals. A policy-based framework for automated SLA negotiation for a virtual computing environment is described in [379].

3.9 Responsibility sharing between user and cloud service provider

After reviewing cloud services provided by Amazon, Google, and Microsoft, we are in a better position to understand the differences among *SaaS*, *IaaS*, and *PaaS*. There is no confusion about *SaaS*; the service provider supplies both the hardware and the application software, and the user has direct access to these services through a Web interface and has no control over cloud resources. Typical examples are Google with Gmail, Google Docs, Google Calendar, Google Groups, and Picasa and Microsoft with the Online Services.

In the case of *IaaS*, the service provider supplies the hardware (servers, storage, networks) and system software (operating systems, databases); in addition, the provider ensures system attributes such as security, fault tolerance, and load balancing. The representative of *IaaS* is Amazon *AWS*.

PaaS provides only a platform, including the hardware and system software, such as operating systems and databases; the service provider is responsible for system updates, patches, and software maintenance. *PaaS* does not allow any user control of the operating system, security features, or the ability to install applications. Typical examples are *Google App Engine, Microsoft Azure*, and `Force.com`, provided by `Salesforce.com`.

The level of user control over the system in *IaaS* is different form *PaaS*. *IaaS* provides total control, whereas *PaaS* typically provides no control. Consequently, *IaaS* incurs administration costs similar to a traditional computing infrastructure, whereas the administrative costs are virtually zero for *PaaS*.

It is critical for a cloud user to carefully `read` the SLA and to understand the limitations of the liability a cloud provider is willing to accept. In many instances the liabilities do not apply to damages caused by a third party or to failures attributed either to the customer's hardware and software or to hardware and software from a third party.

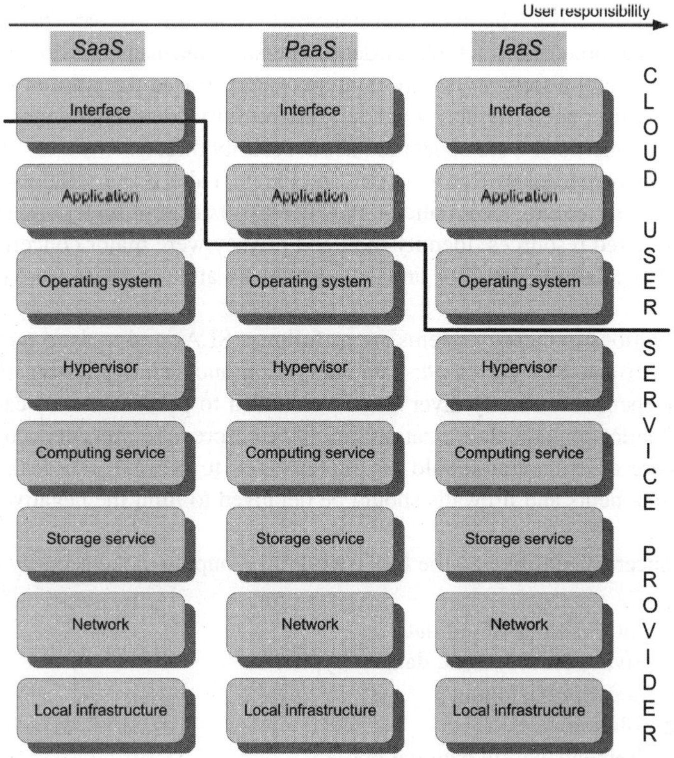

FIGURE 3.7

The limits of responsibility between a cloud user and the cloud service provider.

The limits of responsibility between the cloud user and the cloud service provider are different for the three service-delivery models, as we can see in Figure 3.7. In the case of *SaaS* the user is partially responsible for the interface; the user responsibility increases in the case of *PaaS* and includes the interface and the application. In the case of *IaaS* the user is responsible for all the events occurring in the virtual machine running the application.

For example, if a distributed denial-of-service attack (DDoS) causes the entire *IaaS* infrastructure to fail, the cloud service provider is responsible for the consequences of the attack. The user is responsible if the DDoS affects only several instances, including the ones running the user application. A recent posting describes the limits of responsibility illustrated in Figure 3.7 and argues that security should be a major concern for *IaaS* cloud users, (see `www.sans.org/cloud/2012/07/19/can-i-outsource-my-security-to-the-cloud`).

3.10 User experience

There have been a few studies of user experience based on a large population of cloud computing users. An empirical study of the experience of a small group of users of the Finish Cloud Computing

Consortium is reported in [279]. The main user concerns are security threats, the dependence on fast Internet connections that forced version updates, data ownership, and user behavior monitoring. All users reported that trust in the cloud services is important, two-thirds raised the point of fuzzy boundaries of liability between cloud user and provider, about half did not fully comprehend the cloud functions and its behavior, and about one-third were concerned about security threats.

The security threats perceived by this group of users are: (i) abuse and villainous use of the cloud; (ii) APIs that are not fully secure; (iii) malicious insiders; (iv) account hijacking; (iv) data leaks; and (v) issues related to shared resources. Identity theft and privacy were major concerns for about half of the users questioned; availability, liability, and data ownership and copyright were raised by a third of respondents.

The suggested solutions to these problems are as follows: SLAs and tools to monitor usage should be deployed to prevent abuse of the cloud; data encryption and security testing should enhance the API security; an independent security layer should be added to prevent threats caused by malicious insiders; strong authentication and authorization should be enforced to prevent account hijacking; data decryption in a secure environment should be implemented to prevent data leakage; and compartmentalization of components and firewalls should be deployed to limit the negative effect of resource sharing.

A broad set of concerns identified by the NIST working group on cloud security includes:

- Potential loss of control/ownership of data.
- Data integration, privacy enforcement, data encryption.
- Data remanence after deprovisioning.
- Multitenant data isolation.
- Data location requirements within national borders.
- Hypervisor security.
- Audit data integrity protection.
- Verification of subscriber policies through provider controls.
- Certification/accreditation requirements for a given cloud service.

A 2010 study conducted by IBM [176] aims to identify barriers to public and private cloud adoption. The study is based on interviews with more than 1,000 individuals responsible for IT decision making around the world. Seventy-seven percent of the respondents cited cost savings as the key argument in favor of public cloud adoption, though only 30% of them believed that public clouds are "very appealing or appealing" for their line of business, versus 64% for private clouds and 34% for hybrid ones.

The reasons driving the decision to use public clouds and the percentage of responders who considered each element critical are shown in Table 3.6. In view of the high energy costs for operating a data center (discussed in Section 3.7), it seems strange that only 29% of the respondents seem to be concerned about lower energy costs.

The top workloads mentioned by the users involved in this study are data mining and other analytics (83%), application streaming (83%), help desk services (80%), industry-specific applications (80%), and development environments (80%).

The study also identified workloads that are not good candidates for migration to a public cloud environment:

Table 3.6 The reasons driving the decision to use public clouds.

Reason	Respondents Who Agree
Improved system reliability and availability	50%
Pay only for what you use	50%
Hardware savings	47%
Software license savings	46%
Lower labor costs	44%
Lower maintenance costs	42%
Reduced IT support needs	40%
Ability to take advantage of the latest functionality	40%
Less pressure on internal resources	39%
Solve problems related to updating/upgrading	39%
Rapid deployment	39%
Ability to scale up resources to meet needs	39%
Ability to focus on core competencies	38%
Take advantage of the improved economies of scale	37%
Reduced infrastructure management needs	37%
Lower energy costs	29%
Reduced space requirements	26%
Create new revenue streams	23%

- Sensitive data such as employee and health care records.
- Multiple codependent services (e.g., online transaction processing).
- Third-party software without cloud licensing.
- Workloads requiring auditability and accountability.
- Workloads requiring customization.

Such studies help identify the concerns of potential cloud users and the critical issues for cloud research.

3.11 Software Licensing

Software licensing for cloud computing is an enduring problem without a universally accepted solution at this time. The license management technology is based on the old model of computing centers with licenses given on the basis of named users or as site licenses. This licensing technology, developed for a centrally managed environment, cannot accommodate the distributed service infrastructure of cloud computing or of grid computing.

Only very recently IBM reached an agreement allowing some of its software products to be used on *EC2*. Furthermore, MathWorks developed a business model for the use of MATLAB in grid environments [63]. The *Software-as-a-Service (SaaS)* deployment model is gaining acceptance because it allows users to pay only for the services they use.

There is significant pressure to change the traditional software licensing model and find nonhardware-based solutions for cloud computing. The increased negotiating power of users, coupled with the increase in software piracy, has renewed interest in alternative schemes such as those proposed by the *SmartLM* research project (`www.smartlm.eu`). *SmartLM* license management requires a complex software infrastructure involving SLA, negotiation protocols, authentication, and other management functions.

A commercial product based on the ideas developed by this research project is *elasticLM*, which provides license and billing for Web-based services [63]. The architecture of the *elasticLM* license service has several layers: coallocation, authentication, administration, management, business, and persistency. The authentication layer authenticates communication between the license service and the billing service as well as the individual applications; the persistence layer stores the usage records. The main responsibility of the business layer is to provide the licensing service with the licenses prices, and the management coordinates various components of the automated billing service.

When a user requests a license from the license service, the terms of the license usage are negotiated and they are part of an SLA document. The negotiation is based on application-specific templates and the license cost becomes part of the SLA. The SLA describes all aspects of resource usage, including the ID of application, duration, number of processors, and guarantees, such as the maximum cost and deadlines. When multiple negotiation steps are necessary, the WS-Agreement Negotiation protocol is used.

To understand the complexity of the issues related to software licensing, we point out some of the difficulties related to authorization. To verify the authorization to use a license, an application must have the certificate of an authority. This certificate must be available locally to the application because the application may be executed in an environment with restricted network access. This opens up the possibility for an administrator to hijack the license mechanism by exchanging the local certificate.

3.12 Further reading

Information about cloud computing at Amazon, Google, Microsoft, HP, and Oracle is available from the following sites:

- Amazon: `http://aws.amazon.com/ec2/`
- Google: `http://code.google.com/appengine/`
- Microsoft: `www.microsoft.com/windowsazure/`
- HP: `www.hp.com/go/cloud`
- Oracle: `http://cloud.oracle.com`

Several sites provide additional information about the open-source platforms *Eucalyptus*, *Open-Nebula*, and *Nimbus*:

- Eucalyptus: `www.eucalyptus.com`
- Open-Nebula: `www.opennebula.org`
- Nimbus: `www.nimbusproject.org`

A white paper on SLA specification can be found at `www.itsm.info`, a toolkit at `www.service-level-agreement.net`, and a Web service-level agreement (WSLA) at `www.research.ibm.com/wsla/WSLASpecV1-20030128.pdf`.

Energy use and ecological impact are discussed in [6,158,295,358,364].

Information about the *OpenStack*, an open-source cloud operating system, is available from the project site `www.openstack.org`. The Intercloud is discussed in several papers, including [47–49]. Alternative architectures for cloud computing have been proposed [111].

Several other references including [221,278,283,302,310,378] cover important aspects of the cloud infrastructure.

3.13 History notes

Amazon was one of the first providers of cloud computing. One year after the beta release of *EC2* in 2006, two new instance types (Large and Extra-Large) were added, followed in 2008 by two more types, *High-CPU Medium* and *High-CPU Extra-Large*. New features include static IP addresses, availability zones, and user-selectable kernels as well as the Block Store (EBS). Amazon *EC2* has been in full production mode since October 2008 and supports an SLA and the *Microsoft Windows* operating system as well as the Microsoft SQL Server.

3.14 Exercises and problems

Problem 1. Several desirable properties of a large-scale distributed system were discussed in Section 2.3. The list includes transparency of access, location, concurrency, replication, failure, migration, performance, and scaling. Analyze how each one of these properties applies to *AWS*.

Problem 2. Compare the Oracle Cloud offerings (see `https://cloud.oracle.com`) with the cloud services provided by Amazon, Google, and Microsoft.

Problem 3. Read the IBM report [176] and discuss the workload preferences for private and public clouds and the reasons for the preferences.

Problem 4. In Section 3.7 we introduced the concept of energy-proportional systems and we saw that different system components have different dynamic ranges. Sketch a strategy to reduce the power consumption in a lightly loaded cloud, and discuss the steps for placing a computational server in standby mode and then for bringing it back up to active mode.

Problem 5. Read the paper that introduced the concept of dataspaces [127] and analyze the benefits and the problems with this new idea. Research the literature for potential application of dataspaces for scientific data management in a domain of your choice, be it the search for the Higgs boson at CERN, structural biology, cancer research, or another important research topic that involves data-intensive applications.

Problem 6. In Section 3.7 it was mentioned that *InfiniBand* can be considered an energy-proportional network. The network is used by supercomputers (see `http://i.top500.org/`); the InfiniBand fabric is also used to connect compute nodes, compute nodes with storage servers, and Exadata and Exalogic systems at Oracle data centers. Analyze the features of *InfiniBand* that are critical to reduction of energy consumption.

Problem 7. Many organizations operate one or more computer clusters and contemplate the migration to private clouds. What are the arguments for and against such an effort?

Problem 8. Evaluate the SLA toolkit at `www.service-level-agreement.net`.Is the interactive guide useful? What does it miss? Does the SLA template include all the clauses that are important in your view? If not, what is missing? Are the examples helpful?

Problem 9. Software licensing is a major problem in cloud computing. Discuss several ideas to prevent an administrator from hijacking the authorization to use a software license.

Problem 10. Annotation schemes are widely used by popular services such as the Flickr photo-sharing service, which supports annotation of photos. Sketch the organization of a cloud service used for sharing medical X-ray, tomography, CAT scan, and other medical images and discuss the main challenges for its implementation.

CHAPTER

Cloud Computing: Applications and Paradigms

4

The efforts to support large-scale distributed computing have encountered major difficulties over the years. The users of these systems discovered how difficult it was to locate the systems able to run an application. They soon realized that it is equally difficult to scale up and down to accommodate a dynamic load, to recover after a system failure, and to efficiently support checkpoint or restarting procedures.

At the same time, the providers of computing cycles and storage realized the difficulties in managing a large number of systems and providing guarantees for the quality of service. Any economic advantage offered by resource concentration was offset by the cost of management and the relatively low utilization of costly resources.

Cloud computing is very attractive to users for several economic reasons: It requires a very low infrastructure investment because there is no need to assemble and maintain a large-scale system and it has low *utility-based computing costs* because customers are only billed for the infrastructure used. At the same time, users benefit from the potential to reduce the execution time of compute-intensive and data-intensive applications through parallelization. If an application can partition the workload in n segments and spawn n instances of itself, the execution time could be reduced by a factor close to n.

Moreover, because application developers enjoy the advantages of a *just-in-time infrastructure*, they are free to design an application without being concerned with the system where the application will run. Often, an application becomes the victim of its own success, attracting a user population larger than the system can support. Cloud elasticity allows such an application to absorb the additional workload without any effort from application developers.

Cloud computing is also beneficial for the providers of computing cycles because it typically leads to more efficient resource utilization. The future success of cloud computing rests on the ability of companies promoting utility computing to convince an increasingly large segment of the user population of the advantages of network-centric computing and content. This translates into the ability to provide satisfactory solutions to critical aspects of security, scalability, reliability, quality of service, and the requirements enforced by SLAs.

The appeal of cloud computing is its focus on enterprise applications. This clearly differentiates it from the grid computing effort, which was largely focused on scientific and engineering applications. Of course, the other major advantage of the cloud computing approach over grid computing is the concentration of resources in large data centers in a single administrative domain.

It is expected that utility computing providers such as Amazon, Apple, Google, HP, IBM, Microsoft, Oracle, and others will in the future develop application suites to attract customers. Microsoft seems well positioned in the effort to attract customers to its Azure platform since it already has many applications for enterprise customers, while Red Hat and Amazon may choose to stay with their "infrastructure only" approach [27].

The main attraction of cloud computing is the ability to use as many servers as necessary to optimally respond to the cost and the timing constraints of an application. This is possible only if the workload can be partitioned in segments of arbitrary size and can be processed in parallel by the servers available in the cloud. In Section 4.6 we discuss *arbitrarily divisible* workloads that can be partitioned into an arbitrarily large number of segments; the *arbitrarily divisible load-sharing model* is common to many applications, and these are precisely the applications suitable for cloud computing.

Web services, database services, and transaction-based services are ideal applications for cloud computing. The resource requirements of transaction-oriented services are dependent on the current load, which itself is very dynamic; the cost/performance profile of such applications benefits from an elastic environment in which resources are available when needed and users pay only for the resources they consume.

Not all applications are suitable for cloud computing; applications for which the workload cannot be arbitrarily partitioned or that require intensive communication among concurrent instances are unlikely to perform well on a cloud. An application with a complex workflow and multiple dependencies, as is often the case in high-performance computing, could require longer execution times and higher costs on a cloud. The benchmarks for high-performance computing discussed in Section 4.9 show that communication and memory-intensive applications may not exhibit the performance levels shown when running on supercomputers with low latency and high-bandwidth interconnects.

4.1 Challenges for cloud computing

The development of efficient cloud applications inherits the challenges posed by the natural imbalance among computing, I/O, and communication bandwidths of physical systems. These challenges are greatly amplified due to the scale of the system, its distributed nature, and the fact that virtually all applications are data-intensive. Though cloud computing infrastructures attempt to automatically distribute and balance a load, the application developer is still left with the responsibility of placing the data close to the processing site and identifying optimal storage for the data.

One of the main advantages of cloud computing, the shared infrastructure, could also have a negative impact. Performance isolation[1] is nearly impossible to reach in a real system, especially when the system is heavily loaded. The performance of virtual machines fluctuates based on the load, the infrastructure services, and the environment, including the other users. Security isolation is also challenging on multitenant systems.

Reliability is also a major concern; node failures are to be expected whenever a large number of nodes cooperate for the computations. Choosing an optimal instance (in terms of performance isolation, reliability, and security) from those offered by the cloud infrastructure is another critical factor to be considered. Of course, cost considerations also play a role in the choice of the instance type.

Many applications consist of multiple stages; in turn, each stage may involve multiple instances running in parallel on the systems of the cloud and communicating among them. Thus, efficiency, consistency, and communication scalability are major concerns for an application developer. Indeed,

[1]Performance and security isolation of virtual machines are discussed in Section 5.5.

due to shared networks and unknown topology, cloud infrastructures exhibit internode latency and bandwidth fluctuations that affect application performance.

Data storage plays a critical role in the performance of any data-intensive application; the organization of the storage, the storage location, and the storage bandwidth must be carefully analyzed to lead to optimal application performance. Clouds support many storage options to set up a file system similar to the *Hadoop* file system discussed in Section 8.6; among them are off-instance cloud storage (e.g., *S3*), mountable off-instance block storage (e.g., *EBS*), and storage persistent for the lifetime of the instance.

Many data-intensive applications use metadata associated with individual data records; for example, the metadata for an MPEG audio file may include the name of the song, the singer, recording information, and so on. Metadata should be stored for easy access, and the storage should be scalable and reliable.

Another important consideration for the application developer is logging. Performance considerations limit the amount of data logging, whereas the ability to identify the source of unexpected results and errors is helped by frequent logging. Logging is typically done using instance storage preserved only for the lifetime of the instance. Thus, measures to preserve the logs for a postmortem analysis must be taken. Another challenge awaiting resolution is related to software licensing, discussed in Section 3.11.

4.2 Existing cloud applications and new application opportunities

Existing cloud applications can be divided into several broad categories: (i) processing pipelines; (ii) batch processing systems; and (iii) Web applications [360].

Processing pipelines are data-intensive and sometimes compute-intensive applications and represent a fairly large segment of applications currently running on the cloud. Several types of data processing applications can be identified:

- *Indexing*. The processing pipeline supports indexing of large datasets created by Web crawler engines.
- *Data mining*. The processing pipeline supports searching very large collections of records to locate items of interests.
- *Image processing*. A number of companies allow users to store their images on the cloud (e.g., *Flickr* (`www.flickr.com`) and *Google* (`http://picasa.google.com/`)). The image-processing pipelines support image conversion (e.g., enlarging an image or creating thumbnails). They can also be used to compress or encrypt images.
- *Video transcoding*. The processing pipeline transcodes from one video format to another (e.g., from AVI to MPEG).
- *Document processing*. The processing pipeline converts very large collections of documents from one format to another (e.g., from *Word* to *PDF*), or encrypts the documents. It could also use optical character recognition (OCR) to produce digital images of documents.

Batch processing systems also cover a broad spectrum of data-intensive applications in enterprise computing. Such applications typically have deadlines, and the failure to meet these deadlines could have serious economic consequences. Security is also a critical aspect for many applications of batch processing. A nonexhaustive list of batch processing applications includes:

- Generation of daily, weekly, monthly, and annual activity reports for organizations in retail, manufacturing, and other economic sectors.
- Processing, aggregation, and summaries of daily transactions for financial institutions, insurance companies, and healthcare organizations.
- Inventory management for large corporations.
- Processing billing and payroll records.
- Management of the software development (e.g., nightly updates of software repositories).
- Automatic testing and verification of software and hardware systems.

Finally, and of increasing importance, are cloud applications in the area of Web access. Several categories of Web sites have a periodic or a temporary presence, such as the Web sites for conferences or other events. There are also Web sites that are active during a particular season (e.g., the holiday season) or that support a particular type of activity, such as income tax reporting with the April 15 deadline each year. Other limited-time Web sites used for promotional activities "sleep" during the night and auto-scale during the day.

It makes economic sense to store the data in the cloud close to where the application runs; as we saw in Section 3.1, the cost per GB is low and the processing is much more efficient when the data is stored close to the computational servers. This leads us to believe that several new classes of cloud computing applications could emerge in the years to come – for example, batch processing for decision support systems and other aspects of business analytics. Another class of new applications could be parallel batch processing based on programming abstractions, such as *MapReduce*, discussed in Section 4.6. Mobile interactive applications that process large volumes of data from different types of sensors and services that combine more than one data source (e.g., mashups[2]) are obvious candidates for cloud computing.

Science and engineering could greatly benefit from cloud computing because many applications in these areas are compute- and data-intensive. Similarly, a cloud dedicated to education would be extremely useful. Mathematical software such as *MATLAB* and *Mathematica* could also run on the cloud.

4.3 Architectural styles for cloud applications

Cloud computing is based on the client-server paradigm discussed in Section 2.13. The vast majority of cloud applications take advantage of request/response communication between clients and stateless servers. A *stateless server* does not require a client to first establish a connection to the server. Instead, it views a client request as an independent transaction and responds to it.

The advantages of stateless servers are obvious. Recovering from a server failure requires considerable overhead for a server that maintains the state of all its connections, whereas in the case of a

[2] A *mashup* is an application that uses and combines data, presentation, or functionality from two or more sources to create a service. The fast integration, frequently using open APIs and multiple data sources, produces results not envisioned by the original services. Combination, visualization, and aggregation are the main attributes of mashups.

stateless server a client is not affected while a server goes down and then comes back up between two consecutive requests. A stateless system is simpler, more robust, and scalable. A client does not have to be concerned with the state of the server. If the client receives a response to a request, that means that the server is up and running; if not, it should resend the request later. A connection-based service must reserve spaces to maintain the state of each connection with a client; therefore, such a system is not scalable, and the number of clients a server could interact with at any given time is limited by the storage space available to the server.

For example, a basic Web server is stateless; it responds to an HTTP request without maintaining a history of past interactions with the client. The client, a browser, is also stateless since it sends requests and waits for responses. The *Hypertext Transfer Protocol (HTTP)* used by a browser to communicate with the Web server is a request/response application protocol. *HTTP* uses the *Transport Control Protocol (TCP)*, a connection-oriented and reliable transport protocol. The use of *TCP* ensures reliable delivery of large objects but exposes the Web servers to denial-of-service attacks when malicious clients fake attempts to establish a *TCP* connection and force the server to allocate space for the connection.

A critical aspect of the development of networked applications is how processes and threads running on systems with different architectures and possibly compiled from different programming languages can *communicate structured information with one another*. First, the internal representation of the two structures at the two sites may be different. One system may use *Big-Endian* and the other *Little-Endian* representation. The character representations may also be different. Second, a communication channel transmits a sequence of bits and bytes; thus, the data structure must be serialized at the sending site and reconstructed at the receiving site.

Several other considerations must be analyzed before deciding on the architectural style of an application. The term *neutrality* refers to the ability of the application protocol to use different transport protocols such as *TCP* or *UDP* and, in general, to run on top of a different protocol stack. For example, we shall see that *SOAP* can use *TCP* but also *UDP*, *SMTP*,[3] or *JMS*[4] as transport vehicles. *Extensibility* refers to the ability to incorporate additional functions, such as security. *Independence* refers to the ability to accommodate different programming styles.

Very often the application clients and the servers running on the cloud communicate using RPCs, discussed in Section 2.13, but other styles of communication are possible. RPC-based applications use *stubs* to convert the parameters involved in an RPC call. A stub performs two functions: marshalling the data structures and serialization. A more general concept is that of an *Object Request Broker* (ORB), the middleware that facilitates communication of networked applications. The ORB at the sending site transforms the data structures used internally by a sending process to a byte sequence and transmits this byte sequence over the network. The ORB at the receiving site maps the byte sequence to the data structures used internally by the receiving process.

The *Common Object Request Broker Architecture (CORBA)* was developed in the early 1990s to allow networked applications developed in different programming languages and running on systems with different architectures and system software to work with one another. At the heart of the system is the *Interface Definition Language (IDL)*, used to specify the interface of an object. The *IDL* representation

[3]Simple Mail Transfer Protocol (SMTP) is an application protocol defined in the early 1980s to support email services.
[4]Java Message Service (JMS) is a middleware of the Java Platform for sending messages between two or more clients.

is then mapped to the set of programming languages, including *C, C++, Java, Smalltalk, Ruby, LISP,* and *Python*. Networked applications pass *CORBA* by reference and pass data by value.

The *Simple Object Access Protocol* (SOAP) is an application protocol developed in 1998 for Web applications; its message format is based on the *Extensible Markup Language* (XML). *SOAP* uses *TCP* and, more recently, *UDP* transport protocols. It can also be stacked above other application layer protocols such as *HTTP, SMTP*, or *JMS*. The processing model of *SOAP* is based on a network consisting of senders, receivers, intermediaries, message originators, ultimate receivers, and message paths. *SOAP* is an underlying layer of Web Services.

The *Web Services Description Language (WSDL)* (see `www.w3.org/TR/wsdl`) was introduced in 2001 as an XML-based grammar to describe communication between endpoints of a networked application. The abstract definition of the elements involved include *services*, collections of endpoints of communication; *types*, containers for data type definitions; *operations*, descriptions of actions supported by a service; *port types*, operations supported by endpoints; *bindings*, protocols and data formats supported by a particular port type; and *port*, an endpoint as a combination of a binding and a network address. These abstractions are mapped to concrete message formats and network protocols to define endpoints and services.

Representational State Transfer (REST) is a style of software architecture for distributed hypermedia systems. *REST* supports client communication with stateless servers. It is platform- and language-independent, supports data caching, and can be used in the presence of firewalls.

REST almost always uses *HTTP* to support all four *Create/Read/Update/Delete* (*CRUD*) operations. It uses `GET`, `PUT`, and `DELETE` to `read`, `write`, and delete the data, respectively. *REST* is a much easier-to-use alternative to *RPC, CORBA*, or Web Services such as *SOAP* or *WSDL*. For example, to retrieve the address of an individual from a database, a *REST* system sends a URL specifying the network address of the database, the name of the individual, and the specific attribute in the record the client application wants to retrieve – in this case, the address. The corresponding *SOAP* version of such a request consists of 10 lines or more of *XML*. The *REST* server responds with the address of the individual. This justifies the statement that *REST* is a lightweight protocol. As far as usability is concerned, *REST* is easier to build from scratch and to debug, but *SOAP* is supported by tools that use self-documentation (e.g., *WSDL* to generate the code to connect).

4.4 Workflows: Coordination of multiple activities

Many cloud applications require the completion of multiple interdependent tasks; the description of a complex activity involving such an ensemble of tasks is known as a *workflow*. In this section we discuss workflow models, the life cycle of a workflow, the desirable properties of a workflow description, workflow patterns, reachability of the goal state of a workflow, and dynamic workflows and conclude with a parallel between traditional transaction systems and cloud workflows [230].

Workflow models are abstractions revealing the most important properties of the entities participating in a workflow management system. *Task* is the central concept in workflow modeling; a task is a unit of work to be performed on the cloud, and it is characterized by several attributes, such as:

- *Name*. A string of characters uniquely identifying the task.
- *Description*. A natural language description of the task.

- *Actions*. Modifications of the environment caused by the execution of the task.
- *Preconditions*. Boolean expressions that must be true before the action(s) of the task can take place.
- *Post-conditions*. Boolean expressions that must be true after the action(s) of the task take place.
- *Attributes*. Provide indications of the type and quantity of resources necessary for the execution of the task, the actors in charge of the tasks, the security requirements, whether the task is reversible, and other task characteristics.
- *Exceptions*. Provide information on how to handle abnormal events. The exceptions supported by a task consist of a list of `<event, action>` pairs. The exceptions included in the task exception list are called *anticipated exceptions*, as opposed to unanticipated exceptions. Events not included in the exception list trigger replanning. *Replanning* means restructuring of a process or redefinition of the relationship among various tasks.

A *composite task* is a structure describing a subset of tasks and the order of their execution. A *primitive task* is one that cannot be decomposed into simpler tasks. A composite task inherits some properties from workflows; it consists of tasks and has one start symbol and possibly several end symbols. At the same time, a composite task inherits some properties from tasks; it has a name, preconditions, and post-conditions.

A *routing task* is a special-purpose task connecting two tasks in a workflow description. The task that has just completed execution is called the *predecessor* task; the one to be initiated next is called the *successor task*. A routing task could trigger a sequential, concurrent, or iterative execution. Several types of routing task exist:

- A *fork routing task* triggers execution of several successor tasks. Several semantics for this construct are possible:
  - All successor tasks are enabled.
  - Each successor task is associated with a condition. The conditions for all tasks are evaluated, and only the tasks with a `true` condition are enabled.
  - Each successor task is associated with a condition. The conditions for all tasks are evaluated, but the conditions are mutually exclusive and only one condition may be `true`. Thus, only one task is enabled.
  - Nondeterministic, k out of $n > k$ successors are selected at random to be enabled.
- A *join routing task* waits for completion of its predecessor tasks. There are several semantics for the join routing task:
  - The successor is enabled after all predecessors end.
  - The successor is enabled after k out of $n > k$ predecessors end.
  - Iterative: The tasks between the fork and the join are executed repeatedly.

A *process description*, also called a *workflow schema*, is a structure describing the *tasks* or *activities* to be executed and the order of their execution. A process description contains one start symbol and one end symbol. A process description can be provided in a *workflow definition language (WFDL)*, supporting constructs for choice, concurrent execution, the classical *fork, join* constructs, and iterative execution. Clearly, a workflow description resembles a *flowchart*, a concept we are familiar with from programming.

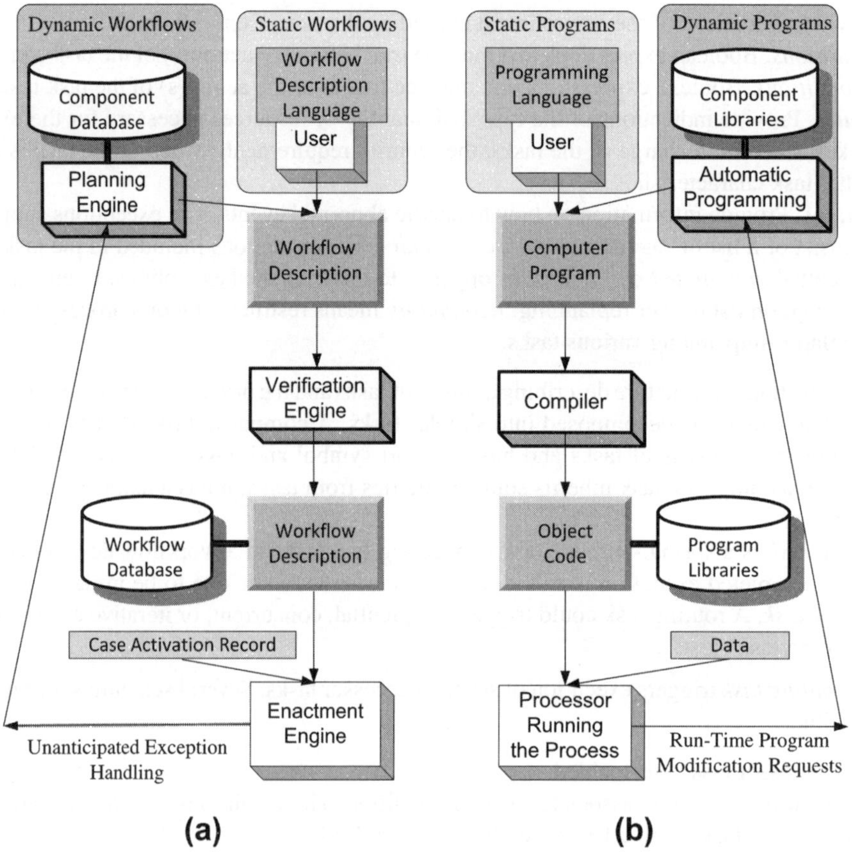

FIGURE 4.1

A parallel between workflows and programs. (a) The life cycle of a workflow. (b) The life cycle of a computer program. The workflow definition is analogous to writing a program. Planning is analogous to automatic program generation. Verification corresponds to syntactic verification of a program. Workflow enactment mirrors the execution of a program. A static workflow corresponds to a static program and a dynamic workflow to a dynamic program.

The phases in the life cycle of a workflow are creation, definition, verification, and enactment. There is a striking similarity between the life cycle of a workflow and that of a traditional computer program, namely, creation, compilation, and execution (see Figure 4.1). The workflow specification by means of a workflow description language is analogous to writing a program. Planning is equivalent to automatic program generation. Workflow verification corresponds to syntactic verification of a program, and workflow enactment mirrors the execution of a compiled program.

A *case* is an instance of a process description. The start and stop symbols in the workflow description enable the creation and the termination of a case, respectively. An *enactment model* describes the steps taken to process a case. When a computer executes all tasks required by a workflow the enactment can be performed by a program called an *enactment engine*.

The *state of a case* at time t is defined in terms of tasks already completed at that time. Events cause transitions between states. Identifying the states of a case consisting of concurrent activities is considerably more difficult than identifying the states of a strictly sequential process. Indeed, when several activities could proceed concurrently, the state has to reflect the progress made on each independent activity.

An alternative description of a workflow can be provided by a transition system describing the possible paths from the current state to a goal state. Sometimes, instead of providing a process description, we may specify only the goal state and expect the system to generate a workflow description that could lead to that state through a set of actions. In this case, the new workflow description is generated automatically, knowing a set of tasks and the preconditions and post-conditions for each one of them. In artificial intelligence (AI) this activity is known as *planning*.

The state space of a process includes one initial state and one goal state; a transition system identifies all possible paths from the initial to the goal state. A case corresponds to a particular path in the transition system. The state of a case tracks the progress made during the enactment of that case.

Among the most desirable properties of a process description are the *safety* and *liveness* of the process. Informally, safety means that nothing "bad" ever happens, and liveness means that something "good" will eventually take place should a case based on the process be enacted. Not all processes are safe and live. For example, the process description in Figure 4.2(a) violates the liveness requirement. As long as task C is chosen after completion of B, the process will terminate. However, if D is chosen, then F will never be instantiated, because it requires the completion of both C and E. The process will never terminate, because G requires completion of both D and F.

A process description language should be unambiguous and should allow a verification of the process description before the enactment of a case. It is entirely possible that a process description may be enacted correctly in some cases but fail for others. Such enactment failures may be very costly and should be prevented by a thorough verification at the process definition time. To avoid enactment errors, we need to verify process description and check for desirable properties such as safety and liveness. Some process description methods are more suitable for verification than others.

A note of caution: Although the original description of a process could be live, the actual enactment of a case may be affected by deadlocks due to resource allocation. To illustrate this situation, consider two tasks, A and B, running concurrently. Each of them needs exclusive access to resources r and q for a period of time. Either of two scenarios is possible:

1. A or B acquires both resources and then releases them and allows the other task to do the same.
2. We face the undesirable situation in Figure 4.2(b) when, at time t_1, task A acquires r and continues its execution; then at time t_2 task B acquires q and continues to run. Then at time t_3 task B attempts to acquire r and it blocks because r is under the control of A. Task A continues to run and at time t_4 attempts to acquire q and it blocks because q is under the control of B.

The deadlock illustrated in Figure 4.2(b) can be avoided by requesting each task to acquire all resources at the same time. The price to pay is underutilization of resources. Indeed, the idle time of each resource increases under this scheme.

Workflow pattern refers to the temporal relationship among the tasks of a process. The workflow description languages and the mechanisms to control the enactment of a case must have provisions

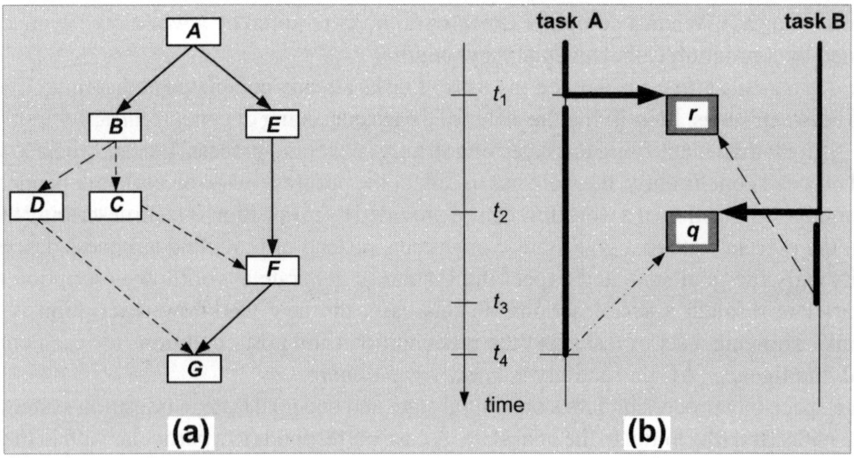

FIGURE 4.2

(a) A process description that violates the liveness requirement. If task C is chosen after completion of B, the process will terminate after executing task G; if D is chosen, then F will never be instantiated, because it requires the completion of both C and E. The process will never terminate, because G requires completion of both D and F. (b) Tasks A and B need exclusive access to two resources r and q, and a deadlock may take place if the following sequence of events occurs. At time t_1 task A acquires r, at time t_2 task B acquires q and continues to run; then at time t_3 task B attempts to acquire r and it blocks because r is under the control of A. Task A continues to run and at time t_4 attempts to acquire q and it blocks because q is under the control of B.

to support these temporal relationships. Workflow patterns are analyzed in [1,382]. These patterns are classified in several categories: basic, advanced branching and synchronization, structural, state-based, cancellation, and patterns involving multiple instances. The basic workflow patterns illustrated in Figure 4.3 are:

- The *sequence* pattern occurs when several tasks have to be scheduled one after the completion of the other [see Figure 4.3(a)].
- The *AND split* pattern requires several tasks to be executed concurrently. Both tasks B and C are activated when task A terminates [see Figure 4.3(b)]. In case of an *explicit AND split*, the activity graph has a routing node and all activities connected to the routing node are activated as soon as the flow of control reaches the routing node. In the case of an *implicit AND split,* activities are connected directly and conditions can be associated with branches linking an activity with the next ones. Only when the conditions associated with a branch are true are the tasks activated.
- The *synchronization* pattern requires several concurrent activities to terminate before an activity can start. In our example, task C can only start after both tasks A and B terminate [see Figure 4.3(c)].
- The *XOR split* requires a decision; after the completion of task A, either B or C can be activated [see Figure 4.3(d)].

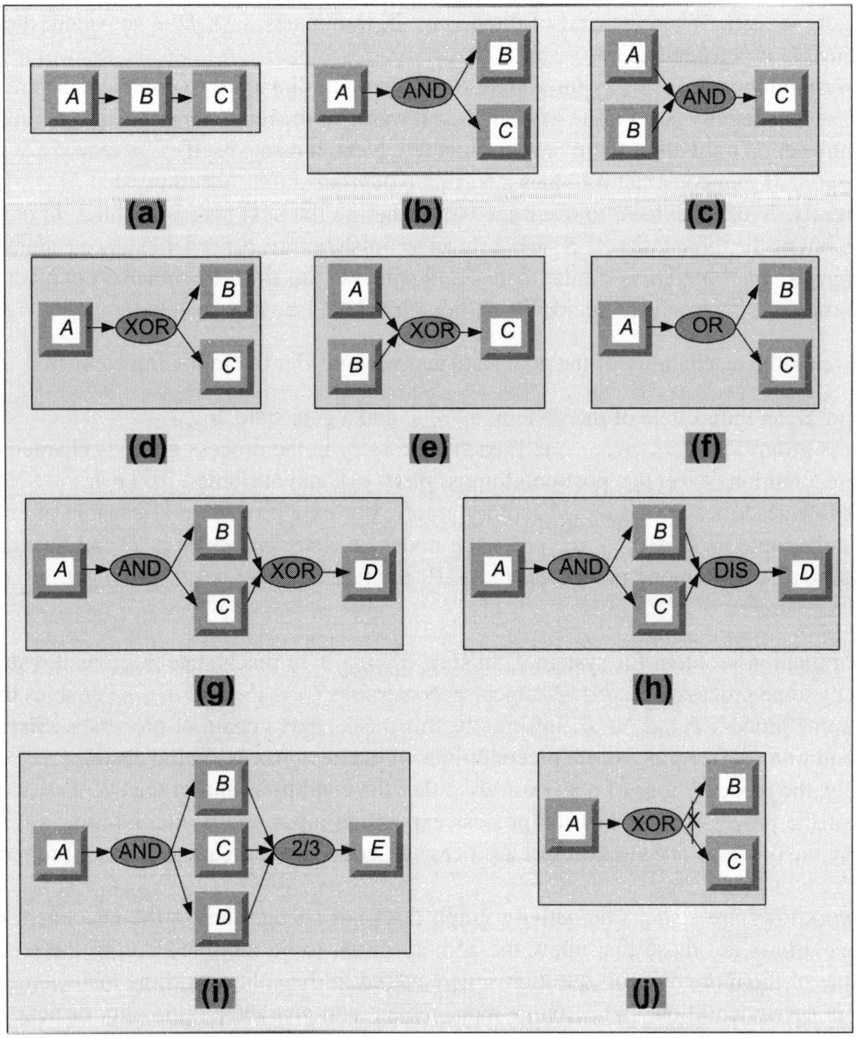

FIGURE 4.3

Basic workflow patterns. (a) *Sequence.* (b) *AND split.* (c) *Synchronization.* (d) *XOR split.* (e) *XOR merge.* (f) *OR split.* (g) *Multiple merge.* (h) *Discriminator.* (i) *N out of M join.* (j) *Deferred choice.*

- In the *XOR join*, several alternatives are merged into one. In our example, task C is enabled when either A or B terminates [see Figure 4.3(e)].
- The *OR split* pattern is a construct to choose multiple alternatives out of a set. In our example, after completion of task A, one could activate either B or C, or both [see Figure 4.3(f)].
- The *multiple merge* construct allows multiple activations of a task and does not require synchronization after the execution of concurrent tasks. Once A terminates, tasks B and C execute concurrently

[see Figure 4.3(g)]. When the first of them, say, B, terminates, task D is activated; then when C terminates, D is activated again.

- The *discriminator* pattern waits for a number of incoming branches to complete before activating the subsequent activity [see Figure 4.3(h)]; then it waits for the remaining branches to finish without taking any action until all of them have terminated. Next, it resets itself.
- The *N out of M join* construct provides a barrier synchronization. Assuming that $M > N$ tasks run concurrently, N of them have to reach the barrier before the next task is enabled. In our example, any two out of the three tasks A, B, and C have to finish before E is enabled [see Figure 4.3(i)].
- The *deferred choice* pattern is similar to the XOR split, but this time the choice is not made explicitly and the run-time environment decides what branch to take [see Figure 4.3(j)].

Next we discuss the reachability of the goal state and we consider the following elements:

- A system Σ, an initial state of the system, $\sigma_{initial}$, and a goal state, σ_{goal}.
- A process group $\mathcal{P} = \{p_1, p_2, \ldots, p_n\}$; each process p_i in the process group is characterized by a set of preconditions, $pre(p_i)$, post-conditions, $post(p_i)$, and attributes, $atr(p_i)$.
- A workflow described by a directed activity graph $\mathcal{A}$ or by a procedure Π capable of constructing $\mathcal{A}$ given the tuple $< \mathcal{P}, \sigma_{initial}, \sigma_{goal} >$. The nodes of $\mathcal{A}$ are processes in $\mathcal{P}$ and the edges define precedence relations among processes. $P_i \rightarrow P_j$ implies that $pre(p_j) \subset post(p_i)$.
- A set of constraints $\mathcal{C} = \{C_1, C_2, \ldots, C_m\}$.

The coordination problem for system Σ in state $\sigma_{initial}$ is to reach state σ_{goal} as a result of post-conditions of some process $P_{final} \in \mathcal{P}$ subject to constraints $C_i \in \mathcal{C}$. Here $\sigma_{initial}$ enables the preconditions of some process $P_{initial} \in \mathcal{P}$. Informally, this means that a chain of processes exists such that the post-conditions of one process are preconditions of the next process in the chain.

Generally, the preconditions of a process are either the conditions and/or the events that trigger the execution of the process or the data the process expects as input; the post-conditions are the results produced by the process. The attributes of a process describe special requirements or properties of the process.

Some workflows are static. The activity graph does not change during the enactment of a case. *Dynamic workflows* are those that allow the activity graph to be modified during the enactment of a case. Some of the more difficult questions encountered in dynamic workflow management refer to (i) how to integrate workflow and resource management and guarantee optimality or near optimality of cost functions for individual cases; (ii) how to guarantee consistency after a change in a workflow; and (iii) how to create a dynamic workflow. Static workflows can be described in WFDL (the workflow definition language), but dynamic workflows need a more flexible approach.

We distinguish two basic models for the mechanics of workflow enactment:

1. *Strong coordination models*, whereby the process group $\mathcal{P}$ executes under the supervision of a *coordinator* process or processes. A coordinator process acts as an enactment engine and ensures a seamless transition from one process to another in the activity graph.
2. *Weak coordination models*, whereby there is no supervisory process.

In the first case, we may deploy a *hierarchical coordination scheme* with several levels of coordinators. A supervisor at level i in a hierarchical scheme with $i+1$ levels coordinates a subset of processes in the process group. A supervisor at level $i-1$ coordinates a number of supervisors at level i and the root provides global coordination. Such a hierarchical coordination scheme may be used to reduce the communication overhead; a coordinator and the processes it supervises may be colocated.

The most important feature of this coordination model is the ability to support dynamic workflows. The coordinator or the global coordinator may respond to a request to modify the workflow by first stopping all the threads of control in a consistent state, then investigating the feasibility of the requested changes, and finally, implementing feasible changes.

Weak coordination models are based on peer-to-peer communication between processes in the process group by means of a societal service such as a *tuple space*. Once a process $p_i \in \mathcal{P}$ finishes, it deposits a token, including possibly a subset of its post-conditions, $post(p_i)$, in a tuple space. The consumer process p_j is expected to visit the tuple space at some point in time, examine the tokens left by its ancestors in the activity graph, and, if its preconditions $pre(p_j)$ are satisfied, commence the execution. This approach requires individual processes to either have a copy of the activity graph or some timetable to visit the tuple space. An alternative approach is using an *active space*, a tuple space augmented with the ability to generate an event awakening the consumer of a token.

There are similarities and some differences between workflows of traditional transaction-oriented systems and *cloud workflows*. The similarities are mostly at the modeling level, whereas the differences affect the mechanisms used to implement workflow management systems. Some of the more subtle differences between the two are:

- The emphasis in a transactional model is placed on the contractual aspect of a transaction; in a workflow the enactment of a case is sometimes based on a "best-effort" model whereby the agents involved will do their best to attain the goal state but there is no guarantee of success.
- A critical aspect of the transactional model in database applications is maintaining a consistent state of the database; however, a cloud is an open system, and thus its state is considerably more difficult to define.
- The database transactions are typically short-lived; the tasks of a cloud workflow could be long-lasting.
- A database transaction consists of a set of well-defined actions that are unlikely to be altered during the execution of the transaction. However, the process description of a cloud workflow may change during the lifetime of a case.
- The individual tasks of a cloud workflow may not exhibit the traditional properties of database transactions. For example, consider durability: At any instance of time, before reaching the goal state, a workflow may roll back to some previously encountered state and continue from there on an entirely different path. A task of a workflow could be either reversible or irreversible. Sometimes, paying a penalty for reversing an action is more profitable in the long run than continuing on a wrong path.
- Resource allocation is a critical aspect of the workflow enactment on a cloud without an immediate correspondent for database transactions.

The relatively simple coordination model discussed next is often used in cloud computing.

4.5 Coordination based on a state machine model: The *ZooKeeper*

Cloud computing elasticity requires the ability to distribute computations and data across multiple systems. Coordination among these systems is one of the critical functions to be exercised in a distributed environment. The coordination model depends on the specific task, such as coordination of data storage, orchestration of multiple activities, blocking an activity until an event occurs, reaching consensus for the next action, or recovery after an error.

The entities to be coordinated could be processes running on a set of cloud servers or even running on multiple clouds. Servers running critical tasks are often replicated, so when one primary server fails, a backup automatically continues the execution. This is only possible if the backup is in a *hot standby* mode – in other words, the standby server shares the same state at all times with the primary.

For example, in the distributed data store model discussed in Section 3.5, the access to data is mitigated by a proxy. This proxy is a single point of failure; thus, an architecture with multiple proxies is desirable. These proxies should be in the same state so that, whenever one of them fails, the client could seamlessly continue to access the data using another proxy.

Consider now an advertising service that involves a large number of servers in a cloud. The advertising service runs on a number of servers specialized for tasks such as database access, monitoring, accounting, event logging, installers, customer dashboards,[5] advertising campaign planners, scenario testing, and so on. A solution to coordinate these activities is through configuration files shared by all systems. When the service starts or after a system failure, all servers use the configuration file to coordinate their actions. This solution is static. Any change requires an update and redistribution of the configuration file. Moreover, in case of a system failure the configuration file does not allow recovery from the state of each server prior to the system crash, which is a more desirable alternative.

A solution for the proxy coordination problem is to consider a proxy as a deterministic finite state machine that performs the commands sent by clients in some sequence. The proxy has thus a definite state and, when a command is received, it transitions to another state. When P proxies are involved, all of them must be synchronized and must execute the same sequence of state machine commands; this can be ensured if all proxies implement a version of the Paxos consensus algorithm described in Section 2.11.

ZooKeeper is a distributed coordination service based on this model. The high-throughput and low-latency service is used for coordination in large-scale distributed systems. The open-source software is written in Java and has bindings for Java and C. Information about the project is available at `http://zookeeper.apache.org/`.

The *ZooKeeper* software must first be downloaded and installed on several servers; then clients can connect to any one of these servers and access the coordination service. The service is available as long as the majority of servers in the pack are available.

The organization of the service is shown in Figure 4.4. The servers in the pack communicate with one another and elect a *leader*. A database is replicated on each one of them and the consistency of the

[5]A customer dashboard provides access to key customer information, such as contact name and account number, in an area of the screen that remains persistent as the user navigates through multiple Web pages.

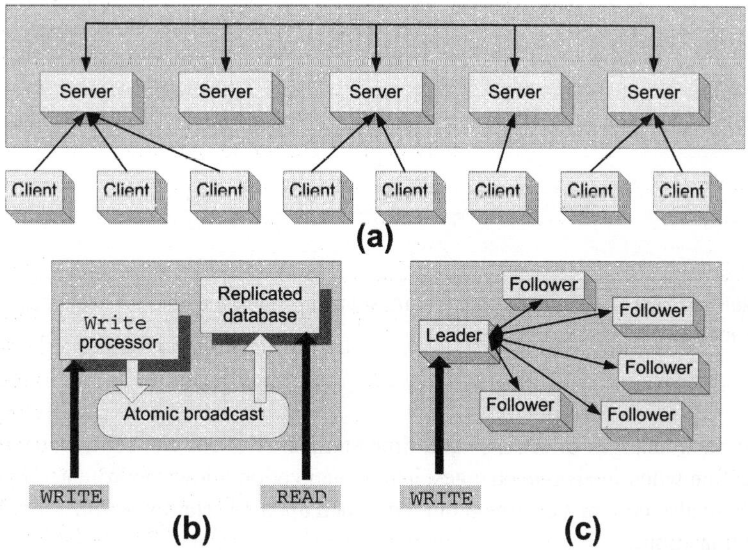

FIGURE 4.4

The *ZooKeeper* coordination service. (a) The service provides a single system image. Clients can connect to any server in the pack. (b) Functional model of the *ZooKeeper* service. The replicated database is accessed directly by `read` commands; `write` commands involve more intricate processing based on atomic broadcast. (c) Processing a `write` command: (1) A server receiving the command from a client forwards the command to the *leader*; (2) the *leader* uses atomic broadcast to reach consensus among all *followers*.

replicas is maintained. Figure 4.4(a) shows that the service provides a single system image. A client can connect to any server of the pack.

A client uses TCP to connect to a single server. Through the TCP connection a client sends requests and receives responses and watches events. A client synchronizes its clock with the server. If the server fails, the TCP connections of all clients connected to it time out and the clients detect the failure of the server and connect to other servers.

Figures 4.4(b) and (c) show that a `read` operation directed to any server in the pack returns the same result, whereas the processing of a `write` operation is more involved; the servers elect a *leader*, and any *follower* receiving a request from one of the clients connected to it forwards it to the leader. The leader uses atomic broadcast to reach consensus. When the leader fails, the servers elect a new leader.

The system is organized as a shared hierarchical namespace similar to the organization of a file system. A name is a sequence of path elements separated by a backslash. Every name in *Zookeper*'s namespace is identified by a unique path (see Figure 4.5).

In *ZooKeeper* the *znodes*, the equivalent of the *inodes* of a file system, can have data associated with them. Indeed, the system is designed to store state information. The data in each node includes version

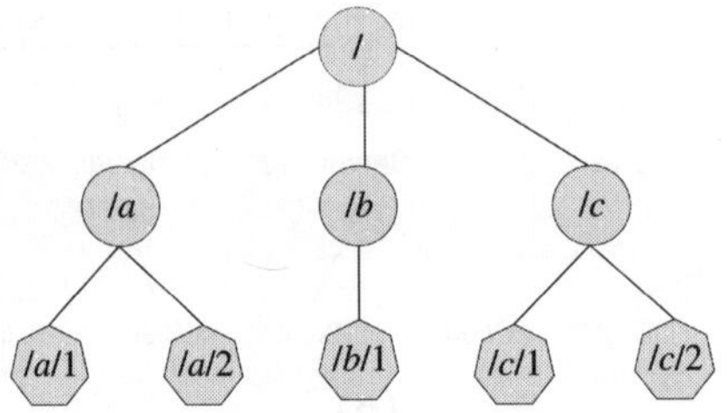

FIGURE 4.5

ZooKeeper is organized as a shared hierarchical namespace in which a name is a sequence of path elements separated by a backslash.

numbers for the data, changes of ACLs,[6] and time stamps. A client can set a watch on a *znode* and receive a notification when the *znode* changes. This organization allows coordinated updates. The data retrieved by a client also contains a version number. Each update is stamped with a number that reflects the order of the transition.

The data stored in each node is `read` and written atomically. A `read` returns all the data stored in a *znode*, whereas a `write` replaces all the data in the *znode*. Unlike in a file system, *Zookeeper* data, the image of the state, is stored in the server memory. Updates are logged to disk for recoverability, and *writes* are serialized to disk before they are applied to the in-memory database that contains the entire tree. The *ZooKeeper* service guarantees:

1. *Atomicity*. A transaction either completes or fails.
2. *Sequential consistency of updates*. Updates are applied strictly in the order in which they are received.
3. *Single system image for the clients*. A client receives the same response regardless of the server it connects to.
4. *Persistence of updates*. Once applied, an update persists until it is overwritten by a client.
5. *Reliability*. The system is guaranteed to function correctly as long as the majority of servers function correctly.

To reduce the response time, `read` requests are serviced from the local replica of the server that is connected to the client. When the leader receives a `write` request, it determines the state of the system where the `write` will be applied and then it transforms the state into a transaction that captures this new state.

The messaging layer is responsible for the election of a new leader when the current leader fails. The messaging protocol uses *packets* (sequences of bytes sent through a FIFO channel), *proposals* (units of agreement), and *messages* (sequences of bytes atomically broadcast to all servers). A message is included in a proposal and it is agreed on before it is delivered. Proposals are agreed on by exchanging packets with a quorum of servers, as required by the Paxos algorithm.

[6]An access control list (ACL) is a list of pairs (subject,value) that defines the list of access rights to an object; for example, `read`, `write`, and execute permissions for a file.

An atomic messaging system keeps all the servers in a pack in synch. This system guarantees (a) reliable delivery: if message *m* is delivered to one server, it will be eventually delivered to all servers; (b) total order: if message *m* is delivered before message *n* to one server, *m* will be delivered before *n* to all servers; and (c) causal order: if message *n* is sent after *m* has been delivered by the sender of *n*, then *m* must be ordered before *n*.

The application programming interface (API) to the *ZooKeeper* service is very simple and consists of seven operations:

- *create* – add a node at a given location on the tree.
- *delete* – delete a node.
- *get data* – `read` data from a node.
- *set data* – `write` data to a node.
- *get children* – retrieve a list of the children of the node.
- *synch* – wait for the data to propagate.

The system also supports the creation of *ephemeral* nodes, which are nodes that are created when a session starts and deleted when the session ends.

This brief description shows that the *ZooKeeper* service supports the finite state machine model of coordination. In this case a *znode* stores the state. The *ZooKeeper* service can be used to implement higher-level operations such as group membership, synchronization, and so on. The system is used by Yahoo!'s Message Broker and by several other applications.

4.6 The *MapReduce* programming model

A main advantage of cloud computing is elasticity – the ability to use as many servers as necessary to optimally respond to the cost and the timing constraints of an application. In the case of transaction processing systems, typically a front-end system distributes the incoming transactions to a number of back-end systems and attempts to balance the load among them. As the workload increases, new back-end systems are added to the pool.

For data-intensive batch applications, partitioning the workload is not always trivial. Only in some cases can the data be partitioned into blocks of arbitrary size and processed in parallel by servers in the cloud. We distinguish two types of divisible workloads:

- *Modularly divisible.* The workload partitioning is defined a priori.
- *Arbitrarily divisible.* The workload can be partitioned into an arbitrarily large number of smaller workloads of equal or very close size.

Many realistic applications in physics, biology, and other areas of computational science and engineering obey the arbitrarily divisible load-sharing model. The Divisible Load Theory (DLT) is analyzed in the literature (see Section 4.12).

MapReduce is based on a very simple idea for parallel processing of data-intensive applications supporting arbitrarily divisible load sharing. First, split the data into blocks, assign each block to an instance or process, and run these instances in parallel. Once all the instances have finished, the computations assigned to them start the second phase: Merge the partial results produced by individual instances. The so-called same program, multiple data (SPMD) paradigm, used since the early days of parallel computing, is based on the same idea but assumes that a *master* instance partitions the data and gathers the partial results.

MapReduce is a programming model inspired by the *Map* and the *Reduce* primitives of the LISP programming language. It was conceived for processing and generating large data sets on computing clusters [100]. As a result of the computation, a set of input $<key, value>$ pairs is transformed into a set of output $<key, value>$ pairs.

Numerous applications can be easily implemented using this model. For example, one can process logs of Web page requests and count the URL access frequency. The *Map* function outputs the pairs $<URL, 1>$ and the *Reduce* function produces the pairs $<URL, totalcount>$. Another trivial example is *distributed sort* when the map function extracts the key from each record and produces a $<key, record>$ pair and the *Reduce* function outputs these pairs unchanged. The following example [100] shows the two user-defined functions for an application that counts the number of occurrences of each word in a set of documents.

```
map(String key, String value):
  //key: document name; value: document contents
  for each word w in value:
  EmitIntermediate (w, "1");

reduce (String key, Iterator values):
  // key: a word; values: a list of counts
  int result = 0;
  for each v in values:
  result += ParseInt (v);
  Emit (AsString (result));
```

Call M and R the number of *Map* and *Reduce* tasks, respectively, and N the number of systems used by the *MapReduce*. When a user program invokes the *MapReduce function*, the following sequence of actions take place (see Figure 4.6):

1. The run-time library splits the input files into M *splits* of 16 to 64 MB each, identifies a number N of systems to run, and starts multiple copies of the program, one of the system being a *master* and the others *workers*. The *master* assigns to each idle system either a *Map* or a *Reduce* task. The *master* makes $\mathcal{O}(M+R)$ scheduling decisions and keeps $\mathcal{O}(M \times R)$ worker state vectors in memory. These considerations limit the size of M and R; at the same time, efficiency considerations require that $M, R \gg N$.
2. A worker being assigned a *Map* task reads the corresponding input split, parses $<key, value>$ pairs, and passes each pair to a user-defined *Map* function. The intermediate $<key, value>$ pairs produced by the *Map* function are buffered in memory before being written to a local disk and partitioned into R regions by the partitioning function.
3. The locations of these buffered pairs on the local disk are passed back to the *master*, who is responsible for forwarding these locations to the *Reduce* workers. A *Reduce* worker uses remote procedure calls to `read` the buffered data from the local disks of the *Map* workers; after reading all the

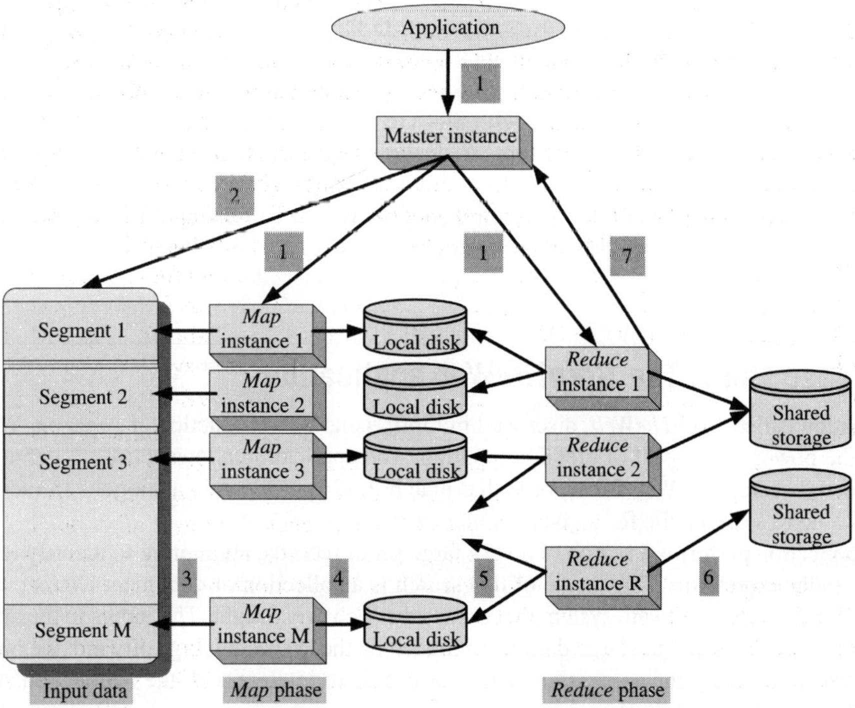

FIGURE 4.6

The *MapReduce* philosophy. (1) An application starts a *master instance* and *M* worker instances for the *Map* phase and, later, *R* worker instances for the *Reduce* phase. (2) The *master* partitions the input data in *M* segments. (3) Each *Map instance* reads its input data segment and processes the data. (4) The results of the processing are stored on the local disks of the servers where the *Map instances* run. (5) When all *Map instances* have finished processing their data, the *R Reduce instances* `read` the results of the first phase and merge the partial results. (6) The final results are written by the *Reduce instances* to a shared storage server. (7) The *master instance* monitors the *Reduce instances* and, when all of them report task completion, the application is terminated.

intermediate data, it sorts it by the intermediate keys. For each unique intermediate key, the key and the corresponding set of intermediate values are passed to a user-defined *Reduce* function. The output of the *Reduce* function is appended to a final output file.

4. When all *Map* and *Reduce* tasks have been completed, the *master* wakes up the user program.

The system is fault tolerant. For each *Map* and *Reduce* task, the *master* stores the state (idle, in-progress, or completed) and the identity of the worker machine. The *master* pings every worker periodically and marks the worker as failed if it does not respond. A task in progress on a failed worker is reset to idle and becomes eligible for rescheduling. The *master* writes periodic checkpoints of its control data structures and, if the task fails, it can be restarted from the last checkpoint. The data is stored using GFS, the Google File System, discussed in Section 8.5.

An environment for experimenting with *MapReduce* is described in [100]: The computers are typically dual-processor *x86* running *Linux*, with 2–4 GB of memory per machine and commodity networking hardware typically 100–1,000 Mbps. A cluster consists of hundreds or thousands of machines. Data is stored on IDE[7] disks attached directly to individual machines. The file system uses replication to provide availability and reliability with unreliable hardware. To minimize network bandwidth, the input data is stored on the local disks of each system.

4.7 A case study: The *GrepTheWeb* application

An application called *GrepTheWeb*, discussed in [360], is now in production at Amazon. We use it to illustrate the power and appeal of cloud computing. The application allows a user to define a regular expression and search the Web for records that match it. *GrepTheWeb* is analogous to the *Unix grep* command used to search a file for a given regular expression.

This application performs a search of a very large set of records, attempting to identify records that satisfy a regular expression. The source of this search is a collection of document URLs produced by the *Alexa Web Search*, a software system that crawls the Web every night. The inputs to the applications are a regular expression and the large data set produced by the Web-crawling software; the output is the set of records that satisfy the expression. The user is able to interact with the application and get the current status [see Figure 4.7(a)].

The application uses message passing to trigger the activities of multiple controller threads that launch the application, initiate processing, shut down the system, and create billing records. *GrepTheWeb* uses *Hadoop MapReduce*, an open-source software package that splits a large data set into chunks, distributes them across multiple systems, launches the processing, and, when the processing is complete, aggregates the outputs from different systems into a final result. *Apache Hadoop* is a software library for distributed processing of large data sets across clusters of computers using a simple programming model.

The details of the workflow of *GrepTheWeb* are captured in Figure 4.7(b) and consist of the following steps [360]:

1. *The startup phase.* Creates several queues – launch, monitor, billing, and shutdown queues. Starts the corresponding controller threads. Each thread periodically polls its input queue and, when a message is available, retrieves the message, parses it, and takes the required actions.
2. *The processing phase.* This phase is triggered by a `StartGrep` user request; then a launch message is enqueued in the launch queue. The launch controller thread picks up the message and executes the launch task; then, it updates the status and time stamps in the Amazon *Simple DB* domain. Finally, it enqueues a message in the monitor queue and deletes the message from the launch queue. The processing phase consists of the following steps:

[7]Integrated Drive Electronics (IDE) is an interface for connecting disk drives. The drive controller is integrated into the drive, as opposed to a separate controller on or connected to the motherboard.

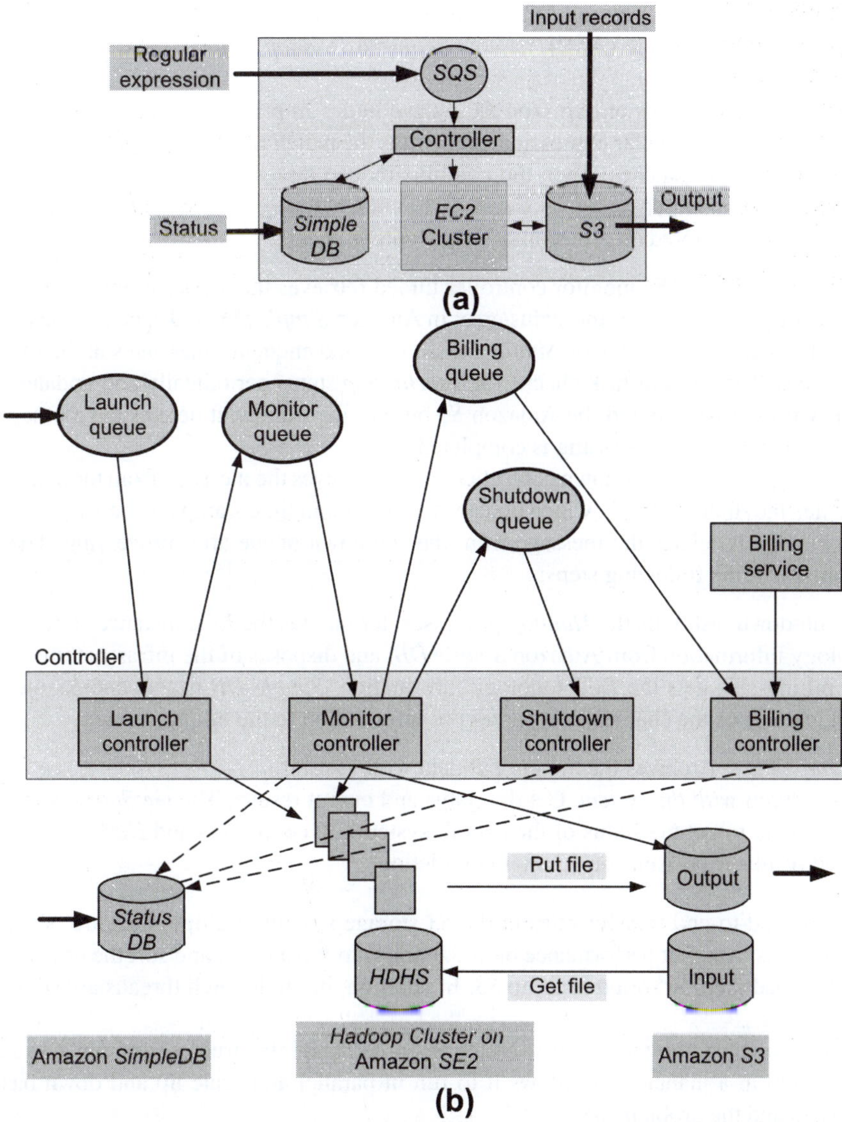

FIGURE 4.7

The organization of the *GrepTheWeb* application. The application uses the *Hadoop MapReduce* software and four Amazon services: *EC2*, *Simple DB*, *S3*, and *SQS*. (a) The simplified workflow showing the two inputs, the regular expression and the input records generated by the Web crawler. A third type of input is the user commands to report the current status and to terminate the processing. (b) The detailed workflow; the system is based on message passing between several queues; four controller threads periodically poll their associated input queues, retrieve messages, and carry out the required actions.

   a. The launch task starts Amazon *EC2* instances. It uses a Java Runtime Environment preinstalled Amazon Machine Image (AMI), deploys required *Hadoop* libraries, and starts a *Hadoop* Job (run *Map/Reduce* tasks).
   b. *Hadoop* runs map tasks on Amazon *EC2* slave nodes in parallel. A map task takes files from Amazon *S3*, runs a regular expression, and writes the match results locally, along with a description of up to five matches. Then the combine/reduce task combines and sorts the results and consolidates the output.
   c. Final results are stored on Amazon *S3* in the output bucket.

3. *The monitoring phase.* The monitor controller thread retrieves the message left at the beginning of the processing phase, validates the status/error in Amazon *Simple DB,* and executes the monitor task. It updates the status in the Amazon *Simple DB* domain and enqueues messages in the shutdown and billing queues. The monitor task checks for the *Hadoop* status periodically and updates the *Simple DB* items with status/error and the Amazon *S3* output file. Finally, it deletes the message from the monitor queue when the processing is completed.
4. *The shutdown phase.* The shutdown controller thread retrieves the message from the shutdown queue and executes the shutdown task, which updates the status and time stamps in the Amazon *Simple DB* domain. Finally, it deletes the message from the shutdown queue after processing. The shutdown phase consists of the following steps:

   a. The shutdown task kills the *Hadoop* processes, terminates the *EC2* instances after getting *EC2* topology information from Amazon *Simple DB,* and disposes of the infrastructure.
   b. The billing task gets the *EC2* topology information, *Simple DB* usage, and *S3* file and query input, calculates the charges, and passes the information to the billing service.

5. *The cleanup phase.* Archives the *Simple DB* data with user info.
6. *User interactions with the system.* Get the status and output results. The *GetStatus* is applied to the service endpoint to get the status of the overall system (all controllers and *Hadoop*) and download the filtered results from Amazon *S3* after completion.

To optimize the end-to-end transfer rates in the *S3* storage system, multiple files are bundled up and stored as *S3* objects. Another performance optimization is to run a script and sort the keys and the URL pointers and upload them in sorted order to *S3*. In addition, multiple fetch threads are started in order to fetch the objects.

This application illustrates the means to create an on-demand infrastructure and run it on a massively distributed system in a manner that allows it to run in parallel and scale up and down based on the number of users and the problem size.

4.8 Clouds for science and engineering

For more than two thousand years of human history, science was empirical. Several hundred years ago theoretical methods based on models and generalization were introduced, allowing substantial progress in human knowledge. In the last few decades, we have witnessed the explosion of computational science based on the simulation of complex phenomena.

In a talk delivered in 2007 and posted on his Web site just before he went missing in January 2007, computer scientist Jim Gray discussed *eScience* as a transformative scientific method [163]. Today, *eScience* unifies experiment, theory, and simulation; data captured from measuring instruments or generated by simulations are processed by software systems, and data and knowledge are stored by computer systems and analyzed using statistical packages.

The generic problems in virtually all areas of science are:

- Collecting experimental data.
- Managing very large volumes of data.
- Building and executing models.
- Integrating data and literature.
- Documenting experiments.
- Sharing the data with others; data preservation for long periods of time.

All these activities require powerful computing systems.

A typical example of a problem faced by agencies and research groups is data discovery in large scientific data sets. Examples of such large collections are the biomedical and genomic data at NCBI,[8] the astrophysics data at NASA,[9] or the atmospheric data at NOAA[10] and NCAR.[11]

The process of online data discovery can be viewed as an ensemble of several phases [282]: (i) recognition of the information problem; (ii) generation of search queries using one or more search engines; (iii) evaluation of the search results; (iv) evaluation of the Web documents; and (v) comparison of information from different sources. The Web search technology allows scientists to discover text documents related to such data, but the binary encoding of many of the documents poses serious challenges.

Metadata is used to describe digital data and provides an invaluable aid for discovering useful information in a scientific data set. A recent paper [282] describes a system for data discovery that supports automated fine-grained metadata extraction and summarization schemes for browsing large data sets and is extensible to different scientific domains. The system, called *Glean*, is designed to run on a computer cluster or on a cloud; its run-time system supports two computational models, one based on *MapReduce* and the other on graph-based orchestration.

4.9 High-performance computing on a cloud

A recent paper [179] describes the set of applications used at the National Energy Research Scientific Computing Center (NERSC) and presents the results of a comparative benchmark of *EC2* and three supercomputers. NERSC is located at Lawrence Berkeley National Laboratory and serves a diverse community of scientists; it has some 3,000 researchers and involves 400 projects based on some 600 codes. Some of the codes used are:

[8]NCBI is the National Center for Biotechnology Information; www.ncbi.nlm.nih.gov.
[9]NASA is the National Aeronautics and Space Administration; www.nasa.gov.
[10]NOAA is the National Oceanic and Atmospheric Administration; www.noaa.gov.
[11]NCAR is the National Center for Atmospheric Research.

Community Atmosphere Mode (CAM), the atmospheric component of Community Climate System Model (CCSM), is used for weather and climate modeling.[12] The code developed at NCAR uses two two-dimensional domain decompositions – one for the dynamics and the other for remapping. The first is decomposed over latitude and vertical level; the second is decomposed over longitude/latitude. The program is communication-intensive; on-node/processor data movement and relatively long *MPI*[13] messages that stress the interconnect point-to-point bandwidth are used to move data between the two decompositions.

General Atomic and Molecular Electronic Structure System (GAMESS) is used for ab initio quantum chemistry calculations. The code, developed by the Gordon Research Group at the U.S. Department of Energy's Ames Lab at Iowa State University, has its own communication library, the Distributed Data Interface (DDI), and is based on the same program multiple data (SPMD) execution model. DDI presents the abstraction of a global shared memory with one-sided data transfers, even on systems with physically distributed memory. On the cluster systems at NERSC the program uses socket communication; on the Cray XT4 the DDI uses *MPI* and only one-half of the processors compute, whereas the other half are data movers. The program is memory- and communication-intensive.

Gyrokinetic[14] (GTC) is a code for fusion research.[15] It is a self-consistent, gyrokinetic tri-dimensional particle-in-cell (PIC)[16] code with a nonspectral Poisson solver. It uses a grid that follows the field lines as they twist around a toroidal geometry representing a magnetically confined toroidal fusion plasma. The version of GTC used at NERSC uses a fixed, one-dimensional domain decomposition with 64 domains and 64 *MPI* tasks. Communication is dominated by nearest-neighbor exchanges that are bandwidth-bound. The most computationally intensive parts of GTC involve gather/deposition of charge on the grid and particle "push" steps. The code is memory-intensive because the charge deposition uses indirect addressing.

Integrated Map and Particle Accelerator Tracking Time (IMPACT-T) is a code for the prediction and performance enhancement of accelerators. It models the arbitrary overlap of fields from beamline elements and uses a parallel, relativistic PIC method with a spectral integrated Green function solver. This object-oriented *Fortran90* code uses a two-dimensional domain decomposition in the $y-z$ directions and dynamic load balancing based on the domains. Hockney's Fast Fourier Transform (FFT) algorithm is used to solve Poisson's equation with open boundary conditions. The code is sensitive to the memory bandwidth and *MPI* collective performance.

---

[12]See `www.nersc.gov/research-and-development/benchmarking-and-workload-characterization`.
[13]*Message Passing Interface* (MPI) is a communication library based on a standard for a portable message-passing system.
[14]The trajectory of charged particles in a magnetic field is a helix that winds around the field line. It can be decomposed into a relatively slow motion of the guiding center along the field line and a fast circular motion called cyclotronic motion. Gyrokinetics describes the evolution of the particles without taking into account the circular motion.
[15]See `www.scidacreview.org/0601/html/news4.html`.
[16]PIC is a technique to solve a certain class of partial differential equations. Individual particles (or fluid elements) in a Lagrangian frame are tracked in continuous phase space, whereas moments of the distribution such as densities and currents are computed simultaneously on Eulerian (stationary) mesh points.

MAESTRO is a low Mach number hydrodynamics code for simulating astrophysical flows.[17] Its integration scheme is embedded in an adaptive mesh refinement algorithm based on a hierarchical system of rectangular, nonoverlapping grid patches at multiple levels with different resolutions; it uses a multigrid solver. Parallelization is via a tridimensional domain decomposition using a coarse-grained distribution strategy to balance the load and minimize communication costs. The communication topology tends to stress simple topology interconnects. The code has a very low computational intensity, it stresses memory latency, and the implicit solver stresses global communications. The message sizes range from short to relatively moderate.

MIMD Lattice Computation (MILC) is a *Quantum Chromo Dynamics* (QCD) code used to study "strong" interactions binding quarks into protons and neutrons and holding them together in the nucleus.[18] The algorithm discretizes the space and evaluates field variables on sites and links of a regular hypercube lattice in four-dimensional space-time. The integration of an equation of motion for hundreds or thousands of time steps requires inverting a large, sparse matrix. The Conjugate Gradient (*CG*) method is used to solve a sparse, nearly singular matrix problem. Many *CG* iteration steps are required for convergence; the inversion translates into tridimensional complex matrix-vector multiplications. Each multiplication requires a dot product of three pairs of tridimensional complex vectors; a dot product consists of five multiply/add operations and one multiply. The MIMD computational model is based on a four-dimensional domain decomposition. Each task exchanges data with its eight nearest neighbors and is involved in the *all-reduce* calls with very small payload as part of the *CG* algorithm. The algorithm requires *gather* operations from widely separated locations in memory. The code is highly memory- and computational-intensive and it is heavily dependent on prefetching.

PARAllel Total Energy Code (PARATEC) is a quantum mechanics code that performs ab initio total energy calculations using pseudo-potentials, a plane wave basis set, and an all-band (unconstrained) Conjugate Gradient (*CG*) approach. Parallel three-dimensional FFTs transform the wave functions between real and Fourier space. The FFT dominates the run-time; the code uses *MPI* and is communication-intensive. The code uses mostly point-to-point short messages. The code parallelizes over grid points, thereby achieving a fine-grain level of parallelism. The BLAS3 and one-dimensional FFT use optimized libraries (e.g., Intel's MKL or AMD's ACML), which results in high cache reuse and a high percentage of per-processor peak performance.

The authors of [179] use the High-Performance Computing Challenge (HPCC) benchmark to compare the performance of *EC2* with the performance of three large systems at NERSC. HPCC[19] is a suite of seven synthetic benchmarks: three targeted synthetic benchmarks that quantify basic system parameters that characterize individually the computation and communication performance and four complex synthetic benchmarks that combine computation and communication and can be considered simple proxy applications. These benchmarks are:

[17] See `www.astro.sunysb.edu/mzingale/Maestro/`.
[18] See `physics.indiana.edu/sg/milc.html`.
[19] For more information see `www.novellshareware.com/info/hpc-challenge.html`.

- DGEMM.[20] The benchmark measures the floating-point performance of a processor/core. The memory bandwidth does little to affect the results, since the code is cache-friendly. Thus, the results of the benchmark are close to the theoretical peak performance of the processor.
- STREAM.[21] The benchmark measures the memory bandwidth.
- The network latency benchmark.
- The network bandwidth benchmark.
- HPL.[22] A software package that solves a (random) dense linear system in double precision arithmetic on distributed-memory computers. It is a portable and freely available implementation of the High-Performance Computing Linpack Benchmark.
- FFTE. Measures the floating-point rate of execution of double precision complex one-dimensional Discrete Fourier Transform (DFT).
- PTRANS. Parallel matrix transpose exercises the communications whereby pairs of processors communicate with each other simultaneously. It is a useful test of the total communications capacity of the network.
- RandomAccess. Measures the rate of integer random updates of memory (GUPS).

The systems used for the comparison with cloud computing are:

Carver. A 400-node IBM iDataPlex cluster with quad-core Intel Nehalem processors running at 2.67 GHz and with 24 GB of RAM (3 GB/core). Each node has two sockets; a single Quad Data Rate (QDR) IB link connects each node to a network that is locally a fat tree with a global two-dimensional mesh. The codes were compiled with the Portland Group suite version 10.0 and Open *MPI* version 1.4.1.

Franklin. A 9,660-node Cray XT4; each node has a single quad-core 2.3 GHz AMD Opteron Budapest processor with 8 GB of RAM (2 GB/core). Each processor is connected through a 6.4 GB/s bidirectional HyperTransport interface to the interconnect via a Cray SeaStar-2 ASIC. The SeaStar routing chips are interconnected in a tridimensional torus topology in which each node has a direct link to its six nearest neighbors. Codes were compiled with the Pathscale or the Portland Group suite version 9.0.4.

Lawrencium. A 198-node (1,584 core) *Linux* cluster; a compute node is a Dell Poweredge 1950 server with two Intel Xeon quad-core 64-bit, 2.66-GHz Harpertown processors with 16 GB of RAM (2 GB/core). A compute node is connected to a Dual Data Rate InfiniBand network configured as a fat tree with a 3:1 blocking factor. Codes were compiled using Intel 10.0.018 and Open *MPI* 1.3.3.

The virtual cluster at Amazon had four *EC2* Compute Units (CUs), two virtual cores with two CUs each, and 7.5 GB of memory (an `m1.large` instance in Amazon parlance). A Compute Unit is approximately equivalent to a 1.0–1.2 GHz 2007 Opteron or 2007 Xeon processor. The nodes are connected with gigabit Ethernet. The binaries were compiled on Lawrencium. The results reported in [179] are summarized in Table 4.1.

[20]For more details see `https://computecanada.org/?pageId=138`.
[21]For more details see `www.streambench.org/`.
[22]For more details see `http://netlib.org/benchmark/hpl/`.

Table 4.1 The results of the measurements reported in [179].

System	DGEMM Gflops	STREAM GB/s	Latency μs	Bndw GB/S	HPL Tflops	FFTE Gflops	PTRANS GB/s	RandAcc GUP/s
Carver	10.2	4.4	2.1	3.4	0.56	21.99	9.35	0.044
Franklin	8.4	2.3	7.8	1.6	0.47	14.24	2.63	0.061
Lawrencium	9.6	0.7	4.1	1.2	0.46	9.12	1.34	0.013
EC2	4.6	1.7	145	0.06	0.07	1.09	0.29	0.004

The results in Table 4.1 give us some ideas about the characteristics of scientific applications likely to run efficiently on the cloud. Communication-intensive applications will be affected by the increased latency (more than 70 times larger then *Carver*) and lower bandwidth (more than 70 times smaller than *Carver*).

4.10 Cloud computing for biology research

Biology, one of the scientific fields that needs vast amounts of computing power, was one of the first to take advantage of cloud computing. Molecular dynamics computations are CPU-intensive, whereas protein alignment is data-intensive.

An experiment carried out by a group from Microsoft Research illustrates the importance of cloud computing for biology research [223]. The authors carried out an "all-by-all" comparison to identify the interrelationship of the 10 million protein sequences (4.2 GB size) in the National Center for Biotechnology Information (NCBI) nonredundant protein database using *AzureBLAST*, a version of the *BLAST*[23] program running on the Azure platform [223].

Azure offers VMs with four levels of computing power, depending on the number of cores: small (1 core), medium (2 cores), large (8 cores), and extra large (>8 cores). The experiment used 8 core CPUs with 14 GB RAM and a 2 TB local disk. It was estimated that the computation would take six to seven CPU-years; thus, the experiment was allocated 3,700 weighted instances or 475 extra-large VMs from three data centers. Each data center hosted three *AzureBLAST* deployments, each with 62 extra-large instances. The 10 million sequences were divided into multiple segments, and each segment was submitted for execution by one *AzureBLAST* deployment. With this vast amount of resources allocated, it took 14 days to complete the computations, which produced 260 GB of compressed data spread across more than 400,000 output files.

A few observations and conclusions useful for many scientific applications running on Azure were drawn after a post-experiment analysis. A first observation is that when a task runs for more than two hours, a message will automatically reappear in the queue requesting the task to be scheduled, thus leading to repeated computations; a simple solution is to check whether the result of a task has

[23]The Basic Local Alignment Search Tool (*BLAST*) finds regions of local similarity between sequences. It compares nucleotide or protein sequences to sequence databases and calculates the statistical significance of matches. It can be used to infer functional and evolutionary relationships between sequences as well as help identify members of gene families. More information is available at `http://blast.ncbi.nlm.nih.gov/Blast.cgi`.

been generated before launching it. Many applications, including *BLAST*, allow for the setting of some parameters, but the computational effort to find optimal parameters is prohibitive. A user is also expected to decide on an optimal balance between the cost and the number of instances to meet budget limitations.

A number of inefficiencies were observed: many VMs were idle for extended periods of time; when a task finished execution, all worker instances waited for the next task; and when all jobs use the same set of instances, resources are either under- or over-utilized. Load imbalance is another source of inefficiency; some of the tasks of a job take considerably longer than others and delay the job's completion time.

The analysis of the logs shows unrecoverable instance failures. Some 50% of active instances lost connection to the storage service but were automatically recovered by the fabric controller. System updates caused several ensembles of instances to fail.

Another observation is that a computational science experiment requires the execution of several binaries; thus the creation of workflows, a challenging task for many domain scientists. To address this challenge, the authors of [215] developed a general platform for executing legacy *Windows* applications on the cloud. In the *Cirrus* system a job has a description consisting of a prologue, a set of commands, and a set of parameters. The prologue sets up the running environment; the commands are sequences of shell scripts, including Azure-storage-related commands to transfer data between Azure blob storage and the instance.

After the *Windows* Live ID service authenticates the user, it can submit and track a job through the portal provided by the Web role (see Figure 4.8). The job is added to a table called *job registry*. The execution of each job is controlled by a *job manager instance* that first scales the size of the worker based on the job configuration; then the parametric engine starts exploring the parameter space. If this is a test run, the parameter-sweeping result is sent to the sampling filter.

Each task is associated with a record in the task table, and this state record is updated periodically by the worker instance running the task. The progress of the task is monitored by the manager. The

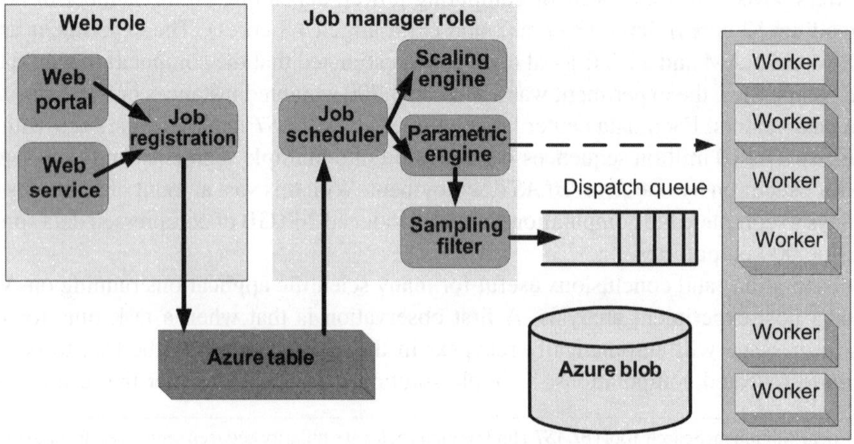

FIGURE 4.8

Cirrus, a general platform for executing legacy *Windows* applications on the cloud.

dispatch queue feeds into a set of worker instances. A worker periodically updates the task state in the task table and listens for any control signals from the manager.

We continue our discussion of biology applications of the *Azure* infrastructure applied to a loosely coupled workload for an ensemble-based simulation reported in [224]. A *role* in Azure is an encapsulation of an application; as noted earlier, there are two kinds of role: (i) the Web roles for Web applications and front-end code and (ii) the worker roles for background processing. Scientific applications such as *AzureBLAST* use worker roles for the compute tasks and to implement their APIs, that provide a run method and an entry point for the application and the state or configuration change notifications. The applications use the Blob Storage (ABS) for large raw data sets, the Table Storage (ATS) for semistructured data, and the Queue Storage (AQS) for message queues. These services provide strong consistency guarantees, but the complexity is moved to the application space.

Figure 4.9 illustrates the use of a software system called *BigJob* to decouple resource allocation from resource binding for the execution of loosely coupled workloads on an Azure platform [224]. This software eliminates the need for the application to manage individual VMs. The results of measurements show a noticeable overhead for starting VMs and for launching the execution of an application task on a remote resource. Increasing the computing power of the VM decreases the completion time for long-running tasks.

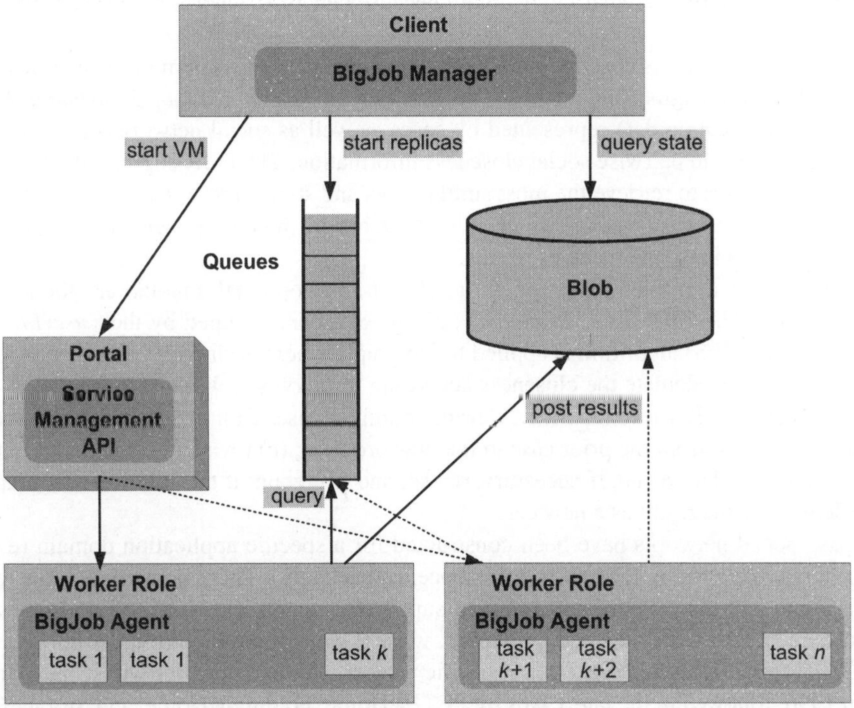

FIGURE 4.9

The execution of loosely coupled workloads using the Azure platform.

4.11 Social computing, digital content, and cloud computing

Social networks play an increasingly important role in people's lives. In recent years they have expanded in terms of the size of the population involved and in terms of the functions performed. A promising solution for analyzing large-scale social network data is to distribute the computation workload over a large number of nodes of a cloud. Traditionally, determining the importance of a node or a relationship in a network is done using sampling and surveying, but in a very large network structural properties cannot be inferred by scaling up the results from small networks. It turns out that the evaluation of social closeness is computationally intensive.

Social intelligence is another area where social and cloud computing intersect. Indeed, the process of knowledge discovery and techniques based on pattern recognition demand high-performance computing and resources that can be provided by computing clouds. Case-based reasoning (CBR), the process of solving new problems based on the solutions of similar past problems, is used by context-aware recommendation systems. It requires similarity-based retrieval. As the case base accumulates, such applications must handle massive amounts of history data, which can be done by developing new reasoning platforms running on the cloud. CBR is preferable to rule-based recommendation systems for large-scale social intelligence applications. Indeed, the rules can be difficult to generalize or apply to some domains. All triggering conditions must be strictly satisfied, scalability is a challenge as data accumulate, and the systems are hard to maintain because new rules have to be added as the amount of data increases.

A system based on CBR is described in [171]. The *BetterLife 2.0* system consists of a cloud layer, a case-based reasoning engine, and an API. The cloud layer uses the *Hadoop Distributed File System* clusters to store application data represented by cases as well as social network information, such as relationship topology and pairwise social closeness information. The CBR engine calculates similarity measures between cases to retrieve the most similar ones and stores new cases back to the cloud layer. The API connects to a master node, which is responsible for handling user queries, distributes the queries to server machines, and receives results.

A case consists of a problem description, a solution, and optional annotations about the path to derive the solution. The CBR uses *MapReduce*; all the cases are grouped by their *userId*, and then a *breadth first search* (BFS) algorithm is applied to the graph, where each node corresponds to one user. *MapReduce* is used to calculate the closeness according to pairwise relationship weight. A reasoning cycle has four steps: (a) Retrieve the most relevant or similar cases from memory to solve the case; (b) reuse: map the solution from the prior case to the new problem; (c) revise: test the new solution in the real world or in a simulation and, if necessary, revise; and (d) retain: if the solution was adapted to the target problem, store the result as a new case.

In the past, social networks have been constructed for a specific application domain (e.g., *MyExperiment* and *nanoHub* for biology and nanoscience, respectively). These networks enable researchers to share data and provide a virtual environment supporting remote execution of workflows. Another form of social computing is *volunteer computing*, when a large population of users donates resources such as CPU cycles and storage space for a specific project – for example, the Mersenne Prime Search initiated in 1996, followed in the late 1990s by SETI@Home, Folding@Home, and Storage@Home, a project to back up and share huge data sets from scientific research. Information about these projects is available online at `www.myExperiment.org`, `www.nanoHub.org`, `www.mersenne.org`, `setiathome.berkeley.edu`, and `folding.stanford.edu`.

Such platforms cannot be used in an environment where users require some level of accountability because there are no SLAs. The *PlanetLab* project is a credit-based system in which users earn credits by contributing resources and then spend those credits when using other resources. The Berkeley Open Infrastructure for Network Computing (BOINC) aims to develop middleware for a distributed infrastructure suitable for different applications.

An architecture designed as a Facebook application for a social cloud is presented in [76]. Methods to get a range of data, including friends, events, groups, application users, profile information, and photos, are available through a Facebook API. The Facebook Markup Language (FBML) is a subset of HTML with proprietary extensions, and the Facebook JavaScript (FBJS) is a version of JavaScript parsed, when a page is loaded, to create a virtual application scope. The prototype uses Web Services to create a distributed and decentralized infrastructure.

There are numerous examples of cloud platforms for social networks. There are scalable cloud applications hosted by commercial clouds (e.g., Facebook applications are hosted by Amazon Web Services). Today some organizations use the Facebook credentials of an individual for authentication.

The new technologies supported by cloud computing favor the creation of digital content. *Data mashups* or *composite services* combine data extracted by different sources; *event-driven mashups*, also called *Svc*, interact through events rather than the request/response traditional method. A recent paper [331] argues that "the *mashup* and the cloud computing worlds are strictly related because very often the services combined to create new *Mashups* follow the *SaaS* model and more, in general, rely on cloud systems." The paper also argues that the *Mashup* platforms rely on cloud computing systems – for example, the IBM *Mashup Center* and the *JackBe Enterprise Mashup* server.

There are numerous examples of monitoring, notification, presence, location, and map services based on the *Svc* approach, including *Monitor Mail, Monitor RSSFeed, Send SMS, Make Phone Call, GTalk, FireEagle,* and *Google Maps*. For example, consider a service to send a phone call when a specific email is received; the *Mail Monitor Svc* uses input parameters such as User Id, Sender Address Filter, and email Subject Filter to identify an email and generates an event that triggers the *Make TTS Call* action of a *Text To Speech Call Svc* linked to it.

The system in [331] supports creation, deployment, activation, execution, and management of event-driven mashups. It has a user interface, a graphics tool called Service Creation Environment that easily supports the creation of new mashups, and a platform called *Mashup Container* that manages mashup deployment and execution. The system consists of two subsystems: the *service execution platform* for mashups execution and the *deployer* module that manages the installation of mashups and *Svcs*. A new mashup is created using the graphical development tool and saved as an XML file. It can then be deployed into a *Mashup Container* following the *Platform-as-a-Service* (PaaS) approach. The *Mashup Container* supports a primitive SLA that allows the delivery of different levels of service.

The prototype uses the *Java Message Service* (JMS), which supports asynchronous communication. Each component sends and receives messages, and the sender does not block while waiting for the recipient to respond. The system's fault tolerance was tested on a system based on the *VMware vSphere*. In this environment, the fault tolerance is provided transparently by the VMM, and neither the VMs nor the applications are aware of the fault-tolerance mechanism. Two VMs, a primary and a secondary one, run on distinct hosts and execute the same set of instructions such that, when the primary fails, the secondary continues the execution seamlessly.

4.12 Further reading

There is a vast literature dedicated to Divisible Load Theory (DLT), including hundreds of papers (see www.ece.sunysb.edu/~tom/dlt.html). *MapReduce* is discussed in [100]. The *GrepTheWeb* application is analyzed in [360]. Metadata generation for large scientific databases is presented in [282]. Cloud applications in biology are analyzed in [223,224], and social applications of cloud computing are presented in [76,171,331]. Benchmarking of cloud services is analyzed in [82,179,133]. High performance computing on the cloud is discussed in [64] and service-level checking is analyzed in [78]. Cloud migration and open-source cloud computing tools are presented in [190] and [234], respectively, while software testing and scientific applications are covered in [305] and [375]. Application and data portability [300], folt-tolerant middleware [388], and a data debugger [330] are also topics of interest for application developers. Workload migration is analyzed in [367], while cost and application performance issues rediscussed in [196] and [381].

4.13 Exercises and Problems

Problem 1. Download and install *Zookeeper* from the site http://zookeeper.apache.org/. Use the API to create the basic workflow patterns shown in Figure 4.3.

Problem 2. Use the *AWS Simple Workflow Service* to create the basic workflow patterns shown in Figure 4.3.

Problem 3. Use the *AWS CloudFormation* service to create the basic workflow patterns shown in Figure 4.3.

Problem 4. Define a set of keywords that are ordered based on their relevance to the topic of cloud security. Then search the Web using these keywords to locate 10–20 papers and store the papers in an *S3* bucket. Create a *MapReduce* application modeled after the one discussed in Section 4.7 to rank the papers based on the incidence of the relevant keywords. Compare your ranking with the rankings of the search engine you used to identify the papers.

Problem 5. Use the *AWS MapReduce* service to rank the papers in Problem 4.

Problem 6. The paper [63] describes the *elasticLM*, a commercial product that provides license and billing Web-based services. Analyze the merits and shortcomings of the system.

Problem 7. Search the Web for reports of cloud system failures and discuss the causes of each incident.

Problem 8. Identify a set of requirements you would like to be included in a service-level agreement. Attempt to express these requirements using the Web Service Agreement Specification (WS-Agreement) [20] and determine whether it is flexible enough to express your options.

Problem 9. Research the power consumption of processors used in mobile devices and their energy efficiency. Rank the components of a mobile device in terms of power consumption. Establish a set of guidelines to minimize the power consumption of mobile applications.

CHAPTER

5

Cloud Resource Virtualization

Three classes of fundamental abstractions – interpreters, memory, and communications links – are necessary to describe the operation of a computing system [312]. The physical realization of each one of these abstractions, such as processors that transform information, primary and secondary memory for storing information, and communication channels that allow different systems to communicate with one another, can vary in terms of bandwidth,[1] latency,[2] reliability, and other physical characteristics. Software systems such as operating systems are responsible for the management of the system resources – the physical implementations of the three abstractions.

Resource management, discussed in depth in Chapter 6, grows increasingly complex as the scale of a system as well as the number of users and the diversity of applications using the system increase. Resource management for a community of users with a wide range of applications running under different operating systems is a very difficult problem. Resource management becomes even more complex when resources are oversubscribed and users are uncooperative. In addition to external factors, resource management is affected by internal factors, such as the heterogeneity of the hardware and software systems, the ability to approximate the global state of the system and to redistribute the load, the failure rates of different components, and many other factors.

The traditional solution for a data center is to install standard operating systems on individual systems and rely on conventional OS techniques to ensure resource sharing, application protection, and performance isolation. System administration, accounting, security, and resource management are very challenging for the providers of service in this setup; application development and performance optimization are equally challenging for the users.

The alternative is *resource virtualization*, a technique analyzed in this chapter. Virtualization is a basic tenet of cloud computing – that simplifies some of the resource management tasks. For example, the state of a virtual machine (VM) running under a virtual machine monitor (VMM) can be saved and migrated to another server to balance the load. At the same time, virtualization allows users to operate in environments with which they are familiar rather than forcing them to work in idiosyncratic environments.

Resource sharing in a virtual machine environment requires not only ample hardware support and, in particular, powerful processors but also architectural support for multilevel control. Indeed, resources

[1] We use the term *bandwidth* in a broad sense to mean the number of operations per unit of time. For example, millions of instructions per second (MIPS) or millions of floating-point instructions per second (MFLOPS) measure the CPU speed and mega bits per second (Mbps) measures the speed of a communication channel.

[2] *Latency* is defined as the time elapsed from the instant an operation is initiated until its effect is sensed. Latency is context-dependent. For example, the latency of a communication channel is the time it takes a bit to traverse the communication channel from its source to its destination; the memory latency is the time elapsed from the instant a memory `read` instruction is issued until the time instant the data becomes available in a memory register.

such as CPU cycles, memory, secondary storage, and I/O and communication bandwidth are shared among several virtual machines; for each VM, resources must be shared among multiple instances of an application.

We start our discussion with a look at virtualization principles and the motivation for virtualization. Then we discuss the interfaces that define the properties of the system at different levels of abstraction: the application programming interface (API), the application binary interface (ABI), and instruction set architecture (ISA). We discuss alternatives for the implementation of virtualization in Sections 5.3 and 5.4, then analyze their impact on performance and security isolation in Section 5.5.

Two distinct approaches for virtualization, the full virtualization and the paravirtualization, are discussed in Section 5.6. Full virtualization is feasible when the hardware abstraction provided by the VMM is an exact replica of the physical hardware. In this case any operating system running on the hardware will run without modifications under the VMM. In contrast, paravirtualization requires some modifications of the guest operating systems because the hardware abstraction provided by the VMM does not support all the functions the hardware does.

Traditional processor architectures were conceived for one level of control because they support two execution modes, the kernel and the user mode. In a virtualized environment all resources are under the control of a VMM and a second level of control is exercised by the guest operating system. Although two-level scheduling for sharing CPU cycles can be easily implemented, sharing of resources such as cache, memory, and I/O bandwidth is more intricate. In 2005 and 2006 the *x86* processor architecture was extended to provide hardware support for virtualization, as discussed in Section 5.7.

We analyze the *Xen* VMM in Section 5.8 and discuss an optimization of its network performance in Section 5.9. High-performance processors (e.g., *Itanium*) have multiple functional units but do not provide explicit support for virtualization, as shown in Section 5.10.

The system functions critical for the performance of a VM environment are cache and memory management, handling of privileged instructions, and input/output (I/O) handling. Important sources for the performance degradation in a VM environment are the cache misses, as we shall see in Section 5.11. We analyze the security advantages of virtualization in Section 9.6 and some of the potential risks in Section 5.12. Finally, we discuss software fault isolation in Section 5.13.

5.1 Virtualization

Virtualization simulates the interface to a physical object by any one of four means:

1. *Multiplexing.* Create multiple virtual objects from one instance of a physical object. For example, a processor is multiplexed among a number of processes or threads.
2. *Aggregation.* Create one virtual object from multiple physical objects. For example, a number of physical disks are aggregated into a RAID disk.
3. *Emulation.* Construct a virtual object from a different type of physical object. For example, a physical disk emulates a random access memory.
4. *Multiplexing and emulation.* Examples: Virtual memory with paging multiplexes real memory and disk, and a Virtual address emulates a real address; TCP emulates a reliable bit pipe and multiplexes a physical communication channel and a processor.

Virtualization abstracts the underlying resources and simplifies their use, isolates users from one another, and supports replication, which, in turn, increases the elasticity of the system. Virtualization is a critical aspect of cloud computing, equally important to the providers and consumers of cloud services, and plays an important role in:

- System security because it allows isolation of services running on the same hardware.
- Performance and reliability because it allows applications to migrate from one platform to another.
- The development and management of services offered by a provider.
- Performance isolation.

Virtualization has been used successfully since the late 1950s. A virtual memory based on paging was first implemented on the Atlas computer at the University of Manchester in the United Kingdom in 1959. In a cloud computing environment a VMM runs on the physical hardware and exports hardware-level abstractions to one or more guest operating systems. A guest OS interacts with the virtual hardware in the same way it would interact with the physical hardware, but under the watchful eye of the VMM which traps all privileged operations and mediates the interactions of the guest OS with the hardware. For example, a VMM can control I/O operations to two virtual disks implemented as two different sets of tracks on a physical disk. New services can be added without the need to modify an operating system.

User convenience is a necessary condition for the success of the utility computing paradigms. One of the multiple facets of user convenience is the ability to run remotely using the system software and libraries required by the application. *User convenience is a major advantage of a VM architecture over a traditional operating system.* For example, a user of the *Amazon Web Services* (AWS) could submit an Amazon Machine Image (AMI) containing the applications, libraries, data, and associated configuration settings. The user could choose the operating system for the application, then start, terminate, and monitor as many instances of the AMI as needed, using the Web Service APIs and the performance monitoring and management tools provided by the *AWS*.

There are side effects of virtualization, notably the *performance penalty* and the *hardware costs*. As we shall see shortly, all privileged operations of a VM must be trapped and validated by the VMM, which ultimately controls system behavior; the increased overhead has a negative impact on performance. The cost of the hardware for a VM is higher than the cost for a system running a traditional operating system because the physical hardware is shared among a set of guest operating systems and it is typically configured with faster and/or multicore processors, more memory, larger disks, and additional network interfaces compared with a system running a traditional operating system.

5.2 Layering and virtualization

A common approach to managing system complexity is to identify a set of *layers* with well-defined *interfaces* among them. The interfaces separate different levels of abstraction. Layering minimizes the interactions among the subsystems and simplifies the description of the subsystems. Each subsystem is abstracted through its interfaces with the other subsystems. Thus, we are able to design, implement, and modify the individual subsystems independently.

The instruction set architecture (ISA) defines a processor's set of instructions. For example, the Intel architecture is represented by the *x86*-32 and *x86*-64 instruction sets for systems supporting 32-bit addressing and 64-bit addressing, respectively. The hardware supports two execution modes, a *privileged*, or *kernel*, mode and a *user* mode. The instruction set consists of two sets of instructions, *privileged* instructions that can only be executed in kernel mode and *nonprivileged* instructions that can be executed in user mode. There are also *sensitive instructions* that can be executed in kernel and in user mode but that behave differently (see Section 5.6).

Computer systems are fairly complex, and their operation is best understood when we consider a model similar to the one in Figure 5.1, which shows the interfaces among the software components and the hardware [325]. The hardware consists of one or more multicore processors, a system interconnect (e.g., one or more buses), a memory translation unit, the main memory, and I/O devices, including one or more networking interfaces. Applications written mostly in high-level languages (HLL) often call library modules and are compiled into *object code*. Privileged operations, such as I/O requests, cannot be executed in user mode; instead, application and library modules issue *system calls* and the operating system determines whether the privileged operations required by the application do not violate system security or integrity and, if they don't, executes them on behalf of the user. The binaries resulting from the translation of HLL programs are targeted to a specific hardware architecture.

The first interface we discuss is the *instruction set architecture (ISA)* at the boundary of the hardware and the software. The next interface is the *application binary interface (ABI)*, which allows the ensemble consisting of the application and the library modules to access the hardware. The ABI does not include privileged system instructions; instead it invokes system calls. Finally, the *application program interface*

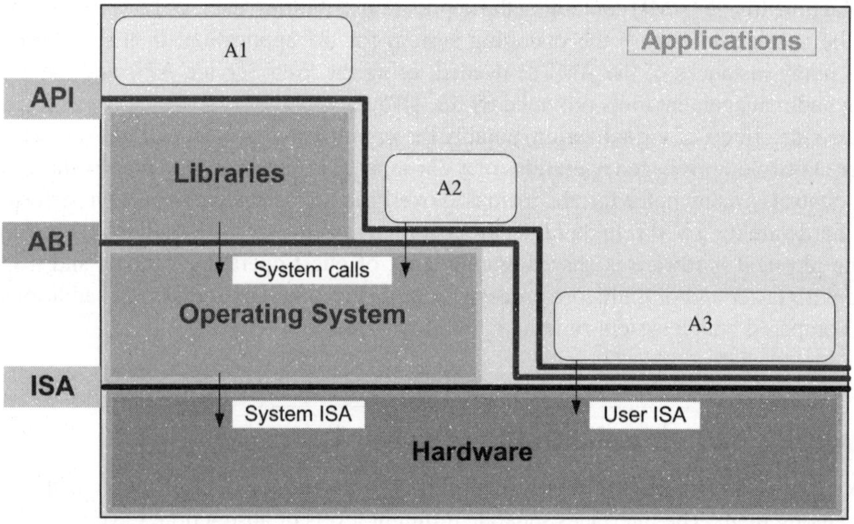

FIGURE 5.1

Layering and interfaces between layers in a computer system. The software components, including applications, libraries, and operating system, interact with the hardware via several interfaces: the *application programming interface* (API), the *application binary interface* (ABI), and the *instruction set architecture* (ISA). An application uses library functions (A1), makes system calls (A2), and executes machine instructions (A3).

(API) defines the set of instructions the hardware was designed to execute and gives the application access to the ISA. It includes HLL library calls, which often invoke system calls. A *process* is the abstraction for the code of an application at execution time; a *thread* is a lightweight process. *The ABI is the projection of the computer system seen by the process, and the API is the projection of the system from the perspective of the HLL program.*

Clearly, the binaries created by a compiler for a specific ISA and a specific operating system are not portable. Such code cannot run on a computer with a different ISA or on computers with the same ISA but different operating systems. However, it is possible to compile an HLL program for a VM environment, as shown in Figure 5.2, where portable code is produced and distributed and then converted by binary translators to the ISA of the host system. A *dynamic binary translation* converts blocks of guest instructions from the portable code to the host instruction and leads to a significant performance improvement as such blocks are cached and reused.

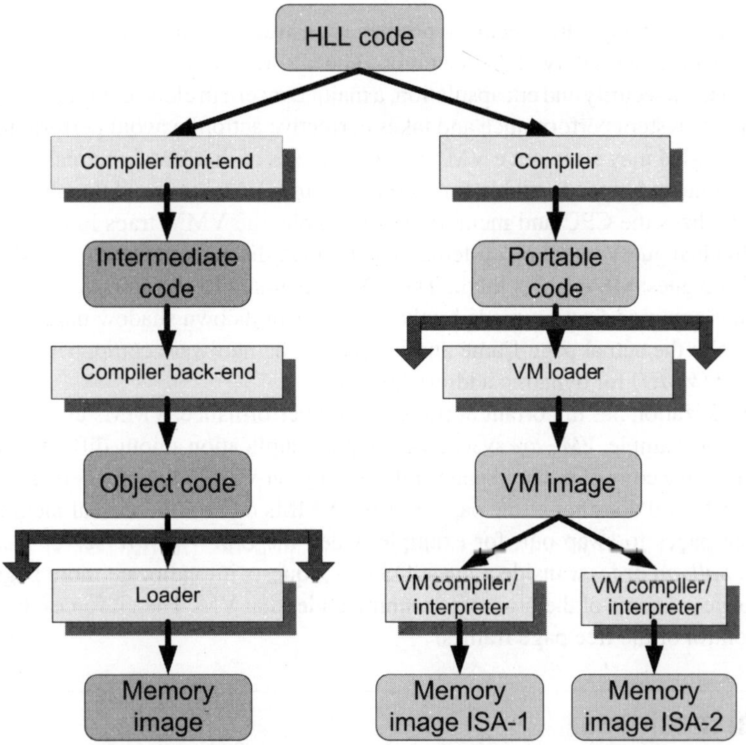

FIGURE 5.2

High-level language (HLL) code can be translated for a specific architecture and operating system. HLL code can also be compiled into portable code and then the portable code translated for systems with different ISAs. The code that is shared/distributed is the object code in the first case and the portable code in the second case.

5.3 Virtual machine monitors

A *virtual machine monitor (VMM)*, also called a *hypervisor*, is the software that securely partitions the resources of a computer system into one or more virtual machines. A *guest operating system* is an operating system that runs under the control of a VMM rather than directly on the hardware. The VMM runs in kernel mode, whereas a guest OS runs in user mode. Sometimes the hardware supports a third mode of execution for the guest OS.

VMMs allow several operating systems to run concurrently on a single hardware platform; at the same time, VMMs enforce isolation among these systems, thus enhancing security. A VMM controls how the guest operating system uses the hardware resources. The events occurring in one VM do not affect any other VM running under the same VMM. At the same time, the VMM enables:

- Multiple services to share the same platform.
- The movement of a server from one platform to another, the so-called live migration.
- System modification while maintaining backward compatibility with the original system.

When a guest OS attempts to execute a privileged instruction, the VMM traps the operation and enforces the correctness and safety of the operation. The VMM guarantees the isolation of the individual VMs, and thus ensures security and encapsulation, a major concern in cloud computing. At the same time, the VMM monitors system performance and takes corrective action to avoid performance degradation; for example, the VMM may swap out a VM (copies all pages of that VM from real memory to disk and makes the real memory frames available for paging by other VMs) to avoid thrashing.

A VMM virtualizes the CPU and memory. For example, the VMM traps interrupts and dispatches them to the individual guest operating systems. If a guest OS disables interrupts, the VMM buffers such interrupts until the guest OS enables them. The VMM maintains a *shadow page table* for each guest OS and replicates any modification made by the guest OS in its own shadow page table. This shadow page table points to the actual page frame and is used by the hardware component called the *memory management unit (MMU)* for dynamic address translation.

Memory virtualization has important implications on performance. VMMs use a range of optimization techniques; for example, *VMware* systems avoid page duplication among different virtual machines; they maintain only one copy of a shared page and use copy-on-write policies whereas Xen imposes total isolation of the VM and does not allow page sharing. VMMs control the virtual memory management and decide what pages to swap out; for example, when the *ESX VMware* server wants to swap out pages, it uses a *balloon process* inside a guest OS and requests it to allocate more pages to itself, thus swapping out pages of some of the processes running under that VM. Then it forces the balloon process to relinquish control of the free page frames.

5.4 Virtual machines

A *virtual machine (VM)* is an isolated environment that appears to be a whole computer but actually only has access to a portion of the computer resources. Each VM appears to be running on the bare hardware, giving the appearance of multiple instances of the same computer, though all are supported by a single physical system. Virtual machines have been around since the early 1970s, when IBM released its VM/370 operating system.

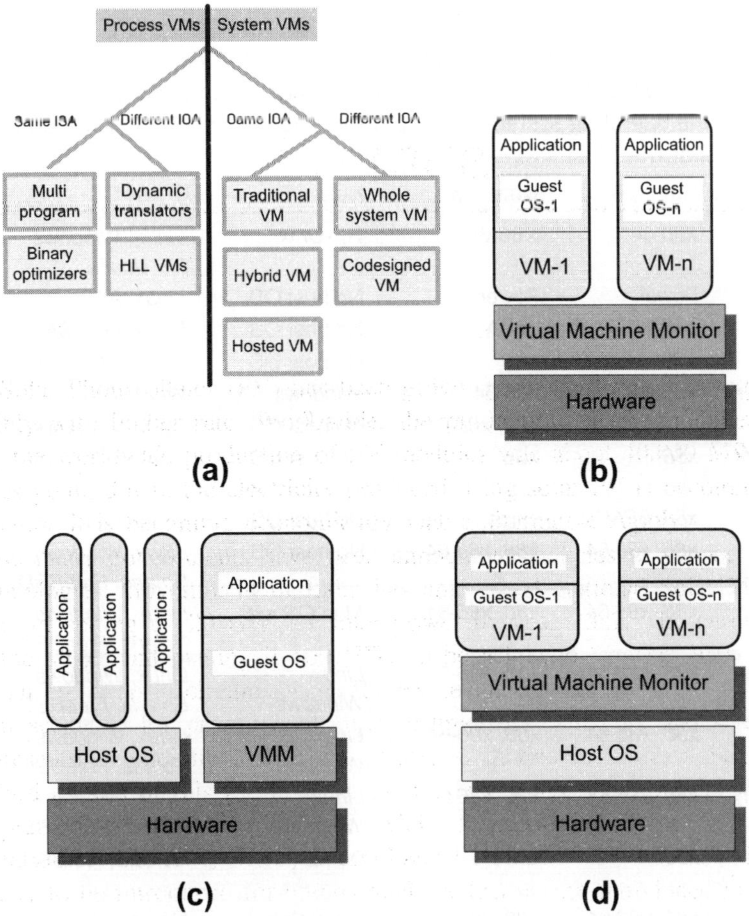

FIGURE 5.3

(a) A taxonomy of process and system VMs for the same and for different ISAs. Traditional, hybrid, and hosted are three classes of VM for systems with the same ISA. (b) Traditional VMs. The VMM supports multiple VMs and runs directly on the hardware. (c) A hybrid VM. The VMM shares the hardware with a host operating system and supports multiple virtual machines. (d) A hosted VM. The VMM runs under a host operating system.

We distinguish two types of VM: process and system VMs [see Figure 5.3(a)]. A *process VM* is a virtual platform created for an individual process and destroyed once the process terminates. Virtually all operating systems provide a process VM for each one of the applications running, but the more interesting process VMs are those that support binaries compiled on a different instruction set. A *system VM* supports an operating system together with many user processes. When the VM runs under the control of a normal OS and provides a platform-independent host for a single application, we have an *application virtual machine* (e.g., Java Virtual Machine [JVM]).

Table 5.1 A nonexhaustive inventory of system virtual machines. The host ISA refers to the instruction set of the hardware; the guest ISA refers to the instruction set supported by the virtual machine. The VM could run under a host OS, directly on the hardware, or under a VMM. The guest OS is the operating system running under the control of a VM, which in turn may run under the control of the VMM.

Name	Host ISA	Guest ISA	Host OS	Guest OS	Company
Integrity VM	*x86-64*	*x86-64*	HP-*Unix*	*Linux, Windows HP Unix*	HP
Power VM	Power	Power	No host OS	*Linux*, AIX	IBM
z/VM	z-ISA	z-ISA	No host OS	*Linux* on z-ISA	IBM
Lynx Secure	*x86*	*x86*	No host OS	*Linux, Windows*	LinuxWorks
Hyper-V Server	*x86-64*	*x86-64*	*Windows*	*Windows*	Microsoft
Oracle VM	*x86, x86-64*	*x86, x86-64*	No host OS	*Linux, Windows*	Oracle
RTS Hypervisor	*x86*	*x86*	No host OS	*Linux, Windows*	Real Time Systems
SUN xVM	*x86*, SPARC	same as host	No host OS	*Linux, Windows*	SUN
VMware EX Server	*x86, x86-64*	*x86, x86-64*	No host OS	*Linux, Windows, Solaris, FreeBSD*	VMware
VMware Fusion	*x86, x86-64*	*x86, x86-64*	*Mac OS x86*	*Linux, Windows, Solaris, FreeBSD*	VMware
VMware Server	*x86, x86-64*	*x86, x86-64*	*Linux, Windows*	*Linux, Windows, Solaris, FreeBSD*	VMware
VMware Workstation	*x86, x86-64*	*x86, x86-64*	*Linux, Windows*	*Linux, Windows, Solaris, FreeBSD*	VMware
VMware Player	*x86, x86-64*	*x86, x86-64*	*Linux, Windows*	*Linux, Windows, Solaris, FreeBSD*	VMware
Denali	*x86*	*x86*	Denali	*ILVACO, NetBSD*	University of Washington
Xen	*x86, x86-64*	*x86, x86-64*	*Linux Solaris*	*Linux, Solaris NetBSD*	University of Cambridge

A literature search reveals the existence of some 60 different virtual machines, many created by the large software companies; Table 5.1 lists a subset of them.

A *system virtual machine* provides a complete system; each VM can run its own OS, which in turn can run multiple applications. Systems such as *Linux Vserver* [214], *OpenVZ* (Open VirtualiZation) [274], *FreeBSD Jails* [124], and *Solaris Zones* [296], based on *Linux, FreeBSD*, and *Solaris*, respectively, implement *operating system-level virtualization technologies*.

Operating system-level virtualization allows a physical server to run multiple isolated operating system instances, subject to several constraints; the instances are known as containers, virtual private servers (VPSs), or virtual environments (VEs). For example, *OpenVZ* requires both the host and the guest OS to be *Linux* distributions. These systems claim performance advantages over the systems based on a VMM such as *Xen* or *VMware*; according to [274], there is only a 1% to 3% performance penalty for *OpenVZ* compared to a stand-alone *Linux* server. *OpenVZ* is licensed under the GPL version 2.

Recall that a VMM allows several virtual machines to share a system. Several organizations of the software stack are possible:

- *Traditional. VM also called a "bare metal" VMM.* A thin software layer that runs directly on the host machine hardware; its main advantage is performance [see Figure 5.3(b)]. Examples: *VMWare ESX, ESXi* Servers, *Xen, OS370,* and *Denali*.
- *Hybrid.* The VMM shares the hardware with the existing OS [see Figure 5.3(c)]. Example: *VMWare Workstation.*
- *Hosted.* The VM runs on top of an existing OS [see Figure 5.3(d)]. The main advantage of this approach is that the VM is easier to build and install. Another advantage of this solution is that the VMM could use several components of the host OS, such as the scheduler, the pager, and the I/O drivers, rather than providing its own. A price to pay for this simplicity is the increased overhead and associated performance penalty; indeed, the I/O operations, page faults, and scheduling requests from a guest OS are not handled directly by the VMM. Instead, they are passed to the host OS. Performance as well as the challenges to support complete isolation of VMs make this solution less attractive for servers in a cloud computing environment. Example: User-mode *Linux*.

A semantic gap exists between the added services and the virtual machine. As pointed out in [79], services provided by the virtual machine "operate below the abstractions provided by the guest operating system .... It is difficult to provide a service that checks file system integrity without the knowledge of on-disk structure."

The VMMs discussed next manage the resource sharing among the VMs sharing a physical system.

5.5 Performance and security isolation

Performance isolation is a critical condition for quality-of-service (QoS) guarantees in shared computing environments. Indeed, if the run-time behavior of an application is affected by other applications running concurrently and, thus, is competing for CPU cycles, cache, main memory, and disk and network access, it is rather difficult to predict the completion time. Moreover, it is equally difficult to optimize the application. Several operating systems, including *Linux*/RK [270], QLinux [343], and SILK [44], support some performance isolation, but problems still exist because one has to account for all resources used and to distribute the overhead for different system activities, including context switching and paging, to individual users – a problem often described as *QoS crosstalk* [348].

Processor virtualization presents multiple copies of the same processor or core on multicore systems. The code is executed directly by the hardware, whereas *processor emulation* presents a model of another hardware system in which instructions are "emulated" in software more slowly than virtualization. An example is Microsoft's VirtualPC, which could run on chip sets other than the *x86* family. It was used on *Mac* hardware until Apple adopted Intel chips.

Traditional operating systems multiplex multiple processes or threads, whereas a virtualization supported by a VMM multiplexes full operating systems. Obviously, there is a performance penalty because an OS is considerably more heavyweight than a process and the overhead of context switching is larger. A VMM executes directly on the hardware a subset of frequently used machine instructions generated by the application and emulates privileged instructions, including device I/O requests. The subset of the instructions executed directly by the hardware includes arithmetic instructions, memory access, and branching instructions.

Operating systems use process abstraction not only for resource sharing but also to support isolation. Unfortunately, this is not sufficient from a security perspective. Once a process is compromised, it is rather easy for an attacker to penetrate the entire system. On the other hand, the software running on a virtual machine has the constraints of its own dedicated hardware; it can only access virtual devices emulated by the software. This layer of software has the potential to provide a level of isolation nearly equivalent to the isolation presented by two different physical systems. Thus, the virtualization can be used to improve security in a cloud computing environment.

A VMM is a much simpler and better specified system than a traditional operating system. For example, the *Xen* VMM discussed in Section 5.8 has approximately 60,000 lines of code, whereas the *Denali* VMM [372] has only about half that, or 30,000 lines of code. The security vulnerability of VMMs is considerably reduced because the systems expose a much smaller number of privileged functions. For example, the *Xen* VMM can be accessed through 28 hypercalls, whereas a standard *Linux* allows hundreds (e.g., *Linux* 2.6.11 allows 289 system calls). In addition to a plethora of system calls, a traditional operating system supports special devices (e.g., `/dev/kmem`) and many privileged programs from a third party (e.g., `sendmail` and `sshd`).

5.6 Full virtualization and paravirtualization

In 1974 Gerald J. Popek and Robert P. Goldberg gave a set of sufficient conditions for a computer architecture to support virtualization and allow a VMM to operate efficiently [293]:

- A program running under the VMM should exhibit a behavior essentially identical to that demonstrated when the program runs directly on an equivalent machine.
- The VMM should be in complete control of the virtualized resources.
- A statistically significant fraction of machine instructions must be executed without the intervention of the VMM.

Another way to identify an architecture suitable for a virtual machine is to distinguish two classes of machine instructions: sensitive instructions, which require special precautions at execution time, and innocuous instructions, which are not sensitive. In turn, sensitive instructions can be:

- *Control sensitive*, which are instructions that attempt to change either the memory allocation or the privileged mode.
- *Mode sensitive*, which are instructions whose behavior is different in the privileged mode.

An equivalent formulation of the conditions for efficient virtualization can be based on this classification of machine instructions. *A VMM for a third-generation (or later) computer can be constructed if the set of sensitive instructions is a subset of the privileged instructions of that machine.* To handle nonvirtualizable instructions, one could resort to two strategies:

- *Binary translation.* The VMM monitors the execution of guest operating systems; nonvirtualizable instructions executed by a guest operating system are replaced with other instructions.

- *Paravirtualization.* The guest operating system is modified to use only instructions that can be virtualized.

There are two basic approaches to processor virtualization: *full virtualization*, in which each virtual machine runs on an exact copy of the actual hardware, and *paravirtualization*, in which each virtual machine runs on a slightly modified copy of the actual hardware (see Figure 5.4). The reasons that paravirtualization is often adopted are (i) some aspects of the hardware cannot be virtualized; (ii) to improve performance; and (iii) to present a simpler interface. *VMware* VMMs are examples of full virtualization. *Xen* [41] and *Denali* [372] are based on paravirtualization; Section 5.8 covers the strategies to overcome hardware limitations for paravirtualization in *Xen*.

Full virtualization requires a virtualizable architecture; the hardware is fully exposed to the guest OS, which runs unchanged, and this ensures that this direct execution mode is efficient. On the other hand, paravirtualization is done because some architectures such as *x86* are not easily virtualizable. Paravirtualization demands that the guest OS be modified to run under the VMM; furthermore, the guest OS code must be ported for individual hardware platforms.

Systems such as *VMware EX Server* support full virtualization on *x86* architecture. The virtualization of the memory management unit (MMU) and the fact that privileged instructions executed by a guest OS fail silently pose some challenges; for example, to address the latter problem, one has to insert traps whenever privileged instructions are issued by a guest OS. The system must also maintain shadow copies of system control structures, such as page tables, and trap every event affecting the state of these control structures; the overhead of many operations is substantial .

Application performance under a virtual machine is critical; generally, virtualization adds some level of overhead that negatively affects the performance. In some cases an application running under a VM

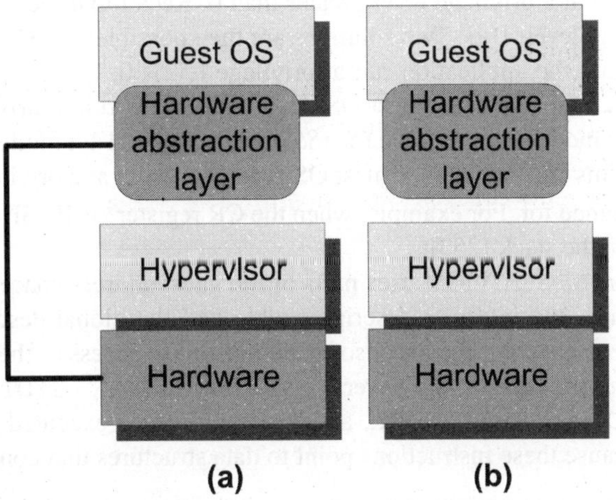

FIGURE 5.4

(a) Full virtualization requires the hardware abstraction layer of the guest OS to have some knowledge about the hardware. (b) Paravirtualization avoids this requirement and allows full compatibility at the application binary interface (ABI).

performs better than one running under a classical OS. This is the case of a policy called *cache isolation*. The cache is generally not partitioned equally among processes running under a classical OS, since one process may use the cache space better than the other. For example, in the case of two processes, one `write`-intensive and the other `read`-intensive, the cache may be aggressively filled by the first. Under the *cache isolation* policy the cache is divided between the VMs and it is beneficial to run workloads competing for cache in two different VMs [324]. The application I/O performance running under a VM depends on factors such as the disk partition used by the VM, the CPU utilization, the I/O performance of the competing VMs, and the I/O block size. On a *Xen* platform, discrepancies between the optimal choice and the default are as high as 8% to 35% [324].

5.7 Hardware support for virtualization

In early 2000 it became obvious that hardware support for virtualization was necessary, and Intel and AMD started work on the first-generation virtualization extensions of the *x86* [3] architecture. In 2005 Intel released two Pentium 4 models supporting *VT-x*, and in 2006 AMD announced *Pacifica* and then several *Athlon 64* models.

A 2006 paper [253] analyzes the challenges to virtualizing Intel architectures and then presents *VT-x* and *VT-i* virtualization architectures for *x86* and *Itanium* architectures, respectively. Software solutions at that time addressed some of the challenges, but hardware solutions could improve not only performance but also security and, at the same time, simplify the software systems. We first examine the problems faced by virtualization of the *x86* architecture:

- *Ring deprivileging.* This means that a VMM forces the guest software, the operating system, and the applications to run at a privilege level greater than 0. Recall that the *x86* architecture provides four protection rings at levels 0–3. Two solutions are then possible: (a) The *(0/1/3) mode*, in which the VMM, the OS, and the application run at privilege levels 0, 1, and 3, respectively; or (b) the *(0,3,3) mode*, in which the VMM, a guest OS, and applications run at privilege levels 0, 3, and 3, respectively. The first mode is not feasible for *x86* processors in 64-bit mode, as we shall see shortly.
- *Ring aliasing.* Problems created when a guest OS is forced to run at a privilege level other than that it was originally designed for. For example, when the CR register[4] is PUSHed, the current privilege level is also stored on the stack [253].
- *Address space compression.* A VMM uses parts of the guest address space to store several system data structures, such as the interrupt-descriptor table and the global-descriptor table. Such data structures must be protected, but the guest software must have access to them.
- *Nonfaulting access to privileged state.* Several instructions, `LGDT`, `SIDT`, `SLDT`, and `LTR` that load the registers `GDTR`, `IDTR`, `LDTR`, and `TR`, can only be executed by software running at privilege level 0, because these instructions point to data structures that control the CPU operation.

[3]The names *x86*-32, *i386*, *x86*, and *IA*-32 all refer to the Intel CISC-based instruction architecture, now supplanted by *x86*-64, which supports vastly larger physical and virtual address spaces. The *x86*-64 specification is distinct from the *Itanium*, initially known as *IA*-64 architecture.

[4]The *x86* architecture supports memory segmentation with a segment size of 64K. The code-segment register (CR) points to the code segment. MOV, POP, and PUSH instructions serve to load and store segment registers, including CR.

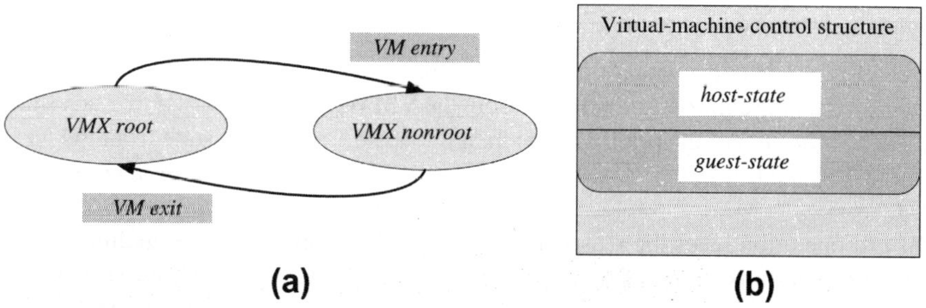

FIGURE 5.5

(a) The two modes of operation of *VT-x*, and the two operations to transit from one to another. (b) The VMCS includes *host-state* and *guest-state* areas that control the *VM entry* and *VM exit* transitions.

Nevertheless, instructions that store from these registers fail silently when executed at a privilege level other than 0. This implies that a guest OS executing one of these instructions does not realize that the instruction has failed.

- *Guest system calls.* Two instructions, `SYSENTER` and `SYSEXIT`, support low-latency system calls. The first causes a transition to privilege level 0, whereas the second causes a transition from privilege level 0 and fails if executed at a level higher than 0. The VMM must then emulate every guest execution of either of these instructions, which has a negative impact on performance.
- *Interrupt virtualization.* In response to a physical interrupt, the VMM generates a "virtual interrupt" and delivers it later to the target guest OS. But every OS has the ability to mask interrupts[5]; thus the virtual interrupt could only be delivered to the guest OS when the interrupt is not masked. Keeping track of all guest OS attempts to mask interrupts greatly complicates the VMM and increases the overhead.
- *Access to hidden state.* Elements of the system state (e.g., descriptor caches for segment registers) are hidden; there is no mechanism for saving and restoring the hidden components when there is a context switch from one VM to another.
- *Ring compression.* Paging and segmentation are the two mechanisms to protect VMM code from being overwritten by a guest OS and applications. Systems running in 64-bit mode can only use paging, but paging does not distinguish among privilege levels 0, 1, and 2, so the guest OS must run at privilege level 3, the so-called (0/3/3) mode. Privilege levels 1 and 2 cannot be used; thus the name *ring compression*.
- *Frequent access to privileged resources increases VMM overhead.* The task-priority register (`TPR`) is frequently used by a guest OS. The VMM must protect the access to this register and trap all attempts to access it. This can cause a significant performance degradation.

Similar problems exist for the *Itanium* architecture discussed in Section 5.10.

A major architectural enhancement provided by the *VT-x* is the support for two modes of operations and a new data structure called the virtual machine control structure (VMCS), including *host-state* and *guest-state* areas (see Figure 5.5):

- *VMX root.* Intended for VMM operations and very close to the *x86* without *VT-x*.

[5]The interrupt flag (IF) in the `EFLAGS` register is used to control interrupt masking.

- *VMX nonroot.* Intended to support a VM.

When executing a *VM entry* operation, the processor state is loaded from the *guest-state* of the VM scheduled to run; then the control is transferred from the VMM to the VM. A *VM exit* saves the processor state in the *guest-state* area of the running VM; then it loads the processor state from the *host-state* area and finally transfers control to the VMM. Note that all *VM exit* operations use a common entry point to the VMM.

Each *VM exit* operation saves the reason for the exit and, eventually, some qualifications in VMCS. Some of this information is stored as bitmaps. For example, the *exception bitmap* specifies which one of 32 possible exceptions caused the exit. The *I/O bitmap* contains one entry for each port in a 16-bit I/O space.

The VMCS area is referenced with a physical address and its layout is not fixed by the architecture but can be optimized by a particular implementation. The VMCS includes control bits that facilitate the implementation of virtual interrupts. For example, *external-interrupt exiting*, when set, causes the execution of a *VM exit* operation; moreover, the guest is not allowed to mask these interrupts. When the *interrupt window exiting* is set, a *VM exit* operation is triggered if the guest is ready to receive interrupts.

Processors based on two new virtualization architectures, *VT-d* [6] and *VT-c*, have been developed. The first supports the I/O memory management unit (I/O MMU) virtualization and the second supports network virtualization.

Also known as *PCI pass-through*, I/O MMU virtualization gives VMs direct access to peripheral devices. *VT-d* supports:

- DMA address remapping, which is address translation for device DMA transfers.
- Interrupt remapping, which is isolation of device interrupts and VM routing.
- I/O device assignment, in which an administrator can assign the devices to a VM in any configuration.
- Reliability features, which report and record DMA and interrupt errors that may otherwise corrupt memory and impact VM isolation.

Next we discuss *Xen*, a widely used VMM or hypervisor.

5.8 Case study: *Xen*, a VMM based on paravirtualization

Xen is a VMM or hypervisor developed by the Computing Laboratory at the University of Cambridge, United Kingdom, in 2003. Since 2010 *Xen* has been free software, developed by the community of users and licensed under the GNU General Public License (GPLv2). Several operating systems, including *Linux, Minix, NetBSD, FreeBSD, NetWare*, and *OZONE*, can operate as paravirtualized *Xen* guest operating systems running on *x86*, *x86*-64, *Itanium*, and *ARM* architectures.

The goal of the Cambridge group, led by Ian Pratt, was to design a VMM capable of scaling to about 100 VMs running standard applications and services without any modifications to the application binary interface (ABI). Fully aware that the *x86* architecture does not support efficiently full virtualization, the designers of *Xen* opted for paravirtualization.

Next we analyze the original implementation of *Xen* for the *x86* architecture discussed in [41]. The creators of *Xen* used the concept of *domain* (*Dom*) to refer to the ensemble of address spaces hosting a

[6] The corresponding AMD architecture is called *AMD-Vi*.

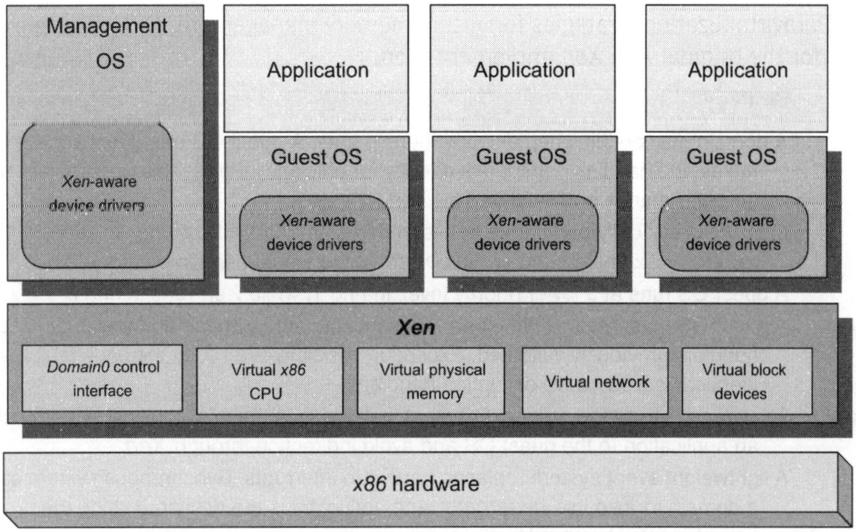

FIGURE 5.6

Xen for the *x86* architecture. In the original *Xen* implementation [41] a guest OS could be *XenoLinix*, *XenoBSD*, or *XenoXP*. The management OS dedicated to the execution of *Xen* control functions and privileged instructions resides in *Dom0*; guest operating systems and applications reside in *DomU*.

guest OS and address spaces for applications running under this guest OS. Each domain runs on a virtual *x86* CPU. *Dom0* is dedicated to the execution of *Xen* control functions and privileged instructions, and *DomU* is a user domain (see Figure 5.6) .

The most important aspects of the *Xen* paravirtualization for virtual memory management, CPU multiplexing, and I/O device management are summarized in Table 5.2 [41]. Efficient management of the translation look-aside buffer (TLB), a cache for page table entries, requires either the ability to identify the OS and the address space of every entry or to allow software management of the TLB. Unfortunately, the *x86* architecture does not support either the tagging of TLB entries or the software management of the TLB. As a result, address space switching, when the VMM activates a different OS, requires a complete TLB flush. This has a negative impact on performance.

The solution that was adopted was to load *Xen* in a 64 MB segment at the top of each address space and delegate the management of hardware page tables to the guest OS with minimal intervention from *Xen*. The 64 MB region occupied by *Xen* at the top of every address space is not accessible or not remappable by the guest OS. When a new address space is created, the guest OS allocates and initializes a page from its own memory, registers it with *Xen*, and relinquishes control of the `write` operations to the VMM. Thus, a guest OS could only map pages it owns. On the other hand, it has the ability to batch multiple page-update requests to improve performance. A similar strategy is used for segmentation.

The *x86* Intel architecture supports four protection rings or privilege levels; virtually all OS kernels run at Level 0, the most privileged one, and applications at Level 3. In *Xen* the VMM runs at Level 0, the guest OS at Level 1, and applications at Level 3.

Table 5.2 Paravirtualization strategies for virtual memory management, CPU multiplexing, and I/O devices for the original *x86 Xen* implementation.

Function	Strategy
Paging	A domain may be allocated discontinuous pages. A guest OS has direct access to page tables and handles page faults directly for efficiency. Page table updates are batched for performance and validated by *Xen* for safety.
Memory	Memory is statically partitioned between domains to provide strong isolation. `XenoLinux` implements a *balloon driver* to adjust domain memory.
Protection	A guest OS runs at a lower priority level, in ring 1, while *Xen* runs in ring 0.
Exceptions	A guest OS must register with *Xen* a description table with the addresses of exception handlers previously validated. Exception handlers other than the page fault handler are identical to *x*86 native exception handlers.
System calls	To increase efficiency, a guest OS must install a "fast" handler to allow system calls from an application to the guest OS and avoid indirection through *Xen*.
Interrupts	A lightweight event system replaces hardware interrupts. Synchronous system calls from a domain to *Xen* use *hypercalls*, and notifications are delivered using the asynchronous event system.
Multiplexing	A guest OS may run multiple applications.
Time	Each guest OS has a timer interface and is aware of "real" and "virtual" time.
Network and I/O devices	Data is transferred using asynchronous I/O rings. A ring is a circular queue of descriptors allocated by a domain and accessible within *Xen*.
Disk access	Only *Dom0* has direct access to IDE and SCSI disks. All other domains access persistent storage through the virtual block device (VBD) abstraction.

Applications make system calls using the so-called *hypercalls* processed by *Xen*. Privileged instructions issued by a guest OS are *paravirtualized* and must be validated by *Xen*. When a guest OS attempts to execute a privileged instruction directly, the instruction fails silently.

Memory is statically partitioned between domains to provide strong isolation. To adjust domain memory, `XenoLinux` implements a *balloon driver*, which passes pages between *Xen* and its own page allocator. For the sake of efficiency, page faults are handled directly by the guest OS.

Xen schedules individual domains using the borrowed virtual time (BVT) scheduling algorithm discussed in Section 6.11. BVT is a work conserving[7] and low-latency wake-up scheduling algorithm. BVT uses a virtual-time warping mechanism to support low-latency dispatch to ensure timely execution when this is needed – for example, for timely delivery of TCP acknowledgments.

A guest OS must register with *Xen* a *description table* with the addresses of exception handlers for validation. Exception handlers are identical to the native *x86* handlers. The only one that does not follow this rule is the page fault handler, which uses an extended stack frame to retrieve the faulty address because the privileged register `CR2`, where this address is found, is not available to a guest OS. Each

[7] A work-conserving scheduling algorithm does not allow the processor to be idle when there is work to be done.

guest OS can validate and then register a "fast" exception handler executed directly by the processor without the interference of *Xen*. A lightweight event system replaces hardware interrupts. Notifications are delivered using this asynchronous event system. Each guest OS has a timer interface and is aware of "real" and "virtual" time.

XenStore is a *Dom0* process that supports a system-wide registry and naming service. It is implemented as a hierarchical key-value storage; a *watch* function of the process informs listeners of changes to the key in storage to which they have subscribed. *XenStore* communicates with guest VMs via shared memory using *Dom0* privileges rather than grant tables.

The *Toolstack* is another *Dom0* component responsible for creating, destroying, and managing the resources and privileges of VMs. To create a new VM a user provides a configuration file describing memory and CPU allocations as well as device configuration. Then the *Toolstack* parses this file and writes this information in the *XenStore*. *Toolstack* takes advantage of *Dom0* privileges to map guest memory, to load a kernel and virtual BIOS, and to set up initial communication channels with the *XenStore* and with the virtual console when a new VM is created.

Xen defines abstractions for networking and I/O devices. *Split drivers* have a front-end in the *DomU* and a back-end in *Dom0*; the two communicate via a ring in shared memory. *Xen* enforces access control for the shared memory and passes synchronization signals. Access control lists (ACLs) are stored in the form of *grant tables*, with permissions set by the owner of the memory.

Data for I/O and network operations move vertically through the system very efficiently using a set of I/O rings (see Figure 5.7). A *ring* is a circular queue of descriptors allocated by a domain and accessible within *Xen*. Descriptors do not contain data; the data buffers are allocated off-band by the guest OS. Memory committed for I/O and network operations is supplied in a manner designed to avoid "cross-talk," and the I/O buffers holding the data are protected by preventing page faults of the corresponding page frames.

Each domain has one or more virtual network interfaces (VIFs) that support the functionality of a network interface card. A VIF is attached to a virtual firewall-router (VFR). Two rings of buffer descriptors, one for packet sending and one for packet receiving, are supported. To transmit a packet, a guest OS enqueues a buffer descriptor to the send ring, then *Xen* copies the descriptor and checks safety and finally copies only the packet header, not the payload, and executes the matching rules.

The rules of the form (<*pattern*>, <*action*>) require the *action* to be executed if the *pattern* is matched by the information in the packet header. The rules can be added or removed by *Dom0*; they ensure the demultiplexing of packets based on the destination IP address and port and, at the same time, prevent spoofing of the source IP address. *Dom0* is the only one allowed to directly access the physical IDE (Integrated Drive Electronics) or SCSI (Small Computer System Interface) disks. All domains other than *Dom0* access persistent storage through a virtual block device (VBD) abstraction created and managed under the control of *Dom0*.

Xen includes a device emulator, *Qemu*, to support unmodified commodity operating systems. *Qemu* emulates a DMA[8] and can map any page of the memory in a *DomU*. Each VM has its own instance of *Qemu* that can run either as a *Dom0* process or as a process of the VM.

[8]Direct Memory Access (DMA) is a hardware feature that allows I/O devices and other hardware subsystems direct access to system memory without CPU involvement.

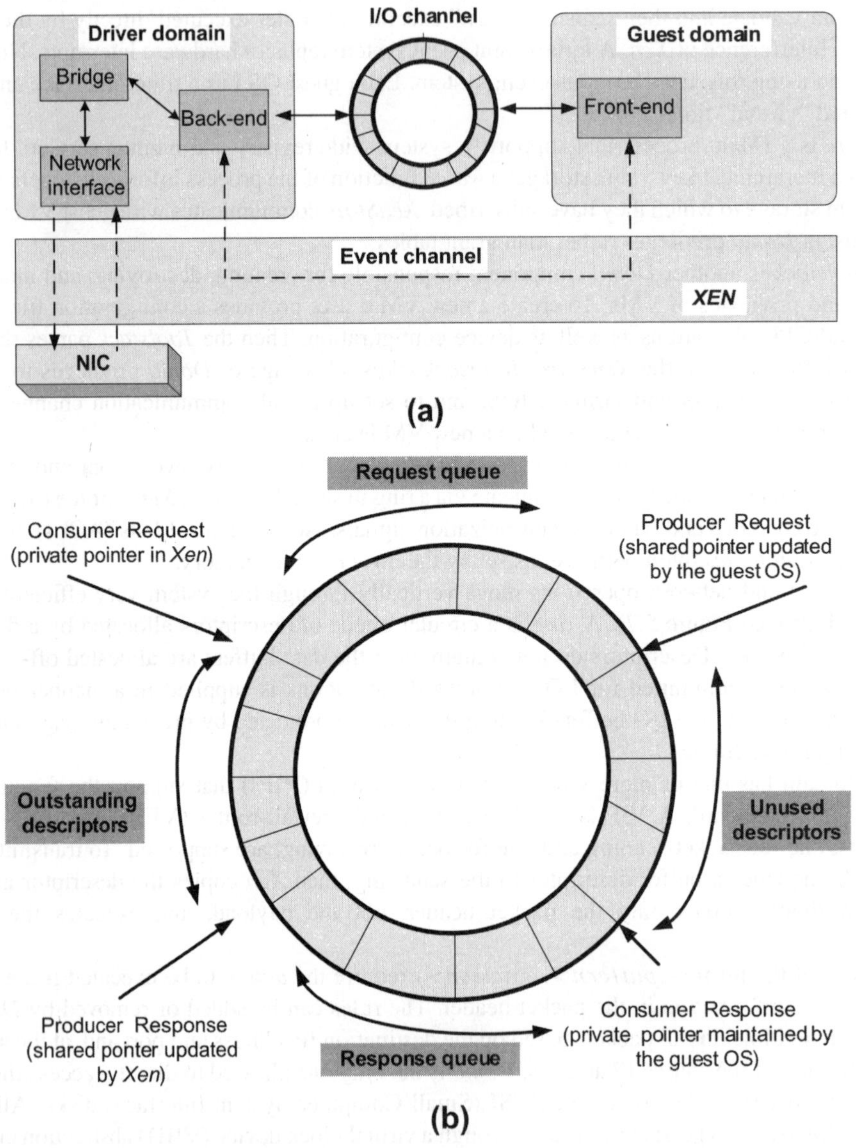

FIGURE 5.7

Xen zero-copy semantics for data transfer using I/O rings. (a) The communication between a guest domain and the driver domain over an I/O and an event channel; NIC is the Network Interface Controller. (b) The circular ring of buffers.

Xen, initially released in 2003, underwent significant changes in 2005, when Intel released the *VT-x* processors. In 2006 *Xen* was adopted by Amazon for its *EC2* service, and in 2008 *Xen* running on Intel's *VT-d* passed the *ACPI S3* [9] test. *Xen* support for *Dom0* and *DomU* was added to the *Linux* kernel in 2011.

In 2008 the PCI pass-through was incorporated for *Xen* running on *VT-d* architectures. The PCI[10] pass-through allows a PCI device, whether a disk controller, network interface card (NIC), graphic card, or Universal Serial Bus (USB), to be assigned to a VM. This avoids the overhead of copying and allows setting up of a ***driver domain*** to increase security and system reliability. A guest OS can exploit this facility to access the 3D acceleration capability of a graphics card. To prepare a device for pass-through, one must know its BDF.[11]

An analysis of VM performance for I/O-bound applications under *Xen* is reported in [298]. Two Apache Web servers, each under a different VM, share the same server running *Xen*. The workload generator sends requests for files of fixed size ranging from 1 KB to 100 KB. When the file size increases from 1 KB to 10 KB and to 100 KB, the CPU utilization, throughput, data rate, and response time are, respectively: (97.5%; 70.44%; 44.4%), (1,900; 1,104; 112) requests/s, (2,018; 11,048; 11,208) KBps, and (1.52; 2.36; 2.08) msec. From the first group of results we see that for files 10 KB or larger the system is I/O bound; the second set of results shows that the throughput measured in requests/s decreases by less than 50% when the system becomes I/O bound, but the data rate increases by a factor of five over the same range. The variation of the response time is quite small; it increases about 10% when the file size increases by two orders of magnitude.

The paravirtualization strategy in *Xen* is different from the one adopted by a group at the University of Washington, the creators of the `Denali` system [372]. `Denali` was designed to support a number of virtual machines running network services one or more orders of magnitude larger than *Xen*. The design of the `Denali` system did not target existing ABI. It does not support some features of potential guest operating systems – for example, it does not support segmentation. `Denali` does not support application multiplexing, running multiple applications under a guest OS, whereas *Xen* does.

Finally, a few words regarding the complexity of porting commodity operating systems to *Xen*. It is reported that a total of about 3,000 lines of *Linux* code, or 1.36%, had to be modified; for *Windows XP* this figure is 4,620, or about 0.04% [41].

5.9 Optimization of network virtualization in *Xen* 2.0

A virtual machine monitor introduces a significant network communication overhead. For example, it is reported that the CPU utilization of a *VMware Workstation 2.0* system running *Linux* 2.2.17 was 5 to 6 times higher than that of the native system (*Linux* 2.2.17) in saturating a 100 Mbps network [338].

[9]The Advanced Configuration and Power Interface (ACPI) specification is an open standard for device configuration and power management by the operating system. It defines four Global "Gx" states and six Sleep "Sx" states. "S3" is referred to as Standby, Sleep, or Suspend to RAM.

[10]PCI stands for Peripheral Component Interconnect and describes a computer bus for attaching hardware devices to a computer. The PCI bus supports the functions found on a processor bus, but in a standardized format independent of any particular processor. At startup time the operating system queries all PCI buses to identify the devices connected to the system and the memory space, I/O space, interrupt lines, and so on needed by each device present.

[11]BDF stands for Bus:Device.Function and is used to describe PCI devices.

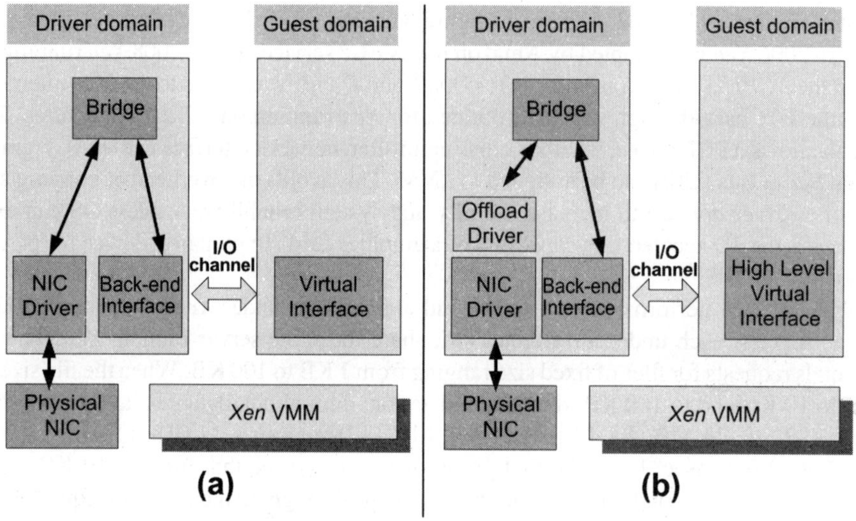

FIGURE 5.8

Xen network architecture. (a) The original architecture. (b) The optimized architecture.

In other words, handling the same amount of traffic as the native system to saturate the network, the VMM executes a much larger number of instructions – 5 to 6 times larger.

Similar overheads are reported for other VMMs and, in particular, for *Xen* 2.0 [241,242]. To understand the sources of the network overhead, we examine the basic network architecture of *Xen* [see Figure 5.8(a)]. Recall that privileged operations, including I/O, are executed by *Dom0* on behalf of a guest operating system. In this context we shall refer to it as the *driver domain* called to execute networking operations on behalf of the *guest domain*. The *driver domain* uses the native *Linux* driver for the network interface controller, which in turn communicates with the physical NIC, also called the network adapter. Recall from Section 5.8 that the *guest domain* communicates with the *driver domain* through an I/O channel; more precisely, the guest OS in the *guest domain* uses a virtual interface to send/receive data to/from the back-end interface in the *driver domain*.

Recall that a *bridge* in a LAN uses broadcast to identify the *MAC* address of a destination system. Once this address is identified, it is added to a table. When the next packet for the same destination arrives, the bridge uses the link layer protocol to send the packet to the proper *MAC* address rather than broadcast it. The bridge in the driver domain performs a multiplexing/demultiplexing function; packets received from the NIC have to be demultiplexed and sent to different VMs running under the VMM. Similarly, packets arriving from multiple VMs have to be multiplexed into a single stream before being transmitted to the network adaptor. In addition to bridging, *Xen* supports IP routing based on network address translation (NAT).

Table 5.3 shows the ultimate effect of this longer processing chain for the *Xen* VMM as well as the effect of optimizations [242]. The receiving and sending rates from a guest domain are roughly 30% and 20%, respectively, of the corresponding rates of a native *Linux* application. Packet multiplexing/

Table 5.3 A comparison of send and receive data rates for a native *Linux* system, the *Xen* driver domain, an original *Xen* guest domain, and an optimized *Xen* guest domain.

System	Receive Data Rate (Mbps)	Send Data Rate (MBPS)
Linux	2,508	3,760
Xen driver	1,728	3,760
Xen guest	820	750
Optimized *Xen* guest	970	3,310

demultiplexing accounts for about 40% and 30% of the communication overhead for the incoming traffic and for the outgoing traffic, respectively.

The *Xen* network optimization discussed in [242] covers optimization of (i) the virtual interface; (ii) the I/O channel; and (iii) the virtual memory. The effects of these optimizations are significant for the send data rate from the optimized *Xen* guest domain, an increase from 750 to 3, 310 Mbps, and rather modest for the receive data rate, 970 versus 820 Mbps.

Next we examine briefly each optimization area, starting with the virtual interface. There is a tradeoff between generality and flexibility on one hand and performance on the other hand. The original virtual network interface provides the guest domain with the abstraction of a simple low-level network interface supporting sending and receiving primitives. This design supports a wide range of physical devices attached to the driver domain but does not take advantage of the capabilities of some physical NICs such as checksum offload (e.g., TSO[12]) and scatter-gather DMA support.[13] These features are supported by the high-level virtual interface of the optimized system [see Figure 5.8(b)].

The next target of the optimization effort is the communication between the guest domain and the driver domain. Rather than copying a data buffer holding a packet, each packet is allocated in a new page and then the physical page containing the packet is remapped into the target domain. For example, when a packet is received, the physical page is remapped to the guest domain. The optimization is based on the observation that there is no need to remap the entire packet; for example, when sending a packet, the network bridge needs to know only the *MAC* header of the packet. As a result, the optimized implementation is based on an "out-of-band" channel used by the guest domain to provide the bridge with the packet *MAC* header. This strategy contributed to a better than four times increase in the send data rate compared with the nonoptimized version.

The third optimization covers virtual memory. Virtual memory in *Xen* 2.0 takes advantage of the *superpage* and *global page-mapping* hardware features available on Pentium and Pentium Pro processors. A superpage increases the granularity of the dynamic address translation; a superpage entry covers 1, 024 pages of physical memory, and the address translation mechanism maps a set of contiguous pages to a set of contiguous physical pages. This helps reduce the number of TLB misses. Obviously,

[12]TSO stands for TCP segmentation offload. This option enables the network adapter to compute the TCP checksum on transmit and receive and save the host CPU the overhead for computing the checksum. Large packets have larger savings.

[13]Direct Memory Access (DMA) can also be used for memory-to-memory copying and can offload expensive memory operations, such as scatter-gather operations, from the CPU to the dedicated DMA engine. Intel includes such engines on high-end servers, called I/O Acceleration Technology (I/OAT).

all pages of a superpage belong to the same guest OS. When new processes are created, the guest OS must allocate *read-only* pages for the page tables of the address spaces running under the guest OS, and that forces the system to use traditional page mapping rather than superpage mapping. The optimized version uses a special memory allocator to avoid this problem.

5.10 *vBlades*: paravirtualization targeting an *x86*-64 Itanium processor

To understand the impact of computer architecture on the ability to efficiently virtualize a given architecture, we discuss some of the findings of the *vBlades* project at HP-Laboratories [228]. The goal of the *vBlades* project was to create a VMM for the *Itanium* family of *IA64* Intel processors,[14] capable of supporting the execution of multiple operating systems in isolated protection domains with security and privacy enforced by the hardware. The VMM was also expected to support optimal server utilization and allow comprehensive measurement and monitoring for detailed performance analysis.

The discussion in Section 5.4 shows that to be fully virtualizable, the ISA of a processor must conform to a set of requirements, but unfortunately the *IA64* architecture does not meet these requirements, and that fact made the *vBlades* project more challenging. We first review the features of the *Itanium* processor that are important for virtualization, starting with the observation that the hardware supports four *privilege rings*, PL0, PL1, PL2, and PL3. Privileged instructions can only be executed by the kernel running at level PL0, whereas applications run at level PL3 and can only execute nonprivileged instructions; PL2 and PL4 rings are generally not used. The VMM uses *ring compression* and runs itself at PL0 and PL1 while forcing a guest OS to run at PL2. A first problem, called *privilege leaking*, is that several nonprivileged instructions allow an application to determine the current privilege level (CPL); thus, a guest OS may not accept to boot or run or may itself attempt to make use of all four privilege rings.

Itanium was selected because of its multiple functional units and multithreading support. The *Itanium* processor has 30 functional units: six general-purpose ALUs, two integer units, one shift unit, four data cache units, six multimedia units, two parallel shift units, one parallel multiply, one population count, three branch units, two 82-bit floating-point multiply-accumulate units, and two SIMD floating-point multiply-accumulate units. A 128-bit instruction word contains three instructions; the fetch mechanism can `read` up to two instruction words per clock from the L1 cache into the pipeline. Each unit can execute a particular subset of the instruction set.

The hardware supports 64-bit addressing; it has 32 64-bit general-purpose registers numbered from R0 to R31 and 96 automatically renumbered registers, R32 through R127, used by procedure calls. When a procedure is entered, the `alloc` instruction specifies the registers the procedure can access by setting the bits of a 7-bit field that controls the register usage. An illegal `read` operation from such a register out of range returns a zero value, whereas an illegal `write` operation to it is trapped as an illegal instruction.

The *Itanium* processor supports isolation of the address spaces of different processes with eight privileged *region* registers. The *Processor Abstraction Layer (PAL)* firmware allows the caller to set the

[14] *Itanium* is a processor developed jointly by HP and Intel and based on a new architecture, explicitly parallel instruction computing (EPIC), that allows the processor to execute multiple instructions in each clock cycle. EPIC implements a form of very long instruction word (VLIW) architecture in which a single instruction word contains multiple instructions. For more information see `www.dig64.org/about/Itanium2_white_paper_public.pdf`.

values in the region register. The VMM intercepts the privileged instruction issued by the guest OS to its PAL and partitions the set of address spaces among the guest OSs to ensure isolation. Each guest is limited to 2^{18} address spaces.

The hardware has an *IVA register* to maintain the address of the *interruption vector table*. The entries in this table control both the interrupt delivery and the interrupt state collection. Different types of interrupts activate different interrupt handlers pointed from this table, provided that the particular interrupt is not disabled. Each guest OS maintains its own version of this vector table and has its own IVA register. The hypervisor uses the guest OS IVA register to give control to the guest interrupt handler when an interrupt occurs.

First, let's discuss *CPU virtualization*. When a guest OS attempts to execute a privileged instruction, the VMM traps and emulates the instruction. For example, when the guest OS uses the `rsm psr.i` instruction to turn off delivery of a certain type of interrupt, the VMM does not disable the interrupt but records the fact that interrupts of that type should not be delivered to the guest OS, and in this case the interrupt should be masked. There is a slight complication related to the fact that the *Itanium* does not have an instruction register (IR) and the VMM has to use state information to determine whether an instruction is privileged. Another complication is caused by the *register stack engine (RSE)*, which operates concurrently with the processor and may attempt to access memory (load or store) and generate a page fault. Normally, the problem is solved by setting up a bit indicating that the fault is due to RSE and, at the same time, the RSE operations are disabled. The handling of this problem by the VMM is more intricate.

A number of *privileged-sensitive* instructions behave differently as a function of the privilege level. The VMM replaces each one of them with a privileged instruction during the dynamic transformation of the instruction stream. Among the instructions in this category are:

- `cover`, which saves stack information into a privileged register. The VMM replaces it with a `break.b` instruction.
- `thash` and `ttag`, which access data from privileged virtual memory control structures and have two registers as arguments. The VMM takes advantage of the fact that an illegal `read` returns a zero and an illegal `write` to a register in the range 32 to 127 is trapped and translates these instructions as:
  `thash Rx=Ry -> tpa Rx=R(y+64)` and `ttag Rx=Ry -> tak Rx=R(y+64)`, where $0 \leqslant y \leqslant 64$.
- Access to performance data from performance data registers is controlled by a bit in the *processor status register* with the `PSR.sp` instruction.

Memory virtualization is guided by the realization that a VMM should not be involved in most memory `read` and `write` operations to prevent a significant degradation of performance, but at the same time the VMM should exercise tight control and prevent a guest OS from acting maliciously. The *vBlades* VMM does not allow a guest OS to access the memory directly. It inserts an additional layer of indirection called *metaphysical addressing* between virtual and real addressing. A guest OS is placed in metaphysical addressing mode. If the address is virtual, the VMM first checks to see whether the guest OS is allowed to access that address and, if it is, it provides the regular address translation. If the address is physical the VMM is not involved. The hardware distinguishes between virtual and real addresses using bits in the processor status register.

5.11 A performance comparison of virtual machines

We have seen that a VMM such as *Xen* introduces additional overhead and negatively affects performance [41,241,242]. The topic of this section is a quantitative analysis of the performance of VMs. We compare the performance of two virtualization techniques with a standard operating system: a plain-vanilla *Linux* referred to as "the base" system. The two VM systems are *Xen*, based on paravirtualization, and *OpenVZ* [281].

First we take a closer look at *OpenVZ*, a system based on OS-level virtualization. *OpenVZ* uses a single patched *Linux* kernel. The guest operating systems in different containers[15] may be different distributions but must use the same *Linux* kernel version that the host uses. The lack of flexibility of the approach for virtualization in *OpenVZ* is compensated by lower overhead.

The memory allocation in *OpenVZ* is more flexible than in the case of paravirtualization; memory not used in one virtual environment can be used by others. The system uses a common file system. Each virtual environment is a directory of files isolated using `chroot`. To start a new virtual machine, one needs to copy the files from one directory to another, create a `config` file for the virtual machine, and launch the VM.

OpenVZ has a two-level scheduler: At the first level, the fair-share scheduler allocates CPU time slices to containers based on `cpuunits` values; the second level is a standard *Linux* scheduler that decides what process to run in that container. The I/O scheduler also has two levels; each container has an I/O priority, and the scheduler distributes the available I/O bandwidth according to the priorities.

The discussion in [281] is focused on the user's perspective, thus the performance measures analyzed are the throughput and the response time. The general question is whether consolidation of the applications and servers is a good strategy for cloud computing. The specific questions examined are:

- How does the performance scale up with the load?
- What is the impact of a mix of applications?
- What are the implications of the load assignment on individual servers?

There is ample experimental evidence that the load placed on system resources by a single application varies significantly in time. A time series displaying CPU consumption of a single application in time clearly illustrates this fact. As we all know, this phenomenon justifies the need for CPU multiplexing among threads/processes supported by an operating system. The concept of *application and server consolidation* is an extension of the idea of creating an aggregate load consisting of several applications and aggregating a set of servers to accommodate this load. Indeed, the peak resource requirements of individual applications are very unlikely to be synchronized, and the aggregate load tends to lead to a better average resource utilization.

The application used in [281] is a two-tier system consisting of an Apache Web server and a MySQL database server. A client of this application starts a session as the user browses through different items in the database, requests information about individual items, and buys or sells items. Each session requires the creation of a new thread; thus, an increased load means an increased number of threads. To understand the potential discrepancies in performance among the three systems, a performance-monitoring tool

[15] A container in *OpenVZ* emulates a separate physical server. It has its own files, users, process tree, IP address, shared memory, semaphores, and messages. Each container can have its own disk quotas.

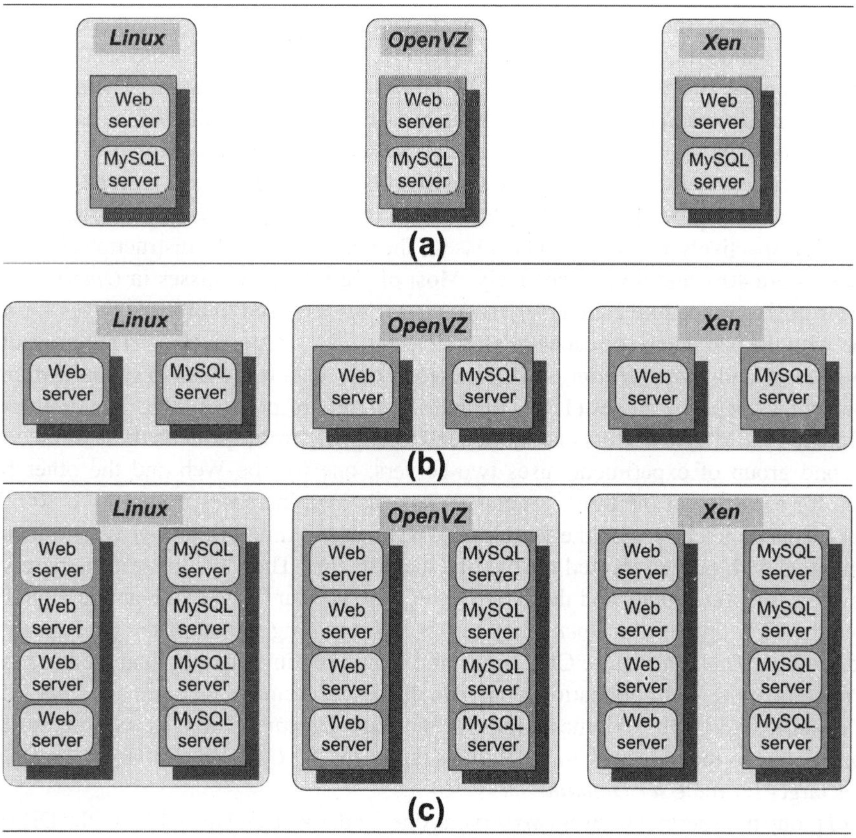

FIGURE 5.9

The setup for the performance comparison of a native `Linux` system with the *OpenVZ* and *Xen* systems. The applications are a Web server and a MySQL database server. (a) In the first experiment, the Web and the DB share a single system. (b) In the second experiment, the Web and the DB run on two different systems. (c) In the third experiment, the Web and the DB run on two different systems and each has four instances.

reports the counters that allow the estimation of (i) the CPU time used by a binary; (ii) the number of L2-cache misses; and (iii) the number of instructions executed by a binary.

The experimental setups for three different experiments are shown in Figure 5.9 . In the first group of experiments the two tiers of the application, the Web and the DB, run on a single server for the *Linux*, the *OpenVZ*, and the *Xen* systems. When the workload increases from 500 to 800 threads, the throughput increases linearly with the workload. The response time increases only slightly for the base system and for the *OpenVZ* system, whereas it increases 600% for the *Xen* system. For 800 threads the response time of the *Xen* system is four times longer than the time for *OpenVZ*. The CPU consumption grows linearly with the load in all three systems; the DB consumption represents only 1–4% of it.

For a given workload, the Web-tier CPU consumption for the *OpenVZ* system is close to that of the base system and is about half of that for the *Xen* system. The performance analysis tool shows that the *OpenVZ* execution has two times more L2-cache misses than the base system, whereas the *Xen Dom0* has 2.5 times more and the *Xen* application domain has 9 times more. Recall that the base system and the *OpenVZ* run a *Linux* OS and the sources of cache misses can be compared directly, whereas *Xen* runs a modified *Linux* kernel. For the *Xen*-based system the procedure *hypervisor_callback*, invoked when an event occurs, and the procedure *evtchn_do_upcall*, invoked to process an event, are responsible for 32% and 44%, respectively, of the L2-cache misses. The percentage of the instructions invoked by these two procedures are 40% and 8%, respectively. Most of the L2-cache misses in *OpenVZ* and the base system occur in (i) a procedure called *do_anonymous_pages*, used to allocate pages for a particular application with the percentage of cache misses 32% and 25%, respectively; (ii) the procedures called *_copy_to_user_ll* and *_copy_from_user_ll*, used to copy data from *user* to *system* buffers and back with the percentage of cache misses $(12+7)\%$ and $(10+1)\%$, respectively. The first figure refers to the copying from *user* to *system* buffers and the second to copying from *system* buffers to the *user* space.

The second group of experiments uses two servers, one for the Web and the other for the DB application, for each one of the three systems. When the load increases from 500 to 800 threads the throughput increases linearly with the workload. The response time of the *Xen* system increases only 114%, compared with 600% reported for the first experiments. The CPU time of the base system, the *OpenVZ* system, the *Xen Dom0*, and the *User Domain* are similar for the Web application. For the DB application, the CPU time of the *OpenVZ* system is twice as long as that of the base system, whereas *Dom0* and the *User Domain* require CPU times of 1.1 and 2.5 times longer than the base system. The L2-cache misses for the Web application relative to the base system are the same for *OpenVZ*, 1.5 times larger for *Dom0* of *Xen*, and 3.5 times larger for the *User Domain*. The L2-cache misses for the DB application relative to the base system are 2 times larger for the *OpenVZ*, 3.5 larger for *Dom0* of *Xen*, and 7 times larger for the *User Domain*.

The third group of experiments uses two servers, one for the Web and the other for the DB application, for each one of the three systems but runs four instances of the Web and the DB application on the two servers. The throughput increases linearly with the workload for the range used in the previous two experiments, from 500 to 800 threads. The response time remains relatively constant for *OpenVZ* and increases 5 times for *Xen*.

The main conclusion drawn from these experiments is that the virtualization overhead of *Xen* is considerably higher than that of *OpenVZ* and that this is due primarily to L2-cache misses. The performance degradation when the workload increases is also noticeable for *Xen*. Another important conclusion is that hosting multiple tiers of the same application on the same server is not an optimal solution.

5.12 The darker side of virtualization

Can virtualization empower the creators of malware[16] to carry out their mischievous activities with impunity and with minimal danger of being detected? How difficult is it to implement such a system?

[16]Malware, an abbreviation of *malicious software*, is software designed specifically to circumvent authorization mechanisms and gain access to a computer system, gather private information, block access to a system, or disrupt the normal operation of a system. Computer viruses, worms, spyware, and Trojan horses are examples of malware.

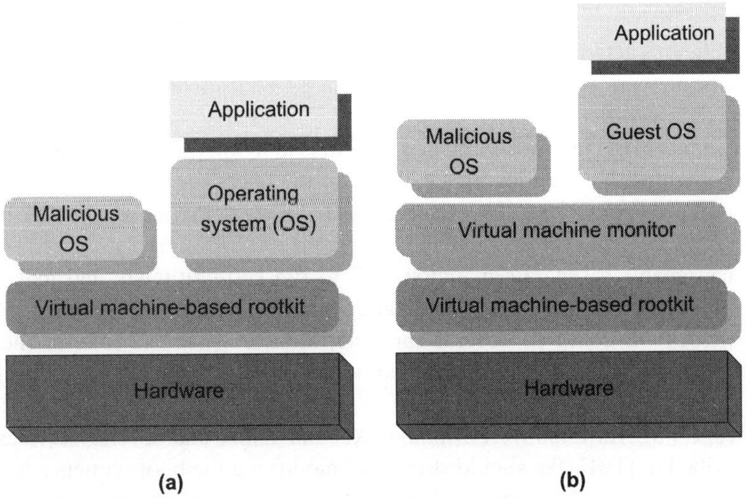

FIGURE 5.10

The insertion of a *virtual machine-based rootkit* (VMBR) as the lowest layer of the software stack running on the physical hardware. (a) Below an operating system; (b) Below a legitimate virtual machine monitor. The VMBR enables a malicious OS to run surreptitiously and makes it invisible to the genuine or the guest OS and to the application.

What are the means to prevent this type of malware to be put in place? The answers to these questions are discussed in this section.

It is well understood that in a layered structure a defense mechanism at some layer can be disabled by malware running a layer below it. Thus, the winner in the continuous struggle between the attackers and the defenders of a computing system is the one in control of the lowest layer of the software stack – the one that controls the hardware (see Figure 5.10).

Recall that a VMM allows a guest operating system to run on virtual hardware. The VMM offers to the guest operating systems a hardware abstraction and mediates its access to the physical hardware. We argued that a VMM is simpler and more compact than a traditional operating system; thus, it is more secure. But what if the VMM itself is forced to run above another software layer so that it is prevented from exercising direct control of the physical hardware?

A 2006 paper [194] argues that it is feasible to insert a "rogue VMM" between the physical hardware and an operating system. Such a rogue VMM is called a *virtual machine-based rootkit* (VMBR). The term *rootkit* refers to malware with privileged access to a system. The name comes from *root*, the most privileged account on a *Unix* system, and *kit*, a set of software components.

It is also feasible to insert the VMBR between the physical hardware and a "legitimate VMM." As a virtual machine running under a legitimate VMM sees virtual hardware, the guest OS will not notice any change of the environment; so the only trick is to present the legitimate VMM with a hardware abstraction, rather than allow it to run on the physical hardware.

Before we address the question of how such an insertion is possible, we should point out that in this approach the malware runs either inside a VMM or with the support of a VMM; but a VMM is a very potent engine for the malware. It prevents the software of the guest operating system or the application from detecting malicious activities. A VMBR can record key strokes, system state, data buffers sent to or received from the network, and data to be written to or `read` from the disk with impunity; moreover, it can change any data at will.

The only way for a VMBR to take control of a system is to modify the boot sequence and to first load the malware and only then load the legitimate VMM or the operating system. This is only possible if the attacker has root privileges. Once the VMBR is loaded it must also store its image on the persistent storage.

The VMBR can enable a separate malicious OS to run surreptitiously and make this malicious OS invisible to the guest OS and to the application running under it. Under the protection of the VMBR, the malicious OS could (i) observe the data, the events, or the state of the target system; (ii) run services such as spam relays or distributed denial-of-service attacks; or (iii) interfere with the application.

Proof-of-concept VMBRs to subvert *Windows XP* and *Linux* and several services based on this platform are described in [194]. We should stress that modifying the boot sequence is by no means an easy task, and once an attacker has root privileges he or she is in total control of a system.

5.13 Software fault isolation

Software fault isolation (SFI) offers a technical solution for sandboxing binary code of questionable provenance that can affect security in cloud computing. Insecure and tampered VM images are one of the security threats because binary codes of questionable provenance for native plug-ins to a Web browser can pose a security threat when Web browsers are used to access cloud services.

A recent paper [322] discusses the application of the sandboxing technology for two modern CPU architectures, *ARM* and 64-bit *x86*. *ARM* is a load/store architecture with 32-bit instruction and 16 general-purpose registers. It tends to avoid multicycle instructions, and it shares many RISC architecture features, but (a) it supports a "thumb" mode with 16-bit instruction extensions; (b) it has complex addressing modes and a complex barrel shifter; and (c) condition codes can be used to predicate most instructions. In the *x86*-64 architecture, general-purpose registers are extended to 64 bits, with an `r` replacing the `e` to identify the 64 versus 32-bit registers (e.g., `rax` instead of `eax`). There are eight new general-purpose registers, named r8–r15. To allow legacy instructions to use these additional registers, *x86*-64 defines a set of new prefix bytes to use for register selection.

This SFI implementation is based on the previous work of the same authors on Google Native Client (NC) and assumes an execution model in which a trusted run-time shares a process with an untrusted multithreaded plug-in. The rules for binary code generation of the untrusted plug-in are: (i) the code section is *read-only* and is statically linked; (ii) the code is divided into 32-byte *bundles*, and no instruction or pseudo-instruction crosses the bundle boundary; (iii) the disassembly starting at the bundle boundary reaches all valid instructions; and (iv) all indirect flow-control instructions are replaced by pseudo-instructions that ensure address alignment to bundle boundaries.

The features of the SFI for the Native Client on the *x86*-32, *x86*-64, and *ARM* are summarized in Table 5.4 [322]. The control flow and store sandboxing for the *ARM* SFI incur less then 5% average overhead, and those for *x86*-64 SFI incur less than 7% average overhead.

Table 5.4 The features of the SFI for the native client on the *x86*-32, *x86*-64, and *ARM*. ILP stands for instruction-level parallelism.

Feature/Architecture	*x86*-32	*x86*-64	*ARM*
Addressable memory	1 GB	4 GB	1 GB
Virtual base address	Any	44 GB	0
Data model	ILP 32	ILP 32	ILP 32
Reserved registers	0 of 8	1 of 16	0 of 16
Data address mask	None	Implicit in result width	Explicit instruction
Control address mask	Explicit instruction	Explicit instruction	Explicit instruction
Bundle size (bytes)	32	32	16
Data in text segment	Forbidden	Forbidden	Allowed
Safe address registers	All	RSP, RBP	SP
Out-of-sandbox store	Trap	Wraps mod 4 GB	No effect
Out-of-sandbox jump	Trap	Wraps mod 4 GB	Wraps mod 1 GB

5.14 Further reading

A good introduction to virtualization principles can be found in a recent text of Saltzer and Kaashoek [312] and in [141]. Virtual machines are dissected in a paper by Smith and Nair [325]. An insightful discussion of virtual machine monitors is provided by the paper of Rosenblum and Garfinkel [308]. Several papers [41,84,241,242] discuss in depth the *Xen* VMM and analyze its performance. The `Denali` system is presented in [372]. Modern systems such as *Linux Vserver* [214], *OpenVZ* (Open VirtualiZation) [274], *FreeBSD Jails* [124], and *Solaris Zones* [296] implement *operating system-level virtualization technologies.*

A paper [281] compares the performance of two virtualization techniques with a standard operating system. The *vBlades* project at HP-Laboratories is presented in [228].

A 2001 paper [79] argues that virtualization allows new services to be added without modifying the operating system. Such services are added below the operating system level, but this process creates a semantic gap between the virtual machine and these services. A survey of security issues in virtual systems is provided by [389]. Object-oriented VMM design is discussed [80]. Several references including [165,199,271,301,342,371] discuss virtualization and system architecture.

5.15 History notes

Virtual memory was the first application of virtualization concepts to commercial computers. It allowed multiprogramming and eliminated the need for users to tailor their applications to the physical memory available on individual systems. Paging and segmentation are the two mechanisms supporting virtual memory. Paging was developed for the Atlas Computer, built in 1959 at the University of Manchester. Independently, the Burroughs Corporation developed the B5000, the first commercial computer with virtual memory, and released it in 1961. The virtual memory of the B5000 used segmentation rather than paging.

In 1967 IBM introduced the 360/67, the first IBM system with virtual memory, expected to run on a new operating system called TSS. Before TSS was released, an operating system called CP-67 was created. CP-67 gave the illusion of several standard IBM 360 systems without virtual memory. The first VMM supporting full virtualization was the CP-40 system, which ran on a S/360-40 that was modified at the IBM Cambridge Scientific Center to support Dynamic Address Translation, a key feature that allowed virtualization. In CP-40, the hardware's supervisor state was virtualized as well, allowing multiple operating systems to run concurrently in separate virtual machine contexts.

In this early age of computing, virtualization was driven by the need to share very expensive hardware among a large population of users and applications. The VM/370 system, released in 1972 for large IBM mainframes, was very successful. It was based on a reimplementation of CP/CMS. In the VM/370 a new virtual machine was created for every user, and this virtual machine interacted with the applications. The VMM managed hardware resources and enforced the multiplexing of resources. Modern-day IBM mainframes, such as the zSeries line, retain backward compatibility with the 1960s-era IBM S/360 line.

The production of microprocessors, coupled with advancements in storage technology, contributed to the rapid decrease of hardware costs and led to the introduction of personal computers at one end of the spectrum and large mainframes and massively parallel systems at the other end. The hardware and the operating systems of the 1980s and 1990s gradually limited virtualization and focused instead on efficient multitasking, user interfaces, the support for networking, and security problems brought in by interconnectivity.

The advancements in computer and communication hardware and the explosion of the Internet, partially due to the success of the World Wide Web at the end of the 1990s, renewed interest in virtualization to support server security and isolation of services. In their review paper, Rosenbloom and Grafinkel write [308]: "VMMs give operating system developers another opportunity to develop functionality no longer practical in today's complex and ossified operating systems, where innovation moves at a geologic pace."

5.16 Exercises and problems

Problem 1. Identify the milestones in the evolution of operating systems during the half century from 1960 to 2010 and comment on this statement from [308]: "VMMs give operating system developers another opportunity to develop functionality no longer practical in today's complex and ossified operating systems, where innovation moves at a geologic pace."

Problem 2. Virtualization simplifies the use of resources, isolates users from one another, and supports replication and mobility, but exacts a price in terms of performance and cost. Analyze each one of these aspects for (i) memory virtualization, (ii) processor virtualization, and (iii) virtualization of a communication channel.

Problem 3. Virtualization of the processor combined with virtual memory management poses multiple challenges. Analyze the interaction of interrupt handling and paging.

Problem 4. In Section 5.5 we stated that a VMM is a much simpler and better-specified system than a traditional operating system. The security vulnerability of VMMs is considerably reduced because the systems expose a much smaller number of privileged functions. Research the literature to gather arguments in support of these affirmations. Compare the number of lines of code and system calls for several operating systems, including *Linux*, Solaris, FreeBSD, *Ubuntu*, AIX, and *Windows*, with the corresponding figures for several system virtual machines in Table 5.1.

Problem 5. In Section 5.6 we state that a VMM for a processor can be constructed if the set of *sensitive instructions* is a subset of the privileged instructions of that processor. Identify the set of sensitive instructions for the *x86* architecture and discuss the problem each one of these instructions poses.

Problem 6. Table 5.3 summarizes the effects of *Xen* network performance optimization reported in [242]. The send data rate of a guest domain is improved by a factor of more than 4, whereas the improvement of the receive data rate is very modest. Identify several possible reasons for this discrepancy.

Problem 7. In Section 5.8 we note that several operating systems, including *Linux*, Minix, NetBSD, FreeBSD, NetWare, and OZONE, can operate as paravirtualized *Xen* guest operating systems running on *x86*, *x86*-64, *Itanium*, and *ARM* architectures, whereas *VMware EX Server* supports full virtualization of *x86* architecture. Analyze how *VMware* provides the functions discussed in Table 5.2 for *Xen*.

Problem 8. In 2012 Intel and HP announced that the *Itanium* architecture will be discontinued. Review the architecture, discussed in Section 5.10, and identify several possible reasons for this decision.

Problem 9. Read [281] and analyze the results of the performance comparison discussed in Section 5.11.

CHAPTER

Cloud Resource Management and Scheduling

6

Resource management is a core function of any man-made system. It affects the three basic criteria for the evaluation of a system: performance, functionality, and cost. An inefficient resource management has a direct negative effect on performance and cost and an indirect effect on the functionality of a system. Indeed, some functions provided by the system may become too expensive or may be avoided due to poor performance.

A cloud is a complex system with a very large number of shared resources subject to unpredictable requests and affected by external events it cannot control. Cloud resource management requires complex policies and decisions for multi-objective optimization. Cloud resource management is extremely challenging because of the complexity of the system, which makes it impossible to have accurate global state information, and because of the unpredictable interactions with the environment.

The strategies for resource management associated with the three cloud delivery models, *IaaS, PaaS*, and *SaaS*, differ from one another. In all cases the cloud service providers are faced with large, fluctuating loads that challenge the claim of cloud elasticity. In some cases, when a spike can be predicted, the resources can be provisioned in advance, e.g., for Web services subject to seasonal spikes. For an unplanned spike, the situation is slightly more complicated. *Auto Scaling* can be used for unplanned spike loads, provided that (a) there is a pool of resources that can be released or allocated on demand and (b) there is a monitoring system that allows a control loop to decide in real time to reallocate resources. Auto Scaling is supported by *PaaS* services such as Google App Engine. *Auto Scaling* for *IaaS*, discussed in Section 6.14, is complicated due to the lack of standards.

It has been argued for some time that in a cloud, where changes are frequent and unpredictable, centralized control is unlikely to provide continuous service and performance guarantees. Indeed, centralized control cannot provide adequate solutions to the host of cloud management policies that have to be enforced. Autonomic policies are of great interest due to the scale of the system, the large number of service requests, the large user population, and the unpredictability of the load. The ratio of the mean to the peak resource needs can be very large.

We start our discussion with an overview of policies and mechanisms for cloud resource management in Section 6.1. A control theoretic approach to resource allocation is discussed in Sections 6.2, 6.3, and 6.4. A machine learning algorithm for coordination of specialized autonomic performance managers is presented in Section 6.5. In Section 6.6 we discuss a utility model for resource allocation for a Web service. Next we present resource bundling and combinatorial auctions in Section 6.7. The fair queuing, start-time fair queuing, and borrowed virtual time scheduling algorithms are analyzed in Sections 6.9, 6.10, and 6.11, respectively. Scheduling with deadlines and the impact of application scaling on resource management are presented in Sections 6.12, 6.13, and 6.14, respectively.

6.1 Policies and mechanisms for resource management

A policy typically refers to the principal guiding decisions, whereas mechanisms represent the means to implement policies. Separation of policies from mechanisms is a guiding principle in computer science. Butler Lampson [208] and Per Brinch Hansen [154] offer solid arguments for this separation in the context of operating system design.

Cloud resource management policies can be loosely grouped into five classes:

1. Admission control.
2. Capacity allocation.
3. Load balancing.
4. Energy optimization.
5. Quality-of-service (QoS) guarantees.

The explicit goal of an admission control policy is to prevent the system from accepting workloads in violation of high-level system policies; for example, a system may not accept an additional workload that would prevent it from completing work already in progress or contracted. Limiting the workload requires some knowledge of the global state of the system. In a dynamic system such knowledge, when available, is at best obsolete. Capacity allocation means to allocate resources for individual instances; an instance is an activation of a service. Locating resources subject to multiple global optimization constraints requires a search of a very large search space when the state of individual systems changes rapidly.

Load balancing and energy optimization can be done locally, but global load-balancing and energy optimization policies encounter the same difficulties as the one we have already discussed. Load balancing and energy optimization are correlated and affect the cost of providing the services. Indeed, it was predicted that by 2012 up to 40% of the budget for IT enterprise infrastructure would be spent on energy [104].

The common meaning of the term *load balancing* is that of evenly distributing the load to a set of servers. For example, consider the case of four identical servers, A, B, C, and D, whose relative loads are 80%, 60%, 40%, and 20%, respectively, of their capacity. As a result of perfect load balancing, all servers would end with the same load – 50% of each server's capacity. In cloud computing a critical goal is minimizing the cost of providing the service and, in particular, minimizing the energy consumption. This leads to a different meaning of the term *load balancing*; instead of having the load evenly distributed among all servers, we want to concentrate it and use the smallest number of servers while switching the others to standby mode, a state in which a server uses less energy. In our example, the load from D will migrate to A and the load from C will migrate to B; thus, A and B will be loaded at full capacity, whereas C and D will be switched to standby mode. Quality of service is that aspect of resource management that is probably the most difficult to address and, at the same time, possibly the most critical to the future of cloud computing.

As we shall see in this section, often resource management strategies jointly target performance and power consumption. *Dynamic voltage and frequency scaling (DVFS)*[1] techniques such as Intel's

[1] DVFS is a power management technique to increase or decrease the operating voltage or frequency of a processor in order to increase the instruction execution rate and, respectively, reduce the amount of heat generated and to conserve power.

Table 6.1 The normalized performance and energy consumption function of the processor speed. The performance decreases at a lower rate than does the energy when the clock rate decreases.

CPU Speed (GHz)	Normalized Energy (%)	Normalized Performance (%)
0.6	0.44	0.61
0.8	0.48	0.70
1.0	0.52	0.79
1.2	0.58	0.81
1.4	0.62	0.88
1.6	0.70	0.90
1.8	0.82	0.95
2.0	0.90	0.99
2.2	1.00	1.00

SpeedStep and AMD's PowerNow lower the voltage and the frequency to decrease power consumption.[2] Motivated initially by the need to save power for mobile devices, these techniques have migrated to virtually all processors, including the ones used for high-performance servers.

As a result of lower voltages and frequencies, the performance of processors decreases, but at a substantially slower rate [213] than the energy consumption. Table 6.1 shows the dependence of the normalized performance and the normalized energy consumption of a typical modern processor on clock rate. As we can see, at 1.8 GHz we save 18% of the energy required for maximum performance, whereas the performance is only 5% lower than the peak performance, achieved at 2.2 GHz. This seems a reasonable energy-performance tradeoff!

Virtually all optimal – or near-optimal – mechanisms to address the five classes of policies do not scale up and typically target a single aspect of resource management, e.g., admission control, but ignore energy conservation. Many require complex computations that cannot be done effectively in the time available to respond. The performance models are very complex, analytical solutions are intractable, and the monitoring systems used to gather state information for these models can be too intrusive and unable to provide accurate data. Many techniques are concentrated on system performance in terms of throughput and time in system, but they rarely include energy tradeoffs or QoS guarantees. Some techniques are based on unrealistic assumptions; for example, capacity allocation is viewed as an optimization problem, but under the assumption that servers are protected from overload.

Allocation techniques in computer clouds must be based on a disciplined approach rather than ad hoc methods. The four basic mechanisms for the implementation of resource management policies are:

- *Control theory.* Control theory uses the feedback to guarantee system stability and predict transient behavior [185,202], but can be used only to predict local rather than global behavior. Kalman filters have been used for unrealistically simplified models.

[2] The power consumption P of a CMOS-based circuit is $P = \alpha \cdot C_{eff} \cdot V^2 \cdot f$, with α = the switching factor, C_{eff} = the effective capacitance, V = the operating voltage, and f = the operating frequency.

- *Machine learning.* A major advantage of machine learning techniques is that they do not need a performance model of the system [353]. This technique could be applied to coordination of several autonomic system managers, as discussed in [187].
- *Utility-based.* Utility-based approaches require a performance model and a mechanism to correlate user-level performance with cost, as discussed in [9].
- *Market-oriented/economic mechanisms.* Such mechanisms do not require a model of the system, e.g., combinatorial auctions for bundles of resources discussed in [333].

A distinction should be made between interactive and noninteractive workloads. The management techniques for interactive workloads, e.g., Web services, involve flow control and dynamic application placement, whereas those for noninteractive workloads are focused on scheduling. A fair amount of work reported in the literature is devoted to resource management of interactive workloads, some to noninteractive, and only a few, e.g., [344], to heterogeneous workloads, a combination of the two.

6.2 Applications of control theory to task scheduling on a cloud

Control theory has been used to design adaptive resource management for many classes of applications, including power management [187], task scheduling [222], QoS adaptation in Web servers [3], and load balancing. The classical feedback control methods are used in all these cases to regulate the key operating parameters of the system based on measurement of the system output; the feedback control in these methods assumes a linear time-invariant system model and a closed-loop controller. This controller is based on an open-loop system transfer function that satisfies stability and sensitivity constraints.

A technique to design self-managing systems based on concepts from control theory is discussed in [369]. The technique allows multiple QoS objectives and operating constraints to be expressed as a cost function and can be applied to stand-alone or distributed Web servers, database servers, high-performance application servers, and even mobile/embedded systems. The following discussion considers a single processor serving a stream of input requests. We attempt to minimize a cost function that reflects the response time and the power consumption. Our goal is to illustrate the methodology for optimal resource management based on control theory concepts. The analysis is intricate and cannot be easily extended to a collection of servers.

Control Theory Principles. We start our discussion with a brief overview of control theory principles one could use for optimal resource allocation. Optimal control generates a sequence of control inputs over a look-ahead horizon while estimating changes in operating conditions. A convex cost function has arguments $x(k)$, the state at step k, and $u(k)$, the control vector; this cost function is minimized, subject to the constraints imposed by the system dynamics. The discrete-time optimal control problem is to determine the sequence of control variables $u(i), u(i+1), \ldots, u(n-1)$ to minimize the expression

$$J(i) = \Phi(n, x(n)) + \sum_{k=i}^{n-1} L^k(x(k), u(k)), \tag{6.1}$$

where $\Phi(n, x(n))$ is the cost function of the final step, n, and $L^k(x(k), u(k))$ is a time-varying cost function at the intermediate step k over the horizon $[i, n]$. The minimization is subject to the constraints

$$x(k+1) = f^k(x(k), u(k)), \tag{6.2}$$

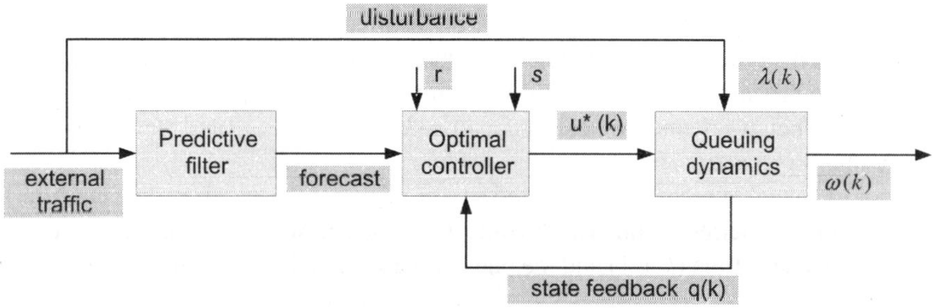

FIGURE 6.1

The structure of an optimal controller described in [369]. The controller uses the feedback regarding the current state as well as the estimation of the future disturbance due to environment to compute the optimal inputs over a finite horizon. The two parameters r and s are the weighting factors of the performance index.

where $x(k+1)$, the system state at time $k+1$, is a function of $x(k)$, the state at time k, and of $u(k)$, the input at time k; in general, the function f^k is time-varying; thus, its superscript.

One of the techniques to solve this problem is based on the *Lagrange multiplier* method of finding the extremes (minima or maxima) of a function subject to constrains. More precisely, if we want to maximize the function $g(x, y)$ subject to the constraint $h(x, y) = k$, we introduce a Lagrange multiplier λ. Then we study the function

$$\Lambda(x, y, \lambda) = g(x, y) + \lambda \times [h(x, y) - k]. \tag{6.3}$$

A necessary condition for the optimality is that (x, y, λ) is a stationary point for $\Lambda(x, y, \lambda)$. In other words,

$$\nabla_{x,y,\lambda}\Lambda(x, y, \lambda) = 0 \text{ or } \left(\frac{\partial\Lambda(x, y, \lambda)}{\partial x}, \frac{\partial\Lambda(x, y, \lambda)}{\partial y}, \frac{\partial\Lambda(x, y, \lambda)}{\partial \lambda}\right) = 0. \tag{6.4}$$

The Lagrange multiplier at time step k is λ_k and we solve Eq. (6.4) as an unconstrained optimization problem. We define an adjoint cost function that includes the original state constraints as the Hamiltonian function H, then we construct the adjoint system consisting of the original state equation and the *costate equation* governing the Lagrange multiplier. Thus, we define a two-point boundary problem[3]; the state x_k develops forward in time whereas the costate occurs backward in time.

A Model Capturing Both QoS and Energy Consumption for a Single-Server System. Now we turn our attention to the case of a single processor serving a stream of input requests. To compute the optimal inputs over a finite horizon, the controller in Figure 6.1 uses feedback regarding the current state, as well as an estimation of the future disturbance due to the environment. The control task is solved as a state regulation problem updating the initial and final states of the control horizon.

We use a simple queuing model to estimate the response time. Requests for service at processor P are processed on a first-come, first-served (FCFS) basis. We do not assume a priori distributions of the arrival

[3]A boundary value problem has conditions specified at the extremes of the independent variable, whereas an initial value problem has all the conditions specified at the same value of the independent variable in the equation.

process and of the service process; instead, we use the estimate $\hat{\Lambda}(k)$ of the arrival rate $\Lambda(k)$ at time k. We also assume that the processor can operate at frequencies $u(k)$ in the range $u(k) \in [u_{min}, u_{max}]$ and call $\hat{c}(k)$ the time to process a request at time k when the processor operates at the highest frequency in the range, u_{max}. Then we define the scaling factor $\alpha(k) = u(k)/u_{max}$ and we express an estimate of the processing rate $N(k)$ as $\alpha(k)/\hat{c}(k)$.

The behavior of a single processor is modeled as a nonlinear, time-varying, discrete-time state equation. If T_s is the sampling period, defined as the time difference between two consecutive observations of the system, e.g., the one at time $(k+1)$ and the one at time k, then the size of the queue at time $(k+1)$ is

$$q(k+1) = \max\left\{\left[q(k) + \left(\hat{\Lambda}(k) - \frac{u(k)}{\hat{c}(k) \times u_{max}}\right) \times T_s\right], 0\right\}. \tag{6.5}$$

The first term, $q(k)$, is the size of the input queue at time k, and the second one is the difference between the number of requests arriving during the sampling period, T_s, and those processed during the same interval.

The response time $\omega(k)$ is the sum of the waiting time and the processing time of the requests

$$\omega(k) = (1 + q(k)) \times \hat{c}(k). \tag{6.6}$$

Indeed, the total number of requests in the system is $(1 + q(k))$ and the departure rate is $1/\hat{c}(k)$.

We want to capture both the QoS and the energy consumption, since both affect the cost of providing the service. A utility function, such as the one depicted in Figure 6.4, captures the rewards as well as the penalties specified by the service-level agreement for the response time. In our queuing model the utility is a function of the size of the queue; it can be expressed as a quadratic function of the response time

$$S(q(k)) = 1/2(s \times (\omega(k) - \omega_0)^2), \tag{6.7}$$

with ω_0, the response time set point and $q(0) = q_0$, the initial value of the queue length. The energy consumption is a quadratic function of the frequency

$$R(u(k)) = 1/2(r \times u(k)^2). \tag{6.8}$$

The two parameters s and r are weights for the two components of the cost, the one derived from the utility function and the second from the energy consumption. We have to pay a penalty for the requests left in the queue at the end of the control horizon, a quadratic function of the queue length

$$\Phi(q(N)) = 1/2(v \times q(n)^2). \tag{6.9}$$

The performance measure of interest is a cost expressed as

$$J = \Phi(q(N)) + \sum_{k=1}^{N-1}[S(q(k)) + R(u(k))]. \tag{6.10}$$

The problem is to find the optimal control u^* and the finite time horizon $[0, N]$ such that the trajectory of the system subject to optimal control is q^*, and the cost J in Eq. (6.10) is minimized subject to the following constraints

$$q(k+1) = \left[q(k) + \left(\hat{\Lambda}(k) - \frac{u(k)}{\hat{c}(k) \times u_{max}} \right) \times T_s \right], \ q(k) \geqslant 0, \text{ and } u_{min} \leqslant u(k) \leqslant u_{max}. \quad (6.11)$$

When the state trajectory $q(\cdot)$ corresponding to the control $u(\cdot)$ satisfies the constraints

$$\Gamma 1 : q(k) > 0, \quad \Gamma 2 : u(k) \geqslant u_{min}, \quad \Gamma 3 : u(k) \leqslant u_{max}, \quad (6.12)$$

then the pair $[q(\cdot), u(\cdot)]$ is called a *feasible state*. If the pair minimizes Eq. (6.10), then the pair is *optimal*.

The Hamiltonian H in our example is

$$\begin{aligned} H = & S(q(k)) + R(u(k)) + \lambda(k+1) \times \left[q(k) + \left(\Lambda(k) - \frac{u(k)}{c \times u_{max}} \right) T_s \right] \\ & + \mu_1(k) \times (-q(k)) + \mu_2(k) \times (-u(k) + u_{min}) + \mu_3(k) \times (u(k) - u_{max}). \end{aligned} \quad (6.13)$$

According to Pontryagin's minimum principle,[4] the necessary condition for a sequence of feasible pairs to be optimal pairs is the existence of a sequence of costates λ and a Lagrange multiplier $\mu = [\mu_1(k), \mu_2(k), \mu_3(k)]$ such that

$$H(k, q^*, u^*, \lambda^*, \mu^*) \leqslant H(k, q, u^*, \lambda^*, \mu^*), \quad \forall q \geqslant 0 \quad (6.14)$$

where the Lagrange multipliers, $\mu_1(k), \mu_2(k), \mu_3(k)$, reflect the sensitivity of the cost function to the queue length at time k and the boundary constraints and satisfy several conditions

$$\mu_1(k) \geqslant 0, \ \mu_1(k)(-q(k)) = 0, \quad (6.15)$$

$$\mu_2(k) \geqslant 0, \ \mu_2(k)(-u(k) + u_{min}) = 0, \quad (6.16)$$

$$\mu_3(k) \geqslant 0, \ \mu_3(k)(u(k) - u_{max}) = 0. \quad (6.17)$$

A detailed analysis of the methods to solve this problem and the analysis of the stability conditions is beyond the scope of our discussion and can be found in [369].

The extension of the techniques for optimal resource management from a single system to a cloud with a very large number of servers is a rather challenging area of research. The problem is even harder when, instead of transaction-based processing, the cloud applications require the implementation of a complex workflow.

6.3 Stability of a two-level resource allocation architecture

In Section 6.2 we saw that we can assimilate a server with a closed-loop control system and we can apply control theory principles to resource allocation. In this section we discuss a two-level resource

[4]Pontryagin's principle is used in the optimal control theory to find the best possible control that leads a dynamic system from one state to another, subject to a set of constraints.

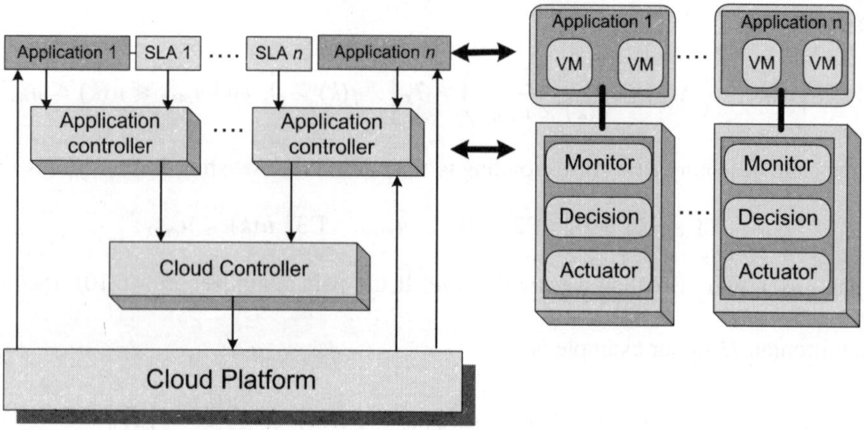

FIGURE 6.2

A two-level control architecture. Application controllers and cloud controllers work in concert.

allocation architecture based on control theory concepts for the entire cloud. The automatic resource management is based on two levels of controllers, one for the service provider and one for the application, see Figure 6.2.

The main components of a control system are the inputs, the control system components, and the outputs. The inputs in such models are the offered workload and the policies for admission control, the capacity allocation, the load balancing, the energy optimization, and the QoS guarantees in the cloud. The system components are *sensors* used to estimate relevant measures of performance and *controllers* that implement various policies; the output is the resource allocations to the individual applications .

The controllers use the feedback provided by sensors to stabilize the system; stability is related to the change of the output. If the change is too large, the system may become unstable. In our context the system could experience thrashing, the amount of useful time dedicated to the execution of applications becomes increasingly small and most of the system resources are occupied by management functions.

There are three main sources of instability in any control system:

1. The delay in getting the system reaction after a control action.
2. The granularity of the control, the fact that a small change enacted by the controllers leads to very large changes of the output.
3. Oscillations, which occur when the changes of the input are too large and the control is too weak, such that the changes of the input propagate directly to the output.

Two types of policies are used in autonomic systems: (i) threshold-based policies and (ii) sequential decision policies based on Markovian decision models. In the first case, upper and lower bounds on performance trigger adaptation through resource reallocation. Such policies are simple and intuitive but require setting per-application thresholds.

Lessons learned from the experiments with two levels of controllers and the two types of policies are discussed in [109]. A first observation is that the actions of the control system should be carried out in a rhythm that does not lead to instability. Adjustments should be carried out only after the performance of the system has stabilized. The controller should measure the time for an application to stabilize and adapt to the manner in which the controlled system reacts.

If upper and lower thresholds are set, instability occurs when they are too close to one another if the variations of the workload are large enough and the time required to adapt does not allow the system to stabilize. The actions consist of allocation/deallocation of one or more virtual machines; sometimes allocation/deallocation of a single VM required by one of the thresholds may cause crossing of the other threshold and this may represent, another source of instability.

6.4 Feedback control based on dynamic thresholds

The elements involved in a control system are sensors, monitors, and actuators. The *sensors* measure the parameter(s) of interest, then transmit the measured values to a *monitor*, which determines whether the system behavior must be changed, and, if so, it requests that the *actuators* carry out the necessary actions. Often the parameter used for admission control policy is the current system load; when a threshold, e.g., 80%, is reached, the cloud stops accepting additional load.

In practice, the implementation of such a policy is challenging or outright infeasible. First, due to the very large number of servers and to the fact that the load changes rapidly in time, the estimation of the current system load is likely to be inaccurate. Second, the ratio of average to maximal resource requirements of individual users specified in a service-level agreement is typically very high. Once an agreement is in place, user demands must be satisfied; user requests for additional resources within the SLA limits cannot be denied.

Thresholds. A *threshold* is the value of a parameter related to the state of a system that triggers a change in the system behavior. Thresholds are used in control theory to keep critical parameters of a system in a predefined range. The threshold could be *static*, defined once and for all, or it could be *dynamic*. A dynamic threshold could be based on an average of measurements carried out over a time interval, a so-called *integral control*. The dynamic threshold could also be a function of the values of multiple parameters at a given time or a mix of the two.

To maintain the system parameters in a given range, a *high* and a *low* threshold are often defined. The two thresholds determine different actions; for example, a high threshold could force the system to limit its activities and a low threshold could encourage additional activities. *Control granularity* refers to the level of detail of the information used to control the system. *Fine control* means that very detailed information about the parameters controlling the system state is used, whereas *coarse control* means that the accuracy of these parameters is traded for the efficiency of implementation.

Proportional Thresholding. Application of these ideas to cloud computing, in particular to the *IaaS* delivery model, and a strategy for resource management called *proportional thresholding* are discussed in [217]. The questions addressed are:

- Is it beneficial to have two types of controllers, (1) *application controllers* that determine whether additional resources are needed and (2) *cloud controllers* that arbitrate requests for resources and allocate the physical resources?
- Is it feasible to consider *fine control*? Is *course control* more adequate in a cloud computing environment?

- Are dynamic thresholds based on time averages better than static ones?
- Is it better to have a high and a low threshold, or it is sufficient to define only a high threshold?

The first two questions are related to one another. It seems more appropriate to have two controllers, one with knowledge of the application and one that's aware of the state of the cloud. In this case a coarse control is more adequate for many reasons. As mentioned earlier, the cloud controller can only have a very rough approximation of the cloud state. Moreover, to simplify its resource management policies, the service provider may want to hide some of the information it has. For example, it may not allow a VM to access information available to VMM-level sensors and actuators.

To answer the last two questions, we have to define a measure of "goodness." In the experiments reported in [217], the parameter measured is the average CPU utilization, and one strategy is better than another if it reduces the number of requests made by the application controllers to add or remove virtual machines to the pool of those available to the application.

Devising a control theoretical approach to address these questions is challenging. The authors of [217] adopt a pragmatic approach and provide qualitative arguments; they also report simulation results using a synthetic workload for a transaction-oriented application, a Web server.

The essence of the proportional thresholding is captured by the following algorithm:

1. Compute the integral value of the high and the low thresholds as averages of the maximum and, respectively, the minimum of the processor utilization over the process history.
2. Request additional VMs when the average value of the CPU utilization over the current time slice exceeds the high threshold.
3. Release a VM when the average value of the CPU utilization over the current time slice falls below the low threshold.

The conclusions reached based on experiments with three VMs are as follows: (a) dynamic thresholds perform better than static ones and (b) two thresholds are better than one. Though conforming to our intuition, such results have to be justified by experiments in a realistic environment. Moreover, convincing results cannot be based on empirical values for some of the parameters required by integral control equations.

6.5 Coordination of specialized autonomic performance managers

Can specialized autonomic performance managers cooperate to optimize power consumption and, at the same time, satisfy the requirements of SLAs? This is the question examined by a group from IBM Research in a 2007 paper [187]. The paper reports on actual experiments carried out on a set of blades mounted on a chassis (see Figure 6.3 for the experimental setup). Extending the techniques discussed in this report to a large-scale farm of servers poses significant problems; computational complexity is just one of them.

Virtually all modern processors support dynamic voltage scaling (DVS) as a mechanism for energy saving. Indeed, the energy dissipation scales quadratically with the supply voltage. The power management controls the CPU frequency and, thus, the rate of instruction execution. For some compute-intensive workloads the performance decreases linearly with the CPU clock frequency, whereas for others the effect of lower clock frequency is less noticeable or nonexistent. The clock frequency of individual

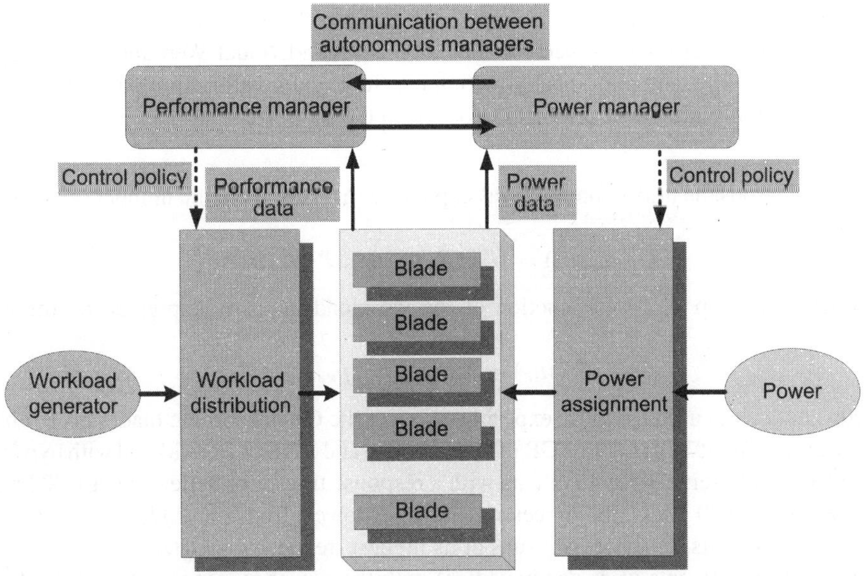

FIGURE 6.3

Autonomous performance and power managers cooperate to ensure SLA prescribed performance and energy optimization. They are fed with performance and power data and implement the performance and power management policies, respectively.

blades/servers is controlled by a power manager, typically implemented in the firmware; it adjusts the clock frequency several times a second.

The approach to coordinating power and performance management in [187] is based on several ideas:

- Use a joint utility function for power and performance. The joint performance-power utility function, $U_{pp}(R, P)$, is a function of the response time, R, and the power, P, and it can be of the form

$$U_{pp}(R, P) = U(R) - \epsilon \times P \quad \text{or} \quad U_{pp}(R, P) = \frac{U(R)}{P}, \tag{6.18}$$

  with $U(R)$ the utility function based on response time only and ϵ a parameter to weight the influence of the two factors, response time and power.
- Identify a minimal set of parameters to be exchanged between the two managers.
- Set up a power cap for individual systems based on the utility-optimized power management policy.
- Use a standard performance manager modified only to accept input from the power manager regarding the frequency determined according to the power management policy. The power manager consists of Tcl (Tool Command Language) and C programs to compute the per-server (per-blade) power caps and send them via IPMI[5] to the firmware controlling the blade power. The power manager and the performance manager interact, but no negotiation between the two agents is involved.

[5]Intelligent Platform Management Interface (IPMI) is a standardized computer system interface developed by Intel and used by system administrators to manage a computer system and monitor its operation.

- Use standard software systems. For example, use the WebSphere Extended Deployment (WXD), middleware that supports setting performance targets for individual Web applications and for the monitor response time, and periodically recompute the resource allocation parameters to meet the targets set. Use the Wide-Spectrum Stress Tool from the IBM Web Services Toolkit as a workload generator.

For practical reasons the utility function was expressed in terms of n_c, the number of clients, and p_κ, the powercap, as in

$$U'(p_\kappa, n_c) = U_{pp}(R(p_\kappa, n_c), P(p_\kappa, n_c)). \tag{6.19}$$

The optimal powercap p_κ^{opt} is a function of the workload intensity expressed by the number of clients, n_c,

$$p_\kappa^{opt}(n_c) = \arg\max U'(p_\kappa, n_c). \tag{6.20}$$

The hardware devices used for these experiments were the Goldensbridge blades each with an Intel Xeon processor running at 3 GHz with 1 GB of level 2 cache and 2 GB of DRAM and with hyperthreading enabled. A blade could serve 30 to 40 clients with a response time at or better than a 1,000 msec limit. When p_k is lower than 80 Watts, the processor runs at its lowest frequency, 375 MHz, whereas for p_k at or larger than 110 Watts, the processor runs at its highest frequency, 3 GHz.

Three types of experiments were conducted: (i) with the power management turned off; (ii) when the dependence of the power consumption and the response time were determined through a set of exhaustive experiments; and (iii) when the dependency of the powercap p_κ on n_c was derived via reinforcement-learning models.

The second type of experiment led to the conclusion that both the response time and the power consumed are nonlinear functions of the powercap, p_κ, and the number of clients, n_c; more specifically, the conclusions of these experiments are:

- At a low load the response time is well below the target of 1,000 msec.
- At medium and high loads the response time decreases rapidly when p_k increases from 80 to 110 watts.
- For a given value of the powercap, the consumed power increases rapidly as the load increases.

The machine learning algorithm used for the third type of experiment was based on the Hybrid Reinforcement Learning algorithm described in [349]. In the experiments using the machine learning model, the powercap required to achieve a response time lower than 1,000 msec for a given number of clients was the lowest when $\epsilon = 0.05$ and the first utility function given by Eq. (6.18) was used. For example, when $n_c = 50$, then $p_\kappa = 109$ Watts when $\epsilon = 0.05$, whereas $p_\kappa = 120$ when $\epsilon = 0.01$.

6.6 A utility-based model for cloud-based Web services

A *utility function* relates the "benefits" of an activity or service with the "cost" to provide the service. For example, the benefit could be revenue and the cost could be the power consumption.

A service-level agreement (SLA) often specifies the rewards as well as the penalties associated with specific performance metrics. Sometimes the quality of services translates into average response time; this is the case of cloud-based Web services when the SLA often explicitly specifies this requirement.

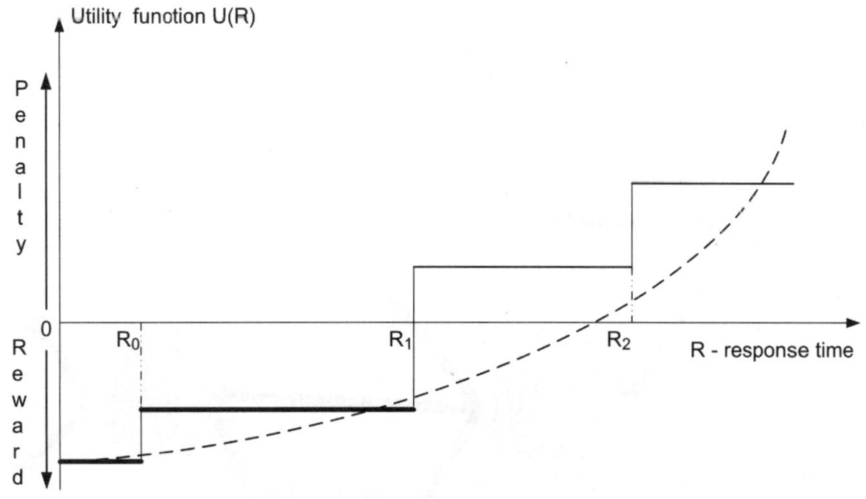

FIGURE 6.4

The utility function $U(R)$ is a series of step functions with jumps corresponding to the response time, $R = R_0|R_1|R_2$, when the reward and the penalty levels change according to the SLA. The dotted line shows a quadratic approximation of the utility function.

For example, Figure 6.4 shows the case when the performance metrics is R, the response time. The largest reward can be obtained when $R \leqslant R_0$; a slightly lower reward corresponds to $R_0 < R \leqslant R_1$. When $R_1 < R \leqslant R_2$, instead of gaining a reward, the provider of service pays a small penalty; the penalty increases when $R > R_2$. A utility function, $U(R)$, which captures this behavior, is a sequence of step functions. The utility function is sometimes approximated by a quadratic curve, as we shall see in Section 6.2.

In this section we discuss a utility-based approach for autonomic management. The goal is to maximize the total profit computed as the difference between the revenue guaranteed by an SLA and the total cost to provide the services. Formulated as an optimization problem, the solution discussed in [9] addresses multiple policies, including QoS. The cloud model for this optimization is quite complex and requires a fair number of parameters.

We assume a cloud providing $|K|$ different classes of service, each class k involving N_k applications. For each class $k \in K$ call v_k the revenue (or the penalty) associated with a response time r_k and assume a linear dependency for this utility function of the form $v_k = v_k^{max}\left(1 - r_k/r_k^{max}\right)$, see Figure 6.5(a). Call $m_k = -v_k^{max}/r_k^{max}$ the slope of the utility function.

The system is modeled as a network of queues with multiqueues for each server and with a delay center that models the think time of the user after the completion of service at one server and the start of processing at the next server [see Figure 6.5(b)]. Upon completion, a class k request either completes with probability $(1 - \sum_{k' \in K} \pi_{k,k'})$ or returns to the system as a class k' request with transition probability $\pi_{k,k'}$. Call λ_k the external arrival rate of class k requests and Λ_k the aggregate rate for class k, where $\Lambda_k = \lambda_k + \sum_{k' \in K} \Lambda_{k'} \pi_{k,k'}$.

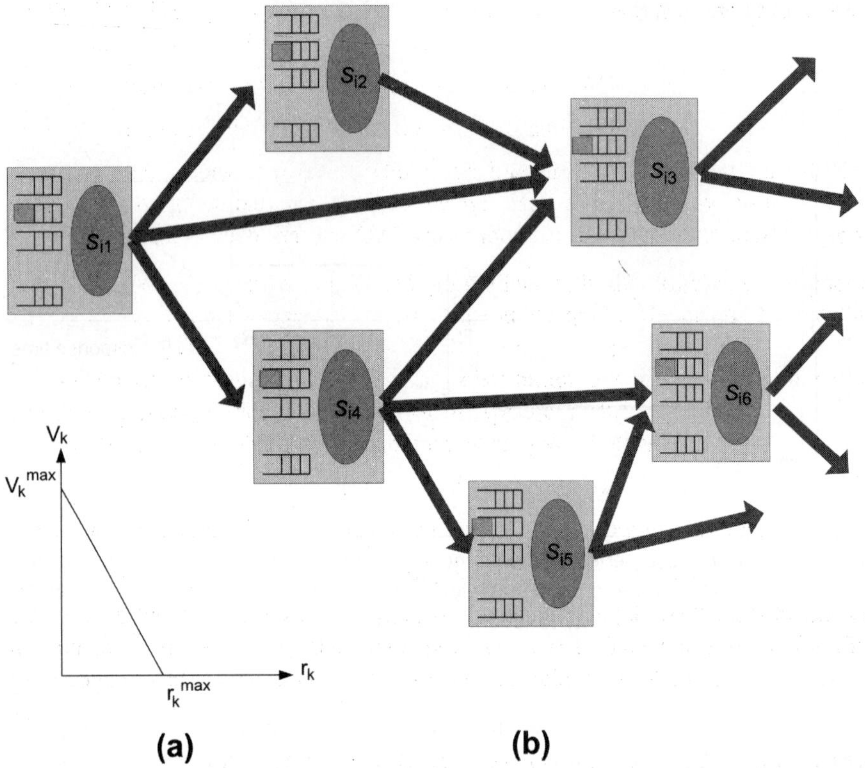

FIGURE 6.5

(a) The utility function, v_k the revenue (or the penalty) associated with a response time r_k for a request of class $k \in K$. The slope of the utility function is $m_k = -v_k^{max}/r_k^{max}$. (b) A network of multiqueues. At each server S_i there are $|K|$ queues for each one of the $k \in K$ classes of requests. A tier consists of all requests of class $k \in K$ at all servers $S_{ij} \in I, 1 \leqslant j \leqslant 6$.

Typically, CPU and memory are considered representative for resource allocation; for simplicity we assume a single CPU that runs at a discrete set of clock frequencies and a discrete set of supply voltages according to a Dynamic Voltage and Frequency Scaling (DVFS) model. The power consumption of a server is a function of the clock frequency. The scheduling of a server is work-conserving[6] and is modeled as a Generalized Processor Sharing (GPS) scheduling [385]. Analytical models [4,280] are too complex for large systems.

The optimization problem formulated in [9] involves five terms: A and B reflect revenues; C the cost of servers in a low-power, stand-by mode; D the cost of active servers, given their operating frequency; E, the cost of switching servers from low-power, stand-by mode to active state, and F, the cost of migrating VMs from one server to another. There are nine constraints $\Gamma_1, \Gamma_2, \ldots, \Gamma_9$ for this mixed-integer, nonlinear programming problem. The decision variables for this optimization problem are listed in Table 6.2 and the parameters used are shown in Table 6.3.

[6] A scheduling policy is work-conserving if the server cannot be idle while there is work to be done.

Table 6.2 Decision variables for the optimization problem.

Name	Description
x_i	$x_i = 1$ if server $i \in I$ is running, $x_i = 0$ otherwise
$y_{i,h}$	$y_{i,h} = 1$ if server i is running at frequency h, $y_{i,h} = 0$ otherwise
$z_{i,k,j}$	$z_{i,k,j} = 1$ if application tier j of a class k request runs on server i, $z_{i,k,j} = 0$ otherwise
$w_{i,k}$	$w_{i,k} = 1$ if at least one class k request is assigned to server i, $w_{i,k} = 0$ otherwise
$\lambda_{i,k,j}$	Rate of execution of applications tier j of class k requests on server i
$\phi_{i,k,j}$	Fraction of capacity of server i assigned to tier j of class k requests

Table 6.3 The parameters used for the A, B, C, D, E, and F terms and the constraints Γ_i of the optimization problem.

Name	Description
I	The set of servers
K	The set of classes
Λ_k	The aggregate rate for class $k \in K$, $\Lambda_k = \lambda_k + \sum_{k' \in K} \Lambda_{k'} \pi_{k,k'}$
a_i	The availability of server $i \in I$
A_k	Minimum level of availability for request class $k \in K$ specified by the SLA
m_k	The slope of the utility function for a class $k \in K$ application
N_k	Number of applications in class $k \in K$
H_i	The range of frequencies of server $i \in I$
$C_{i,h}$	Capacity of server $i \in I$ running at frequency $h \in H_i$
$c_{i,h}$	Cost for server $i \in I$ running at frequency $h \in H_i$
$\bar{c}_i$	Average cost of running server i
$\mu_{k,j}$	Maximum service rate for a unit capacity server for tier j of a class k request
cm	The cost of moving a virtual machine from one server to another
cs_i	The cost for switching server i from the stand-by mode to an active state
$RAM_{k,j}$	The amount of main memory for tier j of class k request
$\overline{RAM}_i$	The amount of memory available on server i

The expression to be maximized is:

$$(A + B) - (C + D + E + F) \tag{6.21}$$

with

$$A = \max \sum_{k \in K} \left(-m_k \sum_{i \in I, j \in N_k} \frac{\lambda_{i,k,j}}{\sum_{h \in H_i} \left(C_{i,h} \times y_{i,h} \right) \mu_{k,j} \times \phi_{i,k,j} - \lambda_{i,k,j}} \right),$$

$$B = \sum_{k \in K} u_k \times \Lambda_k, \tag{6.22}$$

$$C = \sum_{i \in I} \bar{c}_i, \quad D = \sum_{i \in I, h \in H_i} c_{i,h} \times y_{i,h}, \quad E = \sum_{i \in I} cs_i \max(0, x_i - \bar{x}_i), \tag{6.23}$$

and

$$F = \sum_{i \in I, k \in K, j \in N_j} cm \max(0, z_{i,j,k} - \bar{z}_{i,j,k}). \tag{6.24}$$

The nine constraints are:

(Γ_1) $\sum_{i \in I} \lambda_{i,k,j} = \Lambda_k, \ \forall k \in K, \ j \in N_k \Rightarrow$ the traffic assigned to all servers for class k requests equals the predicted load for the class.

(Γ_2) $\sum_{k \in K, j \in N_k} \phi_{i,k,j} \leqslant 1 \, \forall i \in I \Rightarrow$ server i cannot be allocated an workload more than its capacity.

(Γ_3) $\sum_{h \in H_i} y_{i,h} = x_i, \ \forall i \in I \Rightarrow$ if server $i \in I$ is active it runs at one frequency in the set H_i, and only one $y_{i,h}$ is nonzero.

(Γ_4) $z_{i,k,j} \leqslant x_i, \ \forall i \in I, \ k \in K, \ j \in N_k \Rightarrow$ requests can only be assigned to active servers.

(Γ_5) $\lambda_{i,k,j} \leqslant \Lambda_k \times z_{i,k,j}, \ \forall i \in I, \ k \in K, \ j \in N_k \Rightarrow$ requests may run on server $i \in I$ only if the corresponding application tier has been assigned to server i.

(Γ_6) $\lambda_{i,k,j} \leqslant \left(\sum_{h \in H_i} C_{i,h} \times y_{i,h}\right) \mu_{k,j} \times \phi_{i,k,j}, \ \forall i \in I, \ k \in K, \ j \in N_k \Rightarrow$ resources cannot be saturated.

(Γ_7) $RAM_{k,j} \times z_{i,k,j} \leqslant \overline{RAM}_i, \ \forall i \in I, \ k \in K \Rightarrow$ the memory on server i is sufficient to support all applications running on it.

(Γ_8) $\Pi_{j=1}^{N_k} \left(1 - \Pi_{i=1}^{M}(1 - a_i^{w_{i,k}}\right) \geqslant A_k, \ \forall k \in K \Rightarrow$ the availability of all servers assigned to class k request should be at least equal to the minimum required by the SLA.

(Γ_9) $\sum_{j=1}^{N_k} z_{i,k,j} \geqslant N_k \times w_{i,k}, \ \forall i \in I, \ k \in K$
$\lambda_{i,j,k}, \phi_{i,j,k} \geqslant 0, \ \forall i \in I, \ k \in K, \ j \in N_k$
$x_i, y_{i,h}, z_{i,k,j}, w_{i,k} \in \{0, 1\}, \ \forall i \in I, \ k \in K, \ j \in N_k \Rightarrow$ constraints and relations among decision variables.

Clearly, this approach is not scalable to clouds with a very large number of servers. Moreover, the large number of decision variables and parameters of the model make this approach infeasible for a realistic cloud computing resource management strategy.

6.7 Resource bundling: Combinatorial auctions for cloud resources

Resources in a cloud are allocated in *bundles*, allowing users get maximum benefit from a specific combination of resources. Indeed, along with CPU cycles, an application needs specific amounts of main memory, disk space, network bandwidth, and so on. Resource bundling complicates traditional resource allocation models and has generated interest in economic models and, in particular, auction algorithms. In the context of cloud computing, an auction is the allocation of resources to the highest bidder.

Combinatorial Auctions. Auctions in which participants can bid on combinations of items, or *packages*, are called *combinatorial auctions* [93]. Such auctions provide a relatively simple, scalable, and tractable solution to cloud resource allocation. Two recent combinatorial auction algorithms are the *simultaneous clock auction* [29] and the *clock proxy auction* [30]. The algorithm discussed in this chapter and introduced in [333] is called the *ascending clock auction (ASCA)*. In all these algorithms the current price for each resource is represented by a "clock" seen by all participants at the auction.

We consider a strategy in which prices and allocation are set as a result of an auction. In this auction, users provide bids for desirable bundles and the price they are willing to pay. We assume a population of U users, $u = \{1, 2, \ldots, U\}$, and R resources, $r = \{1, 2, \ldots, R\}$. The bid of user u is $\mathcal{B}_u = \{\mathcal{Q}_u, \pi_u\}$ with $\mathcal{Q}_i = (q_u^1, q_u^2, q_u^3, \ldots)$ an R-component vector; each element of this vector, q_u^i, represents a bundle of resources user u would accept and, in return, pay the total price π_u. Each vector component q_u^i is a positive quantity and encodes the quantity of a resource desired or, if negative, the quantity of the resource offered. A user expresses her desires as an *indifference set* $\mathcal{I} = (q_u^1 \text{ XOR } q_u^2 \text{ XOR } q_u^3 \text{ XOR} \ldots)$.

The final auction prices for individual resources are given by the vector $p = (p^1, p^2, \ldots, p^R)$ and the amounts of resources allocated to user u are $x_u = (x_u^1, x_u^2, \ldots, x_u^R)$. Thus, the expression $[(x_u)^T p]$ represents the total price paid by user u for the bundle of resources if the bid is successful at time T. The scalar $[\min_{q \in \mathcal{Q}_u} (q^T p)]$ is the final price established through the bidding process.

The bidding process aims to optimize an *objective function* $f(x, p)$. This function could be tailored to measure the net value of all resources traded, or it can measure the *total surplus* – the difference between the maximum amount users are willing to pay minus the amount they pay. Other optimization functions could be considered for a specific system, e.g., the minimization of energy consumption or of security risks.

Pricing and Allocation Algorithms. A pricing and allocation algorithm partitions the set of users into two disjoint sets, winners and losers, denoted as $\mathcal{W}$ and $\mathcal{L}$, respectively. The algorithm should:

1. Be computationally tractable. Traditional combinatorial auction algorithms such as Vickey-Clarke-Groves (VLG) fail this criteria, because they are not computationally tractable.
2. Scale well. Given the scale of the system and the number of requests for service, scalability is a necessary condition.
3. Be objective. Partitioning in winners and losers should only be based on the price π_u of a user's bid. If the price exceeds the threshold, the user is a winner; otherwise the user is a loser.
4. Be fair. Make sure that the prices are *uniform*. All winners within a given resource pool pay the same price.
5. Indicate clearly at the end of the auction the unit prices for each resource pool.
6. Indicate clearly to all participants the relationship between the supply and the demand in the system.

The function to be maximized is

$$\max_{x,p} f(x, p). \tag{6.25}$$

The constraints in Table 6.4 correspond to our intuition: (a) the first one states that a user either gets one of the bundles it has opted for or nothing; no partial allocation is acceptable. (b) The second constraint expresses the fact that the system awards only available resources; only offered resources can be allocated. (c) The third constraint is that the bid of the winners exceeds the final price. (d) The fourth constraint states that the winners get the least expensive bundles in their indifference set. (e) The fifth constraint states that losers bid below the final price. (f) The last constraint states that all prices are positive numbers.

Table 6.4 The constraints for a combinatorial auction algorithm.

$x_u \in \{0 \cup \mathcal{Q}_u\},\ \forall u$	A user gets all resources or nothing.
$\sum_u x_u \leqslant 0$	Final allocation leads to a net surplus of resources.
$\pi_u \geqslant (x_u)^T p,\ \forall u \in \mathcal{W}$	Auction winners are willing to pay the final price.
$(x_u)^T p = \min_{q \in \mathcal{Q}_u} (q^T p),\ \forall u \in \mathcal{W}$	Winners get the cheapest bundle in $\mathcal{I}$.
$\pi_u < \min_{q \in \mathcal{Q}_u} (q^T p),\ \forall u \in \mathcal{L}$	The bids of the losers are below the final price.
$p \geqslant 0$	Prices must be nonnegative.

The ASCA Combinatorial Auction Algorithm. Informally, in the ASCA algorithm [333] the participants at the auction specify the resource and the quantities of that resource offered or desired at the price listed for that time slot. Then the *excess vector*

$$z(t) = \sum_u x_u(t) \tag{6.26}$$

is computed. If all its components are negative, the auction stops; negative components mean that the demand does not exceed the offer. If the demand is larger than the offer, $z(t) \geqslant 0$, the auctioneer increases the price for items with a positive excess demand and solicits bids at the new price. Note that the algorithm satisfies conditions 1 through 6; from Table 6.3 all users discover the price at the same time and pay or receive a "fair" payment relative to uniform resource prices, the computation is tractable, and the execution time is linear in the number of participants at the auction and the number of resources. The computation is robust and generates plausible results regardless of the initial parameters of the system.

There is a slight complication as the algorithm involves user bidding in multiple rounds. To address this problem the user proxies automatically adjust their demands on behalf of the actual bidders, as shown in Figure 6.6. These proxies can be modeled as functions that compute the "best bundle" from each $\mathcal{Q}_u$ set given the current price

$$\mathcal{Q}_u = \begin{cases} \hat{q}_u & \text{if } \hat{q}_u^T p \leqslant \pi_u \quad \text{with} \quad \hat{q}_u \in \arg\min\,(q_u^T p) \\ 0 & \text{otherwise} \end{cases}.$$

The input to the ASCA algorithm: U users, R resources, $\bar{p}$ the starting price, and the update increment function, $g : (x, p) \mapsto \mathbb{R}^{\mathbb{R}}$. The pseudocode of the algorithm is:

set $t = 0$, $p(0) = \bar{p}$
loop
  collect bids $x_u(t) = \mathcal{G}_u(p(t)),\ \forall u$
  calculate excess demand $z(t) = \sum_u x_u(t)$
  if z(t) <0 **then**
    break
  else

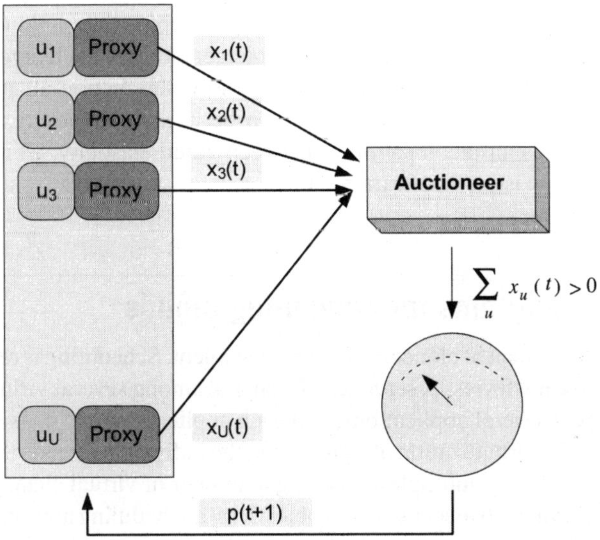

FIGURE 6.6

The schematics of the ASCA algorithm. To allow for a single round, auction users are represented by proxies that place the bids $x_U(t)$. The auctioneer determines whether there is an excess demand and, in that case, raises the price of resources for which the demand exceeds the supply and requests new bids.

```
8:      update prices p(t + 1) = p(t) + g(x(t), p(t))
9:      t ← t + 1
10:  end if
11: end loop
```

In this algorithm $g(x(t), p(t))$ is the function for setting the price increase. This function can be correlated with the excess demand $z(t)$, as in $g(x(t), p(t)) = \alpha z(t)^+$ (the notation x^+ means max $(x, 0)$) with α a positive number. An alternative is to ensure that the price does not increase by an amount larger than δ. In that case $g(x(t), p(t)) = \min(\alpha z(t)^+, \delta e)$ with $e = (1, 1, \ldots, 1)$ is an R-dimensional vector and minimization is done componentwise.

The convergence of the optimization problem is guaranteed *only if* all participants at the auction are either providers of resources or consumers of resources, but not both providers and consumers at the same time. Nevertheless, the clock algorithm only finds a feasible solution; it does not guarantee its optimality.

The authors of [333] have implemented the algorithm and allowed internal use of it within Google. Their preliminary experiments show that the system led to substantial improvements. One of the most interesting side effects of the new resource allocation policy is that users were encouraged to make their applications more flexible and mobile to take advantage of the flexibility of the system controlled by the ASCA algorithm.

An auctioning algorithm is very appealing because it supports resource bundling and does not require a model of the system. At the same time, a practical implementation of such algorithms is challenging. First, requests for service arrive at random times, whereas in an auction all participants must react to a bid at the same time. Periodic auctions must then be organized, but this adds to the delay of the response. Second, there is an incompatibility between cloud elasticity, which guarantees that the demand for resources of an existing application will be satisfied immediately, and the idea of periodic auctions.

6.8 Scheduling algorithms for computing clouds

Scheduling is a critical component of cloud resource management. Scheduling is responsible for resource sharing/multiplexing at several levels. A server can be shared among several virtual machines, each virtual machine could support several applications, and each application may consist of multiple threads. CPU scheduling supports the virtualization of a processor, the individual threads acting as virtual processors; a communication link can be multiplexed among a number of virtual channels, one for each flow.

In addition to the requirement to meet its design objectives, a scheduling algorithm should be efficient, fair, and starvation-free. The objectives of a scheduler for a batch system are to maximize the throughput (the number of jobs completed in one unit of time, e.g., in one hour) and to minimize the turnaround time (the time between job submission and its completion). For a real-time system the objectives are to meet the deadlines and to be predictable. Schedulers for systems supporting a mix of tasks – some with hard real-time constraints, others with soft, or no timing constraints – are often subject to contradictory requirements. Some schedulers are *preemptive*, allowing a high-priority task to interrupt the execution of a lower-priority one; others are *nonpreemptive*.

Two distinct dimensions of resource management must be addressed by a scheduling policy: (a) the amount or quantity of resources allocated and (b) the timing when access to resources is granted. Figure 6.7 identifies several broad classes of resource allocation requirements in the space defined by these two dimensions: best-effort, soft requirements, and hard requirements. Hard-real time systems are the most challenging because they require strict timing and precise amounts of resources.

There are multiple definitions of a fair scheduling algorithm. First, we discuss the *max-min fairness criterion* [128]. Consider a resource with bandwidth B shared among n users who have equal rights. Each user requests an amount b_i and receives B_i. Then, according to the max-min criterion, the following conditions must be satisfied by a fair allocation:

C_1. The amount received by any user is not larger than the amount requested, $B_i \leqslant b_i$.

C_2. If the minimum allocation of any user is B_{min} no allocation satisfying condition C_1 has a higher B_{min} than the current allocation.

C_3. When we remove the user receiving the minimum allocation B_{min} and then reduce the total amount of the resource available from B to $(B - B_{min})$, the condition C_2 remains recursively true.

A fairness criterion for CPU scheduling [142] requires that the amount of work in the time interval from t_1 to t_2 of two runnable threads a and b, $\Omega_a(t_1, t_2)$ and $\Omega_b(t_1, t_2)$, respectively, minimize the expression

$$\left| \frac{\Omega_a(t_1, t_2)}{w_a} - \frac{\Omega_b(t_1, t_2)}{w_b} \right|, \tag{6.27}$$

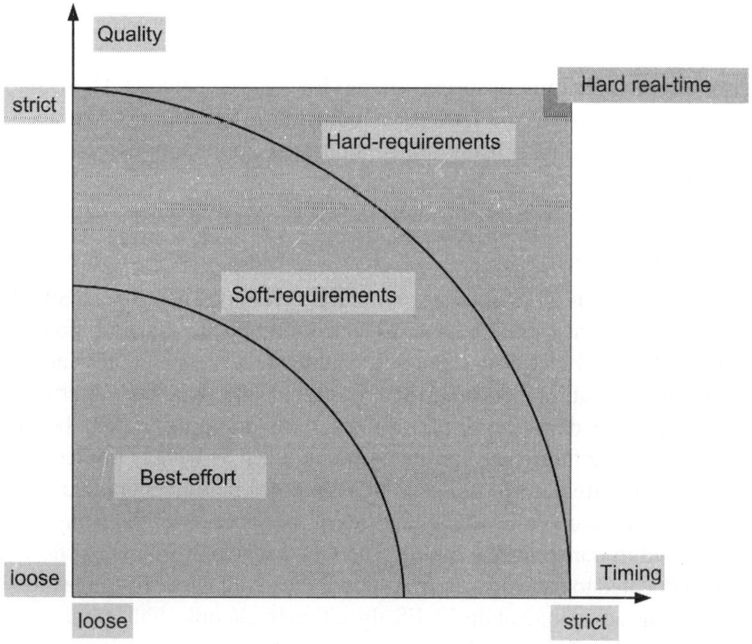

FIGURE 6.7

Best-effort policies do not impose requirements regarding either the amount of resources allocated to an application or the timing when an application is scheduled. Soft-requirements allocation policies require statistically guaranteed amounts and timing constraints; hard-requirements allocation policies demand strict timing and precise amounts of resources.

where w_a and w_b are the weights of the threads a and b, respectively.

The quality-of-service (QoS) requirements differ for different classes of cloud applications and demand different scheduling policies. Best-effort applications such as batch applications and analytics[7] do not require QoS guarantees. Multimedia applications such as audio and video streaming have soft real-time constraints and require statistically guaranteed maximum delay and throughput. Applications with hard real-time constraints do not use a public cloud at this time but may do so in the future.

Round-robin, FCFS, shortest-job-first (SJF), and priority algorithms are among the most common scheduling algorithms for best-effort applications. Each thread is given control of the CPU for a definite period of time, called a *time-slice*, in a circular fashion in the case of round-robin scheduling. The algorithm is fair and starvation-free. The threads are allowed to use the CPU in the order in which they arrive in the case of the FCFS algorithms and in the order of their running time in the case of SJF algorithms. Earliest deadline first (EDF) and rate monotonic algorithms (RMA) are used for real-time applications. Integration of scheduling for the three classes of application is discussed in [56], and two

[7]The term *analytics* is overloaded; sometimes it means discovery of patterns in the data, but it could also mean statistical processing of the results of a commercial activity.

new algorithms for integrated scheduling, resource allocation/dispatching (RAD) and rate-based earliest deadline (RBED) are proposed.

Next we discuss several algorithms of special interest for computer clouds. These algorithms illustrate the evolution in thinking regarding the fairness of scheduling and the need to accommodate multi-objective scheduling – in particular, scheduling for multimedia applications.

6.9 Fair queuing

Computing and communication on a cloud are intimately related. Therefore, it should be no surprise that the first algorithm we discuss can be used for scheduling packet transmission as well as threads. Interconnection networks allow cloud servers to communicate with one another and with users. These networks consist of communication links of limited bandwidth and switches/routers/gateways of limited capacity. When the load exceeds its capacity, a switch starts dropping packets because it has limited input buffers for the switching fabric and for the outgoing links, as well as limited CPU cycles.

A switch must handle multiple flows and pairs of source-destination endpoints of the traffic. Thus, a scheduling algorithm has to manage several quantities at the same time: the *bandwidth*, the amount of data each flow is allowed to transport; the *timing* when the packets of individual flows are transmitted; and the *buffer space* allocated to each flow. A first strategy to avoid network congestion is to use a FCFS scheduling algorithm. The advantage of the FCFS algorithm is a simple management of the three quantities: bandwidth, timing, and buffer space. Nevertheless, the FCFS algorithm does not guarantee fairness; greedy flow sources can transmit at a higher rate and benefit from a larger share of the bandwidth.

To address this problem, a fair queuing algorithm proposed in [252] requires that separate queues, one per flow, be maintained by a switch and that the queues be serviced in a round-robin manner. This algorithm guarantees the fairness of buffer space management, but does not guarantee fairness of bandwidth allocation. Indeed, a flow transporting large packets will benefit from a larger bandwidth (see Figure 6.8).

The *fair queuing (FQ)* algorithm in [102] proposes a solution to this problem. First, it introduces a *bit-by-bit round-robin (BR)* strategy; as the name implies, in this rather impractical scheme a single bit from each queue is transmitted and the queues are visited in a round-robin fashion. Let $R(t)$ be the number of rounds of the BR algorithm up to time t and $N_{active}(t)$ be the number of active flows through the switch. Call t_i^a the time when the packet i of flow a, of size P_i^a bits arrives, and call S_i^a and F_i^a the values of $R(t)$ when the first and the last bit, respectively, of the packet i of flow a are transmitted. Then,

$$F_i^a = S_i^a + P_i^a \quad \text{and} \quad S_i^a = \max\left[F_{i-1}^a, R(t_i^a)\right]. \tag{6.28}$$

The quantities $R(t)$, $N_{active}(t)$, S_i^a, and F_i^a depend only on the arrival time of the packets, t_i^a, and not on their transmission time, provided that a flow a is active as long as

$$R(t) \leqslant F_i^a \quad \text{when} \quad i = \max\left(j | t_i^a \leqslant t\right). \tag{6.29}$$

The authors of [102] use for packet-by-packet transmission time the following nonpreemptive scheduling rule, which emulates the BR strategy: *The next packet to be transmitted is the one with the smallest* F_i^a. A preemptive version of the algorithm requires that the transmission of the current packet be interrupted as soon as one with a shorter finishing time, F_i^a, arrives.

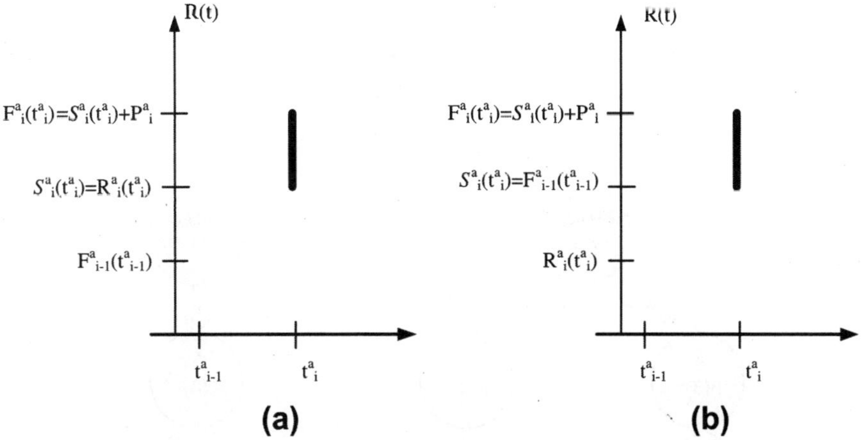

FIGURE 6.8

Transmission of a packet i of flow a arriving at time t_i^a of size P_i^a bits. The transmission starts at time $S_i^a = \max[F_{i-1}^a, R(t_i^a)]$ and ends at time $F_i^a = S_i^a + P_i^a$ with $R(t)$ the number of rounds of the algorithm. (a) The case $F_{i-1}^a < R(t_i^a)$. (b) The case $F_{i-1}^a \geqslant R(t_i^a)$.

A fair allocation of the bandwidth does not have an effect on the timing of the transmission. A possible strategy is to allow less delay for the flows using less than their fair share of the bandwidth. The same paper [102] proposes the introduction of a quantity called the *bid*, B_i^a, and scheduling the packet transmission based on its value. The bid is defined as

$$B_i^a = P_i^a + \max\left[F_{i-1}^a, \left(R\left(t_i^a\right) - \delta\right)\right], \tag{6.30}$$

with δ a nonnegative parameter. The properties of the FQ algorithm, as well as the implementation of a nonpreemptive version of the algorithms, are analyzed in [102].

6.10 Start-time fair queuing

A hierarchical CPU scheduler for multimedia operating systems was proposed in [142]. The basic idea of the *start-time fair queuing (SFQ)* algorithm is to organize the consumers of the CPU bandwidth in a tree structure; the root node is the processor and the leaves of this tree are the threads of each application. A scheduler acts at each level of the hierarchy. The fraction of the processor bandwidth, B, allocated to the intermediate node i is

$$\frac{B_i}{B} = \frac{w_i}{\sum_{j=1}^{n} w_j} \tag{6.31}$$

with w_j, $1 \leqslant j \leqslant n$, the weight of the n children of node i; see the example in Figure 6.9.

When a virtual machine is not active, its bandwidth is reallocated to the other VMs active at the time. When one of the applications of a virtual machine is not active, its allocation is transferred to the other

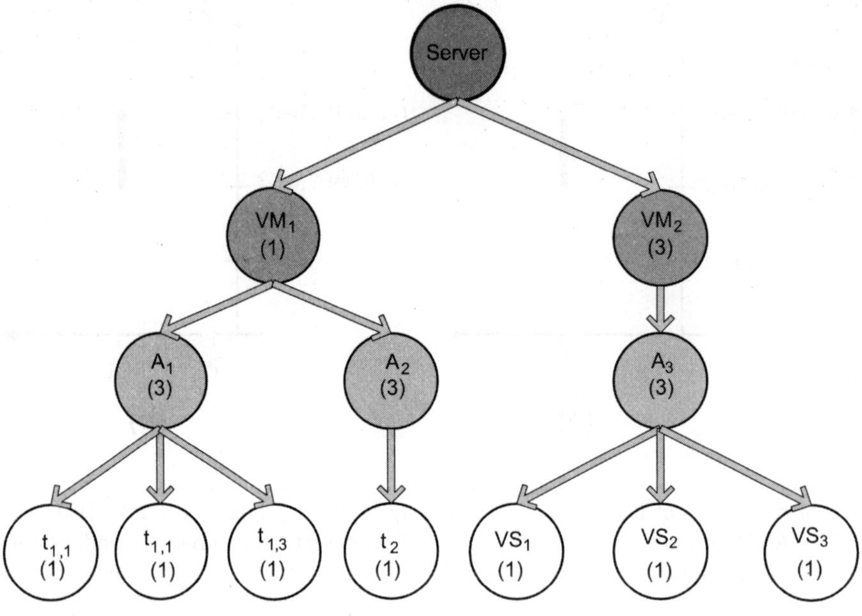

FIGURE 6.9

The SFQ tree for scheduling when two virtual machines, VM_1 and VM_2, run on a powerful server. VM_1 runs two best-effort applications A_1, with three threads $t_{1,1}$, $t_{1,2}$, and $t_{1,3}$, and A_2 with a single thread, t_2. VM_2 runs a video-streaming application, A_3, with three threads vs_1, vs_2, and vs_3. The weights of virtual machines, applications, and individual threads are shown in parenthesis.

applications running on the same VM. Similarly, if one of the threads of an application is not runnable, its allocation is transferred to the other threads of the applications.

Call $v_a(t)$ and $v_b(t)$ the virtual time of threads a and b, respectively, at real time t. The virtual time of the scheduler at time t is denoted by $v(t)$. Call q the time quantum of the scheduler in milliseconds. The threads a and b have their time quanta, q_a and q_b, weighted by w_a and w_b, respectively; thus, in our example, the time quanta of the two threads are q/w_a and q/w_b, respectively. The i-th activation of thread a will start at the virtual time S_a^i and will finish at virtual time F_a^i. We call τ^j the real time of the j-th invocation of the scheduler.

An SFQ scheduler follows several rules:

R1. The threads are serviced in the order of their virtual start-up time; ties are broken arbitrarily.

R2. The virtual startup time of the i-th activation of thread x is

$$S_x^i(t) = \max\left[v\left(\tau^j\right), F_x^{(i-1)}(t)\right] \quad \text{and} \quad S_x^0 = 0. \tag{6.32}$$

The condition for thread i to be started is that thread $(i-1)$ has finished and that the scheduler is active.

R3. The virtual finish time of the i-th activation of thread x is

$$F_x^i(t) = S_x^i(t) + \frac{q}{w_x}. \tag{6.33}$$

A thread is stopped when its time quantum has expired; its time quantum is the time quantum of the scheduler divided by the weight of the thread.

R4. The virtual time of all threads is initially zero, $v_x^0 = 0$. The virtual time $v(t)$ at real time t is computed as follows:

$$v(t) = \begin{cases} \text{Virtual start time of the thread in service at time } t, & \text{if CPU is busy} \\ \text{Maximum finish virtual time of any thread,} & \text{if CPU is idle.} \end{cases} \tag{6.34}$$

In this description of the algorithm we have included the real time t to stress the dependence of all events in virtual time on the real time. To simplify the notation we use in our examples the real time as the index of the event. In other words, S_a^6 means the virtual start-up time of thread a at real time $t = 6$.

Example. The following example illustrates the application of the SFQ algorithm when there are two threads with the weights $w_a = 1$ and $w_b = 4$ and the time quantum is $q = 12$ (see Figure 6.10.)

Initially $S_a^0 = 0$, $S_b^0 = 0$, $v_a(0) = 0$, and $v_b(0) = 0$. Thread b blocks at time $t = 24$ and wakes up at time $t = 60$.

The scheduling decisions are made as follows:

1. $t = 0$: We have a tie, $S_a^0 = S_b^0$, and arbitrarily thread b is chosen to run first. The virtual finish time of thread b is

$$F_b^0 = S_b^0 + q/w_b = 0 + 12/4 = 3. \tag{6.35}$$

2. $t = 3$: Both threads are runnable and thread b was in service; thus, $v(3) = S_b^0 = 0$; then

$$S_b^1 = \max[v(3), F_b^0] = \max(0, 3) = 3. \tag{6.36}$$

But $S_a^0 < S_b^1$, thus thread a is selected to run. Its virtual finish time is

$$F_a^0 = S_a^0 + q/w_a = 0 + 12/1 = 12. \tag{6.37}$$

3. $t = 15$: Both threads are runnable, and thread a was in service at this time; thus,

$$v(15) = S_a^0 = 0 \tag{6.38}$$

and

$$S_a^1 = \max[v(15), F_a^0] = \max[0, 12] = 12. \tag{6.39}$$

As $S_b^1 = 3 < 12$, thread b is selected to run; the virtual finish time of thread b is now

$$F_b^1 = S_b^1 + q/w_b = 3 + 12/4 = 6. \tag{6.40}$$

4. $t = 18$: Both threads are runnable, and thread b was in service at this time; thus,

$$v(18) = S_b^1 = 3 \tag{6.41}$$

and

$$S_b^2 = \max[v(18), F_b^1] = \max[3, 6] = 6. \tag{6.42}$$

As $S_b^2 < S_a^1 = 12$, thread b is selected to run again; its virtual finish time is

$$F_b^2 = S_b^2 + q/w_b = 6 + 12/4 = 9. \tag{6.43}$$

5. $t = 21$: Both threads are runnable, and thread b was in service at this time; thus,

$$v(21) = S_b^2 = 6 \tag{6.44}$$

and

$$S_b^3 = \max[v(21), F_b^2] = \max[6, 9] = 9. \tag{6.45}$$

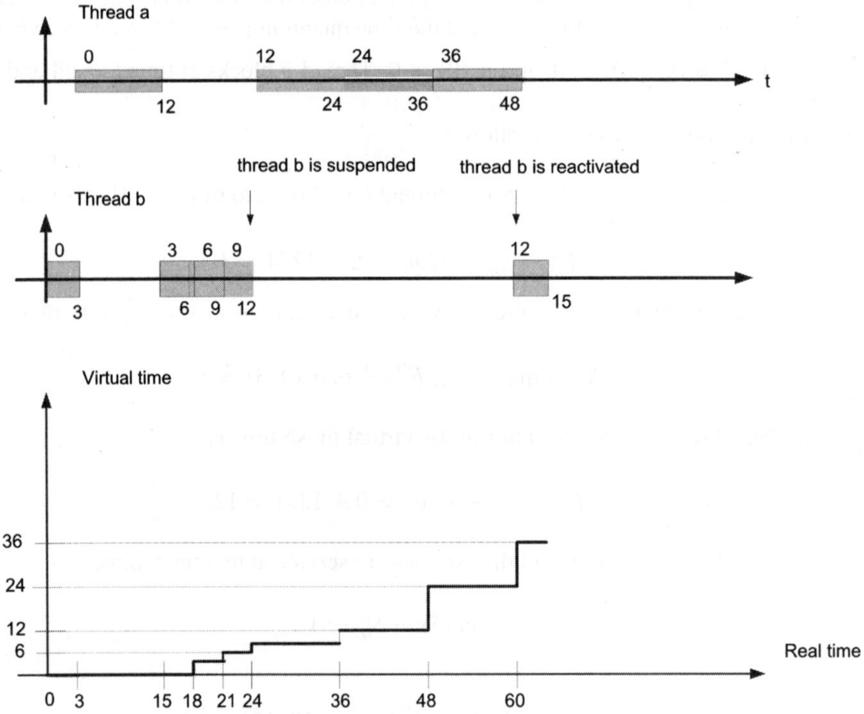

FIGURE 6.10

Top, the virtual start-up time $S_a(t)$ and $S_b(t)$ and the virtual finish time $F_a(t)$ and $F_b(t)$ function of the real time t for each activation of threads a and b, respectively, are marked at the top and bottom of the box representing a running thread. The virtual time of the scheduler $v(t)$ function of the real time is shown on the bottom graph.

As $S_b^2 < S_a^1 = 12$, thread b is selected to run again; its virtual finish time is

$$F_b^3 = S_b^3 + q/w_b = 9 + 12/4 = 12. \quad (6.46)$$

6. $t = 24$: Thread b was in service at this time; thus,

$$v(24) = S_b^3 = 9 \quad (6.47)$$
$$S_b^4 = \max[v(24), F_b^3] = \max[9, 12] = 12. \quad (6.48)$$

Thread b is suspended till $t = 60$; thus, thread a is activated. Its virtual finish time is

$$F_a^1 = S_a^1 + q/w_a = 12 + 12/1 = 24. \quad (6.49)$$

7. $t = 36$: Thread a was in service and the only runnable thread at this time; thus,

$$v(36) = S_a^1 = 12 \quad (6.50)$$

and

$$S_a^2 = \max[v(36), F_a^2] = \max[12, 24] = 24. \quad (6.51)$$

Then,

$$F_a^2 = S_a^2 + q/w_a = 24 + 12/1 = 36. \quad (6.52)$$

8. $t = 48$: Thread a was in service and is the only runnable thread at this time; thus,

$$v(48) = S_a^2 = 24 \quad (6.53)$$

and

$$S_a^3 = \max[v(48), F_a^2] = \max[24, 36] = 36. \quad (6.54)$$

Then,

$$F_a^3 = S_a^3 + q/w_a = 36 + 12/1 = 48. \quad (6.55)$$

9. $t = 60$: Thread a was in service at this time; thus,

$$v(60) = S_a^3 = 36 \quad (6.56)$$

and

$$S_a^4 = \max[v(60), F_a^3] = \max[36, 48] = 48. \quad (6.57)$$

But now thread b is runnable and $S_b^4 = 12$.
Thus, thread b is activated and

$$F_b^4 = S_b^4 + q/w_b = 12 + 12/4 = 15. \quad (6.58)$$

Several properties of the SFQ algorithm are proved in [142]. The algorithm allocates CPU fairly when the available bandwidth varies in time and provides throughput as well as delay guarantees. The algorithm schedules the threads in the order of their virtual start-up time, the shortest one first; the length of the time quantum is not required when a thread is scheduled but only after the thread has finished its current allocation. The authors of [142] report that the overhead of the SFQ algorithms is comparable to that of the Solaris scheduling algorithm.

6.11 Borrowed virtual time

The objective of the *borrowed virtual time (BVT)* algorithm is to support low-latency dispatching of real-time applications as well as a weighted sharing of the CPU among several classes of applications [107]. Like SFQ, the BVT algorithm supports scheduling of a mix of applications, some with hard, some with soft real-time constraints, and applications demanding only a best effort.

Thread i has an *effective virtual time*, E_i, an *actual virtual time*, A_i, and a *virtual time warp*, W_i. The scheduler thread maintains its own *scheduler virtual time (SVT)*, defined as the minimum actual virtual time A_j of any thread. The threads are dispatched in the order of their effective virtual time, E_i, a policy called the earliest virtual time (EVT).

The virtual time warp allows a thread to acquire an earlier effective virtual time – in other words, to borrow virtual time from its future CPU allocation. The virtual warp time is enabled when the variable *warpBack* is set. In this case a latency-sensitive thread gains dispatching preference as

$$E_i \leftarrow \begin{cases} A_i & \text{if } \; warpBack = OFF \\ A_i - W_i & \text{if } \; warpBack = ON. \end{cases} \tag{6.59}$$

The algorithm measures the time in *minimum charging units* (*mcu*) and uses a time quantum called *context switch allowance (C)*, which measures the real time a thread is allowed to run when competing with other threads, measured in multiples of *mcu*. Typical values for the two quantities are $mcu = 100\ \mu sec$ and $C = 100\ msec$. A thread is charged an integer number of *mcu*.

Context switches are triggered by traditional events, the running thread is blocked waiting for an event to occur, the time quantum expires, and an interrupt occurs. Context switching also occurs when a thread becomes runnable after sleeping. When the thread τ_i becomes runnable after sleeping, its actual virtual time is updated as follows:

$$A_i \leftarrow \max[A_i, SVT]. \tag{6.60}$$

This policy prevents a thread sleeping for a long time to claim control of the CPU for a longer period of time than it deserves.

If there are no interrupts, threads are allowed to run for the same amount of virtual time. Individual threads have weights; a thread with a larger weight consumes its virtual time more slowly. In practice, each thread τ_i maintains a constant k_i and uses its weight w_i to compute the amount Δ used to advance its actual virtual time upon completion of a run:

$$A_i \leftarrow A_i + \Delta. \tag{6.61}$$

Given two threads a and b,

$$\Delta = \frac{k_a}{w_a} = \frac{k_b}{w_b}. \tag{6.62}$$

The EVT policy requires that every time the actual virtual time is updated, a context switch from the current running thread τ_i to a thread τ_j occurs if

$$A_j \leqslant A_i - \frac{C}{w_i}. \tag{6.63}$$

Example 1. The following example illustrates the application of the BVT algorithm for scheduling two threads a and b of best-effort applications. The first thread has a weight twice that of the second, $w_a = 2w_b$; when $k_a = 180$ and $k_b = 90$, then $\Delta = 90$.

We consider periods of real-time allocation of $C = 9$ *mcu*. The two threads a and b are allowed to run for $2C/3 = 6$ *mcu* and $C/3 = 3$ *mcu*, respectively.

Threads a and b are activated at times

$$\begin{aligned} a &: 0, 5, 5+9 = 14, 14+9 = 23, 23+9 = 32, 32+9 = 41, \ldots \\ b &: 2, 2+9 = 11, 11+9 = 20, 20+9 = 29, 29+9 = 38, \ldots \end{aligned} \tag{6.64}$$

The context switches occur at real times:

$$2, 11, 14, 20, 23, 29, 32, 38, 41, \ldots \tag{6.65}$$

The time is expressed in units of *mcu*. The initial run is a shorter one, consists of only 3 *mcu*; a context switch occurs when a, which runs first, exceeds b by 2 *mcu*.

Table 6.5 shows the effective virtual time of the two threads at the time of each context switch. At that moment, its actual virtual time is incremented by an amount equal to Δ if the thread was allowed

Table 6.5 The real time of the context switch and the effective virtual time $E_a(t)$ and $E_b(t)$ at the time of a context switch. There is no time warp, so the effective virtual time is the same as the actual virtual time. At time $t = 0$, $E_a(0) = E_b(0) = 0$ and we choose thread a to run.

Context Switch	Real Time	Running Thread	Effective Virtual Time of the Running Thread
1	$t = 2$	a	$E_a(2) = A_a(2) = A_a(0) + \Delta/3 = 30$ *b runs next as* $E_b(2) = 0 < E_a(2) = 30$
2	$t = 5$	b	$E_b(5) = A_b(5) = A_b(0) + \Delta = 90$ *a runs next as* $E_a(5) = 30 < E_b(5) = 90$
3	$t = 11$	a	$E_a(11) = A_a(11) = A_a(2) + \Delta = 120$ *b runs next as* $E_b(11) = 90 < E_a(11) = 120$
4	$t = 14$	b	$E_b(14) = A_b(14) = A_b(5) + \Delta = 180$ *a runs next as* $E_a(14) = 120 < E_b(14) = 180$
5	$t = 20$	a	$E_a(20) = A_a(20) = A_a(11) + \Delta = 210$ *b runs next as* $E_b(20) = 180 < E_a(20) = 210$
6	$t = 23$	b	$E_b(23) = A_b(23) = A_b(14) + \Delta = 270$ *a runs next as* $E_a(23) = 210 < E_b(23) = 270$
7	$t = 29$	a	$E_a(29) = A_a(29) = A_a(20) + \Delta = 300$ *b runs next as* $E_b(29) = 270 < E_a(29) = 300$
8	$t = 32$	b	$E_b(32) = A_b(32) = A_b(23) + \Delta = 360$ *a runs next as* $E_a(32) = 300 < E_b(32) = 360.$
9	$t = 38$	a	$E_a(38) = A_a(38) = A_a(29) + \Delta = 390$ *b runs next as* $E_b(11) = 360 < E_a(11) = 390$
10	$t = 41$	b	$E_b(41) = A_b(41) = A_b(32) + \Delta = 450$ *a runs next as* $E_a(41) = 390 < E_b(41) = 450$

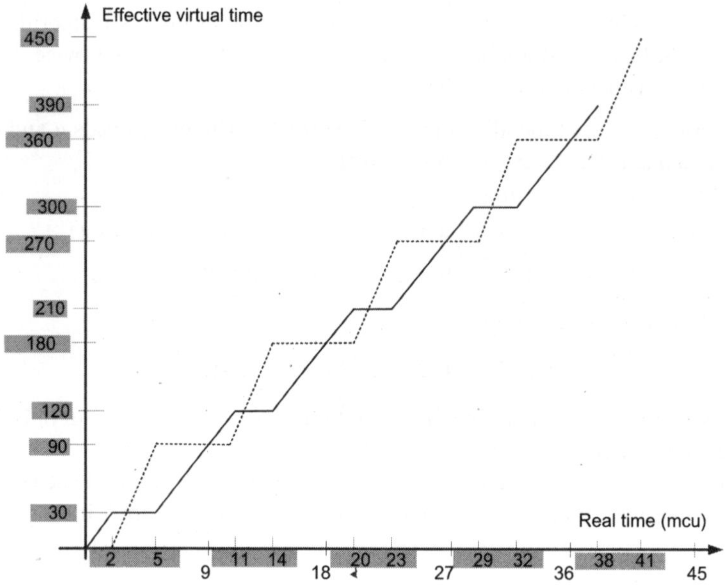

FIGURE 6.11

Example 1, the effective virtual time and the real time of threads *a* (solid line) and *b* (dotted line) with weights $w_a = 2w_b$ when the actual virtual time is incremented in steps of $\Delta = 90$ *mcu*. The real time the two threads are allowed to use the CPU is proportional to their weights. The virtual times are equal, but thread *a* consumes it more slowly. There is no time warp. The threads are dispatched based on their actual virtual time.

to run for its time allocation. The scheduler compares the effective virtual time of the threads and first runs the one with the minimum effective virtual time.

Figure 6.11 displays the effective virtual time and the real time of threads *a* and *b*. When a thread is running, its effective virtual time increases as the real time increases; a running thread appears as a diagonal line. When a thread is runnable but not running, its effective virtual time is constant. A runnable period is displayed as a horizontal line. We see that the two threads are allocated equal amounts of virtual time, but thread *a*, with a larger weight, consumes its real time more slowly.

Example 2. Next we consider the previous example, but this time there is an additional thread, *c*, with real-time constraints. Thread *c* wakes up at time $t = 9$ and then periodically at times $t = 18, 27, 36, \ldots$ for 3 units of time.

Table 6.6 summarizes the evolution of the system when the real-time application thread *c* competes with the two best-effort threads *a* and *b*. Context switches occur now at real times

$$t = 2, 5, 9, 12, 14, 18, 21, 23, 27, 30, 32, 36, 39, 41, \ldots \tag{6.66}$$

The context switches at times

$$t = 9, 18, 27, 36, \ldots \tag{6.67}$$

Table 6.6 A real-time thread c with a time warp $W_c = -60$ is waking up periodically at times $t = 18, 27, 36, \ldots$ for 3 units of time and is competing with the two best-effort threads a and b. The real time and the effective virtual time of the three threads of each context switch are shown.

Context Switch	Real Time	Running Thread	Effective Virtual Time of the Running Thread
1	$t = 2$	a	$E_a(2) = A_a(2) = A_a(0) + \Delta/3 = 0 + 90/3 = 30$
2	$t = 5$	b	$E_b^1 = A_b^1 = A_b^0 + \Delta = 0 + 90 = 90 \Rightarrow$ *a runs next*
3	$t = 9$	a	c wakes up $E_a^1 = A_a^1 + 2\Delta/3 = 30 + (-60) = 90$ $[E_a(9), E_b(9), E_c(9)] = (90, 90, -60) \Rightarrow$ *c runs next*
4	$t = 12$	c	$SVT(12) = \min(90, 90)$ $E_c^s(12) = SVT(12) + W_c = 90 + (-60) = 30$ $E_c(12) = E_c^s(12) + \Delta/3 = 30 + 30 = 60 \Rightarrow$ *b runs next*
5	$t = 14$	b	$E_b^2 = A_b^2 = A_b^1 + 2\Delta/3 = 90 + 60 = 150 \Rightarrow$ *a runs next*
6	$t = 18$	a	c wakes up $E_a^3 = A_a^3 = A_a^2 + 2\Delta/3 = 90 + 60 = 150$ $[E_a(18), E_b(18), E_c(18)] = (150, 150, 60) \Rightarrow$ *c runs next*
7	$t = 21$	c	$SVT = \min(150, 150)$ $E_c^s(21) = SVT + W_c = 150 + (-60) = 90$ $E_c(21) = E_c^s(21) + \Delta/3 = 90 + 30 = 120 \Rightarrow$ *b runs next*
8	$t = 23$	b	$E_b^3 = A_b^3 = A_b^2 + 2\Delta/3 = 150 + 60 = 210 \Rightarrow$ *a runs next*
9	$t = 27$	a	c wakes up $E_a^4 = A_a^4 = A_a^3 + 2\Delta/3 = 150 + 60 = 210$ $[E_a(27), E_b(27), E_c(27)] = (210, 210, 120) \Rightarrow$ *c runs next*
10	$t = 30$	c	$SVT = \min(210, 210)$ $E_c^s(30) = SVT + W_c = 210 + (-60) = 150$ $E_c(30) = E_c^s(30) + \Delta/3 = 150 + 30 = 180 \Rightarrow$ *b runs next*
11	$t = 32$	b	$E_b^4 = A_b^4 = A_b^3 + 2\Delta/3 = 210 + 60 = 270 \Rightarrow$ *a runs next*
10	$t = 36$	a	c wakes up $E_a^5 = A_a^5 = A_a^4 + 2\Delta/3 = 210 + 60 = 270$ $[E_a(36), E_b(36), E_c(36)] = (270, 270, 180) \Rightarrow$ *c runs next*
12	$t = 39$	c	$SVT = \min(270, 270)$ $E_c^s(39) = SVT + W_c = 270 + (-60) = 210$ $E_c(39) = E_c^s(39) + \Delta/3 = 210 + 30 = 240 \Rightarrow$ *b runs next*
13	$t = 41$	b	$E_b^5 = A_b^5 = A_b^4 + 2\Delta/3 = 270 + 60 = 330 \Rightarrow$ *a runs next*

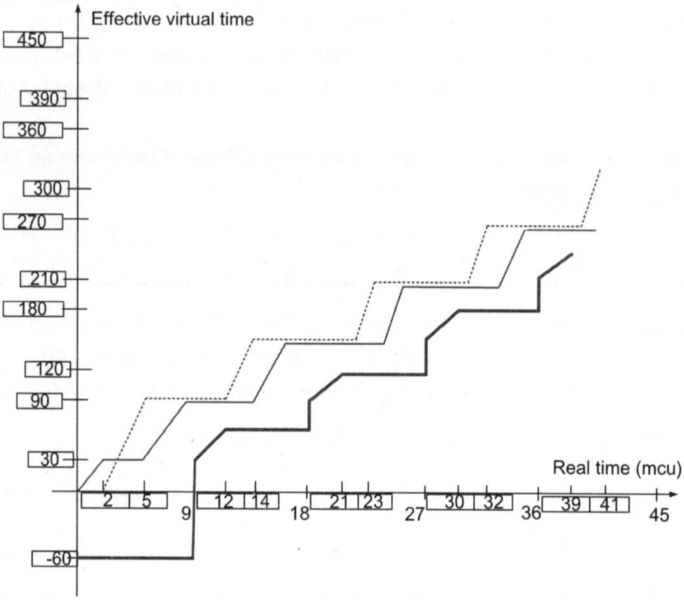

FIGURE 6.12

Example 2, the effective virtual time and the real time of threads *a* (thin solid line), *b* (dotted line), and *c*, with real-time constraints (thick solid line). *c* wakes up periodically at times $t = 9, 18, 27, 36, \ldots$, is active for 3 units of time, and has a time warp of 60 *mcu*.

are triggered by the waking up of thread c, which preempts the currently running thread. At $t = 9$ the time warp $W_c = -60$ gives priority to thread c. Indeed,

$$E_c(9) = A_c(9) - W_c = 0 - 60 = -60 \tag{6.68}$$

compared with $E_a(9) = 90$ and $E_b(9) = 90$. The same conditions occur every time the real-time thread c wakes up. The best-effort application threads have the same effective virtual time when the real-time application thread finishes and the scheduler chooses b to be dispatched first. Note that the ratio of real times used by a and b is the same, as $w_a = 2w_b$.

Figure 6.12 shows the effective virtual times for the three threads a, b, and c. Every time thread c wakes up, it preempts the current running thread and is immediately scheduled to run.

6.12 Cloud scheduling subject to deadlines

Often, an SLA specifies the time when the results of computations done on the cloud should be available. This motivates us to examine cloud scheduling subject to deadlines, a topic drawing on a vast body of literature devoted to real-time applications.

Task Characterization and Deadlines. Real-time applications involve periodic or aperiodic tasks with deadlines. A task is characterized by a tuple (A_i, σ_i, D_i), where A_i is the arrival time, $\sigma_i > 0$ is the data size of the task, and D_i is the *relative deadline*. Instances of a *periodic task*, Π_i^q, with period q are identical, $\Pi_i^q = \Pi^q$, and arrive at times $A_0, A_1, \ldots A_i, \ldots$, with $A_{i+1} - A_i = q$. The deadlines satisfy the constraint $D_i \leqslant A_{i+1}$ and generally the data size is the same, $\sigma_i = \sigma$. The individual instances of *aperiodic tasks*, Π_i, are different. Their arrival times A_i are generally uncorrelated, and the amount of data σ_i is different for different instances. The *absolute deadline* for the aperiodic task Π_i is $(A_i + D_i)$.

We distinguish *hard deadlines* from *soft deadlines*. In the first case, if the task is not completed by the deadline, other tasks that depend on it may be affected and there are penalties; a hard deadline is strict and expressed precisely as milliseconds or possibly seconds. Soft deadlines play more of a guideline role and, in general, there are no penalties. Soft deadlines can be missed by fractions of the units used to express them, e.g., minutes if the deadline is expressed in hours, or hours if the deadlines is expressed in days. The scheduling of tasks on a cloud is generally subject to soft deadlines, though occasionally applications with hard deadlines may be encountered.

System Model. In our discussion we consider only aperiodic tasks with arbitrarily divisible workloads. The application runs on a partition of a cloud, a virtual cloud with a *head node* called S_0 and n *worker nodes* $S_1, S_2, \ldots, S_n$. The system is homogeneous, all workers are identical, and the communication time from the head node to any worker node is the same. The head node distributes the workload to worker nodes, and this distribution is done sequentially. In this context there are two important problems:

1. The order of execution of the tasks Π_i.
2. The workload partitioning and the task mapping to worker nodes.

Scheduling Policies. The most common scheduling policies used to determine the order of execution of the tasks are:

- First in, first out (FIFO). The tasks are scheduled for execution in the order of their arrival.
- Earliest deadline first (EDF). The task with the earliest deadline is scheduled first.
- Maximum workload derivative first (MWF).

The *workload derivative* $DC_i(n^{min})$ of a task Π_i when n^{min} nodes are assigned to the application, is defined as

$$DC_i(n^{min}) = W_i\left(n_i^{min} + 1\right) - W_i\left(n_i^{min}\right), \tag{6.69}$$

with $W_i(n)$ the workload allocated to task Π_i when n nodes of the cloud are available; if $\mathcal{E}(\sigma_i, n)$ is the execution time of the task, then $W_i(n) = n \times \mathcal{E}(\sigma_i, n)$. The MWF policy requires that:

1. The tasks are scheduled in the order of their derivatives, the one with the highest derivative DC_i first.
2. The number n of nodes assigned to the application is kept to a minimum, n_i^{min}.

We discuss two workload partitioning and task mappings to worker nodes, optimal and the equal partitioning.

Optimal Partitioning Rule (OPR). The optimality in OPR refers to the execution time; in this case, the workload is partitioned to ensure the earliest possible completion time, and all tasks are required to

Table 6.7 The parameters used for scheduling with deadlines.

Name	Description
Π_i	The aperiodic tasks with arbitrary divisible load of an application $\mathcal{A}$
A_i	Arrival time of task Π_i
D_i	The relative deadline of task Π_i
σ_i	The workload allocated to task Π_i
S_0	Head node of the virtual cloud allocated to $\mathcal{A}$
S_i	Worker nodes $1 \leqslant i \leqslant n$ of the virtual cloud allocated to $\mathcal{A}$
σ	Total workload for application $\mathcal{A}$
n	Number of nodes of the virtual cloud allocated to application $\mathcal{A}$
n^{min}	Minimum number of nodes of the virtual cloud allocated to application $\mathcal{A}$
$\mathcal{E}(n, \sigma)$	The execution time required by n worker nodes to process the workload σ
τ	Cost of transferring a unit of workload from the head node S_0 to worker S_i
ρ	Cost of processing a unit of workload
α	The load distribution vector $\alpha = (\alpha_1, \alpha_2, \ldots, \alpha_n)$
$\alpha_i \times \sigma$	The fraction of the workload allocated to worker node S_i
Γ_i	Time to transfer the data to worker S_i, $\Gamma_i = \alpha_i \times \sigma \times \tau$, $1 \leqslant i \leqslant n$
Δ_i	Time the worker S_i needs to process a unit of data, $\Delta_i = \alpha_i \times \sigma \times \rho$, $1 \leqslant i \leqslant n$
t_0	Start time of the application $\mathcal{A}$
A	Arrival time of the application $\mathcal{A}$
D	Deadline of application $\mathcal{A}$
$C(n)$	Completion time of application $\mathcal{A}$

complete at the same time. EPR, as the name suggests, means that the workload is partitioned in equal segments. In our discussion we use the derivations and some of the notations in [218]; these notations are summarized in Table 6.7.

The timing diagram in Figure 6.13 allows us to determine the execution time $\mathcal{E}(n, \sigma)$ for the OPR as

$$
\begin{aligned}
\mathcal{E}(n, \sigma) &= \Gamma_1 + \Delta_1 \\
&= \Gamma_1 + \Gamma_2 + \Delta_2 \\
&= \Gamma_1 + \Gamma_2 + \Gamma_3 + \Delta_3 \\
&\ \ \vdots \\
&= \Gamma_1 + \Gamma_2 + \Gamma_3 + \cdots + \Gamma_n + \Delta_n.
\end{aligned}
\tag{6.70}
$$

We substitute the expressions of $\Gamma_i, \Delta_i, 1 \leqslant i \leqslant n$, and rewrite these equations as

$$
\begin{aligned}
\mathcal{E}(n, \sigma) &= \alpha_1 \times \sigma \times \tau + \alpha_1 \times \sigma \times \rho \\
&= \alpha_1 \times \sigma \times \tau + \alpha_2 \times \sigma \times \tau + \alpha_2 \times \sigma \times \rho \\
&= \alpha_1 \times \sigma \times \tau + \alpha_2 \times \sigma \times \tau + \alpha_3 \times \sigma \times \tau + \alpha_3 \times \sigma \times \rho \\
&= \vdots \\
&= \alpha_1 \times \sigma \times \tau + \alpha_2 \times \sigma \times \tau + \alpha_3 \times \sigma \times \tau + \cdots + \alpha_n \times \sigma \times \tau + \alpha_n \times \sigma \times \rho.
\end{aligned}
\tag{6.71}
$$

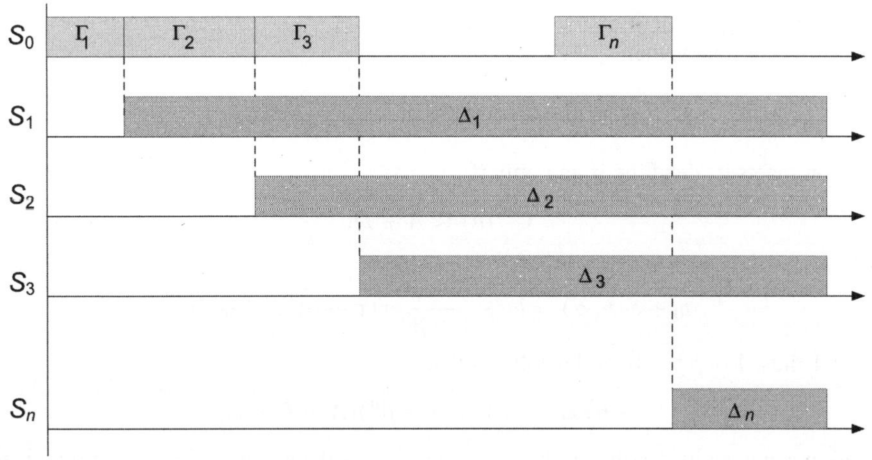

FIGURE 6.13

The timing diagram for the optimal partitioning rule. The algorithm requires worker nodes to complete execution at the same time. The head node, S_0, distributes sequentially the data to individual worker nodes. The communication time is $\Gamma_i = \alpha_i \times \sigma \times \tau, 1 \leqslant i \leqslant n$. Worker node S_i starts processing the data as soon as the transfer is complete. The processing time is $\Delta_i = \alpha_i \times \sigma \times \rho, 1 \leqslant i \leqslant n$.

From the first two equations we find the relation between α_1 and α_2 as

$$\alpha_1 = \frac{\alpha_2}{\beta} \quad \text{with} \quad \beta = \frac{\rho}{\tau + \rho}, \quad 0 \leqslant \beta \leqslant 1. \tag{6.72}$$

This implies that $\alpha_2 = \beta \times \alpha_1$. It is easy to see that in the general case

$$\alpha_i = \beta \times \alpha_{i-1} = \beta^{i-1} \times \alpha_1. \tag{6.73}$$

But α_i are the components of the load distribution vector; thus,

$$\sum_{i=1}^{n} \alpha_i = 1. \tag{6.74}$$

Next, we substitute the values of α_i and obtain the expression for α_1:

$$\alpha_1 + \beta \times \alpha_1 + \beta^2 \times \alpha_1 + \beta^3 \times \alpha_1 \ldots \beta^{n-1} \times \alpha_1 = 1 \quad \text{or} \quad \alpha_1 = \frac{1-\beta}{1-\beta^n}. \tag{6.75}$$

We have now determined the load distribution vector and we can now determine the execution time as

$$\mathcal{E}(n, \sigma) = \alpha_1 \times \sigma \times \tau + \alpha_1 \times \sigma \times \rho = \frac{1-\beta}{1-\beta^n}\sigma(\tau + \rho). \tag{6.76}$$

Call $C^{\mathcal{A}}(n)$ the completion time of an application $\mathcal{A} = (A, \sigma, D)$, which starts processing at time t_0 and runs on n worker nodes; then

$$C^{\mathcal{A}}(n) = t_0 + \mathcal{E}(n, \sigma) = t_0 + \frac{1-\beta}{1-\beta^n}\sigma(\tau + \rho). \tag{6.77}$$

The application meets its deadline if and only if

$$C^{\mathcal{A}}(n) \leqslant A + D, \tag{6.78}$$

or

$$t_0 + \mathcal{E}(n, \sigma) = t_0 + \frac{1-\beta}{1-\beta^n}\sigma(\tau + \rho) \leqslant A + D. \tag{6.79}$$

But $0 < \beta < 1$ thus, $1 - \beta^n > 0$, and it follows that

$$(1-\beta)\sigma(\tau + \rho) \leqslant (1-\beta^n)(A + D - t_0). \tag{6.80}$$

The application can meet its deadline only if $(A + D - t_0) > 0$, and under this condition this inequality becomes

$$\beta^n \leqslant \gamma \quad \text{with} \quad \gamma = 1 - \frac{\sigma \times \tau}{A + D - t_0}. \tag{6.81}$$

If $\gamma \leqslant 0$, there is not enough time even for data distribution and the application should be rejected. When $\gamma > 0$, then $n \geqslant \frac{\ln \gamma}{\ln \beta}$. Thus, the minimum number of nodes for the OPR strategy is

$$n^{min} = \lceil \frac{\ln \gamma}{\ln \beta} \rceil. \tag{6.82}$$

Equal Partitioning Rule (EPR). EPR assigns an equal workload to individual worker nodes, $\alpha_i = 1/n$. From the diagram in Figure 6.14 we see that

$$\mathcal{E}(n, \sigma) = \sum_{i=1}^{n} \Gamma_i + \Delta_n = n \times \frac{\sigma}{n} \times \tau + \frac{\sigma}{n} \times \rho = \sigma \times \tau + \frac{\sigma}{n} \times \rho. \tag{6.83}$$

The condition for meeting the deadline, $C^{\mathcal{A}}(n) \leqslant A + D$, leads to

$$t_0 + \sigma \times \tau + \frac{\sigma}{n} \times \rho \leqslant A + D \text{ or } n \geqslant \frac{\sigma \times \rho}{A + D - t_0 - \sigma \times \tau}. \tag{6.84}$$

Thus,

$$n^{min} = \left\lceil \frac{\sigma \times \rho}{A + D - t_0 - \sigma \times \tau} \right\rceil. \tag{6.85}$$

The pseudocode for a general schedulability test for FIFO, EDF, and MWF scheduling policies, for two-node allocation policies, MN (minimum number of nodes) and AN (all nodes), and for OPR and EPR partitioning rules is given in reference [218]. The same paper reports on a simulation study for 10 algorithms. The generic format of the names of the algorithms is **Sp-No-Pa**, with **Sp** = FIFO/EDF/MWF, **No** = MN/AN, and **Pa** = OPR/EPR. For example, MWF-MN-OPR uses MWF scheduling, minimum number of nodes, and OPR partitioning. The relative performance of the algorithms depends on the relations between the unit cost of communication τ and the unit cost of computing ρ.

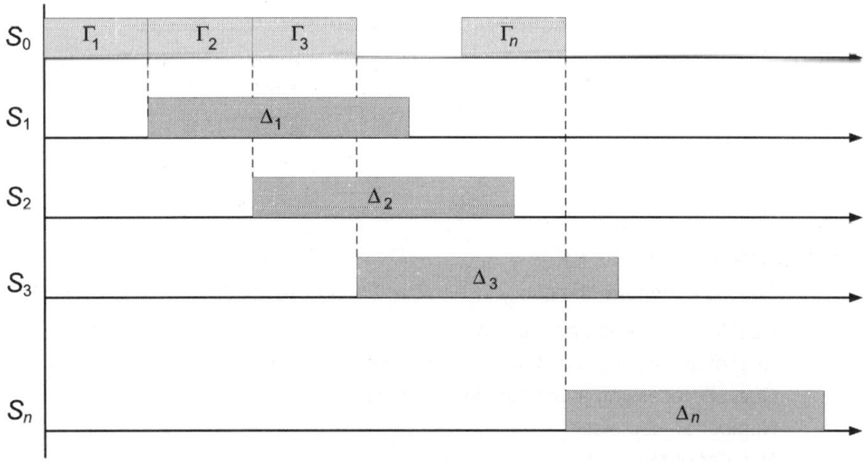

FIGURE 6.14

The timing diagram for the equal partitioning rule. The algorithm assigns an equal workload to individual worker nodes, $\alpha_i = 1/n$. The head node, S_0, distributes sequentially the data to individual worker nodes. The communication time is $\Gamma_i = (\sigma/n) \times \tau, 1 \leqslant i \leqslant n$. Worker node S_i starts processing the data as soon as the transfer is complete. The processing time is $\Delta_i = (\sigma/n) \times \rho, 1 \leqslant i \leqslant n$.

6.13 Scheduling *MapReduce* applications subject to deadlines

Now we turn our attention to applications of the analysis in Section 6.12 and discuss scheduling of *MapReduce* applications on the cloud subject to deadlines. Several options for scheduling Apache *Hadoop*, an open-source implementation of the *MapReduce* algorithm, are:

- The default FIFO schedule.
- The Fair Scheduler [383].
- The Capacity Scheduler.
- The Dynamic Proportional Scheduler [315].

A recent paper [186] applies the deadline scheduling framework analyzed to *Hadoop* tasks. Table 6.8 summarizes the notations used for the analysis of *Hadoop*; the term *slots* is equivalent with *nodes* and means the number of instances.

We make two assumptions for our initial derivation:

- The system is homogeneous; this means that ρ_m and ρ_r, the cost of processing a unit data by the *map* and the *reduce* task, respectively, are the same for all servers.
- Load equipartition.

Under these conditions the duration of the job J with input of size σ is

$$\mathcal{E}(n_m, n_r, \sigma) = \sigma \left[\frac{\rho_m}{n_m} + \phi \left(\frac{\rho_r}{n_r} + \tau \right) \right]. \tag{6.86}$$

Table 6.8 The parameters used for scheduling with deadlines.

Name	Description
Q	The query $Q = (A, \sigma, D)$
A	Arrival time of query Q
D	Deadline of query Q
Π_m^i	A map task, $1 \leqslant i \leqslant u$
Π_r^j	A reduce task, $1 \leqslant j \leqslant v$
J	The job to perform the query $Q = (A, \sigma, D)$, $J = \left(\Pi_m^1, \Pi_m^2, \ldots, \Pi_m^u, \Pi_r^1, \Pi_r^2, \ldots, \Pi_r^v\right)$
τ	Cost for transferring a data unit
ρ_m	Cost of processing a unit data in map task
ρ_r	Cost of processing a unit data in reduce task
n_m	Number of map slots
n_r	Number of reduce slots
n_m^{min}	Minimum number of slots for the map task
n	Total number of slots, $n = n_m + n_r$
t_m^0	Start time of the map task
t_r^{max}	Maximum value for the start time of the reduce task
α	Map distribution vector; the EPR strategy is used and, $\alpha_i = 1/u$
ϕ	Filter ratio, the fraction of the input produced as output by the map process

Thus, the condition that query $Q = (A, \sigma, D)$ with arrival time A meets the deadline D can be expressed as

$$t_m^0 + \sigma\left[\frac{\rho_m}{n_m} + \phi\left(\frac{\rho_r}{n_r} + \tau\right)\right] \leqslant A + D. \tag{6.87}$$

It follows immediately that the maximum value for the start-up time of the *reduce* task is

$$t_r^{max} = A + D - \sigma\phi\left(\frac{\rho_r}{n_r} + \tau\right). \tag{6.88}$$

We now plug the expression of the maximum value for the start-up time of the *reduce* task into the condition to meet the deadline

$$t_m^0 + \sigma\frac{\rho_m}{n_m} \leqslant t_r^{max}. \tag{6.89}$$

It follows immediately that n_m^{min}, the minimum number of slots for the *map* task, satisfies the condition

$$n_m^{min} \geqslant \frac{\sigma\rho_m}{t_r^{max} - t_m^0}, \quad \text{thus,} \quad n_m^{min} = \left\lceil \frac{\sigma\rho_m}{t_r^{max} - t_m^0} \right\rceil. \tag{6.90}$$

The assumption of homogeneity of the servers can be relaxed and we assume that individual servers have different costs for processing a unit workload $\rho_m^i \neq \rho_m^j$ and $\rho_t^i \neq \rho_t^j$. In this case we can use the minimum values $\rho_m = \min \rho_m^i$ and $\rho_r = \min \rho_r^i$ in the expression we derived.

A Constraints Scheduler based on this analysis and an evaluation of the effectiveness of this scheduler are presented in [186].

6.14 Resource management and dynamic application scaling

The demand for computing resources, such as CPU cycles, primary and secondary storage, and network bandwidth, depends heavily on the volume of data processed by an application. The demand for resources can be a function of the time of day, can monotonically increase or decrease in time, or can experience predictable or unpredictable peaks. For example, a new Web service will experience a low request rate when the service is first introduced and the load will exponentially increase if the service is successful. A service for income tax processing will experience a peak around the tax filling deadline, whereas access to a service provided by Federal Emergency Management Agency (FEMA) will increase dramatically after a natural disaster.

The elasticity of a public cloud, the fact that it can supply to an application precisely the amount of resources it needs and that users pay only for the resources they consume are serious incentives to migrate to a public cloud. The question we address is: How scaling can actually be implemented in a cloud when a very large number of applications exhibit this often unpredictable behavior [62,233,357]. To make matters worse, in addition to an unpredictable external load the cloud resource management has to deal with resource reallocation due to server failures.

We distinguish two scaling modes: vertical and horizontal. *Vertical scaling* keeps the number of VMs of an application constant, but increases the amount of resources allocated to each one of them. This can be done either by migrating the VMs to more powerful servers or by keeping the VMs on the same servers but increasing their share of the CPU time. The first alternative involves additional overhead; the VM is stopped, a snapshot of it is taken, the file is transported to a more powerful server, and, finally, the VM is restated at the new site.

Horizontal scaling is the most common mode of scaling on a cloud; it is done by increasing the number of VMs as the load increases and reducing the number of VMs when the load decreases. Often, this leads to an increase in communication bandwidth consumed by the application. Load balancing among the running VMs is critical to this mode of operation. For a very large application, multiple load balancers may need to cooperate with one another. In some instances the load balancing is done by a front-end server that distributes incoming requests of a transaction-oriented system to back-end servers.

An application should be designed to support scaling. As we saw in Section 4.6 in the case of a *modularly divisible* application, the workload partitioning is static, it is decided a priori, and cannot be changed; thus, the only alternative is vertical scaling. In the case of an *arbitrarily divisible* application the workload can be partitioned dynamically; as the load increases, the system can allocate additional VMs to process the additional workload. Most cloud applications belong to this class, which justifies our statement that horizontal scaling is the most common scaling mode.

Mapping a computation means to assign suitable physical servers to the application. A very important first step in application processing is to identify the type of application and map it accordingly. For example, a communication-intensive application should be mapped to a powerful server to minimize the network traffic. This may increase the cost per unit of CPU usage, but it will decrease the computing time and probably reduce the overall cost for the user. At the same time, it will reduce the network traffic, a highly desirable effect from the perspective of the cloud service provider. To scale up and down a compute-intensive application, a good strategy is to increase or decrease the number of VMs or instances. Because the load is relatively stable, the overhead of starting up or terminating an instance does not increase significantly the computing time or the cost.

There are several strategies to support scaling. *Automatic VM scaling* uses predefined metrics, e.g., CPU utilization, to make scaling decisions. Automatic scaling requires *sensors* to monitor the state of VMs and servers; *controllers* make decisions based on the information about the state of the cloud, often using a state machine model for decision making. Amazon and Rightscale (`www.rightscale.com`) offer automatic scaling. In the case of *AWS* the *CloudWatch* service supports applications monitoring and allows a user to set up conditions for automatic migrations.

Nonscalable or single-load balancers are also used for horizontal scaling. The *Elastic Load Balancing* service from Amazon automatically distributes incoming application traffic across multiple *EC2* instances. Another service, the *Elastic Beanstalk*, allows dynamic scaling between a low and a high number of instances specified by the user (see Section 3.1). The cloud user usually has to pay for the more sophisticated scaling services such as *Elastic Beanstalk*.

6.15 Further reading

Cloud resource management poses new and extremely challenging problems, so it should be no surprise that it is a very active area of research. A fair number of papers, including [22,65,75,77,113,114,115,120, 138,139,151,155,162,184,238,275,307,313] are dedicated to various resource management policies. Several papers are concerned with SLA and QoS; e.g., [4] covers SLA-driven capacity management and [23] covers SLA-based resource allocation policies. Dynamic request scheduling of applications subject to SLA requirements is presented in [54]. The QoS in clouds is analyzed in [121].

Autonomic computing [130] is the subject of papers such as [24], which covers energy-aware resource allocation in autonomic computing; [188], which analyzes policies for autonomic computing based on utility functions; [187], which discusses coordination of multiple autonomic managers and power-performance tradeoffs; and [9], which presents autonomic management of cloud services subject to availability guarantees.

Auctions in which participants can bid on combinations of items or *packages* are called *combinatorial auctions* [93]. Such auctions provide a relatively simple, scalable, and tractable solution to cloud resource allocation. Two recent combinatorial auction algorithms are the *simultaneous clock auction* [29] and the *clock proxy auction* [30]; the algorithm discussed in this chapter and introduced in [333] is called the *ascending clock auction (ASCA)*.

An authoritative reference on fault tolerance is [31]; applications of control theory to resource allocation discussed in [70,109] cover resource multiplexing in data centers. Admission control policies are discussed in [150]. Power and performance management are the subject of [202], and performance management for cluster-based Web services is covered in [280]. Autonomic management of heterogeneous workloads is discussed in [344], and application placement controllers are the topic of [346].

Scheduling and resource allocation are also covered by numerous papers: a batch queuing system on clouds with *Hadoop and HBase* is presented in [387]; data flow-driven scheduling for business applications is covered in [106]. Scalable thread scheduling is the topic of [374]. Scheduling of real-time services in cloud computing is presented in [220]. The Open Grid Forum (OGF) Open Cloud

Computing Interface (OCCI) is involved in the definition of virtualization formats and APIs for *IaaS* [175] presents a performance analyzer.

6.16 Exercises and problems

Problem 1. Analyze the benefits and the problems posed by the four approaches to the implementation of resource management policies: control theory, machine learning, utility-based, and market-oriented.

Problem 2. Can optimal strategies for the five classes of policy – admission control, capacity allocation, load balancing, energy optimization, and QoS guarantees – be actually implemented in a cloud? The term *optimal* is used in the sense of control theory. Support your answer with solid arguments. Optimal strategies for one could be in conflict with optimal strategies for one or more of the other classes. Identify and analyze such cases.

Problem 3. Analyze the relationship between the scale of a system and the policies and the mechanisms for resource management. In your arguments, consider also the geographic scale of the system.

Problem 4. What are the limitations of the control theoretic approach discussed in Section 6.2? Do the approaches discussed in Sections 6.3 and 6.4 remove or relax some of these limitations? Justify your answers.

Problem 5. Multiple controllers are probably necessary due to the scale of a cloud. Is it beneficial to have system and application controllers? Should the controllers be specialized – for example, some to monitor performance, others to monitor power consumption? Should all the functions we want to base the resource management policies on be integrated in a single controller and one such controller be assigned to a given number of servers or a geographic region? Justify your answers.

Problem 6. In a scale-free network, the nodes have an exponential degree distribution (see Section 7.11). A scale-free network could be used as a virtual network infrastructure for cloud computing. *Controllers* represent a dedicated class of nodes tasked with resource management. In a scale-free network, nodes with high connectivity can be designated as controllers. Analyze the potential benefit of such a strategy.

Problem 7. Use the start-time fair queuing (SFQ) scheduling algorithm to compute the virtual start-up and the virtual finish time for two threads a and b with weights $w_a = 1$ and $w_b = 5$ when the time quantum is $q = 15$ and thread b blocks at time $t = 24$ and wakes up at time $t = 60$. Plot the virtual time of the scheduler function of the real time.

Problem 8. Apply the borrowed virtual time (BVT) scheduling algorithm to the problem in Example 2 of Section 6.11 but with a time warp of $W_c = -30$.

Problem 9. Consider the workflow for your favorite cloud application. Use XML to describe this workflow, including the instances and the storage required for each task. Translate this description into a file that can be used for the *Elastic Beanstalk AWS*.

CHAPTER

Networking Support

7

Cloud computing and delivery of content stored on a cloud are feasible only due to the interconnectivity supported by a continually evolving Internet and by the access to remote resources provided by the World Wide Web. A cloud is built around a high-performance interconnect; the servers in a cloud communicate through high-bandwidth and low-latency specialized networks. It is thus obvious why networking will continue to play a crucial role in the evolution of cloud computing and a content-centric world.

This chapter starts with a review of basic concepts related to packet switching and the Internet in Sections 7.1 and 7.2. The need to accommodate a very large address space is discussed in Section 7.3; then the transformational changes suffered by the Internet under the pressure of applications are surveyed in Section 7.4. Section 7.5 covers statistics regarding Web metrics and the arguments for increasing the initial congestion control window in TCP. Models for network resource management are analyzed in Section 7.6. Efficient topologies for computer clouds and storage area networks are discussed in Sections 7.7 and 7.8, respectively. Overlay networks, small-world networks, and scale-free networks are presented in Sections 7.10 and 7.11. Finally, Section 7.12 is devoted to a discussion of epidemic algorithms.

7.1 Packet-switched networks

The access to a cloud is provided by the Internet, a packet-switched network; thus, we start our discussion with an overview of this important concept. A *packet-switched network* transports data units called *packets* through a maze of *switches*, where packets are queued and routed toward their destination. Packets are subject to a variable delay and loss and possibly arrive at their final destination out of order. A *datagram* is a basic transfer unit in a packet-switched network; it consists of a header, which contains control information necessary for its transport through the network, and a payload or data.

A packet-switched network has a *network core* consisting of routers and control systems interconnected by very high-bandwidth communication channels and a *network edge* where the end-user systems reside. A *network architecture* describes the protocol stack used for communication. A *protocol* is a discipline for communication that specifies the actions taken by the sender and the receiver of a data unit. We use the term *host* to describe a system located at the network edge and capable of initiating and receiving communication, whether a computer, a mobile device such as an phone, or a sensor.

This very concise description hints that a packet-switched network is a complex system consisting of a very large number of autonomous components and subject to complex and sometimes contradictory requirements. Basic strategies for implementing a complex system are *layering* and *modularization*; this means decomposing a complex function into components that interact through well-defined channels (e.g., a layer can only communicate with its two adjacent layers).

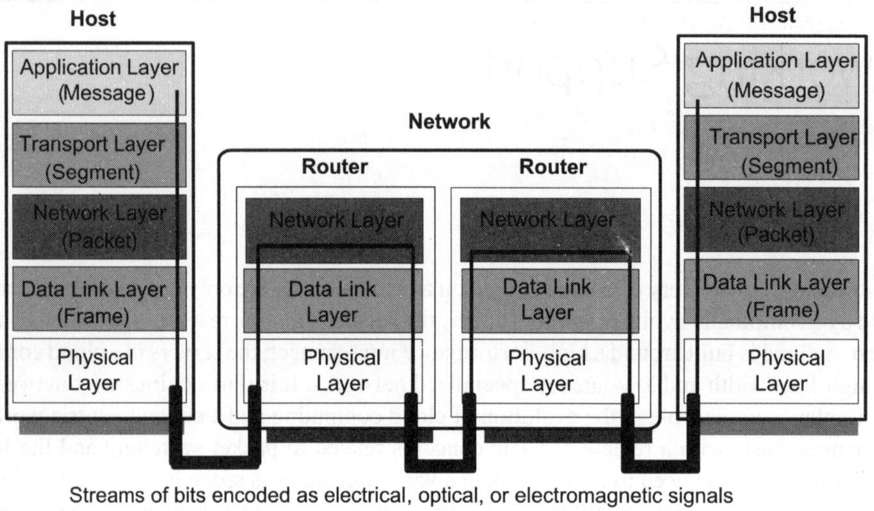

FIGURE 7.1

Protocol stacks. Applications running on hosts at the edge of the network communicate using application layer protocols. The transport layer deals with end-to-end delivery. The network layer is responsible for routing a packet through the network. The data link layer ensures reliable communication between adjacent nodes of the network, and the physical layer transports streams of bits encoded as electrical, optical, or electromagnetic signals (the thick lines represent such bit pipes). The corresponding data units for the five-layer architecture are messages, segments, packets, frames, and encoded bits, respectively.

All network architectures are based on layering; this justifies the term *protocol stack*, as shown in Figure 7.1. In the Internet architecture the *network layer* is responsible for routing packets through the packet-switched network from the source to the destination. The *transport layer* is responsible for end-to-end communication, from an application running on the sending host to its peer running on the destination host.

Physically, at the sender site the data flows down the protocol stack from the application layer to the transport, network, and data link layers; the streams of bits are pushed through a physical communication link encoded as electrical, optical, or electromagnetic signals. Once they reach a router, the bits are passed to the data link and then to the network layer.

The network layer decides where the packet should be sent, either to another router or to a destination host connected to a local area network connected to the router. Then the data link layer encapsulates the packet for the communication link to the next hop, and then the bit stream is passed to the next physical channel (see Figure 7.1). At the receiving end the data flows upward from the data link to the application layer.

A protocol on one system *communicates logically* with its *peer* on another system. For example, the transport protocol on the sender, host A, communicates with the transport protocol on the receiver, host B. On the sending side, A, the transport protocol encapsulates the data from the application layer and adds control information as headers that can only be understood by its peer, the transport layer on host B.

When the peer receives the data unit, it carries out a decapsulation, retrieves the control information, removes the headers, then passes the payload to the next layer up, the application layer on host B.

The payload for the data link layer at the sending side includes the network header and the payload at the network layer. In turn, the network layer payload includes a transport layer header and its payload, consisting of the application layer header and application data.

7.2 The Internet

The Internet is a collection of separate and distinct networks, each one operating under a common framework consisting of globally unique IP addressing and using IP routing and global Border Gateway Routing (BGP) protocols.[1] An *IP address* is a string of integers uniquely identifying every host connected to the Internet; the IP address allows the network to identify first the destination network and then the host in that network to which a datagram should be delivered.

In addition to the IP or logical address, each network interface, the hardware connecting a host with a network, has a unique *physical* or *MAC address*. Although the MAC address is permanently assigned to a network interface of the device, the IP address may be dynamically assigned and changes depending on the network. For example, a laptop will get a different IP address when it is connected to different networks and a phone will get different IP addresses in different Wi-Fi networks. A host may have multiple network interfaces and, consequently, multiple IP addresses when it is connected to multiple networks.

The Internet is based on a hourglass network architecture and the TCP/IP protocol family (see Figure 7.2). The hourglass model captures the fact that all packets transported through the Internet use Internet Protocol (IP) to reach the destination. IP ensures datagrams' delivery from the source host to the destination host based on their IP addresses. A host could be a supercomputer, a workstation, a laptop, a mobile phone, a network printer, or any other physical device with a network interface.

IP only provides *best-effort delivery* and its service is characterized as unreliable. Best-effort delivery means that any router on the path from the source to the destination may drop a packet when it is overloaded.

The Internet uses two transport protocols: a connectionless datagram protocol, User Datagram Protocol (UDP), and a connection-oriented protocol, Transport Control Protocol (TCP). The header of a datagram contains information sufficient for routing through the network from the source to the destination.

To ensure efficient communication, the UDP transport protocol assumes that error checking and error correction are either not necessary or performed by the application. Datagrams may arrive out of order or duplicated, or may not arrive at all. Applications using UDP include the Domain Name System (DNS), Voice over IP (VoIP), Trivial File Transfer Protocol (TFTP), streaming media applications such as Internet Protocol television (IPTV), and online games.

Once a packet reaches the destination host, it is delivered to the proper transport protocol daemon, which, in turn, delivers it to the application that listens to an abstraction of the endpoint of a logical communication channel called a *port* (see Figure 7.3). The processes or threads running an application

[1] The Border Gateway Protocol (BGP) is a path vector reachability protocol that makes the core routing decisions on the Internet. It maintains a table of networks that designate network reachability among autonomous systems. BGP makes routing decisions based on path, network policies, and/or rule sets.

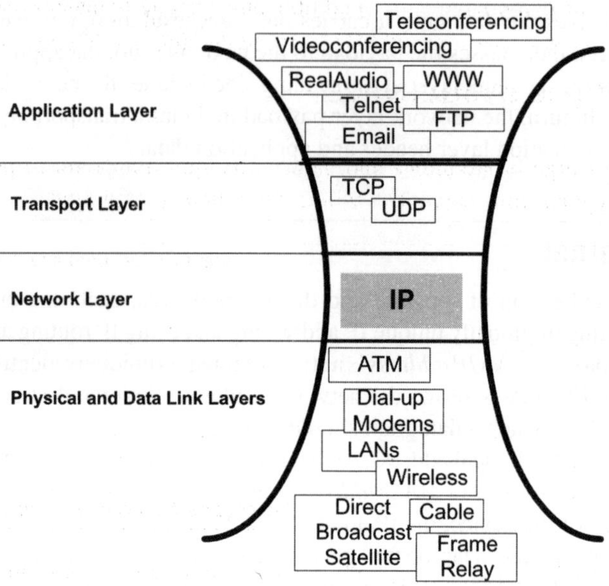

FIGURE 7.2

The hourglass network architecture of the Internet. Regardless of the application, the transport protocol, and the physical network, all packets are routed through the Internet from the source to the destination by the IP protocol, and routing is based on the destination IP address.

use an abstraction called *socket* to send and receive data through the network. A socket manages a queue of incoming messages and one of outgoing messages.

TCP provides reliable, ordered delivery of a stream of bytes from an application on one system to its peer on the destination system. An application sends/receives data units called *segments* to/from a specific port, an abstraction of and endpoint of a logical communication link. TCP is the transport protocol used by the World Wide Web, email, file transfer, remote administration, and many other important applications.

TCP uses an end-to-end *flow control mechanism* based on a sliding window, a range of packets the sender can send before receiving an acknowledgment from the receiver. This mechanism allows the receiver to control the rate of segments sent and process them reliably.

A network has a finite capacity to transport data, and when its load is approaching this capacity, we witness undesirable effects: The routers start dropping packets, and the delays and the jitter increase. An obvious analogy is a highway on which the time to travel from point A to point B increases dramatically when the highway becomes congested; a solution for traffic management is to introduce traffic lights limiting the rate at which new traffic is allowed to enter the highway, and this is precisely what the TCP emulates.

TCP uses several mechanisms for *congestion control* (see Section 7.5). These mechanisms control the rate of data entering the network, keeping the data flow below a rate that would lead to a network

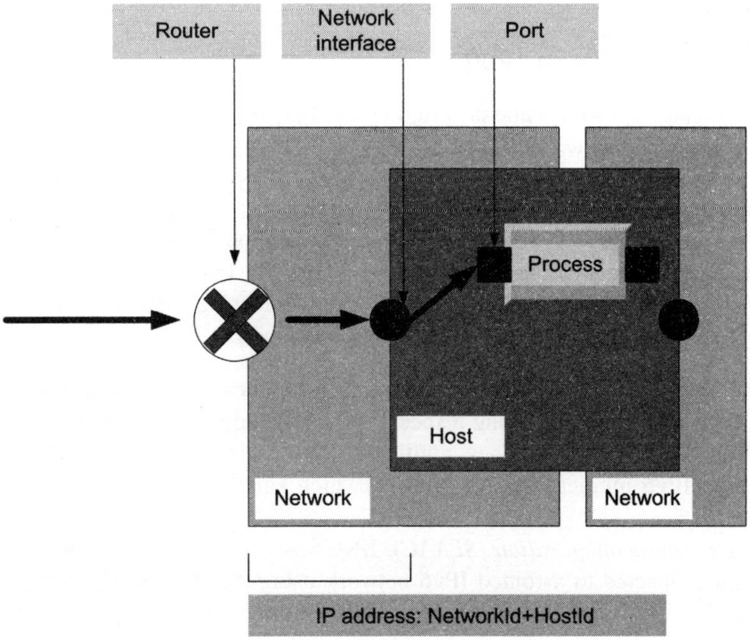

FIGURE 7.3

Packet delivery to processes and threads. The packet is first routed by the IP protocol to the destination network and then to the host specified by the IP address. Each application listens to an abstraction of the endpoint of a logical communication channel called a *port*.

collapse and enforce a max/min fair allocation between flows. Section acknowledgment coupled to timers is used to infer network conditions between the sender and receiver.

TCP congestion control policies are based on four algorithms: *slow-start, congestion avoidance, fast retransmit*, and *fast recovery*. These algorithms use local information, such as the retransmission timeout (RTO) based on the estimated round-trip time (RTT) between the sender and receiver as well as the variance in this round-trip time to implement the congestion control policies. UDP is a connectionless protocol, so there are no means to control the UDP traffic.

The review of basic networking concepts in this section shows why process-to-process communication incurs a significant overhead. Though raw speed of fiber optic channels can reach Tbps,[2] the actual transmission rate for end-to-end communication over a wide area network can only be of the order of tens of Mbps and the latency is of the order of milliseconds. This has important consequences for the development of computer clouds.

[2]Nippon Telegraph and Telephone (NTT) achieved a speed of 69.1 Tbps in 2010; to do so it used wavelength division multiplex (WDM) of 432 wavelengths with a capacity of 171 Gbps over a single 240-km-long optical fiber. Note that the term *speed* is used informally to describe the maximum data transmission rate, or the capacity of a communication channel. This capacity is determined by the physical bandwidth of the channel and explains why the term *channel bandwidth* is also used to measure the channel capacity, or the maximum data rate.

7.3 Internet migration to IPv6

The Internet addressing capabilities and the migration of IPv6 are important for cloud computing, as we shall see in this section. The Internet Protocol, Version 4 (IPv4), provides an addressing capability of 2^{32}, or approximately 4.3 billion addresses, a number that proved to be insufficient. Indeed, the Internet Assigned Numbers Authority (IANA) assigned the last batch of five address blocks to the Regional Internet Registries in February 2011, officially depleting the global pool of completely fresh blocks of addresses. Each of the address blocks represents approximately 16.7 million possible addresses.

The Internet Protocol, Version 6 (IPv6), provides an addressing capability of 2^{128}, or 3.4×10^{38} addresses. There are other major differences between IPv4 and IPv6:

- *Multicasting.* IPv6 does not implement traditional IP broadcast, (i.e., the transmission of a packet to all hosts on the attached link using a special broadcast address) and, therefore, does not define broadcast addresses. IPv6 supports new multicast solutions, including embedding rendezvous point addresses in an IPv6 multicast group address, which simplifies the deployment of interdomain solutions.
- *Stateless address autoconfiguration (SLAAC).* IPv6 hosts can configure themselves automatically when they are connected to a routed IPv6 network using the Internet Control Message Protocol version 6 (ICMPv6) router discovery messages. When first connected to a network, a host sends a link-local router solicitation multicast request for its configuration parameters; if configured suitably, routers respond to such a request with a router advertisement packet that contains network-layer configuration parameters.
- *Mandatory support for network security.* Internet Network Security (IPsec) is an integral part of the base protocol suite in IPv6; it is optional for IPv4. IPsec is a protocol suite operating at the IP layer. Each IP packet is authenticated and encrypted. Other security protocols operate at the upper layers of the TCP/IP suite (e.g., the Secure Sockets Layer (SSL), the Transport Layer Security (TLS), and the Secure Shell (SSH)). IPsec uses several protocols: (1) Authentication Headers (AH) – supports connectionless integrity, data origin authentication for IP datagrams, and protection against replay attacks; (2) Encapsulating Security Payloads (ESP) – supports confidentiality, data-origin authentication, connectionless integrity, an anti-replay service, and limited traffic-flow confidentiality; and (3) Security Associations (SA) – provides the parameters necessary to operate the AH and/or ESP operations.

Unfortunately, migration to IPv6 is a very challenging and costly proposition. A simple analogy allows us to explain the difficulties related to migration to IPv6. The telephone numbers in North America consist of 10 decimal digits; this scheme supports up to 10 billion phones, but, in practice, we have fewer available numbers than that. Indeed, some phone numbers are wasted because we use area codes based on geographic proximity and, on the other hand, not all available numbers in a given area are allocated.

To overcome the limited number of phone numbers in this scheme, large organizations use private phone extensions of typically three to five digits. Thus, a single public phone number can translate to 1,000 phones for an organization using a three-digit extension. Analogously, Network Address Translation (NAT) allows a single public IP address to support hundreds or even thousands of private IP addresses. In the past NAT did not work well with applications such as VoIP and virtual private networking (VPN). Nowadays Skype and STUN VoIP applications work well with NAT and NAT-T, and SSLVPN supports VPN NAT.

If the telephone companies decide to promote a new system based on 40-decimal-digit phone numbers, we will need new telephones; at the same time we will need new phone books that are much thicker because each phone number is 40 characters instead of 10. Each individual will need a new personal address book, and virtually all the communication and switching equipment and software will need to be updated. Similarly, the IPv6 migration involves upgrading all applications, hosts, routers, and DNS infrastructure. Also, moving to IPv6 requires backward compatibility, because any organization migrating to IPv6 should maintain a complete IPv4 infrastructure.

In 2009 a group from Google investigated the adoption of IPv6 [89] and concluded that "... the IPv6 deployment is small but growing steadily, and that adoption is still heavily influenced by a small number of large deployments. While we see IPv6 adoption in research and education networks, IPv6 deployment is, with one notable exception, largely absent from consumer access networks."

7.4 The transformation of the Internet

There is no doubt that the decades-long evolution of microprocessor and storage technologies, computer architecture and software systems, and parallel algorithms and distributed control strategies paved the way for cloud computing. Yet we have to recognize that the fascinating developments in networking are at the heart of this new technology. In this section we only discuss those features of the Internet affecting cloud computing.

The Internet is continually evolving under the pressure of its own success and the need to accommodate new applications and a larger number of users; initially conceived as a data network, a network supporting only the transport of data files, it has morphed into today's network for data with real-time constraints for multimedia applications. To understand the architectural consequences of this evolution, we examine first the relations between two networks:

- Peering, in which the two networks freely exchange traffic between each other's customers.
- Transit, in which a network pays another one to access the Internet.
- Customer, in which a network is paid money to allow Internet access.

Based on these relations the networks are commonly classified as Tier 1, 2, and 3 (Figure 7.4). A *Tier 1 network* can reach every other network on the Internet without purchasing IP transit or paying settlements; examples of Tier 1 networks are Verizon, ATT, NTT and Deutsche Telecom.

A *Tier 2 network* is an Internet service provider (ISP) that engages in the practice of peering with other networks but that still purchases IP transit to reach some portion of the Internet. Tier 2 providers are the most common providers on the Internet. A *Tier 3 network* purchases transit rights from other networks (typically Tier 2 networks) to reach the Internet. A *point-of-presence (POP)* is an access point from one place to the rest of the Internet.

An *Internet exchange point (IXP)* is a physical infrastructure allowing ISPs to exchange Internet traffic. The primary purpose of an IXP is to allow networks to interconnect directly via the exchange rather than through one or more third-party networks. The advantages of the direct interconnection are numerous, but the primary reasons to implement an IXP are cost, latency, and bandwidth. Traffic

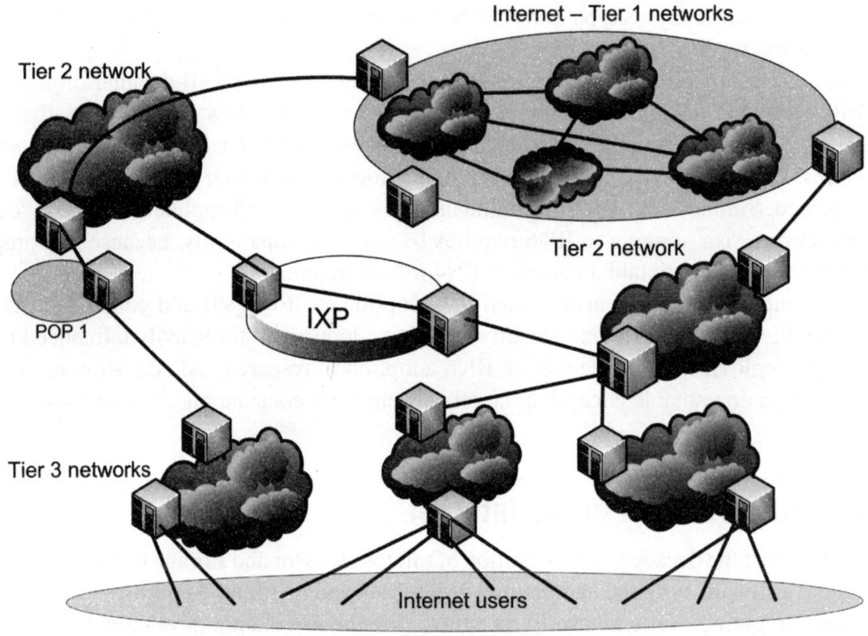

FIGURE 7.4

The relation of Internet networks based on the transit and paying settlements. There are three classes of networks: Tier 1, 2, and 3. An IXP is a physical infrastructure that allows ISPs to exchange Internet traffic.

passing through an exchange is typically not billed by any party, whereas traffic to an ISP's upstream provider is.

IXPs reduce the portion of an ISP's traffic that must be delivered via their upstream transit providers, thereby reducing the average per-bit delivery cost of their service. Furthermore, the increased number of paths through the IXP improves routing efficiency and fault tolerance. A typical IXP consists of one or more network switches, to which each of the participating ISPs connects.

New technologies such as Web applications, cloud computing, and content-delivery networks are reshaping the definition of a network, as shown in Figure 7.5 [203]. The Web, gaming, and entertainment are merging, and more computer applications are moving to the cloud. Data streaming consumes an increasingly large fraction of the available bandwidth as high-definition TV (HDTV) sets become less expensive and content providers such as Netflix and Hulu offer customers services that require a significant increase in network bandwidth.

Does the network infrastructure keep up with the demand for bandwidth? The Internet infrastructure in the United States is falling behind in terms of network bandwidth, as illustrated in Figure 7.6. A natural question to ask is: Where is the actual bottleneck that limits the bandwidth available to a typical Internet broadband user? The answer is: the "last mile," the link connecting the home to the ISP network.

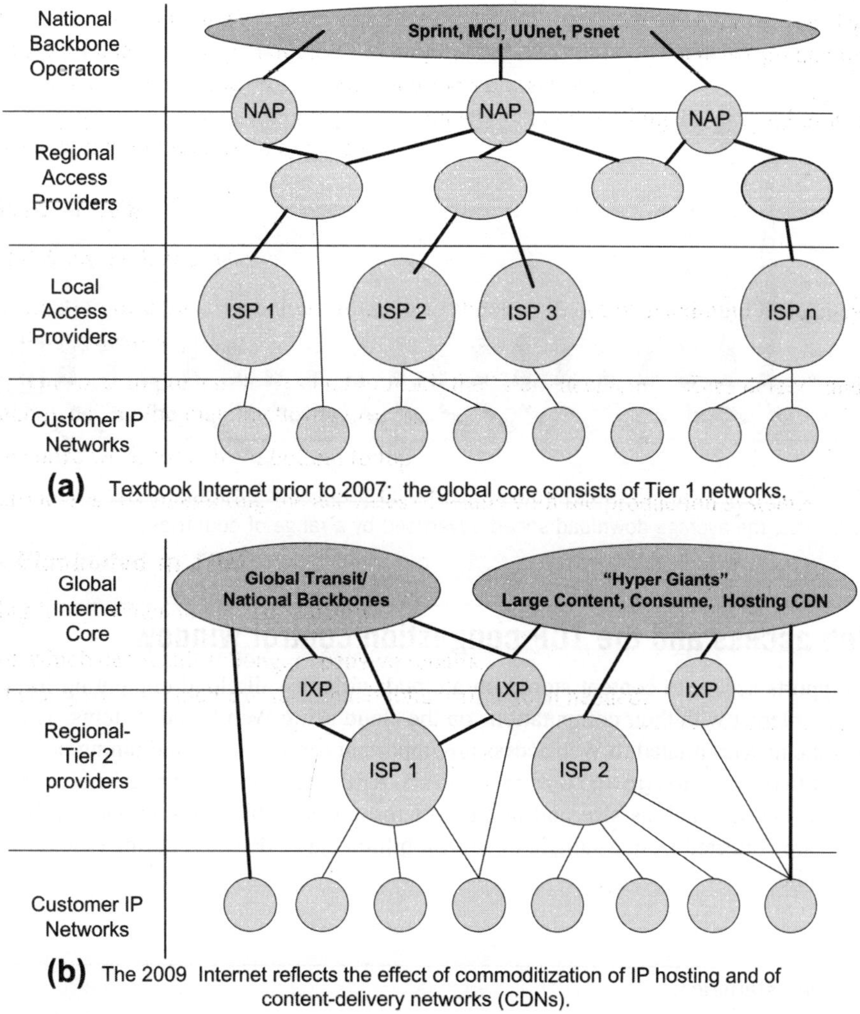

FIGURE 7.5

The transformation of the Internet. The traffic carried by Tier 3 networks increased from 5.8% in 2007 to 9.4% in 2009. Google applications accounted for 5.2% of the traffic in 2009 [203].

Recognizing that the broadband access infrastructure ensures continual growth of the economy and allows people to work from any site, Google has initiated the Google Fiber Project, which aims to provide 1 Gb/s access speed to individual households through FTTH.[3]

[3]Fiber-to-the-home (FTTH) is a broadband network architecture that uses optical fiber to replace the copper-based local loop used for the last mile of network access to the home.

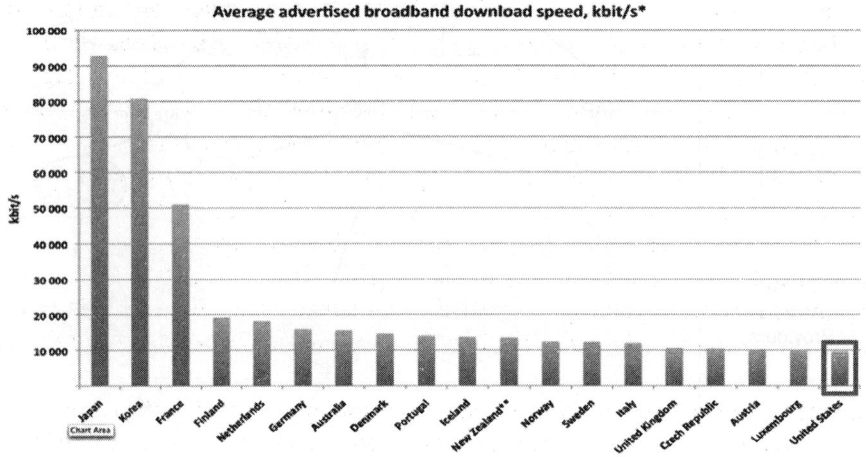

FIGURE 7.6

Broadband access, the average download speed advertised by a range of countries.

7.5 Web access and the TCP congestion control window

The Web supports access to content stored on a cloud; virtually all cloud computing infrastructures allow users to interact with their computations on the cloud using Web-based systems. Thus, it should be clear that the metrics related to Web access are important for designing and tuning networks.

The site `http://code.google.com/speed/articles/web-metrics.html` provides statistics about metrics such as size and number of resources; Table 7.1 summarizes these metrics. The statistics are collected from a sample of several billion pages detected during Google's crawl and indexing pipeline.

Table 7.1 Web statistics.

Metric	Value
Number of sample pages analyzed	4.2×10^9
Average number of resources per page	44
Average number of GETs per page	44.5
Average number of unique host names encountered per page	7
Average size transferred over the network per page, including HTTP headers	320 KB
Average number of unique images per page	29
Average size of the images per page	206 KB
Average number of external scripts per page	7
Number of sample SSL (HTTPS) pages analyzed	17×10^6

Such statistics are useful for tuning the transport protocols to deliver optimal performance in terms of latency and throughput. HTTP, the application protocol for Web browsers, uses TCP, which supports mechanisms to limit the amount of data transported over the network to avoid congestion. Metrics, such as the average size of a page or the number of GET operations, are useful to explain the results of performance measurements carried out on existing systems and to propose changes to optimize the performance, as discussed next.

Another example illustrating the need for the networking infrastructure to adapt to new requirements is the TCP initial congestion window. Before we analyze this problem in depth, we review two important mechanisms to control data transport, called flow control and congestion control. TCP seeks to achieve high channel utilization, avoid congestion, and, at the same time, ensure a fair sharing of the network bandwidth.

TCP uses a sliding window flow control protocol. If W is the window size, then the data rate S of the sender is:

$$S = \frac{W \times \text{MSS}}{\text{RTT}} \text{bps} = \frac{W}{\text{RTT}} \text{ packets/second},$$

where MSS and RTT denote the maximum segment size and the round-trip time, respectively. If S is too, small, the transmission rate is smaller than the channel capacity, whereas a large S leads to congestion. The channel capacity in the case of communication over the Internet is not a fixed quantity, but, as different physical channels are shared among many flows, it depends on the load of the network.

The actual window size W is affected by two factors: (a) the ability of the receiver to accept new data and (b) the sender's estimation of the available network capacity. The receiver specifies the amount of additional data it is willing to accept in the *receive window* field of every frame; the receive window shifts when the receiver receives and acknowledges a new segment of data. When a receiver advertises a window size of zero, the sender stops sending data and starts the persist timer; this timer is used to avoid the deadlock when a subsequent window size update from the receiver is lost. When the persist timer expires, the sender sends a small packet and the receiver responds by sending another acknowledgment containing the new window size. In addition to the flow control provided by the receiver, the sender attempts to infer the available network capacity and to avoid overloading the network. The source uses the losses and the delay to determine the level of congestion. If *awnd* denotes the receiver window and *cwnd* the congestion window set by the sender, the actual window should be:

$$W = \min (cwnd,\ awnd).$$

Several algorithms are used to calculate *cwnd*, including Tahoe and Reno, developed by Jacobson in 1988 and 1990. Tahoe was based on slow-start (SS), congestion avoidance (CA), and fast retransmit (FR); the sender probes the network for spare capacity and detects congestion based on loss. The slow start means that the sender starts with a window of two times MSS, $init\_cwnd = 1$; for every packet acknowledged, the congestion window increases by 1 MSS so that the congestion window effectively doubles for every RTT. When the congestion window exceeds the threshold, $cwnd \geqslant ssthresh$, the algorithm enters the congestion avoidance state; in CA state, on each successful acknowledgment $cwnd \leftarrow cwnd + 1/cwnd$ and on each RTT $cwnd \leftarrow cwnd + 1$. The fast retransmit is motivated by the fact that the time out is too long, so a sender retransmits immediately after three duplicate acknowledgments without waiting for a timeout; two adjustments are then made:

$$flightsize = \min(awnd,\ cwnd) \quad \text{and} \quad ssthresh \leftarrow \max(flightsize/2, 2)$$

and the system enters in the slow-start state, $cwnd = 1$.

The pseudocode describing the Tahoe algorithm is:

```
for every ACK {
        if (W < ssthresh) then W++   (SS)
          else     W += 1/W   (CA)
      }
      for every loss {
          ssthresh = W/2
             W = 1
      }
```

The pattern of usage of the Internet has changed. Measurements reported by different sources [108] show that in 2009 the average bandwidth of an Internet connection was 1.7 Mbps; more than 50% of the traffic required more than 2 Mbps and could be considered broadband, whereas only about 5% of the flows required less that 256 Kbps and could be considered narrowband. Recall that the average Web page size is in the range of 384 KB.

Although the majority of Internet traffic is due to long-lived, bulk data transfer (e.g., video streaming and audio streaming), the majority of transactions are short lived (e.g., Web requests). So a major challenge is to ensure some fairness for short-lived transactions.

To overcome the limitations of the slow-start application, strategies have been developed to reduce the time to download data over the Internet. For example, two browsers, Firefox 3 and Google Chrome, open up to six TCP connections per domain to increase the parallelism and to boost startup performance in downloading a Web page. Internet Explorer 8 opens 180 connections. Clearly, these strategies circumvent the mechanisms for congestion control and incur a considerable overhead. It is argued that a better solution is to increase the initial congestion window of TCP, and the arguments presented in [108] are:

- The TCP latency is dominated by the number of RTTs during the slow-start phase[4]; increasing the *init_cwnd* parameter allows the data transfer to be completed with fewer RTTs.
- Given that the average page size is 384 KB, a single TCP connection requires multiple RTTs to download a single page.
- It ensures fairness between short-lived transactions that are the majority of Internet transfers and the long-lived transactions that transfer very large amounts of data.
- It allows faster recovery after losses through fast retransmission.

In the experiments reported in [108] the TCP latency was reduced from about 490 msec when $init\_cwnd = 3$ to about 466 msec for $init\_cwnd = 16$.

[4]It can be shown that the latency of a transfer completing during the slow start without losses is given by the expression

$$\lceil \log_\gamma \left(\frac{L(\gamma - 1)}{init\_cwnd} + 1 \right) \rceil \times RTT + \frac{L}{C}$$

with L the transfer size, C the bottleneck-link rate, and γ a constant equal to 1.5 or 2, depending on whether the acknowledgments are delayed; $L/init\_cwnd \geqslant 1$.

7.6 Network resource management

As mentioned repeatedly, cloud computing is intrinsically dependent on communication; thus, network resource management is a very important aspect of the management of computer clouds. A critical aspect of resource management in cloud computing is to guarantee the communication bandwidth required by an application as specified by a service-level agreement (SLA). The solutions to this problem are based on the strategies used for some time on the Internet to support the quality-of-service (QoS) requirements of data streaming.

First, we discuss the stochastic fairness queuing (SFQ) algorithm [240], which takes into account data packet sizes to ensure that each flow has the opportunity to transmit an equal amount of data. SFQ is a simpler and less accurate implementation of fair queuing algorithms and thus requires fewer calculations. The fair queuing (FQ) algorithm discussed in Section 6.9 ensures that a high-data-rate flow cannot use more than its fair share of the link capacity. Packets are first classified into flows by the system and then assigned to a queue dedicated to the flow; queues are serviced one packet at a time in round-robin order, as shown in Figure 7.7. FQ's objective is *max–min* fairness; this means that first, it maximizes the minimum data rate of any of the data flows, then it maximizes the second minimum data rate, etc. Starvation of expensive flows is avoided, but the throughput is lower.

Next we review a widely used strategy for link sharing, the class-based queuing (CBQ) method proposed by Sally Floyd and Van Jacobson in 1995 [125]. The objective of CBQ is to support flexible link sharing for applications that require bandwidth guarantees such as VoIP, video streaming, and audio streaming. At the same time, CBQ supports some balance between short-lived network flows, such as Web searches, and long-lived ones, such as video streaming or file transfers.

CBQ aggregates the connections and constructs a hierarchy of classes with different priorities and throughput allocations. To accomplish link sharing, CBQ uses several functional units: (i) a *classifier* that uses the information in the packet header to assign arriving packets to classes; (ii) an *estimator* of

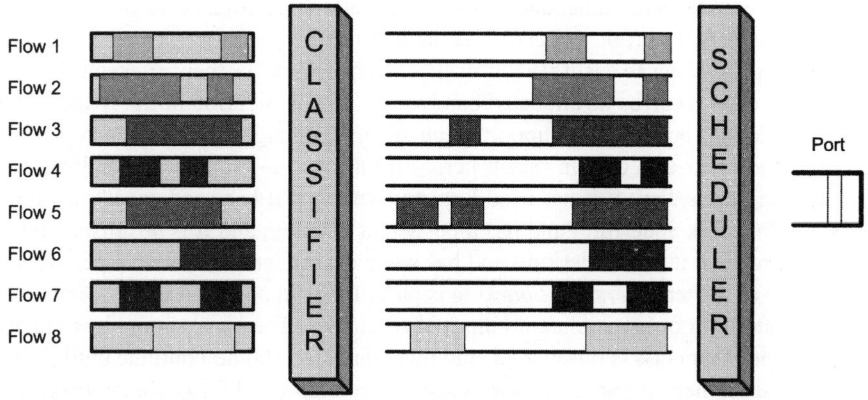

FIGURE 7.7

Fair queuing (FQ), in which packets are first classified into flows by the system and then assigned to a queue dedicated to the flow. Queues are serviced one packet at a time in round-robin order, and empty queues are skipped.

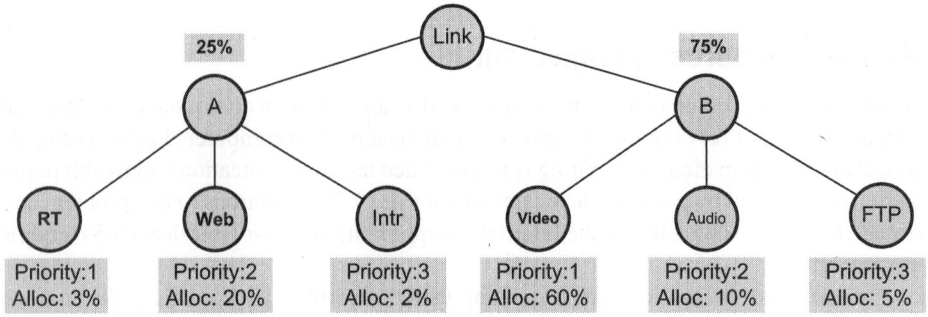

FIGURE 7.8

CBQ link sharing for two groups: A, of short-lived traffic, and B, of long-lived traffic, allocated 25% and 75% of the link capacity, respectively. There are three classes with priorities 1, 2, and 3. The RT (real-time) and the video-streaming classes have priority one and are allocated 3% and 60%, respectively. Web transactions and audio streaming have priority 2 and are allocated 20% and 10%, respectively, and Intr (interactive applications) and FTP (file transfer protocols) have priority 3 and are allocated 2% and 5%, respectively, of the link capacity.

the short-term bandwidth for the class; (iii) a *selector*, or scheduler, which identifies the highest-priority class to send next and, if multiple classes have the same priority, to schedule them on a round-robin basis; and (iv) a *delayer* to compute the next time when a class that has exceeded its link allocation is allowed to send.

The classes are organized in a tree-like hierarchy; for example, in Figure 7.8 we see two types of traffic: group *A* corresponding to short-lived traffic and group *B* corresponding to long-lived traffic. The leaves of the tree are considered Level 1 and in this example include six classes of traffic: real time, Web, interactive, video streaming, audio streaming, and file transfer. At Level 2 there are the two classes of traffic, *A* and *B*. The root, at Level 3, is the link itself.

The link-sharing policy aims to ensure that if sufficient demand exists, then, after some time intervals, each interior or leaf class receives its allocated bandwidth. The distribution of the "excess" bandwidth follows a set of guidelines but does not support mechanisms for congestion avoidance.

A class is *overlimit* if over a certain recent period it has used more than its bandwidth allocation (in bytes per second), *underlimit* if it has used less, and *atlimit* if it has used exactly its allocation. A leaf class is *satisfied* if it is underlimit and has a persistent backlog, and it is *unsatisfied* otherwise. A nonleaf class is unsatisfied if it is underlimit and has some descendent class with a persistent backlog. A precise definition of the term *persistent backlog* is part of a local policy. A class does not need to be *regulated* if it is underlimit or if there are no unsatisfied classes. The class should be regulated if it is overlimit and if some other class is unsatisfied, and this regulation should continue until the class is no longer overlimit or until there are no unsatisfied classes (see Figure 7.9 for two examples).

The *Linux* kernel implements a link-sharing algorithm called *hierarchical token buckets* (HTB) inspired by CBQ. In CBQ every class has an *assured rate* (AR); in addition to the AR every class in HTB has also a *ceil rate* (CR) (see Figure 7.10). The main advantage of HTB over CBQ is that it allows *borrowing*. If a class C needs a rate above its AR, it tries to borrow from its parent; then the parent

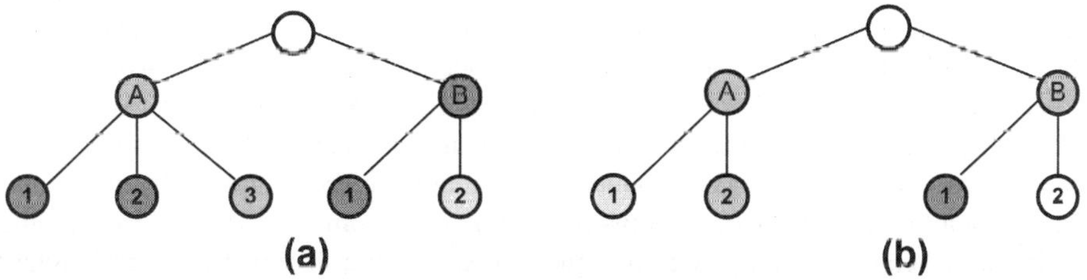

FIGURE 7.9

There are two groups, *A* and *B*, and three types of traffic, (e.g., Web, real time, and interactive) denoted 1, 2, and 3. (a) Group *A* and class *A*.3 traffic are underlimit and unsatisfied. Classes *A*.1, *A*.2, and *B*.1 are overlimit, unsatisfied, and with persistent backlog and have to be regulated. Type *A*.3 is underlimit and unsatisfied. Group *B* is overlimit. (b) Group *A* is underlimit and unsatisfied. Group *B* is overlimit and needs to be regulated. Class *A*.1 traffic is underlimit. Class *A*.2 is overlimit and with persistent backlog. Class *B*.1 traffic is overlimit and with persistent backlog and needs to be regulated.

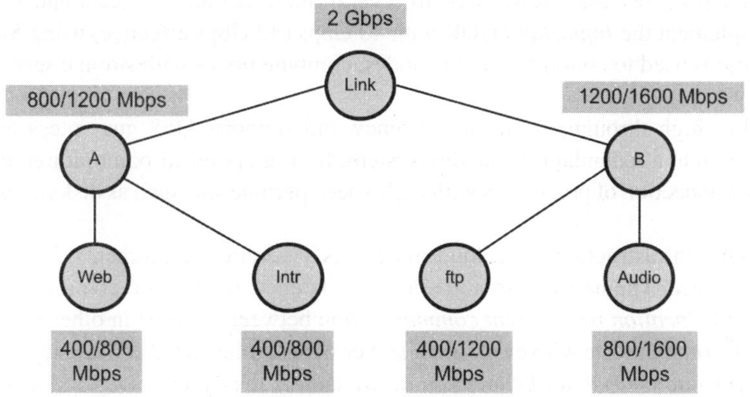

FIGURE 7.10

HTB packet scheduling uses a ceil rate for every node in addition to the allocated rate.

examines its children and, if there are classes running at a rate lower than their AR, the parent can borrow from them and reallocate it to class C.

7.7 Interconnection networks for computer clouds

This section presents high-speed interconnects for cloud computing. A cloud, sometimes referred to as a *warehouse-scale computer* (WSC), has an infrastructure consisting of a very large number of servers interconnected by high-speed networks. This infrastructure is homogeneous in terms of the hardware and software running on individual servers.

Although processor and memory technology have followed Moore's law (i.e., that computer processors double in complexity every two years), the interconnection networks have evolved at a slower pace and have become a major factor in determining the overall performance and cost of the system. The speed of the Ethernet has increased from 1 Gbps in 1997 to 100 Gbps in 2010; this increase is slightly slower than Moore's law for traffic [251], which would require 1 Tbps Ethernet by 2013.

InfiniBand is another interconnection network used by supercomputers as well as computer clouds. *InfiniBand* has a switched fabric topology designed to be scalable. It supports several signaling rates, and the energy consumption depends on the throughput. Links can be bonded together for additional throughput; *InfiniBand*'s architectural specification defines multiple operational data rates: single data rate (SDR), double data rate (DDR), quad data rate (QDR), fourteen data rate (FDR), and enhanced data rated (EDR). The signaling rates are: 2.5 Gbps in each direction per connection for an SDR connection; 5 Gbps for DDR; 10 Gbps for QDR; 14.0625 Gbps for FDR; and 25.78125 Gbps per lane for EDR . SDR, DDR, and QDR link encoding is 8 B/10 B, every 10 bits sent carry 8 bits of data. Thus single, double, and quad data rates carry 2, 4, or 8 Gbps useful data, respectively. The effective data transmission rate is four-fifths of the raw rate.

InfiniBand allows links to be configured for a specified speed and width; the reactivation time of the link can vary from several nanoseconds to several microseconds. Exadata and Exalogic systems from Oracle implement the *InfiniBand* QDR with 40 Gbps (32 Gbps effective) using Sun switches; the *InifiniBand* fabric is used to connect compute nodes, compute nodes with storage servers, and Exadata and Exalogic systems.

InfiniBand has high throughput and low latency and supports QoS guarantees and failover, the capability to switch to a redundant or standby system. It offers point-to-point bidirectional serial links intended for the connection of processors with high-speed peripherals, such as disks, as well as multicast operations.

The networking infrastructure of a cloud must satisfy several requirements, including scalability, cost, and performance. The network should allow low-latency, high-speed communication and, at the same time, provide *location transparent communication* between servers; in other words, every server should be able to communicate with every other server with similar speed and latency. This requirement ensures that *applications need not be location aware* and, at the same time, it reduces the complexity of the system management.

Important elements of the interconnection fabric are routers and switches. Routers are switches with a very specific function: joining multiple networks, LANs, and WANs. They receive IP packets, look inside each packet to identify the source and target IP addresses, then forward these packets as needed to ensure that data reaches its final destination.

Typically, the networking infrastructure is organized hierarchically. The servers are packed into racks and interconnected by a top-of-the-rack router; then rack routers are connected to cluster routers, which in turn are interconnected by a local communication fabric. Finally, interdata center networks connect multiple WSCs [197]. The switching fabric must have sufficient bidirectional bandwidth for cloud computing. Clearly, in a hierarchical organization, true location transparency is not feasible and cost considerations ultimately decide the actual organization and performance of the communication fabric.

The cost of routers and the number of cables interconnecting the routers are major components of the overall cost of the interconnection network. We should note that the wire density has scaled up at a slower rate than processor speed, and the wire delay has remained constant over time; thus, better performance and lower costs can only be achieved with innovative router architecture. This motivates us to take a closer look at the actual design of routers.

The number of ports of a router distinguishes *low-radix* routers, with a small number of ports, from *high-radix* routers, with a large number of ports. High-radix chips divide the bandwidth into a larger number of narrow ports; low-radix chips divide the bandwidth into a smaller number of wide ports.

The number of intermediate routers in high-radix networks is greatly reduced, and such networks enjoy a lower latency and reduced power consumption. As a result of the increase in the signaling rate and in the number of signals, the pin bandwidth of the chips used for switching has increased by approximately an order of magnitude every five years during the past two decades.

The topology of an interconnection network determines the *network diameter*[5] and its *bisection bandwidth*[6], as well as the cost and power consumption [193]. First, we introduce informally the *Clos* and the *flattened butterfly* topologies. The name *butterfly* comes from the pattern of inverted triangles created by the interconnections, which look like butterfly wings. A butterfly network transfers the data using the most efficient route, but it is blocking, so it cannot handle a conflict between two packets attempting to reach the same port at the same time.

A *Clos network* is a multistage nonblocking network with an odd number of stages (see Figure 7.11(a)). The network consists of two butterfly networks, and the last stage of the input is fused with the first stage of the output. In a *Clos network* all packets overshoot their destination and then hop back to it. Most of the time the overshoot is not necessary and increases the latency, meaning that a packet takes twice as many hops as it really needs. In a *folded Clos* topology the input and output networks share switch modules Figure 7.11(b). Such networks are sometimes called *fat tree*; many commercial high-performance interconnects such as *Myrinet*, *InfiniBand*, and *Quadrics* implement a fat-tree topology. Some folded Clos networks use low-radix routers (e.g., the Cray XD1 uses radix-24 routers). The latency and the cost of the network can be lowered using high-radix routers.

The *Black Widow* topology extends the folded Clos topology and has a lower cost and latency. It adds side links, which permit a statical partitioning of the global bandwidth among peer subtrees [321]. The Black Widow topology is used in Cray computers.

The *flattened butterfly* topology [192] is similar to the *generalized hypercube* that was proposed in the early 1980s, but the wiring complexity is reduced and this topology is able to exploit high-radix routers. When constructing a *flattened butterfly*, we start with a conventional butterfly and combine the switches in each row into a single, higher-radix one; each router is linked to more processors, and this halves the number of router-to-router connections.

The latency is reduced because data from one processor can reach another processor with fewer hops, though the physical path may be longer. For example, in Figure 7.12(b) we see a 2-ary 4-fly butterfly. We combine the four switches S_0, S_1, S_2, and S_3 in the first row into a single switch S'_0. The *flattened butterfly* adaptively senses congestion and overshoots only when it needs to. On adversarial traffic patterns, the *flattened butterfly* has similar performance to that of the *folded Clos* but provides over an order of magnitude increase in performance compared to the conventional butterfly.

[5]The diameter of a network is the average distance between each pair of two nodes. If a network is fully connected, its diameter is equal to one.

[6]When a network is partitioned into two networks of the same size, the bisection bandwidth measures the communication bandwidth between the two.

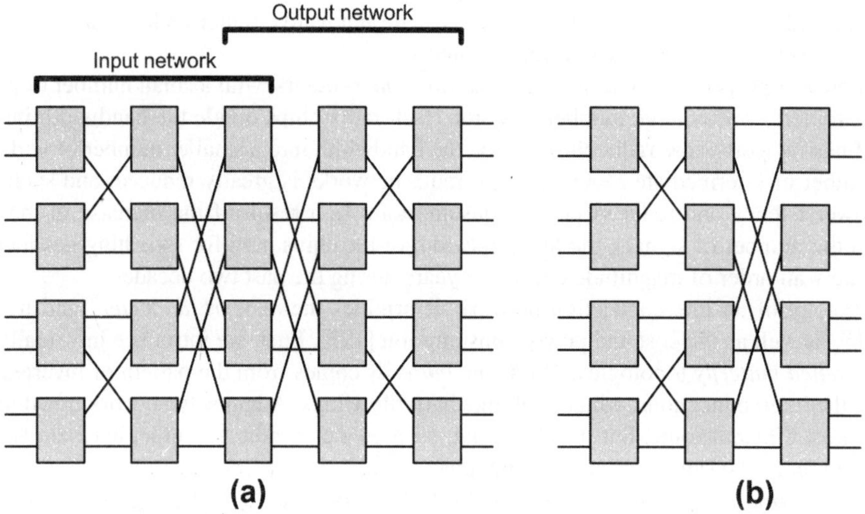

FIGURE 7.11

(a) A five-stage *Clos network* with radix-2 routers and unidirectional channels. The network is equivalent to two back-to-back butterfly networks. (b) The corresponding *folded-Clos network* with bidirectional channels. The input and output networks share switch modules.

The authors of [193] argue that the cost of the networks in storage area networks (SANs) and computer clusters can be reduced by a factor of two when high-radix routers (radix-64 or higher) and the *flattened butterfly* topology are used. The *flattened butterfly* does not reduce the number of local cables, (e.g., backplane wires from the processors to routers), but it reduces the number of global cables. The cost of the cables represents as much as 80% of the total network cost (e.g., for a 4 K system the cost savings of the *flattened butterfly* exceed 50%).

7.8 Storage area networks

A *storage area network* (SAN) is a specialized, high-speed network for data-block transfers between computer systems and storage elements; thus, it is a critical element of a cloud infrastructure (see Figure 7.13). A SAN consists of a communication infrastructure and a management layer. The Fibre Channel (FC) is the dominant architecture of SANs.

FC is a layered protocol with several layers, as depicted in Figure 7.14:

A. The lower three layer protocols: FC-0, the physical interface; FC-1, the transmission protocol responsible for encoding/decoding; and FC-2, the signaling protocol responsible for framing and flow control.

FC-0 uses laser diodes as the optical source and manages the point-to-point fiber connections. When the fiber connection is broken, the ports send a series of pulses until the physical connection is reestablished and the necessary handshake procedures are followed.

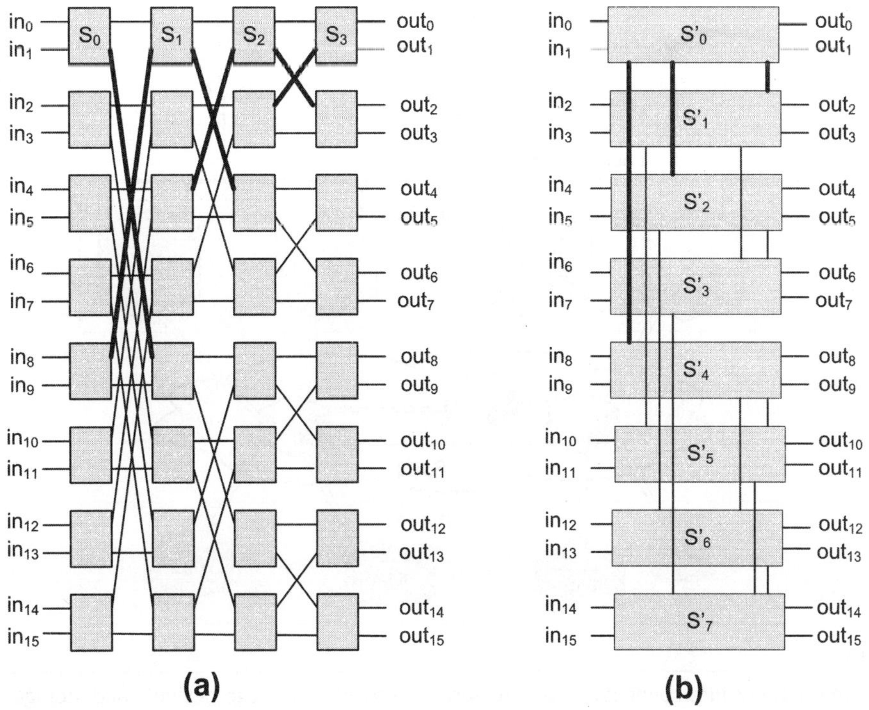

FIGURE 7.12

(a) A 2-ary 4-fly butterfly with unidirectional links. (b) The corresponding 2-ary 4-fly *flattened butterfly* is obtained by combining the four switches S_0, S_1, S_2, and S_3 in the first row of the traditional butterfly into a single switch S'_0 and adding connections between switches [192].

FC-1 controls the serial transmission and integrates data with clock information. It ensures encoding to the maximum length of the code, maintains DC balance, and provides word alignment.

FC-2 provides the transport methods for data transmitted in 4-byte ordered sets containing data and control characters. It handles the topologies based on the presence or absence of a fabric, the communication models, the classes of service provided by the fabric and the nodes, sequence and exchange identifiers, and segmentation and reassembly.

B. Two upper layer protocols: FC-3, the common services layer; and FC-4, the protocol mapping layer. FC-3 supports multiple ports on a single node or fabric using:

- Hunt groups-sets of associated ports assigned an alias identifier that allows any frames containing that alias to be routed to any available port within the set.
- Striping to multiply bandwidth, using multiple ports in parallel to transmit a single information unit across multiple links.
- Multicast and broadcast to deliver a single transmission to multiple destination ports or to all nodes.

To accommodate various application needs, FC supports several classes of service:

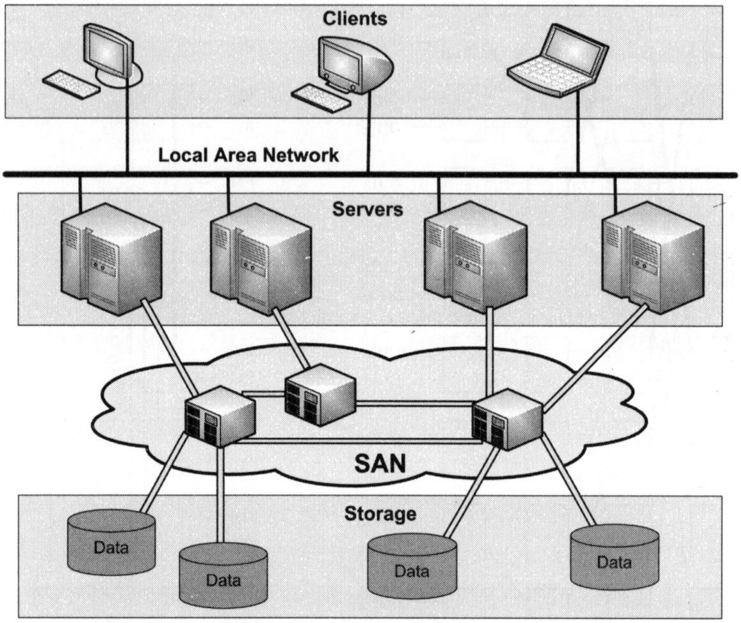

FIGURE 7.13

A storage area network interconnects servers to servers, servers to storage devices, and storage devices to storage devices. Typically it uses fiber optics and the FC protocol.

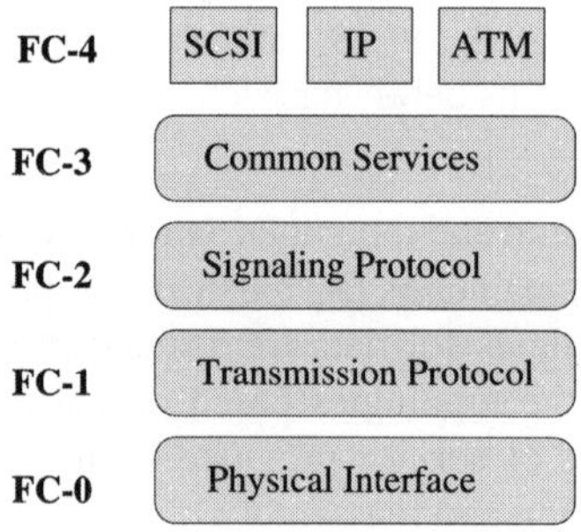

FIGURE 7.14

FC protocol layers.

Class 1. Rarely used blocking connection-oriented service. Acknowledgments ensure that the frames are received in the same order in which they are sent and reserve full bandwidth for the connection between the two devices.

Class 2. Acknowledgments ensure that the frames are received. Allows the fabric to multiplex several messages on a frame-by-frame basis. Because frames can take different routes, it does not guarantee in-order delivery; it relies on upper layer protocols to take care of frame sequence.

Class 3. Datagram connection; no acknowledgments.

Class 4. Supports connection-oriented service. Virtual circuits (VCs) established between ports guarantee in-order delivery and acknowledgment of delivered frames, but the fabric is responsible for multiplexing frames of different VCs. Guaranteed QoS, including bandwidth and latency; intended for multimedia applications.

Class 5. Supports isochronous service for applications requiring immediate delivery without buffering.

Class 6. Supports dedicated connections for a reliable multicast.

Class 7. Similar to Class 2 but used for the control and management of the fabric. A connectionless service with notification of nondelivery.

Although each device connected to a LAN has a unique physical address, also called a Media Access Control (MAC) address, each FC device has a unique ID called the World Wide Name (WWN), a 64-bit address. Each port in the switched fabric has its own unique 24-bit address consisting of the domain (bits 23–16), the area (bits 15–08), and the port physical address (bits 07–00).

The switch of a switched fabric environment assigns dynamically and maintains the port addresses. When a device with a WWN logs into the switch on a port, the switch assigns the port address to that port and maintains the correlation between that port address and the WWN address of the device using the Name Server, a component of the fabric operating system, which runs inside the switch.

The format of an FC frame is shown in Figure 7.15. Zoning permits finer segmentation of the switched fabric. Only the members of the same zone can communicate within that zone. It can be used to separate different environments (e.g., a *Microsoft Windows NT* from a *UNIX* environment).

Several other protocols are used for SANs. Fibre Channel over IP (FCIP) allows transmission of Fibre Channel information through the IP network using *tunneling*. Tunneling is a technique for network protocols to encapsulate a different payload protocol. It allows a network protocol to carry a payload over an incompatible delivery network or to provide a secure path through an untrusted network. Tunneling allows a protocol that a firewall would normally block to cross it wrapped inside a protocol that the firewall does not block. For example, an HTTP tunnel can be used for communication from network locations with restricted connectivity (e.g., behind NATs, firewalls, or proxy servers) and most often with applications that lack native support for communication in such conditions of restricted connectivity. Restricted connectivity is a commonly used method to lock down a network to secure it against internal and external threats.

Internet Fibre Channel Protocol (iFCP) is a gateway-to-gateway protocol that supports communication among FC storage devices in a SAN or on the Internet using TCP/IP. iFCP replaces the lower-layer

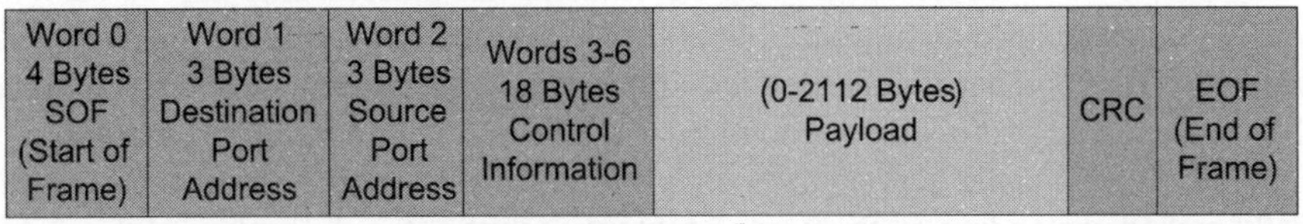

FIGURE 7.15

The format of an FC frame. The payload can be, at most, 2112 bytes. Larger data units are carried by multiple frames. CRC – Cyclic Redundancy Check.

Fibre Channel transport with TCP/IP and Gigabit Ethernet. With iFCP, Fibre Channel devices connect to an iFCP gateway or switch, and each Fibre Channel session is terminated at the local gateway and converted to a TCP/IP session via iFCP.

7.9 Content-delivery networks

Computer clouds support not only network-centric computing, but also network-centric content. For example, we shall see in Chapter 8 that in 2013 Internet video is expected to generate over 18 exabytes of data per month. The vast amount of data stored on the cloud has to be delivered efficiently to a large user population.

Content-delivery networks (CDNs) offer fast and reliable content delivery and reduce the communication bandwidth by caching and replication. A CDN receives the content from an *origin* server, then replicates it to its *edge* cache servers. The content is delivered to an end user from the "closest" edge server.

CDNs are designed to support scalability, increase reliability and performance, and provide better security. The volume of transactions and data transported by the Internet increases dramatically every year. Additional resources are necessary to accommodate the additional load placed on communication and storage systems and to improve the end-user experience. CDNs place additional resources provisioned to absorb the traffic caused by *flash crowds*[7] and, in general, to provide capacity on demand.

The additional resources are placed strategically throughout the Internet to ensure scalability. The resources provided by a CDN are replicated, and when one of the replicas fails, the content is available from another one. The replicas are "close" to the consumers of the content, and this placement reduces the startup time and the communication bandwidth. A CDN uses two types of server: the *origin* server updated by the content provider and *replica* servers that cache the content and serve as an authoritative reference for client requests. Security is a critical aspect of the services provided by a CDN; the replicated content should be protected from the increased risk of cyber fraud and unauthorized access.

A CDN can deliver static content and/or live or on-demand streaming media. *Static content* refers to media that can be maintained using traditional caching technologies because changes are infrequent. Examples of static content are HTML pages, images, documents, software patches, and audio and/or video files. *Live media* refers to live events during which the content is delivered in real time from the encoder to the media server. On-demand delivery of audio and/or video streams, movie files, and music clips provided to end users is content-encoded and then stored on media servers. Virtually all CDN providers support static content delivery, whereas live or on-demand streaming media are considerably more challenging.

The first CDN was set up by *Akamai*, a company evolved from a Massachusetts Institute of Technology (MIT) project to optimize network traffic. *Akamai* has placed some 20,000 servers in 1,000 networks in 71 countries since its inception. In 2009 it controlled some 85% of the market [285].

Akamai mirrors the contents of clients on multiple systems placed strategically through the Internet. Though the domain name (but not the subdomain) is the same, the IP address of the resource requested by a user points to an *Akamai* server rather than the customer's server. Then the *Akamai* server is automatically picked, depending on the type of content and the network location of the end user.

[7]The term *flash crowds* refers to an event that disrupts the life of a very significant segment of the population, such as an earthquake in a very populated area, and causes Internet traffic to increase dramatically.

There are several other active commercial CDNs, including *EdgeStream*, which provides video streaming, and *Limelight Networks*, which provides distributed on-demand and live delivery of video, music, and games. There are several academic CDNs: *Coral* is a freely available network designed to mirror Web content, hosted on PlanetLab; *Globule* is an open-source collaborative CDN developed at the Vrije Universiteit in Amsterdam.

The communication infrastructure among different CDN components uses a fair number of protocols, including *Network Element Control Protocol* (NECP), *Web Cache Coordination Protocol* (WCCP), *SOCKS*, *Cache Array Routing Protocol* (CARP), *Internet Cache Protocol* (ICP), *Hypertext Caching Protocol* (HTCP), and *Cache Digest*, described succinctly in [285]. For example, caches exchange ICP queries and replies to locate the best sites from which to retrieve an object; HTCP is used to discover HTTP caches, cache data, or manage sets of HTTP caches and monitor cache activity.

There are two strategies for CDN organization. In the so-called *overlay*, the network core does not play an active role in content delivery. On the other hand, the *network* approach requires the routers and the switches to use dedicated software to identify specific application types and to forward user requests based on predefined policies.

The first strategy is based exclusively on content replication on multiple caches and redirection based on proximity to the end user. In the second approach, the network core elements redirect content requests to local caches or redirect data center incoming traffic to servers optimized for specific content type access. Some CDNs, including *Akamai*, use both strategies.

Important design and policy decisions for a CDN are:

- The placement of the edge servers.
- The content selection and delivery.
- The content management.
- The request routing policies.

The placement problem is often solved with suboptimal heuristics using workload patterns and network topology as inputs. The simplest, but a costly, approach for content selection and delivery is *full-site* replication, suitable for static content. The edge servers replicate the entire content of the origin server. On the other hand, *partial-site* selection and delivery retrieve the base HTML page from the origin server and the objects referenced by this page from the edge caches. The objects can be replicated based on their popularity or on some heuristics.

Content management depends on the caching techniques, cache maintenance, and cache update policies. CDNs use several strategies to manage the consistency of content at replicas: periodic updates, updates triggered by the content change, and on-demand updates.

The request routing in a CDN directs users to the closest edge server that can best serve the request; metrics such as network proximity, client perceived latency, distance, and replica server load are taken into account in routing a request. Round-robin is a nonadaptive request-routing method that aims to balance the load; it assumes that all edge servers have similar characteristics and can deliver the content.

Adaptive algorithms perform considerably better but are more complex and require some knowledge of the current state of the system. The algorithm used by *Akamai* takes into consideration metrics such as the load of the edge server, the bandwidth currently available to a replica server, and the reliability of the client's connection to the edge servers.

CDN routing can exploit an organization in which several edge servers are connected to a service node that's aware of the load and the information about each edge server connected to it and attempts to implement a *global load-balancing policy*. An alternative is *DNS-based routing*, in which a domain name has multiple IP addresses associated with it and the service provider's DNS server returns the IP addresses of the edge servers holding the replica of the requested object; then the client's DNS server chooses one of them.

Another alternative is *HTTP redirection*; in this case a Web server includes in the HTTP header of a response to a client the address of another edge server. Finally, *IP anycasting* requires that the same IP address is assigned to several hosts, and the routing table of a router contains the address of the host closest to it.

The critical metrics of CDN performance are:

- Cache hit ratio, which is the ratio of the number of cached objects versus total number of objects requested.
- Reserved bandwidth for the origin server.
- Latency, which is based on the perceived response time by the end users.
- Edge server utilization.
- Reliability, which is based on packet-loss measurements.

CDNs will face considerable challenges in the future due to increased appeal of data streaming and to the proliferation of mobile devices such as smartphones and tablets. On-demand video streaming requires enormous bandwidth and storage space as well as powerful servers. CDNs for mobile networks must be able to dynamically reconfigure the system in response to spatial and temporal demand variations.

The concept of a *content service network (CSN)* was introduced in [226]. CSNs are overlay networks built around CDNs to provide an infrastructure service for processing and transcoding.

7.10 Overlay networks and small-world networks

An *overlay network*, or virtual network, is a network built on top of a physical network. The nodes of an overlay network are connected by virtual links that can traverse multiple physical links. Overlay networks are widely used in many distributed systems such as peer-to-peer systems, content-delivery systems, and client-server systems; in all these cases the distributed systems communicate through the Internet.

An overlay network can support QoS guarantees for data-streaming applications through improved routing over the Internet. It can also support routing of messages to destinations not specified by an IP address; in this case, distributed hash tables can be used to route messages based on their logical addresses. For example, *Akamai* is a company that manages an overlay network to provide reliable and efficient content delivery.

Virtualization is a central concept in cloud computing. We have discussed extensively the virtualization of processors, and it makes sense to consider also the virtualization of the cloud interconnect. Indeed, communication is a critical function of a cloud, and overlay networks can be used to support more efficient resource management. In this section we discuss several possible candidates as virtual cloud interconnects and algorithms to construct such networks. Such networks are modeled as graphs; we start our discussion with a few concepts from graph theory.

The topology of a network used to model the interactions in complex biological, social, economic, and computing systems is described by means of graphs in which vertices represent the entities and the edges represent their interactions. The number of edges incident upon a vertex is called the *degree of the vertex*.

Several types of graphs have been investigated, starting with the Erdös-Rény model [53,116,117], in which the number of vertices is fixed and the edges connecting vertices are created randomly. This model produces a homogeneous network with an exponential tail, and connectivity follows a Poisson distribution peaked at the average degree $\bar{k}$ and decaying exponentially for $k \gg \bar{k}$. An evolving network, in which the number of vertices increases linearly and a newly introduced vertex is connected to m existing vertices according to a preferential attachment rule, is described by Barabási and Albert in [10–12,39].

Regular graphs in which a fraction of edges are rewired with a probability p have been proposed by Watts and Strogatz and are called *small-world networks* [370]. Networks for which the degree distribution follows a power law, $p(k) \sim k^{-\gamma}$, are called *scale-free networks*. The four models are sometimes referred to as Erdös-Rény (ER), Barabási-Albert (BA), Watts-Strogatz (WS), and Scale-free (SF) models, respectively [140].

Small-World Networks. Traditionally, the connection topology of a network was assumed to be either completely regular or completely random. Regular graphs are highly clustered and have large characteristic path length, whereas random graphs exhibit low clustering and have small characteristic path length.

The *characteristic path length, L*, is the number of edges in the shortest path between two vertices averaged over all pairs of vertices. The *clustering coefficient* C is defined as follows: If vertex a has m_a neighbors, then a fully connected network of its neighbors could have at most $E_a = m_a(m_a - 1)/2$ edges. Call C_a the fraction of the E_a edges that actually exist; C is the average of C_a over all vertices. Clearly, C measures the degree of clusterings of the network.

In 1998, D. Watts and S. H. Strogatz studied the graphs combining the two desirable features, high clustering and small path length, and introduced the Watts-Strogatz graphs [370]. They proposed the following procedure to interpolate between regular and random graphs: Starting from a ring lattice with n vertices and m edges per node, rewire each edge at random with probability $0 \leqslant p \leqslant 1$; when $p = 0$ the graph is regular, and when $p = 1$ the graph is random.

When $0 < p < 1$, the structural properties of the graph are quantified by:

1. The characteristic path length, $L(p)$.
2. The clustering coefficient, $C(p)$.

If the condition

$$n \gg m \gg \ln(n) \gg 1 \tag{7.1}$$

is satisfied, then

$$p \to 0 \Rightarrow L_{regular} \approx n/2m \gg 1 \quad \text{and} \quad C_{regular} \approx 3/4, \tag{7.2}$$

whereas

$$p \to 1 \Rightarrow L_{random} \approx \ln(n)/\ln(m) \quad \text{and} \quad C_{random} \approx m/n \ll 1. \tag{7.3}$$

Small-world networks have many vertices with sparse connections but are not in danger of getting disconnected. Moreover, there is a broad range of the probability p such that $L(p) \approx L_{random}$ and, at the same time, $C(p) \gg C_{random}$. The significant drop of $L(p)$ is caused by the introduction of a few shortcuts that connect vertices that otherwise would be much further apart. For small p, the addition of a shortcut has a highly nonlinear effect; it affects not only the distance between the pair of vertices it connects but also the distance between their neighbors. If the shortcut replaces an edge in a clustered neighborhood, $C(p)$ remains practically unchanged, because it is a linear function of m.

7.11 Scale-free networks

Scale-free networks may prove to be a very useful type of overlay networks for cloud computing. The degree distribution of scale-free networks follows a power law. We only consider the discrete case when the probability density function is $p(k) = af(k)$ with $f(k) = k^{-\gamma}$ and the constant a is $a = 1/\zeta(\gamma, k_{min})$. Thus,

$$p(k) = \frac{1}{\zeta(\gamma, k_{min})} k^{-\gamma}. \tag{7.4}$$

In this expression, k_{min} is the smallest degree of any vertex, and for the applications we discuss in this chapter $k_{min} = 1$; ζ is the Hurvitz zeta function[8]

$$\zeta(\gamma, k_{min}) = \sum_{n=0}^{\infty} \frac{1}{(k_{min} + n)^{\gamma}} = \sum_{n=0}^{\infty} \frac{1}{(1 + n)^{\gamma}}. \tag{7.5}$$

Many physical and social systems are interconnected by a scale-free network. Indeed, empirical data available for power grids, the Web, the citation of scientific papers, or social networks confirm this trend: The power grid of the Western United States has some 5,000 vertices representing power-generating stations, and in this case $\gamma \approx 4$. For the World Wide Web the probability that m pages point to one page is $p(k) \approx k^{-2.1}$ [40]. Recent studies indicate that $\gamma \approx 3$ for the citation of scientific papers. The collaborative graph of movie actors in which links are present if two actors were ever cast in the same movie follows the power law with $\gamma \approx 2.3$. The larger the network, the closer a power law with $\gamma \approx 3$ approximates the distribution [39].

A scale-free network is *nonhomogeneous*; the majority of the vertices have a low degree, and only a few vertices are connected to a large number of edges (see Figure 7.16). On the other hand, an exponential network is homogeneous since most of the vertices have the same degree. The average distance d between the N vertices, also referred to as the *diameter* of the scale-free network, scales as $\ln N$; in fact, it has been shown that when $k_{min} > 2$, a lower bound on the diameter of a network with $2 < \gamma < 3$ is $\ln N$ [88]. A number of studies have shown that scale-free networks have remarkable properties such as robustness against random failures [40], favorable scaling [10,11], resilience to congestion [140], tolerance to attacks [352], small diameter [88], and small average path length [39].

The moments of a power-law distribution play an important role in the behavior of a network. It has been shown that the *giant connected component* (GCC) of networks with a finite average vertex degree and divergent variance can only be destroyed if all vertices are removed; thus, such networks are highly resilient against faulty constituents [249]. These properties make scale-free networks very attractive for

[8]The Hurvitz zeta function $\zeta(s, q) = \sum_{n=0}^{\infty} \frac{1}{(q+n)^s}$ for $s, q \in \mathbb{C}$ and $\Re e(s) > 1$ and $\Re e(q) > 0$. The Riemann zeta function is $\zeta(s, 1)$.

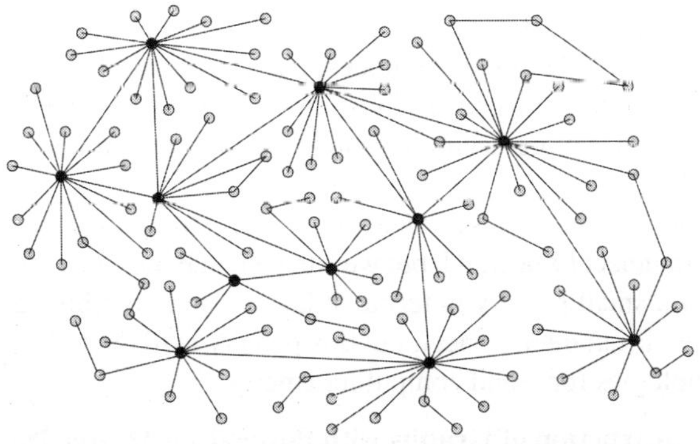

FIGURE 7.16

A scale-free network is nonhomogeneous. The majority of the vertices have a low degree and only a few vertices are connected to a large number of edges. The majority of the vertices are directly connected to the vertices with the highest degree.

interconnection networks in many applications, including social systems [256], peer-to-peer systems [8,318], sensor networks [231], and cloud computing.

As an example, consider the case $\gamma = 2.5$ and the minimum vertex degree, $x_{min} = 1$. We first determine the value of the zeta function $\zeta(\gamma, x_{min})$ and approximate $\zeta(2.5, 1) = 1.341$; thus, the distribution function is $p(k) = k^{-2.5}/1.341 = 0.745 \times (1/k^{2.5})$, where k is the degree of each vertex. The probability of vertices with degree $k > 10$ is $\text{Prob}(k > 10) = 1 - \text{Prob}(k \leqslant 10) = 0.015$. This means that at most 1.5% of the total number of vertices will have more than 10 edges connected to them. We also see that 92.5% of the vertices have degree 1, 2, or 3. Table 7.2 shows the number of vertices of degrees 1 to 10 for a very large network, $N = 10^8$.

Another important property is that the majority of the vertices of a scale-free network are directly connected to the vertices with the highest degree. For example, in a network with $N = 130$ vertices and $m = 215$ edges, 60% of the nodes are directly connected to the five vertices with the highest degree, whereas in a random network fewer than half, 27%, of the nodes have this property [11].

Table 7.2 A power-law distribution with degree $\gamma = 2.5$. The probability, $p(k)$, and N_k, the number of vertices with degree k, for a network with a total number of vertices $N = 10^8$.

k	$p(k)$	N_k	k	$p(k)$	N_k
1	0.745	74.5×10^6	6	0.009	0.9×10^6
2	0.131	13.1×10^6	7	0.006	0.6×10^6
3	0.049	4.9×10^6	8	0.004	0.4×10^6
4	0.023	2.3×10^6	9	0.003	0.3×10^6
5	0.013	1.3×10^6	10	0.002	0.2×10^6

Thus, the nodes of a scale-free network with a degree larger than a given threshold (e.g., $k = 4$ in our example) could assume the role of control nodes, and the remaining 92.5% of the nodes could be servers; this partition is autonomic. Moreover, most of the server nodes are at distance 1, 2, or 3 from a control node that could gather more accurate state information from these nodes and with minimal communication overhead.

We conclude that a scale-free network is an ideal interconnect for a cloud. It is not practical to construct a scale-free physical interconnect for a cloud, but we can generate instead a virtual interconnect with the desired topology. We pay a small penalty in terms of latency and possibly bandwidth when the nodes communicate through the virtual interconnect, but this penalty is likely to become smaller and smaller as new networking technologies for cloud computing emerge.

An Algorithm for the Construction of Graphs with Power-Law Degree Distribution. Consider an Erdös-Rényi (ER) graph G_{ER} with N vertices. Vertex i has a unique label from a compact set $i \in \{1, N\}$. We want to rewire this graph and produce a new graph G_{SF} in which the degrees of the vertices follow a power-law distribution. The procedure we discuss consists of the following steps [212]:

1. We assign to each node i a probability:

$$p_i = \frac{i^{-\alpha}}{\sum_{j=1}^{N} j^{-\alpha}} = \frac{i^{-\alpha}}{\zeta_N(\alpha)} \quad \text{with} \quad 0 < \alpha < 1 \quad \text{and} \quad \zeta_N(\alpha) = \sum_{i=1}^{N} i^{-\alpha}. \tag{7.6}$$

2. We select a pair of vertices i and j and create an edge between them with probability

$$p_{ij} = p_i p_j = \frac{(ij)^{-\alpha}}{\zeta_N^2(\alpha)} \tag{7.7}$$

   and repeat this process n times.

Then the probability that a given pair of vertices i and j is not connected by an edge h_{ij} is

$$p_{ij}^{NC} = (1 - p_{ij})^n \approx e^{-2np_{ij}} \tag{7.8}$$

and the probability that they are connected is

$$p_{ij}^{C} = \left(1 - p_{ij}^{NC}\right) = 1 - e^{-2np_{ij}}. \tag{7.9}$$

Call k_i the degree of vertex i; then the moment-generating function of k_i is

$$g_i(t) = \prod_{j \neq i} \left[p_{ij}^{NC} + t p_{ij}^{C}\right]. \tag{7.10}$$

The average degree of vertex i is

$$\bar{k}_i = t\frac{d}{dt} g_i(t)|_{t=1} = \sum_{j \neq i} p_{ij}^{C}. \tag{7.11}$$

Thus,

$$\bar{k}_i = \sum_{j\neq i}(1-e^{-2np_{ij}}) = \sum_{j\neq i}\left(1-e^{-2n\frac{(ij)^{-\alpha}}{\zeta_N^2(\alpha)}}\right) \approx \sum_{j\neq i} 2n\frac{(ij)^{-\alpha}}{\zeta_N^2(\alpha)} = \frac{2n}{\zeta_N^2(\alpha)}\sum_{j\neq i}(ij)^{-\alpha}. \tag{7.12}$$

This expression can be transformed as

$$\bar{k}_i = \frac{2n}{\zeta_N^2(\alpha)}\sum_{j\neq i}(ij)^{-\alpha} = \frac{2ni^{-\alpha}\sum_{j\neq i} j^{-\alpha}}{\zeta_N^2(\alpha)} = \frac{2ni^{-\alpha}\left(\zeta_N(\alpha)-i^{-\alpha}\right)}{\zeta_N^2(\alpha)}. \tag{7.13}$$

The moment-generating function of k_i can be written as

$$\begin{aligned} g_i(t) &= \prod_{j\neq i}\left[p_{ij}^{NC}+tp_{ij}^{C}\right] = e^{(1-t)\bar{k}_i} = \prod_{j\neq i} e^{-(1-t)p_{ij}^C} \\ &\approx \prod_{j\neq i}[1-(1-t)p_{ij}^C = e^{(1-t)\sum_{j\neq i} p_{ij}^C} = e^{(1-t)\bar{k}_i}. \end{aligned} \tag{7.14}$$

We conclude that the probability that $k_i = k$ is given by

$$p_{d,i}(k) = \frac{1}{k!}\frac{d^k}{dt^k}g_i(t)|_{t=0} \approx \frac{\bar{k}_i}{k!}e^{-\bar{k}_i}. \tag{7.15}$$

When $N\to\infty$ then $\zeta_N(\alpha)=\sum_{i=1}^N i^{-\alpha}$ converges to the Riemann zeta function $\zeta(\alpha)$ for $\alpha>1$ and diverges as $\frac{N^{1-\alpha}}{1-\alpha}$ if $0<\alpha<1$. For $0<\alpha<1$ Eq. (7.6) becomes

$$p_i = \frac{i^{-\alpha}}{\zeta_N(\alpha)} = \frac{1-\alpha}{N^{1-\alpha}}i^{-\alpha}. \tag{7.16}$$

When $N\to\infty$, $0<\alpha<1$, and the average degree of the vertices is $2m$, then the degree of vertex i is

$$k = p_i\times mN = 2mN\frac{1-\alpha}{N^{1-\alpha}}i^{-\alpha} = 2m(1-\alpha)\left(\frac{i}{N}\right)^{-\alpha}. \tag{7.17}$$

Indeed, the total number of edges in the graph is mN and the graph has a power-law distribution. Then

$$i = N\left(\frac{k}{2m(1-\alpha)}\right)^{-\frac{1}{\alpha}}. \tag{7.18}$$

From this expression we see that there is a one-to-many correspondence between the unique label of the node i in the G_{ER} graph and the degree k of the vertices in the G_{SF} graph. This reflects the fact that multiple vertices may have the same degree k. The number of vertices of degree k is

$$\begin{aligned} n(k) &= N\left(\frac{k}{2m(1-\alpha)}\right)^{-\frac{1}{\alpha}} - N\left(\frac{k-1}{2m(1-\alpha)}\right)^{-\frac{1}{\alpha}} \\ &= N\left(\frac{k-1}{2m(1-\alpha)}\right)^{-\frac{1}{\alpha}}\left(\left(1+\frac{1}{k}\right)^{-\frac{1}{\alpha}}-1\right). \end{aligned} \tag{7.19}$$

We denote $\gamma = 1 + \frac{1}{\alpha}$ and observe that

$$\left(1+\frac{1}{k}\right)^{-\frac{1}{\alpha}} = 1 + \left(-\frac{1}{\alpha}\right)\left(\frac{1}{k}\right)^{-\frac{1}{\alpha}} + \frac{1}{2}\left(-\frac{1}{\alpha}\right)\left(-\frac{1}{\alpha}-1\right)\left(\frac{1}{k}\right)^{-\frac{1}{\alpha}-1} + \cdots. \tag{7.20}$$

We see that

$$n(k) = N\left(\frac{(k-1)(\gamma-1)}{2m(\gamma-2)}\right)^{-\gamma+1}\left((1-\gamma)\left(\frac{1}{k}\right)^{-\gamma+1} - \frac{\gamma(1-\gamma)}{2}\left(\frac{1}{k}\right)^{-\gamma} + \cdots\right). \tag{7.21}$$

We conclude that to reach the value predicted by the theoretical model for the number of vertices of degree k, the number of iterations is a function of N, of the average degree $2m$, and of γ, the degree of the power law. Next we discuss an algorithm for constructing scale-free networks using biased random walks.

Biased Random Walks. A strategy used successfully to locate systems satisfying a set of conditions in applications such as peer-to-peer systems is based on *biased random walks* [33]. Random walks are reported to be more efficient in searching for nodes with desirable properties than other methods, such as flooding [135].

Unfortunately, the application of random walks in a large network with an irregular topology is unfeasible because a central authority could not maintain accurate information about a dynamic set of members. A solution is to exploit the fact that sampling with a given probability distribution can be simulated by a discrete-time Markov chain. Indeed, consider an irreducible Markov chain with states $(i, j) \in \{0, 1, \ldots, S\}$, and let $P = [p_{ij}]$ denote its probability transition matrix, where

$$p_{ij} = \text{Prob}[X(t+1) = j | X(t) = i], \tag{7.22}$$

with $X(t)$ the state at time t. Let $\pi = (\pi_0, \pi_1, \ldots, \pi_S)$ be a probability distribution with nonzero probability for every state, $\pi_i > 0, 0 \leqslant i \leqslant S$. The transition matrix P is chosen so that π is its unique stationary distribution; thus, the reversibility condition $\pi = \pi P$ holds. When $g(\cdot)$ is a function defined on the states of the Markov chain and we want to estimate

$$E = \sum_{i=0}^{S} g(i)\pi_i, \tag{7.23}$$

we can simulate the Markov chain at times $t = 1, 2, \ldots, N$, and the quantity

$$\widehat{E} = \sum_{i=1}^{N} \frac{f(X(t))}{N} \tag{7.24}$$

is a good estimate of E – more precisely, $\widehat{E} \mapsto E$ when $N \mapsto \infty$. Hastings [160] generalizes the sampling method of Metropolis [243] to construct the transition matrix given the distribution π. He starts by imposing the reversibility condition $\pi_i p_{ij} = \pi_j p_{ji}$. If $Q = [q_{ij}]$ is the transition matrix of an arbitrary Markov chain on the states $\{0, 1, \ldots, S\}$, it is assumed that

$$p_{ij} = q_{ij}\alpha_{ij} \quad \text{if} \quad i \neq j \quad \text{and} \quad p_{ii} = 1 - \sum_{j \neq i} p_{ij}. \tag{7.25}$$

Two versions of sampling are discussed in [160]: that of Metropolis and one proposed by Baker[36]. The quantities α_{ij} are, respectively,

$$\alpha_{ij}^{M} = \begin{cases} 1 & \text{if } \frac{\pi_j}{\pi_i} \geqslant 1 \\ \frac{\pi_j}{\pi_i} & \text{if } \frac{\pi_j}{\pi_i} < 1 \end{cases} \quad \text{and} \quad \alpha_{ij}^{B} = \frac{\pi_j}{\pi_i + \pi_j}. \tag{7.26}$$

For example, consider a Poisson distribution $\pi_i = \lambda^i e^{-\lambda}/i!$. We choose $q_{ij} = 1/2$ if $j = i - 1, i \neq 0$ or $j = i + 1, i \neq 0$ and $q_{00} = q_{01} = 1/2$. Then, using Baker's approach, we have

$$p_{ij} = \begin{cases} \lambda/(\lambda + i + 1) & \text{if } \ j = i + 1, i \neq 0 \\ i/(i + \lambda) & \text{if } \ j = i - 1, i \neq 0 \end{cases} \tag{7.27}$$

and $p_{00} = 1/2$, and $p_{01} = \lambda e^{-\lambda}/(1 + \lambda e^{-\lambda})$.

The algorithm to construct scale-free overlay topologies with an adjustable exponent presented in [319] adopts the equilibrium model discussed in [140]. The algorithm is based on random walks in a connected overlay network $G(V, E)$, viewed as a Markov chain with state space V and a stationary distribution with a random walk bias configured according to a Metropolis–Hastings chain [160]. In this case

$$p_i = i^{-\alpha}, \quad \text{with} \quad 1 \leqslant i \leqslant N, \quad \alpha \in [0, 1) \tag{7.28}$$

and add an edge between two vertices a and b with probability

$$p_a \Big/ \sum_{i=1}^{N} p_i \times p_b \Big/ \sum_{i=1}^{N} p_i \tag{7.29}$$

if none exists; they repeat the process until mN edges are created and the mean degree is $2m$. Then the degree distribution is

$$p(k) \sim k^{-\gamma}, \quad \text{with} \quad \gamma = (1 + \alpha)/\alpha. \tag{7.30}$$

The elements of the transition matrix $P = [p_{ij}]$ are

$$p_{ij} = \begin{cases} \frac{1}{k_i} \min\left\{ \left(\frac{1}{j}\right)^{\frac{1}{\gamma - 1}} \frac{k_i}{k_j}, 1 \right\} & (i, j) \in E \\ 1 - \frac{1}{k_i} \sum_{(l,i) \in E} c_{il} & i = j \\ 0 & (i, j) \notin E \end{cases} \tag{7.31}$$

with k_i the degree of vertex i. An upper bound for the number of random walk steps can be determined from a lower bound for the second smallest eigenvalue of the transition matrix, a nontrivial problem.

A distributed rewiring scheme for constructing a scale-free overlay topology with an adjustable exponent is presented in [319]. An alternative method of creating the scale-free overlay network could be based on the gossip-based peer sampling discussed in [181]. The distributed algorithm for constructing a scale-free network in [319] is based on the method of constructing a random graph with a power-law distribution sketched in [140,212].

Estimation of the Degree of a Power-Law Network. The question we address next is how to estimate the degree distribution of any scheme for the construction of a power-law network [43]. The estimation of the degree distribution from empirical data is analyzed in [86]. According to this study, a good approximation for γ for a discrete power-law distribution for a network with P vertices and $k_{min} = 1$ is

$$\hat{\gamma} \approx 1 + P \left[\sum_{i=1}^{P} \ln \frac{k_i}{k_{min} - 1/2} \right]^{-1} = 1 + \frac{P}{\sum_{i=1}^{P} 2k_i}. \tag{7.32}$$

Several measures exist for the similarity and dissimilarity of two probability density functions of discrete random variables, including the trace distance, fidelity, mutual information, and relative entropy [92,198]. The *trace distance* (also called Kolmogorov or L1 distance) of two probability density functions, $p_X(x)$ and $p_Y(y)$, and their *fidelity* are defined as

$$D(p_X(x), p_Y(x)) = \frac{1}{2} \sum_x |p_X(x) - p_Y(x)| \tag{7.33}$$

and

$$F(p_X(x), p_Y(x)) = \sum_x \sqrt{p_X(x) p_Y(x)}. \tag{7.34}$$

The trace distance is a metric: It is easy to prove nonnegativity, symmetry, the identity of indiscernibles, and the triangle inequality. On the other hand, the fidelity is not a metric, since it fails to satisfy the identity of indiscernibles,

$$F(p_X(x), p_X(x)) = \sum_x \sqrt{p_X(x) p_X(x)} = 1 \neq 0, \tag{7.35}$$

respectively. Determining either the $L1$ distance between the distribution calculated based on Eq. (7.4) or the one produced by the algorithm discussed earlier requires information about the degree of all vertices. From Table 7.2 we see that the degree-one vertices represent a very large fraction of the vertices of a power-law network and may provide a reasonable approximation of the actual degree distribution.

7.12 Epidemic algorithms

Epidemic algorithms mimic the transmission of infectious diseases and are often used in distributed systems to accomplish tasks such as:

- Disseminating information (e.g., topology information).
- Compute aggregates (e.g., arrange the nodes in a gossip overlay into a list sorted by some attributes in logarithmic time).
- Manage data replication in a distributed system [149,180,181].

The *game of life* is a very popular epidemic algorithm invented by John Conway [46].

Several classes of epidemic algorithm exist; the concepts used to classify these algorithms as *susceptible, infective*, or *recovered* refer to the state of the individual in the population subject to infectious disease and, by extension, to the recipient of information in a distributed system:

- *Susceptible.* The individual is healthy but can get infected; the system does not know the specific information but can get it.
- *Infective.* The individual is infected and able to infect others; the system knows the specific information and uses the rules to disseminate it.
- *Recovered.* The individual is infected but does not infect others; the system knows the specific information and does not disseminate it.

7.12.1 Susceptible-Infective (SI)

The SI algorithms apply when the entire population is susceptible to be infected. Once an individual becomes infected, it remains in that state until the entire population is infected. If $I(t)$ is the number of individuals infected, $S(t)$ is the number of individuals susceptible to be infected, and $R(t)$ the number of those infected and then recovered at time t, and if all individuals have an equal probability β of contracting the disease, then

$$\frac{I(0)}{2[1 - I(0)]} \leqslant I(t) \leqslant \frac{I(0)}{1 - I(0)} e^{-\beta t} \tag{7.36}$$

and

$$\frac{1}{2}\left(\frac{1}{S(0) - 1}\right) e^{-\beta t} \leqslant S(t) \leqslant \left(\frac{1}{S(0) - 1}\right) e^{-\beta t} \tag{7.37}$$

when we assume that $I(t)$ and $S(t)$ are continuous variables rather than natural numbers.

7.12.2 Susceptible-Infectious-Recover (SIR)

SIR algorithms are based on the model developed by Kermack and McKendrik in 1927 [189]. The model assumes the following transition from one state to another: $S \mapsto I \mapsto R$. It also assumes that $1/\gamma$ is the average infectious period and that the size of the population is fixed:

$$S(t) + I(t) + R(t) = N. \tag{7.38}$$

The dynamics of the model are captured by the following equations:

$$\frac{dS(t)}{dt} = -\beta S(t)I(t), \quad \frac{dI(t)}{dt} = \beta S(t)I(t) - \gamma I(t), \quad \text{and} \quad \frac{dR(t)}{dt} = \gamma I(t). \tag{7.39}$$

7.12.3 Susceptible-Infective-Susceptible (SIS)

SIS algorithms [57] are particular cases of SIR models in which individuals recover from the disease without immunity. If $p = R(r)/I(r)$, then the number of newly infected grows until $(1 - p)/2$ are infected and then decreases exponentially to $(1 - p)$ according to the expression

$$I(r) = \frac{1 - p}{1 + \left(\frac{(1-p)N}{I(0)} - 1\right)} \times N. \tag{7.40}$$

Recall that the m-th moment of the power-law distribution of a discrete random variable X, $P_X(x = k) = k^{-\gamma}$, is

$$E\left[X^m\right] = \sum_{k=1}^{\infty} k^m P_X(x = k) = \sum_{k=1}^{\infty} k^m k^{-\gamma} = \sum_{k=1}^{\infty} \frac{1}{k^{\gamma - m}}. \tag{7.41}$$

For power-law networks, the epidemic threshold λ for the *Susceptible–Infectious–Recovered* (SIR) and *Susceptible–Infectious–Susceptible* (SIS) epidemic models can be expressed as [112]

$$\lambda = \frac{E\left[X\right]}{E\left[X^2\right]}. \tag{7.42}$$

The *epidemic threshold* is defined as the minimum ratio of infected nodes to the cured nodes per time such that it still allows the epidemics to continue without outside infections. It follows that $\lambda \mapsto 0$ if $\gamma \in (2, 3)$; in other words, such networks become infinitely susceptible to epidemic algorithms. This property is very important for dissemination of control information in such networks.

7.13 Further reading

"A Brief History of the Internet," written by Barry Leiner, Vinton Cerf, David Clark, Robert Kahn, Leonard Kleinrock, Daniel Lynch, Jon Postel, Larry Roberts, and Stephen Wolff, can be accessed at `http://www.internetsociety.org/internet/what-internet/history-internet/brief-history-internet`.

The widely used text of Kurose and Ross [201] is an excellent introduction to basic networking concepts. The book by Bertsekas and Gallagher [50] gives insights into the performance evaluation of computer networks. The classic texts on queuing theory of Kleinrock [195] are required reading for those interested in network analysis.

Moore's law for traffic is discussed in [251]. The class-based queuing algorithm was introduced by Floyd and Van Jacobson in [125]. The *Black Widow* topology for system interconnects is analyzed in [321]. An extensive treatment of storage area networks can be found in [347].

Erdös-Rény random graphs are analyzed in [53,116]. Scale-free networks and their applications are described by Barabási and Albert by [10 – 12,39]. Small-world networks were introduced by Watts and Strogatz in [370]. Epidemic algorithms and their applications are presented in [149,180,181]. Additional references for the topics covered in this chapter are [204,232,248,257].

7.14 History notes

The Internet is a global network based on the Internet Protocol Suite (TCP/IP); its origins can be traced back to 1965, when Ivan Sutherland, the head of the Information Processing Technology Office (IPTO) at the Advanced Research Projects Agency (ARPA), encouraged Lawrence Roberts, who had worked previously at MIT's Lincoln Laboratories, to become the chief scientist at ISTO Technologies and to initiate a networking project based on packet switching rather than circuit switching.

In the early 1960s Leonard Kleinrock at the University of California at Los Angeles (UCLA) developed the theoretical foundations of packet networks and, in the early 1970s, for hierarchical routing in packet-switching networks. Kleinrock published the first paper on packet-switching theory in 1961 and the first book on the subject in 1964.

In August 1968 DARPA released a request for quotation (RFQ) for the development of packet switches called interface message processors (IMPs). A group from Bolt Beranek and Newman (BBN) won the contract. Several researchers and their teams including Robert Kahn from BBN, Lawrence Roberts from DARPA, Howard Frank from Network Analysis Corporation, and Leonard Kleinrock from UCLA, played a major role in the overall ARPANET architectural design. The idea of open-architecture networking was first introduced by Kahn in 1972, and his collaboration with Vint Cerf from Stanford led to the design of TCP/IP. Three groups, one at Stanford, one at BBN, and one at UCLA, won the DARPA contract to implement TCP/IP.

In 1969 BBN installed the first IMP at UCLA. The first two nodes the ARPANET interconnected were the Network Measurement Center at UCLA's School of Engineering and Applied Science and SRI International in Menlo Park, California. Two more nodes were added at UC Santa Barbara and the University of Utah. By the end of 1971 there were 15 sites interconnected by ARPANET.

Ethernet technology, developed by Bob Metcalfe at Xerox PARC in 1973, and other local area network technologies, such as token-passing rings, allowed the personal computers and workstations to be connected to the Internet in the 1980s. As the number of Internet hosts increased, it was no longer feasible to have a single table of all hosts and their addresses. The Domain Name System (DNS) was invented by Paul Mockapetris of USC/ISI. The DNS permitted a scalable distributed mechanism for resolving hierarchical host names into an Internet address.

UC Berkeley, with support from DARPA, rewrote the TCP/IP code developed at BBN and incorporated it into the *Unix* BSD system. In 1985 Dennis Jennings started the NSFNET program at NSF to support the general research and academic communities.

7.15 Exercises and problems

Problem 1. Four ground rules for open-architecture principles are cited in "A Brief History of the Internet." Read the paper and analyze the implication of each one of these rules.

Problem 2. The paper in Problem 1 also lists several key issues for the design of a network:

- Algorithms to prevent lost packets from permanently disabling communications and enabling them to be successfully retransmitted from the source.
- Providing for host-to-host "pipelining" so that multiple packets can be en route from source to destination at the discretion of the participating hosts, if the intermediate networks allow.
- The need for end-to-end checksums, reassembly of packets from fragments, and detection of duplicates, if any.
- The need for global addressing.
- Techniques for host-to-host flow control.

Discuss how these issues were addressed by the TCP/IP network architecture.

Problem 3. Analyze the challenges of a transition to IPv6. What, in your view, will be the effect of this transition on cloud computing?

Problem 4. Discuss the algorithms used to compute TCP window size.

Problem 5. Creating a virtual machine (VM) reduces ultimately to copying a file. Therefore, the explosion in the number of VMs cannot be prevented (see Section 9.7). Because each VM needs its own IP address, virtualization could drastically lead to an exhaustion of the IPv4 address space. Analyze the solution to this potential problem that was adopted by the *IaaS* cloud service delivery model.

Problem 6. Read the paper describing the stochastic fair-queuing algorithm [125]. Analyze the similarities and dissimilarities of this algorithm and the start-time fair queuing discussed in Section 6.10.

Problem 7. Small-world networks were introduced by D. Watts and S. H. Strogatz. These networks have two desirable features: high clustering and small path length. Read [370] and design an algorithm to construct a small-world network.

Problem 8. The properties of scale-free networks are discussed in [10 – 12,39]. Discuss the important features of systems interconnected by scale-free networks as discussed in these papers.

Problem 9. Discuss the three models for the propagation of an infectious disease in a finite population: *SI, SIR*, and *SIS*. Justify the formulas describing the dynamics of the system for each model.

CHAPTER

Storage Systems

8

A cloud provides the vast amounts of storage and computing cycles demanded by many applications. The network-centric content model allows a user to access data stored on a cloud from any device connected to the Internet. Mobile devices with limited power reserves and local storage take advantage of cloud environments to store audio and video files. Clouds provide an ideal environment for multimedia content delivery.

A variety of sources feed a continuous stream of data to cloud applications. An ever-increasing number of cloud-based services collect detailed data about their services and information about the users of these services. Then the service providers use the clouds to analyze that data.

Storage and processing on the cloud are intimately tied to one another; indeed, sophisticated strategies to reduce the access time and to support real-time multimedia access are necessary to satisfy the requirements of content delivery. On the other hand, most cloud applications process very large amounts of data; effective data replication and storage management strategies are critical to the computations performed on the cloud.

A new concept, "*big data*," reflects the fact that many applications use data sets so large that they cannot be stored and processed using local resources. The consensus is that "big data" growth can be viewed as a three-dimensional phenomenon; it implies an increased volume of data, requires an increased processing speed to process more data and produce more results, and at the same time it involves a diversity of data sources and data types.

Applications in many areas of science, including genomics, structural biology, high-energy physics, astronomy, meteorology, and the study of the environment, carry out complex analysis of data sets, often of the order of terabytes.[1] In 2010, the four main detectors at the Large Hadron Collider (LHC) produced 13 PB of data; the Sloan Digital Sky Survey (SDSS) collects about 200 GB of data per night. As a result of this increasing appetite for data, file systems such as Btrfs, XFS, ZFS, exFAT, NTFS, HFS Plus, and ReFS support disk formats with theoretical volume sizes of several exabytes.

Several figures can help us place in context the amount of data associated with various human activities. The global data volume at the end of 2009 reached 800 EB, according to `www.genevaassociation.org`. Internet video will generate over 18 EB/month in 2013 and global mobile data traffic will reach 2 EB/month by 2013 according to a report from Cisco Systems (`www.cisco.com/en/US/netsol/ns827/networking_solutions_sub_solution.html`).

Our discussion of cloud storage starts with a review of the storage technology in Section 8.1, followed by an overview of storage models in Section 8.2. Then we follow the evolution of file systems, from distributed to parallel file systems, then to the file systems capable of handling massive amounts of data. In Sections 8.3 and 8.4 we discuss distributed file systems, General Parallel File Systems, and the Google

[1]Terabyte, 1 TB = 10^{12} bytes; petabyte, 1 PB = 10^{15} bytes; exabyte, 1 EB = 10^{18} bytes; zettabyte, 1 ZB = 10^{21} bytes.

File System, respectively. A locking service, *Chubby*, based on the Paxos algorithm, is presented in Section 8.7, followed by a discussion of transaction-processing systems and *NoSQL* databases in Section 8.8. The next two sections, Sections 8.9 and 8.10, analyze *BigTable* and *Megastore* systems.

8.1 The evolution of storage technology

The technological capacity to store information has grown over time at an accelerated pace [164,178]:

- 1986: 2.6 EB; equivalent to less than one 730 MB CD-ROM of data per computer user.
- 1993: 15.8 EB; equivalent to four CD-ROMs per user.
- 2000: 54.5 EB; equivalent to 12 CD-ROMs per user.
- 2007: 295 EB; equivalent to almost 61 CD-ROMs per user.

Though it pales in comparison with processor technology, the evolution of storage technology is astounding. A 2003 study [251] shows that during the 1980–2003 period the storage density of hard disk drives (HDD) increased by four orders of magnitude, from about 0.01 Gb/in^2 to about 100 Gb/in^2. During the same period the prices fell by five orders of magnitude, to about 1 cent/Mbyte. HDD densities are projected to climb to 1,800 Gb/in^2 by 2016, up from 744 Gb/in^2 in 2011.

The density of Dynamic Random Access Memory (DRAM) increased from about 1 Gb/in^2 in 1990 to 100 Gb/in^2 in 2003. The cost of DRAM tumbled from about $80/MB to less than $1/MB during the same period. In 2010 Samsung announced the first monolithic, 4 gigabit, low-power, double-data-rate (LPDDR2) DRAM using a 30 nm process.

These rapid technological advancements have changed the balance between initial investment in storage devices and system management costs. Now the cost of storage management is the dominant element of the total cost of a storage system. This effect favors the centralized storage strategy supported by a cloud; indeed, a centralized approach can automate some of the storage management functions, such as replication and backup, and thus reduce substantially the storage management cost.

While the density of storage devices has increased and the cost has decreased dramatically, the access time has improved only slightly. The performance of I/O subsystems has not kept pace with the performance of computing engines, and that affects multimedia, scientific and engineering, and other modern applications that process increasingly large volumes of data.

The storage systems face substantial pressure because the volume of data generated has increased exponentially during the past few decades; whereas in the 1980s and 1990s data was primarily generated by humans, nowadays machines generate data at an unprecedented rate. Mobile devices, such as smart-phones and tablets, record static images, as well as movies and have limited local storage capacity, so they transfer the data to cloud storage systems. Sensors, surveillance cameras, and digital medical imaging devices generate data at a high rate and dump it onto storage systems accessible via the Internet. Online digital libraries, ebooks, and digital media, along with reference data,[2] add to the demand for massive amounts of storage.

As the volume of data increases, new methods and algorithms for data mining that require powerful computing systems have been developed. Only a concentration of resources could provide the CPU

[2]The term *reference data* is used for infrequently accessed data such as archived copies of medical or financial records, customer account statements, and so on.

cycles along with the vast storage capacity necessary to perform such intensive computations and access the very large volume of data.

Although we emphasize the advantages of a concentration of resources, we have to be acutely aware that a cloud is a large-scale distributed system with a very large number of components that must work in concert. The management of such a large collection of systems poses significant challenges and requires novel approaches to systems design. Case in point: Although the early distributed file systems used custom-designed reliable components, nowadays large-scale systems are built with off-the-shelf components. The emphasis of the design philosophy has shifted from *performance at any cost* to *reliability at the lowest possible cost*. This shift is evident in the evolution of ideas, from the early distributed file systems of the 1980s, such as the Network File System (NFS) and the Andrew File System (AFS), to today's Google File System (GFS) and the *Megastore*.

8.2 Storage models, file systems, and databases

A *storage model* describes the layout of a data structure in physical storage; a *data model* captures the most important logical aspects of a data structure in a database. The physical storage can be a local disk, a removable media, or storage accessible via a network.

Two abstract models of storage are commonly used: *cell storage* and *journal storage*. Cell storage assumes that the storage consists of cells of the same size and that each object fits exactly in one cell. This model reflects the physical organization of several storage media; the primary memory of a computer is organized as an array of memory cells, and a secondary storage device (e.g., a disk) is organized in sectors or blocks `read` and written as a unit. `read/write` *coherence* and *before-or-after atomicity* are two highly desirable properties of any storage model and in particular of cell storage (see Figure 8.1).

Journal storage is a fairly elaborate organization for storing composite objects such as records consisting of multiple fields. Journal storage consists of a *manager* and *cell storage*, where the entire

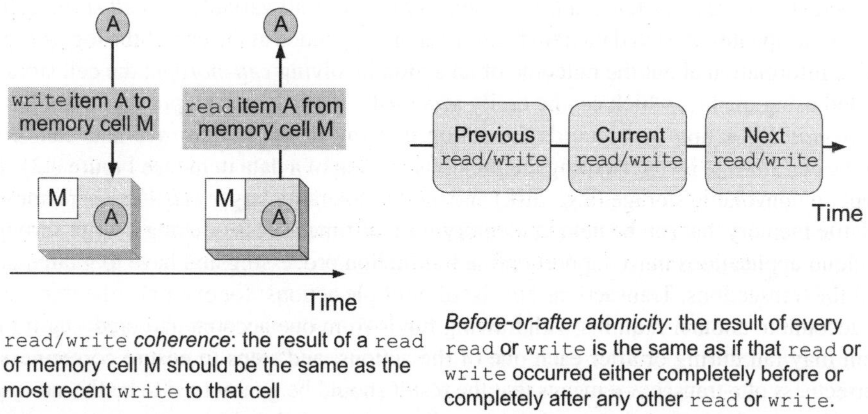

FIGURE 8.1

Illustration capturing the semantics of `read/write` *coherence* and *before-or-after atomicity.*

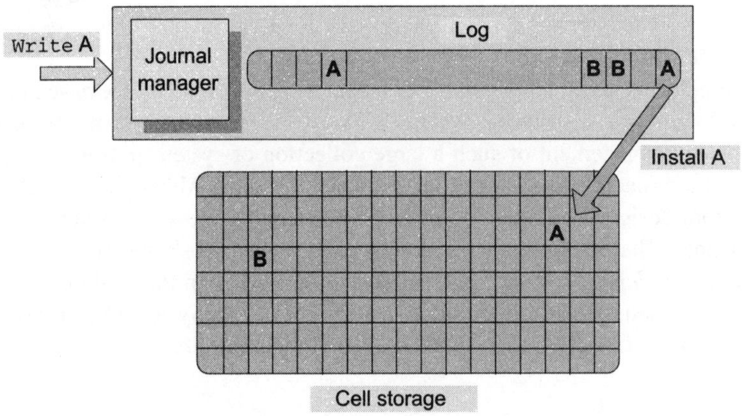

FIGURE 8.2

A *log* contains the entire history of all variables. The log is stored on nonvolatile media of *journal storage*. If the system fails after the new value of a variable is stored in the log but before the value is stored in cell memory, then the value can be recovered from the log. If the system fails while writing the log, the cell memory is not updated. This guarantees that all actions are *all-or-nothing*. Two variables, **A** and **B**, in the log and cell storage are shown. A new value of **A** is written first to the *log* and then *installed* on cell memory at the unique address assigned to **A**.

history of a variable is maintained, rather than just the current value. The user does not have direct access to the *cell storage*; instead the user can request the *journal manager* to (i) start a new action; (ii) `read` the value of a cell; (iii) `write` the value of a cell; (iv) commit an action; or (v) abort an action. The *journal manager* translates user requests to commands sent to the cell storage: (i) `read` a cell; (ii) `write` a cell; (iii) allocate a cell; or (iv) deallocate a cell.

In the context of storage systems, a *log* contains a history of all variables in *cell storage*. The information about the updates of each data item forms a record appended at the end of the log. A log provides authoritative information about the outcome of an action involving *cell storage*; the cell storage can be reconstructed using the log, which can be easily accessed – we only need a pointer to the last record.

An *all-or-nothing* action first records the action in a *log* in *journal storage* and then *installs* the change in the *cell storage* by overwriting the previous version of a data item (see Figure 8.2). The *log* is always kept on nonvolatile storage (e.g., disk) and the considerably larger *cell storage* resides typically on nonvolatile memory, but can be held in memory for real-time access or using a write-through cache.

Many cloud applications must support online transaction processing and have to guarantee the correctness of the transactions. Transactions consist of multiple actions; for example, the transfer of funds from one account to another requires withdrawing funds from one account and crediting it to another. The system may fail during or after each one of the actions, and steps to ensure correctness must be taken. Correctness of a transaction means that the result should be guaranteed to be the same as though the actions were applied one after another, regardless of the order. More stringent conditions must sometimes be observed; for example, banking transactions must be processed in the order in which they are issued, the so-called *external time consistency*. To guarantee correctness, a transaction-processing system supports *all-or-nothing atomicity*, discussed in Section 2.10.

A *file system* consists of a collection of *directories*. Each directory provides information about a set of files. Today high-performance systems can choose among three classes of file system: network file systems (NFSs), storage area networks (SANs), and parallel file systems (PFSs). The NFS is very popular and has been used for some time, but it does not scale well and has reliability problems; an NFS server could be a single point of failure.

Advances in networking technology allow the separation of storage systems from computational servers; the two can be connected by a SAN. SANs offer additional flexibility and allow cloud servers to deal with nondisruptive changes in the storage configuration. Moreover, the storage in a SAN can be *pooled* and then allocated based on the needs of the servers; pooling requires additional software and hardware support and represents another advantage of a centralized storage system. A SAN-based implementation of a file system can be expensive, since each node must have a Fibre Channel adapter to connect to the network.

Parallel file systems are scalable, are capable of distributing files across a large number of nodes, and provide a global naming space. In a parallel data system, several I/O nodes serve data to all computational nodes and include a metadata server that contains information about the data stored in the I/O nodes. The interconnection network of a parallel file system could be a SAN.

Most cloud applications do not interact directly with file systems but rather through an application layer that manages a database. A *database* is a collection of logically related records. The software that controls the access to the database is called a *database management system (DBMS)*. The main functions of a DBMS are to enforce data integrity, manage data access and concurrency control, and support recovery after a failure.

A DBMS supports a *query language,* a dedicated programming language used to develop database applications. Several database models, including the navigational model of the 1960s, the relational model of the 1970s, the object-oriented model of the 1980s, and the *NoSQL* model of the first decade of the 2000s, reflect the limitations of the hardware available at the time and the requirements of the most popular applications of each period.

Most cloud applications are data intensive and test the limitations of the existing infrastructure. For example, they demand DBMSs capable of supporting rapid application development and short time to market. At the same time, cloud applications require low latency, scalability, and high availability and demand a consistent view of the data.

These requirements cannot be satisfied simultaneously by existing database models; for example, relational databases are easy to use for application development but do not scale well. As its name implies, the *NoSQL* model does not support SQL as a query language and may not guarantee the *atomicity, consistency, isolation, durability* (ACID) properties of traditional databases. *NoSQL* usually guarantees the eventual consistency for transactions limited to a single data item. The *NoSQL* model is useful when the structure of the data does not require a relational model and the amount of data is very large. Several types of *NoSQL* database have emerged in the last few years. Based on the way the *NoSQL* databases store data, we recognize several types, such as key-value stores, *BigTable* implementations, document store databases, and graph databases.

Replication, used to ensure fault tolerance of large-scale systems built with commodity components, requires mechanisms to guarantee that all replicas are consistent with one another. This is another example of increased complexity of modern computing and communication systems due to physical characteristics of components, a topic discussed in Chapter 10. Section 8.7 contains an in-depth analysis of a service implementing a consensus algorithm to guarantee that replicated objects are consistent.

8.3 Distributed file systems: The precursors

In this section we discuss the first distributed file systems, developed in the 1980s by software companies and universities. The systems covered are the Network File System developed by Sun Microsystems in 1984, the Andrew File System developed at Carnegie Mellon University as part of the Andrew project, and the Sprite Network File System developed by John Osterhout's group at UC Berkeley as a component of the *Unix*-like distributed operating system called Sprite. Other systems developed at about the same time are Locus [365], Apollo [211], and the Remote File System (RFS) [35]. The main concerns in the design of these systems were scalability, performance, and security (see Table 8.1.)

In the 1980s many organizations, including research centers, universities, financial institutions, and design centers, considered networks of workstations to be an ideal environment for their operations. Diskless workstations were appealing due to reduced hardware costs and because of lower maintenance and system administration costs. Soon it became obvious that a distributed file system could be very useful for the management of a large number of workstations. Sun Microsystems, one of the main promoters of distributed systems based on workstations, proceeded to develop the NFS in the early 1980s.

Network File System (NFS). NFS was the first widely used distributed file system; the development of this application based on the client-server model was motivated by the need to share a file system among a number of clients interconnected by a local area network.

Table 8.1 A comparison of several network file systems [250].

File System	Cache Size and Location	Writing Policy	Consistency Guarantees	Cache Validation
NFS	Fixed, memory	On close or 30 s delay	Sequential	On open, with server consent
AFS	Fixed, disk	On close	Sequential	When modified server asks client
Sprite	Variable, memory	30 s delay	Sequential, concurrent	On open, with server consent
Locus	Fixed, memory	On close	Sequential, concurrent	On open, with server consent
Apollo	Variable, memory	Delayed or on unlock	Sequential	On open, with server consent
RFS	Fixed, memory	Write-through	Sequential, concurrent	On open, with server consent

A majority of workstations were running under *Unix*; thus, many design decisions for the NFS were influenced by the design philosophy of the *Unix File System* (UFS). It is not surprising that the NFS designers aimed to:

- Provide the same semantics as a local UFS to ensure compatibility with existing applications.
- Facilitate easy integration into existing UFS.
- Ensure that the system would be widely used and thus support clients running on different operating systems.
- Accept a modest performance degradation due to remote access over a network with a bandwidth of several Mbps.

Before we examine NFS in more detail, we have to analyze three important characteristics of the *Unix* File System that enabled the extension from local to remote file management:

- The layered design provides the necessary *flexibility* for the file system; layering allows separation of concerns and minimization of the interaction among the modules necessary to implement the system. The addition of the *vnode* layer allowed the *Unix* File System to treat local and remote file access uniformly.
- The hierarchical design supports *scalability* of the file system; indeed, it allows grouping of files into special files called *directories* and supports multiple levels of directories and collections of directories and files, the so-called *file systems*. The hierarchical file structure is reflected by the file-naming convention.
- The metadata supports a systematic rather than an ad hoc design philosophy of the file system. The so called *inodes* contain information about individual files and directories. The inodes are kept on persistent media, together with the data. Metadata includes the file owner, the access rights, the creation time or the time of the last modification of the file, the file size, and information about the structure of the file and the persistent storage device cells where data is stored. Metadata also supports device independence, a very important objective due to the very rapid pace of storage technology development.

The *logical organization* of a file reflects the data model – the view of the data from the perspective of the application. The *physical organization* reflects the storage model and describes the manner in which the file is stored on a given storage medium. The layered design allows UFS to separate concerns for the physical file structure from the logical one.

Recall that a *file* is a linear array of cells stored on a persistent storage device. The *file pointer* identifies a cell used as a starting point for a `read` or `write` operation. This linear array is viewed by an application as a collection of logical records; the file is stored on a physical device as a set of physical records, or blocks, of a size dictated by the physical media.

The lower three layers of the UFS hierarchy – the block, the file, and the inode layer – reflect the physical organization. The block layer allows the system to locate individual blocks on the physical device; the file layer reflects the organization of blocks into files; and the inode layer provides the metadata for the objects (files and directories). The upper three layers – the path name, the absolute path name, and the symbolic path name layer – reflect the logical organization. The file-name layer mediates between the machine-oriented and the user-oriented views of the file system (see Figure 8.3).

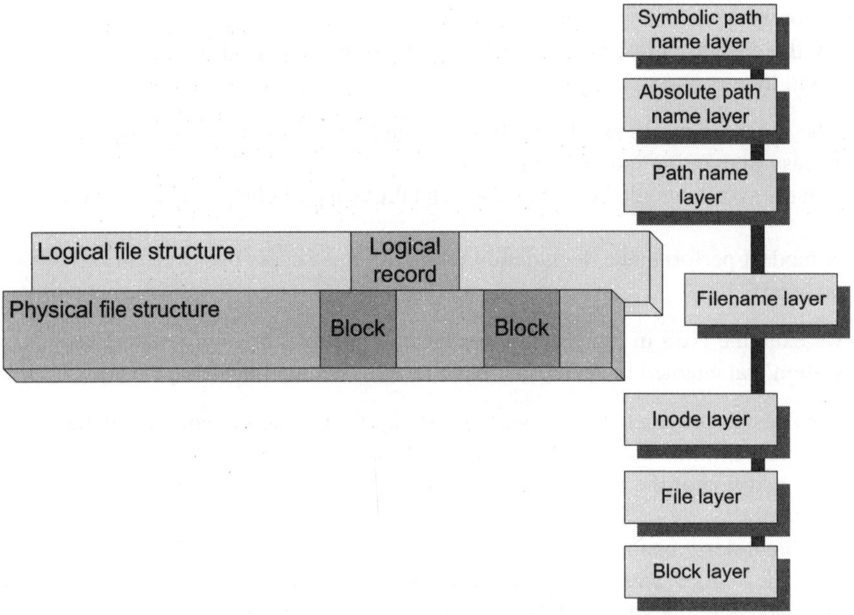

FIGURE 8.3

The layered design of the *Unix* File System separates the physical file structure from the logical one. The lower three layers – block, file, and inode – are related to the physical file structure, while the upper three layers – path name, absolute path name, and symbolic path name – reflect the logical organization. The filename layer mediates between the two.

Several *control structures* maintained by the kernel of the operating system support file handling by a running process. These structures are maintained in the user area of the process address space and can only be accessed in kernel mode. To access a file, a process must first establish a connection with the file system by opening the file. At that time a new entry is added to the *file description table*, and the meta-information is brought into another control structure, the *open file table*.

A *path* specifies the location of a file or directory in a file system; a *relative path* specifies this location relative to the current/working directory of the process, whereas a *full path*, also called an *absolute path*, specifies the location of the file independently of the current directory, typically relative to the root directory. A local file is uniquely identified by a *file descriptor (fd)*, generally an index in the open file table.

The Network File System is based on the client-server paradigm. The client runs on the local host while the server is at the site of the remote file system, and they interact by means of remote procedure calls (RPCs) (see Figure 8.4). The API interface of the local file system distinguishes file operations on a local file from the ones on a remote file and, in the latter case, invokes the RPC client. Figure 8.5 shows the API for a *Unix* File System, with the calls made by the RPC client in response to API calls issued by a user program for a remote file system as well as some of the actions carried out by the NFS

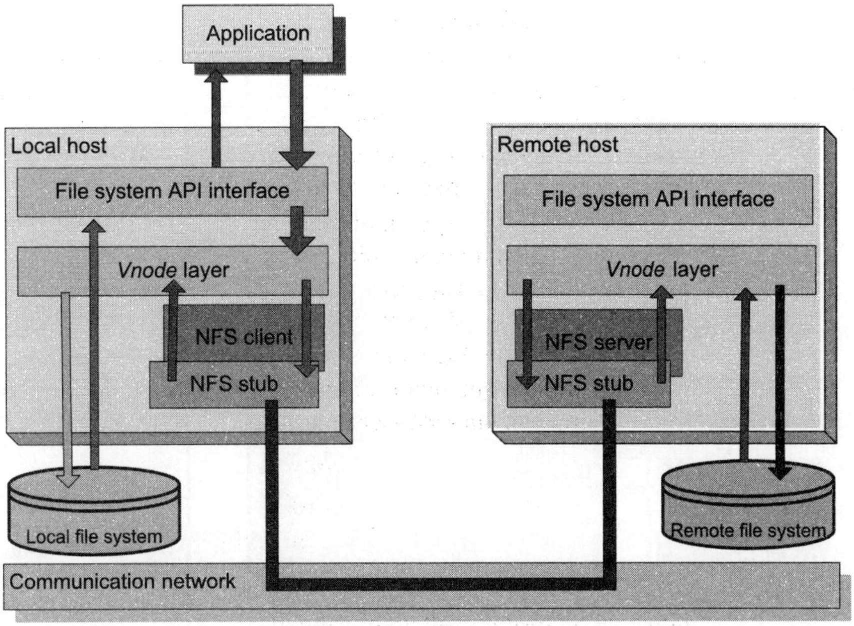

FIGURE 8.4

The NFS client-server interaction. The *vnode* layer implements file operation in a uniform manner, regardless of whether the file is local or remote. An operation targeting a local file is directed to the local file system, whereas one for a remote file involves NFS. An NSF client packages the relevant information about the target and the NFS server passes it to the *vnode* layer on the remote host, which, in turn, directs it to the remote file system.

server in response to an RPC call. NFS uses a *vnode* layer to distinguish between operations on local and remote files, as shown in Figure 8.4.

A remote file is uniquely identified by a *file handle (fh)* rather than a file descriptor. The file handle is a 32-byte internal name, a combination of the file system identification, an inode number, and a generation number. The file handle allows the system to locate the remote file system and the file on that system; the generation number allows the system to reuse the inode numbers and ensures correct semantics when multiple clients operate on the same remote file.

Although many RPC calls, such as `read`, are idempotent,[3] communication failures could sometimes lead to unexpected behavior. Indeed, if the network fails to deliver the response to a `read` RPC, then the call can be repeated without any side effects. By contrast, when the network fails to deliver the response to the `rmdir` RPC, the second call returns an error code to the user if the call was successful the first time. If the server fails to execute the first call, the second call returns normally. Note also that there is no `close` RPC because this action only makes changes in the process open file structure and does not affect the remote file.

[3] An action is idempotent if repeating it several times has the same effect as though the action were executed only once.

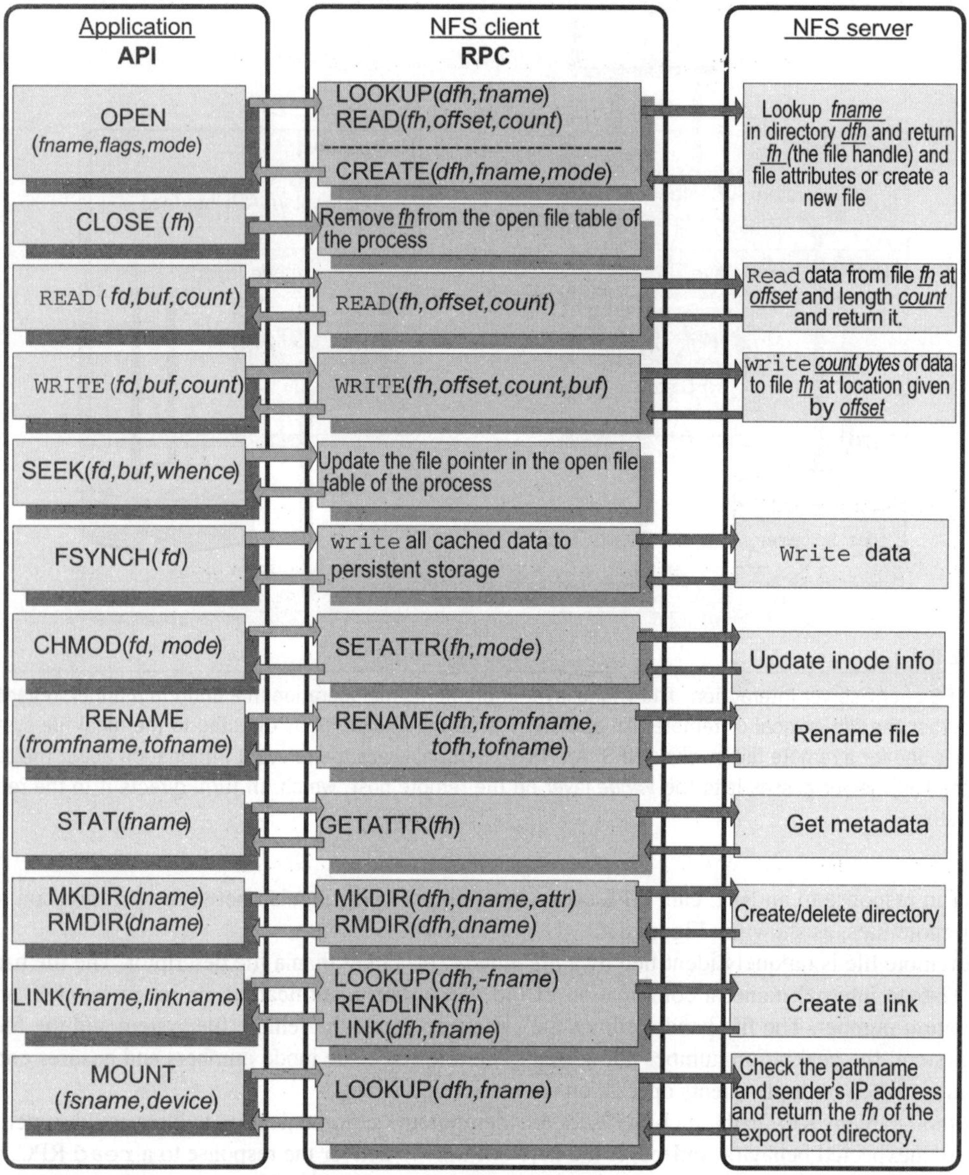

FIGURE 8.5

The API of the *Unix* File System and the corresponding RPC issued by an NFS client to the NFS server. The actions of the server in response to an RPC issued by the NFS client are too complex to be fully described. *fd* stands for file descriptor, *fh* for file handle, *fname* for filename, *dname* for directory name, *dfh* for the directory where the file handle can be found, *count* for the number of bytes to be transferred, *buf* for the buffer to transfer the data to/from, and *device* for the device on which the file system is located *fsname* (stands for files system name).

The NFS has undergone significant transformations over the years. It has evolved from Version 2 [314], discussed in this section, to Version 3 [286] in 1994 and then to Version 4 [287] in 2000 (see Section 8.11).

Andrew File System (AFS). AFS is a distributed file system developed in the late 1980s at Carnegie Mellon University (CMU) in collaboration with IBM [250]. The designers of the system envisioned a very large number of workstations interconnected with a relatively small number of servers; it was anticipated that each individual at CMU would have an Andrew workstation, so the system would connect up to 10,000 workstations. The set of trusted servers in AFS forms a structure called Vice. The OS on a workstation, 4.2 BSD *Unix*, intercepts file system calls and forwards them to a user-level process called Venus, which caches files from Vice and stores modified copies of files back on the servers they came from. Reading and writing from/to a file are performed directly on the cached copy and bypass Venus; only when a file is opened or closed does Venus communicate with Vice.

The emphasis of the AFS design was on performance, security, and simple management of the file system [170]. To ensure scalability and to reduce response time, the local disks of the workstations are used as persistent cache. The master copy of a file residing on one of the servers is updated only when the file is modified. This strategy reduces the load placed on the servers and contributes to better system performance.

Another major objective of the AFS design was improved security. The communications between clients and servers are encrypted, and all file operations require secure network connections. When a user signs into a workstation, the password is used to obtain security tokens from an authentication server. These tokens are then used every time a file operation requires a secure network connection.

The AFS uses *access control lists* (ACLs) to allow control sharing of the data. An ACL specifies the access rights of an individual user or group of users. A set of tools supports ACL management. Another facet of the effort to reduce user involvement in file management is *location transparency*. The files can be accessed from any location and can be moved automatically or at the request of system administrators without user involvement and/or inconvenience. The relatively small number of servers drastically reduces the efforts related to system administration because operations, such as backups, affect only the servers, whereas workstations can be added, removed, or moved from one location to another without administrative intervention.

Sprite Network File System (SFS). SFS is a component of the Sprite network operating system [165]. SFS supports non-write-through caching of files on the client as well as the server systems [255]. Processes running on all workstations enjoy the same semantics for file access as they would if they were run on a single system. This is possible due to a cache consistency mechanism that flushes portions of the cache and disables caching for shared files opened for `read/write` operations.

Caching not only hides the network latency, it also reduces server utilization and obviously improves performance by reducing response time. A file access request made by a client process could be satisfied at different levels. First, the request is directed to the local cache; if it's not satisfied there, it is passed to the local file system of the client. If it cannot be satisfied locally then the request is sent to the remote server. If the request cannot be satisfied by the remote server's cache, it is sent to the file system running on the server.

The design decisions for the Sprite system were influenced by the resources available at a time when a typical workstation had a 1–2 MIPS processor and 4–14 Mbytes of physical memory. The main-memory caches allowed diskless workstations to be integrated into the system and enabled the development of unique caching mechanisms and policies for both clients and servers. The results of a file-intensive benchmark report [255] show that SFS was 30–35% faster than either NFS or AFS.

The file cache is organized as a collection of 4 KB blocks; a cache block has a virtual address consisting of a unique file identifier supplied by the server and a block number in the file. Virtual addressing allows the clients to create new blocks without the need to communicate with the server. File servers map virtual to physical disk addresses. Note that the page size of the virtual memory in Sprite is also 4K.

The size of the cache available to an SFS client or a server system changes dynamically as a function of the needs. This is possible because the Sprite operating system ensures optimal sharing of the physical memory between file caching by SFS and virtual memory management.

The file system and the virtual memory manage separate sets of physical memory pages and maintain a time of last access for each block or page, respectively. Virtual memory uses a version of the clock algorithm [254] to implement a least recently used (LRU) page replacement algorithm, and the file system implements a strict LRU order, since it knows the time of each `read` and `write` operation. Whenever the file system or the virtual memory management experiences a file cache miss or a page fault, it compares the age of its oldest cache block or page, respectively, with the age of the oldest one of the other system; the oldest cache block or page is forced to release the real memory frame.

An important design decision related to the SFS was to *delay write-backs;* this means that a block is first written to cache, and the writing to the disk is delayed for a time of the order of tens of seconds. This strategy speeds up writing and avoids writing when the data is discarded before the time to `write` it to the disk. The obvious drawback of this policy is that data can be lost in case of a system failure. *Write-through* is the alternative to the delayed write-back; it guarantees reliability because the block is written to the disk as soon as it is available on the cache, but it increases the time for a write operation.

Most network file systems guarantee that once a file is closed, the server will have the newest version on persistent storage. As far as concurrency is concerned, we distinguish *sequential write sharing*, when a file cannot be opened simultaneously for reading and writing by several clients, from *concurrent write sharing*, when multiple clients can modify the file at the same time. Sprite allows both modes of concurrency and delegates the cache consistency to the servers. In case of concurrent `write` sharing, the client caching for the file is disabled; all `reads` and `writes` are carried out through the server.

Table 8.1 presents a comparison of caching, writing strategy, and consistency of NFS, AFS [250], Sprite [165], Locus [365], Apollo [211], and the Remote File System (RFS) [35].

8.4 General Parallel File System

Parallel I/O implies execution of multiple input/output operations concurrently. Support for parallel I/O is essential to the performance of many applications [236]. Therefore, once distributed file systems became ubiquitous, the natural next step in the evolution of the file system was to support parallel access. Parallel file systems allow multiple clients to `read` and `write` concurrently from the same file.

Concurrency control is a critical issue for parallel file systems. Several semantics for handling the shared access are possible. For example, when the clients share the file pointer, successive reads issued by multiple clients advance the file pointer; another semantic is to allow each client to have its own

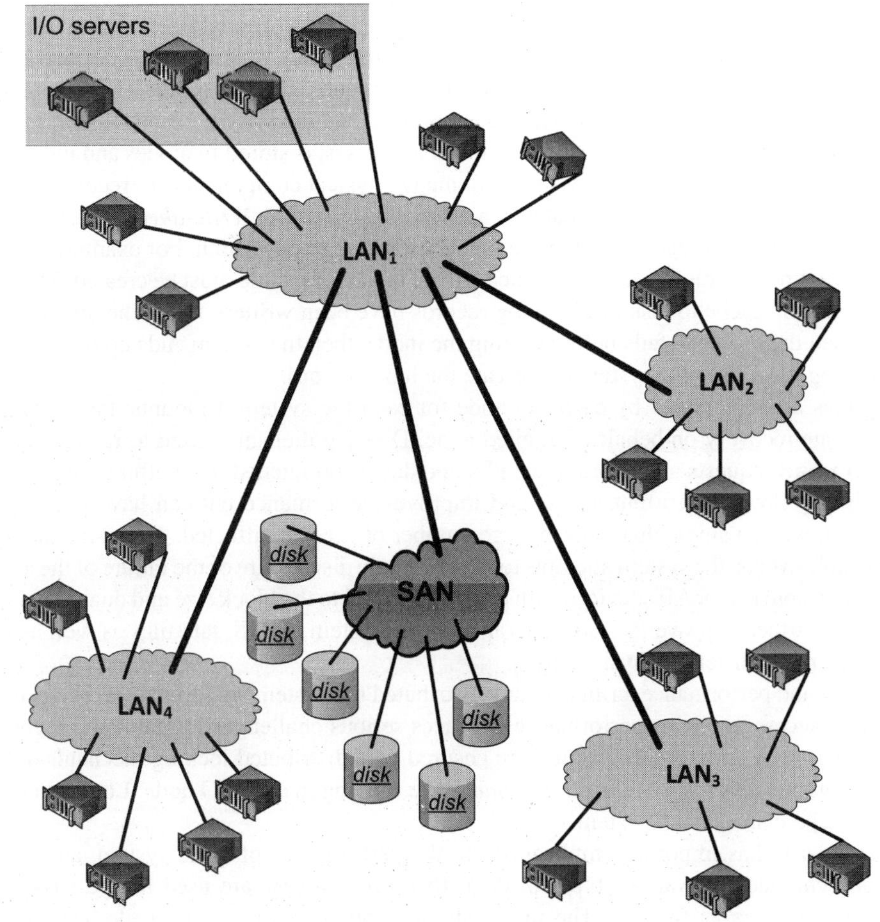

FIGURE 8.6

A GPFS configuration. The disks are interconnected by a SAN and compute servers are distributed in four LANs, LAN_1–LAN_4. The I/O nodes/servers are connected to LAN_1.

file pointer. Early supercomputers such as the Intel Paragon[4] took advantage of parallel file systems to support applications based on the same program, multiple data (SPMD) paradigm.

The General Parallel File System (GPFS) [317] was developed at IBM in the early 2000s as a successor to the TigerShark multimedia file system [159]. GPFS is a parallel file system that emulates closely the behavior of a general-purpose POSIX system running on a single system. GPFS was designed for optimal performance of large clusters; it can support a file system of up to 4 PB consisting of up to 4, 096 disks of 1 TB each (see Figure 8.6).

[4]The Paragon series of superconductors launched in 1992 were based on the Touchstone Delta system. Up to 4,000 i860s Intel microprocessors were connected in a 2D grid. A parallel file system was available for the Paragon.

The maximum file size is $(2^{63}-1)$ bytes. A file consists of blocks of equal size, ranging from 16 KB to 1 MB striped across several disks. The system could support not only very large files but also a very large number of files. The directories use *extensible hashing* techniques[5] to access a file. The system maintains user data, file metadata such as the time when last modified, and file system metadata such as allocation maps. Metadata, such as file attributes and data block addresses, is stored in inodes and indirect blocks.

Reliability is a major concern in a system with many physical components. To recover from system failures, GPFS records all metadata updates in a *write-ahead* log file. *Write-ahead* means that updates are written to persistent storage only after the log records have been written. For example, when a new file is created, a directory block must be updated and an inode for the file must be created. These records are transferred from cache to disk after the log records have been written. When the directory block is written and then the I/O node fails before writing the inode, then the system ends up in an inconsistent state and the log file allows the system to recreate the inode record.

The log files are maintained by each I/O node for each file system it mounts; thus, any I/O node is able to initiate recovery on behalf of a failed node. Disk parallelism is used to reduce access time. Multiple I/O `read` requests are issued in parallel and data is prefetched in a buffer pool.

Data striping allows concurrent access and improves performance but can have unpleasant side-effects. Indeed, when a single disk fails, a large number of files are affected. To reduce the impact of such undesirable events, the system attempts to mask a single disk failure or the failure of the access path to a disk. The system uses RAID devices with the stripes equal to the block size and dual-attached RAID controllers. To further improve the fault tolerance of the system, GPFS data files as well as metadata are replicated on two different physical disks.

Consistency and performance, critical to any distributed file system, are difficult to balance. Support for concurrent access improves performance but faces serious challenges in maintaining consistency. In GPFS, consistency and synchronization are ensured by a distributed locking mechanism; a *central lock manager* grants *lock tokens* to *local lock managers* running in each I/O node. Lock tokens are also used by the cache management system.

Lock granularity has important implications in the performance of a file system, and GPFS uses a variety of techniques for various types of data. *Byte-range tokens* are used for `read` and `write` operations to data files as follows: The first node attempting to `write` to a file acquires a token covering the entire file, $[0, \infty]$. This node is allowed to carry out all `reads` and `writes` to the file without any need for permission until a second node attempts to write to the same file. Then the range of the token given to the first node is restricted. More precisely, if the first node writes sequentially at offset fp_1 and the second one at offset $fp_2 > fp_1$, the range of the tokens for the two tokens are $[0, fp_2]$ and $[fp_2, \infty]$, respectively, and the two nodes can operate concurrently, without the need for further negotiations. Byte-range tokens are rounded to block boundaries.

Byte-range token negotiations among nodes use the *required range* and the *desired range* for the offset and for the length of the current and future operations, respectively. *Data shipping*, an alternative to byte-range locking, allows fine-grained data sharing. In this mode the file blocks are controlled by the I/O nodes in a round-robin manner. A node forwards a `read` or `write` operation to the node controlling the target block, the only one allowed to access the file.

---

[5]A hash function is applied to the name of the file; then the n low-order bits of the hash value give the block number of the directory where the file information can be found. n is a function of the number of files in the directory. Extensible hashing is used to add a new directory block.

A *token manager* maintains the state of all tokens; it creates and distributes tokens, collects tokens once a file is closed, and downgrades or upgrades tokens when additional nodes request access to a file. Token management protocols attempt to reduce the load placed on the token manager; for example, when a node wants to revoke a token, it sends messages to all the other nodes holding the token and forwards the reply to the token manager.

Access to metadata is synchronized. For example, when multiple nodes `write` to the same file, the file size and the modification dates are updated using a *shared write lock* to access an inode. One of the nodes assumes the role of a *metanode*, and all updates are channeled through it. The file size and the last update time are determined by the metanode after merging the individual requests. The same strategy is used for updates of the indirect blocks. GPFS global data such as access control lists (ACLs), quotas, and configuration data are updated using the distributed locking mechanism.

GPFS uses *disk maps* to manage the disk space. The GPFS block size can be as large as 1 MB, and a typical block size is 256 KB. A block is divided into 32 subblocks to reduce disk fragmentation for small files; thus, the block map has 32 bits to indicate whether a subblock is free or used. The system disk map is partitioned into n regions, and each disk map region is stored on a different I/O node. This strategy reduces conflicts and allows multiple nodes to allocate disk space at the same time. An *allocation manager* running on one of the I/O nodes is responsible for actions involving multiple disk map regions. For example, it updates free space statistics and helps with deallocation by sending periodic hints of the regions used by individual nodes.

A detailed discussion of system utilities and the lessons learned from the deployment of the file system at several installations in 2002 can be found in [317]; the documentation of the GPFS is available from [177].

8.5 Google File System

The Google File System (GFS) was developed in the late 1990s. It uses thousands of storage systems built from inexpensive commodity components to provide petabytes of storage to a large user community with diverse needs [136]. It is not surprising that a main concern of the GFS designers was to ensure the reliability of a system exposed to hardware failures, system software errors, application errors, and last but not least, human errors.

The system was designed after a careful analysis of the file characteristics and of the access models. Some of the most important aspects of this analysis reflected in the GFS design are:

- Scalability and reliability are critical features of the system; they must be considered from the beginning rather than at some stage of the design.
- The vast majority of files range in size from a few GB to hundreds of TB.
- The most common operation is to `append` to an existing file; random `write` operations to a file are extremely infrequent.
- Sequential `read` operations are the norm.
- The users process the data in bulk and are less concerned with the response time.
- The consistency model should be relaxed to simplify the system implementation, but without placing an additional burden on the application developers.

Several design decisions were made as a result of this analysis:

1. Segment a file in large chunks.
2. Implement an atomic file `append` operation allowing multiple applications operating concurrently to `append` to the same file.
3. Build the cluster around a high-bandwidth rather than low-latency interconnection network. Separate the flow of control from the data flow; schedule the high-bandwidth data flow by pipelining the data transfer over TCP connections to reduce the response time. Exploit network topology by sending data to the closest node in the network.
4. Eliminate caching at the client site. Caching increases the overhead for maintaining consistency among cached copies at multiple client sites and it is not likely to improve performance.
5. Ensure consistency by channeling critical file operations through a *master*, a component of the cluster that controls the entire system.
6. Minimize the involvement of the *master* in file access operations to avoid hot-spot contention and to ensure scalability.
7. Support efficient checkpointing and fast recovery mechanisms.
8. Support an efficient garbage-collection mechanism.

GFS files are collections of fixed-size segments called *chunks*; at the time of file creation each chunk is assigned a unique *chunk handle*. A chunk consists of 64 KB blocks and each block has a 32-bit checksum. Chunks are stored on *Linux* files systems and are replicated on multiple sites; a user may change the number of the replicas from the standard value of three to any desired value. The chunk size is 64 MB; this choice is motivated by the desire to optimize performance for large files and to reduce the amount of metadata maintained by the system.

A large chunk size increases the likelihood that multiple operations will be directed to the same chunk; thus it reduces the number of requests to locate the chunk and, at the same time, it allows the application to maintain a persistent network connection with the server where the chunk is located. Space fragmentation occurs infrequently because the chunk for a small file and the last chunk of a large file are only partially filled.

The architecture of a GFS cluster is illustrated in Figure 8.7. A *master* controls a large number of *chunk servers*; it maintains metadata such as filenames, access control information, the location of all the replicas for every chunk of each file, and the state of individual chunk servers. Some of the metadata is stored in persistent storage (e.g., the *operation log* records the file namespace as well as the file-to-chunk mapping).

The locations of the chunks are stored only in the control structure of the *master*'s memory and are updated at system startup or when a new chunk server joins the cluster. This strategy allows the *master* to have up-to-date information about the location of the chunks.

System reliability is a major concern, and the operation log maintains a historical record of metadata changes, enabling the *master* to recover in case of a failure. As a result, such changes are atomic and are not made visible to the clients until they have been recorded on multiple replicas on persistent storage. To recover from a failure, the *master* replays the operation log. To minimize the recovery time, the *master* periodically checkpoints its state and at recovery time replays only the log records after the last checkpoint.

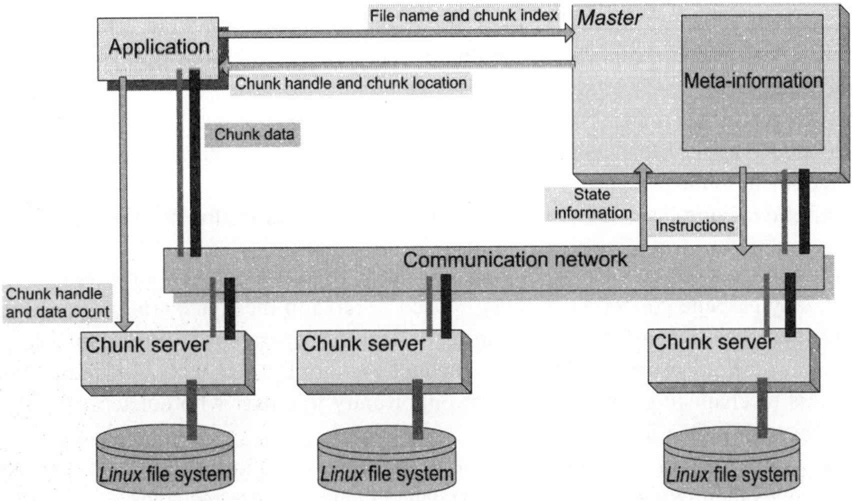

FIGURE 8.7

The architecture of a GFS cluster. The *master* maintains state information about all system components; it controls a number of *chunk servers*. A chunk server runs under *Linux*; it uses metadata provided by the *master* to communicate directly with the application. The data flow is decoupled from the control flow. The data and the control paths are shown separately, data paths with thick lines and control paths with thin lines. Arrows show the flow of control among the application, the *master*, and the chunk servers.

Each chunk server is a commodity *Linux* system; it receives instructions from the *master* and responds with status information. To access a file, an application sends to the *master* the filename and the chunk index, the offset in the file for the `read` or `write` operation; the *master* responds with the chunk handle and the location of the chunk. Then the application communicates directly with the chunk server to carry out the desired file operation.

The consistency model is very effective and scalable. Operations, such as file creation, are atomic and are handled by the *master*. To ensure scalability, the *master* has minimal involvement in file mutations and operations such as `write` or `append` that occur frequently. In such cases the *master* grants a lease for a particular chunk to one of the chunk servers, called the *primary*; then, the primary creates a serial order for the updates of that chunk.

When data for a `write` straddles the chunk boundary, two operations are carried out, one for each chunk. The steps for a `write` request illustrate a process that buffers data and decouples the control flow from the data flow for efficiency:

1. The client contacts the *master*, which assigns a lease to one of the chunk servers for a particular chunk if no lease for that chunk exists; then the *master* replies with the ID of the primary as well as secondary chunk servers holding replicas of the chunk. The client caches this information.
2. The client sends the data to all chunk servers holding replicas of the chunk; each one of the chunk servers stores the data in an internal LRU buffer and then sends an acknowledgment to the client.

3. The client sends a `write` request to the primary once it has received the acknowledgments from all chunk servers holding replicas of the chunk. The primary identifies mutations by consecutive sequence numbers.
4. The primary sends the `write` requests to all secondaries.
5. Each secondary applies the mutations in the order of the sequence numbers and then sends an acknowledgment to the primary.
6. Finally, after receiving the acknowledgments from all secondaries, the primary informs the client.

The system supports an efficient checkpointing procedure based on *copy-on-write* to construct system snapshots. A lazy garbage collection strategy is used to reclaim the space after a file deletion. In the first step the filename is changed to a hidden name and this operation is time stamped. The *master* periodically scans the namespace and removes the metadata for the files with a hidden name older than a few days; this mechanism gives a window of opportunity to a user who deleted files by mistake to recover the files with little effort.

Periodically, chunk servers exchange with the *master* the list of chunks stored on each one of them; the *master* supplies them with the identity of orphaned chunks whose metadata has been deleted, and such chunks are then deleted, Even when control messages are lost, a chunk server will carry out the housecleaning at the next *heartbeat* exchange with the *master*. Each chunk server maintains in core the checksums for the locally stored chunks to guarantee data integrity.

CloudStore is an open-source C++ implementation of GFS that allows client access not only from C++ but also from Java and Python.

8.6 *Apache Hadoop*

A wide range of data-intensive applications such as marketing analytics, image processing, machine learning, and Web crawling use *Apache Hadoop*, an open-source, Java-based software system.[6] *Hadoop* supports distributed applications handling extremely large volumes of data. Many members of the community contributed to the development and optimization of *Hadoop* and several related Apache projects such as *Hive* and *HBase*.

Hadoop is used by many organizations from industry, government, and research; the long list of *Hadoop* users includes major IT companies such as Apple, IBM, HP, Microsoft, Yahoo!, and Amazon; media companies such as The New York Times and Fox; social networks, including Twitter, Facebook, and LinkedIn; and government agencies, such as the U.S. Federal Reserve. In 2011, the Facebook *Hadoop* cluster had a capacity of 30 PB.

A *Hadoop* system has two components, a *MapReduce* engine and a database (see Figure 8.8). The database could be the *Hadoop File System (HDFS)*, Amazon *S3*, or *CloudStore*, an implementation of the Google File System discussed in Section 8.5. *HDFS* is a distributed file system written in Java; it is portable, but it cannot be directly mounted on an existing operating system. *HDFS* is not fully POSIX compliant, but it is highly performant.

The *Hadoop* engine on the master of a multinode cluster consists of a *job tracker* and a *task tracker*, whereas the engine on a slave has only a *task tracker*. The *job tracker* receives a *MapReduce* job

[6] *Hadoop* requires Java Runtime Environment (JRE) 1.6 or higher.

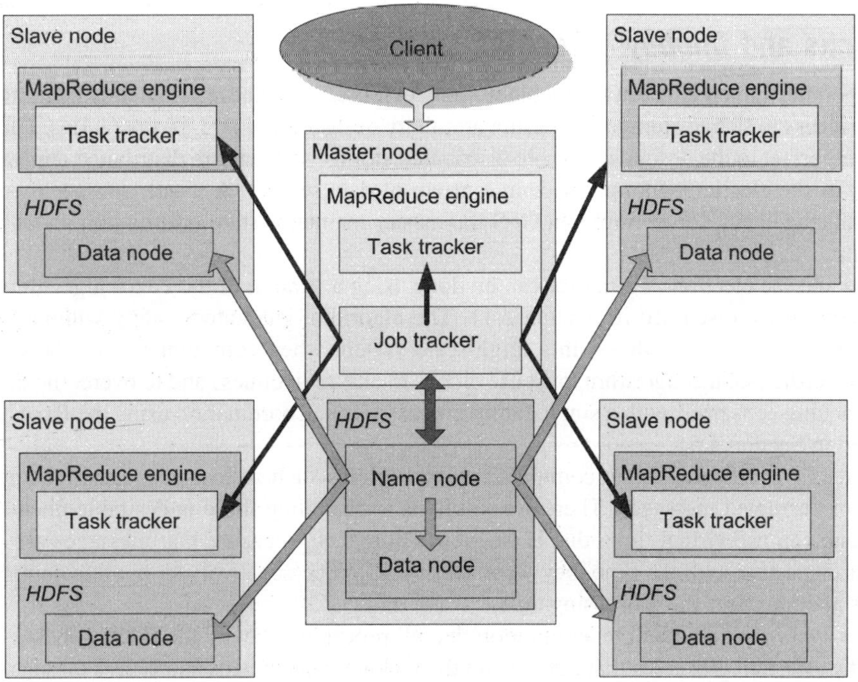

FIGURE 8.8

A *Hadoop* cluster using *HDFS*. The cluster includes a master and four slave nodes. Each node runs a *MapReduce* engine and a database engine, often *HDFS*. The *job tracker* of the master's engine communicates with the *task trackers* on all the nodes and with the *name node* of *HDFS*. The *name node* of *HDFS* shares information about data placement with the *job tracker* to minimize communication between the nodes on which data is located and the ones where it is needed.

from a client and dispatches the work to the *task trackers* running on the nodes of a cluster. To increase efficiency, the *job tracker* attempts to dispatch the tasks to available slaves closest to the place where it stored the task data. The *task tracker* supervises the execution of the work allocated to the node. Several scheduling algorithms have been implemented in *Hadoop* engines, including Facebook's fair scheduler and Yahoo!'s capacity scheduler; see Section 6.8 for a discussion of cloud scheduling algorithms.

HDFS replicates data on multiple nodes. The default is three replicas; a large dataset is distributed over many nodes. The *name node* running on the master manages the data distribution and data replication and communicates with *data nodes* running on all cluster nodes; it shares with the *job tracker* information about data placement to minimize communication between the nodes on which data is located and the ones where it is needed. Although *HDFS* can be used for applications other than those based on the *MapReduce* model, its performance for such applications is not at par with the ones for which it was originally designed.

8.7 Locks and *Chubby*: A locking service

Locks support the implementation of reliable storage for loosely coupled distributed systems; they enable controlled access to shared storage and ensure atomicity of `read` and `write` operations. Furthermore, critically important to the design of reliable distributed storage systems are distributed consensus problems, such as the election of a master from a group of data servers. A master has an important role in system management; for example, in GFS the master maintains state information about all system components.

Locking and the election of a master can be done using a version of the Paxos algorithm for asynchronous consensus, discussed in Section 2.11. The algorithm guarantees safety without any timing assumptions, a necessary condition in a large-scale system when communication delays are unpredictable. Nevertheless, the algorithm must use clocks to ensure liveliness and to overcome the impossibility of reaching consensus with a single faulty process [123]. Coordination using the Paxos algorithm is discussed in Section 4.5.

Distributed systems experience communication problems such as lost messages, messages out of sequence, or corrupted messages. There are solutions for handling these undesirable phenomena; for example, one can use virtual time, that is, sequence numbers, to ensure that messages are processed in an order consistent with the time they were sent by all processes involved, but this complicates the algorithms and increases the processing time.

Advisory locks are based on the assumption that all processes play by the rules. Advisory locks do not have any effect on processes that circumvent the locking mechanisms and access the shared objects directly. *Mandatory locks* block access to the locked objects to all processes that do not hold the locks, regardless of whether they use locking primitives.

Locks that can be held for only a very short time are called *fine-grained*, whereas *coarse-grained* locks are held for a longer time. Some operations require meta-information about a lock, such as the name of the lock, whether the lock is shared or held in exclusivity, and the generation number of the lock. This meta-information is sometimes aggregated into an opaque byte string called a *sequencer*.

The question of how to most effectively support a locking and consensus component of a large-scale distributed system demands several design decisions. A first design decision is whether the locks should be mandatory or advisory. *Mandatory locks* have the obvious advantage of enforcing access control; a traffic analogy is that a mandatory lock is like a drawbridge. Once it is up, all traffic is forced to stop.

An *advisory lock* is like a stop sign; those who obey the traffic laws will stop, but some might not. The disadvantages of mandatory locks are added overhead and less flexibility. Once a data item is locked, even a high-priority task related to maintenance or recovery cannot access the data unless it forces the application holding the lock to terminate. This is a very significant problem in large-scale systems where partial system failures are likely.

A second design decision is whether the system should be based on fine-grained or coarse-grained locking. *Fine-grained locks* allow more application threads to access shared data in any time interval, but they generate a larger workload for the lock server. Moreover, when the lock server fails for a period of time, a larger number of applications are affected. Advisory locks and *coarse-grained locks* seem to be a better choice for a system expected to scale to a very large number of nodes distributed in data centers that are interconnected via wide area networks.

A third design decision is how to support a systematic approach to locking. Two alternatives come to mind: (i) delegate to the clients the implementation of the consensus algorithm and provide a library of functions needed for this task, or (ii) create a locking service that implements a version of the asynchronous Paxos algorithm and provide a library to be linked with an application client to support service calls. Forcing application developers to invoke calls to a Paxos library is more cumbersome and more prone to errors than the service alternative. Of course, the lock service itself has to be scalable to support a potentially heavy load.

Another design consideration is flexibility, the ability of the system to support a variety of applications. A name service comes immediately to mind because many cloud applications `read` and `write` small files. The names of small files can be included in the namespace of the service to allow atomic file operations. The choice should also consider the performance; a service can be optimized and clients can cache control information. Finally, we should consider the overhead and resources for reaching consensus. Again, the service seems to be more advantageous because it needs fewer replicas for high availability.

In the early 2000s, when Google started to develop a lock service called *Chubby* [61], it was decided to use advisory and coarse-grained locks. The service is used by several Google systems, including the GFS discussed in Section 8.5 and *BigTable* (see Section 8.9).

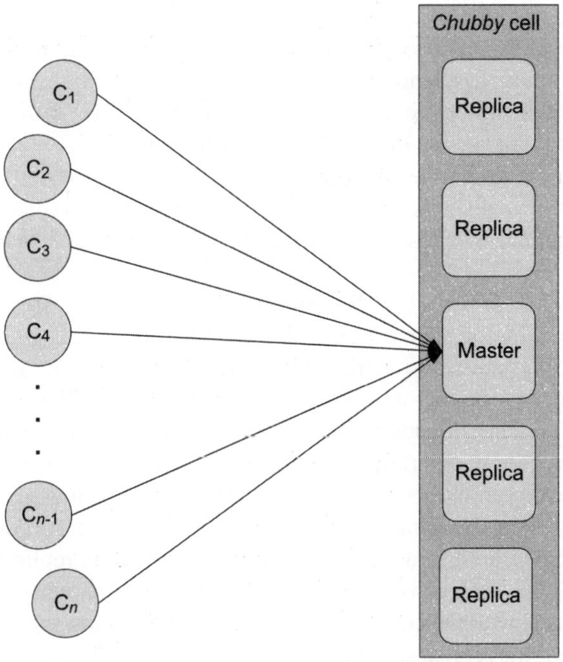

FIGURE 8.9

A *Chubby* cell consisting of five replicas, one of which is elected as a master; *n* clients use RPCs to communicate with the master.

The basic organization of the system is shown in Figure 8.9. A *Chubby* cell typically serves one data center. The cell server includes several *replicas*, the standard number of which is five. To reduce the probability of correlated failures, the servers hosting replicas are distributed across the campus of a data center.

The replicas use a distributed consensus protocol to elect a new *master* when the current one fails. The master is elected by a majority, as required by the asynchronous Paxos algorithm, accompanied by the commitment that a new master will not be elected for a period called a *master lease*. A *session* is a connection between a client and the cell server maintained over a period of time; the data cached by the client, the locks acquired, and the handles of all files locked by the client are valid for only the duration of the session.

Clients use RPCs to request services from the master. When it receives a `write` request, the master propagates the request to all replicas and waits for a reply from a majority of replicas before responding. When it receives a `read` request the master responds without consulting the replicas. The client interface of the system is similar to, yet simpler than, the one supported by the *Unix* File System. In addition, it includes notification of events related to file or system status. A client can subscribe to events such as file content modification, change or addition of a child node, master failure, lock acquired, conflicting lock requests, and invalid file handle.

The files and directories of the *Chubby* service are organized in a tree structure and use a naming scheme similar to that of *Unix*. Each file has a *file handle* similar to the file descriptor. The master of a cell periodically writes a snapshot of its database to a GFS file server.

Each file or directory can act as a lock. To `write` to a file the client must be the only one holding the file handle, whereas multiple clients may hold the file handle to `read` from the file. Handles are created by a call to *open ()* and destroyed by a call to *close ()*. Other calls supported by the service are *GetContentsAndStat ()*, to get the file data and meta-information, *SetContents*, and *Delete ()* and several calls allow the client to acquire and release locks. Some applications may decide to create and manipulate a sequencer with calls to *SetSequencer ()*, which associates a sequencer with a handle, *GetSequencer ()* to obtain the sequencer associated with a handle, or check the validity of a sequencer with *CheckSequencer ()*.

The sequence of calls *SetContents()*, *SetSequencer()*, *GetContentsAndStat()*, and *CheckSequencer()* can be used by an application for the election of a master as follows: all candidate threads attempt to open a lock file, call it *lfile*, in exclusive mode; the one that succeeds in acquiring the lock for *lfile* becomes the master, writes its identity in *lfile*, creates a sequencer for the lock of *lfile*, call it *lfseq*, and passes it to the server. The other threads read the *lfile* and discover that they are replicas; periodically they check the sequencer *lfseq* to determine whether the lock is still valid. The example illustrates the use of *Chubby* as a name server. In fact, this is one of the most frequent uses of the system.

We now take a closer look at the actual implementation of the service. As pointed out earlier, *Chubby* locks and *Chubby* files are stored in a database, and this database is replicated. The architecture of these replicas shows that the stack consists of the Chubby component, which implements the Chubby protocol for communication with the clients, and the active components, which `write` log entries and files to the local storage of the replica see (Figure 8.10).

Recall that an *atomicity log* for a transaction-processing system allows a crash recovery procedure to undo all-or-nothing actions that did not complete or to finish all-or-nothing actions that committed

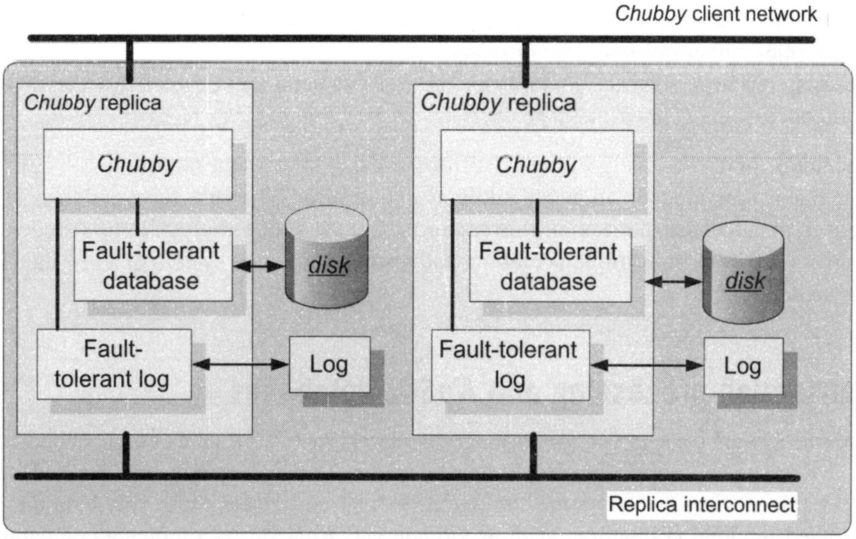

FIGURE 8.10

Chubby replica architecture. The *Chubby* component implements the communication protocol with the clients. The system includes a component to transfer files to a fault-tolerant database and a fault-tolerant log component to `write` log entries. The fault-tolerant log uses the Paxos protocol to achieve consensus. Each replica has its own local file system; replicas communicate with one another using a dedicated interconnect and communicate with clients through a client network.

but did not record all of their effects. Each replica maintains its own copy of the log; a new log entry is appended to the existing log and the Paxos algorithm is executed repeatedly to ensure that all replicas have the same sequence of log entries.

The next element of the stack is responsible for the maintenance of a fault-tolerant database – in other words, making sure that all local copies are consistent. The database consists of the actual data, or the *local snapshot* in *Chubby* speak, and a *replay log* to allow recovery in case of failure. The state of the system is also recorded in the database.

The Paxos algorithm is used to reach consensus on sets of values (e.g., the sequence of entries in a replicated log). To ensure that the Paxos algorithm succeeds in spite of the occasional failure of a replica, the following three phases of the algorithm are executed repeatedly:

1. Elect a replica to be the master/coordinator. When a master fails, several replicas may decide to assume the role of a master. To ensure that the result of the election is unique, each replica generates a sequence number larger than any sequence number it has seen, in the range $(1, r)$, where r is the number of replicas, and broadcasts it in a *propose* message. The replicas that have not seen a higher sequence number broadcast a *promise* reply and declare that they will reject proposals from other candidate masters. If the number of respondents represents a majority of replicas, the one that sent the *propose* message is elected master.

2. The master broadcasts to all replicas an *accept* message, including the value it has selected, and waits for replies, either *acknowledge* or *reject*.
3. Consensus is reached when the majority of the replicas send an *acknowledge* message; then the master broadcasts the *commit* message.

Implementation of the Paxos algorithm is far from trivial. Although the algorithm can be expressed in as few as ten lines of pseudocode, its actual implementation could be several thousand lines of C++ code [71]. Moreover, practical use of the algorithm cannot ignore the wide variety of failure modes, including algorithm errors and bugs in its implementation, and testing a software system of a few thousands lines of codes is challenging.

8.8 Transaction processing and *NoSQL* databases

Many cloud services are based on *online transaction processing* (OLTP) and operate under tight latency constraints. Moreover, these applications have to deal with extremely high data volumes and are expected to provide reliable services for very large communities of users. It did not take very long for companies heavily involved in cloud computing, such as Google and Amazon, e-commerce companies such as eBay, and social media networks such as Facebook, Twitter, or LinkedIn, to discover that traditional relational databases are not able to handle the massive amount of data and the real-time demands of online applications that are critical for their business models.

The search for alternate models with which to store the data on a cloud is motivated by the need to decrease the latency by caching frequently used data in memory on dedicated servers, rather than fetching it repeatedly. In addition, distributing the data on a large number of servers allows multiple transactions to occur at the same time and decreases the response time. The relational schema are of little use for such applications in which conversion to key-value databases seems a much better approach. Of course, such systems do not store meaningful metadata information, unless they use extensions that cannot be exported easily.

A major concern for the designers of OLTP systems is to reduce the response time. The term *memcaching* refers to a general-purpose distributed memory system that caches objects in main memory (RAM); the system is based on a very large hash table distributed across many servers. The *memcached* system is based on a client-server architecture and runs under several operating systems, including *Linux*, *Unix*, *Mac OS X*, and *Windows*. The servers maintain a key-value associative array. The API allows the clients to add entries to the array and to query it. A key can be up to 250 bytes long, and a value can be no larger than 1 MB. The *memcached* system uses an LRU cache-replacement strategy.

Scalability is the other major concern for cloud OLTP applications and implicitly for datastores. There is a distinction between *vertical scaling*, where the data and the workload are distributed to systems that share resources such as cores and processors, disks, and possibly RAM, and *horizontal scaling*, where the systems do not share either primary or secondary storage [66].

Cloud stores such as *document stores* and *NoSQL* databases are designed to scale well, do not exhibit a single point of failure, have built-in support for consensus-based decisions, and support partitioning and replication as basic primitives. Systems such as Amazon's *SimpleDB*, discussed in Section 3.1; *CouchDB* (see `http://couchdb.apache.org/`), or *Oracle NoSQL database* [277] are very popular, though they provide less functionality than traditional databases. The *key-value* data model is very popular. Several such systems, including Voldemort, Redis, Scalaris, and Tokyo cabinet, are discussed in [66].

The "soft-state" approach in the design of *NoSQL* allows data to be inconsistent and transfers the task of implementing only the subset of the ACID properties required by a specific application to the application developer. The *NoSQL* systems ensure that data will be "eventually consistent" at some future point in time instead of enforcing consistency at the time when a transaction is "committed." Data partitioning among multiple storage servers and data replication are also tenets of the *NoSQL* philosophy[7]; they increase availability, reduce response time, and enhance scalability.

The name *NoSQL* given to this storage model is misleading. Michael Stonebreaker notes [335] that "blinding performance depends on removing overhead. Such overhead has nothing to do with SQL, but instead revolves around traditional implementations of ACID transactions, multi-threading, and disk management."

The overhead of OLTP systems is due to four sources with equal contribution: logging, locking, latching, and buffer management. Logging is expensive because traditional databases require transaction durability; thus, every `write` to the database can be completed only after the log has been updated. To guarantee atomicity, transactions lock every record, and this requires access to a lock table. Many operations require multithreading, and the access to shared data structures, such as lock tables, demands short-term latches[8] for coordination. The breakdown of the instruction count for these operations in existing DBMSs is as follows: 34.6% for buffer management, 14.2% for latching, 16.3% for locking, 11.9% for logging, and 16.2% for hand-coded optimization [157].

Today OLTP databases could exploit the vast amounts of resources of modern computing and communication systems to store the data in main memory rather than rely on disk-resident B-trees and heap files, locking-based concurrency control, and support for multithreading optimized for the computer technology of past decades [157]. Logless, single-threaded, and transaction-less databases could replace the traditional ones for some cloud applications.

Data replication is critical not only for system reliability and availability, but also for its performance. In an attempt to avoid catastrophic failures due to power blackouts, natural disasters, or other causes (see also Section 1.6), many companies have established multiple data centers located in different geographic regions. Thus, data replication must be done over a *wide area network* (WAN). This could be quite challenging, especially for log data, metadata, and system configuration information, due to increased probability of communication failure and larger communication delays. Several strategies are possible, some based on master/slave configurations, others based on homogeneous replica groups.

Master/slave replication can be asynchronous or synchronous. In the first case the master replicates write-ahead log entries to at least one slave, and each slave acknowledges appending the log record as soon as the operation is done. In the second case the master must wait for the acknowledgments from all slaves before proceeding. Homogeneous replica groups enjoy shorter latency and higher availability than master/slave configurations. Any member of the group can initiate mutations that propagate asynchronously.

[7]It was suggested in the literature that a *NoSQL* database could be associated with the BASE acronym constructed from its relevant properties: *basically available*, *soft state*, and *eventually consistent*. This is in contrast with traditional databases characterized by ACID properties: *atomicity*, *consistency*, *isolation*, and *durability*.

[8]A *latch* is a counter that triggers an event when it reaches zero. For example, a master thread initiates a counter with the number of worker threads and waits to be notified when all of them have finished.

In summary, the "one-size-fits-all" approach to traditional storage system design is replaced by a flexible one tailored to the specific requirements of the applications. Sometimes the data management ecosystem of a cloud computing environment integrates multiple databases; for example, Oracle integrates its *NoSQL* database with the *HDFS* discussed in Section 8.6, with the Oracle Database, and with the Oracle Exadata. Another approach, discussed in Section 8.10, is to partition the data and to guarantee full ACID semantics within a partition, while supporting eventual consistency among partitions.

8.9 *BigTable*

BigTable is a distributed storage system developed by Google to store massive amounts of data and to scale up to thousands of storage servers [73]. The system uses the Google File System discussed in Section 8.5 to store user data as well as system information. To guarantee atomic `read` and `write` operations, it uses the *Chubby* distributed lock service (see Section 8.7); the directories and the files in the namespace of *Chubby* are used as locks.

The system is based on a simple and flexible data model. It allows an application developer to exercise control over the data format and layout and reveals data locality information to the application clients. Any `read` or `write` row operation is atomic, even when it affects more than one column. The column keys identify *column families*, which are units of access control. The data in a column family is of the same type. Client applications written in C++ can add or delete values, search for a subset of data, and look up data in a row.

A row key is an arbitrary string of up to 64 KB, and a row range is partitioned into *tablets* serving as units for load balancing. The time stamps used to index various versions of the data in a cell are 64-bit integers; their interpretation can be defined by the application, whereas the default is the time of an event in microseconds. A column key consists of a string defining the family name, a set of printable characters, and an arbitrary string as qualifier.

The organization of a *BigTable* (see Figure 8.11) shows a sparse, distributed, multidimensional map for an email application. The system consists of three major components: a library linked to application clients to access the system, a master server, and a large number of tablet servers. The master server controls the entire system, assigns tablets to tablet servers and balances the load among them, manages garbage collection, and handles table and column family creation and deletion.

Internally, the space management is ensured by a three-level hierarchy: the *root tablet*, the location of which is stored in a *Chubby* file, points to entries in the second element, the *metadata* tablet, which, in turn, points to *user* tablets, collections of locations of users' tablets. An application client searches through this hierarchy to identify the location of its tablets and then caches the addresses for further use.

The performance of the system reported in [73] is summarized in Table 8.2. The table shows the number of random and sequential `read` and `write` and scan operations for $1,000$ bytes, when the number of servers increases from 1 to 50, then to 250, and finally to 500. Locking prevents the system from achieving a linear speed-up, but the performance of the system is still remarkable due to a fair number of optimizations. For example, the number of scans on 500 tablet servers is $7{,}843/2 \times 10^3$ instead of $15{,}385/2 \times 10^3$. It is reported that only 12 clusters use more than 500 tablet servers, whereas some 259 clusters use between 1 and 19 tablet servers.

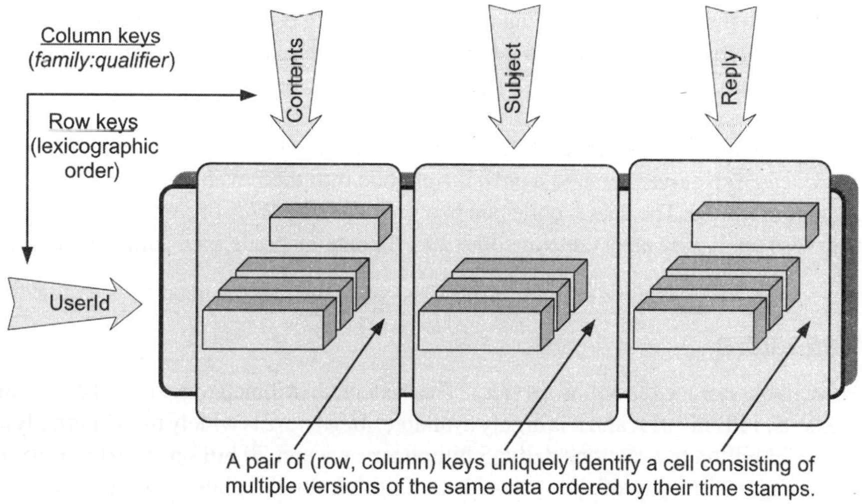

FIGURE 8.11

A *BigTable* example. The organization of an email application as a sparse, distributed, multidimensional map. The slice of the *BigTable* shown consists of a row with the key "UserId" and three family columns. The "Contents" key identifies the cell holding the contents of emails received, the cell with key "Subject" identifies the subject of emails, and the cell with the key "Reply" identifies the cell holding the replies. The versions of records in each cell are ordered according to their time stamps. The row keys of this *BigTable* are ordered lexicographically. A column key is obtained by concatenating the *family* and the *qualifier* fields. Each value is an uninterpreted array of bytes.

Table 8.2 *BigTable* performance: the number of operations per tablet server.

Number of Tablet Servers	Random Read	Sequential Read	Random Write	Sequential Write	Scan
1	1,212	4,425	8,850	8,547	15,385
50	593	2,463	3,745	3,623	10,526
250	479	2,625	3,425	2,451	9,524
500	241	2,469	2,000	1,905	7,843

BigTable is used by a variety of applications, including *Google Earth*, *Google Analytics*, *Google Finance*, and Web crawlers. For example, *Google Earth* uses two tables, one for preprocessing and one for serving client data. The preprocessing table stores raw images; the table is stored on disk because it contains some 70 TB of data. Each row of data consists of a single image; adjacent geographic segments are stored in rows in close proximity to one another. The column family is very sparse; it contains a column for every raw image. The preprocessing stage relies heavily on *MapReduce* to clean and consolidate the data for the serving phase. The serving table stored on GFS is "only" 500 GB, and it is distributed across several hundred tablet servers, which maintain in-memory column families. This organization enables the serving phase of *Google Earth* to provide a fast response time to tens of thousands of queries per second.

Google Analytics provides aggregate statistics such as the number of visitors to a Web page per day. To use this service, Web servers embed a *JavaScript* code into their Web pages to record information every time a page is visited. The data is collected in a *raw-click BigTable* of some 200 TB, with a row for each end-user session. A *summary* table of some 20 TB contains predefined summaries for a Website.

8.10 *Megastore*

Megastore is scalable storage for online services. The system, distributed over several data centers, has a very large capacity, 1 PB in 2011, and it is highly available. *Megastore* is widely used internally at Google; it handles some 23 billion transactions daily: 3 billion `write` and 20 billion `read` transactions [37].

The basic design philosophy of the system is to partition the data into *entity groups* and replicate each partition independently in data centers located in different geographic areas. The system supports full ACID semantics within each partition and provides limited consistency guarantees across partitions (see Figure 8.12). *Megastore* supports only those traditional database features that allow the system to scale well and that do not drastically affect the response time.

Another distinctive feature of the system is the use of the Paxos consensus algorithm, discussed in Section 2.11, to replicate primary user data, metadata, and system configuration information across data centers and for locking. The version of the Paxos algorithm used by *Megastore* does not require a single master. Instead, any node can initiate `read` and `write` operations to a write-ahead log replicated to a group of symmetric peers.

The entity groups are application-specific and store together logically related data. For example, an email account could be an entity group for an email application. Data should be carefully partitioned to avoid excessive communication between entity groups. Sometimes it is desirable to form multiple entity groups, as in the case of blogs [37].

The middle ground between traditional and *NoSQL* databases taken by the *Megastore* designers is also reflected in the data model. The data model is declared in a *schema* consisting of a set of *tables* composed of *entries*, each entry being a collection of named and typed *properties*. The unique primary key of an entity in a table is created as a composition of entry properties. A *Megastore* table can be a *root* or a *child* table. Each *child entity* must reference a special entity, called a *root entity* in its root table. An entity group consists of the primary entity and all entities that reference it.

The system makes extensive use of *BigTable*. Entities from different *Megastore* tables can be mapped to the same *BigTable* row without collisions. This is possible because the *BigTable* column name is a concatenation of the *Megastore* table name and the name of a property. A *BigTable* row for the root entity stores the transaction and all metadata for the entity group. As we saw in Section 8.9, multiple versions of the data with different time stamps can be stored in a cell. *Megastore* takes advantage of this feature to implement *multi-version concurrency control* (MVCC); when a mutation of a transaction occurs, this mutation is recorded along with its time stamp, rather than marking the old data as obsolete

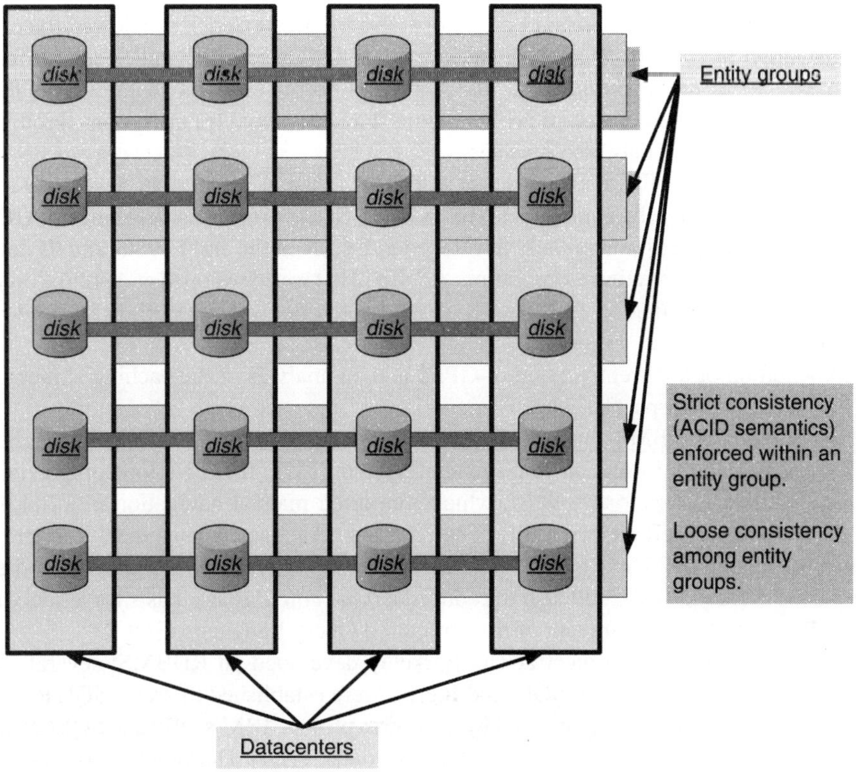

FIGURE 8.12

Megastore organization. The data is partitioned into *entity groups*; full ACID semantics within each partition and limited consistency guarantees across partitions are supported. A partition is replicated across data centers in different geographic areas.

and adding the new version. This strategy has several advantages: `read` and `write` operations can proceed concurrently, and a `read` always returns the last fully updated version.

A `write` transaction involves the following steps: (1) Get the timestamp and the log position of the last committed transaction. (2) Gather the `write` operations in a log entry. (3) Use the consensus algorithm to `append` the log entry and then commit. (4) Update the *BigTable* entries. (5) Clean up.

8.11 History notes

A 1989 survey of distributed file systems can be found in [316]. NFS Versions 2, 3, and 4 are defined in RFCs 1094, 1813, and 3010, respectively. NFS Version 3 added a number of features, including support for 64-bit file sizes and offsets, support for asynchronous writes on the server, additional file attributes in many replies, and a `readdirplus` operation. These extensions allowed the new version to handle files larger than 2 GB, to improve performance, and to get file handles and attributes along with file names when scanning a directory. NFS Version 4 borrowed a few features from the Andrew File System. WebNFS is an extension of NFS Versions 2 and 3; it enables operations through firewalls and is more easily integrated into Web browsers.

AFS was developed at CMU in collaboration with IBM [250]; it was further developed as an open-source system by IBM under the name OpenAFS in 2000. Sprite [165] was developed at UC Berkeley in the mid-1980s. Locus [365] was initially developed at UCLA in the early 1980s and its development was continued by Locus Computing Corporation. Apollo [211] was developed at Apollo Computer Inc., established in 1980 and acquired in 1989 by HP. The Remote File System (RFS) [35] was developed at Bell Labs in the mid-1980s.

The documentation of a current version of GPFS and an analysis of the caching strategy are given in GPFS [177] and [317], respectively.

Several generations of DBMSs based on different models have been developed through the years. In 1968 IBM released the Information Management System (IMS) for IBM 360 computers; IMS was based on the so-called *navigational model*, which supported manual navigation in a linked data set where the data was organized hierarchically. The relational database management system (RDBMS) model was introduced in 1970 by Codd [87]; in this model related records are linked together and can be accessed using a unique *key*. Codd also introduced a *tuple calculus* as a basis for a query model for an RDBMS; this led to the development of the Structured Query Language (SQL).

In 1973, the Ingres research project at UC Berkeley developed an RDBMS; several companies, including Sybase, Informix, NonStop SQL, and Ingres, were established to create SQL RDBMS commercial products based on the ideas generated by the Ingres project. IBM's DB2 and SQL/DS dominated the RDBMS market for mainframes during the later years of the 1980s. The Oracle Corporation, founded in 1977, was also involved in the development of RDBMS.

The ACID properties of database transactions were defined by Jim Gray in 1981 [143] and the term ACID was introduced in [156].

The object-oriented programming ideas of the 1980s led to the development of *object-oriented database management systems (OODBMSs)* in which the information is packaged as objects. The ideas developed by several research projects, including Encore-Ob/Server at Brown University, Exodus at the University of Wisconsin at Madison, Iris at HP, ODE at Bell Labs, and the Orion project at MCC-Austin, helped the development of several OODBMS commercial products [191].

The so-called *NoSQL* database management systems emerged in the 2000s. They do not follow the RDBMS model, do not use SQL as a query language, may not give ACID grantees, and have a distributed, fault-tolerant architecture.

8.12 Further reading

A 2011 article in the journal *Science* [164] discusses the volume of information stored, processed, and transferred through networks. [251] is a comprehensive study of the storage technology until 2003.

Network File System Versions 2, 3, and 4 are discussed in [314], [286], and [287], respectively. References [250] and [170] provide a wealth of information about the Andrew File System; [165]

and [255] discuss in detail the Sprite File System. Other file systems such as Locus, Apollo, and the Remote File System (RFS) are discussed in [365], [211], and [35], respectively. Storage systems are also discussed in [103,105].

The General Parallel File System (GPFS) developed at IBM and its precursor, the TigerShark multimedia file system, are presented in [317] and [159]. A good source for information about the Google File System is [136].

The development of *Chubby* is covered in [61]. *NoSQL* databases are analyzed in several papers, including [335], [157], and [66]. *BigTable* and *Megastore*, developed at Google, are discussed in [73] and [37]. Evaluation of datastores is presented in [59] and a cloud storage abstraction for portable applications is introduced in [166].

Oracle's Lustre file system is discussed in [276], a cost storage analysis in [299], and an overview of cloud storage is covered in [327].

8.13 Exercises and problems

Problem 1. Analyze the reasons for the introduction of storage area networks (SANs) and their properties. *Hint:* Read [251].

Problem 2. *Block virtualization* simplifies the storage management tasks in SANs. Provide solid arguments in support of this statement. *Hint:* Read [251].

Problem 3. Analyze the advantages of memory-based checkpointing. *Hint:* Read [183].

Problem 4. Discuss the security of distributed file systems including those from Sun NFS, Apollo Domain, Andrew, IBM AIX, RFS, and Sprite. *Hint:* Read [316].

Problem 5. The designers of the Google File System (GFS) have reexamined the traditional choices for a File System. Discuss the four observations regarding these choices that have guided the design of GFS. *Hint:* Read [136].

Problem 6. In his seminal paper on the virtues and limitations of the transaction concept [143], Jim Gray analyzes logging and locking. Discuss the main conclusions of his analysis.

Problem 7. Michael Stonebreaker argues that "blinding performance depends on removing overhead." Discuss his arguments regarding the *NoSQL* concept. *Hint:* Read [335].

Problem 8. Discuss the *Megastore* data model. *Hint:* Read [37].

Problem 9. Discuss the use of locking in *BigTable*. *Hint:* Read [73] and [61].

CHAPTER

Cloud Security

9

Security has been a concern since the early days of computing, when a computer was isolated in a room and a threat could be posed only by malicious insiders. The Pandora's box[1] of threats opened wide once computers were able to communicate with one another. In an interconnected world, various embodiments of malware can migrate easily from one system to another, cross national borders, and infect systems all over the globe.

The security of computing and communication systems takes on a new urgency as society becomes increasingly dependent on the information infrastructure. Nowadays, even the critical infrastructure of a nation can be attacked by exploiting flaws in computer security. Malware, such as the Stuxnet virus, targets industrial control systems controlled by software [81]. Recently, the term *cyberwarfare* has entered the dictionary with the meaning "actions by a nation-state to penetrate another nation's computers or networks for the purposes of causing damage or disruption" [85].

A computer cloud is a target-rich environment for malicious individuals and criminal organizations. It is thus no surprise that security is a major concern for existing users and for potential new users of cloud computing services. In Section 3.10 we identified some of the security threats perceived by cloud users; in Section 9.1 we elaborate on this topic. Some of these risks are shared with other systems supporting network-centric computing and network-centric content, e.g., service-oriented architectures (SOAs), grids, and Web-based services.

Cloud computing is an entirely new approach to computing based on a new technology. It is therefore reasonable to expect that new methods to deal with some of the security threats will be developed, whereas other perceived threats will prove to be exaggerated. Indeed, "early on in the life cycle of a technology, there are many concerns about how this technology will be used ... they represent a barrier to the acceptance ... over the time, however, the concerns fade, especially if the value proposition is strong enough" [174].

The idea that moving to a cloud liberates an organization from many technical concerns related to computer security and eliminates internal threats is accepted by some members of the IT community. As we shall see throughout this chapter, this seems a rather naïve point of view, because outsourcing computing to a cloud generates major new security and privacy concerns. Moreover, service-level agreements do not provide adequate legal protection for cloud computer users, who are often left to deal with events beyond their control.

[1]In Greek mythology, Pandora was the first woman on Earth. When Prometheus stole fire from heaven, Zeus took vengeance by presenting Pandora to Epimetheus, the brother of Prometheus. Pandora was given a beautiful box and told not to open it under any circumstance. Impelled by curiosity, a trait given to her by the mischievous gods, Pandora opened the box, and all evil contained therein escaped, except for one item at the bottom of the box: Elpis, the Spirit of Hope.

One of the consequences of the breathtaking pace of development of information science and technology is that standards, regulations, and laws governing the activities of organizations supporting the new computing services, and in particular utility computing, have yet to be devised or adopted. As a result, many issues related to privacy, security, and trust in cloud computing are far from settled. The pool of resources of a cloud service provider can be dispersed over several countries or even several continents. Since information can freely cross national borders there is a need for international regulations to be adopted by the countries where data centers of cloud computing providers are located.

9.1 Cloud security risks

Some believe that it is very easy, possibly too easy, to start using cloud services without a proper understanding of the security risks and without the commitment to follow the ethics rules for cloud computing. A first question is: What are the security risks faced by cloud users? There is also the possibility that a cloud could be used to launch large-scale attacks against other components of the cyber infrastructure. The next question is: How can the nefarious use of cloud resources be prevented?

There are multiple ways to look at the security risks for cloud computing. A recent paper identifies three broad classes of risk [83]: traditional security threats, threats related to system availability, and threats related to third-party data control.

Traditional threats are those experienced for some time by any system connected to the Internet, but with some cloud-specific twists. The impact of traditional threats is amplified due to the vast amount of cloud resources and the large user population that can be affected. The fuzzy bounds of responsibility between the providers of cloud services and users and the difficulties in accurately identifying the cause of a problem add to cloud users' concerns.

The traditional threats begin at the user site. The user must protect the infrastructure used to connect to the cloud and to interact with the application running on the cloud. This task is more difficult because some components of this infrastructure are outside the firewall protecting the user.

The next threat is related to the authentication and authorization process. The procedures in place for one individual do not extend to an enterprise. In this case the cloud access of the members of an organization must be nuanced; individuals should be assigned distinct levels of privilege based on their roles in the organization. It is also nontrivial to merge or adapt the internal policies and security metrics of an organization with the ones of the cloud.

Moving from the user to the cloud, we see that the traditional types of attack have already affected cloud service providers. The favorite means of attack are distributed denial-of-service (DDoS) attacks, which prevent legitimate users accessing cloud services; phishing;[2] SQL injection;[3] or cross-site scripting.[4]

[2]Phishing is an attack aiming to gain information from a site database by masquerading as a trustworthy entity. Such information could be names and credit card numbers, Social Security Numbers (SSN), or other personal information stored by online merchants or other service providers.

[3]SQL injection is a form of attack typically used against a Web site. An SQL command entered in a Web form causes the contents of a database used by the Web site to be dumped to the attacker or altered. SQL injection can be used against other transaction-processing systems and is successful when the user input is not strongly typed and/or rigorously filtered.

[4]Cross-site scripting is the most popular form of attack against Web sites. A browser permits the attacker to insert client scripts into the Web pages and thus bypass the access controls at the Web site.

Cloud servers host multiple VMs, and multiple applications may run under each VM. Multitenency in conjunction with VMM vulnerabilities could open new attack channels for malicious users. Identifying the path followed by an attacker is much more difficult in a cloud environment. Traditional investigation methods based on digital forensics cannot be extended to a cloud, where the resources are shared among a large user population and the traces of events related to a security incident are wiped out due to the high rate of `write` operations on any storage media.

Availability of cloud services is another major concern. System failures, power outages, and other catastrophic events could shut down cloud services for extended periods of time. When such an event occurs, data lock-in, discussed in Section 3.5, could prevent a large organization whose business model depends on that data from functioning properly.

Clouds could also be affected by phase transition phenomena and other effects specific to complex systems (see Chapter 10). Another critical aspect of availability is that users cannot be assured that an application hosted on the cloud will return correct results.

Third-party control generates a spectrum of concerns caused by the lack of transparency and limited user control. For example, a cloud provider may subcontract some resources from a third party whose level of trust is questionable. There are examples when subcontractors failed to maintain the customer data. There are also examples when the third party was not a subcontractor but a hardware supplier and the loss of data was caused by poor-quality storage devices [83].

Storing proprietary data on a cloud is risky because cloud provider espionage poses real dangers. The terms of contractual obligations usually place all responsibilities for data security with the user. The Amazon Web Services customer agreement, for example, does not help boost user confidence as it states: "We . . . will not be liable to you for any direct, indirect, incidental . . . damages . . . nor . . . be responsible for any compensation, reimbursement, arising in connection with: (A) your inability to use the services . . . (B) the cost of procurement of substitute goods or services . . . or (D) any unauthorized access to, alteration of, or deletion, destruction, damage, loss or failure to store any of your content or other data."

It is very difficult for a cloud user to prove that data has been deleted by the service provider. The lack of transparency makes auditability a very difficult proposition for cloud computing. Auditing guidelines elaborated by the National Institute of Standards and Technology (NIST), such as the Federal Information Processing Standard (FIPS) and the Federal Information Security Management Act (FISMA), are mandatory for U.S. government agencies.

The first release of the Cloud Security Alliance (CSA) report in 2010 identifies seven top threats to cloud computing. These threats are the abuse of the cloud, APIs that are not fully secure, malicious insiders, shared technology, account hijacking, data loss or leakage, and unknown risk profiles [97]. According to this report, the *IaaS* delivery model can be affected by all threats. *PaaS* can be affected by all but the shared technology, whereas *SaaS* is affected by all but abuse and shared technology.

The term *abuse of the cloud* refers to the ability to conduct nefarious activities from the cloud – for example, using multiple *AWS* instances or applications supported by *IaaS* to launch DDoS attacks or to distribute spam and malware. *Shared technology* considers threats due to multitenant access supported by virtualization. VMMs can have flaws allowing a guest operating system to affect the security of the platform shared with other virtual machines.

Insecure APIs may not protect users during a range of activities, starting with authentication and access control to monitoring and control of the application during runtime. The cloud service providers do not disclose their hiring standards and policies; thus, the risks of *malicious insiders* cannot be ignored. The potential harm due to this particular form of attack is great.

Data loss or leakage are two risks with devastating consequences for an individual or an organization using cloud services. Maintaining copies of the data outside the cloud is often unfeasible due to the sheer volume of data. If the only copy of the data is stored on the cloud, sensitive data is permanently lost when cloud data replication fails and is followed by a storage media failure. Because some of the data often includes proprietary or sensitive data, access to such information by third parties could have severe consequences.

Account or service hijacking is a significant threat, and cloud users must be aware of and guard against all methods of stealing credentials. Finally, *unknown risk profile* refers to exposure to the ignorance or underestimation of the risks of cloud computing.

The 2011 version of the CSA report, "Security Guidance for Critical Area of Focus in Cloud Computing V3.0," provides a comprehensive analysis of and makes recommendations to minimize the risks inherent in cloud computing [98].

An attempt to identify and classify the attacks in a cloud computing environment is presented in [147]. The three actors involved in the model considered are the user, the service, and the cloud infrastructure, and there are six types of attacks possible (see Figure 9.1). The user can be attacked from two directions:

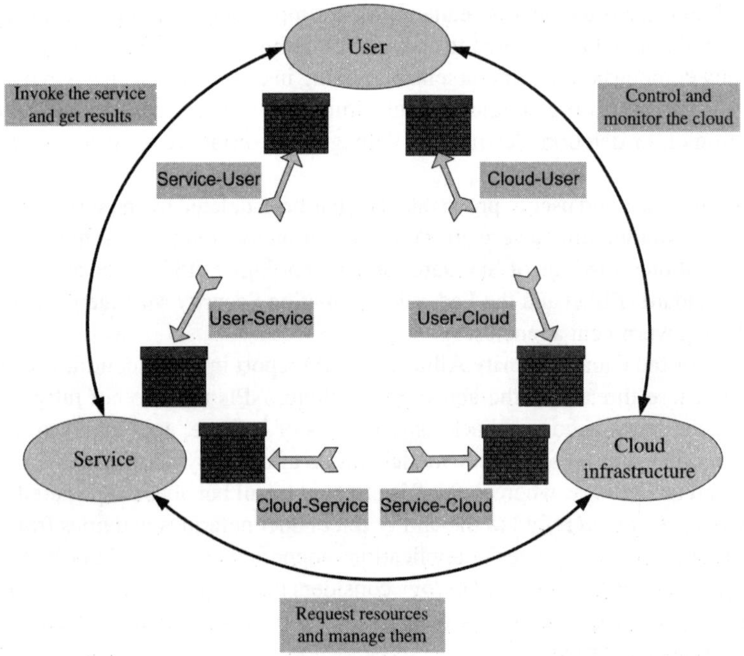

FIGURE 9.1

Surfaces of attacks in a cloud computing environment.

from the service and from the cloud. SSL certificate spoofing, attacks on browser caches, or phishing attacks are examples of attacks that originate at the service. The user can also be a victim of attacks that either originate at the cloud or spoofs that originate from the cloud infrastructure.

The service can be attacked from the user. Buffer overflow, SQL injection, and privilege escalation are the common types of attacks from the service. The service can also be subject to attack by the cloud infrastructure; this is probably the most serious line of attack. Limiting access to resources, privilege-related attacks, data distortion, and injecting additional operations are only a few of the many possible lines of attack originated at the cloud.

The cloud infrastructure can be attacked by a user who targets the cloud control system. The types of attack are the same ones that a user directs toward any other cloud service. The cloud infrastructure may also be targeted by a service requesting an excessive amount of resources and causing the exhaustion of the resources.

9.2 Security: The top concern for cloud users

Virtually all surveys report that security is the top concern for cloud users, who are accustomed to having full control of all systems on which sensitive information is stored and processed. Users typically operate inside a secure perimeter protected by a corporate firewall. In spite of the potential threats, users have to extend their trust to the cloud service provider if they want to benefit from the economical advantages of utility computing. This is a fairly difficult transition, yet it is a critical one for the future of cloud computing. To support this transition, some argue that cloud security is in the hands of experts, so users are even better protected than when they are in charge of their own security.

Major user concerns are unauthorized access to confidential information and data theft. Data is more vulnerable in storage than while it is being processed. Data is kept in storage for extended periods of time, whereas it is exposed to threats during processing for relatively short periods of time. Hence, close attention should be paid to the security of storage servers and to data in transit.

This does not mean that threats during processing can be ignored; such threats can originate from flaws in the VMM, rogue VMs, or a VMBR, as discussed in Section 5.12. There is also the risk of unauthorized access and data theft posed by rogue employees of a cloud service provider (CSP). The hiring and security screening policies of the CSP personnel are totally opaque processes to users, and this justifies users' concern about insider attacks.

The next concerns regard user control over the life cycle of data. It is virtually impossible for a user to determine whether data that should have been deleted is actually deleted. Even if it was deleted, there is no guarantee that the media was wiped and the next user is not able to recover confidential data. This problem is exacerbated because the CSPs rely on seamless backups to prevent accidental data loss. Such backups are done without users' consent or knowledge. During this exercise data records can be lost, accidentally deleted, or accessible to an attacker.

Lack of standardization is next on the list of concerns. Today there are no interoperability standards, as we discussed in Section 3.5. Many questions do not have satisfactory answers at this time. For example: What can be done when the service provided by the CSP is interrupted? How can we access our critically needed data in case of a blackout? What if the CSP drastically raises its prices? What is the cost of moving to a different CSP?

It is undeniable that auditing and compliance pose an entirely different set of challenges in cloud computing. These challenges are not yet resolved. A full audit trail on a cloud is an infeasible proposition at this time.

Another, less analyzed user concern is that cloud computing is based on a new technology expected to evolve in the future. Case in point: autonomic computing is likely to enter the scene. When this happens, self-organization, self-optimization, self-repair, and self-healing could generate additional security threats. In an autonomic system it will be even more difficult than at present to determine when an action occurred, what was the reason for that action, and how it created the opportunity for an attack or for data loss. It is still unclear how autonomic computing can be compliant with privacy and legal issues.

There is no doubt that multitenancy is the root cause of many user concerns. Nevertheless, multitenancy enables a higher server utilization thus, lower costs. Because it is one of the pillars of utility computing, users have to learn to live with multitenancy. The threats caused by multitenancy differ from one cloud delivery model to another. For example, in the case of *SaaS*, private information such as name, address, phone numbers, and possibly credit card numbers of many users is stored on one server, and when the security of that server is compromised, a large number of users are affected. We have already mentioned that multitenancy threats during processing time cannot be ignored.

Users are also greatly concerned about the legal framework for enforcing cloud computing security. The cloud technology has moved much faster than cloud security and privacy legislation, so users have legitimate concerns regarding the ability to defend their rights. Because the datacenters of a CSP may be located in several countries, it is difficult to understand which laws apply – the laws of the country where information is stored and processed, the laws of the countries where the information crossed from the user to the datacenter, or the laws of the country where the user is located.

To make matters even more complicated, a CSP may outsource the handling of personal and/or sensitive information. Existing laws stating that the CSP must exercise reasonable security may be difficult to implement in a case where there is a chain of outsourcing to companies in different countries. Finally, a CSP may be required by law to share private data with law enforcement agencies.

Now we examine briefly what cloud users can and should do to minimize security risks regarding data handling by the CSP. First, users should evaluate the security policies and the mechanisms the CSP has in place to enforce these policies. Then users should analyze the information that would be stored and processed on the cloud. Finally, the contractual obligations should be clearly spelled out.

The contract between the user and the CSP should do the following [290]:

1. State explicitly the CSP's obligations to securely handle sensitive information and its obligation to comply with privacy laws.
2. Spell out CSP liabilities for mishandling sensitive information.
3. Spell out CSP liabilities for data loss.
4. Spell out the rules governing the ownership of the data.
5. Specify the geographical regions where information and backups can be stored.

To minimize security risks, a user may try to avoid processing sensitive data on a cloud. The Secure Data Connector from Google carries out an analysis of the data structures involved and allows users to access data protected by a firewall. This solution is not feasible for several classes of application, e.g., processing of medical or personnel records. It may not be feasible when the cloud processing workflow requires cloud access to the entire volume of user data.

When the volume of sensitive data or the processing workflow requires sensitive data to be stored on a public or hybrid cloud, then, whenever feasible, data should be encrypted. This poses a dilemma because encryption prevents indexing and searching the data. For some applications it is possible to scramble the data to make it unintelligible to an intruder. Though this system is extremely inefficient, hence impractical at this time, it is possible to process encrypted data using either a fully homomorphic encryption scheme [134] or secure two-party computations [380].

9.3 Privacy and privacy impact assessment

The term *privacy* refers to the right of an individual, a group of individuals, or an organization to keep information of a personal or proprietary nature from being disclosed to others. Many nations view privacy as a basic human right. The Universal Declaration of Human Rights, Article 12, states: "No one shall be subjected to arbitrary interference with his privacy, family, home or correspondence, nor to attacks upon his honor and reputation. Everyone has the right to the protection of the law against such interference or attacks."

The U.S. Constitution contains no express right to privacy; however, the Bill of Rights reflects the concern of the framers for protecting specific aspects of privacy.[5] In the United Kingdom privacy is guaranteed by the Data Protection Act. The European Court of Human Rights has developed many documents defining the right to privacy.

At the same time, the right to privacy is limited by laws. For example, taxation laws require individuals to share information about personal income or earnings. Individual privacy may conflict with other basic human rights, e.g., freedom of speech. Privacy laws differ from country to country; laws in one country may require public disclosure of information considered private in other countries and cultures.

The digital age has confronted legislators with significant challenges related to privacy as new threats have emerged. For example, personal information voluntarily shared, but stolen from sites granted access to it or misused, can lead to *identity theft.*

Some countries have been more aggressive than others in addressing the new privacy concerns. For example, the countries of the European Union (EU) have very strict laws governing handling of personal data in the digital age. A sweeping new privacy right, the "right to be forgotten," is codified as part of a broad new proposed data protection regulation in the EU. This right addresses the following problem: Today it is very hard to escape your past when every photo, status update, and tweet lives forever on some Web site.

Our discussion targets primarily public clouds where privacy has an entirely new dimension because the data, often in an unencrypted form, resides on servers owned by a CSP. Services based on individual preferences, the location of individuals, membership in social networks, or other personal information

[5]The First Amendment covers the protection of beliefs, the Third Amendment privacy of homes, the Fourth Amendment the privacy of person and possessions against unreasonable searches, the Fifth Amendment the privilege against self-incrimination and thus, the privacy of personal information. According to some Justices, the Ninth Amendment, which reads, "The enumeration in the Constitution, of certain rights, shall not be construed to deny or disparage others retained by the people," can be viewed as a protection of privacy in ways not explicitly specified by the first eight amendments in the Bill of Rights.

present a special risk. The owner of the data cannot rely exclusively on the CSP to guarantee the privacy of the data.

Privacy concerns are different for the three cloud delivery models and also depend on the actual context. For example, consider Gmail, a widely used *SaaS* delivery model. Gmail privacy policy reads (see `www.google.com/policies/privacy/`, accessed on October 6, 2012): "We collect information in two ways: information you give us ... like your name, email address, telephone number or credit card; information we get from your use of our services such as: ... device information, ... log information, ... location information, ... unique application numbers, ... local storage, ... cookies and anonymous identifiers ... We will share personal information with companies, organizations or individuals outside of Google if we have a good-faith belief that access, use, preservation or disclosure of the information is reasonably necessary to: meet any applicable law, regulation, legal process or enforceable governmental request ... protect against harm to the rights, property or safety of Google, our users or the public as required or permitted by law. We may share aggregated, nonpersonally identifiable information publicly and with our partners like publishers, advertisers or connected sites. For example, we may share information publicly to show trends about the general use of our services."

The main aspects of privacy are: the lack of user control, potential unauthorized secondary use, data proliferation, and dynamic provisioning [290]. The lack of user control refers to the fact that user-centric data control is incompatible with cloud usage. Once data is stored on the CSP's servers, the user loses control of the exact location, and in some instances the user could lose access to the data. For example, in case of the Gmail service, the account owner has no control over where the data is stored or how long old emails are stored in some backups of the servers.

A CSP may obtain revenues from unauthorized secondary usage of the information, e.g., for targeted advertising. There are no technological means to prevent this use. Dynamic provisioning refers to threats due to outsourcing. A range of issues is very fuzzy; for example, how to identify the subcontractors of a CSP, what rights to the data they have, and what rights to data are transferable in case of bankruptcy or merger.

There is a need for legislation addressing the multiple aspects of privacy in the digital age. A document elaborated by the Federal Trade Commission for the U.S. Congress states [122]: "Consumer-oriented commercial Web sites that collect personal identifying information from or about consumers online would be required to comply with the four widely accepted fair information practices:

1. *Notice.* Web sites would be required to provide consumers clear and conspicuous notice of their information practices, including what information they collect, how they collect it (e.g., directly or through nonobvious means such as cookies), how they use it, how they provide Choice, Access, and Security to consumers, whether they disclose the information collected to other entities, and whether other entities are collecting information through the site.
2. *Choice.* Web sites would be required to offer consumers choices as to how their personal identifying information is used beyond the use for which the information was provided (e.g., to consummate a transaction). Such choice would encompass both internal secondary uses (such as marketing back to consumers) and external secondary uses (such as disclosing data to other entities).
3. *Access.* Web sites would be required to offer consumers reasonable access to the information a Web site has collected about them, including a reasonable opportunity to review information and to correct inaccuracies or delete information.

4. *Security*. Web sites would be required to take reasonable steps to protect the security of the information they collect from consumers. The Commission recognizes that the implementation of these practices may vary with the nature of the information collected and the uses to which it is put, as well as with technological developments. For this reason, the Commission recommends that any legislation be phrased in general terms and be technologically neutral. Thus, the definitions of fair information practices set forth in the statute should be broad enough to provide flexibility to the implementing agency in promulgating its rules or regulations."

There is a need for tools capable of identifing privacy issues in information systems, the so-called *Privacy Impact Assesment (PIA)*. As of mid-2012 there were no international standards for such a process, though different countries and organizations require PIA reports. An example of an analysis is to assess the legal implications of the U.K.-U.S. Safe Harbor process to allow U.S. companies to comply with the European Directive 95/46/EC[6] on the protection of personal data.

Such an assessment forces a proactive attitude toward privacy. An ab-initio approach to embedding privacy rules in new systems is preferable to painful changes that could affect the functionality of existing systems.

A PIA tool that could be deployed as a Web-based service is proposed in [345]. The inputs to the tool includes project information, an outline of project documents, privacy risks, and stakeholders. The tool will produce a PIA report consisting of a summary of findings, a risk summary, security, transparency, and cross-border data flows.

The centerpiece of the PIA tool is a knowledge base (KB) created and maintained by domain experts. The users of the *SaaS* service providing access to the PIA tool must fill in a questionnaire. The system uses templates to generate additional questions necessary and to fill in the PIA report. An expert system infers which rules are satisfied by the facts in the database and provided by the users and executes the rule with the highest priority.

9.4 Trust

Trust in the context of cloud computing is intimately related to the general problem of trust in online activities. In this section we first discuss the traditional concept of trust and then the trust necessary to online activities.

According to the Merriam-Webster dictionary, *trust* means "assured reliance on the character, ability, strength, or truth of someone or something." Trust is a complex phenomenon; it enables cooperative behavior, promotes adaptive organizational forms, reduces harmful conflict, decreases transaction costs, facilitates formulation of ad hoc workgroups, and promotes effective responses to crisis [309].

Two conditions must exist for trust to develop. The first condition is *risk*, the perceived probability of loss; indeed, trust would not be necessary if there were no risk involved, if there is a certainty that an action can succeed. The second condition is *interdependence*, the idea that the interests of one entity cannot be achieved without reliance on other entities. A trust relationship goes though three phases: (1) a building phase, when trust is formed; (2) a stability phase, when trust exists; and (3) a dissolution phase, when trust declines.

[6]See eur-lex.europa.eu/LexUriServ/LexUriServ.do?uri=CELEX:31995L0046:en:HTML.

There are different reasons for and forms of trust. Utilitarian reasons could be based on the belief that the costly penalties for breach of trust exceed any potential benefits from opportunistic behavior. This is the essence of *deterrence-based* trust. Another reason is the belief that the action involving the other party is in the self-interest of that party. This is the so-called *calculus-based* trust. After a long sequence of interactions, *relational trust* between entities can develop based on the accumulated experience of dependability and reliance on each other.

The common wisdom is that an entity must work very hard to build trust but may lose that trust very easily; a single violation of trust can lead to irreparable damage. *Persistent trust* is trust based on the long-term behavior of an entity, whereas *dynamic trust* is based on a specific context, e.g., a state of the system or the effect of technological developments.

The trust in the Internet "obscures or lacks entirely the dimensions of character and personality, nature of relationship, and institutional character" of traditional trust [258]. The missing identity, personal characteristics, and role definitions are elements we have to deal with in the context of online trust.

The Internet offers individuals the ability to obscure or conceal their identities. The resulting anonymity reduces the cues normally used in judgments of trust. The identity is critical for developing trust relations; it allows us to base our trust on the past history of interactions with an entity. Anonymity causes mistrust because identity is associated with accountability and, in the absence of identity, accountability cannot be enforced. The opacity extends immediately from identity to personal characteristics. It is impossible to infer whether the entity or individual we transact with is who it pretends to be, since the transactions occur between entities separated in time and distance. Finally, there are no guarantees that the entities we transact with fully understand the role they have assumed.

To remedy the loss of clues, we need security mechanisms for access control, transparency of identity, and surveillance. The mechanisms for access control are designed to keep intruders and mischievous agents out. Identity transparency requires that the relationship between a virtual agent and a physical person should be carefully checked through methods such as biometric identification. Digital signatures and digital certificates are used for identification. Surveillance could be based on *intrusion detection* or on logging and auditing. The first option is based on real-time monitoring, the second on offline sifting through audit records.

Credentials are used when an entity is not known. Credentials are issued by a trusted authority and describe the qualities of the entity using the credential. A Doctor of Dental Surgery diploma hanging on the wall of a dentist's office is a credential that the individual has been trained by an accredited university and hence is capable of performing a set of dental procedures; similarly, a digital signature is a credential used in many distributed applications.

Policies and *reputation* are two ways of determining trust. Policies reveal the conditions to obtain trust and the actions to take when some of the conditions are met. Policies require the verification of credentials. Reputation is a quality attributed to an entity based on a relatively long history of interactions with or possibly observations of the entity. Recommendations are based on trust decisions made by others and filtered through the perspective of the entity assessing the trust.

In a computer science context, "trust of a party A to a party B for a service X is the measurable belief of A in that B behaves dependably for a specified period within a specified context (in relation to service X)" [272]. An assurance about the operation of a particular hardware or software component leads to persistent social-based trust in that component. A comprehensive discussion of trust in computer services in the semantic Web can be found in [26]. In Section 11.10 we discuss the concept of trust in the context of cognitive radio networks where multiple transmitters compete for free communication channels. In Section 11.11 we present a cloud-based trust management service.

9.5 Operating system security

An operating system (OS) allows multiple applications to share the hardware resources of a physical system, subject to a set of policies. A critical function of an OS is to protect applications against a wide range of malicious attacks such as unauthorized access to privileged information, tempering with executable code, and spoofing. Such attacks can now target even single-user systems such as personal computers, tablets, or smartphones. Data brought into the system may contain malicious code; this could occur via a Java applet, or data imported by a browser from a malicious Web site.

The *mandatory security* of an OS is considered to be "any security policy where the definition of the policy logic and the assignment of security attributes is tightly controlled by a system security policy administrator" [209]. Access control, authentication usage, and cryptographic usage policies are all elements of mandatory OS security. The first policy specifies how the OS controls the access to different system objects, the second defines the authentication mechanisms the OS uses to authenticate a principal, and the last specifies the cryptographic mechanisms used to protect the data. A necessary but not sufficient condition for security is that the subsystems tasked with performing security-related functions are temper-proof and cannot be bypassed. The OS should confine an application to a unique security domain.

Applications with special privileges that perform security-related functions are called *trusted applications*. Such applications should only be allowed the lowest level of privileges required to perform their functions. For example, type enforcement is a mandatory security mechanism that can be used to restrict a trusted application to the lowest level of privileges.

Enforcing mandatory security through mechanisms left to the discretion of users could lead to a breach of security due not only to malicious intent but also carelessness or lack of understanding. Discretionary mechanisms place the burden of security on individual users. Moreover, an application may change a carefully defined discretionary policy without the consent of the user, whereas a mandatory policy can only be changed by a system administrator.

Unfortunately, commercial operating systems do not support multilayered security; such systems only distinguish between a completely privileged security domain and a completely unprivileged one. Some operating systems, such as *Windows NT*, allow a program to inherit all the privileges of the program invoking it, regardless of the level of trust in that program.

The existence of *trusted paths*, mechanisms supporting user interactions with trusted software, is critical to system security. If such mechanisms do not exist, malicious software can impersonate trusted software. Some systems provide trust paths for a few functions such as login authentication and password changing and allow servers to authenticate their clients.

The solution discussed in [209] is to decompose a complex mechanism into several components with well-defined roles. For example, the access control mechanism for the application space could consist of *enforcer* and *decider* components. To access a protected object, the enforcer will gather the required information about the agent attempting the access and will pass this information to the decider, together with the information about the object and the elements of the policy decision. Finally, it will carry out the actions requested by the decider.

A trusted-path mechanism is required to prevent malicious software invoked by an authorized application to tamper with the attributes of the object and/or with the policy rules. A trusted path is also required to prevent an impostor from impersonating the decider agent. A similar solution is proposed for cryptography usage, which should be decomposed into an analysis of the invocation mechanisms and an analysis of the cryptographic mechanism.

Another question is how an OS can protect itself and the applications running under it from malicious mobile code attempting to gain access to the data and the other resources and compromise system confidentiality and/or integrity. Java Security Manager uses the type-safety attributes of Java to prevent unauthorized actions of an application running in a "sandbox." Yet, the Java Virtual Machine (JVM) accepts byte code in violation of language semantics; moreover, it cannot protect itself from tampering by other applications.

Even if all these security problems could be eliminated, good security relies on the ability of the file system to preserve the integrity of Java class code. The approach to require digitally signed applets and accept them only from trusted sources could fail due to the all-or-nothing security model. A solution to securing mobile communication could be to confine a browser to a distinct security domain.

Specialized *closed-box platforms* such as the ones on some cellular phones, game consoles, and automated teller machines (ATMs) could have embedded cryptographic keys that allow themselves to reveal their true identity to remote systems and authenticate the software running on them. Such facilities are not available to *open-box platforms*, the traditional hardware designed for commodity operating systems.

A highly secure operating system is necessary but not sufficient unto itself; application-specific security is also necessary. Sometimes security implemented above the operating system is better. This is the case for electronic commerce that requires a digital signature on each transaction.

We conclude that commodity operating systems offer low assurance. Indeed, an OS is a complex software system consisting of millions of lines of code, and it is vulnerable to a wide range of malicious attacks. An OS poorly isolates one application from another, and once an application is compromised, the entire physical platform and all applications running on it can be affected. The platform security level is thus reduced to the security level of the most vulnerable application running on the platform.

Operating systems provide only weak mechanisms for applications to authenticate to one another and do not have a trusted path between users and applications. These shortcomings add to the challenges of providing security in a distributed computing environment. For example, a financial application cannot determine whether a request comes from an authorized user or from a malicious program; in turn, a human user cannot distinguish a response from a malicious program impersonating the service from the response provided by the service itself.

9.6 Virtual machine security

The hybrid and the hosted VM models in Figures 5.3(c) and (d), respectively, expose the entire system to the vulnerability of the host operating system; thus, we will not analyze these models. Our discussion of virtual machine security is restricted to the traditional system VM model in Figure 5.3(b), where the VMM controls access to the hardware.

Virtual security services are typically provided by the VMM, as shown in Figure 9.2(a). Another alternative is to have a dedicated security services VM, as shown in Figure 9.2(b). A secure *trusted*

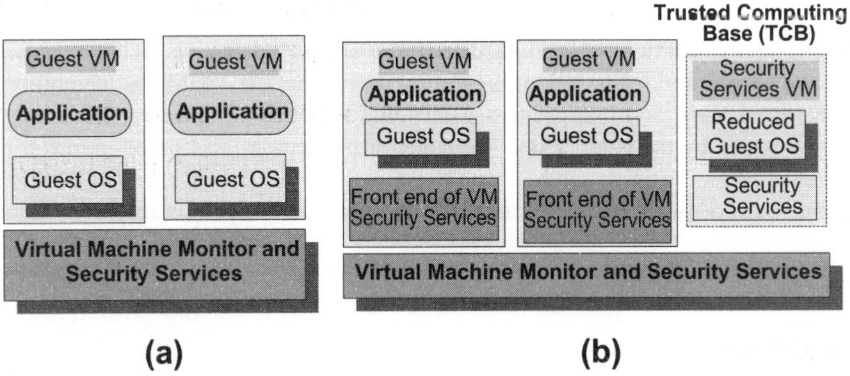

FIGURE 9.2

(a) Virtual security services provided by the VMM. (b) A dedicated security VM.

computing base (TCB) is a necessary condition for security in a virtual machine environment; if the TCB is compromised, the security of the entire system is affected.

The analysis of *Xen* and *vBlades* in Sections 5.8 and 5.10 shows that VM technology provides a stricter isolation of virtual machines from one another than the isolation of processes in a traditional operating system. Indeed, a VMM controls the execution of privileged operations and can thus enforce memory isolation as well as disk and network access. The VMMs are considerably less complex and better structured than traditional operating systems; thus, they are in a better position to respond to security attacks. A major challenge is that a VMM sees only raw data regarding the state of a guest operating system, whereas security services typically operate at a higher logical level, e.g., at the level of a file rather than a disk block.

A guest OS runs on simulated hardware, and the VMM has access to the state of all virtual machines operating on the same hardware. The state of a guest virtual machine can be saved, restored, cloned, and encrypted by the VMM. Not only can replication ensure reliability, it can also support security, whereas cloning could be used to recognize a malicious application by testing it on a cloned system and observing whether it behaves normally. We can also clone a running system and examine the effect of potentially dangerous applications. Another interesting possibility is to have the guest VM's files moved to a dedicated VM and thus, protect it from attacks [389]; this is possible because inter-VM communication is faster than communication between two physical machines.

Sophisticated attackers are able to fingerprint virtual machines and avoid VM *honeypots* designed to study the methods of attack. They can also attempt to access VM-logging files and thus recover sensitive data; such files have to be very carefully protected to prevent unauthorized access to cryptographic keys and other sensitive data.

There is no free lunch; thus, we expect to pay some price for the better security provided by virtualization. This price includes: higher hardware costs, because a virtual system requires more resources, such as CPU cycles, memory, disk, and network bandwidth; the cost of developing VMMs and modifying the host operating systems in case of paravirtualization; and the overhead of virtualization because the VMM is involved in privileged operations.

A recent paper [389] surveys VM-based intrusion detection systems such as `Livewire` and `Siren`, which exploit the three capabilities of a virtual machine for intrusion detection: isolation, inspection, and interposition. We have examined isolation; inspection means that the VMM has the ability to review the state of the guest VMs, and interposition means that the VMM can trap and emulate the privileged instruction issued by the guest VMs. The paper also discusses VM-based intrusion prevention systems such as `SVFS`, `NetTop`, and `IntroVirt` and surveys `Terra`, a VM-based trust computing platform. `Terra` uses a *trusted virtual machine monitor* to partition resources among virtual machines.

The security group involved with the NIST project has identified the following VMM- and VM-based threats:

- VMM-based threats:
  1. Starvation of resources and denial of service for some VMs. Probable causes: (a) badly configured resource limits for some VMs; (b) a rogue VM with the capability to bypass resource limits set in the VMM.
  2. VM side-channel attacks. Malicious attacks on one or more VMs by a rogue VM under the same VMM. Probable causes: (a) lack of proper isolation of inter-VM traffic due to misconfiguration of the virtual network residing in the VMM; (b) limitation of packet inspection devices to handle high-speed traffic, e.g., video traffic; (c) presence of VM instances built from insecure VM images, e.g., a VM image having a guest OS without the latest patches.
  3. Buffer overflow attacks.
- VM-based threats:
  1. Deployment of rogue or insecure VM. Unauthorized users may create insecure instances from images or may perform unauthorized administrative actions on existing VMs. Probable cause: improper configuration of access controls on VM administrative tasks such as instance creation, launching, suspension, reactivation, and so on.
  2. Presence of insecure and tampered VM images in the VM image repository. Probable causes: (a) lack of access control to the VM image repository; (b) lack of mechanisms to verify the integrity of the images, e.g., digitally signed image.

Sections 9.7, 9.8, 9.9, and 9.10 discuss in depth various aspects related to virtualization and security.

9.7 Security of virtualization

The relationship between virtualization and security is a complex one and has two distinct aspects: virtualization for security and the security of virtualization [215]. In Section 5.1 we praised the virtues of virtualization. We also discussed two of the problems associated with virtual environments: (a) the negative effect on performance due to the additional overhead; and (b) the need for more powerful systems to run multiple virtual machines. In this section we take a closer look at the security of virtualization.

One of the most important virtues of virtualization is that the complete state of an operating system running under a virtual machine is captured by the VM. *This state can be saved in a file and then the file can be copied and shared.* There are several useful implications regarding this fact:

1. Ability to support the *IaaS* delivery model. In this model a user selects an image matching the local environment used by the application and then uploads and runs the application on the cloud using this image.
2. Increased reliability. An operating system with all the applications running under it can be replicated and switched to a hot standby[7] in case of a system failure.
3. Straightforward mechanisms to implement resource management policies:
   - To balance the load of a system, an OS and the applications running under it can be moved to another server when the load on the current server exceeds a high-water mark.
   - To reduce power consumption, the load of lightly loaded servers can be moved to other servers and then these servers can be turned off or set on standby mode.
4. Improved intrusion prevention and detection. In a virtual environment a clone can look for known patterns in system activity and detect intrusion. The operator can switch to a hot standby when suspicious events are detected.
5. Secure logging and intrusion protection. Intrusion detection can be disabled and logging can be modified by an intruder when implemented at the OS level. When these services are implemented at the VMM/hypervisor layer, the services cannot be disabled or modified. In addition, the VMM may be able to log *only* events of interest for a post-attack analysis.
6. More efficient and flexible software testing. Instead of a very large number of dedicated systems running under different operating systems, different versions of each operating system, and different patches for each version, virtualization allows the multitude of OS instances to share a small number of physical systems.

Is there a price to pay for the benefits of virtualization outlined here? There is always the other side of a coin, so we should not be surprised that the answer to this question is a resounding "yes." In a 2005 paper [132] Garfinkel and Rosenblum argued that the serious implications of virtualization on system security cannot be ignored. This theme was revisited in 2008 by Price [297], who reaches similar conclusions.

A first type of undesirable effects of virtualization leads to the diminished ability of an organization to manage its systems and track their status:

- The number of physical systems in the inventory of an organization is limited by cost, space, energy consumption, and human support. Creating a VM reduces ultimately to copying a file; therefore the explosion in the number of VMs is a fact of life. The only limitation for the number of VMs is the amount of storage space available.
- In addition to quantity, there is also a qualitative aspect to the explosion in the number of VMs. Traditionally, organizations install and maintain the same version of system software. In a virtual environment such homogeneity cannot be enforced; thus, the number of different operating systems, their versions, and the patch status of each version will be very diverse, and this heterogeneity will tax the support team.
- Probably one of the most critical problems posed by virtualization is related to the software life cycle. The traditional assumption is that the software life cycle is a straight line, so patch management

[7] A hot standby is a method of achieving redundancy. The primary and the secondary or backup systems run simultaneously. The data is mirrored to the secondary in real time so that both systems contain identical information.

is based on a monotonic forward progress. However, the virtual execution model *maps to a tree structure* rather than a line; indeed, at any point in time multiple instances of the VM can be created and then each one of them can be updated, different patches installed, and so on. This problem has serious implications for security, as we shall see shortly.

Let us now concentrate our discussion on direct implications of virtualization on security. A first question is: How can the support team deal with the consequences of an attack in a virtual environment? Do we expect the infection from a computer virus or a worm to be less manageable in a virtual environment? The surprising answer to this question is that an infection may last indefinitely.

Some of the infected VMs may be dormant at the time when the measures to clean up the systems are taken and then, at a later time, they could wake up and infect other systems. This scenario can repeat itself and guarantee that infection will last indefinitely. This is in stark contrast to the manner in which an infection is treated in nonvirtual environments; once an infection is detected, the infected systems are quarantined and then cleaned up. The systems will then behave normally until the next episode of infection occurs.

The more general observation is that in a traditional computing environment a steady state can be reached. In this steady state all systems are brought up to a "desirable" state, whereas "undesirable" states – states in which some of the systems are either infected by a virus or display an undesirable pattern of behavior – are only transient. This desirable state is reached by installing the latest version of the system software and then applying the latest patches to all systems. Due to the lack of control, a virtual environment may never reach such a steady state. In a nonvirtual environment the security can be compromised when an infected laptop is connected to the network protected by a firewall or when a virus is brought in on removable media. But unlike a virtual environment, the system can still reach a steady state.

A side effect of the ability to record in a file the complete state of a VM is the possibility to roll back a VM. This opens wide the door for a new type of vulnerability caused by events recorded in the memory of an attacker. Two such situations are discussed in [132]. The first is that one-time passwords are transmitted in the clear and the protection is guaranteed only if the attacker does not have the possibility to access passwords used in previous sessions. If a system runs the S/KEY password system[8] an attacker can replay rolled-back versions and access past sniffed passwords.

The second situation is related to the requirement of some cryptographic protocols, and even noncryptographic protocols, regarding the "freshness" of the random-number source used for session keys and nonces.[9] This situation occurs when a VM is rolled back to a state in which a random number has been generated but not yet used.

Even noncryptographic use of random numbers may be affected by the rollback scenario. For example, the initial sequence number for a new TCP connection must be "fresh"; when it is not, the door to TCP hijacking is left open.

[8]S/KEY is a password system based on Leslie Lamport's scheme. It is used by several operating systems, including *Linux*, OpenBSD, and NetBSD. The real password of the user is combined with a short set of characters and a counter that is decremented at each use to form a single-use password.

[9]A *nonce* is a random or pseudo-random number issued in an authentication protocol to ensure that old communications cannot be reused in replay attacks. For example, nonces are used to calculate an *MD5* of the password for *HTTP* digest access authentication. Each time the authentication challenge response code is presented, the nonces are different; thus replay attacks are virtually impossible. This guarantees that an online order to Amazon or other online store cannot be replayed.

Another undesirable effect of the virtual environment affects the trust. Recall from Section 9.4 that *trust is conditioned by the ability to guarantee the identity of entities involved.* Each computer system in a network has a unique physical, or *MAC*, address; the uniqueness of this address guarantees that an infected or malicious system can be identified and then cleaned, shut down, or denied network access. This process breaks down for virtual systems when VMs are created dynamically. Often, to avoid name collision, a random *MAC* address is assigned to a new VM. The other effect discussed at length in Section 9.8 is that popular VM images are shared by many users.

The ability to guarantee confidentiality of sensitive data is yet another pillar of security affected by virtualization. Virtualization undermines the basic principle that the time-sensitive data stored on any system should be reduced to a minimum. First, the owner has very limited control over where sensitive data is stored; it could be spread across many servers and may be left on some of them indefinitely. To be able to roll it back, a VMM records the state of a VM. This process allows an attacker to access sensitive data the owner attempted to destroy.

9.8 Security risks posed by shared images

Even when we assume that a cloud service provider is trustworthy, many users either ignore or underestimate the danger posed by other sources of concern. One of them, especially critical to the *IaaS* cloud delivery model, is image sharing. For example, a user of *AWS* has the option to choose between Amazon Machine Images (AMIs), accessible through the *Quick Start* or the *Community AMI* menus of the *EC2* service. The option of using one of these AMIs is especially tempting for a first-time or less sophisticated user.

First, let's review the process to create an AMI. We can start from a running system, from another AMI, or from the image of a VM and copy the contents of the file system to the *S3*, the so-called *bundling*. The first of the three steps in bundling is to create an image, the second step is to compress and encrypt the image, and the last step is to split the image into several segments and then upload the segments to the *S3*.

Two procedures for the creation of an image are available: `ec2-bundle-image` and `ec2-bundle-volume`. The first is used for images prepared as loopback files[10] when the data is transferred to the image in blocks. To bundle a running system, the creator of the image can use the second procedure when bundling works at the level of the file system and files are copied recursively to the image.

To use an image, a user has to specify the resources, provide the credentials for login, provide a firewall configuration, and specify the region, as discussed in Section 3.1. Once instantiated, the user is informed about the public DNS and the virtual machine is made available. A *Linux* system can be accessed using `ssh` at port 22, whereas the Remote Desktop at port 3389 is used for *Windows*.

A recent paper reports on the results of an analysis carried out over a period of several months, from November 2010 to May 2011, of over 5,000 AMIs available through the public catalog at Amazon [38].

[10]A *loopback file system* (LOFS) is a virtual file system that provides an alternate path to an existing file system. When other file systems are mounted onto an LOFS file system, the original file system does not change. One useful purpose of LOFS is to take a CD-ROM image file, a file of type iso, and mount it on the file system and then access it without the need to record a CD-R. It is somewhat equivalent to the *Linux* `mount -o loop` option but adds a level of abstraction; most commands that apply to a device can be used to handle the mapped file.

Many of the analyzed images allowed a user to *undelete* files and recover credentials, private keys, or other types of sensitive information with little effort and using standard tools. The results of this study were shared with Amazon's Security Team, which acted promptly to reduce the threats posed to *AWS* users.

The details of the testing methodology can be found in [38]. Here we only discuss the results. The study was able to audit some 5,303 images out of the 8,448 *Linux* AMIs and 1,202 *Windows* AMIs at Amazon sites in the United States, Europe, and Asia. The audit covered software vulnerabilities and security and privacy risks.

The average duration of an audit was 77 minutes for a *Windows* image and 21 minutes for a *Linux* image; the average disk space used was about 1 GB and 2.7 GB, respectively. The entire file system of a *Windows* AMI was audited because most malware targets *Windows* systems. Only directories containing executables for *Linux* AMIs were scanned; this strategy and the considerably longer start-up time of *Windows* explain the time discrepancy of the audits across the types of AMIs.

The *software vulnerability* audit revealed that 98% of the *Windows* AMIs (249 out of 253) and 58% of *Linux* AMIs (2,005 out of 3,432) audited had critical vulnerabilities. The average number of vulnerabilities per AMI were 46 for *Windows* and 11 for *Linux*. Some of the images were rather old; 145, 38, and 2 *Windows* AMIs and 1,197, 364, and 106 *Linux* were older than two, three, and four years, respectively. The tool used to detect vulnerabilities, *Nessus*, available from `www.tenable.com/productus/nessus`, classifies the vulnerabilities based on their severity in four groups, at levels 0–3. The audit reported only vulnerabilities of the highest severity level, e.g., remote code execution.

Three types of *security risks* were analyzed: (1) backdoors and leftover credentials, (2) unsolicited connections, and (3) malware. An astounding finding is that about 22% of the scanned *Linux* AMIs contained credentials allowing an intruder to remotely log into the system. Some 100 passwords, 995 `ssh` keys, and 90 cases in which both passwords and keys could be retrieved were identified.

To rent a *Linux* AMI, a user must provide the public part of the `ssh` key, and this key is stored in the `authorized_keys` in the home directory. This opens a backdoor for a malicious creator of an AMI who does not remove his own public key from the image and can remotely log into any instance of this AMI. Another backdoor is opened when the `ssh` server allows password-based authentication and the malicious creator of an AMI does not remove his own password. This backdoor is opened even wider as one can extract the password hashes and then crack the passwords using a tool such as John the Ripper (see `www.openwall.com/john`).

Another threat is posed by the omission of the `cloud-init` script that should be invoked when the image is booted. This script, provided by Amazon, regenerates the host key an `ssh` server uses to identify itself; the public part of this key is used to authenticate the server. When this key is shared among several systems, these systems become vulnerable to *man-in-the middle*[11] attacks. When this

[11]In a *man-in-the-middle* an attacker impersonates the agents at both ends of a communication channel and makes them believe that they communicate through a secure channel. For example, if B sends her public key to A, but C is able to intercept it, such an attack proceeds as follows: C sends a forged message to A claiming to be from B but instead includes C's public key. Then A encrypts his message with C's key, believing that he is using B's key, and sends the encrypted message to B. The intruder, C, intercepts, deciphers the message using her private key, possibly alters the message, and re-encrypts the public key B originally sent to A. When B receives the newly encrypted message, she believes it came from A.

script does not run, an attacker can use the *NMap* tool[12] to match the ssh keys discovered in the AMI images with the keys obtained via *NMap*. The study reports that the authors were able to identify more than 2,100 instances following this procedure.

Unsolicited connections pose a serious threat to a system. Outgoing connections allow an outside entity to receive privileged information, e.g., the IP address of an instance and events recorded by a *syslog* daemon to files in the *var/log* directory of a *Linux* system. Such information is available only to users with administrative privileges. The audit detected two *Linux* instances with modified *syslog* daemons, which forwarded to an outside agent information about events such as login and incoming requests to a Web server. Some of the unsolicited connections are legitimate – for example, connections to a software update site. It is next to impossible to distinguish legitimate from malicious connections.

Malware, including viruses, worms, spyware, and trojans, were identified using *ClamAV*, a software tool with a database of some 850,000 malware signatures, available from www.clamav.net. Two infected *Windows* AMIs were discovered, one with a *Trojan-Spy* (variant 50112) and a second one with a *Trojan-Agent* (variant 173287). The first trojan carries out keylogging and allows stealing data from the files system and monitoring processes; the AMI also included a tool called *Trojan.Firepass* to decrypt and recover passwords stored by the *Firefox* browser.

The creator of a shared AMI assumes some *privacy risks*; his private keys, IP addresses, browser history, shell history, and deleted files can be recovered from the published images. A malicious agent can recover the *AWS* API keys that are not password protected. Then the malicious agent can start AMIs and run cloud applications at no cost to herself, since the computing charges are passed on to the owner of the API key. The search can target files with names such as $pk - [0-9A-Z]^*.pem$ or $cert - [0-9A-Z]^*.pem$ used to store API keys.

Another avenue for a malicious agent is to recover ssh keys stored in files named *id_dsa* and *id_rsa*. Though ssh keys can be protected by a *passphrase*,[13] the audit determined that the majority of *ssh* keys (54 out of 56) were not password protected.

Recovery of IP addresses of other systems owned by the same user requires access to the *lastlog* or the *lastb* databases. The audit found 187 AMIs with a total of more than 66,000 entries in their *lastb* databases. Nine AMIs contained Firefox browser history and allowed the auditor to identify the domains contacted by the user.

In addition, 612 AMIs contained at least one shell history file. The audit analyzed 869 history files named *~/.history*, *~/.bash_history*, and *~/.sh_history*, containing some, 160,000 lines of command history, and identified 74 identification credentials. Users should be aware that when *HTTP* is used to transfer information from a user to a Web site, the *GET* requests are stored in the logs of the Web server. Passwords and credit card numbers communicated via a *GET* request can be exploited by a malicious agent with access to such logs. When remote credentials such as the DNS management password are available, a malicious agent can redirect traffic from its original destination to her own system.

---

[12]*NMap* is a security tool running on most operating systems, including *Linux, Microsoft Windows, Solaris, HP-UX, SGI-IRIX*, and BSD variants such as *Mac OS X*, to map the network. *Mapping the network* means discovering hosts and services in a network.

[13]A *passphrase* is a sequence of words used to control access to a computer system; it is the analog of a password but provides added security. For high-security nonmilitary applications, NIST recommends an 80-bit-strength passphrase. Hence a secure passphrase should consist of at least 58 characters, including uppercase and alphanumeric characters. The entropy of written English is less than 1.1 bits per character.

Recovery of deleted files containing sensitive information poses another risk for the provider of an image. When the sectors on the disk containing sensitive information are actually overwritten by another file, recovery of sensitive information is much harder. To be safe, the creator of the image effort should use utilities such as `shred`, `scrub`, `zerofree`, or `wipe` to make recovery of sensitive information next to impossible. If the image is created with the block-level tool discussed at the beginning of this section, the image will contain blocks of the file system marked as free; such blocks may contain information from deleted files. The audit process was able to recover files from 98% of the AMIs using the `exundelete` utility. The number of files recovered from an AMI was as low as 6 and as high as 40,000.

We conclude that the users of published AMIs as well as the providers of images may be vulnerable to a wide range of security risks and must be fully aware of the dangers posed by image sharing.

9.9 Security risks posed by a management OS

We often hear that virtualization enhances security because a virtual machine monitor or hypervisor is considerably smaller than an operating system. For example, the *Xen* VMM discussed in Section 5.8 has approximately 60,000 lines of code, one to two orders of magnitude fewer than a traditional operating system.[14]

A hypervisor supports stronger isolation between the VMs running under it than the isolation between processes supported by a traditional operating system. Yet the hypervisor must rely on a management OS to create VMs and to transfer data in and out from a guest VM to storage devices and network interfaces.

A small VMM can be carefully analyzed; thus, one could conclude that the security risks in a virtual environment are diminished. We have to be cautious with such sweeping statements. Indeed, the trusted computer base (TCB)[15] of a cloud computing environment includes not only the hypervisor but also the management OS. The management OS supports administrative tools, live migration, device drivers, and device emulators.

For example, the TCB of an environment based on *Xen* includes not only the hardware and the hypervisor but also the management operating system running in the so-called *Dom0* (see Figure 9.3). System vulnerabilities can be introduced by both software components, *Xen*, and the management operating system. An analysis of *Xen* vulnerabilities reports that 21 of the 23 attacks were against service components of the control VM [90]; 11 attacks were attributed to problems in the guest OS caused by buffer overflow[16] and 8 were denial-of-service attacks.

Dom0 manages the building of all user domains (*DomU*), a process consisting of several steps:

1. Allocate memory in the *Dom0* address space and load the kernel of the guest operating system from secondary storage.
2. Allocate memory for the new VM and use foreign mapping[17] to load the kernel to the new VM.

[14]The number of lines of code of the *Linux* operating system evolved in time from 176,250 for *Linux 1.0.0*, released in March 1995, to 1,800,847 for *Linux 2.2.0*, released in January 1999; 3,377,902 for *Linux 2.4.0*, released in January 2001; and to 5,929,913 for *Linux 2.6.0*, released in December 2003.

[15]The TCB is defined as the totality of protection mechanisms within a computer system, including hardware, firmware, and software, the combination of which is responsible for enforcing a security policy.

[16]Buffer overflow allows execution of arbitrary code in a privileged mode.

[17]The foreign mapping mechanism of *Xen* is used by *Dom0* to map arbitrary memory frames of a VM into its page tables.

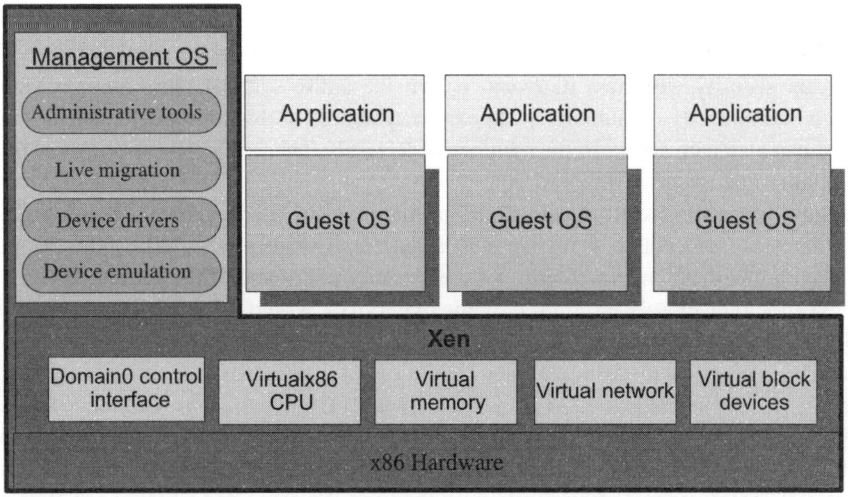

FIGURE 9.3

The trusted computing base of a *Xen*-based environment includes the hardware, *Xen*, and the management operating system running in *Dom0*. The management OS supports administrative tools, live migration, device drivers, and device emulators. A guest operating system and applications running under it reside in a *DomU*.

3. Set up the initial page tables for the new VM.
4. Release the foreign mapping on the new VM memory, set up the virtual CPU registers, and launch the new VM.

A malicious *Dom0* can play several nasty tricks at the time when it creates a *DomU* [215]:

- Refuse to carry out the steps necessary to start the new VM, an action that can be considered a *denial-of-service* attack.
- Modify the kernel of the guest operating system in ways that will allow a third party to monitor and control the execution of applications running under the new VM.
- Undermine the integrity of the new VM by setting the wrong page tables and/or setting up incorrect virtual CPU registers.
- Refuse to release the foreign mapping and access the memory while the new VM is running.

Let us now turn our attention to the run-time interaction between *Dom0* and a *DomU*. Recall that *Dom0* exposes a set of abstract devices to the guest operating systems using *split drivers*. The front end of such a driver is in the *DomU* and its back end in *Dom0*, and the two communicate via a ring in shared memory (see Section 5.8).

In the original implementation of *Xen* a service running in a *DomU* sends data to or receives data from a client located outside the cloud using a network interface in *Dom0*; it transfers the data to I/O devices using a device driver in *Dom0*.[18] Therefore, we have to ensure that run-time communication

[18]Later implementations of *Xen* offer the pass-through option.

through *Dom0* is encrypted. Yet, *Transport Layer Security* (TLS) does not guarantee that *Dom0* cannot extract cryptographic keys from the memory of the OS and applications running in *DomU*.

A significant security weakness of *Dom0* is that the entire state of the system is maintained by *XenStore* (see Section 5.8). A malicious VM can deny access to this critical element of the system to other VMs; it can also gain access to the memory of a *DomU*. This brings us to additional requirements for confidentiality and integrity imposed on *Dom0*.

Dom0 should be prohibited from using foreign mapping for sharing memory with a *DomU* unless a *DomU* initiates the procedure in response to a hypercall from *Dom0*. When this happens, *Dom0* should be provided with an encrypted copy of the memory pages and of the virtual CPU registers. The entire process should be closely monitored by the hypervisor, which, after the access, should check the integrity of the affected *DomU*.

A virtualization architecture that guarantees confidentiality, integrity, and availability for the TCB of a *Xen*-based system is presented in [215]. A secure environment when *Dom0* cannot be trusted can only be ensured if the guest application is able to store, communicate, and process data safely. Thus, the guest software should have access to secure secondary storage on a remote storage server for keeping sensitive data and network interfaces to communicate with the user. We also need a secure run-time system.

To implement a secure run-time system we have to intercept and control the hypercalls used for communication between a *Dom0* that cannot be trusted and a *DomU* we want to protect. Hypercalls issued by *Dom0* that do not `read` or `write` to the memory of a *DomU* or to its virtual registers should be allowed. Other hypercalls should be restricted either completely or during specific time *windows*. For example, hypercalls used by *Dom0* for debugging or for the control of the IOMMU[19] should be prohibited.

We cannot restrict some of the hypercalls issued by *Dom0*, even though they can be harmful to the security of a *DomU*. For example, foreign mapping and access to the virtual registers are needed to save and restore the state of a *DomU*. We should check the integrity of a *DomU* after the execution of such security-critical hypercalls.

New hypercalls are necessary to protect:

- The privacy and integrity of the virtual CPU of a VM. When *Dom0* wants to save the state of the VM, the hypercall should be intercepted and the contents of the virtual CPU registers should be encrypted. When a *DomU* is restored, the virtual CPU context should be decrypted and then an integrity check should be carried out.
- The privacy and integrity of the VM virtual memory. The *page table update* hypercall should be intercepted and the page should be encrypted so that *Dom0* handles only encrypted pages of the VM. To guarantee integrity, the hypervisor should calculate a hash of all the memory pages before they are saved by *Dom0*. Because a restored *DomU* may be allocated a different memory region, an address translation is necessary (see [215]).
- The freshness of the virtual CPU and the memory of the VM. The solution is to add to the hash a version number.

As expected, the increased level of security and privacy leads to increased overhead. Measurements reported in [215] show increases by factors of 1.7 to 2.3 for the domain build time, 1.3 to 1.5 for the domain save time, and 1.7 to 1.9 for the domain restore time.

---

[19] An input/output memory management unit (IOMMU) connects main memory with a DMA-capable I/O bus. It maps device-visible virtual addresses to physical memory addresses and provides memory protection from misbehaving devices.

9.10 *Xoar*: Breaking the monolithic design of the TCB

Xoar is a modified version of *Xen* that is designed to boost system security [90]. The security model of *Xoar* assumes that the system is professionally managed and that privileged access to the system is granted only to system administrators. The model also assumes that the administrators have neither financial incentives nor the desire to violate the trust of the user. The security threats come from a guest VM that could attempt to violate the data integrity or the confidentiality of another guest VM on the same platform or exploit the code of the guest. Another source of threats are bugs in the initialization code of the management virtual machine.

Xoar is based on microkernel[20] design principles. *Xoar* modularity makes exposure to risk explicit and allows guests to configure access to services based on their needs. Modularity allows the designers of *Xoar* to reduce the size of the system's permanent footprint and increase the level of security of critical components. The ability to record a secure audit log is another critical function of a hypervisor facilitated by a modular design. The design goals of *Xoar* are:

- Maintain the functionality provided by *Xen*.
- Ensure transparency with existing management and VM interfaces.
- Maintain tight control of privileges; each component should only have the privileges required by its function.
- Minimize the interfaces of all components to reduce the possibility that a component can be used by an attacker.
- Eliminate sharing and make sharing explicit whenever it cannot be eliminated to allow meaningful logging and auditing.
- Reduce the opportunity of an attack targeting a system component by limiting the time window when the component runs.

These design principles aim to break the monolithic TCB design of a *Xen*-based system. Inevitably, this strategy has an impact on performance, but the implementation attempted to keep the modularization overhead to a minimum.

A close analysis shows that booting the system is a complex activity, but the fairly large modules used during booting are no longer needed once the system is up and running. In Section 5.8 we saw that *XenStore* is a critical system component because it maintains the state of the system; thus, it is a prime candidate for hardening. The *ToolStack* is only used for management functions and can only be loaded upon request.

The *Xoar* system has four types of components: permanent, self-destructing, restarted upon request, and restarted on timer (see Figure 9.4):

1. Permanent components. *XenStore-State* maintains all information regarding the state of the system.
2. Components used to boot the system. These components self-destruct before any user VM is started. Two components discover the hardware configuration of the server, including the PCI drivers, and then boot the system:

[20]A microkernel (μ-kernel) supports only the basic functionality of an operating system kernel, including low-level address space management, thread management, and inter-process communication. Traditional operating system components such as device drivers, protocol stacks, and file systems are removed from the microkernel and run in the user space.

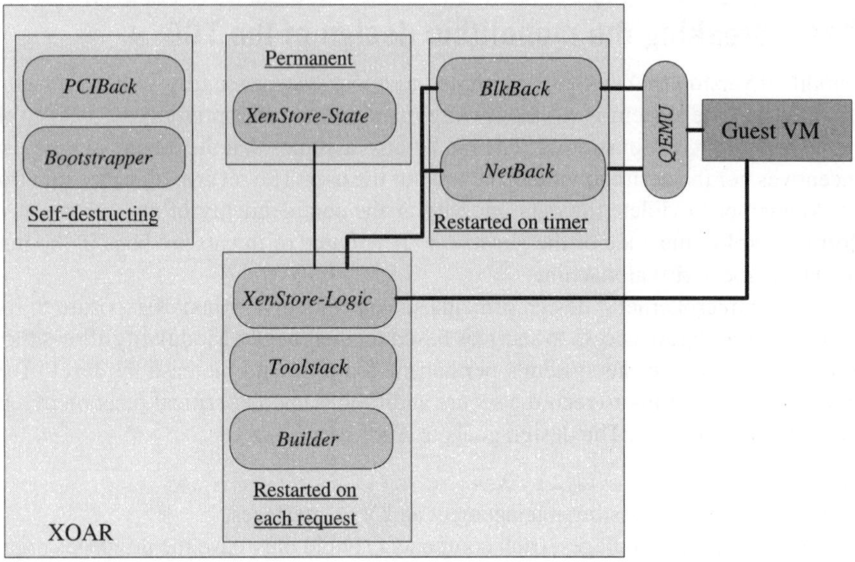

FIGURE 9.4

Xoar has nine classes of components of four types: permanent, self-destructing, restarted upon request, and restarted on timer. A guest VM is started using the *Toolstack* by the *Builder*, and it is controlled by the *XenStore-Logic*. The devices used by the guest VM are emulated by the *QEMU* component.

- *PCIBack*. Virtualizes access to PCI bus configuration.
- *Bootstrapper*. Coordinates booting of the system.

3. Components restarted on each request:
   - *XenStore-Logic*.
   - *Toolstack*. Handles VM management requests, e.g., it requests the *Builder* to create a new guest VM in response to a user request.
   - *Builder*. Initiates user VMs.
4. Components restarted on a timer. Two components export physical storage device drivers and the physical network driver to a guest VM:
   - *Blk-Back*. Exports physical storage device drivers using *udev*[21] rules.
   - *NetBack*. Exports the physical network driver.

Another component, `QEMU`, is responsible for device emulation. *Bootstrapper, PCIBack*, and *Builder* are the most privileged components, but the first two are destroyed once *Xoar* is initialized, and the

[21] *udev* is the device manager for the *Linux* kernel.

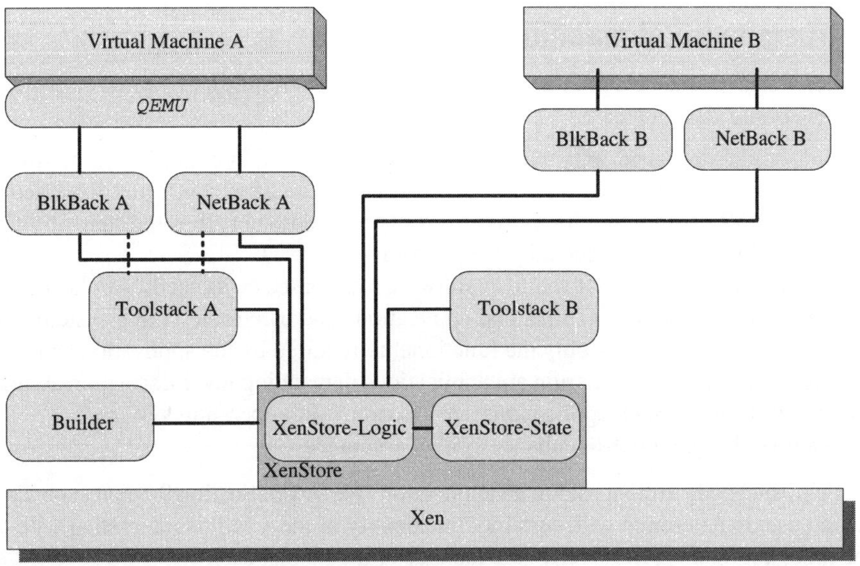

FIGURE 9.5

Component sharing between guest VMs in *Xoar*. Two VMs share only the *XenStore* components. Each one has a private version of the *BlkBack: NetBack* and *Toolstack*.

Builder is very small; it consists of only 13,000 lines of code. *XenStore* is broken into two components: *XenStore-Logic* and *XenStore-State*. Access control checks are done by a small monitor module in *XenStore-State*. Guest virtual machines share only the *Builder*, *XenStore-Logic*, and *XenStore-State* (see Figure 9.5).

Users of *Xoar* are able to only share service VMs with guest VMs that they control. To do so, they specify a tag on all the devices of their hosted VMs. Auditing is more secure; whenever a VM is created, deleted, stopped, or restarted by *Xoar*, the action is recorded in an append-only database on a different server accessible via a secure channel.

Rebooting provides the means to ensure that a virtual machine is in a known-good state. To reduce the overhead and the increased start-up time demanded by a reboot, *Xoar* uses *snapshots* instead of rebooting. The service VM snapshots itself when it is ready to service a request; similarly, snapshots of all components are taken immediately after their initialization and before they start interacting with other services or guest VMs. Snapshots are implemented using a *copy-on-write* mechanism[22] to preserve any page about to be modified.

[22]Copy-on-write (COW) is used by virtual memory operating systems to minimize the overhead of copying the virtual memory of a process when a process creates a copy of itself. Then the pages in memory that might be modified by the process or by its copy are marked as COW. When one process modifies the memory, the operating system's kernel intercepts the operation and copies the memory, so that changes in one process's memory are not visible to the other.

9.11 A trusted virtual machine monitor

Now let's briefly analyze the design of a trusted virtual machine monitor (TVMM) called *Terra* [131]. The novel ideas of this design are:

- The TVMM should support not only traditional operating systems, by exporting the hardware abstraction for open-box platforms, but also the abstractions for closed-box platforms discussed in Section 9.5. Note that the VM abstraction for a closed-box platform does not allow the contents of the system to be either manipulated or inspected by the platform owner.
- An application should be allowed to build its software stack based on its needs. Applications requiring a very high level of security, e.g., financial applications and electronic voting systems, should run under a very thin OS supporting only the functionality required by the application and the ability to boot. At the other end of the spectrum are applications demanding low information assurance[23] but a rich set of OS features; such applications need a commodity operating system.
- Support additional capabilities to enhance system assurance:
  - Provide trusted paths from a user to an application. We saw in Section 9.5 that such a path allows a human user to determine with certainty the identity of the VM it is interacting with and, at the same time, allows the VM to verify the identity of the human user.
  - Support attestation, which is the ability of an application running in a closed box to gain trust from a remote party by cryptographically identifying itself.
  - Provide airtight isolation guarantees for the TVMM by denying the platform administrator root access.

The management VM is selected by the owner of the platform but makes a distinction between a *platform owner* and a *platform user*. The management VM formulates limits to the number of guest VMs running on the platform, denies access to guest VMs that are deemed unsuitable to run, and grants access to I/O devices to running VMs and limits their CPU, memory, and disk usage. Guest VMs expose a raw hardware interface, including virtual network interfaces to virtual devices. The TVMM runs at the highest privilege level and is secure even from the actions of the platform owner; it provides application developers with the semantics of a closed-box platform.

A significant challenge to the security of a TVMM comes from the device drivers used by different VMs running on the platform. Device drivers are large or very large software components, especially the drivers for high-end wireless cards and video cards. There is also a large variety of such drivers, many hastily written to accommodate new hardware features. Typically, the device drivers are the lowest-quality software components found in the kernel of an operating system; thus, they pose the highest security risks. To protect a TVMM, the device drivers should not be allowed to access sensitive information and their memory access should be limited by different hardware protection mechanisms. Malicious I/O devices can use different hardware capabilities, such as DMA, to modify the kernel.

[23] Information assurance (IA) involves managing the risks related to the use, processing, storage, and transmission of information, as well as protecting the systems and processes used for those purposes. IA implies protection of the integrity, availability, authenticity, nonrepudiation, and confidentiality of the application data.

9.12 Further reading

The Cloud Security Alliance (CSA) is an organization with more than 100 corporate members. It aims to address all aspects of cloud security and serve as a cloud security standards incubator. The reports, available from the organization's Web site, are periodically updated; the original report was published in 2009 [96] and subsequent reports followed ([97,98]).

A seminal paper on the negative implications of virtualization on system security, "When Virtual Is Harder Than Real: Security Challenges in Virtual Machine-Based Computing Environments," by Garfinkel and Rosenblum [132], was published in 2005, followed by another one that reaches similar conclusions [297].

A 2010 paper [147] presents a taxonomy of attacks on computer clouds, and [101] covers management of the security services life cycle. Security issues vary depending on the cloud model, as discussed in [273]. The privacy impact on cloud computing is the topic of [345]. A 2011 book [373] gives a comprehensive look at cloud security. Privacy and protection of personal data in the European Community is discussed in a document available at `ec.europa.eu/justice/policies/privacy`.

One paper [28] analyzes the inadequacies of current risk controls for a cloud. Intercloud security is the theme of [48]. Secure collaborations are discussed in [51]. Another paper [216] presents an approach to secure VM execution under untrusted management OS. The social impact of privacy in cloud computing is analyzed in [118]. An anonymous access control scheme is presented in [182].

An empirical study into the security exposure to hosts of hostile virtualized environments can be found at `taviso.decsystem.org/virtsec.pdf`. A model-based security-testing approach to cloud computing is presented in [384]. Several other relevant aspects of security are covered in [152, 268, 341].

9.13 Exercises and problems

Problem 1. Identify the main security threats for the *SaaS* cloud delivery model on a public cloud. Discuss the different aspects of these threats on a public cloud vis-à-vis the threats posed to similar services provided by a traditional service-oriented architecture running on a private infrastructure.

Problem 2. Analyze how the six attack surfaces discussed in Section 9.1 and illustrated in Figure 9.1 apply to the *SaaS*, *PaaS*, and *IaaS* cloud delivery models.

Problem 3. Analyze Amazon's privacy policies and design a service-level agreement you would sign if you were to process confidential data using *AWS*.

Problem 4. Analyze the implications of the lack of trusted paths in commodity operating systems and give one or more examples showing the effects of this deficiency. Analyze the implications of the two-level security model of commodity operating systems.

Problem 5. Compare the benefits and the potential problems due to virtualization on public, private, and hybrid clouds.

Problem 6. Read [38] and discuss the measures taken by Amazon to address the problems posed by shared images available from *AWS*. Would it be useful to have a cloud service to analyze images and sign them before being listed and made available to the general public?

Problem 7. Analyze the risks posed by foreign mapping and the solution adopted by *Xoar*. What is the security risk posed by *XenStore*?

Problem 8. Read [90] and discuss the performance of the system. What obstacles to its adoption by the providers of *IaaS* services can you foresee?

Problem 9. Discuss the impact of international agreements regarding privacy laws on cloud computing.

CHAPTER

Complex Systems and Self-Organization

10

This chapter emphasizes the need to adopt a systemic approach to the engineering of modern computing and communication systems. Such an approach is critical to the future of large-scale systems such as clouds. A systemic approach is also critical to the development of other complex systems such as cyberphysical and sociotechnical systems, which are increasingly important in the modern computing landscape, along with computer clouds.

Complex systems exhibit different patterns of behavior than traditional systems and require new design principles based on a deeper understanding of the physical properties of their components and of the manner in which they interact with one another and with the environment. The new thinking in complex system design has to be an ab-initio concern rather than an afterthought.

10.1 Complex systems

A March 16, 2012, posting on *ZDNet* reveals that *EC2* was made up of 454,600 servers; if we add the number of servers supporting other *AWS* services, the total number of Amazon systems dedicated to cloud computing is much larger. An unofficial estimate puts the number of servers used by Google in January 2012 close to 1.8 million; this number is expected to be close to 2.4 million by early 2013 [289].

The complexity of such systems is unquestionable and raises questions such as: What are the generic properties of complex systems? How can we manage such systems? Do we have to consider radically new ideas, such as self-management and self-repair, for future clouds consisting of millions of components? Should we migrate from a strictly deterministic view of such systems to a nondeterministic one when the desirable properties of a system are statistically assured? These are some of the questions examined in this chapter.

When we think about complex systems, the human brain comes immediately to mind; the number of neurons in the human brain is estimated to be between 80 and 120 billion. Technology systems with a very large number of components, such as the space shuttle,[1] a modern microprocessor with several

[1] "The main elements of the space shuttle ... are assembled from more than 2.5 million parts, 230 miles of wire, 1,040 valves and 1,440 circuit breakers" (Columbia Accident Investigation Board, Report, vol. I, pp. 14, August 2003, at `www.nasa.gov/columbia/caib/html/report.html`).

million transistors,[2] or the Internet with some 800 million hosts as of January 2010, are examples of complex man-made systems.

A very large number of interaction channels among the components of a system is another defining characteristic of a complex system. Indeed, the behavior of any system cannot be explained without precise knowledge of the interactions among its components. Even systems with a relatively small number of components can be complex; for example, the complexity of interactions between the gravitational fields of the planets make our solar system a very complex one.

Discovering all possible interactions among the components of a system is a formidable task. Such an effort is undertaken whenever we need to make progress in our understanding of the behavior of a system we engineer or of the physical world surrounding us. Sometimes we are forced to discover such interactions to build better systems. For example, the investigations following the failure of an aircraft, the space shuttle, or any other system aim to discover the interaction channels that contributed to the failure.

Predicting all possible interactions among the components of a system during the design process is an even more daunting task. A good illustration of this problem is the so-called "death grip" effect manifested by a smartphone released not long ago. The signal suffered a significant attenuation when the device was gripped in a certain way, because the gain of the antenna embedded in the smartphone's case was drastically reduced. In retrospect, such an effect should have been foreseen, but during the design process it was either overlooked or considered very unlikely.

Discovery of the interactions among the basic building blocks of a physical system is required for the advancement of our knowledge. A major step in understanding the human brain is the development of a comprehensive map of neural connections in the brain. The goal of the *Human Connectome Project* sponsored by the National Institutes of Health (NIH) is to build a network map of the human brain in healthy individuals.

Can we increase the number of components of a system while limiting the number of interaction paths among its components? Though there is no positive answer to this question for most complex systems, a solution applicable in the case of some computing and communication systems exists. In Section 7.10 we showed that systems interconnected by scale-free networks have this highly desirable property. Because the degrees of the nodes enjoy a power-law distribution, the number of highly connected components is very small, whereas the vast majority of components have one or a few connections. Thus, scalability of large-scale systems can, in principle, be assured.

Interaction with the environment is an important dimension of system complexity; unfortunately this dimension is often ignored. The more complex the interactions with the environment, the more difficult it is to satisfy the often contradictory requirements of a dynamic environment, and the more complex the system becomes. Moreover, changes in a dynamic environment are difficult to predict and to accommodate in the original design of a system. For example, a system might not be able to perform additional checks when the environment acquires new capabilities to challenge the system's integrity.

Whenever we simulate a system, the complexity of the simulation increases with the number of components and with the number of interaction paths among them. Indeed, the simulation program has

[2]The number of transistors for several processors announced in 2011 are as follows: 2.5×10^6 for the 10-core Xeon Westmere-EX produced by Intel, 4.3×10^6 for the Tahiti GPU of Advanced Micro Devices (AMD), and 6.8×10^6 for the Virtex-7 FPGA of Xilinx.

to describe the properties of each component as well as the effect of each interaction on all components involved. Symmetry and regularity help decrease the complexity of the simulation as multiple components and multiple interactions share the same description; irregularities have the opposite effect. The length of the description of all the system components is captured by the concept of Kolmogorov complexity, discussed in Section 10.3.

Symmetry and regularity of computing and communication systems imply homogeneity; the hardware and the software of individual components are identical or very similar. Large-scale systems designed as collections of homogeneous systems are easier to assemble, their properties are better understood, and they are more effectively managed than collections of heterogeneous systems. In Section 1.3 we cited the hardware and software homogeneity of a cloud as one of the reasons we believe that cloud computing could be successful, whereas heterogeneous large-scale distributed computing systems could not be.

Because we want to increase the versatility and usefulness, as well as the performance of man-made systems, we add new features and we increase the complexity of the system. This is especially true whenever we try to accommodate changes that were not envisioned by the original design. For example, the Internet was originally designed as a data network based on a best-effort model where routers could freely discard packets. Major changes were necessary to support data streaming and other types of communication with real-time delivery constraints when the retransmission of discarded packets could not be tolerated. These changes have increased the complexity of the Internet. We also saw in Chapter 6 that the management of cloud resources increases in complexity when we attempt to mix best-effort applications with applications that have soft real-time constraints and when we add to the mix applications with real-time constraints.

10.2 Abstraction and physical reality

Abstraction is one of the means to cope with system complexity, but abstractions could drive us away from physical reality. We should not forget that our objective is to build systems that store, transform, and transport information and that the physical properties of such systems must be well understood.

Three fundamental abstractions are sufficient to describe all possible elements of computing and communication systems: storage, interpreter, and communication channel. An interpreter is an active element of a system that transforms information; we distinguish hardware interpreters, such as a processor or a disk controller, from software interpreters, such as scripting languages and text-processing systems. In all the possible embodiments of this abstraction, the interpreter, we recognize three elements [312]: (i) an action reference, which tells the interpreter where to find the next action; (ii) a repertoire, which defines the set of actions the interpreter is able to perform; and (iii) an environment reference, which points to the environment and the state in which the interpreter should be when executing the next action. The physical properties of actual embodiments of an interpreter span a very large spectrum; for example, when we design an application for a mobile device, a major concern in selecting the processor should be its power consumption, whereas the main concern for the browser should be the size of the screen.

Information has a physical support, and each one of these three processes acts on a property of that physical system. For example, to transport information from a sender to a receiver, we can encode it in the amplitude, the frequency, or the phase of electromagnetic waves, and we have to well understand the interaction of the electromagnetic waves with the communication media. Indeed, if we want to have error-free communication channels we have to determine the error rate and use error-correcting or error-detecting code designed to cope with the error rate.

We have to maintain a delicate balance between the abstractions that are critical to the development of algorithms and the physical characteristics of the systems used to store, transform, and transport information. This balance has shifted in recent years due to the widespread use of *cyberphysical systems*. In such systems there is a tight relationship between the computational elements and the physical elements. Embedded systems are ubiquitous, and sensors allow them to react to the properties of the physical systems they control and, at the same time, to monitor their own properties and adapt to changes in the environment.

One dimension of the design of modern complex systems is related to their operational environment. The recently introduced concept of *sociotechnical systems* (see, for example, [329]) captures the fact that the design of modern systems should consider not only the technological aspect but also the environment – more precisely, the humans who use a system.

From this informal discussion of several attributes of complex systems we move to quantitative measures of system complexity, the topic of the next section.

10.3 Quantifying complexity

Abstract questions about systems consisting of an ensemble of components have preoccupied the minds of humans for millennia. For example, the Greek philosopher Aristotle stated that "... the whole is something over and above its parts, and not just the sum of them all." In *The Republic*, fellow Greek philosopher Plato introduced the concept of "level of knowledge," ranging from total ignorance to total knowledge. "True knowledge" exists only if a foundation of axioms or a priori knowledge exists [172], and this cannot be the case for complex systems.

At first we can turn for guidance on how to measure system complexity to thermodynamics, a branch of physics concerned with heat and its relation with energy and work. Thermodynamics defines macroscopic properties such as temperature, pressure, and entropy to characterize large assemblies of microscopic particles, e.g., gases, and establishes laws governing the behavior of such systems. The analogy to large-scale systems is inescapable; indeed, we are interested in high-level properties such as reliability; performance measured by throughput and response time, security, and elasticity; and the ability to respond to a sudden increase of the load of very large collections of servers, each one powered by many processors, each processor with millions of transistors. From the "microscopic" properties of these elements we have to estimate the "macroscopic" properties of the system.

The concepts of thermodynamic entropy, von Neumann entropy, and Shannon entropy are related to the number of states of a system; thus, they reflect to some extent the system's complexity [92]. The thermodynamic entropy of a microscopic system, e.g., N molecules of gas, is

$$S = k_B \ln \Omega, \tag{10.1}$$

with k_B the Boltzmann's constant and Ω the number of microstates of the system. When the N molecules are grouped together in m macrostates depending on their energy, then the number of bits required to label the individual microstates is

$$Q = H(p_1, p_2, \ldots, p_m), \tag{10.2}$$

with $H(p_1, p_2, \ldots, p_m)$ the Shannon entropy of a system with m states. If n_i is the number of molecules in state i, then $p_i = n_i/N$ is the probability of the system being in state i.

In turn, the von Neumann entropy of a quantum system with the density matrix ρ

$$S(\rho) = -\mathrm{tr}[\rho \log \rho] \tag{10.3}$$

is equal to the Shannon entropy if the system is prepared in a *maximally mixed state*, a state where all pure states are equally likely.

A measure of complexity is the *relative predictive efficiency*, denoted by e and defined as

$$e = E/C \tag{10.4}$$

with E the excess entropy and C the statistical complexity [95]. The *excess entropy* measures the complexity of the stochastic process and can be regarded as the fraction of historical information about the process that allows us to predict the future behavior of that process. The *statistical complexity* reflects the size of the model of the system at a certain level of abstraction.

The scale of organization considered by an external observer plays a critical role in assessing the relative predictive efficiency. For example, at the microscopic level the calculation of e for a volume of gas requires very complex molecular dynamic computations in order to accurately predict the excess entropy; both E and C are very high and the predictive efficiency is low. On the other hand, at the macroscopic level the relationship among the pressure P, the volume V, and the temperature T is a very simple $PV = nRT$, with n the number of moles of gas and R the universal gas constant. In this case, E maintains a high value, but now C is low and the predictive efficiency E/C is large.

Physical systems in equilibrium display their most complex behavior at *critical points*. In thermodynamics a critical point specifies the conditions of temperature and pressure at which a phase boundary, e.g., between liquid and gas, ceases to exist. The time to reach equilibrium becomes very high at critical points, a phenomenon called *critical slowing*. Wolpert and Macready [377] argue that *self-similarity* can be used to quantify complexity; the patterns exhibited by complex systems at different scales are very different, whereas the patterns exhibited by simple systems such as gases and crystals do not vary significantly from one scale to another.

As discussed earlier, we could use the complexity of a program that simulates the system as a measure of complexity of the system. This will reflect not only the number of states but also the pattern of transitions among states. This idea has its own limitations because, generally, in our simulations we use approximate models of a system rather than exact ones.

This measure of complexity is consistent with the concept of *depth*, defined as the number of computational steps needed to simulate a system's state. The author of [225] argues that the emergence of complexity requires a long history, but we need a measure stricter than physical time to reflect this history. The depth reflects not how long the system remains in equilibrium but *how many steps are necessary to reach equilibrium following some efficient process.* The rate of change of the system state and the communication time do not reflect the complexity of a system. Indeed, two rotating structures involving very different physical processes, a hurricane and a spiral celestial galaxy, are at the limit of today's realistic computer simulations, thus, are of similar depth and, consequently, of similar complexity. Yet, galaxy formation occurs at a scale of millions of light years and is bounded by communication at the speed of light, whereas the time for hurricane formation is measured in days, the atmospheric disturbances propagate more slowly, and the scale is only hundreds of kilometers.

Complexity could be related to the description of a system and may consist of structural, functional, and, possibly, other important properties of the system. The question of how to measure the descriptive complexity of an object was addressed by Kolmogorov [198] and, independently, by Solomonoff [328] and Chaitin [69]. An application of Kolmogorov complexity to the characterization of scheduling on a computational grid is discussed in [229].

The Kolmogorov complexity $K_{\mathcal{V}}(s)$ of the string s with respect to the universal computer $\mathcal{V}$ is defined as the minimal length over all programs $Prog_{\mathcal{V}}$ that print s and halt

$$K_{\mathcal{V}}(s) = min[Length(s)] \quad \text{over all} \quad \text{Prog: } \mathcal{V}(Prog_{\mathcal{V}}) = s. \tag{10.5}$$

The intuition behind Kolmogorov complexity is to provide the shortest possible description of any object or phenomenon, and its roots can be traced back to wisdom formulated centuries ago. "Nunquam ponenda est pluritas sine necesitate," the famous principle formulated by William of Ockham (1290–1349), states; it means that an explanation should not be extended beyond what is necessary [351]. Bertrand Russell translates this as "It is vain to do with more what can be done with fewer."

10.4 Emergence and self-organization

Two most important concepts for understanding complex systems are *emergence* and *self-organization*. *Emergence* lacks a clear and widely accepted definition, but it is generally understood as *a property of a system that is not predictable from the properties of individual system components.* There is a continuum of emergence spanning multiple scales of organization. Halley and Winkler argue that simple emergence occurs in systems at or near thermodynamic equilibrium, whereas complex emergence occurs only in nonlinear systems driven far from equilibrium by the input of matter or energy [153].

Physical phenomena that do not manifest themselves at microscopic scales but occur at macroscopic scale are manifestations of emergence. For example, temperature is a manifestation of the microscopic behavior of large ensembles of particles. For such systems at equilibrium, the temperature is proportional with the average kinetic energy per degree of freedom. This is not true for ensembles of a small number of particles. Even the laws of classical mechanics can be viewed as limiting cases of quantum mechanics applied to large objects.

Emergence could be critical for complex systems such as financial systems, the air-traffic system, and the power grid. The May 6, 2010, event in which the Dow Jones Industrial Average dropped 600 points in a short period of time is a manifestation of emergence. The cause of this failure of the trading systems was attributed to interactions of trading systems developed independently and owned by organizations that work together, but their actions were motivated by self-interest.

A recent paper [329] points out that dynamic coalitions of software-intensive systems used for financial activities pose serious challenges because there is no central authority and there are no means to control the behavior of the individual trading systems. The failures of the power grid (for example, the Northeastern U.S. blackout of 2003) can also be attributed to emergence; indeed, during the first few

Table 10.1 Attributes associated with self-organization and complexity.

Simple Systems; No Self-Organization	Complex Systems; Self-Organization
Mostly linear	Nonlinear
Close to equilibrium	Far from equilibrium
Tractable at component level	Intractable at component level
One or few scales of organization	Many scales of organization
Similar patterns at different scales	Different patterns at different scales
Do not require a long history	Require a long history
Simple emergence	Complex emergence
Unaffected by phase transitions	Affected by phase transitions
Limited scalability	Scale-free

hours of this event, the cause of the failure could not be identified due to the large number of independent systems involved. Only later was it established that multiple causes, including the deregulation of the electricity market and the inadequacy of the transmission lines of the power grid, contributed to this failure.

Informally, self-organization means synergetic activities of elements, when no single element acts as a coordinator and the global patterns of behavior are distributed [137,320]. The intuitive meaning of self-organization is captured by this observation of mathematician Alan Turing [355]: "Global order can arise from local interactions."

Self-organization is prevalent in nature; for example, in chemistry this process is responsible for molecular self-assembly, for self-assembly of monolayers, for the formation of liquid and colloidal crystals, and in many other instances. Spontaneous folding of proteins and other biomacromolecules, the formation of lipid bilayer membranes, the flocking behavior of various species, the creation of structures by social animals – all are manifestations of self-organization of biological systems.

Inspired by biological systems, self-organization was proposed for the organization of different types of computing and communication systems [169,231], including sensor networks, space exploration [167], or even economic systems [200].

The generic attributes of complex systems exhibiting self-organization are summarized in Table 10.1. Nonlinearity of physical systems used to build computing and communication systems has countless manifestations and consequences. For example, when the clock rate of a microprocessor doubles, the power dissipation increases from $2^2 = 4$ to $2^3 = 8$ times, depending of the solid-state technology used. This means that the heat-removal system of much faster microprocessors has to use a different technology when we double the speed. This nonlinearity is ultimately the reason that in the last few years we have seen the clock rate of general-purpose microprocessors increasing only slightly,[3] while the increased number of transistors postulated by Moore's law, allow companies such as Intel and AMD (Advanced Micro Devices) to build multicore chips. This example also illustrates the so-called *incommensurate scaling,* another attribute of complex systems. Incommensurate scaling means that,

[3]In 1975, the Intel 8080 had a clock rate of 2 MHz. The HP PA-7100, a RISC microprocessor released in 1992, and the Intel P5 Pentium, released in 1995, had a 100 MHz clock rate. In 2002 the Intel Pentium 4 had a clock rate of 3 GHz.

when the size of the system or one of its important attributes such as speed increases, different system components are subject to different scaling rules.

The fact that computing and communication systems operate far from equilibrium is clearly illustrated by the traffic carried by the Internet. There are patterns of traffic specific to the time of the day, but there is no steady-state. The many scales of the organization and the fact that there are different patterns at different scales is also clear in the Internet, which is a collection of networks where, in turn, each network is also a collection of smaller networks, each one with its own specific traffic patterns.

The concept of *phase transition* comes from thermodynamics and describes the transformation, often discontinuous, of a system from one phase or state to another, as a result of a change in the environment. Examples of phase transitions are *freezing*, which is a transition from liquid to solid, and its reverse, *melting*; *deposition*, which is a transition from gas to solid, and its reverse, *sublimation*; and *ionization*, which is a transition from gas to plasma, and its reverse, *recombination*.

Phase transitions can occur in computing and communication systems due to avalanche phenomena, when the process designed to eliminate the cause of an undesirable behavior leads to a further deterioration of the system state. A typical example is thrashing due to competition among several memory-intensive processes, which leads to excessive page faults. Another example is acute congestion, which can cause a total collapse of a network; the routers start dropping packets and, unless congestion avoidance and congestion control means are in place and operate effectively, the load increases as senders retransmit packets and the congestion increases. To prevent such phenomena, some form of *negative feedback* has to be built into the system.

A defining attribute of *self-organization* is scalability – the ability of the system to grow without affecting its global function(s). Complex systems, encountered in nature or man-made, exhibit an intriguing property: They enjoy a *scale-free organization* [39,40]. This property reflects one of the few attributes of self-organization that can be precisely quantified. The scale-free organization can best be explained in terms of the network model of the system, a random graph [53] with vertices representing the entities and the links representing the relationships among them. In a scale-free organization, the probability $P(m)$ that a vertex interacts with m other vertices decays as a power law, $P(m) \approx m^{-\gamma}$, with γ a real number, regardless of the type and function of the system, the identity of its constituents, and the relationships among them.

Empirical data available for social networks, power grids, the Web, or the citation of scientific papers confirm this trend. As an example of a social network, consider a collaborative graph of movie actors on which links are present if two actors were ever cast in the same movie; in this case, $\gamma \approx 2.3$. The power grid of the Western United States has some 5,000 vertices representing power-generating stations, and in this case, $\gamma \approx 4$. For the World Wide Web the exponent is $\gamma \approx 2.1$; this means that the probability that m pages point to one page is $P(m) \approx m^{-2.1}$ [40]. Recent studies indicate that $\gamma \approx 3$ for the citation of scientific papers. The larger the network, the closer a power law with $\gamma \approx 3$ approximates the distribution [39].

10.5 Composability bounds and scalability

Nature creates complex systems from simple components. For example, a vast variety of proteins are linear chains assembled from 21 amino acids, the building blocks of proteins. Twenty amino acids are naturally incorporated into polypeptides and are encoded in the genetic code.

Imitating nature, man-made systems are assembled from subassemblies; in turn, a subassembly is made from several modules, each of which could consist of submodules, and so on. Composability has natural bounds imposed by the laws of physics, as we saw when discussing heat dissipation of solid-state devices. As the number of components increases, the complexity of a system also increases for the reasons discussed in Section 10.1.

The limits of composability can be reached because new physical phenomena could affect the system when the physical size of the individual components changes. A recent paper with the suggestive title, "When Every Atom Counts" [245], discusses the fact that even the most modern solid-state fabrication facilities cannot produce chips with consistent properties. The percentage of defective or substandard chips has been constantly increasing as the components have become smaller and smaller.

The lack of consistency in the manufacturing process of solid-state devices is attributed to the increasingly small size of the physical components of a chip. This problem is identified by the International Technology Roadmap for Semiconductors as "a red brick," a problem without a clear solution – a wall that could prevent further progress. Chip consistency is no longer feasible because the transistors and "wires" on a chip are so small that random differences in the placement of an atom can have a devastating effect, e.g., can increase power consumption by an order of magnitude and slow the chip by as much as 30%.

As the features become smaller and smaller, the range of the *threshold voltage* – the voltage needed to turn a transistor on and off – has been widening, and many transistors have this threshold voltage at or near zero. Thus, they cannot operate as switches. Although the range for 28 nm technology was approximately between +0.01 and +0.4 V, the range for 20 nm technology is between −0.05 and +0.45 V, and the range becomes even wider, from −0.18 to +0.55, for 14 nm technology.

There are physical bounds on the composition of analog systems; noise accumulation, heat dissipation, cross-talk, the interference of signals on multiple communication channels, and several other factors limit the number of components of an analog system. Digital systems have more distant bounds, but composability is still limited by physical laws.

There are virtually no bounds on composition of digital computing and communication systems controlled by software. The Internet is a network of networks and a prime example of composability with distant bounds. Computer clouds are another example; a cloud is composed of a very large number of servers and interconnects with each server made up of multiple processors and each processor made up of multiple cores. Software is the ingredient that pushes the composability bounds and liberates computer and communication systems from the limits imposed by physical laws.

In the physical world the laws that are valid at one scale break down at a different scale, e.g., the laws of classical mechanics are replaced at atomic and subatomic scales by quantum mechanics. Thus, we should not be surprised that scale really matters in the design of computing and communication systems. Indeed, architectures, algorithms, and policies that work well for systems with a small number of components very seldom scale up.

For example, many computer clusters have a front-end that acts as the nerve center of a system, manages communication with the outside world, monitors the entire system, and supports system administration and software maintenance. A computer cloud has multiple nerve centers of this kind, and new algorithms to support collaboration among these centers must be developed. Scheduling algorithms that work well within the confines of a single system cannot be extended to collections of autonomous systems where each system manages local resources; in this case, as in the previous example, entities must collaborate with one another, and this requires communication and consensus.

Another manifestation of this phenomenon is in the vulnerabilities of large-scale distributed systems. The implementation of Google *BigTable* revealed that many distributed protocols designed to protect against network partitions and fail-stop are unable to cope with failures due to scale [73]. Memory and network corruption, extended and asymmetric network partitions, systems that fail to respond, and large clock skews occur with increased frequency in a large-scale system and interact with one another in a manner that greatly affects overall system availability.

Scaling has other dimensions than just the number of components. The space plays an important role; the communication latency is small when the component systems are clustered together within a small area and allows us to implement efficient algorithms for global decision making, e.g., consensus algorithms. When, for the reasons discussed in Section 1.6, the data centers of a cloud provider are distributed over a large geographic area, transactional database systems are of little use for most online transaction-oriented systems, and a new type of data store must be introduced in the computational ecosystem, as shown in Section 8.8.

Societal scaling means that a service is used by a very large segment of the population and/or is a critical element of the infrastructure. There is no better example to illustrate how societal scaling affects system complexity than communication supported by the Internet. The infrastructure supporting the service must be highly available. A consequence of redundancy and of the measures to maintain consistency is increased system complexity.

At the same time, the popularity of the service demands simple and intuitive means to access the infrastructure. Again, system complexity increases due to the need to hide the intricate mechanisms from a layperson who has little understanding of the technology. Another consequence of the desire to design wireless devices that operate efficiently in terms of power consumption and present the user with a simple interface and few choices and satisfy a host of other popular attributes is an increased vulnerability to attacks from a few individuals who can discover and exploit system weaknesses. Few smartphone and tablet users understand the security risks of wireless communication.

10.6 Modularity, layering, and hierarchy

Modularity, layering, and hierarchy represent some of the means to cope with the complexity of a system. Modularity is a technique to build a complex system from a set of components built and tested independently. A strong requirement for modularity is to define very clearly the interfaces between modules and enable the modules to work together.

Modularity has been used extensively since the industrial revolution for building every imaginable product, from weaving looms to steam engines, watches to automobiles, and electronic devices to airplanes. Individual modules are often made of subassemblies; for example, the power train of a car includes the engine assembly, the gear box, and the transmission.

Modularity can reduce costs for manufacturers and consumers. The same module may be used by a manufacturer in multiple products; to repair a defective product a consumer only needs to replace the module causing the malfunction rather than the entire product. Modularity encourages specialization because individual modules can be developed by experts with deep understanding of a particular field.

It also supports innovation, allowing a module to be replaced with a better one without affecting the rest of the system.

Layering and hierarchy have been present in social systems since ancient times. For example, the Spartan Constitution, called Politeia, described a Dorian society based on a rigidly layered social system and a strong military. Nowadays, in a modern society, we are surrounded by organizations that are structured hierarchically. We have to recognize that layering and hierarchical organization have their own problems, could negatively affect society, impose a rigid structure and affect social interactions, increase the overhead of activities, and prevent the system from acting promptly when such actions are necessary.

Layering demands modularity because each layer fulfills a well-defined function, but the communication patterns in the case of layering are more restrictive. A layer is expected to communicate only with adjacent layers. This restriction, the limitation of communication patterns, clearly reduces the complexity of a system and makes it easier to understand its behavior.

It is no surprise that modularity, layering, and hierarchy are critical to computer and communication systems. Since the early days of computing, large programs have been split into modules, each with a well-defined functionality. Modules with related functionalities have then been grouped together into numerical, graphical, statistical, and many other types of libraries.

Layering helps us deal with complicated problems when we have to separate concerns that prevent us from making optimal design decisions. To do so, we define layers that address each concern and design the clear interfaces between the layers.

Probably the best example is layering of communication protocols. In this case it was recognized that we have to accommodate a variety of physical communication channels that carry electromagnetic, optical, and acoustic signals; thus, we need a *physical* layer. The next concern is how to transport bits, not signals, between two points joined to one another by a communication channel; thus, the need for a *data link* layer. Next we decided that we need networks with multiple intermediate nodes when bits have to traverse a chain of intermediate nodes from a source to the destination; the concern here is how to forward the bits from one intermediate node to the next, so we had to introduce the *network* layer. Then we recognized that the source and the recipient of information are in fact outside the network and they are not interested in how the information crosses the network, but we want the information to reach its destination unaltered; the *transport* layer was then deemed necessary. Finally, the information sent and received has a meaning only in the context of an application; thus, we needed an *application* layer.

Layering could prevent some optimizations; for example, cross-layer communication (communication between non-adjacent layers) could allow wireless applications to take advantage of information available at the Media Access Control (*MAC*) sublayer of the data link layer. This example shows that layering gives us insight as to where to place the basic mechanisms for error control, flow control, and congestion control on the protocol stack.

An interesting question is whether a layered cloud architecture that has practical implications for the future development of computing clouds could be implemented. One could argue that it may be too early for such an endeavor, that we need time to fully understand how to better organize a cloud infrastructure, and we need to gather data to support the advantages of one approach over another.

On the other hand, there are other systems in which it is difficult to envision a layered organization because of the complexity of the interaction between the individual modules. Consider, for example, an operating system that has a set of well-defined functional components:

- The processor management subsystem, responsible for processor virtualization, scheduling, interrupt handling, and execution of privileged operations and system calls.
- The virtual memory management subsystem, responsible for translating virtual addresses to physical addresses.
- The multilevel memory management subsystem, responsible for transferring storage blocks between different memory levels, most commonly between primary and secondary storage.
- The I/O subsystem, responsible for transferring data between the primary memory and the I/O devices.
- The networking subsystem, responsible for network communication.

The processor management interacts with all other subsystems. There are also multiple interactions between the other subsystems; therefore, it seems unlikely that a layered organization is feasible in this case.

10.7 More on the complexity of computing and communication systems

In addition to the laws of physics, several other factors limit in practice the complexity of man-made systems; among them are cost, reliability, performance, and functionality. Assembling reliable systems from unreliable components is quite challenging; as the number of components grows, the mean time to failure (MTTF) of the entire system becomes smaller and smaller. As the number of components increases, so does the complexity of coordination; then the fraction of system resources dedicated to coordination increases and limits the performance.

Modularity allows us to develop individual system components independently and then assemble them into more complex structures. In many instances the laws of physics place a limit on the composition process; for example, the number of gates in a solid-state circuit is limited by the ability to remove the heat generated during switching. A new technology could extend these limits until other physical laws, e.g., the finite speed of light, expose a new limit.

Computing and communication systems have a unique characteristic: the physical limitations of composability can be pushed further and further as the software allows us to overcome the physical limitations of the hardware. For example, though there are limits on the number of cores on a chip, the software allows us to build multiprocessor systems in which each processor has multiple cores. Such systems can then be interconnected using networking hardware under the control of another layer of software to form a computer cluster; in turn, multiple clusters can be interconnected to build a computer cloud controlled by the next layer of software, and so on.

Our limited understanding of system complexity and the highly abstract concepts developed in the context of natural sciences do not lend themselves to straightforward development of design principles for modern computing and communication systems. Nevertheless, the physical nature and the physical properties of computing and communication systems must be well understood because the system design must obey the laws of physics.

Some of the specific factors affecting the complexity of computing and communication systems are [2]:

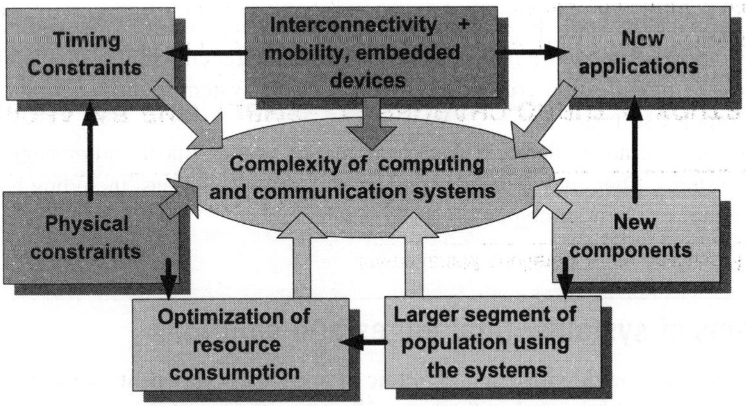

FIGURE 10.1

Factors contributing to the complexity of modern computing and communication systems. The slim black arrows show a causality relation between individual factors; for example, physical constraints demand optimization of resource consumption.

- The behavior of the systems is controlled by phenomena that occur at multiple scales or levels. As levels form or disintegrate, phase transitions and/or chaotic phenomena may occur.
- Systems have no predefined bottom level; it is never known when a lower-level phenomenon will affect how the system works.
- Abstractions of the system that are useful for a particular aspect of the design may have unwanted consequences at another level.
- Systems are entangled with their environment. A system depends on its environment for its persistence; therefore, it is far from equilibrium. The environment is man-made and the selection required by the evolution can either result in innovation or generate unintended consequences, or both.
- Systems are expected to function simultaneously as individual systems and as groups of systems (systems of systems).
- Typically, computing and communication systems are both deployed and under development at the same time.

A number of factors contribute to the complexity of modern computing and communication systems, as shown in Figure 10.1. Some of these factors are:

- The rapid pace of technological developments and the availability of relatively cheap and efficient new system components such as multicore processors, sensors, retina displays, and high-density storage devices.
- The development of new applications that take advantage of the new technological developments.
- The ubiquitous use of the systems in virtually every area of human endeavor, which, in turn, demands a faster pace for hardware and software development.
- The need for interconnectivity and the support for mobility.
- The need to optimize the resource consumption.
- The constraints imposed by the laws of physics, such as heat dissipation and finite speed of light.

Each one of these factors could have side effects. For example, the very large number of transistors on a chip allows hiding of *hardware trojan horses (HTH)*,[4] malignant circuits that are extremely hard to detect. Wireless communication creates new challenges for system security, and increased security demands more complex software.

These factors will continue to demand changes in the way we engineer and manage computing and communication systems. They may require paradigm shifts in many areas, including hardware design, software engineering, and new strategies for systems integration.

10.8 Systems of systems: Challenges and solutions

Large-scale systems could be classified as monolithic when all the components work in concert under the control of a supervising authority and as *Systems of Systems* (SoS) collections of independent systems with limited interactions. An analysis of the defining characteristics of an SoS appeared in 1998 [237]. According to this study, a system of systems has five important attributes:

1. The individual components of an SoS, are independent and can be operated alone, disconnected from the other system components.
2. The components enjoy managerial independence and in fact do operate independently for some periods of time.
3. The system of systems continually evolves in time as new functions are added while others are removed.
4. The system is able to perform functions that cannot be performed by any of its components alone; in other words, it has an emergent behavior.
5. The components exchange only information; thus, they can be geographically distributed over a large area. As the performance of interconnection networks improves, this geographic spread becomes less and less noticeable and does not affect the function or the performance of the SoS. This is in contrast to systems that exchange mass or energy when the distance between components plays a significant role.

Managerial control distinguishes several classes of systems of systems. A *direct system* has a central management that steers the long-term operation of the ensemble of systems; these systems operate independently most of the time but are subordinated to the common goal. The example of a direct system given in [237] is an air-defense system in which the individual components can operate independently but are subject to the requirement to defend the air space.

In the case of *collaborative systems* such as the Internet, the component systems collaborate voluntarily, subject to a previously agreed set of rules and objectives. Finally, *virtual systems* do not have a central authority to manage their operations. The World Wide Web is an example of a virtual system; individual sites may or may not follow policies regarding the structure or the contents of the documents, the naming conventions, or the site navigation rules.

[4]The HTH is said to be *functional* when gates are added to or deleted from the original design; a *parametric* HTH reduces the reliability of the chip.

10.9 Further reading

A recent textbook on principles of computer systems design, coauthored by J. H. Saltzer and M. F. Kaashoek [312], devotes its first chapter to system complexity and to the means of coping with system complexity. This is a refreshing departure from traditional operating systems textbooks that largely ignore this topic and focus on how existing systems operate.

10.10 Exercises and problems

Problem 1. Search the literature for papers proposing a layered architecture for computing clouds and analyze critically the practicality of each of these approaches.

Problem 2. Discuss means to cope with the complexity of computer and communication systems other than modularity, layering, and hierarchy.

Problem 3. Discuss the implications of the exponential improvement of computer and communication technologies on system complexity.

Problem 4. In Section 5.12 we discussed a side effect of abstractions, yet another method to cope with complexity. We showed how a virtual machine-based rootkit (VMBK) could pose serious security problems. Give other examples demonstrating how abstraction of a physical system could be exploited for nefarious activities.

Problem 5. Give examples of undesirable behavior of computing and communication systems that can be characterized as phase transitions. Can you imagine a phase transition in a computing cloud?

Problem 6. Can you attribute the limited success of the grid movement to causes that can be traced to emergence?

Problem 7. Hardware trojan horses (HTHs), malicious modifications of the circuitry of an integrated circuit, are very difficult to detect. What in your view are the main challenges for detecting HTHs? Discuss how various conceptual methods to detect HTHs are impractical due to the complexity of the integrated circuits.

Problem 8. Kolmogorov complexity seems to be a theoretical concept that is fairly remote from any practical application. Yet the simulation of a computer and/or communication system seems to be informally related to Kolmogorov complexity. Can you explain why?

Problem 9. If you define the entropy of a system based on the probability of being in each of the states it can reach in the phase space[5] and you accept as a measure of system complexity the uncertainty in the system and, thus, the entropy, can you justify why modularization decreases the system complexity?

[5]The phase space is an abstraction in which all possible states of a system are represented, with each possible state corresponding to one unique point in the space.

10.9 Further reading

A recent textbook on principles of computer systems design, coauthored by J. H. Saltzer and M. F. Kaashoek [432], devotes its first chapter to system complexity and to the means of coping with system complexity. This is a refreshing departure from traditional operating systems textbooks that largely ignore this topic and focus on how existing systems operate.

10.10 Exercises and problems

Problem 1. Search the literature for papers proposing a layered architecture for computing clouds and analyze critically the practicality of each of these approaches.

Problem 2. Discuss means to cope with the complexity of computer and communication systems other than modularity, layering, and hierarchy.

Problem 3. Discuss the implications of the exponential improvement of computer and communication technologies on system complexity.

Problem 4. In Section [illegible] we discussed a side effect of abstractions, yet another method to cope with complexity. We showed how a virtual machine-based rootkit (VMBR) could pose serious security problems. Give other examples demonstrating how abstraction of a physical system could be exploited for nefarious activities.

Problem 5. Give examples of undesirable behavior of computing and communication systems that can be characterized as phase transitions. Can you imagine a phase transition in a computing cloud?

Problem 6. Can you attribute the limited success of the grid movement to causes that can be traced to emergence?

Problem 7. Hardware trojan horses (HTHs), malicious modifications of the circuitry of an integrated circuit, are very difficult to detect. What in your view are the main challenges for detecting HTHs? Discuss how various conceptual methods to detect HTHs are impractical due to the complexity of the integrated circuits.

Problem 8. Kolmogorov complexity seems to be a theoretical concept that is fairly remote from any practical application. Yet the simulation of a computer and/or communication system seems to be informally related to Kolmogorov complexity. Can you explain why?

Problem 9. If you define the entropy of a system based on the probability of being in each of the states it can reach in the phase space[1] and you accept it as a measure of system complexity, the uncertainty of the system and, thus, the entropy, can you justify why modularization decreases the system complexity?

[1] The phase space is an abstraction in which all possible states of a system are represented, with each possible state corresponding to one unique point of the space.

CHAPTER

Cloud Application Development

11

In the previous chapters our discussion was focused on research issues in cloud computing. Now we examine computer clouds from the perspective of an application developer. This chapter presents a few recipes that are useful in assembling a cloud computing environment on a local system and in using basic cloud functions.

It is fair to assume that the population of application developers and cloud users is and will continue to be very diverse. Some cloud users have developed and run parallel applications on clusters or other types of systems for many years and expect an easy transition to the cloud. Others are less experienced but willing to learn and expect a smooth learning curve. Many view cloud computing as an opportunity to develop new businesses with minimum investment in computing equipment and human resources.

The questions we address here are: How easy is it to use the cloud? How knowledgeable should an application developer be about networking and security? How easy is it to port an existing application to the cloud? How easy is it to develop a new cloud application?

The answers to these questions are different for the three cloud delivery models, *SaaS, PaaS*, and *IaaS*; the level of difficulty increases as we move toward the base of the cloud service pyramid, as shown in Figure 11.1. Recall that *SaaS* applications are designed for end users and are accessed over the Web; in this case, users must be familiar with the API of a particular application. *PaaS* provides a set of tools and services designed to facilitate application coding and deploying; *IaaS* provides the hardware and the software for servers, storage, and networks, including operating systems and storage management software. The *IaaS* model poses the most challenges; thus, we restrict our discussion to the *IaaS* cloud computing model and concentrate on the most popular services offered at this time, the *Amazon Web Services* (AWS).

Though the *AWS* are well documented, the environment they provide for cloud computing requires some effort to benefit from the full spectrum of services offered. In this section we report on lessons learned from the experience of a group of students with a strong background in programming, networking, and operating systems; each of them was asked to develop a cloud application for a problem of interest in his or her own research area. Here we first discuss several issues related to cloud security, a major stumbling block for many cloud users; then we present a few recipes for the development of cloud applications, and finally we analyze several cloud applications developed by individuals in this group over a period of less than three months.

In the second part of this chapter we discuss several applications. Cognitive radio networks (CRNs) and a cloud-based simulation of a distributed trust management system are investigated in Section 11.10. In Section 11.11 we discuss a cloud service for CRN trust management using a history-based algorithm, and we analyze adaptive audio streaming from a cloud in Section 11.12. A cloud-based optimal FPGA

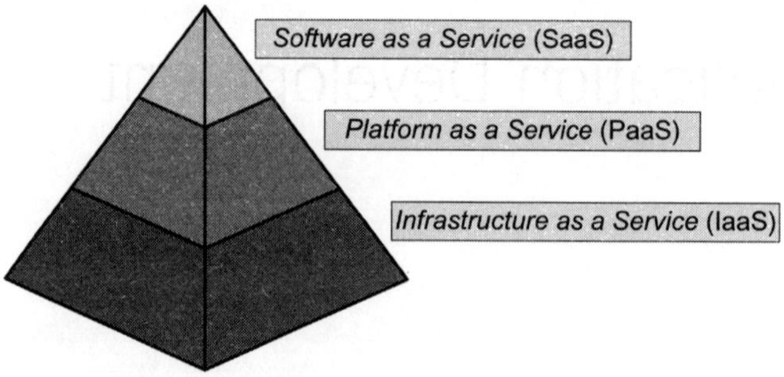

FIGURE 11.1

A pyramid model of cloud computing paradigms. The infrastructure provides the basic resources, the platform adds an environment to facilitate the use of these resources, while software allows direct access to services.

(Field-Programmable Gate Arrays) synthesis with multiple instances running different design options is presented in Section 11.13.

11.1 *Amazon Web Services*: *EC2* instances

Figure 11.2 displays the *Amazon Management Console* (AMC) window listing the Amazon Web Services offered at the time of this writing. The services are grouped into several categories: computing and networking, storage and content delivery, deployment and management, databases, and application services.

In spite of the wealth of information available from the providers of cloud services, the learning curve of an application developer is still relatively steep. The examples discussed in this chapter are designed to help overcome some of the hurdles faced when someone first attempts to use the *AWS*. Due to space limitations we have chosen to cover only a few of the very large number of combinations of services, operating systems, and programming environments supported by *AWS*.

In Section 3.1 we mentioned that new services are continually added to *AWS*; the look and feel of the Web pages changes over time. The screen shots we've selected reflect the state of the system at the time of the writing of this book, the second half of 2012.

To access *AWS* one must first create an account at `http://aws.amazon.com/`. Once the account is created, the AMC allows the user to select one of the services, e.g., *EC2*, and then start an instance.

Recall that an *AWS EC2 instance* is a virtual server started in a region and the availability zone is selected by the user. Instances are grouped into a few classes, and each class has available to it a specific amount of resources, such as: CPU cycles, main memory, secondary storage, and communication and I/O bandwidth. Several operating systems are supported by *AWS*, including *Amazon Linux, Red Hat Enterprise Linux, 6.3, SUSE Linux Enterprise Server 11, Ubuntu Server 12.04.1*, and several versions of *Microsoft Windows* (see Figure 11.3).

The next step is to create an (AMI)[1] on one of the platforms supported by *AWS* and start an instance using the *RunInstance* API. If the application needs more than 20 instances, a special form must be

[1]An AMI is a unit of deployment. It is an environment that includes all information necessary to set up and boot an instance.

FIGURE 11.2

Amazon Web Services accessible from the *Amazon Management Console*.

filled out. The local instance store persists only for the duration of an instance; the data will persist if an instance is started using the Amazon Elastic Block Storage (EBS) and then the instance can be restarted at a later time.

Once an instance is created, the user can perform several actions – for example, connect to the instance, launch more instances identical to the current one, or create an EBS AMI. The user can also terminate, reboot, or stop the instance (see Figure 11.4). The *Network & Security* panel allows the creation of *Security Groups, Elastic IP addresses, Placement Groups, Load Balancers*, and *Key Pairs* (see the discussion in Section 11.3), whereas the EBS panel allows the specification of volumes and the creation of snapshots.

11.2 Connecting clients to cloud instances through firewalls

A firewall is a software system based on a set of rules for filtering network traffic. Its function is to protect a computer in a local area network from unauthorized access. The first generation of firewalls, deployed in the late 1980s, carried out *packet filtering*; they discarded individual packets that did not match a set of acceptance rules. Such firewalls operated below the transport layer and discarded packets based on the information in the headers of physical, data link, and transport layer protocols.

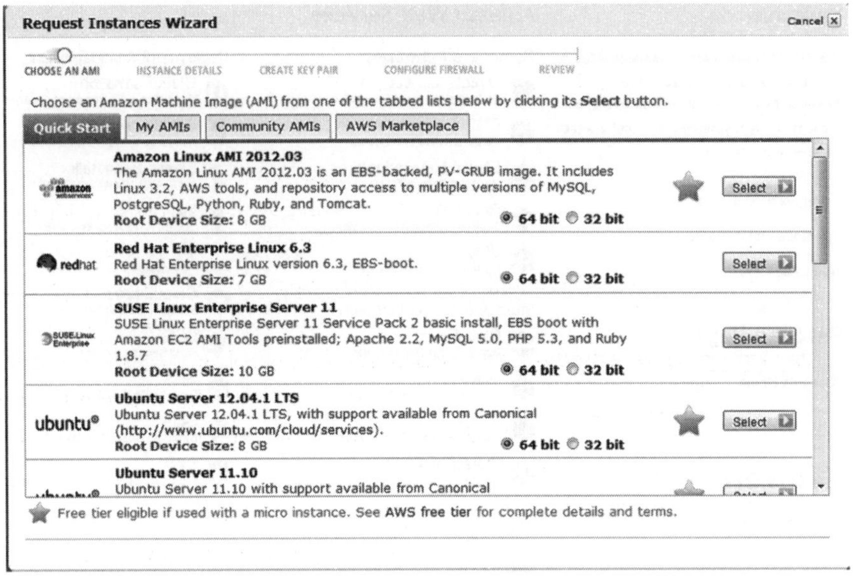

FIGURE 11.3

The Instance menu allows the user to select from existing AMIs.

The second generation of firewalls operate at the transport layer and maintain the state of all connections passing through them. Unfortunately, this traffic-filtering solution opened the possibility of *denial-of-service (DoS) attacks.* A DoS attack targets a widely used network service and forces the operating system of the host to fill the connection tables with illegitimate entries. DoS attacks prevent legitimate access to the service.

The third generation of firewalls "understand" widely used application layer protocols such as *FTP, HTTP, TELNET, SSH,* and *DNS*. These firewalls examine the header of application layer protocols and support *intrusion detection systems* (IDSs).

Firewalls screen incoming traffic and sometimes filter outgoing traffic as well. A first filter encountered by the incoming traffic in a typical network is a firewall provided by the operating system of the router; the second filter is a firewall provided by the operating system running on the local computer (see Figure 11.5).

Typically, the local area network (LAN) of an organization is connected to the Internet via a router. A router firewall often hides the true address of hosts in the local network using the Network Address Translation (NAT) mechanism. The hosts behind a firewall are assigned addresses in a "private address range," and the router uses the NAT tables to filter the incoming traffic and translate external IP addresses to private ones.[2]

[2]The mapping between the (*external address, external port*) pair and the (*internal address, internal port*) tuple carried by the Network Address Translation function of the router firewall is also called a *pinhole*.

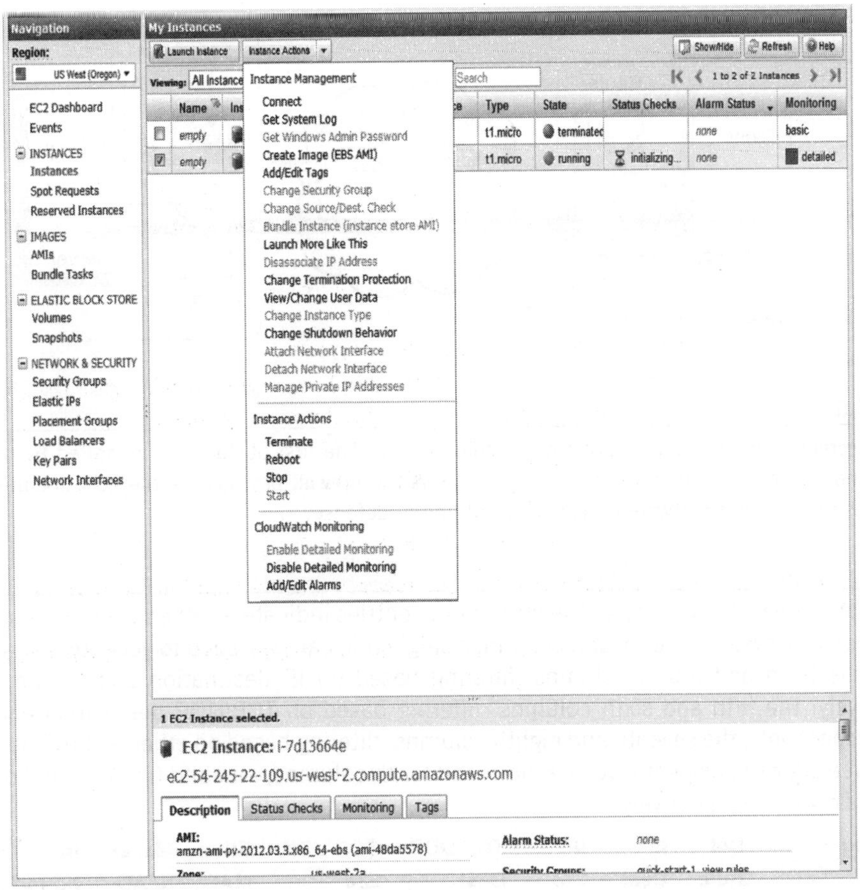

FIGURE 11.4

The *Instance Action* pull-down menu of the *Instances* panel of the *AWS Management Console* allows the user to interact with an instance, e.g., *Connect, Create an EBS AMI Image*, and so on.

If one tests a client-server application with the client and the server in the same LAN, the packets do not cross a router. Once a client from a different LAN attempts to use the service, the packets may be discarded by the router's firewall. The application may no longer work if the router is not properly configured.

Now let's examine the firewall support in several operating systems. Table 11.1 summarizes the options supported by various operating systems running on a host or on a router.

A *rule* specifies a filtering option at (i) the network layer, when filtering is based on the destination/source IP address; (ii) the transport layer, when filtering is based on destination/source port number; or (iii) the MAC layer, when filtering is based on the destination/source MAC address.

In *Linux* or *Unix* systems the firewall can be configured only as a *root* using the *sudo* command. The firewall is controlled by a kernel data structure, the *iptables*. The *iptables* command is used to set up,

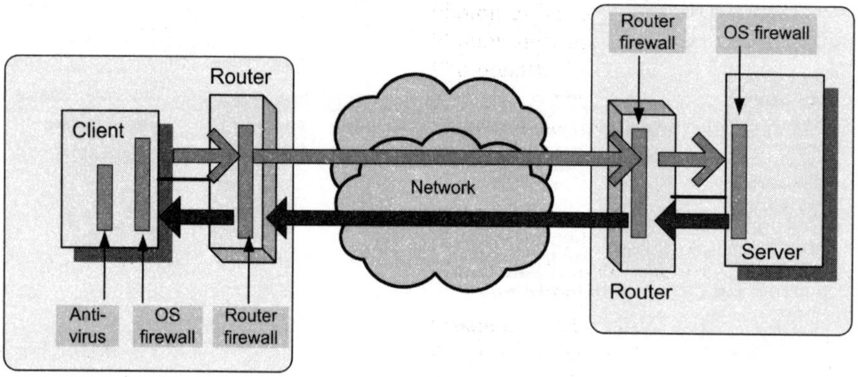

FIGURE 11.5

Firewalls screen incoming and sometimes outgoing traffic. The first obstacle encountered by the inbound or outbound traffic is a router firewall. The next one is the firewall provided by the host operating system. Sometimes the antivirus software provides a third line of defense.

Table 11.1 Firewall rule setting. The first column entries indicate whether a feature is supported by an operating system; the second column, a single rule can be issued to accept/reject a default policy; the third and fourth columns, filtering based on IP destination and source address, respectively; the fifth and sixth columns, filtering based on TCP/UDP destination and source ports, respectively; the seventh and eighth columns, filtering based on ethernet MAC destination and source address, respectively; the ninth and tenth columns, inbound (ingress) and outbound (egress) firewalls, respectively.

Operating System	Def Rule	IP Dest Addr	IP Src Addr	TCP/UDP Dest Port	TCP/UDP Src Port	Ether MAC Dest	Ether MAC Src	In-bound Fwall	Out-bound Fwall
Linux iptables	Yes	Yes	Yes	Yes	Yes	Yes	Yes	Yes	Yes
OpenBSD	Yes	Yes	Yes	Yes	Yes	Yes	Yes	Yes	Yes
Windows 7	Yes	Yes	Yes	Yes	Yes	Yes	Yes	Yes	Yes
Windows Vista	Yes	Yes	Yes	Yes	Yes	No	No	Yes	Yes
Windows XP	No	No	Yes	Partial	No	No	No	Yes	No
Cisco Access List	Yes	Yes	Yes	Yes	Yes	Yes	Yes	Yes	Yes
Juniper Networks	Yes	Yes	Yes	Yes	Yes	Yes	Yes	Yes	Yes

maintain, and inspect the tables of the *IPv4* packet filter rules in the *Linux* kernel. Several tables may be defined; each table contains a number of built-in chains and may also contain user-defined chains. A *chain* is a list of rules that can match a set of packets: The *INPUT* rule controls all incoming connections; the *FORWARD* rule controls all packets passing through this host; and the *OUTPUT* rule controls all outgoing connections from the host. A *rule* specifies what to do with a packet that matches: *Accept*, let the packet pass; *Drop*, discharge the packet; *Queue*, pass the packet to the user space; or *Return*, stop traversing this chain and resume processing at the head of the next chain. For complete information on the *iptables*, see `http://linux.die.net/man/8/iptables`.

To get the status of the firewall, specify the L (List) action of the *iptables* command:

```
sudo iptables -L
```

As a result of this command the status of the *INPUT, FORWARD,* and *OUTPUT* chains will be displayed.

To change the default behavior for the entire chain, specify the action P (Policy), the chain name, and the target name; e.g., to allow all outgoing traffic to pass unfiltered, use

```
sudo iptables -P OUTPUT ACCEPT s
```

To add a new security rule, specify: the action, A (add), the chain, the transport protocol, TCP or UDP, and the target ports, as in:

```
sudo iptables -A INPUT -p -tcp -dport ssh -j ACCEPT
sudo iptables -A OUTPUT -p -udp -dport 4321 -j ACCEPT
sudo iptables -A FORWARD -p -tcp -dport 80 -j DROP
```

To delete a specific security rule from a chain, set the action D (Delete) and specify the chain name and the rule number for that chain. The top rule in a chain has number 1:

```
sudo iptables -D INPUT 1
sudo iptables -D OUTPUT 1
sudo iptables -D FORWARD 1
```

By default, the *Linux* virtual machines on Amazon's *EC2* accept all incoming connections.

The ability to access that virtual machine will be permanently lost when a user accesses an *EC2* virtual machine using *ssh* and then issues the following command:

```
sudo iptables -P INPUT DROP.
```

The access to the *Windows 7* firewall is provided by a GUI accessed as follows:

```
Control Panel -> System & Security -> Windows Firewall -> Advanced
Settings
```

The default behavior for incoming and/or outgoing connections can be displayed and changed from the window *Windows Firewall with Advanced Security on Local Computer*.

Access to the *Windows XP* firewall is provided by a graphical user interface (GUI) accessed by selecting *Windows Firewall* in the *Control Panel*. If the status is *ON*, incoming traffic is blocked by default and a list of Exceptions (as noted on the *Exceptions* tab) defines the connections allowed. The user can only define exceptions for TCP on a given port, UDP on a given port, and a specific program. *Windows XP* does not provide any control over outgoing connections.

Antivirus software running on a local host may provide an additional line of defense. For example, the *Avast* antivirus software (see `www.avast.com`) supports several real-time shields. The *Avast network shield* monitors all incoming traffic; it also blocks access to known malicious Web sites. The *Avast Web shield* scans the HTTP traffic and monitors all Web browsing activities. The antivirus also provides statistics related to its monitoring activities.

11.3 Security rules for application and transport layer protocols in *EC2*

A client must know the IP address of a virtual machine in the cloud to be able to connect to it. The Domain Name Service (DNS) is used to map human-friendly names of computer systems to IP addresses in the Internet or in private networks. DNS is a hierarchical distributed database and plays a role reminiscent of a phone book on the Internet. In late 2010 Amazon announced a DNS service called *Route 53* to route users to *AWS* services and to infrastructure outside of *AWS*. A network of DNS servers is scattered across the globe, which enables customers to gain reliable access to *AWS* and place strict controls over who can manage their DNS system by allowing integration with *AWS* Identity and Access Management (IAM).

For several reasons, including security and the ability of the infrastructure to scale up, the IP addresses of instances visible to the outside world are mapped internally to private IP addresses. A virtual machine running under Amazon's *EC2* has several IP addresses:

1. *EC2 Private IP Address.* The internal address of an instance; it is only used for routing within the *EC2* cloud.
2. *EC2 Public IP Address.* Network traffic originating outside the *AWS* network must use either the public IP address or the elastic IP address of the instance. The public IP address is translated using Network Address Translation (NAT) to the private IP address when an instance is launched and it is valid until the instance is terminated. Traffic to the public address is forwarded to the private IP address of the instance.
3. *EC2 Elastic IP Address.* The IP address allocated to an *AWS* account and used by traffic originated outside *AWS*. NAT is used to map an elastic IP address to the private IP address. Elastic IP addresses allow the cloud user to mask instance or availability zone failures by programmatically remapping public IP addresses to any instance associated with the user's account. This allows fast recovery after a system failure. For example, rather than waiting for a cloud maintenance team to reconfigure or replace the failing host or waiting for DNS to propagate the new public IP to all of the customers of a Web service hosted by *EC2*, the Web service provider can remap the elastic IP address to a replacement instance. Amazon charges a fee for unallocated Elastic IP addresses.

Amazon Web Services use *security groups* to control access to users' virtual machines. A virtual machine instance belongs to one and only one security group, which can only be defined before the instance is launched. Once an instance is running, the security group the instance belongs to cannot be changed. However, more than one instance can belong to a single security group.

Security group rules control inbound traffic to the instance and have no effect on outbound traffic from the instance. The inbound traffic to an instance, either from outside the cloud or from other instances running on the cloud, is blocked unless a rule stating otherwise is added to the security group of the instance. For example, assume a client running on instance A in the security group Σ_A is to connect to a server on instance B listening on TCP port P, where B is in security group Σ_B. A new rule must be added to security group Σ_B to allow connections to port P; to accept responses from server B, a new rule must be added to security group Σ_A.

The following steps allow the user to add a security rule:

1. Sign in to the *AWS* Management Console at `http://aws.amazon.com` using your email address and password and select *EC2* service.
2. Use the *EC2 Request Instance Wizard* to specify the instance type, whether it should be monitored, and specify a key/value pair for the instance to help organize and search (see Figures 11.6 and 11.7).
3. Provide a name for the key pair. Then on the left-side panel, choose *Security Groups* under *Network & Security*, select the desired security group, and click on the *Inbound* tab to enter the desired rule (see Figure 11.6).

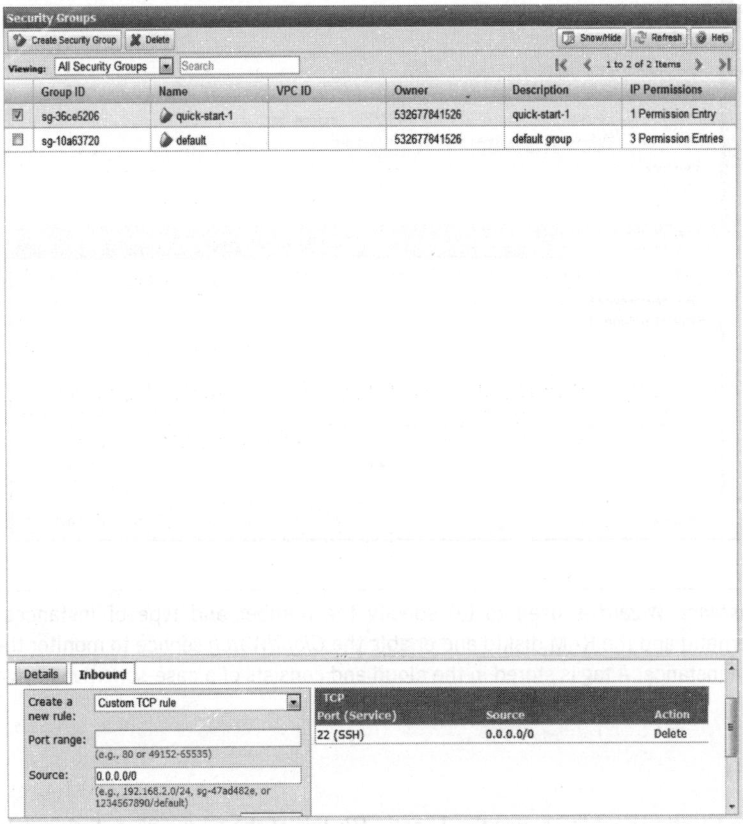

FIGURE 11.6

AWS security. Choose *Security Groups* under *Network & Security*, select the desired security group, and click on the *Inbound* tab to enter the desired rule.

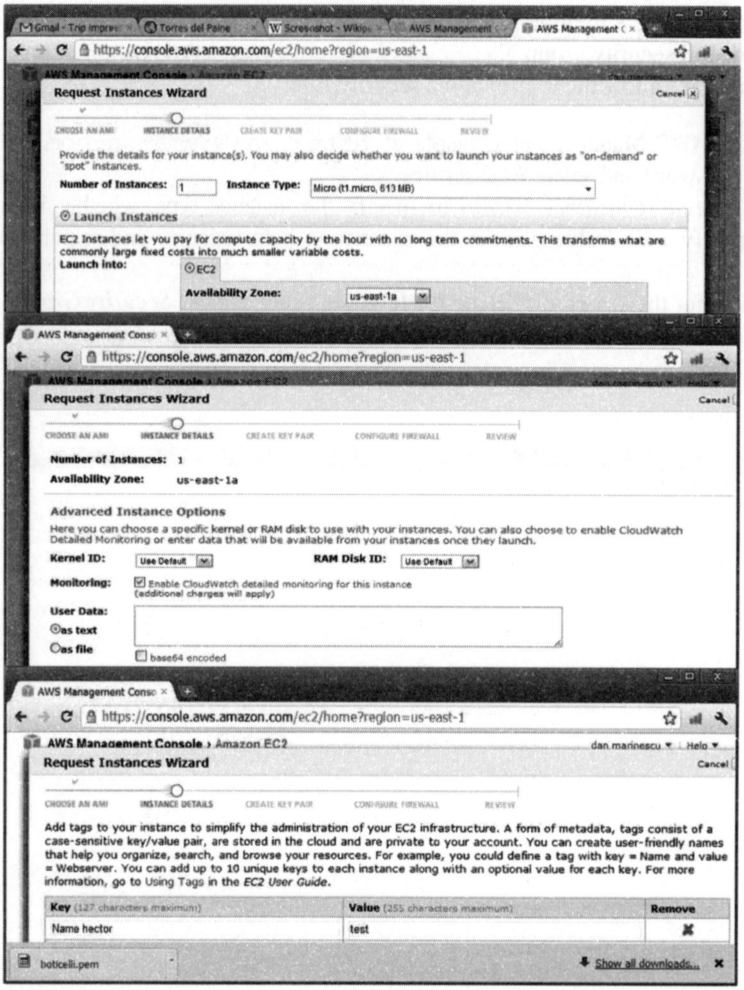

FIGURE 11.7

EC2 Request Instance Wizard is used to (a) specify the number and type of instances and the zone; (b) specify the kernelId and the RAM diskId and enable the *CloudWatch* service to monitor the *EC2* instance; (c) add tags to the instance. A tag is stored in the cloud and consists of a case-sensitive key/value pair private to the account.

To allocate an Elastic IP address, use the *Elastic IPs* tab of the *Network & Security* left-side panel.

On *Linux* or *Unix* systems the port numbers below 1,024 can only be assigned by the *root*. The plain ASCII file called *services* maps friendly textual names for Internet services to their assigned port numbers and protocol types, as in the following example:

```
netstat 15/tcp
ftp 21/udp
ssh 22/tcp
telnet 23/tcp
http 80/tcp
```

11.4 How to launch an *EC2 Linux* instance and connect to it

This section gives a step-by-step process to launch an *EC2 Linux* instance from a *Linux* platform.

A. Launch an instance

1. From the *AWS Management Console*, select *EC2* and, once signed in, go to *Launch Instance Tab.*
2. To determine the processor architecture when you want to match the instance with the hardware, enter the command

   ```
   uname -m
   ```

   and choose an appropriate *Amazon Linux AMI* by pressing *Select.*
3. Choose *Instance Details* to control the number, size, and other settings for instances.
4. To learn how the system works, press *Continue* to select the default settings.
5. Define the instance's security, as discussed in Section 11.3: In the *Create Key Pair* page enter a name for the pair and then press *Create and Download Key Pair.*
6. The key-pair file downloaded in the previous step is a *.pem* file, and it *must* be hidden to prevent unauthorized access. If the file is in the directory *awcdir/dada.pem* enter the commands

   ```
   cd awcdir
   chmod 400 dada.pem
   ```

7. Configure the firewall. Go to the page *Configure firewall*, select the option *Create a New Security Group*, and provide a *Group Name*. Normally we use `ssh` to communicate with the instance; the default port for communication is port 8080, and we can change the port and other rules by creating a new rule.
8. Press *Continue* and examine the review page, which gives a summary of the instance.
9. Press *Launch* and examine the confirmation page, then press *Close* to end the examination of the confirmation page.
10. Press the *Instances* tab on the navigation panel to view the instance.
11. Look for your *Public DNS* name. Because by default some details of the instance are hidden, click on the *Show/Hide* tab on the top of the console and select *Public DNS.*
12. Record the *Public DNS* as *PublicDNSname*; it is needed to connect to the instance from the *Linux* terminal.
13. Use the *ElasticIP* panel to assign an Elastic IP address if a permanent IP address is required.

B. Connect to the instance using *ssh* and the TCP transport protocol.

1. Add a rule to the *iptables* to allow `ssh` traffic using the TCP *protocol.* Without this step, either an *access denied* or *permission denied* error message appears when you're trying to connect to the instance.

```
sudo iptables -A iptables -p -tcp -dport ssh -j ACCEPT
```

2. Enter the *Linux* command:

```
ssh -i abc.pem ec2-user@PublicDNSname
```

If you get the prompt *You want to continue connecting?* respond *Yes*. A warning that the DNS name was added to the list of known hosts will appear.
3. An icon of the `Amazon Linux AMI` will be displayed.

C. Gain root access to the instance

By default the user does not have *root* access to the instance; thus, the user cannot install any software. Once connected to the *EC2* instance, use the following command to gain *root* privileges:

```
sudo -i
```

Then use `yum` install commands to install software, e.g., *gcc* to compile C programs on the cloud.

D. Run the service ServiceName

If the instance runs under *Linux* or *Unix*, the service is terminated when the *ssh* connection is closed. To avoid the early termination, use the command

```
nohup ServiceName
```

To run the service in the background and redirect *stdout* and *stderr* to files *p.out* and *p.err*, respectively, execute the command

```
nohup ServiceName > p.out 2 > p.err &
```

11.5 How to use *S3* in Java

The Java API for Amazon Web Services is provided by the *AWS* SDK.[3]
Create an S3 client. S3 access is handled by the class *AmazonS3Client* instantiated with the account credentials of the *AWS* user:

```
AmazonS3Client s3 = new AmazonS3Client(
new BasicAWSCredentials("your_access_key", "your_secret_key"));
```

[3] A software development kit (SDK) is a set of software tools for the creation of applications in a specific software environment. Java Development Kit (JDK) is an SDK for Java developers available from Oracle; it includes a set of programming tools such as: *javac*, the Java compiler that converts Java source code into Java bytecode; *java*, the loader for Java applications, which can interpret the class files generated by the Java compiler; *javadoc*, the documentation generator; *jar*, the archiver for class libraries; *jdb*, the debugger; *JConsole*, the monitoring and management console; *jstat*, for JVM statistics monitoring; *jps*, a JVM process status tool; *jinfo*, the utility to get configuration information from a running Java process; *jrunscript*, the command-line script shell for Java; the *appletviewer* tool to debug Java applets without a Web browser; and *idlj*, the IDL-to-Java compiler. The *Java Runtime Environment* is also a component of the JDK, consisting of a Java Virtual Machine (JVM) and libraries.

The access and the secret keys can be found on the user's *AWS* account homepage, as mentioned in Section 11.3.

Buckets. An *S3 bucket* is analogous to a file folder or directory, and it is used to store *S3 objects*. Bucket names must be *globally unique*; hence, it is advisable to check first to see whether the name exists:

```
s3.doesBucketExist("bucket_name");
```

This function returns "true" if the name exists and "false" otherwise. Buckets can be created and deleted either directly from the *AWS* Management Console or programmatically as follows:

```
s3.createBucket("bucket_name");
s3.deleteBucket("bucket_name");
```

S3 objects. An *S3 object* stores the actual data and it is indexed by a key string. A single key points to only one *S3* object in one bucket. Key names do not have to be globally unique, but if an existing key is assigned to a new object, the original object indexed by that key is lost. To upload an object in a bucket, we can use the *AWS Management Console* or, programmatically, a file *local_file_name* can be uploaded from the local machine to the bucket *bucket_name* under the key *key* using

```
File f = new File("local_file_name");
s3.putObject("bucket_name", "key", f);
```

A versioning feature for the objects in *S3* was made available recently; it allows us to preserve, retrieve, and restore every version of an *S3* object. To avoid problems in uploading large files, e.g., dropped connections, use the *.initiateMultipartUpload()* with an API described at the *AmazonS3Client*. To access this object with key *key* from the bucket *bucket_name* use:

```
S3Object myFile = s3.getObject("bucket_name", "key");
```

To `read` this file, you must use the S3Object's *InputStream*:

```
InputStream in = myFile.getObjectContent();
```

The *InputStream* can be accessed using *Scanner, BufferedReader*, or any other supported method. Amazon recommends closing the stream as early as possible, since the content is not buffered and it is streamed directly from the *S3*. An open *InputStream* means an open connection to *S3*. For example, the following code will `read` an entire object and print the contents to the screen:

```
AmazonS3Client s3 = new AmazonS3Client(
    new BasicAWSCredentials("access_key", "secret_key"));
    InputStream input = s3.getObject("bucket_name", "key")
      .getObjectContent();
    Scanner in = new Scanner(input);
    while (in.hasNextLine())
```

```
        {
         System.out.println(in.nextLine());
        }
    in.close();
    input.close();
```

Batch upload/download. Batch upload requires repeated calls of *s3.putObject()* while iterating over local files.

To view the keys of all objects in a specific bucket, use

```
ObjectListing listing = s3.listObjects("bucket_name");
```

ObjectListing supports several useful methods, including *getObjectSummaries(). S3ObjectSummary* encapsulates most of an *S3* object properties (excluding the actual data), including the key to access the object directly,

```
List<S3ObjectSummary> summaries = listing.getObjectSummaries();
```

For example, the following code will create a list of all keys used in a particular bucket and all of the keys will be available in string form in *List < String >allKeys*:

```
AmazonS3Client s3 = new AmazonS3Client(
  new BasicAWSCredentials("access_key", "secret_key"));
  List<String> allKeys = new ArrayList<String>();
  ObjectListing listing = s3.listObjects("bucket_name");
  for (S3ObjectSummary summary:listing.getObjectSummaries())
   {
    allKeys.add(summary.getKey());
  }
```

Note that if the bucket contains a very large number of objects, then *s3.listObjects()* will return a truncated list. To test if the list is truncated, we could use *listing.isTruncated()*; to get the next batch of objects, use

```
s3.listNextBatchOfObjects(listing)};
```

To account for a large number of objects in the bucket, the previous example becomes

```
AmazonS3Client s3 = new AmazonS3Client(
new BasicAWSCredentials("access_key", "secret_key"));
List<String> allKeys = new ArrayList<String>();
ObjectListing listing = s3.listObjects("bucket_name");
while (true)
  {
   for (S3ObjectSummary summary :
    listing.getObjectSummaries())
```

```
        {
        allKeys.add(summary.getKey());
        }
      if (!listing.isTruncated())
        {
        break;
        }
      listing = s3.listNextBatchOfObjects(listing);
    }
```

11.6 How to manage *SQS* services in C#

Recall from Section 3.1 that *SQS* is a system for supporting automated workflows; multiple components can communicate with messages sent and received via *SQS* . An example showing the use of message queues is presented in Section 4.7. Figure 11.8 shows the actions available for a given queue in *SQS*.

The following steps can be used to create a queue, send a message, receive a message, and delete a message, and delete the queue in C#:

1. Authenticate an *SQS* connection:

```
NameValueCollection appConfig =
   ConfigurationManager.AppSettings;
AmazonSQS sqs = AWSClientFactory.CreateAmazonSQSClient
  (appConfig["AWSAccessKey"], appConfig["AWSSecretKey"]);
```

2. Create a queue:

```
CreateQueueRequest sqsRequest = new CreateQueueRequest();
sqsRequest.QueueName = "MyQueue";
CreateQueueResponse createQueueResponse =
   sqs.CreateQueue(sqsRequest);
String myQueueUrl;
```

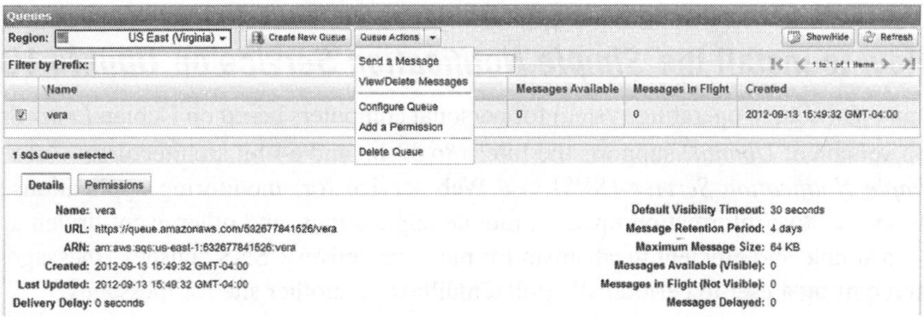

FIGURE 11.8

Queue actions in *SQS*.

```
myQueueUrl = createQueueResponse.CreateQueueResult.QueueUrl;
```

3. Send a message:

```
SendMessageRequest sendMessageRequest =
   new SendMessageRequest();
sendMessageRequest.QueueUrl =
   myQueueUrl; //URL from initial queue
sendMessageRequest.MessageBody = "This is my message text.";
sqs.SendMessage(sendMessageRequest);
```

4. Receive a message:

```
ReceiveMessageRequest receiveMessageRequest =
   new ReceiveMessageRequest();
receiveMessageRequest.QueueUrl = myQueueUrl;
ReceiveMessageResponse receiveMessageResponse =
   sqs.ReceiveMessage(receiveMessageRequest);
```

5. Delete a message:

```
DeleteMessageRequest deleteRequest =
   new DeleteMessageRequest();
deleteRequest.QueueUrl = myQueueUrl;
deleteRequest.ReceiptHandle = messageRecieptHandle;
DeleteMessageResponse DelMsgResponse =
   sqs.DeleteMessage(deleteRequest);
```

6. Delete a queue:

```
DeleteQueueRequest sqsDelRequest = new DeleteQueueRequest();
sqsDelRequest.QueueUrl =
   CreateQueueResponse.CreateQueueResult.QueueUrl;
DeleteQueueResponse delQueueResponse =
sqs.DeleteQueue(sqsDelRequest);
```

11.7 How to install the *Simple Notification Service* on *Ubuntu* 10.04

Ubuntu is an open-source operating system for personal computers based on Debian *Linux* distribution; the desktop version of *Ubuntu*[4] supports the Intel *x86* 32-bit and 64-bit architectures.

The *Simple Notification Service (SNS)* is a Web service for: monitoring applications, workflow systems, time-sensitive information updates, mobile applications, and other event-driven applications that require a simple and efficient mechanism for message delivery. SNS "pushes" messages to clients rather than requiring a user to periodically poll a mailbox or another site for messages.

[4] *Ubuntu* is an African humanist philosophy; "*Ubuntu*" is a word in the Bantu language of South Africa that means "humanity toward others."

SNS is based on the publish/subscribe paradigm; it allows a user to define the topics, the transport protocol used (HTTP/HTTPS, email, SMS, *SQS*), and the endpoint (URL, email address, phone number, *SQS* queue) for notifications to be delivered. It supports the following actions:

- Add/Remove Permission.
- Confirm Subscription.
- Create/Delete Topic.
- Get/Set Topic Attributes.
- List Subscriptions/Topics/Subscriptions by Topic.
- Publish/Subscribe/Unsubscribe.

The document at `http://awsdocs.s3.amazonaws.com/SNS/latest/sns-qrc.pdf` provides detailed information about each one of these actions.

To install the *SNS* client the following steps must be taken:

1. Install Java in the *root* directory and then execute the commands:

```
deb http://archive.canonical.com/lucidpartner
update
install sun-java6-jdk
```

Then change the default Java settings:

```
update-alternatives -config java
```

2. Download the *SNS* client, unzip the file, and change permissions:

```
wget http://sns-public-resources.s3.amazonaws.com/
    SimpleNotificationServiceCli-2010-03-31.zip
chmod 775 /root/ SimpleNotificationServiceCli-1.0.2.3/bin
```

3. Start the *AWS* Management Console and go to *Security Credentials.* Check the *Access Key ID* and the *Secret Access Key* and create a text file */root/credential.txt* with the following content:

```
AWSAccessKeyId= your_Access_Key_ID
AWSSecretKey= your_Secret_Access_Key
```

4. Edit the *.bashrc* file and add:

```
export AWS_SNS_HOME=~/SimpleNotificationServiceCli-1.0.2.3/
export AWS_CREDENTIAL_FILE=$HOME/credential.txt
export PATH=$AWS_SNS_HOME/bin
export JAVA_HOME=/usr/lib/jvm/java-6-sun/
```

5. Reboot the system.

6. Enter on the command line:

```
sns.cmd
```

If the installation was successful, the list of *SNS* commands will be displayed.

11.8 How to create an *EC2 Placement Group* and use *MPI*

An *EC2 Placement Group* is a logical grouping of instances that allows the creation of a virtual cluster. When several instances are launched as an *EC2 Placement Group*, the virtual cluster has a high-bandwidth interconnect system suitable for network-bound applications. The cluster computing instances require a hardware virtual machine (HVM) ECB-based machine image, whereas other instances use a paravirtual machine (PVM) image. Such clusters are particularly useful for high-performance computing when most applications are communication intensive.

Once a placement group is created, *MPI* (Message Passing Interface) can be used for communication among the instances in the placement group. *MPI* is a de facto standard for parallel applications using message passing, designed to ensure high performance, scalability, and portability; it is a language-independent "message-passing application programmer interface, together with a protocol and the semantic specifications for how its features must behave in any implementation" [146]. *MPI* supports point-to-point as well as collective communication; it is widely used by parallel programs based on the same program multiple data (SPMD) paradigm.

The following *C* code [146] illustrates the startup of *MPI* communication for a process group *MPI_COM_PROCESS_GROUP* consisting of a number of *nprocesses*; each process is identified by its *rank*. The run-time environment *mpirun* or *mpiexec* spawns multiple copies of the program, with the total number of copies determining the number of process ranks in *MPI_COM_PROCESS_GROUP*.

```
#include <mpi.h>
#include <stdio.h>
#include <string.h>

#define TAG 0
#define BUFSIZE 128

int main(int argc, char *argv[])
{
 char idstr[32];
 char buff[BUFSIZE];
 int nprocesses;
 int my_processId;
 int i;
 MPI_Status stat;

 MPI_Init(&argc,&argv);
 MPI_Comm_size(MPI_COM_PROCESS_GROUP,&nprocesses);
 MPI_Comm_rank(MPI_COM_PROCESS_GROUP,&my_processId);
```

MPI_SEND and *MPI_RECEIVE* are blocking send and blocking receive, respectively; their syntax is:

```
int MPI_Send(void *buf, int count, MPI_Datatype datatype,
          int dest, int tag,MPI_Comm comm)
```

```
int MPI_Recv(void *buf, int count, MPI_Datatype datatype,
          int source, int tag, MPI_Comm comm, MPI_Status *status)
```

with

`buf`	– initial address of send buffer (choice).
`count`	– number of elements in send buffer (nonnegative integer).
`datatype`	– data type of each send buffer element (handle).
`dest`	– rank of destination (integer).
`tag`	– message tag (integer).
`comm`	– communicator (handle).

Once started, every process other than the coordinator, the process with $rank = 0$, sends a message to the entire group and then receives a message from all the other members of the process group.

```
  if(my_processId == 0)
  {
   printf("%d: We have %d processes\n", my_processId, nprocesses);
   for(i=1;i<nprocesses;i++)
   {
    sprintf(buff, "Hello %d! ", i);
    MPI_Send(buff, BUFSIZE, MPI_CHAR, i, TAG, MPI_COMM_PROCESS_
    GROUP);
   }
   for(i=1;i<nprocesses;i++)
   {
    MPI_Recv(buff, BUFSIZE, MPI_CHAR, i, TAG, MPI_COMM_PROCESS_
    GROUP,&stat);
    printf("%d: %s\n", my_processId, buff);
   }
  }
  else
  {
   /* receive from rank 0: */
   MPI_Recv(buff, BUFSIZE, MPI_CHAR, 0, TAG, MPI_COMM_PROCESS_
   GROUP, &stat);
   sprintf(idstr, "Processor %d ", my_processId);
   strncat(buff, idstr, BUFSIZE-1);
   strncat(buff, "reporting for duty\n' BUFSIZE-1);
   /* send to rank 0: */
   MPI_Send(buff, BUFSIZE, MPI_CHAR, 0, TAG, MPI_COM_PROCESS
   _GROUP);
  }
  MPI_Finalize();
  return 0;
}
```

An example of cloud computing using the *MPI* is described in [119]. An example of *MPI* use on *EC2* is located at `http://rc.fas.harvard.edu/faq/amazonec2`.

11.9 How to install *Hadoop* on *Eclipse* on a *Windows* system

The software packages used are:

- *Eclipse* (`www.eclipse.org`) is a software development environment that consists of an integrated development environment (IDE) and an extensible plug-in system. It is written mostly in Java and can be used to develop applications in Java and, by means of various plug-ins, in C, C++, Perl, PHP, Python, R, Ruby, and several other languages. The IDE is often called Eclipse CDT for C/C++, Eclipse JDT for Java, and Eclipse PDT for PHP.
- Apache *Hadoop* is a software framework that supports data-intensive distributed applications under a free license. *Hadoop* was inspired by Google's *MapReduce*. See Section 4.6 for a discussion of *MapReduce* and Section 4.7 for an application using *Hadoop*.
- *Cygwin* is a *Unix*-like environment for *Microsoft Windows*. It is open-source software released under the GNU General Public License version 2. The *cygwin* environment consists of (1) a dynamic-link library (DLL) as an API compatibility layer providing a substantial part of the POSIX API functionality; and (2) an extensive collection of software tools and applications that provide a *Unix*-like look and feel.

A. Prerequisites

- *Java 1.6*; set JAVA_Home = path where *JDK* is installed
- *Eclipse Europa 3.3.2*
  Note: the *Hadoop* plugin was specially designed for Europa and newer releases of *Eclipse* might have some issues with the *Hadoop* plugin.

B. SSH Installation

1. Install *cygwin* using the installer downloaded from `www.cygwin.com`. From the *Select Packages* window, select the *openssh* and *openssl* under Net.
   Note: Create a desktop icon when asked during installation.
2. Display the "Environment Variables" panel:

   ```
   Computer -> System Properties -> Advanced System Settings
   -> Environment Variables
   ```

   Click on the variable named *Path* and press *Edit*; `append` the following value to the path variable:

   ```
   ;c:\cygwin\bin;c:\cygwin\usr\bin
   ```

3. Configure the *ssh daemon* using *cygwin*. Left-click on the *cygwin* icon on the desktop and click "Run as Administrator." Type in the command window of *cygwin*:

   ```
   ssh-host-config.
   ```

4. Answer "Yes" when prompted with *sshd should be installed as a service*; answer "No" to all other questions.
5. Start the *cygwin* service by navigating to:

```
Control Panel -> Administrative Tools -> Services
```

   Look for *cygwin sshd* and start the service.
6. Open the *cygwin* command prompt and execute the following command to generate keys:

```
ssh-keygen
```

7. When prompted for filenames and passphrases, press Enter to accept default values. After the command has finished generating keys, enter the following command to change into your *.ssh* directory:

```
cd~.ssh
```

8. Check to see whether the keys were indeed generated:

```
ls -l
```

9. The two files *id_rsa.pub* and *id_rsa* with recent creation dates contain authorization keys.
10. To register the new authorization keys, enter the following command (note: the sharply-angled double brackets are very important):

```
cat id_rsa.pub ≫ authorized_keys
```

11. Check to see whether the keys were set up correctly:

```
ssh localhost
```

12. Since it is a new *ssh* installation, you will be warned that authenticity of the host could not be established and will be asked whether you really want to connect. Answer Yes and press Enter. You should see the `cygwin` prompt again, which means that you have successfully connected.
13. Now execute again the command:

```
ssh localhost
```

   This time no prompt should appear.

C. Download Hadoop

1. Download *Hadoop 0.20.1* and place it in a directory such as:

```
C:Java
```

2. Open the *cygwin* command prompt and execute:

```
cd
```

3. Enable the home directory folder to be shown in the *Windows* Explorer window:

```
explorer
```

4. Open another *Windows* Explorer window and navigate to the folder that contains the downloaded *Hadoop* archive.
5. Copy the *Hadoop* archive into the home directory folder.

D. Unpack Hadoop

1. Open a new *cygwin* window and execute:

```
tar -xzf hadoop-0.20.1.tar.gz
```

2. List the contents of the home directory:

```
ls -l
```

You should see a newly created directory called *Hadoop-0.20.1*. Execute:

```
cd hadoop-0.20.1
ls -l
```

You should see the files listed in Figure 11.9.

E. Set properties in configuration file

1. Open a new *cygwin* window and execute the following commands:

```
cd hadoop-0.20.1
cd conf
explorer
```

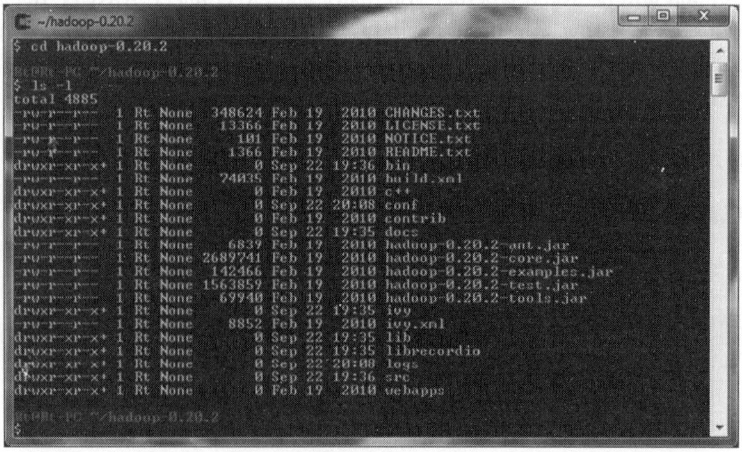

FIGURE 11.9

The result of unpacking *Hadoop*.

FIGURE 11.10

The creation of a *Hadoop* Distributed File System (HDFS).

2. The last command will cause the Explorer window for the *conf* directory to pop up. Minimize it for now or move it to the side.
3. Launch *Eclipse* or a text editor such as *Notepad* ++ and navigate to the *conf* directory. Open the *Hadoop*-site file to insert the following lines between the *<configuration>* and *</configuration>* tags:

```
<property>
<name>fs.default.name</name>
<value>hdfs://localhost:9100</value>
</property> <property>
<name>mapred.job.tracker</name>
<value>localhost:9101</value>
</property> <property>
<name>dfs.replication</name>
<value>1</value>
</property>
```

F. Format the Namenode

Format the *namenode* to create a *Hadoop* Distributed File System (HDFS). Open a new *cygwin* window and execute the following commands:

```
cd hadoop-0.20.1
mkdir logs
bin/hadoop namenode -format
```

When the formatting of the *namenode* is finished, the message in Figure 11.10 appears.

11.10 Cloud-based simulation of a distributed trust algorithm

Mobile wireless applications are likely to benefit from cloud computing, as we discussed in Chapter 4. This expectation is motivated by several reasons:

- The convenience of data access from any site connected to the Internet.
- The data transfer rates of wireless networks are increasing; the time to transfer data to and from a cloud is no longer a limiting factor.

- Mobile devices have limited resources; whereas new generations of smartphones and tablet computers are likely to use multicore processors and have a fair amount of memory, power consumption is, and will continue to be, a major concern in the near future. Thus, it seems reasonable to delegate compute- and data-intensive tasks to an external entity, e.g., a cloud.

The first application we discuss is a cloud-based simulation for trust evaluation in a Cognitive Radio Network (CRN) [52]. The available communication spectrum is a precious commodity, and the objective of a CRN is to use the communication bandwidth effectively while attempting to avoid interference with licensed users. Two main functions necessary for the operation of a CRN are spectrum sensing and spectrum management. The former detects unused spectrum and the latter decides the optimal use of the available spectrum. Spectrum sensing in CRNs is based on information provided by the nodes of the network. The nodes compete for the free channels, and some may supply deliberately distorted information to gain advantage over the other nodes; thus, trust determination is critical for the management of CRNs.

Cognitive Radio Networks. Research over the last decade reveals a significant temporal and spatial underutilization of the allocated spectrum. Thus, there is a motivation to opportunistically harness the vacancies of spectrum at a given time and place.

The original goal of cognitive radio, first proposed at Bell Labs [246,247], was to develop a software-based radio platform that allows a reconfigurable wireless transceiver to automatically adapt its communication parameters to network availability and to user demands. Today the focus of cognitive radio is on spectrum sensing [58,161].

We recognize two types of devices connected to a CRN: primary and secondary. *Primary* nodes/devices have exclusive rights to specific regions of the spectrum; *secondary* nodes/devices enjoy dynamic spectrum access and are able to use a channel, provided that the primary, licensed to use that channel, is not communicating. Once a primary starts its transmission, the secondary using the channel is required to relinquish it and identify another free channel to continue its operation. This mode of operation is called an *overlay mode.*

CRNs are often based on a *cooperative spectrum-sensing* strategy. In this mode of operation, each node determines the occupancy of the spectrum based on its own measurements, combined with information from its neighbors, and then shares its own spectrum occupancy assessment with its neighbors [129,339,340].

Information sharing is necessary because a node alone cannot determine the true spectrum occupancy. Indeed, a secondary node has a limited transmission and reception range; node mobility combined with typical wireless channel impairments, such as multipath fading, shadowing, and noise, add to the difficulty of gathering accurate information by a single node.

Individual nodes of a centralized or infrastructure-based CRN send the results of their measurements regarding spectrum occupancy to a central entity, whether a base station, an access point, or a cluster head. This entity uses a set of *fusion rules* to generate the spectrum occupancy report and then distributes it to the nodes in its jurisdiction. The area covered by such networks is usually small since global spectrum decisions are affected by the local geography.

There is another mode of operation based on the idea that a secondary node operates at a much lower power level than a primary one. In this case the secondary can share the channel with the primary as long as its transmission power is below a threshold, μ, that has to be determined periodically. In this scenario the receivers that want to listen to the primary are able to filter out the "noise" caused by the transmission initiated by secondaries if the signal-to-noise ratio, (S/N), is large enough.

We are only concerned with the overlay mode whereby a secondary node maintains an *occupancy report*, which gives a snapshot of the current status of the channels in the region of the spectrum it is able to access. The occupancy report is a list of all the channels and their state, e.g., 0 if the channel is free for use and 1 if the primary is active. Secondary nodes continually sense the channels available to them to gather accurate information about available channels.

The secondary nodes of an ad hoc CRN compete for free channels, and the information one node may provide to its neighbors could be deliberately distorted. Malicious nodes will send false information to the fusion center in a centralized CRN. Malicious nodes could attempt to deny the service or to cause other secondary nodes to violate spectrum allocation rules. To *deny the service*, a node will report that free channels are used by the primary. To entice the neighbors to commit Federal Communication Commission (FCC) violations, the occupancy report will show that channels used by the primary are free. This attack strategy is called a *secondary spectrum data falsification (SSDF)*, or Byzantine, attack.[5] Thus, trust determination is a critical issue for CR networks.

Trust. The actual meaning of *trust* is domain and context specific. Consider, for example, networking; at the MAC layer the multiple-access protocols assume that all senders follow the channel access policy, e.g., in Carrier Sense Multiple Access with Collision Detection (CSMA-CD) a sender senses the channel and then attempts to transmit if no one else does. In a store-and-forward network, trust assumes that all routers follow a best-effort policy to forward packets toward their destination.

In the context of cognitive radio, trust is based on the quality of information regarding the channel activity provided by a node. The status of individual channels can be assessed by each node based on the results of its own measurements, combined with the information provided by its neighbors, as is the case of several algorithms discussed in the literature [68,339].

The alternative discussed in Section 11.11 is to have a cloud-based service that collects information from individual nodes, evaluates the state of each channel based on the information received, and supplies this information on demand. Evaluation of the trust and identification of untrustworthy nodes are critical for both strategies [284].

A Distributed Algorithm for Trust Management in Cognitive Radio. The algorithm computes the trust of node $1 \leqslant i \leqslant n$ in each node in its vicinity, $j \in V_i$, and requires several preliminary steps. The basic steps executed by a node i at time t are:

1. Determine node i's version of the occupancy report for each one of the K channels:

$$S_i(t) = \{s_{i,1}(t), s_{i,2}(t), \ldots, s_{i,K}(t)\} \tag{11.1}$$

   In this step node i measures the power received on each of the K channels.
2. Determine the set $V_i(t)$ of the nodes in the vicinity of node i. Node i broadcasts a message and individual nodes in its vicinity respond with their `NodeId`.
3. Determine the distance to each node $j \in V_i(t)$ using the algorithm described in this section.

[5] See Section 2.11 for a brief discussion of Byzantine attacks.

4. Infer the power as measured by each node $j \in V_i(t)$ on each channel $k \in K$.
5. Use the location and power information determined in the previous two steps to infer the status of each channel:

$$s_{i,k,j}^{infer}(t), \quad 1 \leqslant k \leqslant K, \quad j \in V_i(t). \tag{11.2}$$

A secondary node j should have determined 0 if the channel is free for use, 1 if the primary node is active, and X if it cannot be determined.

$$s_{i,k,j}^{infer}(t) = \begin{cases} 0 & \text{if secondary node } j \text{ decides that channel } k \text{ is free.} \\ 1 & \text{if secondary node } j \text{ decides that channel } k \text{ is used by the primary.} \\ X & \text{if no inference can be made.} \end{cases} \tag{11.3}$$

6. Receive the information provided by neighbor $j \in V_i(t)$, $S_{i,k,j}^{recv}(t)$.
7. Compare the information provided by neighbor $j \in V_i(t)$:

$$S_{i,k,j}^{recv}(t) = \left\{ s_{i,1,j}^{recv}(t),\ s_{i,2,j}^{recv}(t), \ldots,\ s_{i,K,j}^{recv}(t) \right\} \tag{11.4}$$

with the information inferred by node i about node j:

$$S_{i,k,j}^{infer}(t) = \left\{ s_{i,1,j}^{infer}(t),\ s_{i,2,j}^{infer}(t), \ldots,\ s_{i,K,j}^{infer}(t) \right\}. \tag{11.5}$$

8. Compute the number of matches, mismatches, and cases when no inference is possible, respectively,

$$\alpha_{i,j}(t) = \mathcal{M}\left[S_{i,k,j}^{infer}(t),\quad S_{i,k,j}^{recv}(t) \right], \tag{11.6}$$

with $\mathcal{M}$ the number of matches between the two vectors and

$$\beta_{i,j}(t) = \mathcal{N}\left[S_{i,k,j}^{infer}(t),\quad S_{i,k,j}^{recv}(t) \right], \tag{11.7}$$

with $\mathcal{N}$ the number of mismatches between the two vectors, and $X_{i,j}(t)$ the number of cases where no inference could be made.
9. Use the quantities $\alpha_{i,j}(t)$, $\beta_{i,j}(t)$, and $X_{i,j}(t)$ to assess the trust in node j. For example, compute the trust of node i in node j at time t as

$$\zeta_{i,j}(t) = \left[1 + X_{i,j}(t)\right] \frac{\alpha_{i,j}(t)}{\alpha_{i,j}(t) + \beta_{i,j}(t)}. \tag{11.8}$$

Simulation of the Distributed Trust Algorithm. The cloud application is a simulation of a CRN to assess the effectiveness of a particular trust assessment algorithm. Multiple instances of the algorithm run concurrently on an *AWS* cloud. The area where the secondary nodes are located is partitioned into several overlapping subareas, as shown in Figure 11.11. The secondary nodes are identified by an instance Id, *iId*, as well as a global Id, *gId*. The simulation assumes that the primary nodes cover the entire area; thus, their position is immaterial.

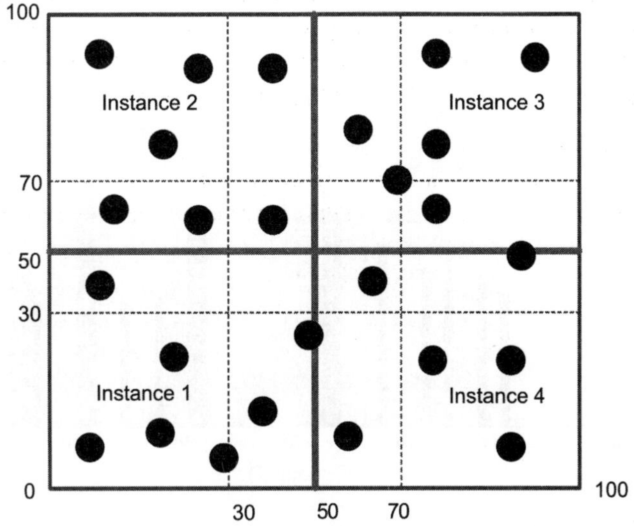

FIGURE 11.11

Data partitioning for the simulation of a trust algorithm. The area covered is of size 100 × 100 units. The nodes in the four subareas of size 70 × 70 units are processed by an instance of the cloud application. The subareas allocated to an instance overlap to allow an instance to have all the information about a node in its coverage area.

The simulation involves a controller and several cloud instances. In its initial implementation, the controller runs on a local system under *Linux Ubuntu* 10.04 LTS. The controller supplies the data, the trust program, and the scripts to the cloud instances; the cloud instances run under the Basic 32-bit *Linux* image on *AWS*, the so-called `t1.micro`. The instances run the actual trust program and compute the instantaneous trust inferred by a neighbor; the results are then processed by an *awk*[6] script to compute the average trust associated with a node as seen by all its neighbors. On the next version of the application the data is stored on the cloud using the *S3* service, and the controller also runs on the cloud.

In the simulation discussed here, the nodes with

$$gId = \{1, 3, 6, 8, 12, 16, 17, 28, 29, 32, 35, 38, 39, 43, 44, 45\} \tag{11.9}$$

were programmed to be dishonest. The results show that the nodes programmed to act maliciously have a trust value lower than that of the honest nodes; their trust value is always lower than 0.6 and, in many instances, lower than 0.5 (see Figure 11.12). We also observe that the node density affects the accuracy of the algorithm; the algorithm predicts more accurately the trust in densely populated areas. As expected, nodes with no neighbors are unable to compute the trust.

[6]The *awk* utility is based on a scripting language and used for text processing; in this application it is used to produce formatted reports.

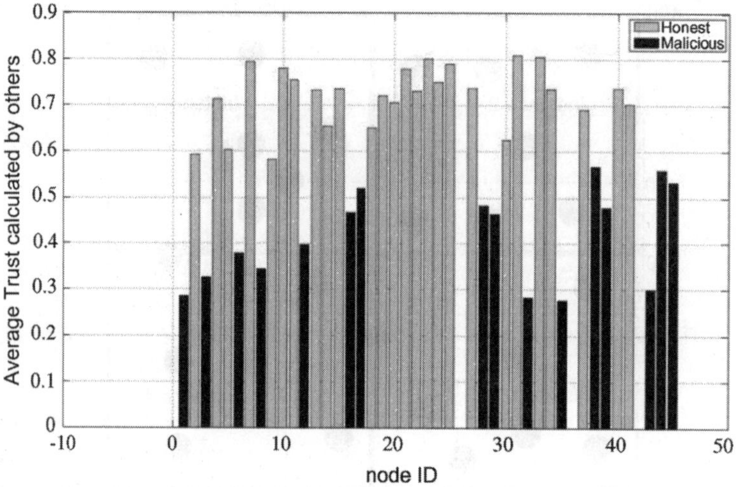

FIGURE 11.12

The trust values computed using the distributed trust algorithm. The secondary nodes programmed to act maliciously have a trust value less than 0.6 and many less than 0.5, lower than that of the honest nodes.

In practice the node density is likely to be nonuniform, high in a crowded area such as a shopping mall, and considerably lower in surrounding areas. This indicates that when the trust is computed using the information provided by all secondary nodes, we can expect higher accuracy of the trust determination in higher density areas.

11.11 A trust management service

The cloud service discussed in this section, see also [52], is an alternative to the distributed trust management scheme analyzed in Section 11.10. mobile devices are ubiquitous nowadays and their use will continue to increase. Clouds are emerging as the computing and storage engines of the future for a wide range of applications. There is a symbiotic relationship between the two; mobile devices can consume as well as produce very large amounts of data, whereas computer clouds have the capacity to store and deliver such data to the user of a mobile device. To exploit the potential of this symbiotic relationship, we propose a new cloud service for the management of wireless networks.

Mobile devices have limited resources; new generations of smartphones and tablet computers are likely to use multicore processors and have a fair amount of memory, but power consumption is still and will continue to be a major concern; thus, it seems reasonable to delegate and data-intensive tasks to the cloud. The motivation for this application is to reduce the power consumption of the mobile devices.

Transferring computations related to CRN management to a cloud supports the development of new, possibly more accurate, resource management algorithms. For example, algorithms to discover communication channels currently in use by a primary transmitter could be based on past history but are not feasible when the trust is computed by the mobile device. Such algorithms require massive amounts of data and can also identify malicious nodes with high probability.

Mobile devices such as smartphones and tablets are able to communicate using two networks: (i) a cellular wireless network; and (ii) a Wi-Fi network. The service we propose assumes that a mobile device uses the cellular wireless network to access the cloud, whereas the communication over the Wi-Fi channel is based on cognitive radio (CR). The amount of data transferred using the cellular network is limited by the subscriber's data plan, but no such limitation exists for the Wi-Fi network. The cloud service, discussed next, will allow mobile devices to use the Wi-Fi communication channels in a cognitive radio network environment and will reduce the operating costs for end users.

Although the focus of our discussion is on trust management for CRNs, the cloud service we propose can be used for tasks other than bandwidth management; for example, routing in mobile ad hoc networks, detection and isolation of noncooperative nodes, and other network management and monitoring functions could benefit from the identification of malicious nodes.

Model Assumptions. The cognitive radio literature typically analyzes networks with a relatively small number of nodes and active in a limited geographic area; thus, all nodes in the network sense the same information on channel occupancy. Channel impairments, such as signal fading, noise, and so on cause errors and lead trustworthy nodes to report false information. We consider networks with a much larger number of nodes distributed over a large geographic area; as the signal strength decays with the distance, we consider several rings around a primary tower. We assume a generic fading model given by the following expression:

$$\gamma_k^i = T_k \times \frac{A^2}{s_{ik}^{\alpha}} \tag{11.10}$$

where γ_k^i is the received signal strength on channel k at location of node i, A is the frequency constant, $2 \leqslant \alpha \leqslant 6$ is path loss factor, s_{ik}^{α} is the distance between primary tower P_k and node i, and T_k is the transition power of primary tower P_k transmitting on channel k.

In our discussion we assume that there are K channels labeled $1, 2, \ldots, K$ and a primary transmitter P^k transmits on channel k. The algorithm is based on several assumptions regarding the secondary nodes, the behavior of malicious nodes, and the geometry of the system. First, we assume that the secondary nodes:

- Are mobile devices; some are slow-moving, others are fast-moving.
- Cannot report their position because they are not equipped with a global positioning system (GPS).
- The clocks of the mobile devices are not synchronized.
- The transmission and reception range of a mobile device can be different.
- The transmission range depends on the residual power of each mobile device.

We assume that the malicious nodes in the network are a minority and their behavior is captured by the following assumptions:

- The misbehaving nodes are malicious rather than selfish; their only objective is to hinder the activity of other nodes whenever possible, a behavior distinct from the one of selfish nodes motivated to gain some advantage.

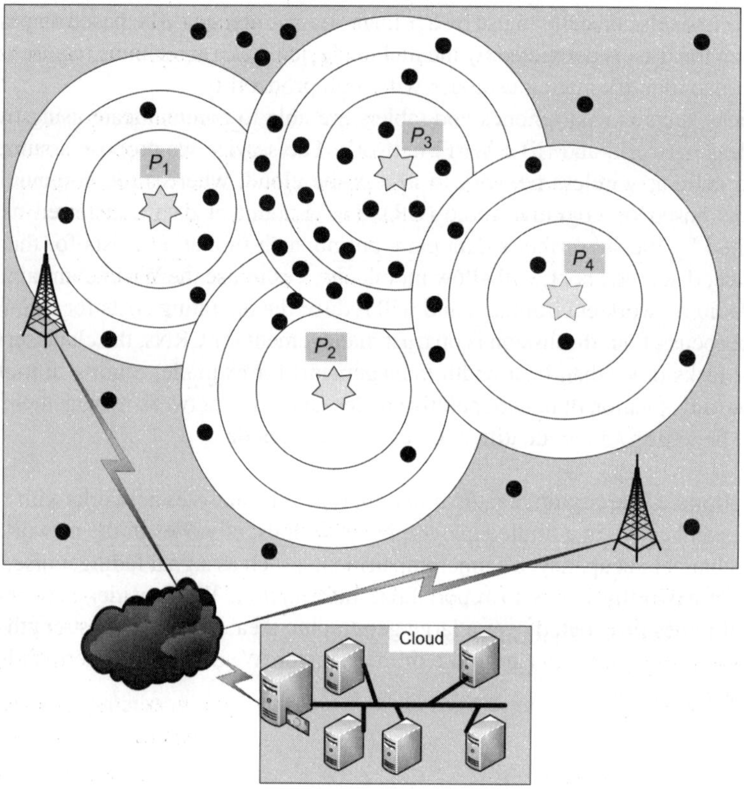

FIGURE 11.13

Schematic representation of a CRN layout: four primary nodes, P_1–P_4, a number of mobile devices, two towers for a cellular network and a cloud are shown. Not shown are the hotspots for the Wi-Fi network.

- The malicious nodes are uniformly distributed in the area we investigate.
- The malicious nodes do not collaborate in their attack strategies.
- The malicious nodes change the intensity of their Byzantine attack in successive time slots. Similar patterns of malicious behavior are easy to detect, and an intelligent attacker is motivated to avoid detection.

The geometry of the system is captured by Figure 11.13. We distinguish primary and secondary nodes and the cell towers used by the secondary nodes to communicate with service running on the cloud.

We use a majority voting rule for a particular ring around a primary transmitter. The global decision regarding the occupancy of a channel requires a majority of the votes. Since the malicious nodes are a minority and they are uniformly distributed, the malicious nodes in any ring are also a minority; thus, a ring-based majority fusion is a representative of accurate occupancy for the channel associated with the ring.

All secondary nodes are required to register first and then to transmit periodically their current power level, as well as their occupancy report for each one of the K channels. As mentioned in the introductory discussion, the secondary nodes connect to the cloud using the cellular network. After a mobile device is registered, the cloud application requests the cellular network to detect its location. The towers of the cellular network detect the location of a mobile device by triangulation with an accuracy that is a function of the environment and is of the order of 10 meters. The location of the mobile device is reported to the cloud application every time it provides an occupancy report.

The nodes that do not participate in the trust computation will not register in this cloud-based version of the resource management algorithm; thus, they do not get the occupancy report and cannot use it to identify free channels. Obviously, if a secondary node does not register, it cannot influence other nodes and prevent them from using free channels, or tempt them to use busy channels.

In the registration phase a secondary node transmits its MAC address and the cloud responds with the tuple (Δ, δ_s). Here, Δ is the time interval between two consecutive reports, chosen to minimize the communication as well as the overhead for sensing the status of each channel. To reduce the communication overhead, secondary nodes should only transmit the changes from the previous status report. $\delta_s < \Delta$ is the time interval to the first report expected from the secondary node. This scheme provides a pseudo-synchronization so that the data collected by the cloud, and used to determine the trust is, based on observations made by the secondary nodes at about the same time.

An Algorithm for Trust Evaluation Based on Historical Information. The cloud computes the probable distance d_i^k of each secondary node i from the known location of a primary transmitter, P^k. Based on signal attenuation properties we conceptualize N circular rings centered at the primary, where each ring is denoted by $\mathcal{R}_r^k$, with $1 \leqslant r \leqslant N$ the ring number. The radius of a ring is based on the distance d_r^k to the primary transmitter P^k. A node at a distance $d_i^k \leqslant d_1^k$ is included in the ring $\mathcal{R}_1^k$, nodes at distance $d_1^k < d_i^k \leqslant d_2^k$ are included in the ring $\mathcal{R}_2^k$, and so on. The closer to the primary, the more accurate the channel occupancy report of the nodes in the ring should be. Call n_r^k the number of nodes in ring $\mathcal{R}_r^k$.

At each report cycle at time t_q, the cloud computes the occupancy report for channel $1 \leqslant k \leqslant K$used by primary transmitter P^k. The status of channel k reported by node $i \in \mathcal{R}_r^k$ is denoted as $s_i^k(t_q)$. Call $\sigma_{one}^k(t_q)$ the count of the nodes in the ring $\mathcal{R}_r^k$ reporting that the channel k is not free (reporting $s_i^k(t_q) = 1$) and $\sigma_{zero}^k(t_q)$ the count of those reporting that the channel is free (reporting $s_i^k(t_q) = 0$):

$$\sigma_{one}^k(t_q) = \Sigma_{i=1}^{n_r^k} s_i^k(t_q) \quad \text{and} \quad \sigma_{zero}^k(t_q) = n_r^k - \sigma_{one}^k(t_q). \tag{11.11}$$

Then, the status of channel k reported by the nodes in the ring R_r^k is determined by majority voting as

$$\sigma_{R_r}^k(t_q) \begin{cases} = 1 \text{ when } \sigma_{one}^k(t_q) \geqslant \sigma_{zero}^k(t_q). \\ = 0 \text{ otherwise.} \end{cases} \tag{11.12}$$

To determine the trust in node i we compare $s_i^k(t_q)$ with $\sigma_{R_r}^k(t_q)$; call $\alpha_{i,r}^k(t_q)$ and $\beta_{i,r}^k(t_q)$ the number of matches and, respectively, mismatches in this comparison for each node in the ring R_r^k. We repeat this procedure for all rings around P^k and construct

$$\alpha_i^k(t_q) = \Sigma_{r=1}^{n_r^k} \alpha_{i,r}^k(t_q) \quad \text{and} \quad \beta_i^k(t_q) = \Sigma_{r=1}^{n_r^k} \beta_{i,r}^k(t_q). \tag{11.13}$$

Node i will report the status of the channels in the set $C_i(t_q)$, the channels with index $k \in C_i(t_q)$; then, the quantities $\alpha_i(t_q)$ and $\beta_i(t_q)$ with $\alpha_i(t_q) + \beta_i(t_q) = |C_i(t_q)|$ are

$$\alpha_i(t_q) = \Sigma_{k \in C_i} \alpha_i^k(t_q) \quad \text{and} \quad \beta_i(t_q) = \Sigma_{k \in C_i} \beta_i^k(t_q). \tag{11.14}$$

Finally, the global trust in node i is

$$\zeta_i(t_q) = \frac{\alpha_i(t_q)}{\alpha_i(t_q) + \beta_i(t_q)}. \tag{11.15}$$

The trust in each node at each iteration is determined using a similar strategy to the one discussed earlier. Its status report, $S_j(t)$, contains only information about the channels it can report on, and only if the information has changed from the previous reporting cycle.

Then, a statistical analysis of the random variables for a window of time W, $\zeta_j(t_q)$, $t_q \in W$ allows us to compute the moments as well as a 95% confidence interval. Based on these results we assess whether node j is trustworthy and eliminate the untrustworthy nodes when we evaluate the occupancy map at the next cycle. We continue to assess the trustworthiness of all nodes and may accept the information from node j when its behavior changes.

Let's now discuss the use of historical information to evaluate trust. We assume a sliding window $W(t_q)$ consists of n_w time slots. Given two decay constants $k_1$and k_2, with $k_1 + k_2 = 1$, we use an exponential averaging that gives decreasing weight to old observations. We choose $k_1 \ll k_2$ to give more weight to the past actions of a malicious node. Such nodes attack only intermittently and try to disguise their presence with occasional good reports; the misbehavior should affect the trust more than the good actions. The history-based trust requires the determination of two quantities:

$$\alpha_i^H(t_q) = \Sigma_{i=0}^{n_w-1} \alpha_i(t_q - i\tau)k_1^i \quad \text{and} \quad \beta_i^H(t_q) = \Sigma_{i=0}^{n_w-1} \beta_i(t_q - i\tau)k_2^i. \tag{11.16}$$

Then, the history-based trust for node i valid only at times $t_q \geqslant n_w\tau$ is:

$$\zeta_i^H(t_q) = \frac{\alpha_i^H(t_q)}{\alpha_i^H(t_q) + \beta_i^H(t_q)}. \tag{11.17}$$

For times $t_q < n_w\tau$ the trust will be based only on a subset of observations rather than a full window on n_w observations.

This algorithm can also be used in regions in which the cellular infrastructure is missing. An ad hoc network could allow the nodes that cannot connect directly to the cellular network to forward their information to nodes closer to the towers and then to the cloud-based service.

Simulation of the History-Based Algorithm for Trust Management. The aim of the history-based trust evaluation is to distinguish between trustworthy and malicious nodes. We expect the ratio of malicious to trustworthy nodes as well as node density to play an important role in this decision. The node density ρ is the number of nodes per unit of the area. In our simulation experiments the size of the area is constant but the number of nodes increases from 500 to 2,000; thus, the node density increases by a factor of four. The ratio of the number of malicious to the total number of nodes varies between $\alpha = 0.2$ and a worst case of $\alpha = 0.6$.

The performance metrics we consider are as follows: the average trust for all nodes, the average trust of individual nodes, and the error of honest/trustworthy nodes. We want to see how the algorithm behaves when the density of the nodes increases, so we consider four cases with 500, 1,000, 1,500, and 2,000 nodes on the same area. Thus, we allow the density to increase by a factor of four. We also investigate the average trust when α, the ratio of malicious nodes to the total number of nodes, increases from $\alpha = 0.2$ to $\alpha = 0.4$ and, finally, to $\alpha = 0.6$.

This straightforward data-partitioning strategy for the distributed trust management algorithm is not a reasonable one for the centralized algorithm, because it would lead to excessive communication among the cloud instances. Individual nodes may contribute data regarding primary transmitters in a different subarea; to evaluate the trust of each node, the cloud instances would have to exchange a fair amount of information. This data partitioning would also complicate our algorithm, which groups together secondary nodes based on their distance from the primary one.

Instead, we allocate to each instance a number of channels, and all instances share the information about the geographic position of each node. The distance of a secondary node to any primary one can then be easily computed. This data-partitioning strategy scales well in the number of primaries. Thus, it is suitable for simulation in large metropolitan areas, but may not be able to accommodate cases when the number of secondaries is on the order of 10^8–10^9.

The objective of our studies is to understand the limitations of the algorithm; the aim of the algorithm is to distinguish between trustworthy and malicious nodes. We expect that the ratio of malicious to trustworthy nodes, as well as the node density should play an important role in this decision. The measures we examine are the average trust for all nodes, as well as the average trust of individual nodes.

The effect of the malicious versus trustworthy node ratio on the average trust. We report the effect of the malicious versus trustworthy node ratio on the average trust when the number of nodes increases. The average trust is computed separately for the two classes of nodes and allows us to determine whether the algorithm is able to clearly separate them.

Recall that the area is constant; thus, when the number of nodes increases, so does the node density. First we consider two extreme cases: the malicious nodes represent only 20% of the total number of nodes and an unrealistically high presence, 60%. Then we report on the average trust when the number of nodes is fixed and the malicious nodes represent an increasing fraction of the total number of nodes.

Results reported in [52] show that when the malicious nodes represent only 20% of all nodes, there is a clear distinction between the two groups. The malicious nodes have an average trust of 0.28 and trustworthy nodes have an average trust index of 0.91, regardless of the number of nodes.

When the malicious nodes represent 60% of all the nodes, the number of nodes plays a significant role; when the number of nodes is small, the two groups cannot be distinguished, so their average trust index is almost equal, 0.55, although the honest nodes have a slightly larger average trust value. When the number of nodes increases to 2,000 and node density increases fourfold, the average trust of the malicious group decreases to 0.45 and for the honest group it increases to about 0.68.

This result is not unexpected; it only shows that the history-based algorithm is able to classify the nodes properly, even when the malicious nodes are a majority, a situation we do not expect to encounter in practice. This effect is somewhat surprising; we did not expect that under these extreme conditions the average of the trust of all nodes would be so different for the two groups. A possible explanation is that our strategy to reward constant good behavior rather than occasional good behavior, designed to mask the true intentions of a malicious node, works well.

Figures 11.14(a) and (b) shows the average trust function of α, the ratio of malicious versus total number of nodes. The results confirm the behavior discussed earlier. We see a clear separation of the two classes only when the malicious nodes are in the minority. When the density of malicious nodes approaches a high value so that they are in the majority, the algorithm still performs, as is evident from the figures. The average trust for honest nodes even at high value of α is larger than the trust of malicious nodes. Thus, the trusts allows the identification of malicious nodes. We also observe that the distinction between the two classes of nodes is more clear when the number of nodes in the network increases.

The benefits of a cloud-based service for trust management. A cloud service for trust management in cognitive networks can have multiple technical as well as economic benefits [74]. The service is likely to have a broader impact than the one discussed here, and it could be used to support a range of important policies in a wireless network where many decisions require the cooperation of all nodes. A history-based algorithm to evaluate the trust and detect malicious nodes with high probability is at the center of the solution we have proposed [52].

A centralized, history-based algorithm for bandwidth management in CRNs has several advantages over the distributed algorithms discussed in the literature:

- Drastically reduces the computations a mobile device is required to carry out to identify free channels and avoid penalties associated with interference with primary transmitters.
- Allows a secondary node to get information about channel occupancy as soon as it joins the system, and later on demand. This information is available even when a secondary node is unable to receive reports from its neighbors, or when it is isolated.
- Does not require the large number of assumptions critical to the distributed algorithms.
- The dishonest nodes can be detected with high probability and their reports can be ignored; thus, over time the accuracy of the results increases. Moreover, historic data could help detect a range of Byzantine attacks orchestrated by a group of malicious nodes.
- Is very likely to produce more accurate results than the distributed algorithm because the reports are based on information from all secondary nodes reporting on a communication channel used by a primary, not only those in its vicinity; a higher node density increases the accuracy of the predictions. The accuracy of the algorithm is a function of the frequency of the occupancy reports provided by the secondary nodes.

The centralized trust management scheme has several other advantages. First, it can be used not only to identify malicious nodes and provide channel occupancy reports, but also to manage the allocation of free channels. In the distributed case, two nodes may attempt to use a free channel and collide; this situation is avoided in the centralized case. At the same time, malicious nodes can be identified with high probability and be denied access to the occupancy report.

The server could also collect historic data regarding the pattern of behavior of the primary nodes and use this information for the management of free channels. For example, when a secondary requests access for a specific length of time, the service may attempt to identify a free channel likely to be available for that time.

The trust management may also be extended to other network operations such as routing in a mobile ad hoc network; the strategy in this case would be to avoid routing through malicious nodes.

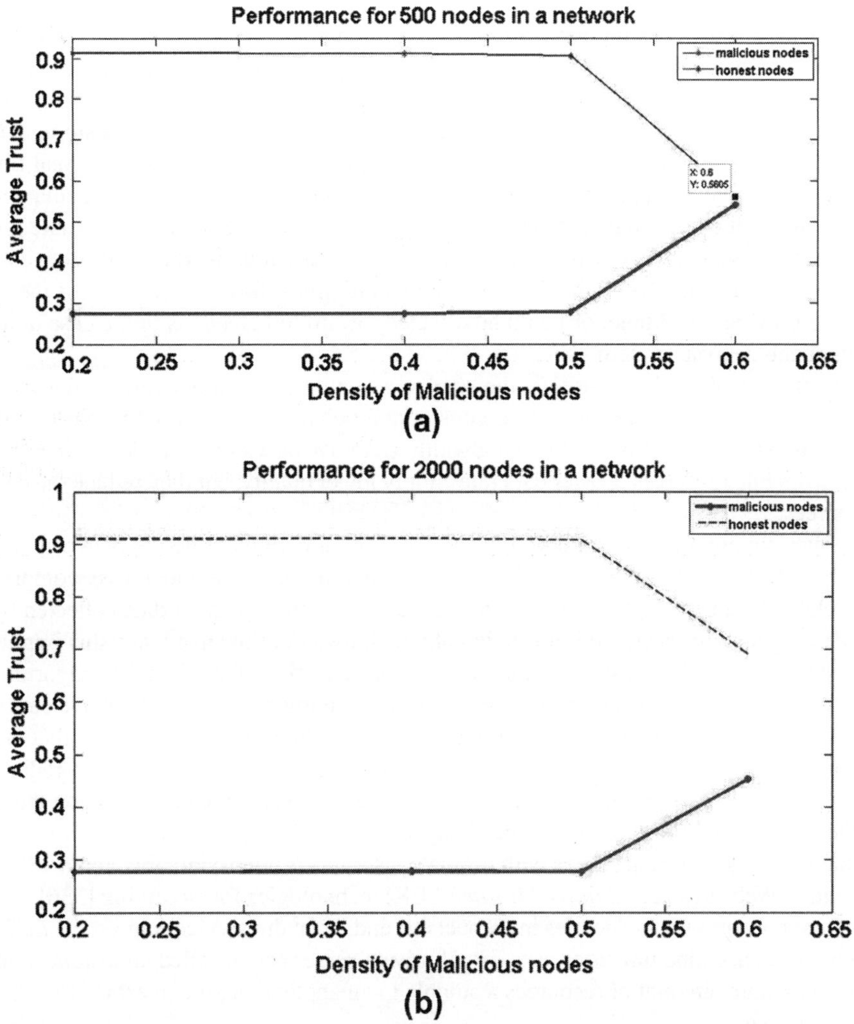

FIGURE 11.14

The average trust function of α when the population size increases: (a) 500; (b) 2,000 nodes. As long as malicious nodes represent 50% or less of the total number of nodes, the average trust of malicious nodes is below 0.3, whereas the average trust of trustworthy nodes is above 0.9 in a scale of 0 to 1.0. As the number of nodes increases, the distance between the average trust of the two classes becomes larger, and even larger when $\alpha > 0.5.$, i.e., when the malicious nodes are in the majority.

11.12 A cloud service for adaptive data streaming

In this section we discuss a cloud application related to data streaming [288]. Data streaming is the name given to the transfer of data at a high rate with real-time constraints. Multimedia applications such as music and video streaming, high-definition television (HDTV), scientific applications that process a continuous stream of data collected by sensors, the continuous backup copying to a storage medium of the data flow within a computer, and many other applications require the transfer of real-time data at a high rate. For example, to support real-time human perception of the data, multimedia applications have to make sure that enough data is being continuously received without any noticeable time lag.

We are concerned with the case when data streaming involves a multimedia application connected to a service running on a computer cloud. The stream could originate from the cloud, as is the case of the iCloud service provided by Apple, or could be directed toward the cloud, as in the case of a real-time data collection and analysis system.

Data streaming involves three entities: the sender, a communication network, and a receiver. The resources necessary to guarantee the timing constraints include CPU cycles and buffer space at the sender and the receiver, as well as network bandwidth. Adaptive data streaming determines the data rate based on the available resources. Lower data rates imply lower quality, but they reduce the demands for system resources.

Adaptive data streaming is possible only if the application permits tradeoffs between quantity and quality. Such tradeoffs are feasible for audio and video streaming, which allow lossy compression, but are not acceptable for many applications that process a continuous stream of data collected by sensors.

Data streaming requires accurate information about all resources involved, and this implies that the network bandwidth has to be constantly monitored; at the same time, the scheduling algorithms should be coordinated with memory management to guarantee the timing constraints. Adaptive data streaming poses additional constraints because the data flow is dynamic. Indeed, once we detect that the network cannot accommodate the data rate required by an audio or video stream, we have to reduce the data rate; thus, to convert to a lower quality audio or video. Data conversion can be done on the fly and, in this case, the data flow on the cloud has to be changed.

Accommodating dynamic data flows with timing constraints is nontrivial; only about 18% of the top 100 global video Web sites use *adaptive bit rate* (ABR) technologies for streaming [336].

This application stores the music files in *S3* buckets, and the audio service runs on the *EC2* platform. In *EC2* each virtual machine functions as a virtual private server and is called an *instance;* an instance specifies the maximum amount of resources available to an application, the interface for that instance, and the cost per hour.

EC2 allows the import of virtual machine images from the user environment to an instance through a facility called *VM import.* It also distributes automatically the incoming application traffic among multiple instances using the *elastic load-balancing* facility. *EC2* associates an *elastic IP address* with an account; this mechanism allows a user to mask the failure of an instance and remap a public IP address to any instance of the account, without the need to interact with the software support team.

Adaptive audio streaming involves a multi-objective optimization problem. We want to convert the highest-quality audio file stored on the cloud to a resolution corresponding to the rate that can be sustained by the available bandwidth; at the same time, we want to minimize the cost on the cloud site and minimize the buffer requirements for the mobile device to accommodate the transmission jitter. Finally, we want to reduce to a minimum the startup time for the content delivery.

A first design decision is whether data streaming should only begin after the conversion from the WAV to MP3 format has been completed or it should proceed concurrently with conversion – in other words, start as soon as several MP3 frames have been generated. Another question is whether the converted music file should be saved for later use or discarded.

To answer these questions, we experimented with conversion from the highest-quality audio files, which require a 320 Kbps data rate, to lower-quality files corresponding to 192, 128, 64, 32, and finally 16 Kbps. If the conversion time is small and constant there is no justification for pipelining data conversion and streaming, a strategy that complicates the processing flow on the cloud. It makes sense to cache the converted copy for a limited period of time with the hope that it will be reused in the future.

Another design decision is how the two services should interact to optimize performance. Two alternatives come to mind:

1. The audio service running on the *EC2* platform requests the data file from the *S3*, converts it, and, eventually, sends it back. The solution involves multiple delays and it is far from optimal.
2. Mount the *S3 bucket* as an *EC2* drive. This solution reduces considerably the start-up time for audio streaming.

The conversion from a high-quality audio file to a lower-quality, thus a lower-bit-rate, file is performed using the LAME library.

The conversion time depends on the desired bitrate and the size of the original file. Tables 11.2, 11.3, 11.4, and 11.5 show the conversion time in seconds when the source MP3 files are of 320 Kbps and 192 Kbps, respectively. The sizes of the input files are also shown.

The platforms used for conversion are (a) the *EC2 t1.micro* server for the measurements reported in Tables 11.2 and 11.3 and (b) the *EC2 c1.medium* for the measurements reported in Tables 11.4 and 11.5. The instances run the *Ubuntu Linux* operating system.

The results of our measurements when the instance is the *t1.micro* server exhibit a wide range of conversion times, 13–80 seconds, for the large audio file of about 6.7 MB when we convert from 320 to 192 Kbps. A wide range, 13–64 seconds, is also observed for an audio file of about 4.5 MB when

Table 11.2 Conversion time in seconds on a *EC2 t1.micro* server platform. The source file is of the highest audio quality, 320 Kbps. The individual conversions are labeled *C1* to *C10*; $\overline{T}_c$ is the mean conversion time.

Bit Rate (Kbps)	Audio File Size (MB)	C1	C2	C3	C4	C5	C6	C7	C8	C9	C10	$\overline{T}_c$
192	6.701974	73	43	19	13	80	42	33	62	66	36	46.7
128	4.467982	42	46	64	48	19	52	52	48	48	13	43.2
64	2.234304	9	9	9	9	10	26	43	9	10	10	14.4
32	1.117152	7	6	14	6	6	7	7	6	6	6	7.1
16	0.558720	4	4	4	4	4	4	4	4	4	4	4

Table 11.3 Conversion time in seconds on a *EC2 t1.micro* server platform. The source file is of high audio quality, 192 Kbps. The individual conversions are labeled *C1* to *C10*; $\overline{T}_c$ is the mean conversion time.

Bit Rate (Kbps)	Audio File Size (MB)	C1	C2	C3	C4	C5	C6	C7	C8	C9	C10	$\overline{T}_c$
128	4.467982	14	15	13	13	73	75	56	59	72	14	40.4
64	2.234304	9	9	9	32	44	9	23	9	45	10	19.9
32	1.117152	6	6	6	6	6	6	20	6	6	6	7.4
16	0.558720	6	6	6	6	6	6	20	6	6	6	5.1

Table 11.4 Conversion time T_c in seconds on a *EC2 c1.medium* platform. The source file is of the highest audio quality, 320 Kbps. The individual conversions are labeled *C1* to *C10*; $\overline{T}_c$ is the mean conversion time.

Bit Rate (Kbps)	Audio File Size (MB)	C1	C2	C3	C4	C5	C6	C7	C8	C9	C10	$\overline{T}_c$
192	6.701974	15	15	15	15	15	15	15	15	15	15	15
128	4.467982	15	15	15	15	15	15	15	15	15	15	15
64	2.234304	11	11	11	11	11	11	11	11	11	11	11
32	1.117152	7	7	7	7	7	7	7	7	7	7	7
16	0.558720	4	4	4	4	4	4	4	4	4	4	4

Table 11.5 Conversion time in seconds on a *EC2 c1.medium* platform. The source file is of high audio quality, 192 Kbps. The individual conversions are labeled *C1* to *C10*; $\overline{T}_c$ is the mean conversion time.

Bit Rate (Kbps)	Audio File Size (MB)	C1	C2	C3	C4	C5	C6	C7	C8	C9	C10	$\overline{T}_c$
128	4.467982	15	15	15	15	15	15	15	15	15	15	15
64	2.234304	10	10	10	10	10	10	10	10	10	10	10
32	1.117152	7	7	7	7	7	7	7	7	7	7	7
16	0.558720	4	4	4	4	4	4	4	4	4	4	4

we convert from 320 to 128 Kbps. For poor-quality audio the file size is considerably smaller, about 0.56 MB, and the conversion time is constant and small, 4 seconds. Figure 11.15 shows the average conversion time for the experiments summarized in Tables 11.2 and 11.3. It is somewhat surprising that

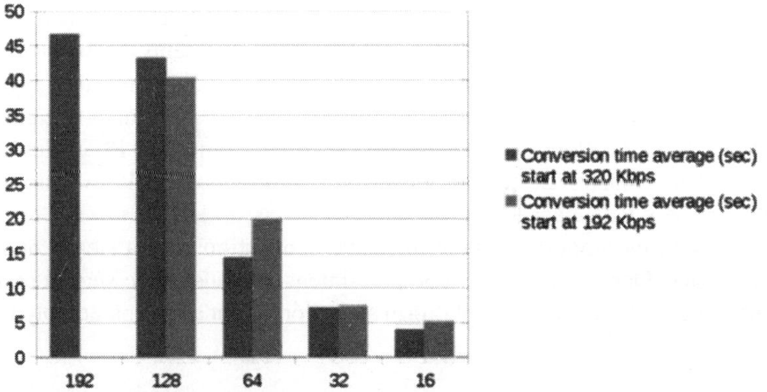

FIGURE 11.15

The average conversion time on a *EC2 t1.micro* platform. The bars at left and right correspond to the original file at the highest resolution (320 Kbps data rate) and next highest resolution (192 Kbps data rate), respectively.

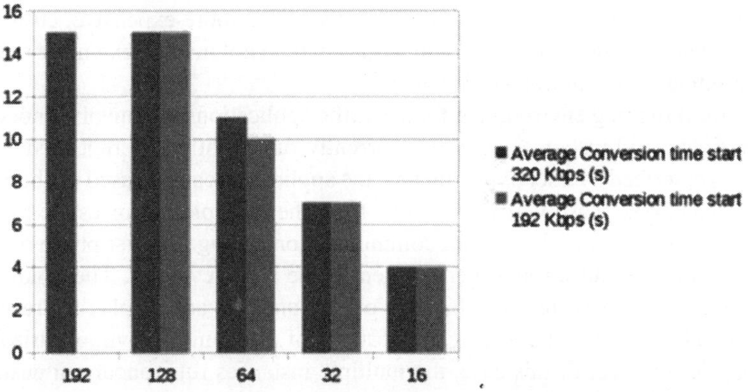

FIGURE 11.16

The average conversion time on a *EC2 c1.medium* platform. The bars at left and right correspond to the original file at the highest resolution (320 Kbps data rate) and next highest resolution (192 Kbps data rate), respectively.

the average conversion time is larger when the source file is smaller, as is the case when the target bit rates are 64, 32, and 16 Kbps.

Figure 11.16 shows the average conversion time for the experiments summarized in Tables 11.4 and 11.5.

The results of our measurements when the instance runs on the *EC2 c1.medium* platform show consistent and considerably lower conversion times; Figure 11.16 presents the average conversion time.

To understand the reasons for our results, we took a closer look at the two types of *AWS EC2* instances, "micro" and "medium," and their suitability for the adaptive data-streaming service. The *t1.micro* supports bursty applications, with a high average-to-peak ratio for CPU cycles, e.g., transaction-processing systems. The Amazon Elastic Block Store (EBS) provides block-level storage volumes; the "micro" instances are only EBS-backed.

The "medium" instances support compute-intensive application with a steady and relatively high demand for CPU cycles. Our application is compute-intensive; thus, there should be no surprise that our measurements for the *EC2 c1.medium* platform show consistent and considerably lower conversion times.

11.13 Cloud-based optimal FPGA synthesis

In this section we discuss another class of application that could benefit from cloud computing. In Chapter 4 we discussed cloud applications in computational science and engineering. The benchmarks presented in Section 4.9 compared the performance of several codes running on a cloud with runs on supercomputers; as expected, the results showed that a cloud is not an optimal environment for applications exhibiting fine- or medium-grained parallelism. Indeed, the communication latency is considerably larger on a cloud than on a supercomputer with a more expensive, custom interconnect. This means that we have to identify cloud applications that do not involve extensive communication or applications exhibiting coarse-grained parallelism.

A cloud is an ideal running environment for scientific applications that involve model development. In this case, multiple cloud instances could concurrently run slightly different models of the system. When the model is described by a set of parameters, the application can be based on the SPMD paradigm combined with an analysis phase when the results from the multiple instances are ranked based on a well-defined metric. In this case there is no communication during the first phase of the application, when partial results are produced and then written to the storage server. Then individual instances signal the completion and a new instance to carry out the analysis and display the results is started. A similar strategy can be used by engineering applications of mechanical, civil, electrical, electronic, or any other system design area. In this case, the multiple instances run concurrent design for different sets of parameters of the system.

A cloud application for optimal design of Field-Programmable Gate Arrays (FPGAs) is discussed next. As the name suggests, an FPGA is an integrated circuit designed to be configured, adapted, or programmed in the field to perform a well-defined function [311]. Such a circuit consists of *logic blocks* and *interconnects* that can be "programmed" to carry out logical and/or combinatorial functions (see Figure 11.17).

The first commercially viable FPGA, the XC2064, was produced in 1985 by Xilinx. Today FPGAs are used in many areas, including digital signal processing, CRNs, aerospace, medical imaging, computer vision, speech recognition, cryptography, and computer hardware emulation. FPGAs are less energy efficient and slower than application-specific integrated circuits (ASICs). The widespread use of FPGAs is due to their flexibility and the ability to reprogram them.

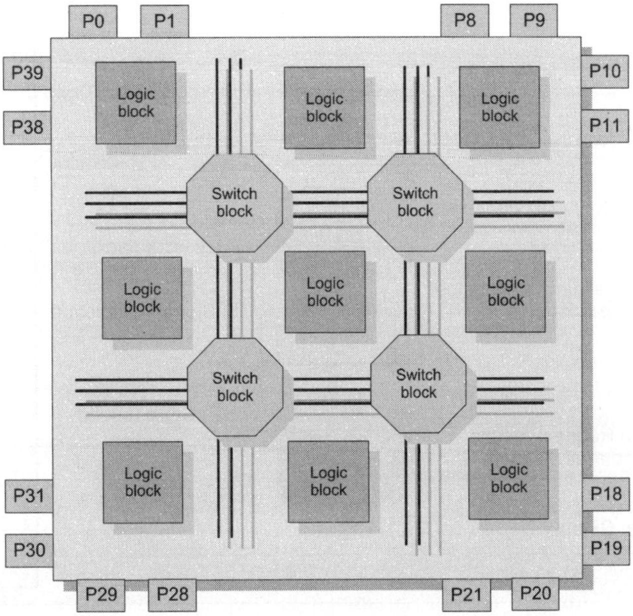

FIGURE 11.17

The structure of an FPGA with 30 pins, P0–P29; nine logic blocks; and four switch blocks.

Hardware description languages (HDLs) such as VHDL and Verilog are used to program FPGAs. HDLs are used to specify a register-transfer level (RTL) description of the circuit. Multiple stages are used to synthesize FPGAs.

A cloud-based system was designed to optimize the routing and placement of components. The basic structure of the tool is shown in Figure 11.18. The system uses the PlanAhead tool from Xilinx (see `www.xilinx.com`) to place system components and route chips on the FPGA logical fabric. The computations involved are fairly complex and take a considerable amount of time; for example, a fairly simple system consisting of a software core processor (Microblaze), a block random access memory (BRAM), and a couple of peripherals can take up to 40 minutes to synthesize on a powerful workstation. Running *N* design options in parallel on a cloud speeds up the optimization process by a factor close to N.

11.14 Exercises and problems

Problem 1. Establish an *AWS* account. Use the *AWS* Management Console to launch an *EC2* instance and connect to it.

Problem 2. Launch three *EC2* instances. The computations carried out by the three instances should consist of two phases, and the second phase should be started only after all instances

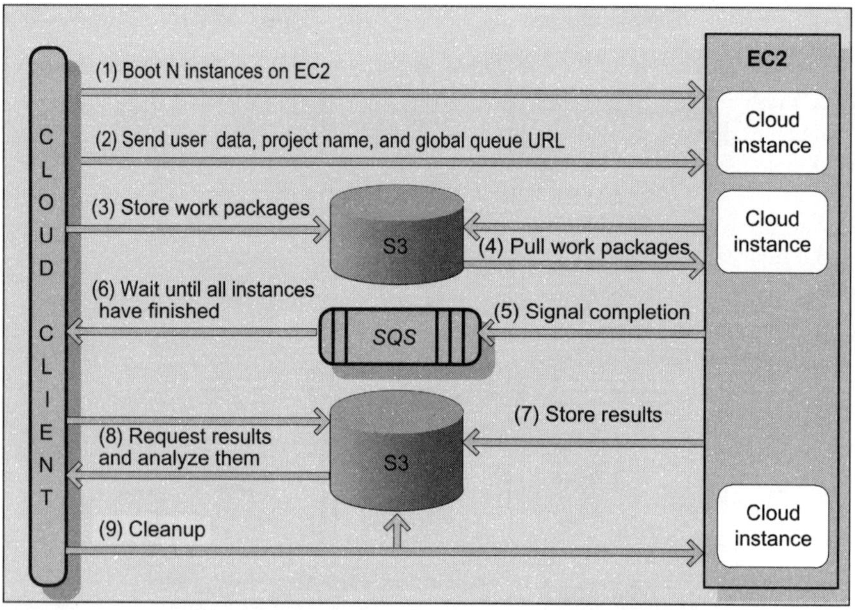

FIGURE 11.18

The architecture of a cloud-based system to optimize the routing and placement of components on an FPGA.

have finished the first stage. Design a protocol and use *Simple Queue Service (SQS)* to implement the barrier synchronization after the first phase.

Problem 3. Use the *Zookeeper* to implement the coordination model in Problem 2.

Problem 4. Use the *Simple Workflow Service (SWF)* to implement the coordination model in Problem 2. Compare the three methods.

Problem 5. Upload several (10 – 20) large image files to an *S3* bucket. Start an instance that retrieves the images from the *S3* bucket and compute the retrieval time. Use the *ElastiCache* service and compare the retrieval time for the two cases.

Problem 6. Numerical simulations are ideal applications for cloud computing. Output data analysis of a simulation experiment requires the computation of confidence intervals for the mean for the quantity of interest [210]. This implies that one must run multiple batches of simulation, compute the average value of the quantity of interest for each batch, and then calculate, say, 95% confidence intervals for the mean. Use the *CloudFormation* service to carry out a simulation using multiple cloud instances that store partial results in *S3* and then another instance that computes the confidence interval for the mean.

Problem 7. Run an application that takes advantage of the *Autoscaling* service.

Problem 8. Use the *Elastic Beanstalk* service to run an application and compare it with the case when the *Autoscaling* service was used.

Problem 9. Design a cloud service and a testing environment. Use the *Elastic Beanstalk* service to support automatic scaling up and down, and use the *Elastic Load Balancer* to distribute the incoming service request to different instances of the application.

Literature

[1] W. M. P. van der Aalst, A. H. ter Hofstede, B. Kiepuszewski, and A. P. Barros. "Workflow patterns." *Technical Report*, Eindhoven University of Technology, 2000.

[2] R. Abbott. "Complex systems engineering: putting complex systems to work," *Complexity*, **13**(2):10–11, 2007.

[3] T. F. Abdelzaher, K. G. Shin, and N. Bhatti. "Performance guarantees for web server end-system: a control theoretic approach." *IEEE Trans. Parallel & Distributed Systems*, **13**(1):80–96, 2002.

[4] B. Abrahao, V. Almeida, J. Almeida, A. Zhang, D. Beyer, and F. Safai. "Self-adaptive SLA-driven capacity management for Internet srvices." *Proc. IEEE/IFIP Network Operations & Management Symposium (NOMS06)*, pp. 557–68, 2006.

[5] H. Abu-Libdeh, L. Princehouse, and H. Weatherspoon. "RACS: A case for cloud storage diversity," *Proc. ACM Symp. on Cloud Computing (SOCC)*, (CD Proceedings) ISBN: 978-1-4503-0036-0.

[6] D. Abts. "The Cray XT4 and Seastar 3-D torus interconnect." *Encyclopedia of Parallel Computing, Part 3*, David Padua, Ed., pp. 470–477, Springer, 2011.

[7] D. Abts, M. R. Marty, P. M. Wells, P. Klausler, and H. Liu. "Energy proportional datacenter networks." *ACM IEEE Int. Symp. on Comp. Arch. (ISCA'10)*, pp. 338–347, 2010.

[8] L. A. Adamic, R. M. Lukose, A. R. Puniyami, and B. A. Huberman. "Search in power-law networks." *Physical Review E*, **64**(4):046135, 2001.

[9] B. Addis, D. Ardagna, B. Panicucci, and L. Zhang. "Autonomic management of cloud service centers with availability guarantees." *Proc. IEEE 3rd Int. Conf. on Cloud Computing*, pp. 220–227, 2010.

[10] R. Albert, H. Jeong, and A.-L. Barabási. "The diameter of the World Wide Web." *Nature*, **401**:130–131, 1999.

[11] R. Albert, H. Jeong, and A.-L. Barabási. "Error and attack tolerance of complex networks." *Nature*, **406**:378–382, 2000.

[12] R. Albert and A.-L. Barabási. "Statistical mechanics of complex networks." *Reviews of Modern Physics*, **72**(1):48–97, 2002.

[13] "Amazon elastic compute cloud." *http://aws.amazon.com/ec2/.*

[14] "Amazon virtual private cloud." *http://aws.amazon.com/vpc/.*

[15] "Amazon Web services: Overview of security processes." *http://s3.amazonaws.com.*

[16] "Amazon CloudWatch." *http://aws.amazon.com/cloudwatch.*

[17] "Amazon elastic block store (EBS)." *http://aws.amazon.com/ebs/.*

[18] "AWS management console." *http://aws.amazon.com/console/.*

[19] T. Andrei. "Cloud computing challenges and related security issues." *http://www1.cse.wustl.edu/jain/ cse571-09/ftp/cloud/index.html.*

[20] A. Andrieux, K. Czajkowski, A. Dan, K. Keahey, H. Ludwing, J. Pruyne, J. Rofrano, S. Tuecke, and M. Xu. "Web Service Agreement Specification." *http://www.gridforum.org/Meetings/GGF11/Documents/ draftggfgraap-agreement.pdf*, 2004.

[21] D. P. Anderson. "BOINC: A system for public-resource computing and storage." *Proc. 5th IEEE/ACM Int. Workshop on Grid Computing*, pp. 4–10, 2004.

[22] R. Aoun, E. A. Doumith, and M. Gagnaire. "Resource provisioning for enriched services in cloud environment." *Proc. IEEE 2nd Int. Conf. on Cloud Computing Technology and Science*, pp. 296–303, 2010.

[23] D. Ardagna, M. Trubian, and L. Zhang. "SLA based resource allocation policies in autonomic environments." *J. Parallel Distrib. Comp.*, **67**(3):259–270, 2007.

[24] D. Ardagna, B. Panicucci, M. Trubian, and L. Zhang. "Energy-aware autonomic resource allocation in multi-tier virtualized environments." *IEEE Trans. on Services Computing*, **5**(1):2–19, 2012.

[25] M. Armbrust, A. Fox, R. Griffith, A. D. Joseph, R. Katz, A. Konwinski, G. Lee, D. Paterson, A. Rabkin, I. Stoica, and M. Zaharia. "Above the clouds: a Berkeley view of cloud computing." *Technical Report UCB/EECS-2009-28*, 2009. Also *http://www.eecs.berkeley.edu/Pubs/TechRpts/2009/EECS-2009-28.pdf.*

[26] D. Artz and Y. Gil. "A survey of trust in computer science and the semantic web." *J. of Web Semantics: Science, Services, and Agents on the World Wide Web*, pp. 58–71, 2007.

[27] M. Asay. "An application war is brewing in the cloud." *http://news.cnet.com/8301-13505_3-10422861-16.html.*

[28] M. Auty, S. Creese, M. Goldsmith, and P. Hopkins. "Inadequacies of current risk controls for the cloud." *Proc. IEEE 2nd Int. Conf. on Cloud Computing Technology and Science*, pp. 659–666, 2010.

[29] L. Ausubel and P. Cramton. "Auctioning many divisible goods." *J. European Economic Assoc.*, **2** (2–3):480–493, 2004.

[30] L. Ausubel, P. Cramton, and P. Milgrom. "The clock-proxy auction: a practical combinatorial auction design." *Chapter 5*, in *Combinatorial Auctions*, P. Cramton, Y. Shoham, and R. Steinberg, Eds., MIT Press, 2006.

[31] A. Avisienis, J. C. Laprie, B. Randell, and C. Landwehr. "Basic concepts and taxonomy of dependable and secure computing." *IEEE Trans. Dependable and Secure Computing*, **1**(1):11–33, 2004.

[32] M. Azambuja, R. Pereira, K. Breitman, and M. Endler. "An architecture for public and open submission systems in the cloud." *Proc. IEEE 3rd Int. Conf. on Cloud Computing*, pp. 513–517, 2010.

[33] Y. Azar, A.Z. Broder, A.R. Karlin, N. Linial, and S. Phillips. "Biased random walks." *Proc STOC92, 24th Annual Symp on Theory of Computing*, pp. 1–9, 1992.

[34] Ö Babaoğlu and K. Marzullo. "Consistent global states." In *Distributed Systems*, Sape Mullender, Ed., Addison Wesley, Reading, Mass., pp. 55–96, 1993.

[35] M. J. Bach, M. W. Luppi, A. S. Melamed, and K. Yueh. "A Remote-file cache for RFS." *Proc. USENIX Summer 1987 Conf.*, pp. 275–280, 1987.

[36] A. A. Baker. "Monte Carlo simulations of radial distribution functions for a proton-electron plasma." *Aust. J. Phys.* **18**:119–133, 1965.

[37] J. Baker, C. Bond, J. C. Corbett, J. J. Furman, A. Khorlin, J. Larson, J.-M. Léon, Y. Li, A. Lloyd, and V. Yushprakh. "Megastore: Providing scalable, highly available storage for interactive services." *Proc. 5th Biennial Conf. on Innovative Data Systems Research (CIDR'11)*, pp. 223–234, 2011.

[38] M. Balduzzi, J. Zaddach, D. Balzarotti, E. Kirda, and S. Loureiro. "A security analysis of Amazon's elastic compute cloud service." *Proc. 27th Annual ACM Symp. on Applied Computing*, pp. 1427–1434, 2012.

[39] A-L. Barabási and R. Albert. "Emergence of scaling in random networks," *Science*, **286**(5439):509–512, 1999.

[40] A-L. Barabási, R. Albert, and H. Jeong. "Scale-free theory of random networks; the topology of World Wide Web." *Physica A*, **281**:69–77, 2000.

[41] P. Barham. B. Dragovic, K. Fraser, S. Hand, T. Harris, A. Ho, R. Neugebauer, I. Pratt, and A. Warfield. "Xen and the art of virtualization." *Proc. 19th ACM Symp. on Operating Systems Principles (SOSP'03)*, pp. 164–177, 2003.

[42] L. A. Barroso and U. Hözle. "The case for energy-proportional computing." *IEEE Computer*, **40**(12):33–7, 2007.

[43] H. Bauke. "Parameter estimation for power-law distributions by maximum likelihood methods." *The European Physical Journal B*, **58**(2):167–173, 2007.

[44] A. Bavier, T. Voigt, M. Wawrzoniak, L. Peterson, and P. Gunningberg. "SILK: Scout paths in the Linux kernel." *Technical Report 2002-009*, Uppsala University, Department of Information Technology, Feb. 2002.

[45] G. Bell. "Massively parallel computers: why not parallel computers for the masses?" *Proc. 4-th Symp. on Frontiers of Massively Parallel Computing*, pp. 292–297, 1992.

[46] E. R. Berlekamp, J. H. Conway, and R. K. Guy. *Winning Ways for your Mathematical Plays* (Second Edition). A K Peters/CRC Press, 2004.

[47] D. Bernstein, E. Ludvigson, K. Sankar, S. Diamond, and M. Morrow. "Blueprint for the Intercloud: protocols and formats for cloud computing interoperability." *Proc. Internet and Web Applications and Services, ICIW '09*, pp. 328–336, 2009.

[48] D. Bernstein and D. Vij. "Intercloud security considerations." *Proc. IEEE 2nd Int. Conf. on Cloud Computing Technology and Science*, pp. 537–544, 2010.

[49] D. Bernstein, D. Vij, and S. Diamond. "An Intercloud cloud computing economy: technology, governance, and market blueprints." *Proc. SRII Global Conference*, pp. 293–299, 2011.

[50] D. Bertsekas and R. Gallagher. *Data Networks* (Second Edition). Prentice Hall, 1992.

[51] S. Bertram, M. Boniface, M. Surridge, N. Briscombe, and M. Hall-May. "On-demand dynamic security for risk-based secure collaboration in clouds." *Proc. IEEE 3rd Int. Conf. on Cloud Computing*, pp. 518–525, 2010.

[52] S. Bhattacharjee and D. C. Marinescu. "A cloud service for trust management in cognitive radio networks." *Int. J. of Cloud Computing*, 2013 (in print).

[53] B. Bollobás. *Random Graphs*, Academic Press, London, 1985.

[54] K. Boloor, R. Chirkova, Y. Viniotis, and T. Salo. "Dynamic request allocation and scheduling for context aware applications subject to a percentile response time SLA in a distributed cloud." *Proc. IEEE 2nd Int. Conf. on Cloud Computing Technology and Science*, pp. 464–472, 2010.

[55] I. Brandic, S. Dustdar, T. Ansett, D. Schumm, F. Leymann, and R. Konrad. "Compliant cloud computing (C3): Architecture and language support for user-driven compliance management in clouds." *Proc. IEEE 3rd Int. Conf. on Cloud Computing*, pp. 244–251, 2010.

[56] S. Brandt, S. Banachowski, C. Lin, and T. Bisson. "Dynamic integrated scheduling of hard real-time, soft real-time, and non-real-time processes." *Proc. IEEE Real-Time Sys. Symp. (RTSS 2003)*, pp. 396–409, 2003.

[57] N. F. Britton. *Essential Mathematical Biology.* Springer, 2004.

[58] M. Buddhikot and K. Ryan. "Spectrum management in coordinated dynamic spectrum access based cellular networks." *Proc. Int. Symp. New Fromtiers in Dynamic Spectrum Access Networks*, pp. 299–307, 2005.

[59] C. Bunch, N. Chohan, C. Krintz, J. Chohan, J. Kupferman, P. Lakhina, Y. Li, and Y. Nomura. "An evaluation of distributed datatstores using the AppScale cloud platform." *Proc. IEEE 3rd Int. Conf. on Cloud Computing*, pp. 305–312, 2010.

[60] A. W. Burks, H. H. Goldstine, and J. von Neumann. "Preliminary Discussion of the Logical Design of an Electronic Computer Instrument." *Report to the U.S. Army Ordnance Department*, 1946. Also in: *Papers of John von Neumann*. W. Asprey and A. W. Burks, Eds., 97–146, MIT Press, Cambridge, MA, 1987.

[61] M. Burrows. "The Chubby lock service for loosely coupled distributed systems." *Proc. Symp. OS Design and Implementation (OSDI06)*, pp. 335–350, 2006.

[62] R. Buyya, R. Ranjan, and R. Calheiros. "Intercloud: Utility-oriented federation of cloud computing environments for scaling of application services." *Proc. Int. Conf. on Algorithms and Architectures for Parallel Processing (ICA3PP-10)*, pp. 19–24, 2010.

[63] C. Cacciari, F. D'Andria, M. Gonzalo, B. Hagemeier, D. Mallmann, J. Martrat, D. G. Perez, A. Rumpl, W. Ziegler, and C. Zsigri. "elasticLM: A novel approach for software licensing in distributed computing infrastructures." *Proc. IEEE 2nd Int. Conf. on Cloud Computing Technology and Science*, pp. 67–74, 2010.

[64] A. G. Carlyle, S. L. Harrell, and P. M. Smith. "Cost-effective HPC: The community or the cloud?" *Proc. IEEE 2nd Int. Conf. on Cloud Computing Technology and Science*, pp. 169–176, 2010.

[65] E. Caron, F. Desprez, and A. Muresan. "Forecasting for grid and cloud computing on-demand resources based on pattern matching." *Proc. IEEE 2nd Int. Conf. on Cloud Computing Technology and Science*, pp. 456–463, 2010.

[66] R. Cattell. "Scalable SQL and NoSQL data stores." *http://cattell.net/datastores/Datastores.pdf*, 2011.

[67] A. Celesti, F. Tusa, M. Villari, and A. Puliafito. "How to enhance cloud architectures to enable cross-federation." *Proc. IEEE 3rd Int. Conf. on Cloud Computing*, pp. 337–345, 2010.

[68] R. Chen, J.-M. Park, and K. Bian. "Robust distributed spectrum sensing in cognitive radio networks." *Proc. IEEE Infocom*, pp. 1876–1884, 2008.

[69] G. J. Chaitin. "On the length of programs for computing binary sequences." *J. Assoc. Comp. Mach.* **13**:547–69, 1966.

[70] A. Chandra, P. Goyal, and P. Shenoy. "Quantifying the benefits of resource multiplexing in on-demand data centers." *Proc. 1st Workshop on Algorithms and Architecture for Self-Managing Systems*, 2003.

[71] T. D. Chandra, R. Griesemer, and J. Redstone. "Paxos made live: an engineering perspectice." *Proc. Symp. Principles of Distributed Computing*, pp. 398–407, 2007.

[72] K. M. Chandy and L. Lamport. "Distributed snapshots: determining global states of distributed systems." *ACM Trans. on Computer Systems*, **3**(1):63–75, 1985.

[73] F. Chang, J. Dean, S. Ghemawat, W. C. Hsieh, D. A. Wallach, M. Burrows, T. Chandra, A. Fikes, and R. E. Gruber. "BigTable: a distributed storage system for structured data." *Proc. Conf. OS Design and Implementation* (OSDI06), pp. 205–218, 2006.

[74] V. Chang, G. Wills, and D. De Roure. "A review of cloud business models and sustainability." *Proc. IEEE 3rd Int. Conf. on Cloud Computing*, pp. 43–50, 2010.

[75] F. Chang, J. Ren, and R. Viswanathan. "Optimal resource allocation in clouds." *Proc. IEEE 3rd Int. Conf. on Cloud Computing*, pp. 418–425, 2010.

[76] K. Chard, S. Caton, O. Rana, and K. Bubendorfer. "Social cloud: Cloud computing in social networks." *Proc. IEEE 3rd Int. Conf. on Cloud Computing*, pp. 99–106, 2010.

[77] J. Chase. "Orca technical note: guests and guest controllers." *http://www.cs.duke.edu/nicl/pub/papers/control.pdf*, 2008.

[78] A. Chazalet. "Service level checking in the cloud computing context." *Proc. IEEE 3rd Int. Conf. on Cloud Computing*, pp. 297–304, 2010.

[79] P. M. Chen and B. D. Noble. "When virtual is better than real." *Proc. 8-th Workshop on Hot Topics in Operating Systems*, pp. 133–141, 2001.

[80] H. Chen, P. Liu, R. Chen, and B. Zang. "When OO meets system software: Rethinking the design of VMMs." *Technical Report PPITR-2007-08003*, pp. 1–9, 2007, Fudan University, Parallel Processing Institute. Also, *http://ppi.fudan.edu.cn/system/publications/paper/OVM-ppi-tr.pdf.*

[81] T. M. Chen and S. Abu-Nimeh. "Lessons from Stuxnet." *Computer*, **44**(4):91–93, 2011.

[82] D. Chiu and G. Agarwal. " Evaluating cache and storage options on the Amazon Web Services cloud." *Proc. CCGRID 2011*, pp. 362 –371, 2011.

[83] R. Chow, P. Golle, M. Jackobsson, E. Shi, J. Staddon, R. Masouka, and J. Mollina. "Controlling data on the cloud: outsourcing computations without outsourcing ccontrol." *Proc. Cloud Computing Security Workshop (CCSW09)*, pp. 85–90, 2009.

[84] B. Clark, T. Deshane, E. Dow, S. Evabchik, M. Finlayson, J. Herne, and J. Neefe Matthews. "Xen and the art of repeated research." *Proc. USENIX Annual Technical Conf. (ATEC'04)*, pp. 135–144, 2004. Also, *http://web2.clarkson.edu/class/cs644/xen/files/repeatedxen-usenix04.pdf.*

[85] R. A. Clarke and R. K. Knake. *Cyber War: The Next Threat to National Security and What to Do About It.* Harper Collins, 2012.

[86] A. Clauset, C. R. Shalizi, and M. E. J. Newman. "Power-law distributions in empirical data." *SIAM Review*, **51**:661–704, 2007.

[87] E. F. Codd. "A Relational model of data for large shared data banks." *Comm. ACM*, **13**(6): 377–387, 1970.

[88] R. Cohen and S. Havlin. "Scale-free networks are ultrasmall." *Physical Review Letters*, **90**(5):058701, 2003.

[89] L. Colitti, S. H. Gunderson, E. Kline, and T. Refice. "Evaluating IPv6 adoption in the Internet." *Proc. Passive and Active Measurement Conference, PAM 2010*, pp. 141–150, 2010.

[90] P. Colp, M. Nanavati, J. Zhu, W. Aiello, G. Coker, T. Deegan, P. Loscocco, and A. Warfield. "Breaking up is hard to do: security and functionality in a commodity hypervisor." *Proc. Symp. Operating Systems Principles*, pp. 189–202, 2011.

[91] F. J. Corbatò and V. A. Vyssotsky. "Introduction and overview of the MULTICS system." *Proc AFIPS, Fall Joint Computer Conference*, pp. 185–196, 1965.

[92] T. M. Cover and J. A. Thomas. *Elements of Information Theory* (Second Edition). Wiley-Interscience, 2006.

[93] P. Cramton, Y. Shoham, and R. Steinberg, Eds., *Combinatorial Auctions*, MIT Press, 2006.

[94] F. Cristian, H. Aghili, R. Strong, and D. Dolev. "Atomic broadcast from simple message diffusion to Byzantine agreement." *Proc. Int. Conf. on Fault Tolerant Computing*, IEEE Press, pp. 200–206, 1985.

[95] J. P. Crutchfield and J. P. Shalizi. "Thermodynamic depth of causal states: objective complexity via minimal representation," *Physical Review E*, **59**:275–83, 1999.

[96] Cloud Security Alliance. "Security guidance for critical areas of focus in cloud computing (v2.1)." *https://cloudsecurityalliance.org/csaguide.pdf*, 2009.

[97] Cloud Security Alliance. "Top threats to cloud computing V1.0." *http://cloudsecurityalliance.org/topthreats/csathreats.v1.0.pdf*, 2010.

[98] Cloud Security Alliance. "Security guidance for critical areas of focus in cloud computing V3.0." *https://cloudsecurityalliance.org/guidance/csaguide.v3.0.pdf*, 2011.

[99] H. A. David. *Order Statistics*, Wiley, 1981.

[100] J. Dean and S. Ghernawat. "MapReduce: simplified data processing on large clusters." *Proc. 6th Symp. on Operating Systems Design and Implementation, OSDI04*, 2004.

[101] Y. Demchenko, C. de Laat, and D. R. Lopes. "Security services lifecycle management in on-demand infrastructure services provisioning." *Proc. IEEE 2nd Int. Conf. on Cloud Computing Technology and Science*, pp. 644–650, 2010.

[102] A. Demers, S. Keshav, and S. Shenker. "Analysis and simulation of a fair queuing algorithm." *Proc. ACM SIGCOMM'89 Symp. on Comm. Architectures & Protocols*, pp. 1–12, 1989.

[103] M. Devarakonda, B. Kish, and A. Mohindra. "Recovery in the Calypso file system." *ACM Trans. Comput. Syst.*, **14**(3):287–310, 1996. Also *http://www.cc.gatech.edu/classes/AY2008/cs6210a_fall/recovery.pdf.*

[104] M. D. Dikaiakos, D. Katsaros, P. Mehra, G. Pallis, and A. Vakali. "Cloud computing: distributed Internet computing for IT and scientific research." *IEEE Internet Computing*, **13**(5):10–13, 2009.

[105] P. Donnelly, P. Bui, and D. Thain. "Attaching cloud storage to a campus grid using Parrot, Chirp, and Hadoop." *Proc. IEEE 2nd Int. Conf. on Cloud Computing Technology and Science*, pp. 488–495, 2010.

[106] T. Dörnemann, E. Juhnke, T. Noll, D. Seiler, and B. Freieleben. "Data flow-driven scheduling of BPEL workflows using cloud resources." *Proc. IEEE 3rd Int. Conf. on Cloud Computing*, pp. 196–203, 2010.

[107] K. J. Duda and R. R. Cheriton. "Borrowed-Virtual-Time (BVT) scheduling: supporting latency-sensitive threads in a general-purpose scheduler." *Proc. 17th Symp. on Op. Sys. Principles*, pp. 261–276, 1999.

[108] N. Dukkipati, T. Refice, Y.-C. Cheng, J. Chu, T. Herbert, A. Agarwal, A. Jain, and N. Sutin. "An argument for increasing TCP's initial congestion window." *ACM SIGCOMM Computer Comm. Review*, **40**(3): 27–33, 2010.

[109] X. Dutreild, N. Rivierre, A. Moreau, J. Malenfant, and I. Truck. "From data center resource allocation to control theory and back." *Proc. IEEE 3rd Int. Conf. on Cloud Computing*, pp. 410–417, 2010.

[110] G. Dyson. *Turing's Cathedral: The Origins of the Digital Universe*, Pantheon, 2012.

[111] D. Ebneter, S. Gatziu Grivas, T. U. Kumar, and H. Wache. "Enterprise architecture frameworks for enabling cloud computing." *Proc. IEEE 3rd Int. Conf. on Cloud Computing*, pp. 542–543, 2010.

[112] V. M. Eguiluz and K. Klemm. "Epidemic threshold in structured scale-free networks." *arXiv:cond-mat/0205439v.1*, 2002.

[113] J. Ejarque, R. Sirvent, and R. M. Badia. "A multi-agent approach for semantic resource allocation." *Proc IEEE 2nd Int. Conf. on Cloud Computing Technology and Science.* pp. 335–342, 2010.

[114] M. Elhawary and Z. J. Haas. "Energy-efficient protocol foe cooperative networks." *IEEE/ACM Trans. on Networking*, **19**(2):561–574, 2011.

[115] Enterprise Management Associates. "How to make the most of cloud computing without sacrificing control." White paper, prepared for IBM, pp. 18, September 2010. *http://www.siliconrepublic.com/reports/partner/26-ibm/report/311-how-to-make-the-most-of-clo/.*

[116] P. Erdös and A. Rényi. "On random graphs." *Publicationes Mathematicae*, **6**:290–7, 1959.

[117] P. Erdös and T. Gallai. "Graphs with points (vertices) of prescribed degree (Gráfok elört fokú pontokkal)." *Mat. Lapok* **11**:264–274, 1961; *Zentralblatt Math.* 103.39701.

[118] R. M. Esteves and C. Rong. "Social impact of privacy in cloud computing." *Proc. IEEE 2nd Int. Conf. on Cloud Computing Technology and Science*, pp. 593–596, 2010.

[119] C. Evanghelinos and C. N. Hill. "Cloud computing for parallel scientic HPC applications: feasibility of running coupled atmosphere-ocean climate models on Amazon's EC2" *Cloud Computing and Its Applications, CCA-08*, http://www.cca08.org/papers/Paper34-Chris-Hill.pdf, 2008.

[120] A. D. H. Farwell, M. J. Sergot, M. Salle, C. Bartolini, D. Tresour, A. Christodoulou. "Performance monitoring of service-level agreements for utility computing." *Proc IEEE. Int. Workshop on Electronic Contracting (WEC04)*, 2004.

[121] S. Ferretti, V. Ghini, F. Panzieri, M. Pellegrini, and E. Turrini. "QoS-aware clouds." *Proc. IEEE 3rd Int. Conf. on Cloud Computing*, pp. 321–328, 2010.

[122] Federal Trade Commission. "Privacy online: fair information practice in the electronic marketplace." *A Federal Trade Commission Report to Congress*, Washington, DC, 2000.

[123] M. J. Fischer, N. A. Lynch, and M. S. Paterson. "Impossibility of distributed consensus with one faulty process." *J. ACM*, **32**(2):374–382, 1985.

[124] *http://www.freebsd.org/doc/handbook/jails.html.*

[125] S. Floyd and Van Jacobson. "Link-sharing and resource management models for packet networks." *IEEE/ACM Trans. on Networking*, **3**(4):365–386, 1995.

[126] B. Ford. "Icebergs in the clouds: the other risks of cloud computing." *Proc. 4th Workshop on Hot Topics in Cloud Computing*, arXiv:1203.1979v2, 2012.

[127] M. Franklin, A. Halevy, and D. Maier. "From databases to dataspaces: A new abstraction for information management." *SIGMOD Record*, **34**(4):27–33, 2005.

[128] E. Gafni and D. Bertsekas. "Dynamic control of session input rates in communication networks." *IEEE Trans. on Automatic Control*, **29**(10):1009–1016, 1984.

[129] G. Ganesan and Y. G. Li. "Cooperative spectrum sensing in cognitive radio networks." *Proc. IEEE Symp. New Frontiers in Dynamic Spectrum Access Networks (DySPAN05)*, pp. 137–143, 2005.

[130] A. G. Ganek and T. A. Corbi. "The dawning of the autonomic computing era." *IBM Systems Journal*, **42**(1):5–18, 2003. Also, *https://www.cs.drexel.edu/jsalvage/Winter2010/CS576/autonomic.pdf.*

[131] T. Garfinkel, B. Pfaff, J. Chow, M. Rosenblum, and D. Boneh. "Terra: a virtual machine-based platform for trusted computing." *Proc. ACM Symp. Operating Systems Principles*, pp. 193–206, 2003.

[132] S. Garfinkel and M. Rosenblum. "When virtual is harder than real: security challenges in virtual machines based computing environments." *Proc. Conf. Hot Topics in Operating Systems*, pp. 20–25, 2005.

[133] S. Garfinkel. "An evaluation of Amazon's grid computing services: EC2, S3, and SQS." *Technical Report, TR-08-07*, Harvard University, 2007.

[134] C. Gentry. "Fully hommomorphic encryption using ideal lattices." *Proc. Symp. on Theory of Computing (STOC)*, pp. 169–178, 2009.

[135] C. Gkantsidis, M. Mihail, and A. Saberi. "Random walks in peer-to-peer networks." *Performance Evaluation*, **63**(3): 241–263, 2006.

[136] S. Ghemawat, H. Gobioff, and S.-T. Leung. "The Google file system." *Proc. 19th ACM Symp. on Operating Systems Principles (SOSP'03)*, p. 15, 2003.
[137] M. Gell-Mann. "Simplicity and complexity in the description of nature." *Engineering and Sciences*, LI, vol. 3, California Institute of Technology, pp. 3–9, 1988.
[138] D. Gmach, S. Kompass, A. Scholz, M. Wimmer, and A. Kemper. "Adaptive quality of service management for entreprize services." *ACM Trans. on the Web (TWEB)*, **2**(1):243–253, 2009.
[139] D. Gmach, J. Rolia, and L. Cerkasova. "Satisfying service-level objectives in a self-managed resource pool." *Proc. 3rd. Int. Conf. on Self-Adaptive and Self-Organizing Systems*, pp. 243–253, 2009.
[140] K. I. Goh, B. Kahang, and D. Kim. "Universal behavior of load distribution in scale-free networks." *Physical Review Letters*, **87**:278701, 2001.
[141] R. P. Goldberg. "Architectural principles for virtual computer systems." *Thesis, Harvard University*, 1973.
[142] P. Goyal, X. Guo, and H. M. Vin. "A hierarchial CPU scheduler for multimedia operating systems." *Proc. OSDI 96, Second USENIX Symp. on Operating Systems Design and Implementation*, pp. 107–121, 1996.
[143] J. Gray. "The transaction concept: virtues and limitations." *Proc. 7 Int. Conf. on Very Large Databases*, pp. 144–154, 1981.
[144] J. Gray and D. Patterson. "A conversation with Jim Gray." *ACM Queue*, **1**(4):8–17, 2003.
[145] T. G. Griffn, F. B. Shepherd, and G. Wilfong. "The stable paths problem and interdomain routing." *IEEE/ACM Trans. on Networking*, 10(2):232–43, 2002.
[146] W. Gropp, E. Lusk, and A. Skjellum. *Using MPI*, MIT Press, 1994.
[147] N. Gruschka and M. Jensen. "Attack surfaces: A taxonomy for attacks on cloud services." *Proc. IEEE 3rd Int. Conf. on Cloud Computing*, pp. 276–279, 2010.
[148] T. Gunarathne, T.-L. Wu, J. Qiu, and G. Fox. "MapReduce in the clouds for science." *Proc IEEE 2nd Int. Conf. on Cloud Computing Technology and Science*, pp. 565–572, 2010.
[149] I. Gupta, A. J. Ganesh, A.-M. Kermarrec. "Efficient and adaptive epidemic-style protocols for reliable and scalable multicast." *IEEE Trans. on Parallel and Distributed Systems*, **17**(7):593–605, 2006.
[150] V. Gupta and M. Harchol-Balter. "Self-adaptive admission control policies for resource-sharing systems." *Proc. 11th Int. Joint Conf. Measurement and Modeling Computer Systems (SIGMETRICS'09)*, pp. 311–322, 2009.
[151] J. O. Gutierrez-Garcia and K.- M. Sim. "Self-organizing agents for service composition in cloud computing." *Proc IEEE 2nd Int. Conf. on Cloud Computing Technology and Science*, pp. 59–66, 2010.
[152] F. A. Halderman, S. D. Schoen, N. Heninger, W. Clarkson, W. Paul, J. A. Calandrino, A. J. Feldman, J. Appelbaum, and E. W. Felten. "Lest we remember: cold boot attacks on encryption keys." *Proc. Usenix, Securitry Symp.*, pp. 45–60, 2008.
[153] J. D. Halley and D. A. Winkler. "Classification of emegence and its relation to self-organization," *Complexity*, **13**(5):10–15, 2008.
[154] P. B. Hansen. "The evolution of operating systems." In *Classic Operating Systems: From Batch Processing to Distributed Systems*, pp. 1–36, Springer Verlag, 2000.
[155] R. F. Hartl, S. P. Sethi, and R. G. Vickson. "Survey of the maximum principles for optimal control problems with state constraints." *SIAM Review*, **37**(2):181–218, 1995.
[156] T. Härder and A. Reuter. "Principles of transaction-oriented database recovery." *ACM Computing Surveys*, **15**(4):287–317, 1983.
[157] S. Harizopoulos, D. J. Abadi, S. Madden, M. Stonebreaker. "OLTP through the looking glass, and what we found there." *Proc. SIGMOD Int. Conf. on Mangement of Data*, pp. 981–992, 2008.
[158] K. Hasebe, T. Niwa, A. Sugiki, and K. Kato. "Power-saving in large-scale storage systems with data migration." *Proc IEEE 2nd Int. Conf. on Cloud Computing Technology and Science*, pp. 266–273, 2010.
[159] R. L. Haskin. "Tiger Shark: a scalable file system for multimedia." *IBM Journal of Research and Development*, **42**(2):185–197, 1998.

[160] W. K. Hastings. "Monte Carlo sampling methods using Markov chains and their applications." *Biometrika*, **57**:97–109, 1970.

[161] S. Haykin. "Cognitive radio: brain empowered wireless communications." *IEEE J. of Selected Areas in Comm.* **23**:201–220, 2005.

[162] J. L. Hellerstein. "Why feedback implementations fail: The importance of systematic testing." *5th Int. Workshop on Feedback Control Implementation and Design in Computing Systems and Networks (FeBID 2010)*, http://eurosys2010-dev.sigops-france.fr/workshops/FeBID2010/hellerstein.pdf.

[163] T. Hey, S. Tansley, and K. Tolle. "Jim Gray on eScience: a transformed scientific method." In *The fourth paradigm: Data-intensive scientific discovery.* Microsoft Research, 2009. Also, *http://research.microsoft.com/en-us/collaboration/fourthparadigm/4th_paradigm_book_complete_lr.pdf.*

[164] M. Hilbert and P. López. "The world's technological capacity to store, communicate, and compute information." *Science*, **332**(6025):60–65, 2011.

[165] M. Hill et al. "Design decisions in SPUR." *Computer*, **9**(11):8–22, 1986.

[166] Z. Hill and M. Humphrey. "CSAL: A cloud storage abstraction layer to enable portable cloud applications." *Proc IEEE 2nd Int. Conf. on Cloud Computing Technology and Science*, pp. 504–511, 2010.

[167] M. Hinchey, R. Sterritt, C. Rouff, J. Rash, and W. Truszkowski. "Swarm-based space exploration." *ERCIM News* 64, 2006.

[168] C. A. R. Hoare. "Communicating sequential processes." *Comm. ACM*, **21**(8):666–677, 1978.

[169] J. Hopfield. "Neural networks and physical systems with emergent collective computational abilities." *Proc. National Academy of Science*, 79, pp. 2554–8, 1982.

[170] J. H. Howard, M. L. Kazer, S. G. Menees, D. A. Nichols, M. Satyanarayanan, R. N. Sidebotham, and M. J. West. "Scale and performance in a distributed file system." *ACM Trans. on Comp. Systems*, **6**(1): 51–81, 1988.

[171] D. H. Hu, Y. Wang, and C.-L. Wang. "BetterLife 2.0: Large-scale social intelligence reasoning on cloud." *Proc IEEE 2nd Int. Conf. on Cloud Computing Technology and Science*, pp. 529–536, 2010.

[172] A. W. Hübler. "Understanding complex systems," *Complexity*, **12**(5):9–11, 2007.

[173] K. Hwang, G. Fox, and J. Dongarra. *Distributed and Cloud Computing*, Morgan-Kaufmann Publishers, 2011.

[174] G. Iachello and J. Hong. "End-user privacy in human-computer interaction." *Foundations and Trends in Human-Computer Interactions*, **1**(1):1–137, 2007.

[175] IBM. "Tivoli performance analyzer." *www.ibm.com/software/tivoli/products/performance-analyzer*, 2008.

[176] IBM Smart Business. "Dispelling the vapor around the cloud computing. Drivers, barriers and considerations for public and private cloud adoption." White Paper, 2010. *//ftp.software.ibm.com/common/ssi/ecm/en/ciw03062usen/CIW03062USEN.PDF.*

[177] IBM. "General parallel file systems (version 3, update 4). Documentation Updates." *http://publib.boulder.ibm.com/infocenter/clresctr/vxrx/topic/com.ibm.cluster.gpfs.doc.*

[178] IBM. "The evolution of storage systems." *IBM Research. Almaden Research Center Publications. http://www.almaden.ibm.com/storagesystems/pubs.*

[179] K. R. Jackson, L. Ramakrishnan, K. Muriki, S. Canon, S. Cholia, J. Shalf, H. Wasserman, and N. J. Wright. "Performance analysis of high-performance computing applications on the Amazon Web Services cloud." *Proc. IEEE Second Int. Conf. on Cloud Computing Technology and Science*, pp. 159–168, 2010.

[180] M. Jelasity, A. Montresor, and O. Babaoglu. "Gossip-based aggregation in large dynamic networks." *ACM Trans. on Computer Systems*, **23**(3):219–252, 2005.

[181] M. Jelasity, S. Voulgaris, R. Guerraoui, A.-M. Kermarrec, and M. van Steen. "Gossip-based peer sampling." *ACM Trans. Comput. Syst.*, **25**(3):8, 2007.

[182] M. Jensen, S. Schäge, and J. Schwenk. "Towards an anonymous access control and accountability scheme for cloud computing." *Proc. IEEE 3rd Int. Conf. on Cloud Computing*, pp. 540–541, 2010.

[183] H. Jin, X.-H. Sun, Y. Chen, and T. Ke. "REMEM: REmote MEMory as checkpointing storage." *Proc IEEE 2nd Int. Conf. on Cloud Computing Technology and Science*, pp. 319–326, 2010.

[184] E. Kalyvianaki, T. Charalambous, and S. Hand. "Self-adaptive and self-configured CPU resource provisioning for virtualized servers using Kalman filters." *Proc. 6th Int. Conf. Autonomic Comp. (ICAC2009)*, pp. 117–126, 2009.

[185] E. Kalyvianaki, T. Charalambous, and S. Hand. "Applying Kalman filters to dynamic resource provisioning of virtualized server applications." *Proc. 3rd Int. Workshop Feedback Control Implementation and Design in Computing Systems and Networks (FeBid)*, p. 6, 2008.

[186] K. Kc and K. Anyanwu. "Scheduling Hadoop jobs to meet deadlines." *Proc IEEE 2nd Int. Conf. on Cloud Computing Technology and Science*, pp. 388–92, 2010.

[187] J. Kephart, H. Chan, R. Das, D. Levine, G. Tesauro, F. Rawson, and C. Lefurgy. "Coordinating multiple autonomic managers to achieve specified power-performance tradeoffs." *Proc. 4th Int. Conf. Autonomic Computing (ICAC2007)*, pp. 100–109, 2007.

[188] J. Kephart. "The utility of utility." *Proc. Policy 2011*; 2011.

[189] W. O. Kermack and A. G. McKendrick. " A contribution to the theory of epidemics." *Proc. Royal Soc. London A*, **115**:700–721, 1927.

[190] A. Khajeh-Hosseini, D. Greenwood, and I. Sommeerville. "Cloud migration: A case study of migrating an enterprise IT system to IaaS." *Proc. IEEE 3rd Int. Conf. on Cloud Computing*, pp. 450–457, 2010.

[191] W. Kim. *Introduction to Object-Oriented Databases.* MIT Press, 1990.

[192] J. Kim, W. J. Dally, and D. Abts. "Flattened butterfly: a cost-efficient topology for high-radix networks." *Proc. Int. Symp. on Comp. Arch. (ISCA)*, pp. 126–137, 2007.

[193] J. Kim, W. J. Dally, and D. Abts. "Efficient topologies for large-scale cluster networks." *Proc. 2010 Optical Fiber Comm. Conf. and National Fiber Optic Engineers Conf. (OFC/NFOEC)*, pp. 1–3, 2010.

[194] S. T. King, P. M. Chen, Y.-M Wang, C. Verbowski, H. J. Wang, and J. R. Lorch. "SubVirt: Implementing malware with virtual machines." *Proc. IEEE Symp. on Security and Privacy*, pp. 314–327, 2006.

[195] L. Kleinrock. *Queuing Systems, Vol I and II.* Wiley, 1965.

[196] F. Koeppe and J. Schneider. "Do you get what you pay for? Using proof-of-work functions to verify performance assertions in the cloud." *Proc IEEE 2nd Int. Conf. on Cloud Computing Technology and Science*, pp. 687–692, 2010.

[197] B. Koley, V. Vusirikala, C. Lam, and V. Gill. "100Gb Ethernet and beyond for warehouse scale computing." *Proc. 15th OptoElectronics and Com. Conf. (OECC2010)*, pp. 106–107, 2010.

[198] A. N. Kolmogorov. "Three approaches to the quantitative definition of information." *Problemy Peredachy Informatzii*, **1**:4–7, 1965.

[199] G. Koslovski, W.-L. Yeow, C. Westphal, T. T.Huu, J. Montagnat, and P. Vicat-Blanc. "Reliability support in virtual infrastructures." *Proc IEEE 2nd Int. Conf. on Cloud Computing Technology and Science*, pp. 49–58, 2010.

[200] P. R. Krugman. *The Self-Organizing Economy*. Blackwell Publishers, 1996.

[201] J. F. Kurose and K. W. Ross. *Computer Networking: A Top-Down Approach* (Sixth Edition). Addison-Wesley, 2013.

[202] D. Kusic, J. O. Kephart, N. Kandasamy, and G. Jiang. "Power and performance management of virtualized computing environments via lookahead control." *Proc. 5th Int. Conf. Autonomic Comp. (ICAC2008)*, pp. 3–12, 2008.

[203] C. Labovitz et. al. "ATLAS Internet Observatory 2009 Annual Report." *http://www.nanog.org/meetings/nanog47/presentations*, 2009.

[204] C. F. Lam. "FTTH look ahead: Technologies and architectures." *Proc. 36th European Conf. on Optical Communications (ECOC'10)*, pp. 1–18, 2010.

[205] L. Lamport and P. M. Melliar-Smith. "Synchronizing clocks in the presence of faults." *J. ACM*, **32**(1):52–78, 1985.

[206] L. Lamport. "The part-time parliament." *ACM Trans. on Computer Systems*, **2**:133–69, 1998.

[207] L. Lamport. "Paxos made simple." *ACM SIGACT News*, **32**(4):51–8, 2001.

[208] B. W. Lampson and H. E. Sturfis. " Reflections on operating system design." *Comm. ACM*, **19**(5): 251–65, 1976.

[209] P. A. Loscocco, S. D. Smalley, P. A. Muckelbauer, R. C. Taylor, S. J. Turner, and J. F. Farrell. "The inevitability of failure: the flawed assumption of security in modern computing environments." *Proc. 21 National. Inf. Sys. Security Conf.*, pp. 303–314, 1998.

[210] A. M. Law and W. D. Kelton. *Simulation Modeling and Analysis*, McGraw-Hill, 1982.

[211] P. J. Leach, P. Levine, B. Douros, J. Hamilton, D. Nelson, and B. Stumpf. "The architecture of an integrated local area network." *IEEE J. of Selected Areas in Comm.* **1**(5):842–857, 1983.

[212] D. S. Lee, K. I. Goh, B. Kahng, and D. Kim. "Evolution of scale-free random graphs: Potts model formulation." *Nuclear Physics B*, **696**:351–380, 2004.

[213] E. Le Sueur and G. Heiser. "Dynamic voltage and frequency scaling: the laws of diminishing returns." *Proc. Workshop on Power Aware Computing and Systems, HotPower'10*, pp. 2–5, 2010.

[214] *http://linux-vserver.org*.

[215] Z. Li, N.-H. Yu, and Z. Hao. "A novel parallel traffic control mechanism for cloud computing." *Proc IEEE 2nd Int. Conf. on Cloud Computing Technology and Science*, pp. 376–382, 2010.

[216] C. Li, A. Raghunathan, and N. K. Jha. "Secure virtual machine execution under an untrusted management OS." *Proc. IEEE 3rd Int. Conf. on Cloud Computing*, pp. 172–179, 2010.

[217] H C. Lim, S. Babu, J. S. Chase, and S. S. Parekh. "Automated control in cloud computing: challenges and opportunities." *Proc. First Workshop on Automated Control for Datacenters and Clouds*, ACM Press, pp. 13–18, 2009.

[218] X. Lin, Y. Lu, J. Deogun, and S. Goddard. "Real-time divisible load scheduling for cluster computing." *Proc. 13th IEEE Real-time and Embedded Technology and Applications Symp.*, pp. 303–314, 2007.

[219] C. Lin and D. C. Marinescu. "Stochastic high level Petri Nets and applications." *IEEE Trans. on Computers*, C-37, **7**:815–825, 1988.

[220] S. Liu, G. Quan, and S. Ren. "On-line scheduling of real-time services for cloud computing." *Proc. SERVICES'2010*, pp. 459–464, 2010.

[221] N. Loutas, V. Peristeras, T. Bouras, E. Kamateri, D. Zeginis, and K. Tarabanis. "Towards a reference architecture for semantically interoperable clouds." *Proc IEEE 2nd Int. Conf. on Cloud Computing Technology and Science*, pp. 143–150, 2010.

[222] C. Lu, J. Stankovic, G. Tao, and S. Son. "Feedback control real-time scheduling: framework, modeling and algorithms." *J. of Real-time Systems*, **23**(1-2):85-126, 2002.

[223] W. Lu, J. Jackson, J. Ekanayake, R. S. Barga, and N. Araujo. "Performing large science experiments on Azure: Pitfalls and solutions." *Proc IEEE 2nd Int. Conf. on Cloud Computing Technology and Science*, pp. 209–217, 2010.

[224] A. Luckow and S. Jha. "Abstractions for loosely-coupled and ensemble-based simulations on Azure." *Proc IEEE 2nd Int. Conf. on Cloud Computing Technology and Science*, pp. 550–6, 2010.

[225] J. Machta. "Complexity, parallel computation, and statistical physics," *Complexity*, **11**(5):46–64, 2006.

[226] W.-Y. Ma, B. Shen, and J. Brassil, "Content service networks: the architecture and protocols." in *Web Caching and Content Delivery*, pp. 83–101, Elsevier, 2001.

[227] J. Madhavan, A. Halevy, S. Cohen, X. Dong, S. R. Jeffery, D. Ko, and C. Yu. "Structured data meets the Web: A few observations." *IEEE Data Engineering Bulletin*, **29**(3):19–26, 2006. Also, *http://research.google.com/pubs/pub32593.html*.

[228] D. J. Magenheimer and T. W. Christian. "vBlades: Optimized paravirtualization for the Itanium processor family." *Proc 3rd VM Research and Technology Workshop*, San Jose, CA, pp. 73–82, 2004.

[229] D. C. Marinescu, G. M. Marinescu, and Y. Ji. "The complexity of scheduling and coordination on computational grids." In *Process Coordination and Ubiquitous Computing*, CRC Press, 2002.

[230] D. C. Marinescu. *Internet-based Workflow Management.* Wiley, 2002.

[231] D. C. Marinescu, C. Yu, and G. M. Marinescu. "Scale-free, self-organizing very large sensor networks." *Journal of Parallel and Distributed Computing (JPDC)*, **50**(5):612–622, 2010.

[232] von der Marlsburg, C. "Network Self-organization." In *An Introduction to Neural and Electronic Networks.* S. Zonetzer, J. L. Davis, and C. Lau, Eds., pp. 421–432, Academic Press, San Diego, CA, 1995.

[233] P. Marshall, K. Keahey, and T. Freeman. "Elastic site: using clouds to elastically extend site resources." *Proc. IEEE Int. Symp. on Cluster Computing and the Grid*, pp. 43–52, 2010.

[234] M. Rodriguez-Martinez, J. Seguel, and M. Greer. "Open source cloud computing tools: A case study with a weather application." *Proc. IEEE 3rd Int. Conf. on Cloud Computing*, pp. 443–449, 2010.

[235] F. Mattern. "Virtual time and global states of distributed systems." *Proc. Int. Workshop on Parallel & Distributed Algorithms*, Elsevier, New York, pp. 215–226, 1989.

[236] J. M. May. *Parallel I/O for High Performance Computing.* Morgan Kaufmann, Burlington, Mass, 2000.

[237] M. W. Mayer. "Architecting principles for system of systems." *Systems Engineering*, **1**(4):267–274, 1998.

[238] M. Mazzucco, D. Dyachuk, and R. Deters. "Maximizing cloud providers revenues via energy-aware allocation policies." *Proc. IEEE 3rd Int. Conf. on Cloud Computing*, pp. 131–138, 2010.

[239] S. McCartney. *ENIAC; The Triumphs and Tragedies of the World's First Computer.* Walker and Company Publishing House, New York, 1999.

[240] P. McKenney. "On the efficient implementation of fair queuing." *Internetworking: Research and Experience*, **2**:113–131, 1991.

[241] A. Menon, J. R. Santos, Y. Turner, G. J. Janakiraman, and W. Zwaenepoel. "Diagnosing performance overheads in Xen virtual machine environments." *Proc. First ACM/USENIX Conf. on Virtual Execution Environments*, 2005.

[242] A. Menon, A. L. Cox, and W. Zwaenepoel. "Optimizing network virtualization in Xen." *Proc. 2006 USENIX Annual Technical Conf.*, pp. 15–28, 2006. Also, *http://www.usenix.org/event/usenix06/tech/menon/menon_html/paper.html.*

[243] N. Metropolis, A. W. Rosenbluth, A. Teller, and E. Teller. "Equation of state calculations by fast computing machines." *J. of Chemical Physics*, **21**(6):1092–7, 1953.

[244] R. Milner. *Lectures on a calculus for communicating systems.* Lecture Notes in Computer Science, Vol. 197, Springer Verlag, Heidelberg, 1984.

[245] M. Miranda. "When every atom counts." *IEEE Spectrum*, July 2012, pp. 32–37, 2012.

[246] J. Mitola and G. Q. Maguire. "Cognitive radio: making software radios more personal." *IEEE Personal Comm.*, **6**:13-8, 1999.

[247] J. Mitola. "Cognitive radio: an integrated agent architecture for software-defined radio," Ph.D. Thesis, KTH, Stockholm 2000.

[248] T. Miyamoto, M. Hayashi, and K. Nishimura. "Sustainable network resource management system for virtual private clouds." *Proc IEEE 2nd Int. Conf. on Cloud Computing Technology and Science*, pp. 512–520, 2010.

[249] A. Mondal, S. K. Madria, and M. Kitsuregawa. "Abide: A bid-based economic incentive model for enticing non-cooperative peers in mobile P2P networks," *Proc. Database Systems for Advanced Applications, DASFAA*, pp. 703–714, 2007.

[250] J. H. Morris, M. Satyanarayanan, M. H. Conner, M. H. Howard, D. S. Rosenthal, and F. D. Smith. "Andrew: a distributed personal computing environment." *Comm. ACM*, **29**(3):184–201, 1986.

[251] R. J. T. Morris and B. J. Truskowski. "The evolution of storage systems." *IBM Systems Journal*, **42**(2): 205–217, 2003.

[252] J. Nagle. "On packet switches with infinite storage." *IEEE Trans. on Communications*, **35**(4):435–8, 1987.

[253] G. Neiger, A. Santoni, F. Leung, D. Rodgers, and R. Uhlig. "Intel virtualization technology: hardware support for efficient processor virtualization." *Intel Technology Journal*, **10**(3):167–177, 2006.

[254] Nelson, M. "Virtual memory for the Sprite operating system." *Technical Report UCB/CSD 86/301*, Computer Science Division (EECS), University of California, Berkeley, 1986.

[255] M. N. Nelson, B. B. Welch, and J. K. Osterhout. "Caching in Sprite network file systems." *ACM Trans. on Computer Systems (TOCS)*, **6**(1):134–54, 1988.

[256] M. E. J. Newman. "The structure of scientific collaboration networks." *Proc. Nat. Academy of Science*, **98**(2):404–409, 2001.

[257] A. J. Nicholson, S. Wolchok, and B. D. Noble. "Juggler: virtual networks for fun and profit." *IEEE Trans. Mobile Computing*, **9**(1):31–43, 2010.

[258] H. Nissenbaum. "Can trust be secured online? A theoretical perspective." *Etica e Politica*, vol. 2, 1999.

[259] NIST. "Cloud architecture reference models: A survey." Document *NIST CCRATWG 004*, v2, pps. 32, 2011. Also, *http://collaborate.nist.gov/twiki-cloud-computing/pub/CloudComputing*.

[260] NIST—Reference Architecture Analysis Team. "Cloud computing reference architecture: Straw man model V2." Document *NIST CCRATWG 0028*, pps. 8, 2011.

[261] NIST—ITLCCP. "NIST cloud computing reference architecture. (version 1)" *NIST—Information Technology Laboratory Cloud Computing Program*, 2011.

[262] NIST. "Cloud specific terms and definitions." *NIST Cloud Computing Collaboration Site. http://collaborate.nist.gov/twiki-cloud-computing/pub/CloudComputing/*.

[263] NIST. "Basic security functional areas." *NIST Cloud Computing Collaboration Site. NIST Reference Architecture: Strawman Model, http://collaborate.nist.gov/twiki-cloud-computing/pub/CloudComputing*.

[264] NIST. "Cloud security services architecture." *NIST Cloud Computing Collaboration Site. http://collaborate.nist.gov/twiki-cloud-computing/pub/CloudComputing*.

[265] NIST. "Threat sources by cloud architecture component." *NIST Cloud Computing Collaboration Site. http://collaborate.nist.gov/twiki-cloud-computing/pub/CloudComputing*.

[266] NIST. "General cloud environments: SWG." *NIST Cloud Computing Collaboration Site. http://collaborate.nist.gov/twiki-cloud-computing/pub/CloudComputing*.

[267] NIST. "Threat analysis of cloud services (initial thoughts for discussion)." *NIST Cloud Computing Collaboration Site. http://collaborate.nist.gov/twiki-cloud-computing/pub/CloudComputing*.

[268] NIST. "Top 10 cloud security concerns (Working list)." *NIST Cloud Computing Collaboration Site. http://collaborate.nist.gov/twiki-cloud-computing/pub/CloudComputing*.

[269] D. Nurmi, R. Wolski, C. Grzegorczyk, G. Obertelli, S. Soman, L. Youseff, and D. Zagorodnov. "The Eucalyptus open-source cloud-computing system." *Proc 9th IEEE/ACM Int Symp. on Cluster Computing and the Grid*, pp. 124–131, 2009.

[270] S. Oikawa and R. Rajkumar. "Portable RK: A portable resource kernel for guaranteed and enfoced timing behavior." In *Proc. IEEE Real Time Technology and Applications Symp.*, pp. 111–120, June 1999.

[271] T. Okuda, E. Kawai, and S. Yamaguchi. "A mechanism of flexible memory exchange in cloud computing environments." *Proc IEEE 2nd Int. Conf. on Cloud Computing Technology and Science*, pp. 75–80, 2010.

[272] D. Olmedilla. "Security and privacy on the semantic web." *Security, Privacy and Trust in Modern Data Management*, M. Petkovic and W. Jonker, Eds., Springer Verlag, 2006.

[273] M. O'Neill. "SaaS, PaaS, and IaaS: a security checklist for cloud models." *http://www.csoonline.com/article/660065/saas-paas-and-iaas-a-security-checklist-for-cloud-models*.

[274] OpenVZ. *http://wiki.openvz.org*.

[275] A. M. Oprescu and T. Kielmann. "Bag-of-tasks scheduling under budget constraints." *Proc IEEE 2nd Int. Conf. on Cloud Computing Technology and Science*, pp. 351–359, 2010.

[276] Oracle Corporation. "Lustre file system." *http://en.wikipedia.org/wiki/Lustre_(file_system)*, 2010.

[277] Oracle Corporation. "Oracle NoSQL Database." *http://www.oracle.com/technetwork/database/nosqldb/learnmore/nosql-database-498041.pdf*, 2011.

[278] OSA. "SP-011: Cloud computing pattern." *http://www.opensecurityarchitecture.org/cms/library/pattern-landscape/251-pattern-cloud-computing.*

[279] N. Oza, K. Karppinen, and R. Savola. "User experience and security in the cloud: An empirical study in the Finnish Cloud Consortium." *Proc IEEE 2nd Int. Conf. on Cloud Computing Technology and Science*, pp. 621–628, 2010.

[280] G. Pacifici, M. Spreitzer, A. N. Tantawi, and A. Youssef. "Performance management for cluster-based web services." *J. Selected Areas in Comm.* **23**(12):2333–43, 2005.

[281] P. Padala, X. Zhu, Z. Wang, S. Singhal, and K. G.Shin. "Performance evaluation of virtualization technologies for server consolidation." *HP Technical Report HPL-2007-59*, 2007. Also, *http://www.hpl.hp.com/techreports/2007/HPL-2007-59R1.pdf.*

[282] S. L. Pallickara, S. Pallickara, M. Zupanski, and S. Sullivan. "Efficient metadata generation to enable interactive data discovery over large-scale scientific data collections." *Proc IEEE 2nd Int. Conf. on Cloud Computing Technology and Science*, pp. 573–580, 2010.

[283] Y. Pan, S. Maini, and E. Blevis. "Framing the issues of cloud computing and sustainability: A design perspective." *Proc IEEE 2nd Int. Conf. on Cloud Computing Technology and Science*, pp. 603–608, 2010.

[284] S. Parvin, S. Han, L. Gao, F. Hussain and E. Chang. "Towards trust establishment for spectrum selection in cognitive radio networks." *Proc. IEEE Int. Conf. on Advanced Inf. Networking and Apps.* pp. 579–583, 2010.

[285] AMK Pathan and R. Buya. "A taxonomy of content delivery networks." *http://cloudbus.org/reports/CDN-Taxonomy.pdf*, 2009.

[286] B. Pawlowski, C. Juszezak, P. Staubach, C. Smith, D. Label, and D. Hitz. "NFS Version 3 design and implementation." *Proc. Summer Usenix, Tech. Conf.*, pp. 137–151, 1994.

[287] B. Pawlowski, S. Shepler, C. Beame, B. Callaghan, M. Eisler, D. Noveck, D. Robinson, and R. Turlow. "The NFS Version 4 protocol." *Proc. 2nd Int. Syst. Admn. Networking (SANE) Conf.*, 2000.

[288] A. Paya and D. C. Marinescu "A cloud service for adaptive digital music streaming." *Proc. 8th Int. Conf. on Signal Image Technology and Internet Systems*, 2012.

[289] J. Pearn. https://plus.google.com/114250946512808775436/posts/VaQu9sNxJuY.

[290] S. Pearson and A. Benameur. "Privacy, securitry, and trust issues arising from cloud computing." *Proc. Cloud Computing and Science*, pp. 693–702, 2010.

[291] C. A. Petri. "Kommunikation mit Automaten." *Schriften des Institutes fur Instrumentelle Mathematik*, Bonn, 1962.

[292] C. A. Petri. *Concurrency theory*. Lecture Notes in Computer Science, Vol. 254, pp. 4–24. Springer–Verlag, Heidelberg, 1987.

[293] G. J. Popek and R. P. Golberg. "Formal requirements for virtualizable third generation architecture." *Comm. of the ACM*, **17**(7):412–421, 1974.

[294] "A framework for hardware-software co-design of embedded systems." *Embedded.eecs.berkeley.edu/Respep/Research/hsc*, 2012.

[295] C. Preist and P. Shabajee. "Energy use in the media cloud." *Proc IEEE 2nd Int. Conf. on Cloud Computing Technology and Science*, pp. 581–586, 2010.

[296] D. Price and A. Tucker. "Solaris Zones: operating systems support for consolidating commercial workloads." *Proc. Large Installation System Administration*, USENIX, pp. 241–54, 2004.

[297] M. Price. "The paradox of security in virtual environments." *Computer*, **41**(11):22–28, 2008.

[298] X. Pu, L. Liu, Y. Mei, S. Sivathanu, Y. Koh, and C. Pu. "Understanding performance interference of I/O workload in viitualized cloud environments." *Proc. IEEE 3rd Int. Conf. on Cloud Computing*, pp. 51–58, 2010.

[299] P. Radzikowski. "SAN vs DAS: A cost analysis of storage in the enterprise." *http://capitalhead.com/articles/san-vs-das-a-cost-analysis-of-storage-in-the-enterprise.aspx* (updated 2010).

[300] A. Ranabahu and A. Sheth. "Semantics-centric solutions for application and data portability in cloud computing." *Proc IEEE 2nd Int. Conf. on Cloud Computing Technology and Science*, pp. 234–241, 2010.

[301] N. Regola and J.-C. Ducom. "Recommendations for virtualization technologies in high performance computing." *Proc IEEE 2nd Int. Conf. on Cloud Computing Technology and Science*, pp. 409–416, 2010.

[302] G. Ren, E. Tune, T. Moseley, Y. Shi, S. Rus, and R. Hundt. "Google-wide profiling: A continuous profiling infrastructure for data centers." *IEEE Micro*, pp. 65–79, July/August 2010. *http://static.googleusercontent.com/external_content/untrusted_dlcp/research.google.com/en/us/pubs/archive/36575.pdf.*

[303] D. M. Ritchie and K. Thompson. "The Unix time-sharing system." *Comm. of the ACM*, **17**(7):365-375, 1974.

[304] D. M. Ritchie. "The evolution of the Unix time-sharing system." *Bell Labs Technical Journal*, **63**(2.2): 1577–1593, 1984.

[305] L. M. Riungu, O. Taipale, and K. Smolander. "Research issues for software testing in the cloud." *Proc IEEE 2nd Int. Conf. on Cloud Computing Technology and Science*, pp. 557–564, 2010.

[306] R. Rodrigues and P. Druschel. "Peer-to-peer systems." *CACM*, **53**(10):72–82, 2010.

[307] J. Rolia, L. Cerkasova, M. Arlit, and A. Andrzejak. "A capacity management service for resource pools." *Proc. 2nd Symp. on Software and Performance*, pp. 224–237, 2005.

[308] M. Rosenblum and T. Garfinkel. "Virtual machine monitors: Current technology and future trends." *Computer*, **38**(5):39–47, 2005.

[309] D. M. Rousseau, S. B. Sitkin, R. S. Burt, and C. Camerer. "Not so different after all: a cross-disciplinary view of trust." *Academy of Management Review*, **23**(3):393–404, 1998.

[310] T. L. Ruthkoski. "Exploratory project: State of the cloud, from University of Michigan and beyond." *Proc IEEE 2nd Int. Conf. on Cloud Computing Technology and Science*, pp. 427–432, 2010.

[311] H. F. -W. Sadrozinski and J. Wu. *Applications of Field-Programmable Gate Arrays in Scientific Research.* Taylor & Francis, 2010.

[312] J. H. Saltzer and M. F. Kaashoek. *Principles of Computer System Design.* Morgan Kaufamnn, NY, 2009.

[313] R. R. Sambasivan, A. X. Zheng, M. De Rosa, E. Krevat, S. Whitman, M. Stroucken, W. Wang, L. Xy, and G. R. Ganger. "Diagnosing performance changes by comparing request flows." *Proc. 8th USENIX Conf. on Networked Systems Design and Implementation (NSDI'11)*, p. 14, 2011.

[314] B. Sandberg, D. Goldberg, S. Kleiman, D. Walsh, and B. Lyon. "Design and implementation of the Sun network file system." *Proc. Summer Usenix, Tech. Conf.*, pp. 119–130, 1986.

[315] T. Sandholm and K. Lai. "Dynamic proportional share scheduling in Hadoop." *Proc. JSSPP 10, 15th Workshop on Job Scheduling Strategies for Parallel Processing*, 2010.

[316] M. Satyanarayanan. "A survey of distributed file systems." *CS Technical Report, CMU, http://www.cs.cmu.edu/satya/docdir/satya89survey.pdf*, 1989.

[317] F. Schmuck and R. Haskin. "GFPS: A shared-disk file system for large computing clusters." *Proc. Conf. on File and Storage Technologies (FAST'02)*, pp. 231–244, 2002.

[318] I. Sholtes, J. Botev, A. Höhfeld, H. Schloss, and M. Esch. "Awareness-driven phase transitions in very large scale distributed systems," *Proc. 2nd IEEE Int. Conf. on Self-Adaptive and Self-Organizing Systems, SASO-08*. IEEE Press, pp. 25–34, 2008.

[319] I. Scholtes. "Distributed creation and adaptation of random scale-free overlay networks." *Proc. 4th IEEE Int. Conf. of Self-Adaptive and Self-Organizing Systems, SASO-10*, pp. 51–63, 2010.

[320] P. Schuster. "Nonlinear dynamics from physics to biology. Self-organization: An 53 old paradigm revisited." *Complexity*, **12**(4):9–11, 2007.

[321] S. Scott, D. Abts, J. Kim, and W. J. Dally. "The Blackwidow highradix Clos network." *Proc. Int. Symp. on Computer Architecture (ISCA)*, pp. 16–28, 2006.

[322] D. Sehr, R. Muth, C. Biffle, V. Khimenko, E. Pasko, K. Schimpf, B. Yee, and B. Chen. "Adapting software fault isolation to contemporary CPU architectures." *Proc. 19th USENIX Conf. on Security (USENIX Security'10)*, pp. 1–11, 2010.

[323] P. Sempolinski and D. Thain. "A comparison and critique of Eucalyptus, OpenNebula and Nimbus." *Proc IEEE 2nd Int. Conf. on Cloud Computing Technology and Science*, pp. 417–426, 2010.

[324] S. Sivathanu, L. Liu, M. Yiduo, and X. Pu. "Storage management in virtualized cloud environment." *Proc. IEEE 3rd Int. Conf. on Cloud Computing*, pp. 204–211, 2010.

[325] J. E. Smith and R. Nair. "The architecture of virtual machines." *Computer*, **38**(5):32–8, 2005.

[326] L. Snyder. "Type architectures, shared memory, and the corolary of modest potential." *Ann. Rev. Comp. Sci.* 1, pp. 289–317, 1986.

[327] SNIA, OGF. "Cloud storage for cloud computing." Joint Paper of *Storage Networking Industry Association* and *Open Grid Forum*, pp. 1–12, *http://forge.gridforum.org/sf/docman/do/downloadDocument/projects.occi-wg*, 2009.

[328] R. J. Solomonoff. "A formal theory of inductive inference." *Inform. and Control (Part I)*, **7**(1):1–22, 1964 and *(Part II)*, **7**(2):224–54, 1964.

[329] I. Sommerville, D. Cliff, R. Calinescu, J, Keen, T. Kelly, M. Kwiatowska, J. McDermid, and R. Paige. "Large-scale IT complex systems." *Comm. ACM*, **55**(7):71–77, 2012.

[330] T. Stanley, T. Close, and M. S. Miller. "Causeway: A message-oriented distributed debugger." *Technical Report HPL-2009-78*, p. 14, 2009. Also, *http://www.hpl.hp.com/techreports*.

[331] M. Stecca and M. Maresca. "An architecture for a mashup container in vizualized environments." *Proc. IEEE 3rd Int. Conf. on Cloud Computing*, pp. 386–393, 2010.

[332] P. Stingley. "Cloud architecture." *http://sites.google.com/site/cloudarchitecture/*.

[333] M. Stokely, J. Winget, E. Keyes, C. Grimes, and B. Yolken. "Using a market economy to provision compute resources across planet-wide clusters." *Proc. Int. Parallel and Distributed Processing Symp. (IPDPS 2009)*, pp. 1–8, 2009.

[334] I. Stoica, R. Morris, D. Karger, M. F. Kaashoek, and H. Balakrishnan. "Chord: A scalable peer-to-peer lookup service for Internet applications." *Proc. SIGCOMM*, pp. 149–160, 2001.

[335] M. Stonebreaker. "The "NoSQL" has nothing to do with SQL.'*http://cacm.acm.org/blogs/blog-cacm/ 50678-the-nosql-discussion-has-nothing-to-do-with-sql/fulltext*, 2009.

[336] StreamingMedia. "Only 18% using adaptive streaming, says Skyfire report." *http://www.streamingmedia.com/Articles/ReadArticle.aspx?ArticleID=79393*.

[337] J. Stribling, J. Li, I. G. Councill, M. F. Kaashoek, and R. Morris. "Overcite: A distributed, cooperative citeseer." *Proc. 3rd Symp. on Networked Systems Design and Implementation*, pp. 69–79, 2006.

[338] J. Sugerman, G. Venkitachalam, and B. Lim. "Virtualizing I/O devices on VMware Workstation's hosted virtual machine monitor." *Proc. USENIX Conf.*, pp. 70–85, 2001.

[339] C. Sun, W. Zhang, and K. B. Letaief. "Cluster-based cooperative spectrum sensing for cognitive radio systems." *Proc. IEEE Int. Conf. on Comm. (ICC07)*, pp. 2511–5, 2007.

[340] C. Sun, W. Zhang, and K. B. Letaief. "Cooperative spectrum sensing for cognitive radios under BW constraints." *Proc. IEEE Intl. Wireless Commun. Networking Conf.*, pp. 1–5, 2007.

[341] Y. Sun, Z. Han, and K. J. Ray Liu. "Defense of trust management vulnerabilities in distributed networks." *IEEE Comm. Magazine*, Special Issue, Security in Mobile Ad Hoc and Sensor Networks, **46**(2):112–119, 2008.

[342] Sun Microsystems. "Introduction to cloud computing architecture." White Paper, June 2009. *http://eresearch.wiki.otago.ac.nz/images/7/75/Cloudcomputing.pdf*.

[343] V. Sundaram, A. Chandra, P. Goyal, P. Shenoy, J. Sahni, and H. M. Vin. "Application performance in the QLinux multimedia operating system." In *Proc. 8th ACM Conf. on Multimedia*, pp. 127–136, 2000.

[344] M. Steinder, I. Walley, and D. Chess. "Server virtualization in autonomic management of heterogeneous workloads." *SIGOPS Oper. Sys. Rev.*, **42**(1):94–5, 2008.

[345] D. Tancock, S. Pearson, and A. Charlesworth. "A privacy impact assessment tool for cloud computing." *Proc IEEE 2nd Int. Conf. on Cloud Computing Technology and Science*, pp. 667–674, 2010.

[346] L. Tang, J. Dong, Y. Zhao, and L.-J. Zhang. "Enterprise cloud service architecture." *Proc. IEEE 3rd Int. Conf. on Cloud Computing*, pp. 27–34, 2010.

[347] J. Tate, F. Lucchese, and R. Moore. *Introduction to Storage Area Networks.* IBM Redbooks, 2006. *http://www.redbooks.ibm.com/redbooks/pdfs/sg245470.pdf.*

[348] D. Tennenhouse. "Layered multiplexing considered harmful." In *Protocols for High-Speed Networks*, H. Rudin and R. C. Williamson, Eds., pp. 143–8, North Holland, 1989.

[349] G. Tesauro, N. K. Jong, R. Das, and M. N. Bennani. " A hybrid reinforcement learning approach to autonomic resource allocation." *Proc. Int Conf. on Autonomic Computing, ICAC-06*, pp. 65–73, 2006.

[350] J. Timmermans, V. Ikonen, B. C. Stahl, and E. Bozdag. "The ethics of cloud computing. A conceptual review." *Proc IEEE 2nd Int. Conf. on Cloud Computing Technology and Science*, pp. 614–620, 2010.

[351] S. C. Tornay. "*Ockham: studies and selections.*" Open Court Publishers. La Salle, IL, 1938.

[352] Z. Toroczkai and K. E. Bassler. "Jamming is limited in scale-free systems." *Nature*, **428**:716, 2004.

[353] C. Tung, M. Steinder, M. Spreitzer, and G. Pacifici. "A scalable application placement controller for enterprise data centers." *Proc. 16th Int. Conf. World Wide Web (WWW2007)*, 2007.

[354] A. M. Turing. "On computable numbers, with an application to the Entscheidungsproblem." *Proc. London Math. Soc., Ser.* 2, **42**:230–265, 1937, and "On computable numbers, with an application to the Entscheidungsproblem: A correction," *Proc. London Math. Soc., Ser.* 2, **43**:544–546. 1937.

[355] A. M. Turing. "The chemical basis of morphogenesis." *Philosophical Trans of the Royal Society of London*, Series B, **237**:37–72, 1952.

[356] J. van Vliet, F. Paganelli, S. van Wel, and D. Dowd. "Elastic Beanstalk: Simple Cloud Scaling for Java Developers." O'Reilly Publishers, Sebastopol, California, 2011.

[357] L. M. Vaquero, L. Rodero-Merino, and R. Buyya. "Dynamically scaling applications in the cloud." *Proc. SIGCOMM Comput. Comm. Rev.*, **41**:45–52, 2011.

[358] H. N. Van, F. D. Tran, and J.-M. Menaud. "Performance and power management for cloud infrastructures." *Proc. IEEE 3rd Int. Conf. on Cloud Computing*, pp. 329–336, 2010.

[359] K. Varadhan, R. Govindan, and D. Estrin. "Persistent route oscillations in interdomain routing." *Computer Networks*, **32**(1):1–16, 2000.

[360] J. Varia. "Cloud architectures." *http://jineshvaria.s3.amazonaws.com/public/cloudarchitectures-varia.pdf.*

[361] P. Veríssimo and L. Rodrigues. "A posteriori agreement for fault-tolerant clock synchronization on broadcast networks." *Proc. 22nd Annual Int. Symp. on Fault-Tolerant Computing*, IEEE Press, Los Alamitos, CA, pp. 527–536, 1992.

[362] J. von Neumann. "Probabilistic Logic and Synthesis of Reliable Organisms from Unreliable Components." In *Automata studies*, C. E. Shannon and J. McCarthy, Eds., Princeton University Press, Princeton, NJ, 1956.

[363] J. von Neumann. "Fourth University of Illinois Lecture." *Theory of Self-Reproduced Automata*, A. W. Burks, Ed., University of Illinois Press, Urbana, IL, 1966.

[364] S. V. Vrbsky, M. Lei, K. Smith, and J. Byrd. "Data replication and power consumption in data grids." *Proc IEEE 2nd Int. Conf. on Cloud Computing Technology and Science*, pp. 288–295, 2010.

[365] B. Walker, G. Popek, E. English, C. Kline, G. Thiel. "The LOCUS distributed operating system." *Proc. 9th ACM Symp. on OS principles*, pp. 49–70, 1983.

[366] K. Walsh and E. G. Sirer. "Experience with an object reputation system for peer-to-peer filesharing." *Proc. 3rd symp. on networked systems design and implementation*, pp. 1–14, 2006.

[367] C. Ward, N. Aravamudan, K. Bhattacharya, K. Cheng, R. Filepp, R. Kearney, B. Peterson, L. Shwartz, and C. C. Young. "Workload migration into clouds: challenges, experiences, opportunities." *Proc. IEEE 3rd Int. Conf. on Cloud Computing*, pp. 164–171, 2010.

[368] L. Wang, L. Park, R. Pang, V. S. Pai, and L. Peterson. "Reliability and security in the CoDeeN content distribution network." *Proc. USENIX 2004*, pp. 2004.

[369] M. Wang, N. Kandasamy, A. Guez, and M. Kam. "Adaptive performance control of computing systems via distributed cooperative control: application to power management in computer clusters." *Proc. 3rd Intl. Conf. on Autonomic Computing*, pp. 165–174, 2006.

[370] D. J. Watts and S. H. Strogatz. "Collective-dynamics of small-world networks," *Nature*, **393**:440–442, 1998.

[371] J. Webster. "Evaluating IBM's SVC and TPC for server virtualization." IBM Evaluator Group, 2010. *ftp://ftp.boulder.ibm.com/software/at/tivoli/analyst_paper_ibm_svc_tpc.pdf.*

[372] A. Whitaker, M. Shaw, and S. D. Gribble. "Denali; lightweight virtual machines for distributed and networked applications." *Technical Report 02-0201*, University of Washington, 2002.

[373] V. Winkler. *Securing the cloud: cloud computer security techniques and tactics.* Elsevier Science and Technologies Books, 2011.

[374] J. A. Winter, D. H. Albonesi, and C. A. Shoemaker. "Scalable thread scheduling and global power management for heterogeneous many-core architectures." *9th Int. Conf. on Parallel Architectures and Compilation Techniques (PACT'10)*, pp. 29–40, 2010.

[375] E. C. Withana and B. Plale. "Usage patterns to provision for scientific experimentation in clouds." *Proc IEEE 2nd Int. Conf. on Cloud Computing Technology and Science*, pp. 226–233, 2010.

[376] M. Witkowski, P. Brenner, R. Jansen, D. B. Go, and E. Ward. "Enabling sustainable clouds via environmentally opportunistic computing." *Proc IEEE 2nd Int. Conf. on Cloud Computing Technology and Science*, pp. 587–592, 2010.

[377] D. H. Wolpert and W. Macready. "Using self-dissimilarity to quantify complexity," *Complexity*, **12**(3):77–85, 2007.

[378] Xen Wiki. http://wiki.xensource.com/xenwiki/CreditScheduler, 2007.

[379] Z. Xiao and D. Cao. "A policy-based framework for automated SLA negotiation for internet-based virtual computing environment." *Proc. IEEE 16th Int. Conf. on Parallel and Distributed Systems*, pp. 694–699, 2010.

[380] A. C. Yao "How to generate and exchange secrets." *Proc. Symp. on Theory of Computing (STOC)*, pp. 162–167, 1986.

[381] S. Yi, D. Kondo, and A. Andrzejak. "Reducing costs of spot instances via checkpointing in the Amazon Elastic Compute Cloud." *Proc. IEEE 3rd Int. Conf. on Cloud Computing*, pp. 236–243, 2010.

[382] M. Zapf and A. Heinzl. "Evaluation of process design patterns: an experimental study." In W. M. P. van der Aalst, J. Desel, and A. Oberweis, Eds., *Business Process Management*. Lecture Notes on Computer Science, Vol. 1806, pp. 83–98, Springer-Verlag, Heidelberg, 2000.

[383] M. Zaharia, D. Borthakur, J. S. Sarma, K. Elmeleegy, S. Shenker, and I. Stoica. "Delay scheduling: a simple technique for achieving locality and fairness in cluster scheduling." *Proc. EuroSys 10 5th European Conf. Computer Systems*, pp. 265–278, 2010.

[384] P. Zech, M. Felderer, R. Breu. "Towards a model-based security testing approach in cloud computing environments." *Proc. IEEE 6th Int. Conf. on Software Security and Reliability Companion*, pp. 47–56, 2012.

[385] Z. L. Zhang, D. Towsley, and J. Kurose. "Statistical analysis of the generalized processor sharing scheduling discipline." *IEEE J. Selected Areas in Comm.* **13**(6):1071–1080, 1995.

[386] X. Zhang, J. Liu, B. Li, and T-S.P Yum. "CoolStreaming/DONet: A data-driven overlay network for peer-to-peer live media streaming." *Proc. INFOCOM '05*, pp. 2102–2111, 2005.

[387] C. Zhang and H. D. Sterck. "CloudBATCH: A batch job queuing system on clouds with Hadoop and HBase." *Proc IEEE 2nd Int. Conf. on Cloud Computing Technology and Science*, pp. 368–375, 2010.

[388] W. Zhao, P. M. Melliar-Smith, and L. E. Moser. "Fault tolerance middleware for cloud computing." *Proc. IEEE 3rd Int. Conf. on Cloud Computing*, pp. 67–74, 2010.

[389] X. Zhao, K. Borders, and A. Prakash. "Virtual machine security systems." In *Advances in Computer Science and Engineering*, pp. 339–365. *http://www.eecs.umich.edu/aprakash/eecs588/handouts/virtual-machinesecurity.pdf*.

Glossary

Cloud security

Authentication credential Something that an entity is, has, or knows that allows that entity to prove its identity to a system.

Cloud subscriber An authenticated person who accesses a cloud system over a network. A cloud subscriber may possess administrative privileges, such as the ability to manage virtual machines or the ability to regulate access by users to cloud resources the cloud subscriber controls.

FedRAMP FedRAMP allows joint authorizations and continuous security monitoring services for government and commercial cloud computing systems intended for multiagency use. The use of this common security risk model provides a consistent baseline for cloud-based technologies and ensures that the benefits of cloud-based technologies are effectively integrated across a variety of cloud computing solutions. The risk model will enable the government to "approve once, and use often" by ensuring that multiple agencies gain the benefit and insight of FedRAMP's authorization and access to service providers' authorization packages.

FISMA-compliant environment An environment that meets the requirements of the Federal Information Security Management Act of 2002. Specifically, the law requires an inventory of information systems, the categorization of information and information systems according to risk level, security controls, a risk assessment, a system security plan, certification and accreditation of the system's controls, and continuous monitoring.

Moderate impact Moderate impact refers to the impact levels defined in FIPS 199. A potential impact is "moderate if the loss of confidentiality, integrity, and availability could be expected to have a serious adverse effect on organizational operations, organizational assets, or individuals."

Security accreditation The organization authorizes (i.e., accredits) the cloud system for processing before operations and updates the authorization or when there is a significant change to the system.

Security assessment Assessing the management, operational, and technical controls of the cloud system with frequency depending on risk, but no less than annually.

Security certification A security certification is conducted for accrediting the cloud system; the security certification is a key factor in all security accreditation (i.e., authorization) decisions and is integrated into and spans the system development life cycle.

Some of the definitions are based on dictionaries of terms from organizations such as NIST and the Cloud Computing Alliance.

Cloud services

Cloud distribution The process of transporting cloud data between providers and the cloud.

Mobile/fixed endpoints A physical device that provides a man/machine interface to cloud services and applications.

Service aggregation An aggregation brokerage service combines multiple services into one or more new services.

Service arbitrage Similar to cloud service aggregation; the difference is that the services being aggregated are not fixed. Arbitrage provides flexibility and opportunistic choices for the service aggregator (e.g., provides multiple email services through one service provider or provides a credit-scoring service that checks multiple scoring agencies and selects the best score).

Service deployment All of the activities and organization needed to make a cloud service available.

Service intermediation An intermediation broker provides a service that directly enhances a given service delivered to one or more service consumers.

Service management All service-related functions necessary for the management and operations of those services required by customers.

Service orchestration The arrangement, coordination, and management of cloud infrastructure to provide a variety of cloud services to meet IT and business requirements.

Desirable characteristics/attributes

Data portability The ability to transfer data from one system to another without being required to recreate or reenter data descriptions or to modify significantly the application being transported.

Interoperability The capability to communicate, execute programs, or transfer data among various functional units under specified conditions.

Maintainability A measure of the ease with which maintenance of a functional unit can be performed using prescribed procedures and resources. Synonymous with serviceability.

Privacy The assured, proper, and consistent collection, processing, communication, use, and disposition of personal information and personally identifiable information throughout its life cycle.

Rapid provisioning Automatically deploying a cloud system based on the requested service, resources, and capabilities.

Reliability A measure of the ability of a functional unit to perform a required function under given conditions for a given time interval.

Resilience The ability to reduce the magnitude and/or duration of events disruptive to a critical infrastructure. The effectiveness of a resilient infrastructure or enterprise depends on its ability to anticipate, absorb, adapt to, and/or rapidly recover from a potentially disruptive event.

Service interoperability The capability to communicate, execute programs, or transfer data among various cloud services under specified conditions.

System portability The ability of a service to run on more than one type or size of cloud.

Usability The extent to which a product can be used by specified users to achieve specified goals with effectiveness, efficiency, and satisfaction in a specified context of use.

General

Auditor A party that can conduct independent assessments of cloud services, information system operations, performance, and security of the cloud implementations.

Audits Systematic evaluation of a cloud system by measuring how well it conforms to a set of established criteria (e.g., security audit if the criteria is security, privacy-impact audit if the criteria is privacy, performance audit if the criteria is performance).

Broker An entity that manages the use, performance, and delivery of cloud services and negotiates relationships between cloud providers and cloud consumers.

Carrier The intermediary that provides connectivity and transport of cloud services between providers and consumers.

Community cloud The infrastructure is shared by several organizations and supports a specific community that has shared concerns (e.g., mission, security requirements, policy, and compliance considerations). It may be managed by the organizations or a third party and may exist on or off their premises.

Data object A logical container of data that can be accessed over a network (e.g., a blob). May be an archive, such as specified by the TAR format.

Hybrid cloud The infrastructure is a composition of two or more clouds (private, community, or public) that remain unique entities but are bound together by standardized or proprietary technology that enables data and application portability (e.g., cloud bursting for load balancing between clouds).

Infrastructure-as-a-Service (IaaS) The capability to provision processing, storage, networks, and other fundamental computing resources where the consumer is able to deploy and run arbitrary software, which can include operating systems and applications. The consumer does not manage or control the underlying cloud infrastructure but has control over operating systems, storage, and deployed applications and, possibly, limited control of select networking components (e.g., host firewalls).

Physical data container A storage device suitable for transferring data between cloud subscribers and clouds (e.g., a hard disk). There must be a standard format that the provider supports (e.g., EIDE,

IDE, SCSI). The physical data container must be formatted with a standard logical organization, such as FAT32, UFS, etc.

Platform-as-a-Service (PaaS) The capability to deploy onto the cloud infrastructure consumer-created or acquired applications created using programming languages and tools supported by the provider. The consumer does not manage or control the underlying cloud infrastructure, including network, servers, operating systems, or storage, but has control over the deployed applications and, possibly, application hosting environment configurations.

Private cloud The infrastructure is operated solely for an organization; it may be managed by the organization or a third party and may exist on or off the organization's premises.

Public cloud The infrastructure is made available to the general public or a large industry group and is owned by an organization selling cloud services.

Service consumer Person or organization that maintains a business relationship with, and uses service from, service providers.

Service-level agreement (SLA) A document explaining expected quality of service and legal guarantees.

Service provider Entity responsible for making a service available to service consumers.

SLA management Includes the SLA contract definition (basic schema with the quality-of-service parameters), SLA monitoring, and SLA enforcement, according to the defined policies.

Software-as-a-Service (SaaS) The capability to use a provider's applications running on a cloud infrastructure. The applications are accessible from various client devices through a thin-client interface such as a Web browser (e.g., Web-based email). The consumer does not manage or control the underlying cloud infrastructure, including network, servers, operating systems, storage, or even individual application capabilities, with the possible exception of limited user-specific application configuration settings.

Layers and functions

Application layer Deployed software applications targeted toward end-user software clients or other programs, and made available via the cloud.

Hardware layer Includes computers (CPU, memory), network (router, firewall, switch, network link and interface) and storage components (hard disk), and other physical computing infrastructure elements.

Facility layer Heating, ventilation, air conditioning (HVAC), power, communications, and other aspects of the physical plant comprise the lowest layer, the facility layer.

Metering Providing a measurement capability at some level of abstraction appropriate to the type of service (e.g., storage, processing, bandwidth, and active user accounts).

Monitoring and reporting Discovering and monitoring the virtual resources, monitoring cloud operations and events, and generating performance reports.

Physical resource layer Includes all physical resources used to provide cloud services.

Platform architecture layer Entails compilers, libraries, utilities, and other software tools and development environments needed to implement applications.

Provisioning/configuration Preparing a cloud to allow it to provide (new) services to its users.

Resource abstraction and control layer Software elements used to realize the infrastructure upon which a cloud service can be established (e.g., hypervisor, virtual machines, virtual data storage).

Resource change Adjusting configuration/resource assignment for repairs and upgrades and joining new nodes into the cloud.

Service layer Defines the basic services provided by cloud providers.

Virtualized infrastructure layer Software elements, such as hypervisors, virtual machines, virtual data storage, and supporting middleware components, used to realize the infrastructure upon which a computing platform can be established. Although virtual machine technology is commonly used at this layer, other means of providing the necessary software abstractions are not precluded.

Virtualization

Full virtualization Each virtual machine runs on an exact copy of the actual hardware.

Guest operating system An operating system that runs on a VMM rather than directly on the hardware.

Hypervisor or virtual machine monitor (VMM) Software that securely partitions a computer's resources into one or more virtual machines. Each virtual machine appears to be running on bare hardware, giving the appearance of multiple instances of the same computer, but all are supported on a single machine.

Paravirtualization Each virtual machine runs on a slightly modified copy of the actual hardware. The reasons for paravirtualization are (i) some aspects of the hardware cannot be virtualized; (ii) to improve performance; (iii) to present a simpler interface.

Process or application virtual machine VM runs under the control of a normal OS and provides a platform-independent host for a single application (e.g., Java Virtual Machine (JVM)).

System virtual machine/hardware virtual machine Provides a complete system. Each VM can run its own OS, which in turn can run multiple applications. There are several approaches:

- *Traditional VM.* A thin software layer that runs directly on the host machine hardware; its main advantage is performance. Examples: VMWare ESX, ESXi Servers, Xen, OS370, Denali.
- *Hosted.* Run on top of an existing OS; its main advantage is that it is easier to build and easier to install. Example: User-mode Linux.
- *Hybrid.* Shares the hardware with an existing OS. Example: VMWare Workstation.

Virtualization An abstraction or simulation of hardware resources (e.g., virtual memory).

Virtual machine (VM) An isolated environment that appears to be a whole computer but actually only has access to a portion of the computer's resources.

Index

A

D

E

F

N

O

P

Q

R

S

T

U

V

W

X

Z